EARLY CHILDHOOD EDUCATION

Edited by

LEONARD H. GOLUBCHICK, Ph.D.
BARRY PERSKY, Ph.D.

In Cooperation with

THE AMERICAN FEDERATION OF TEACHERS

A Doctorate Association of New York Educators Series

AVERY PUBLISHING GROUP INC.
Wayne, New Jersey

Other Titles in the Doctorate Association Series

- URBAN, SOCIAL, AND EDUCATIONAL ISSUES, SECOND EDITION
  Golubchick-Persky
- INNOVATIONS IN EDUCATION
  Golubchick-Persky
- BILINGUAL EDUCATION
  LaFontaine-Golubchick-Persky
- CONTEMPORARY ISSUES IN ABNORMAL PSYCHOLOGY AND MENTAL ILLNESS
  Burke
- TOPICS IN HUMAN BEHAVIOR SERIES
  Belkin-Belkin

Contents

Preface, **xi**

Section **I. Overview**, **1**

A. National Perspectives
Introduction by Anthony Sanfilippo

Chapter **1.** Families and Children: Why Do We Ignore Their Needs?, **2**
Walter F. Mondale

There is no substitute for the family in terms of delivering to a child a sense of love, of support, of confidence, of self-worth, of motivation, and of self-respect. It is to the family we must look for our key source of ethical and moral training in this country. The author proposes a policy which should assist families in doing their job.

2. Public Schools and Preschool Programs: A Natural Connection, **6**
Albert Shanker

Testimony presented by Albert Shanker to a joint meeting of the House Select Subcommittee on Education and the Senate Subcommittee on Children and Youth, on why early childhood programs should be sponsored by public education agencies.

3. Reassessing Our Education Priorities, **11**
Burton White

The author examines the role of the family in the education of a young child. He presents suggestions for the development of a national educational policy for young children.

4. Public Policy and Early Childhood Education: A Buddhist Garden, **17**
Edwin W. Martin

The author proposes specific suggestions for public policy in the areas of preschool and early childhood services.

5. Early Childhood Education: A Field in Search of Itself, **20**
Russell C. Doll and Beth Koelker

In this article, the authors discuss the present confusing range and scope of early childhood theory, training, programs, and multidiscipline bases. Clarifications and future directions are detailed.

6. Day Care: A Look at the Present . . . A Hint of the Future, **25**
Paula Zajan

This article defines and describes some of the day-care services that now exist; it presents the rationale for expanding day care, and it explains educare.

B. Historical Perspectives, **29**
Introduction by Carol Harris
7. A Long Road to an Unresolved Problem: Comprehensive Child Care in the United States
Marilyn Rauth

A review of the history, current conditions, and future prospects of child-care programs in America.

8. Starting off on The Right Foot: The Case for putting Early Childhood Education into the Public Schools, **38**
Eugenia Kemble

A case for placing early childhood programs in the public schools is presented. The author describes the current status of present programs.

9. The Urgency of Child Care
Joyce D. Miller, **46**

A historical view of comprehensive child care in the United States. A description of organized labor's role in setting up and developing child care programs.

10. Historical Origins of Early Childhood Education in the United States, **53**
Laura S. Ellis

A historical review of events leading to our current conceptions and practices in early childhood education is presented. Present-day kindergarten and primary grade education are placed in historical and conceptual contexts.

11. Origins of Early Childhood Education
Barbara Ruth Peltzman, **58**

In this chapter, the author presents the principles and practices of Comenius, Rousseau, Pestalozzi, and Froebel as they relate to modern-day early childhood education.

Section II. Theoretical Bases, 63
Introduction by Helen Robison

12. The Effect Of Day Care on Early Development, **64**
Jerome Kagan

A noted child psychologist reports the findings of a research project which sought to find out, "Do infants attending a nurturant, responsibly administered group-care center five days a week for little over 100 weeks display different patterns of psychological development during or at the end of that period compared with children of the same sex and family background who are being reared in a typical nuclear family?"

13. Socialization and Early Childhood Education, **67**
Eleanor Meyer Rogg

Socialization theory is discussed. The author describes the socialization process in the acquisition of culture and the development of specific roles.

14. Dimensions of Right and Left Brain Learning in Early Childhood, **75**
Rosemarie Harter Kraft and Marlin L. Languis

The authors present current learning theory as it relates to right and left brain learning. Knowing the cognitive developmental level and neural organization of a given child may give educators a powerful tool for facilitating learning by constructing an appropriate learning environment and planning effective teaching strategies.

15. Effective Communication with Children: Movement toward a More Positive Self-Concept, **81**
Jeffrey L. Derevensky

This article is intended to provide an in-depth examination of methods for more effective communication with young children, the underlying premise being that effective communication with the young child fosters a more positive self-concept and heightened self-esteem.

16. Philosophies of Early Childhood Education, **87**
Lillian Oxtoby

This chapter describes the educational philosophies of such individuals as Froebel, Montessori, Piaget, B.F. Skinner, and Ira Gordon, and touches upon the influences of these individuals in the field of early childhood education.

17. Action and Interaction in the Development of Thought in the Young Child, **92**
Loren D. Weybright

The young child through direct action and interaction, grows out of egocentric thinking towards sociocentric thought. This article identifies the caregiver's role in supporting this development.

18. Piaget, Parents, and Young Children: Some Ideas that Work with Youngsters, **97**
Thomas D. Yawkey and Ann M. Burke-Merkle

The authors discuss Piaget's theory of development and describe the four stages of development.

19. Some Experiences Important in the Cognitive Growth of Young Children, **101**
John R. Nevius

A presentation of the relationship between experience and logical thinking. Appropriate experience is a factor of an individual's developmental level which determines the effect of experience. Practical activities to promote logical thinking are discussed.

20. Developmental Humanism: A Growth Approach to the Basics, **106**
Don. W. Rapp

Developmental Humanism blends Maslow's human potential outlook with the time–growth-oriented emergence philosophy of child development. Principles are stated and curriculum is discussed.

Section III. Learning Environments
Introduction by Antonio Bilbao, **112**

21. Helping Young Children to Cope with School, **113**
Josephine S. Gemake and Teresa A. Trimarco

Problems of a young child's adjustment to the school environment are discussed. Techniques are considered which a teacher might employ to help a child make a smooth and pleasant adjustment to school.

22. Learning Centers in the Early Childhood Classroom, **115**
Mary Elizabeth York

A practice which has been traditional in nursery schools, often found in kindergartens, and is seldom seen in primary classrooms is that of providing centers in which children may wish to participate. Learning centers are designed to appeal to children's interest and to elicit their active involvement; it is in these centers that learning occurs.

23. Children, Materials, and Adults in Early Learning Settings, **122**
David S. Kuschner and Peter Y. Clark

Understanding the nature, functions, and learning potentials of materials typically found in early learning settings is crucial. Special attention needs to be given to children's thinking and possible adult involvement in the interaction processes with materials.

24. Alternate Valuing Strategies for Young Children, **128**
Jesse S. Liles

The article defines a dilemma of teaching values to young children. Having teachers use cognitive moral dilemmas and/or value clarifications as possible solutions to the dilemmas are discussed.

25. The Importance of Play, **133**
Allen Sher

The author discusses the importance of play in the development of cognitive and sensory-motor skills.

26. Outdoor Learning Environments and Playgrounds, **137**
Jack L. Mahan, Jr.

This article discusses play, learning, ecology, psychology of environments, motor development, and self-development. These are related to outdoor playgrounds as learning environments.

27. BEEP: A Radical Experiment in Early Childhood Education, **144**
Arnold J. Keller

The Brookline Early Education Project (BEEP) is an experimental educational program which aims to increase children's future intellectual and social competence by providing parents with consultants from birth to kindergarten.

28. Behavior Modification in Early Childhood Classrooms, **148**
Shirley Moore

An examination of behavior modification in early childhood classrooms. Techniques are described.

29. Open Education vs. Traditional: Round Two, **152**
Barbara Ruth Peltzman

The author examines in detail the conflict between advocates of traditional and progressive (open) education. There is a discussion of the underlying principles of open education, with both pros and cons.

30. New Worlds: Experiences for the Young at Science and Technology Centers, **157**
Joan Munzer and John Holst

A description of a unique type of institution, the Science and Technology Center. The authors present experiences which create positive learning environments.

Section IV. Curriculum Methods, 160
Introduction by Frank Scalzo

31. Beginning Reading and the Goal of Literacy, **161**
Jeannette Veatch

A presentation of how to teach reading with children's own language without the use of any commercial program.

32. Language Arts in the Primary Grades, **166**
Jane Hornburger

The author surveys the literature pertaining to the primary language arts and takes a stand for the integrated approach. She treats the "problem" of nonstandard dialect.

33. Science in Early Childhood: Some Whys and Hows, **171**
Mary Ann Porcher

Science is perfectly suited to the way young children learn and what they are interested in. What this means for the teacher of young children is discussed by the author.

34. The Mathematical Knowledge of the Entering School Child, **176**
Rowland Hughes

The article examines preschool experiences which extend a young child's mathematical thinking. Paucity, limitations, and findings of recent research on mathematical abilities of children entering kindergarten and first grade are discussed.

35. Beyond the Workbook: Mathematics and the Young Child, **180**
Helene Silverman

This chapter considers activities related to the world of the child as vehicles for teaching mathematics.

36. "Is Today Tomorrow?" History for Young Children, **183**
Carol Seefeldt

Many of the concepts associated with the study of history are familiar to young children, and other concepts can be easily managed and enjoyed by them when presented in meaningful active ways. The author describes this process of teaching history to young children.

37. Creative dramatics in Early Childhood, **186**
Jean Mandelbaum

The "seeds" or simple beginnings of creative dramatics abound in every nursery, kindergarten, and primary classroom. The author offers suggestions as to how early childhood teachers might develop a creative dramatics program from elements that are in the curriculum and in the children themselves.

38. Genesis: The Art of the Young Child, **191**
Olive R. Francks

The purpose of this chapter is to provide a few insights into the art and thought of the young child.

39. Process and Product Art: New Implications for Education, **195**
Margot Kaplan-Sanoff

The article examines two orientations for the use of art in early childhood education. It traces the origins of process and product art through literature, painting, and film.

40. Musical Expression and the Young Child, **199**
Roberta Frankfort

A discussion of the importance and means of encouraging creative improvisation in young children contrasted with the rigid approach to teaching musical skills.

41. Reinforcing Bilingual-Bicultural Early Childhood Instruction With Music and Movement Activities, **203**
Minerva Benitez Rosario

The author discusses how music and movement activities can be used as a means to convey and strengthen learning in a bilingual early childhood classroom.

Section V. Exceptional Children, 206
Introduction by James L. Shields, Jr.

42. An Examination of Early Identification Procedures, **207**
Richard A. Schere and Adrienne Schere

Techniques for identifying young children who are potential learning problems will be critically reviewed. The review will include programs such as Search, Waldo, and the Frosting Screen.

43. Early Intervention: Its Potential for Reducing the Problems of Special Children, **211**
Richard A. Schere and Rosalind I. Reiss

An examination of the roles early childhood education can play in reducing the problems of special children. These roles include: a) early identification, b) mainstreaming, c) prescriptive intervention. A review of current research is included.

44. Mainstreaming Aggressive and Passive Preschoolers through Play, **216**
Charles H. Wolfgang

The author presents a program to be used by the teacher in working with withdrawn, passive, or aggressive preschoolers (ages 3–6) in an open play environment.

45. Identifying Individual Learning Styles & the Instructional Methods and/Or Resources to which Handicapped Early Childhood Youngsters Respond, **221**
Rita Dunn, Kenneth Dunn, and Gary Price

Variations of learning style are explored in an attempt to narrow the gap between the ability to read and the grade-level expectations of slow achieving youngsters.

46. The Readiness Program: For Young Children with Severe Learning Disabilities, **228**
Laura Shapiro and Susan Shapiro

This chapter describes a model program of early diagnosis and intervention for young children with learning disabilities.

47. An Urban School District Tackles the Problem of Educating Gifted Children in an Early Childhood Setting, **237**
Donald Kaplan

This chapter describes the history of policy, administration, and practical considerations of a Superintendent, a school board, and the administrative staff in pioneering a program for the exceptional high achieving 4½ to 6½-year-old child.

48. Old Myths Are Being Challenged by Down-to-Earth Methods at the University of Washington's Model Preschool for Handicapped Children, **246**
Vivian Hedrich

A description of the methods used at the University of Washington's Preschool Center for Handicapped Children for children with Down's Syndrome (mongolism).

Section VI. Critical Issues, 249
Introduction by Bernard Friedman

49. Education and Deprivation, **250**
Allan C. Ornstein

An examination of some theoretical insights and knowledge educating disadvantaged learners; possible causes and antecedents of observed learning deficits and practical learning problems are presented.

50. Program Considerations for Family and Group Day-Care Facilities for Infants and Toddlers, **258**
Vera Zorn and Irene Shigaki

Extrapolating for the developmental needs of infants and toddlers, a model for program development is presented, including guidelines for the physical setting, materials, staffing, and curriculum.

51. The Education of Early Sex-Role Development, **265**
Kathryn Norcross Black

This chapter is concerned with the development of sex-roles and the generalization made about maleness and femaleness. Boys and girls should be valued equally and fairly given options in behavior.

52. TV's Impact on Children: A Checkerboard Scene, **271**
Rose Mukerji

The second TV generation is upon us, and neither the worst fears nor the rosiest hopes for television have been fulfilled. But we know now that TV's impact is tremendous. Decisions made by concerned adults can make that impact either positive or negative.

53. Goals and Directions of Bilingual Programs in Early Childhood Years, **278**
Richard E. Baecher

Bilinqual programs are viewed within a social systems framework from which are derived specific and unqiue goals and directions for early childhood educators.

54. Early Childhood Education—Native American Style, **285**
Leona M. Foerster and Dale Little Soldier

It is the purpose of this article to acquaint the reader with what is occurring in early childhood education for Native Americans. Some of the most noteworthy trends will be examined and several exemplary programs will be discussed.

55. Child Abuse: Mandate for Teacher Intervention, **290**
Diane Divoky

Teachers are being assigned a major role in the national crusade against child abuse. The author describes the extent of child abuse, how can teachers intervene, and the role the teacher should play.

56. Child Care Needs of Migrant Children
Arnold B. Cheyney and Georgia B. Adams, **297**

The authors describe the child care needs of problems of migrant children.

Section VII. Parent Education and the Family, 300
Introduction by Regina Persky

57. The Changing American Family, **301**
Urie Bronfenbrenner

Until recently, there has been surprisingly little and at best sporadic research on the changes in the U.S. family structure. Yet the past 25 years have seen upheavals as gauged by the number of parents or other adult relatives in the home, the amount of attention parents devote to genuine relationships with their children and the necessity of dealing with the social and economic problems posed by these changes.

58. So What Did You Learn in School Today?
Estelle Wolk, **306**

A description of the interaction of a young child in an educational setting and the parents' attitude toward learning.

59. When a Child Begins School **, 308**
Luleen S. Anderson

An invaluable guide for parents both before a child enters school for the first time and during the crucial first few weeks. It is also an invaluable resource for teachers, who may wish to relate some of the ideas in this article to parents of children who find the opening days of school a frightening and traumatic experience.

60. Rearing Children to Meet the Challenge of Change **, 312**
Dan W. Dodson

The author examines how parents can help their children to meet the challenge of change and differences.

61. The Family: The Young Child's Earliest Educator **, 317**
Jane Attanucci and Barbara Kaban

The Harvard Preschool Project research outlines the development of competence in the first three years, creating recommendations for parents to enhance their child's earliest education.

62. Family–Community Involvement in Teacher Education **, 325**
Dorothy Rich

A description of the Home and School Institute method which is devoted to the development of the home-school-community partnership programs in education to help parents assist their children in the home; learning activities have been designed. These are recipe-style activities.

63. Parents, Teachers, and Early Education **, 331**
Judith A. Schickedanz

The article provides a discussion of the sources of current interest in parent involvement in early education followed by a discussion of levels of parent involvement in programs and suggestions for strategies which match each level.

Section VIII. Professionalism and Teacher Education , 334
Introduction by Arnold Raisner

64. Who Should Work with Young Children? **335**
Lillian B. Graham and Blanche A. Persky

A rationale for the need to educate adults (caregivers) who work with infants and toddlers. This is based upon a recognition of the critical importance of the earliest years of life upon later development and an understanding of the crucial role played by adults in this development.

65. Early Childhood Education and Teacher Education: A Search for Consistency **, 338**
Bernard Spodek

In early childhood education there are a number of program models available. Programs of teacher education need to be consistent in educational view with the programs of childhood education to which they would be related.

66. Goal-Directed Teaching in Action-Based Learning Environments, **342**
Sydney L. Schwartz

Identification of learning goals and teaching roles to serve as a guide for decision-making about teaching interactions with learners in multiactivity learning environments of Day Care and Early Childhood Programs.

67. An Approach to Competency Based Teacher Preparation in Early Childhood Education , **349**
Adelle Jacobs and Laura Bursak

The authors describe a teacher education-program based upon a competency-based model.

68. Just Another Pair of Hands? The Role of the Assistant Teacher in Early Childhood Programs , **352**
Paula L. Zajan

This chapter reviews the role of the assistant teacher in the early childhood classroom.

69. The Need for More Male Early Childhood Teachers , **356**
Bruce R. Shames

This article discusses why there are so few male early childhood teachers, the reasons why more are needed, and suggests how to meet this need.

70. The Role of the Manager of Early Childhood Programs , **359**
Alicia I. Pagano

A new profession is emerging—the manager of early childhood programs—based upon child development theories and principles. Roles, tasks, and skills of the manager in quality child-development organizations are defined and discussed.

Section IX. International Early Childhood Education Programs, 365

Introduction by Carl Erdberg

71. The Kibbutz: An Educational Model for Early Childhood Development Programs, **366**
Leonard H. Golubchick

Group care for young children is one of the United States' most pressing needs. As greater numbers of women enter the labor force and seek to combine family life with a career, a national policy with clear-cut guidelines must be established. The kibbutz exemplifies the kind of programs and techniques which can be utilized in the formation and organization of early childhood development programs in the United States.

72. An International Overview of Child Care Programs, **371**
Barry Persky

In this chapter, the author reviews the universal concerns of child care programs. Problems, goals, and objectives are presented.

73. An Overview of Early Childhood Programs in Some Western European Countries, **373**
Gilbert R. Austin

In this chapter the author discusses the development of early childhood education in Europe.

74. Preschool and Elementary Education in Scandinavia Today, **380**
Adele Davidson

The article is a kaleidoscopic view of the early schooling and care of young children in day-care centers and elementary schools in Finland, Norway, Sweden, and Denmark.

75. Early Childhood Education in the Soviet Union, **384**
Virginia Rederer

The Soviet Union is currently engaged in one of the most extensive programs of early schooling for children in the history of education. The author discusses the prescribed instructional program for young Soviet children.

76. Curriculum Practices in Preschool and Primary Schools in the People's Republic of China, **390**
Alfred L. Karlson

The nature of current preschool and primary school curriculum and teaching practices in the People's Republic of China are described from firsthand observation.

To The Memory of Irwin Price

Preface

Early childhood education and child care are now widely perceived to be among the central social needs of the nation. The ever-growing number of working mothers, the proven value of early childhood training to intellectual development, and the scandalous conditions in profit-making day-care operations provide evidence that this perception is well-founded. Unfortunately, attempts since 1970 to enact major federal legislation which would establish a coordinated system of early childhood and family services have been unsuccessful, and the United States is still without a comprehensive program for very young children.

The need for child-care facilities and early childhood education programs now far outdistances their availability. Limited numbers of children, usually those of welfare mothers or from otherwise impoverished backgrounds, have access to federally-sponsored child care programs. The large majority of children of the working poor and those of middle-class parents do not. The federal government spends over $1 billion a year in direct funds for child-care–related services administered by at least 60 different federal agencies. The result is a confusing maze of services which are fragmented and often overlapping. In many instances, even federally-funded child-care programs fail to meet minimal federal standards and almost all are purely custodial in nature. Consequently, many eligible persons are reluctant to place their chidlren in such facilities. The present federal expenditure is too much to waste as we are now doing, but not enough to meet the actual need.

There are few affordable alternatives for quality care. Currently, the most frequently used type of child care is. in-home with a relative, sibling, or "babysitter" providing the care. Following this in frequency of usage are family day-care homes, of which only about five percent are licensed. Although most day-care centers are licensed, licensing standards are minimal and enforcement of regulations is almost nonexistent.

We face a critical situation. With rapidly increasing numbers of working mothers and single-parent families, expansion of early childhood services becomes a necessity. To cite just one example of need, there are almost seven million children under the age of six whose mothers work. Yet, the Child Welfare League of America estimates that there are only 4.3 million spaces available in child-care facilities and of these, some 77 percent are of such inferior quality that they should not be used. In too many cases, personnel are untrained and transient; safety and health are neglected; and little attention, if any, is given to children's development. This situation is inevitable as long as the welfare of children remains a low priority. Quality programs naturally cost a great deal more than custodial care.

In addition to the problems faced by working parents in finding adequate child care, we must take into consideration the needs of the children themselves. Many parents, working and nonworking alike, would like to give their children the advantage of developmental early childhood education programs but are unable to find or afford them. Numerous research studies in the United States and abroad have concluded that the first six years of a child's life are crucial in determining the nature of future development. Harvard researcher Burton White, for example, believes a child's learning patterns are developing as early as ten months of age. Others, like J. McVicker Hunt, tell us early experience may be even more important for perceptual, cognitive, and intellectual functions than for emotional functions. And research leaves no doubt about the importance of social, emotional, and physical development during these years.

Without parent education programs and comprehensive early childhood services, deficiencies in children's social, emotional, physical, and intellectual growth often go undetected and untreated. With each day and year of delay, the problem becomes more and more difficult to correct.

Because of this, the American Federation of Teachers and the Doctorate Association of New York Educators believe we need comprehensive early childhood services which would be universally accessible on a voluntary basis, regardless of social or economic status. To achieve this goal, AFT supports federal legislation which would fund coordinated services for very young children administered by the public schools, provided they are willing and able to do so. Existing programs which meet appropriate standards probably would continue, but under the administration of the local education agency. The rationale for this position is included in articles in this text.

It should be emphasized, however, that although this book focuses on the role of the public schools and professional personnel in early childhood education, alternative viewpoints are also offered. It should not be assumed that contributing authors necessarily support the AFT and DANYE position nor that the AFT or DANYE are in agreement with all ideas or opinions presented in these readings.

The Doctorate Association of New York Educators, in cooperation with the AFT, carefully chose the articles in this book to give the reader a broad comprehensive overview of the issues surrounding early childhood education. These include discussions of the current debate over what constitutes appropriate services, the past history of early childhood programs, classroom theory and tech-

niques, approaches to meeting special needs, and more. The book is divided into nine sections: I. Overview: National and Historical Perspectives; II. Theoretical Bases; III. Learning Environments; IV. Curriculum Methods; V. Exceptional Children; VI. Critical Issues; VII. Parent Education and the Family; VIII. Professionalism and Teacher Education; IX. International Early Childhood Education Programs.

Special thanks go to the editors, Dr. Leonard Golubchick and Dr. Barry Persky, and members of the DANYE Editorial Review Board for their efforts in preparing this book. Special thanks also go to Sylven Seid for her technical and editorial assistance, as well as to Elaine Morenberg, Judith Golubchick, and Regina Persky for their editorial comments. It is the belief of all of us that *Early Childhood Education* will be a useful and valuable tool to students at the undergraduate and graduate levels and all other concerned with meeting the developmental needs of young children.

Marilyn Rauth
Director
Educational Issues Department
American Federation of Teachers

Section 1
Overview

A. National Perspectives

Introduction by Anthony Sanfilippo*

The early childhood years have long been recognized as the most important period in the educational and emotional development of a human being. The youngster in the early childhood program is being introduced to the educational system for the first time. That youngster will be involved with making the necessary adjustments to living in a classroom environment, working together with other children, following instructions from a teacher who is neither mother nor father, and being required to perform tasks which will be evaluated according to a new set of rules. The trauma of entering school is also a trying experience for parents who must learn to entrust their precious child to the responsibility of trained professionals whom they may regard as intruders into the family setting.

As we look at the activities of preschoolers and kindergarten children, most of us cannot help noticing how wonderfully carefree and happy these children usually appear to be as they express themselves in a creative intuitive way, with little regard for how their actions conform to rigid rules and established norms. It is precisely at this tender age when a child's special talents and innate skills are expressed with naive clarity; they are not embarrassed to act out emotions or play games of fantasy or paint a totally abstract picture at the easel.

The early childhood teacher is more than a teacher in the usual sense; she is the first professional observer to be in a position to evaluate the special talents and creative ability which she observes in the classroom setting. It is at this time that programs can be planned for each individual youngster which will bring out the pupil's true potential in later life.

Basic skills in the early childhood program are noted and developed. Where a child shows erratic behavior or an inability to cope with the school setting, remedial measures can be taken which can head off a disastrous school career for that individual child. Through proper guidance procedures and an early warning system of diagnosis and prescrip-

tion, children can be directed into school programs which are hand-tailored to their individual needs and abilities. To some children, this special assessment of talents may mean an accelerated program of instruction. To others it may mean an emphasis on art, music, dance, and drama where such talents have been indicated. To still other children, this individualized system may mean a special school capable of focusing in on some particular mental or physical impairment which prevents this child from adjusting to the mainstream of educational life. Once we let early childhood slip by, the problems encountered in older children are multiplied to levels which make remediation extremely difficult, if not impossible. How often do we find that a child has suffered for years in the wrong class setting when later tests indicate that his mental level or emotional maturity called for a special educational setting? How often are reading problems discovered too late for proper remediation? In early childhood, the school, teacher, supervisor, and parent are given the opportunity to plan ahead for the child's educational career to formulate a plan which will allow the child to develop according to his/her own potential. This opportunity must not be passed up and left for higher grades where little help can be accomplished. This effort must be seen as a joint responsibility between school and home, between teacher and parent. The early childhood program in any school can become the most vital and crucial one in the school setting. It is the responsibility of parents and educators to make the most of these programs by providing their children with a true steppingstone to later life from the very first step into a classroom.

*Anthony Sanfilippo, Community Superintendent, Community School District #24, New York City.

Chapter 1
Families and Children: Why Do We Ignore Their Needs?

Walter F. Mondale*

I wish to speak, very briefly, about an old subject, but one I think we have taken for granted, namely the American family. I have been privileged to serve in the Senate now for just a decade, and I think I have served on as many or more human-problem subcommittees as any member of the Senate. During that time, I have been on the Hunger Committee, the manpower and poverty subcommittee, the children and youth subcommittee, the housing and urban development subcommittee, the Indian education subcommittee which has expired, the education subcommittee, the labor subcommittee and hosts of others. And, in each of them we tend to look at a category: are people hungry? or, do migrants get paid enough? or, do we have bilingual education for Chicanos, for Indians? or, are civil rights being observed? or, is the proper housing being built? All these are categories, and I suppose in a sense that is necessary. But the longer I look at this problem, the more obvious it is that the central focus must be on the family, because no matter how well we do in the delivery of public and private services, there is no adequate substitute for a healthy family. If our system puts undue pressure upon families, destroying them, making it difficult for them to do their task, then an indispensable and irreplaceable aspect of raising healthy children will be gone and irretrievable. I do not care where you look; there is no substitute for the family in terms of delivering to a child a sense of love, of support, of confidence, of self-worth, of motivation and self-respect. It is the family to which we must look for our key source of ethical and moral training in this country.

Urie Bronfenbrenner, testifying last year before our Senate subcommittee on children and youth, put it this way. He said, "It is no accident that in the million years of evolution we've emerged with a particular form for raising children, and that is the human family. We should be very careful in fiddling with something that has managed to do us well so long before we even had Ph.D.'s, like myself, in child development." I think few Americans would disagree with that statement; yet, American families have come under increasing pressures in recent decades. And I am afraid we are often better at paying lip service to the institution of the family and its importance than we are at actually helping them and pursuing policies that assist them to do a better job in their work.

A few years ago, following the White House Children's Conference in Washington, we set up a subcommittee on children and youth which, to my knowledge, is the first time that the Congress has had a subcommittee with a staff that seeks to provide a forum for young people and their problems. We tried not to begin with the experts, but to hear from families and what they have to say about the problems they confront. While I think most American families are strong and healthy, I think there are warning signs that should cause concern in America that we cannot ignore. Teen-age alcoholism and drug abuse are growing problems. Suicide is the second leading cause of death for young Americans between 15 and 24. One out of nine children will be before juvenile court by age 18. One million young Americans, most of them middle class, run away each year. And child abuse is a growing and widespread phenomenon in American life.

There are some problems that don't show up in the statistics. A few months ago I was at Cornell talking to a seminar on this same issue, and in the question-and-answer period someone stood up in the back of the room and said, "All right, senator, we understand the problems of poverty, but how would you like to grow up in a family where there is great wealth but you never see your father or your mother?" And, you could feel in that room that that was the issue which had affected most of that audience. You might call it the problems of prosperity where, as one of them said, the cocktail hour had replaced the family hour.

I think the message of this is pretty clear. We cannot ignore what is happening to American families, the pressure they are under, the problems they face and the changes that are taking place. Some of the problems that families face may be unavoidable, but we must also recognize that in a host of ways, often unwittingly, government policies are placing destructive burdens on our families. Now, I do not want a Big Brother government running American families. I do not think that is the government's business. But, I do believe the government ought to pursue a course that at the very least does not interfere or place burdens upon families in their efforts to raise healthy children. In many ways I

*Walter F. Mondale, Vice President of the United States. Reprinted with the permission of the Education Commission of the State.

think we have gone beyond that and are in fact interfering with and sometimes making it almost impossible for some families to do their jobs.

Look at current economic policies and the inflation that is now literally a torture for families of low and moderate income. We have rising unemployment, and every expert we have talked to says that when the head of the household cannot find a job or cannot earn enough to take care of the minimum necessities of a home, that household is in serious jeopardy. The pride, the sense of authority, the whole family structure breaks down, when the capacity of a family head to find a job and to pay for the cost of raising children decently does not exist. And yet, I would bet that when the Council of Economic Advisers or the Federal Reserve Board meets, the question of the family and the price it is paying for the twin policies of inflation and unemployment is seldom raised. Yet, in the long run, those costs may be in the hundreds of billions of dollars, just in direct economic cost.

Look at how we deal with our taxes. Take the Social Security payroll tax. That's a dandy. In the last 15 years, corporate and business taxes to the federal government have dropped by almost 40 per cent in terms of their contribution to the cost of maintaining the federal government. The individual income tax has remained about the same in terms of its percentage contribution to the cost of federal government. The payroll tax has doubled. The payroll tax is now a bigger tax for low- and moderate-income workers, in most instances, than the income tax. It is a flat tax; there are no exemptions, there are no deductions for the size of the family or for the cost of medicine or anything else. It is a flat, regressive tax. At those income levels approaching welfare, it is a tax that discourages work. And yet, that tax above all is the one that has been soaring.

Today when a low- or moderate-income family's salary rises to adjust to inflation, it just puts them into a higher tax bracket. So, not only are the dollars worth less, but they are being taxed more. And, I see little or no thought being given to the erosion of income and the devastating impact that these tax policies have today upon the family. A family earning $12,000 last year has to earn $13,300 this year simply to stay even. Of course, most of them have had no such increases, which is why the real purchasing power of families has dropped by nearly five per cent from last year. The real purchasing power of the average family today is actually lower than it was nine years ago.

Now, our economic and our tax policies are only one example of those policies that place pressures on families. Others that might also be included in the list are policies which unnecessarily encourage placement of children in foster homes or institutions, rather than offering families the support they need to stay together. Now, sometimes children have to be placed in those institutions, but I think many times the emphasis is on what someone called "pa-

rentectomy" rather than upon trying to provide help and strengthen that family.

Often, I think, our public housing and urban renewal policies have destroyed neighborhoods and communities or have been built in a way that is destructive to the family. Now, I am for public housing and I am for urban renewal, but I think those policies should be shaped sensitively, with the family in mind. And yet, I would bet, when the architects get together to plan one of those high-rises they never talk to a family who is going to live in one. If they ever did talk to such a family, they would never build those small kitchens. And if you talk to educators or social workers or anybody who has worked with families, they will tell you that the notion of packing a lot of very poor people together with all of their problems has proven to be a policy that has put unnecessary burdens on families.

And yet, some of those policies continue. For example, consider the policy in public housing of separating people on the basis of age. In Boston in 1900, 50 percent of the families were three-generational in the same home. Now, four per cent are. In 1900, when a young couple reared their children, grandmother or grandfather or Aunt Susie was often around, or just down the block, and they could help a young couple with the problems of early marriage and young parenthood. Now, granny and grandfather are 18 miles away in a high-rise. That kind of support and strength that the family depended upon years ago is often gone for young couples.

Another example is the transfer policies of the armed services. We had as witnesses women who testified about what it is like to raise a family in the armed services. It is quite a story. They just keep moving them and moving them. And the divorce rate and the child-abuse rate show that the breakdown of families and the pressure in the armed services is not a very nice story.

Some of our day-care policies, especially those related to work requirements of Aid to Families With Dependent Children, have too often resulted in the placement of young children in understaffed, unlicensed custodial care of the worst kind. It is one of the reasons that I fought so hard for those minimum day-care standards. Some say they are unrealistic, but I am absolutely sure that unless you put some floor under minimum day-care standards, that the emphasis in implementation would be, let's save some money, let's "serve more children," or just, let's get those mothers, out working, with little or no thought given to the welfare of the children. That, too, can destroy a family.

I am not sure that when we say in Washington that it is good for all mothers on welfare to work that we are doing the right thing either. You know, my mother stayed at home with me, and I kind of fell in love with her. I think this notion that it is always best under all circumstances to crowd people onto the payroll and take them away from their children in these tender years is a very, very questionable proposition. It is one that I think we will pay a lot more for in the long run, because I think children can be damaged in those custodial, understaffed programs. Parents ought to make those decisions, not governments.

There are many things we can do to begin to change this situation. One of the steps we hope to take shortly is to introduce a notion that I hope will do some good — a Family Impact Statement, like the Environmental Impact Statement — so that when we act on governmental programs we will be required to hold a hearing to ask if this will help families or weaken them. We need to find a way to introduce into our public debates this often-forgotten dimension of the relationship of governmental policies to families.

Second, I think we need to look at tax reform and tax justice in the context of the average family. You know, we are the only Western industrial society that does not have some kind of children's allowance policy. We have, of course, the tax exemption, and it is quite a deal. The richer you are, the more you get; the poorer you are (and you have to be working, of course, to even get it) the less you get. So that under this exemption, Henry Ford is able to add about $525 more a year per dependent to his meager budget, while the average worker is lucky to get $125 or $150 in real tax relief.

Now, one of the things that we tried, so far without success, was to close some of these loopholes through tax reform and then swing what we gain in revenue through this reform back into the hands of the average working family. We would do this in the form of an optional tax credit, an actual shaving-off of taxes, unrelated to your income. Our first proposal provided a choice between using a $200 credit per dependent or continuing to use the $750 personal exemption. Now, this would bring some relief — about $240 — for a family of four whose income is $8,000 a year. It would also bring more relief for large families.

We'd like to move away from exclusive reliance on the exemption system into a system that includes a tax credit option, based on the number of dependents in the family, that would really bring relief to families during the child-rearing era. I believe this is a form of relief that is long overdue.

We are also hoping to develop a bill to encourage wider experimentation with flexible working hours, so that parents can work on a schedule that is consistent with their family responsibilities, so they can develop their professional skills and increase their earning capacity while working in a way that they deem consistent with the needs of their children.

Finally, and most importantly, we need a program that offers families the kind of help and services they need for children during the early childhood years. A major part of this program must be an effort to upgrade child care available across the country. The facts in this area are well known, and there are dramatic changes under way. In 1971, 43 per cent of the nation's mothers worked outside the home compared to 18 per cent in 1948, and the number is rising. One out of every three mothers with preschool children is working today, compared to one out of eight in 1948. One out of seven children, some eight million, are living in single-parent families. That's an area that has not received sufficient attention. Many single-parent homes are having a great deal of difficulty, many of them living in near-poverty. Moreover, 65 per cent of single parents are working. Yet, there are only 700,000 spaces in licensed day care centers to serve six million preschool children, and many of those centers are in lousy shape. Ken Kenniston, director of the Carnegie Council on Children, said, "Of all the industrialized nations, we have the least adequate public provision for the care are of young children whose mothers work." A child-care program must offer other needed services as well, including the kind of prenatal and postnatal health care that will help us reduce our inexcusably high infant mortality rate.

It is indefensible the way the federal government has failed to deal with the problems of children's health. For a modest investment we could make some dramatic changes in this area. Early childhood is a time when parents and children are most in need of proper care. They need it during the time of the mother's pregnancy; they need it at the time of the delivery; they need it during those first few years after birth. And yet, that is the time when millions of people get absolutely no care whatsoever. I remember holding some hearings in migrant health down in southern Texas where a Field Foundation team of doctors had just tried to conduct what they thought was going to be a scientific survey. But they found so many sick people that they dropped the survey and just worked to try to save lives. Something like 60 or 70 per cent of the migrant mothers deliver their children with no professional care. There are other statistics utterly devastating. And yet, for a few dollars, their health needs could be dealt with and they would rear healthy children who could care for themselves instead of ending up as so many of them do, crippled, cheated children, many of them destined for welfare for the rest of their lives.

We must have part-day or in-the-home preschool educational opportunities that can make the difference between success or failure in school and life. We need to continue to work on nutrition and mental health services, classes in parenthood and all the rest.

One of the things we hope to do is to start again to move for the passage of a child and family services bill. This is, as you know, the measure which we introduced and passed overwhelmingly in the Senate and the House and which was then vetoed by President Nixon in 1971. I re-introduced a revised version of the measure with 23 sponsors in the Senate. Representative John Brademas introduced the companion measure in the House with 50 cosponsors, and then we begin joint House-Senate hearings in Washington. This bill authorizes $1.8 billion over the next three years to provide a wide range of child and family services. I believe you are probably familiar with the measure. It is totally voluntary. It maximizes parental control in decision making. It has a unique phase-in year for planning and training. And it seeks to serve a broad range of economic groups, with free services to families with incomes below $8,100 and a graduated-fee schedule for families with incomes above that level.

Now this measure is not etched in stone. We want to use this remaining period and the early part of the next Congress for hearings. We are soliciting your suggestions and advice. One of the areas that has caused a great deal of controversy is the manner in which we propose to deliver services. We would appreciate suggestions about that point or any others. I am increasingly convinced that progress can

be made in this area: but it can be made only if we define what it is we want, if we make a more powerful and effective case than we have, if we establish lobbies at the local and at the state and federal levels, and if we make justice for children an issue with which the political system must grapple as a priority question.

I believe that can be done. I think this country has shown time and time again that there is enormous honesty and compassion and sense of personal responsibility in Americans. And above all, Americans want to respond to the plea for fairness and justice for children. For, as the French philosopher Camus once wrote, "Perhaps we cannot prevent this world from being a world in which children are tortured, but we can reduce the number of tortured children." And, if you don't help us, who else in the world can help us do it?

Eugenia S. Ware

Chapter 2
Public Schools and Preschool Programs: A Natural Connection

Albert Shanker*

Numerous arguments have already been presented here as to why this country must expand facilities for the care of children. There are many compelling reasons which were spelled out in a resolution by the AFL-CIO in May of 1976:

"The unmet need for child care is greater today than it has ever been because large and growing numbers of women have to work. They are being forced to leave their children without the care and attention they need. Other mothers, on public assistance, want jobs but cannot find adequate child care.

"The statistics clearly show the growing nature of the problem:

—From 1948 to 1973, the percentage of working mothers grew from 18 percent to 44 percent.

—26 million children (6 million under 6 years old) have working mothers.

—12 million children live in female-headed households where the median income is $6,195 if the mother works and $3,760 if she does not.

—5 million children live in single-parent families where the parent is in the labor force and out of the home.

"During this time of massive and still rising unemployment and continuing inflation, the family's real dollar shrinks. As husbands become unemployed, wives seek to replace their income. But to work, they must find decent care for their children.

"More mothers are constantly entering the labor force and many more need and want work. But lack of adequate child care poses a major problem to all of them. In addition, millions of disadvantaged children, whose mothers are home, could benefit from child-care services. There are 5 million children under 6 years of age in poor and near-poor families, many of whom could benefit greatly from child-care services."

In addition, there is increasing recognition of the importance of the early years to the total intellectual and social development of children.

In terms of the Child and Family Services Act, these facts lead us to the central question of how to best frame a program so as to maximize its impact for working women and single parents, for the total development of the child, for the professionals who work with children, and for the social needs of the nation. We believe that the best way to do this is by administering such programs through the public education system.

We are aware that our position in support of the public schools as the presumed prime sponsor for child-development programs represents a major departure from the established organization and substance of existing federal programs and a departure from the direction these committees took in passing the vetoed Comprehensive Child Development Act in 1971. We believe that at that time the use of the public-school system as prime sponsor was not adequately considered, probably because even in 1971 it was not yet clear that the schools were available to administer a program that would serve even more children than they were already responsible for. The whole trend of declining enrollments in education has produced a situation where the school system can now begin to provide and coordinate needed services for children in the prekindergarten age group.

In fact, now is a time when our social policies should be trying to combine the interests of children, parents, and the professionals already working in existing programs to develop a program that will meet the common needs of all. We (AFT) believe that putting responsibility in the schools is the best way to create a program that can grow. This is the case I intend to make here today.

First, the schools are available throughout the country. They exist in urban, suburban, small-town, and rural areas. By being universally available, the school system meets the first, and one of the most important, criteria that the AFT has for a child-development program. Child-development programs should be available to all children whose parents desire to utilize this service. It should not be restricted on the basis of means tests, sliding income scales, or other criteria that prevent the majority of our citizens from utilizing a highly desirable and crucial public service. Second, over the past few years, the school systems of our country have become adept at administering large, complicated federal programs. They already possess the expertise to move immediately to the implementation stage without creation of another layer of bureaucracy.

*Albert Shanker, President, American Federation of Teachers.

Another major criteria the AFT has is that the program should contribute to the intellectual development of young children. Within the last 20 years, the works of educators like Benjamin Bloom, J. McVicker Hunt, Jerome Bruner, and Jean Piaget have pointed to the crucial importance of the early—what are now thought of as preschool—years to the later intellectual potential of children. Their thinking tends to support the idea that the young child should be deliberately exposed to stimulating experiences rather than simply left on his own. The evidence on why the public schools would be better equipped to provide such stimulation includes the following:

1. It is well known that much of a child's development during the early years has to do with the social, emotional, and physical growth that surrounds intellectual development. These areas are just as important to cognitive growth as those activities viewed more strictly as "academic." In view of this, comprehensive public-school services having to do with diagnosis, guidance counseling, health (innoculation, etc.), special-treatment referrals, bilingual education, handicapped education, and the services of dieticians would provide children with more services than the average nursery or day-care center.

2. An Office of Child Development Report called "A Report on Longitudinal Evaluations of Preschool Projects: Is Early Intervention Effective?" which suggests that the gains of program like Head Start are better maintained if there is a continuity of effort between such programs and supplementary, public, school-age programs like Follow Through. It would seem to make sense to administer both through public schools to gain maximum effect from a more comprehensive effort.

3. A report of the Institute for Development of Educational Activities (I/D/E/A) which catalogued all the possible kinds of activities that could take place in preschool and found that most programs which they looked at were heavily concentrated in a few of the more obvious: blocks, naps, outdoor play, etc. (see Appendix). The I/D/E/A researchers also found significantly higher program quality in the public-school kindergarten programs they observed and attributed the difference to the fact that these programs were part of the educational mainstream and not isolated as were many of the preschool programs.

There are other, less obvious, reasons why it makes sense to use the schools for these programs:

1. It would be more efficient to use existing underutilized resources than equip new ones.

2. The public schools would be more able to coordinate the diagnostic, counseling, dietetic, and other services needed by young children, than isolated daycare centers. The schools are performing this function with respect to handicapped children and there is every reason to believe they can do it with young children as well. Some services, such as dental care, which are now provided in public schools, could be provided to children earlier if early childhood programs were part of the public-school system.

3. Qualified personnel: Through the licensing mechanisms already in place in every state and local education agency in the country, a program run through the schools could be sure of using the best available people for its operation. We have heard much about the lack of qualified people in early childhood education and how much lead time and training is needed to reach the fully operative stage. Part of the reason for the teacher shortage of the 1950s and 1960s was the ridiculously low pay that teachers received. With the advent of professional pay scales won through collective bargaining, more and more teachers began to look at their jobs as a lifetime profession. When teacher salaries became competitive with some of those paid in the private sector, many qualified teachers stayed with their jobs and the turnover in education became less of a problem. We wonder how many more qualified people would seek the jobs in these programs if they were available at professional salaries. It might turn out that the shortage is not as great as is currently anticipated and that a real program can be made operative. We do, however, agree that special skills are needed for very young children and we do advocate provision for training professionals both inservice and preservice.

Public Control

In our view, one of the main reasons why new initiatives in child development should come under the jurisdiction of the public schools is that the schools are publicly administered and controlled. Because the schools are so often supported by separate and visible taxation, they must be accountable to parents and the public. And because funding for the schools is so frequently dependent on voted bond issues or voted increases in property-tax millage, the public-education system is one of the most responsive institutions of government. Private profit-making entities in the day-care business, on the other hand, are not subject to democratic policy-making, and their services are always geared to their profit margins. It is our position that the public schools should be the presumed prime sponsor of programs provided for under this bill except in those instances where the public-school system is unwilling or unable to assume this responsibility. Our position on this issue is shared by virtually all of the education community and by the AFL-CIO. In May 1976, a resolution adopted unanimously by the AFL-CIO Executive Council stated:

"In most communities, the school system would be the appropriate prime sponsor of the child-care and early childhood development program, with the responsibility for planning programs, distributing funds and monitoring programs. Where the school system is unwilling or unable to undertake this responsibility in accordance with federal standards, some other appropriate public or nonprofit community organization should be eligible.

"Even where the public-school systems are the prime sponsor, all of the services need not actually be offered in public-school facilities. For instance, communities may want in-home child care, family and group day-care homes for children who are too young or not ready for large school facilities, as well as special services for the emotionally and physically handicapped which may be offered outside the educational system. We support the expansion of these diversified services by educational systems or by an alternative sponsor as they administer these programs.

"Only public and nonprofit groups should be permitted to participate in the program. There is no legitimate role for profitmaking entrepreneurs in child-care programs. The sorry record of profitmaking organizations in the provision of human services, especially in the nursing-home, health-care, and education fields, has led the AFL-CIO to strongly oppose any involvement of profitmakers in human-services programs. Profitmakers were excluded from providing day care under Head Start. They should continue to be excluded in any new early childhood and day-care programs."

Clearly, the time has come to reverse direction. Although current efforts include many programs that meet high standards and provide quality care for the children served, they cannot take the place of a comprehensive program intended for all children. While we support continued funding for these programs, we believe it is time to examine some reasons for the sorry state of child-development programs.

Failure at Implementation and Funding

Overlapping jurisdictions make it impossible to know exactly what is and is not being done, but a few dramatic examples should help to illustrate the problems inherent to multiple administrations:

1. The Early and Periodic Screening, Diagnosis, and Treatment Program has screened only 10 percent of a possible 10 to 13 million children under 21 for possible physical defects. The purpose of the program was to provide children who are eligible for Medicaid with preventive health care. HEW has not been able to persuade the states to implement the program Congress authorized seven years ago.

2. The Supplemental Security Income Program is intended to provide monthly cash payments to disabled children. The payments vary according to a family's income and the nature of the disability. HEW now estimates that only 65,000 out of a possible 250,000 eligible children are now receiving these payments. Children receiving SSI are automatically eligible for Medicaid and would also be provided with vocational training. No effective outreach programs now exist to find these children.

3. $900 million appropriated for state social-service programs went unspent during 1973. The $2.5 billion allocated

to social services through Title IV-A is the largest federal source of day-care money. Only a little more than half the money was actually spent.

Poor Quality of Staff, Physical Plant, Health and Safety, etc.

The well-known study, "Windows on Day Care," published by the National Council of Jewish Women, and "Early Schooling in the United States," a report of I/D/E/A, are among the many studies which thoroughly document the poor conditions found in many day-care establishments and the inadequate professional training received by most staffs. Both these reports place the blame at the feet of the states which, for the most part have inadequate state-licensing provisions and staff qualifications that are set very low. A state-by-state analysis of these provisions, which can be found in "Child Care Data and Materials," a report of the Senate Committee on Finance, shows that day-care staff can range in qualification from such vague stipulations as "equipped for work required" in Idaho, Iowa, and Kentucky to the prerequisite of a B.A. in Hawaii.

Although all but two states require that day-care centers be licensed, many exempt federally operated or regulated centers. And, since the Federal Interagency Day Care Requirements defer to the states in the licensing of centers and staff, there is little to prevent endless buck-passing between the two levels of government when it comes to enforcement.

Lack of Adherence to Licensing Standards Including Child/Adult Ratios

Because of fragmentation, surveys in this field are hard to come by. Yet a recent HEW audit of day-care programs called "The Review of Child-Care Services Provided Under Title IV, Social Security Act" gives enough information to indicate how wide the gap is between licensing demands and reality. Of 552 centers and private homes which provide day care in nine states, the audit found that 425 did not meet minimum health-and-safety requirements while over a third of the sample did not meet child/staff ratio requirements. Such figures are really quite shocking. It is surprising that they have not received more attention in the testimony before these committees.

Inadequate Staff Resources

All of the major studies I have referred to thus far support the observation that most day-care and early childhood centers employ staffs at very low rates of pay. Low wage scale cannot hope to attract the best qualified people. In fact, as our members know, one of the reasons for the teacher shortage of the 1950s was the ridiculously low pay that teachers received. It took some hard battles and col-lective bargaining to make teaching a job anyone would view as a long-term profession. It also meant that teaching came to attract better qualified professionals. The same could come to be true in the day-care field.

At this point, some would argue that all this informa-tion on poor quality care only proves that day care is bad for children and that the federal government is wise not to involve itself.

Nothing could be further from the truth.

Women will go on working regardless of what actions are or are not taken by the Congress. The lack of access to quality child care will not eliminate the economic necessity of supporting a family. Rather, failure to provide quality child care to those who need it will simply force families to settle for custodial care or no care. And it will be the chil-dren who suffer. The problem will not go away by ignoring it. It is not a question of encouraging women to leave home. Rather, women working and leaving the home are facts which have existed. Their numbers continue to in-crease in spite of rising unemployment and in spite of decreases in family size.

America prides itself on being a child-loving society. In reality, we pay only lip-service to this ideal. A simple exam-ination of the status of children today painfully illustrates this fact:

● America must bear the shame of lagging behind 14 other countries in the rate of infant mortality.

● Twenty-nine percent of all children in our inner cities do not see a doctor during a given year.

● Five million children in the U.S. suffer from malnutri-tion.

● Hundreds of thousands of handicapped children re-ceive no services.

● Thousands of retarded children are living in state "warehouses" under what has been rightly called "institu-tionalized child abuse."

TABLE 1

RESULTS OF HEALTH AND SAFETY REVIEW

Care type	Number examined	Number not meeting requirements
Day-care centers	453	363
Family day-care homes (includes care in the home of relatives or friends)	50*	21
In-home care	49	41
Totals	552	425

* Excludes 55 facilities which were examined in Virginia but for which the records available did not disclose compliance with health and safety standards.
Source: "Review of Child Care Service Provided Under Title IX, Social Security Act," HEW Audit Agency, Office of the Assistant Secretary, Comptroller, p. 20.

TABLE 2

RESULTS OF CHILD/STAFF RATIOS REVIEW

Care type	Number examined	Number not meeting requirements
Day-care centers	453	185
Family day-care homes (includes care in the homes of relatives or friends)	105	17
In-home care	49	41
Totals	607	243

Source: "Review of Child Care Service Provided Under Title IV, Social Security Act," HEW Audit Agency, Office of the Assistant Secretary, Comptroller, p. 23.

CHART A

Summary of compliance to day-care center child/staff ratios requirements in Virginia, Missouri, and Washington

State and center	Age Group	Required ratio State	Required ratio Federal*	Ratio Observed
Virginia				
A	2-5	10:1	7:1	19:1
B	2-6	10:1	7:1	20:1
C	2-5	10:1	7:1	12:1
D	2-6	10:1	7:1	15:1
E	2-6	10:1	7:1	11:1
Missouri				
A	3-6	10:1	7:1	12:1
B	2-5	10:1	7:1	15:1
C	3-5	10:1	7:1	17:1
D	3-5	10:1	7:1	19:1
E	3-5	10:1	7:1	25:1
Washington				
A	4	10:1	7:1	16:1
B	3-5	10:1	7:1	14:1
C	4-5	10:1	7:1	16:1
D	5-6	10:1	7:1	15:1

* As previously indicated, FIDCR provides for child/staff ra-tios ranging from 5:1 to 10:1 depending upon the ages of the children—5:1 for 3 to 4 years olds; 7:1 for 4 to 6 years olds, and 10:1 for older children up to age 14. In case of overlapping age groups, we used the more liberal 7:1 ratio.
Source: "Review of Child Care Service Provided Under Title IV, Social Security Act," HEW Audit Agency, Office of the Assistant Secretary, Comptroller, p. 24.

CHART B

States reviewed	Number of facilities reviewed	Number of meeting child/ staff ratios	Number meeting health and safety requirements
Massachusetts	12	0	11
New Jersey	20	8	7
Virginia	75	20	17*
Georgia	12	11	9
Michigan	Compliance waived by SRS Regional Commissioner		
Texas	6	3	5
Missouri	40	7	27
California	330	123	279
Washington	607	71	70
Totals	112	243	425

* Records were not available to permit evaluation of health and safety compliance at 55 facilities.
Source: "Review of Child Care Service Provided Under Title IV, Social Security Act," HEW Audit Agency, Office of the

- Child abuse and neglect are widespread and growing problems among all social and economic groups.
- Teenage alcoholism and drug abuse are growing problems.
- One out of nine children will be in juvenile court before they reach the age of 18.
- Suicide is now the second leading cause of death for young Americans between ages 15 and 24.

And what leadership roles have federal, state, and local governments taken to help alleviate this growing crisis?

- HEW is currently spending only about 14 percent of its total budget on children.
- Children represent 40 percent of our population but receive only 10 percent out of every health-service dollar.
- Less than 1 percent of Revenue Sharing money has been spent by states and localities on children.

The costs of neglect are enormous. For the children, neglect means limited opportunities to develop, poor health, and limited opportunities to lead a happy and fruitful life. For society, neglect means expensive compensatory social-service and income-assisted programs.

The end result of all this is that the nation goes on year after year spending excessive time, money, and effort on the problems of juvenile delinquency and crime. We are looking in the wrong place for solutions to problems resulting from a generation of children growing up without proper supervision. The situation becomes a tragic absurdity when one compares the $4 billion a year cost to U.S. taxpayers of treating juvenile delinquency to the $400 million public investment in preventive child-care programs scattered about government agencies.

While Day Care Legislation cannot bear the entire burden of our problems, it can begin to change the continuing record of non-accomplishment. It can encourage programs such as the one now operating in California through the public schools which offers programs for all children regardless of income. We fully realize that a program of this scope cannot be accomplished overnight, especially in times of such economic hardship and budget shortages, but we should remember that means-tested programs available only to low- and no-income people have never evolved into universal, high quality, nondiscriminatory programs. Such programs have traditionally served poor people poorly and working people not at all. We should avoid the pitfalls of a poverty program and begin with a program open to all children that need the service. The time for these services is now and the institution to sponsor them is the schools.

We know that in a school system serving over 45 million students, there are instances of rigidity and failure, but we believe that critics have greatly distorted the state of education today. A resurgence of inservice and preservice reforms has occurred. Alternative schools, work-study and community-as-school programs, open education—all exist within the public schools. They do not exist everywhere because different communities have different needs. Yet the fact is, where the public wants change and works for change, the schools have responded. Placement of comprehensive child development in the schools would necessarily increase parental involvement and contact, thus enhancing the schools would welcome this opportunity to make the schools an even more integral part of our society. We believe that when the program does operate through the schools, they will.

Chapter 3

Reassessing Our Education Priorities

Burton White*

My purposes are to inform and attempt to influence you about a topic I think is of the highest priority in regard to national educational policy, our national resources and last, but far from least, the solidity of our young families. That topic is the role of the family in the education of a young child, particularly during the first three years of life.

My specialty is the study of what it takes to help each child make the most of whatever potential he brings into the world through the experiences of the first six years of life. That's my special role both as a member of the ECS Early Childhood Task Force and professionally. I believe that our current national educational policy is significantly flawed in this particular problem area, that we're wasting much of our most precious natural resource — the people of the next generation — and that we're allowing the quality of everyday life for many of our young families to be far more stressful and far less rewarding than it could be. An awful lot of our most able young women have a miserable average day with two young children; very few people realize this, and the last ones to know are their husbands.

I've been conducting research on the early educational development of children for about 16 years now. When I say conducting research I don't mean every few weeks for an hour or two; I mean that's *all* I've been doing. Seventy-five per cent of my professional time has been on direct empirical research on this topic. I've come to some central conclusions that cry out for a new look at our national educational policy.

First of all, children start to learn long before they enter our education system. Traditionally, in this country and in every other Western country where there has been any writing on the history of education, the society first puts money into the job when the children get to be about 6 years of age. No society has ever put a lot of money into the first years of life, as far as I can find in the literature. Yet everybody knows that children are learning from the fitst day they come into the world. Although they don't usually learn to read, write or cipher much before 5 or 6 years of age, they do start, or fail to start, to learn in more fundamental areas that seem to determine directly how well they will later learn to read, write and cipher. There are at least four fundamental learning topics that all children cope with before their third birthdays. These are not debatable points, by the way. First of all—language development. We have known for years that language growth starts and, in a large way, develops to a solid working capacity before the third birthday. Two- and three-month-old children don't process the meaning of words at all; at 6, 7, 8 months, they begin to understand the meaning of a few selected words — not surprisingly, words like their own name, Mommy, Daddy, kiss, bottle. That initial vocabulary is reasonably well understood. I think. By the time they're 3 years of age, most children have the capacity to understand most of the language they'll use in ordinary conversation for the rest of their lives.

Now language is at the heart of educational capacity. It has its own primary value and, in addition, an instrumental value of direct relevance to all intellectual learnings. Subtly, but just as importantly, it also underlies healthy social growth. Sociability in the first couple years of life depends for its good development on some capacities in the language area, particularly when it comes to other children.

The second major educational foundation that's undergoing development in this first three-year period is curiosity. What could be more important to whether a child learns anything — not just about academic subjects, but about the world at large, about what makes people tick, about how to become a good listener — than simple curiosity. It's the birthright of every child, with a few exceptions — the badly damaged children, for example, may have less of it. But even if a child comes from a bad home and is beaten regularly, it's very difficult to stamp out strong, basic, simple, pure curiosity in the first eight or nine months of life. It is, unfortunately, not that difficult to stamp it out in the next year or two or, if not stamp it out, suppress it dramatically or move it over into peculiar aberrant patterns. Take for example, the 2-year-old who looks at a new toy and, unlike other 2-year-olds, sizes it up mainly to see how he can use it to badger his mother. That's not sheer unqualified curiosity. That can also be very tough on a young mother, by the way.

*Burton White, Director, Preschool Project, Harvard Graduate School of Education. Reprinted with the permission of the Education Commission of the States.

Third major point — social development. In the last five or six years we've begun to apply a little more serious attention to the value of social goals for our educational system, although we're still limping along in this area. For years we've had soft-hearted early-education people saying a child is more than a brain, but they have seldom been listened to because most of them don't have doctorates and most of them don't have the gift of gab. I personally believe, and have a lot of research evidence to support it, that the social skills that develop in the first preschool years are every bit as important, every bit as instrumental, to the intellectual success of a student, for example, as the directly intellectual skills. Moreover, I think a lot of people in this country would be happier if the children we produced were not only bright but were people with whom they liked to live.

We are pretty clear now on the details of social development; we know that human infants won't survive without some sort of strong, protective attachment to an older, more mature, more capable human. And God or somebody else built into the creature a collection of attributes — tools, actually — that help in the cementing of a relationship to somebody.

For instance, that early social smile of the 3-month-old is not reserved for any particular person. It looks as if the child is using it on everyone who happens by. It's as if the species had a kind of first-stage guarantee of attractiveness. The 3- and 4-month-old child is an incredibly attractive, nice-to-live-with creature. He starts to giggle and becomes ticklish for the first time; he's given to euphoria a great deal. Now that's fun, and the photographers like it a great deal, but I think there's a more serious species-survival virtue to this particular kind of phenomenon.

Then, between 8 months and 24 months or so, there takes place one of the most gorgeous experiences you'll ever see. The child establishes a relationship—usually to the mother, because most of our children are still being brought up in homes by their own families. This is an incredibly complicated relationship, making most contracts pale in simplicity in comparison to it. The child learns thousands of things about what he can and can't do in his home, what he can and can't do in interactions with the primary caretaker, about how to read her different mood states, and an incredible number of other things. After all, little children have relatively little in the way of important obligations other than just enjoying themselves, and one of the few really overpowering interests of the child 8 to 24 months of age is that other key figure.

We have seen children at age 2 who are marvelous people to live with; they are free and easy; they are comfortable with their parents; they have gone by the negativism of the second year pretty well. They can play alone well. They are just a delight. On the other hand, how many times have you heard a mother of a 2-year old say he doesn't play alone

well? That's synonymous for he's hanging onto my skirt or my slacks or my legs all day long. That situation can be very rough, especially if there is another child, 8 months of age, crawling around in the home simultaneously. When we see a child for the first time at 2 years of age, it's too late. They are crystallized into their basic social counters in the next year or two — to other children who come into the home, to older siblings, to other adults. A human personality is being formed during those first two years, and there is no job more important than doing that well.

Over and above that primal social development, we have the foundations of intelligence. There are all sorts of problems children can't solve in the first two or three years of life, but they are learning the tools of the trade, and this process is beautifully and brilliantly explained, in detail, in the work of Jean Piaget, the Swiss student of the growth of intelligence. From the very first years, children are very much interested in cause-and-effect relationships, in learning about simple mechanisms such as jack-in-the-boxes and flipping light switches on and off to see the consequences. Such events are trivial little things on the surface, but they indicate a very deep interest in how things work and in the various characteristics of physical objects. After all, these children haven't had a chance to examine many things first-hand, and most things, therefore, are new to them.

Now, these four topic areas are, I submit, the foundations of educational capacity. I'll repeat them: language development, curiosity, social development and the roots of intelligence. They are all undergoing basic formative development in the first three years of life, and the national education system essentially ignores that fact.

These fundamental learnings do not always go well. Indeed, there's reason to believe that failures in these learnings in the first years lead directly to underachievement in the elementary grades and beyond. We're getting there after the horse has left the barn.

Moreover, poor results or failures in the first years are extremely difficult to correct using any means we now have available. I'll repeat that because it's a very strong statement and I think I can support it — poor results or failures in the first three years are extremely difficult to correct using any means now available, be it $10,000 a year spent in a private tutoring situation or a Head Start or a Follow Through or a special education program.

In addition, relatively few of our children, regardless of the type of family that raises them—and that includes your families and mine, your grandchildren and mine—get as much out of the education of the first years as they might. We are probably wasting substantial amounts of our most precious resource, the developed competencies of each new generation.

Can I back up these claims, or am I just another in a long list of education sensationalists?

Point one: Children who enter the first grade significantly behind their peers are not likely ever to catch up. There are exceptions, but the norm is that they fall further behind. This has been recognized educationally for a long time.

Let me tell you a little story about the origination of the Brookline Early Education Project. The superintendent of schools in Brookline, Mass., who's a very smart and vigorous fellow, called me one day and said, "I've been reading things like Benjamin Bloom's statement that most of intelligence is already developed by the time the child is 8, and that half of it is in by 4. I put that idea together with the experience we have in our school system [where, by the way, next year they have budgeted $2,600 for each child at the high school level and $2,000 for the elementary level]. I think I have a pretty good school system," he went on. "But I know that when I get a child in the first grade who already looks weak, I can't do much for him, even though I have one of the best special ed programs in the country."

Now as a reasonable man, he is driven to consideration of the topic of prevention. He has no choice. In fact, it's the same reasoning that led to the creation of Head Start. But here is a fellow who has no excuses — he has first-rate people, he has more money than God and he still cannot do the job.

He said, "I want to recommend that all kids get into our schools at age 4. What do you think of that as a good way to get into this problem?" I said, "That's a dumb idea." He said, "What do you mean? People have been telling me that public kindergarten is a great thing for all these years." I said, "Look, don't spend all your money on an expensive kindergarten program. Half or more of your kids are not going to get much out of it educationally, in my opinion. Take a look at what is going on in the first six years, not just in the fifth year. Try to get at the origin of educational deficits; try to prevent them. Try to help earlier in the game." And so we built the Brookline program.

Second point: The country has been working on prevention for nine years now in a very substantial way. Head Start's original central purpose, I remind you, was to prevent educational failure. Now, it has had lots of other purposes that have grown in emphasis in the last four or five years—better early health care, better social and emotional development. But don't you forget that the original rhetoric that sold Head Start was to try to prevent educational failure. That has been its core purpose. It has had a budget, most of you know, of several hundred million dollars a year, and it's been politically powerful. It has concentrated on the 3- to 5-year age period.

There are two conclusions I think can be easily drawn from the Head Start experience (so far) that are appropriate to this discussion: First, it doesn't often succeed in its prime goal (no matter what somebody working in a center tells you). The best objective evaluation of Head Start is that by and large, by itself, it hasn't had much success in preventing educational failure in the elementary grades. Second, serious deficits for many children are usually already visible at 3 years of age.

Point three: Except for the fewer than five per cent of our children born with serious defects or subjected to extreme abuse during the first year of life, serious educational deficits are not usually seen before 18 months of age. This point comes out of the educational and psychological research literature. The same children who are going to give you endless problems in the third grade look fine at age 1.

Point four: Educational failure begins to show itself toward the end of the second year of life. It is often very reliably detected at 3 years of age and nearly always detectable well before the first grade. Furthermore, educational underachievement by children who look average or slightly above average is quite likely, but has not really been investigated in a serious way as yet. After all, the emergency situation, as always, comes first.

What causes low achievement levels in children? Can we as educators do anything about this problem, or are genetics, for example, at the root of the problem? The question is a very complicated one, and I can't deal with it elaborately here. But I will summarize my position on the issue. We have no conclusive evidence as yet as to how much achievement is due to heredity and how much is due to environment. We have fragments of evidence, but nothing like the weight of evidence needed to resolve that issue on a scientific basis. My personal judgment is simply that both heredity and environment obviously play a role. Heredity certainly sets upper limits to development, but by itself it doesn't guarantee that those limits will be reached. If a child is seriously brain damaged, no matter how you work on his early education, he is never going to achieve the levels that an intact, well-educated child will. But if a child comes into the world with great genes, he is not going to make the most of that potential irrespective of what happens to him subsequently. By controlling his experiences, I can prevent any child in the world from learning to talk, I can prevent him from acquiring any of his skills.

Of course those are just the extreme cases. But my point is that so far we really haven't thoroughly understood what it takes to help each child make the most of the potential he has. We have no right to assume that, by hook or by crook, children are doing that. In fact, we have plenty of evidence that suggests that they are not. I've done more direct research on the role of experience in early development than all but a handful of people in the country, and I'm convinced of the power and relevance of early experiences in this area. Certainly until we have definite evidence to the contrary, the most sensible policy is to assume that early experience makes important differences and to do everything we can to make such experiences as beneficial as possible.

For now, let me point out that there seem to be at least three major obstacles that families face in doing the best job of educating their young children. But let me digress for just a moment. I very much endorse the concept that we are wasting resources and the need for public education. In terms of developmental day care it generally costs more than $3,000 per year, and it can go higher. I agree that this country is not going to make that kind of money available in the near future for all the kids who ought to have it or who need it.

The three major obstacles, then, that I see families coping with in trying to do the best they can for their children are: First of all, ignorance. They don't know how to do the job. They don't know, for example, about the poison-control data that says that most of our reported poisonings in childhood take place between 10 and 30 months of age. More importantly, they don't know why such poisonings take place at that age. They don't know that babies in that age range are incredibly curious, are inclined to use the mouth as an exploring organ and are unsophisticated about labels that have warnings on them.

Parents don't know the story of social development. They don't know, for example, that to be a 9-month-old *only* child means to live in a world that is full of happiness, sweetness, pleasant interpersonal relations. On the other hand, to have an older sibling at home who is 2 years old almost invariably means being on the receiving end of genuine hatred from time to time.

Now that sounds funny, but boy I'll tell you, it's a sad thing to watch a 9- or 10-month-old baby, when his mother isn't looking, trying to put up with the real physical threats of a 2- or 2½-year-old child who had previously thought the whole world was built for him. Now he's got to share it with this creature that's into his toys, that seems to have first place in his mother's affections, and so forth. It is painful for everybody. The older child is having a very tough time; the younger one is having a tough time and may be experiencing things that I don't think anybody should have to experience, if we can avoid it. The mother may be having the worst time of all. Some women spend the whole day trying to control two such children, trying to avoid the destruction of the baby; and the father comes home at night and wonders why the mother is tired. The simple fact is we don't prepare or assist people for this job. As long as you can mate, you are eligible to have a child and the responsibilities that go along with it. That's absolutely crazy.

The second major obstacle for parents is stress. The 8- to 24-month period is not only educationally critical, in my opinion, but it's also one of the most dangerous periods in life. I would guess that there is no period of life that is more dangerous in terms of maimings and accidental deaths.

Take, for example, an 8-month-old child who, for the previous three months or so, has had mature visual and auditory capacities, but hasn't been able to move his body anywhere. Move him to an upright posture, he can see out into the room. It's a new world for him; no matter how poor it is, it's all new to him, and somehow or other his species requires that he learn as much as he can during his early developmental years. Think of how much curiosity is building up inside that mind. Then all of a sudden he discovers he can get from here to there—and he goes. It's a very rare child who doesn't go. Children at this age are very much like puppies, kittens, even young horses I've been told, in their pure, unadorned curiosity. It's necessary for the species.

They go, but they don't know anything at all about the world. They don't know that if you lean on something very spindly, it will fall; they don't know that those beautiful rose-colored shards of glass from a broken vase are dangerous. Everything looks interesting, and one of the prime ways in which they explore something first hand is to immediately put it to the mouth. They are very impulsive at that age; they do not stop to smell, to savor or to sip; they just bring it quickly to the mouth.

We have to tell parents about these things. Why should they learn these things after they go to the pediatrician to have a child's stomach pumped? These aren't controversial matters. There's a lot of controversy in this field about some topics, such as how you should rear children, whether you should teach them to read at nine months, whether you should be stroking their limbs at four months for "tactile stimulation." There's a lot of controversy in that area, but there isn't any about safety.

Every family should know how to safety-proof a home for the child's first crawling efforts. Every family should know that a baby starts to climb at about 8 or 9 months of age, can generally only climb six or seven inches at that point, but by the time he's a year old will be able to climb units of 12 to 14 inches, which means that he can climb almost anything in a room. That sequence has very powerful everyday consequences for a family. It should be common knowledge. Why is learning to drive a car so much more important than learning how to parent a child? Does the high school curriculum have room for driver ed and no room for these topics?

Not only are the first years a dangerous period of life, but they mean extra work. The child crawling around the home makes a mess, and if your husband likes a neat home, that adds to the stress. In addition, if there's an older child who is less than three years older than the child, it's quite normal for there to be significant resentment on the part of the older child, and that also adds to the stress on the mother. Furthermore, when the child gets to be 16 or 17 months of age he starts testing his power with his mother. That's quite routine; almost everybody goes through it.

Some people find this very tough to take. So, there is a lot of stress involved in raising a young child, and raising two or three closely spaced ones creates almost an intolerable amount. Sometimes it is not tolerated, and women crack up and marriages crack up.

Third obstacle: lack of assistance. Mother usually faces this job alone.

So the three obstacles I see through our research are, first, ignorance—they aren't prepared for the job, they aren't knowledgeable, indeed there's an awful lot of mis-information around; second, stress; and third, lack of assistance. That is a tough collection of obstacles to get through.

If there is a role for education, what is it? We must accept the fact that professional educators, working directly with children, especially children over 6 years of age, have much less influence on development than was previously thought. This is, by the way, the major implication of the 1966 U.S. Office of Education report by James Coleman, *Equality of Educational Opportunity*.

I remember a poignant story about a teacher in IS 201 in the heart of New York about six or seven years ago describing his classroom, a third-grade classroom. He said that at no time could he count on more than 30 per cent of the youngsters to be in their seats, and at no time could he count on more than half of them to even be in the room. And he said, "Somehow or other, I'm not doing well in that class." And I said, "How on earth can you expect to do well in that class?" I think teachers have been taking a terribly bad rap in this country. Educating a child is a partnership between the family and the professional educator. I think the senior partner is the family.

The second thing educators must do is recognize that the family ordinarily is the first educational delivery system for the child and seriously accept and face the consequences of that fact.

Third, we should prepare and assist the family for that fundamental educational job.

How do we prepare and assist the family to give the child a solid educational foundation? Here are a couple of suggestions.

Item one: Long before the child is born, we should teach each and every prospective parent all the known and accepted fundamentals about educational development in the first years of life. How do we do this? I would suggest through required courses in the high schools and, second, through public television. I would also suggest that neither of these vehicles costs a great deal. We might delete the geography of India for a year or for one semester.

Item two: Just before and soon after the baby is born is a special time. A lot of parents are traumatized. They suddenly come face to face with the reality that they've got the responsibility for this fragile little thing and they don't know what they're going to do. That can be a very tough experi-

ence. I've had lots of young parents express that fear spontaneously to me. Suggestion: Teach each and every parent whom you missed the first time around the same information and routinely provide refresher information to the remainder. How? Offer adult education courses, year in and year out, for pregnant women and their husbands. Perhaps provide the video-cassette or filmed minicourses in hospitals during the lying-in period. That's being done in Hawaii, by the way. Most of these things are being done somewhere in the country. Provide high-quality public television material on a continuous basis. There's no reason why it cannot be done. I'm involved in commercial television right now, talking about educating an infant. It works well. The viewing audience is dedicated; they watch that program like hawks. If I say something wrong, they're right on it. It can be done, and it can be fun, too.

In addition, just before or soon after the child is born, provide a low-cost education early detection and referral service to every family, with a promise that if a family participates, its children cannot go through the preschool years with an undetected educational handicap. You can make that promise and you can deliver on it for about $200 per year for a child.

Item three: After the child is born, for his first six years of life, especially the first three, I suggest the following: make available continuing, low-pressure, strictly voluntary training for parents. How? Through resource centers and a home-visiting program. I'm talking, you'll notice, about working through the family, not bypassing it and going directly to the child. Provide for monitoring educational development as an extension of that early detection and referral system, again through medical psychology and educational teamwork in resource centers, for about $200 a year.

Provide general assistance for parenting, again with a focus on education, in the following ways: Lend materials like toys and books out of your resource center. Have films and pamphlets available. Have professionals available for parents to talk with once in a while. Have other parents available so that people can talk to each other about their frustations and their joys.

Provide free baby-sitting for psychological relief for parents. This is not day care; I'm talking about a few hours a week when a mother can just leave her child without guilt, and just get away.

On the other hand, a home-visiting service, especially for families who want it and who have a little more difficulty with their children and fewer resources than average, again does not have to be a frightfully expensive affair. We find if you go very often to a home, more than every two or three weeks, it gets uncomfortable. There is not enough to do for most families; so if you go for an hour or two every six, seven or eight weeks we guess that's plenty. These kinds of programs are nowhere near as expensive as running a conventional center; nothing like it.

Item Four: Provide referral service for special needs, an ombudsman function. How do you do it? Through neighborhood resource centers. Provide remedial assistance as soon as possible. If an early detection program finds a borderline hearing difficulty in a 6-month-old child, we can do things about that today. It's scandalous for this country to continue to let some fraction of our children go through primary language acquisition with untreated, unnoticed hearing deficits. The screening examination can be done for $15 or so and the occasional higher level diagnosis will cost $50 to $75. But what an investment!

I think it's fair to say that the entire task force of the ECS Early Childhood Project agrees with the general desirability of strengthening the family ofr its role as the child's first educational delivery system. Exactly how far to go in

terms of dollars per year, of course, is not fully agreed upon. I suggested to you that for an expenditure of perhaps $300 or $400 per year we probably could do the bulk of what needs doing on this topic for most families (not for the very special-need families; they are a much more expensive proposition). Exactly which ideas to use, again, are not fully agreed upon, but I submit to you that there is a core of fundamental information about safety, about social development, about motor development that most people do agree on, and that such information could be very, very useful to young families. Much needed assistance is feasible today. You could spend $1,000 a year for an average family, but I think you could do it quite nicely for $400 or $500. And there just isn't a better way to spend that money than to invest in improving the quality of our earliest educational system.

Eugenia S. Ware

Chapter 4

Public Policy and Early Childhood Education: A Buddhist Garden

Edwin W. Martin*

Public policy in the area of provision of preschool and early childhood services seems destined to be based on the same assumptions that my wife and I use in what she has called our Buddhist approach to gardening. That is, we begin with a reverence for all living things, and then we allow them to grow around our house as they will. I can report to you that this approach involves a minimum of prior planning, that the results are judged to be uneven at best by third-party evaluators, and that later revisions are costly and difficult.

I am tempted to say that I am here today to raise some questions about delivery systems for early childhood education. For example, who shall be responsible? Should our goal be to develop a publicly supported delivery system, or should we assume an essential role for the private sector in our planning for full services for all children? Should we assign responsibility to a single public agency, or should we assume that employing many agencies will provide "creative pluralism" or will allow "flexibility"?

I am going to resist attempting to pass myself off as a neutral statesman, dispassionately raising these questions, merely to assure that those of you legislators, state executives and board members who create public policy would be sure to attend to these important concerns. Not only do many of you know that I am a constitutionally predetermined advocate-type, but I feel my label as an education official might seem to mar my credibility as a dispassionate observer.

So, here are my propositions:

1. Public policymakers should "bite the bullet" and begin the process of making a specific decision about where the responsibility for early childhood education services should be lodged. No more Buddhist gardening.

2. Public policy must be based on the assumption of equal access for all children and so a public system must be developed based on this "zero reject" concept. Private agencies can offer alternatives for those who can afford them, or serve as subcontractors for the public agency.

3. A single public agency should be charged with the primary responsibility.

4. That agency should be the public education agency.

Now, I am tempted to sit down, or perhaps go home, rather than elaborate, but I warned you about my incurable

advocacy impulses. Actually, lecturing a group of early childhood specialists and policymakers about early childhood policy making, reminds me of the time Robert Kennedy, then attorney general, came to speak at the University of Alabama, soon after the governor had stood in the gymnasium door, (euphemistically known as a schoolhouse, but more accurately the site of registration activities). The governor was incensed by the attorney general's visit—to say nothing of how he felt about the university for inviting him—and said it "was like inviting the fox into the chicken coop," a metaphor that was met with mixed enthusiasm by the university community. When at last Kennedy stood safely on the stage inside the notorious Foster Auditorium, he made note of the governor's remarks, saying that he felt, "more like the chicken in a fox coop." I think you can see the parallel between his feelings and mine.

My first proposition, concerning the need for a decision, is based on the belief that we will have universal preschool and early education, and that we will evolve into it in a somewhat random fashion by extending public school programs by expanding Head Start, by developing new federal initiatives in family and child services such as those proposed by the recently reintroduced Mondale and Brademas bills, by developing new state offices of child or human development, by developing day care centers and community health and mental health programs, and by working with a variety of private profit and nonprofit agencies.

I think such a development process will result in all of the problems we now see in many of our government programs: conflicting responsibilities and assumptions, duplication and overlap, gaps and unevenness of access, wide variations in quality of services, etc.—a litany you surely know as well as I. Further, we are dealing with a tremendously large potential population; 17.2 million children between birth and 5 years of age, and 20 million more between 5 and 9, to mark arbitrary end points. I believe it is accurate to say that no formalized public-service delivery system other than the schools deals with such a large population and its attendant logistical problems.

*Edwin W. Martin, Acting Deputy Commissioner, Bureau of Education for the Handicapped, U.S. Office of Education. Reprinted with the permission of the Education Commission of the States.

Governors, legislators, public officials and even we professionals must face this issue squarely and establish firm patterns for the development of services. Further, every effort must be made to provide a basis for coherent federal planning.

My further propositions merge into the proposal that the public education agency be identified as the lead agency, or primary provider of services. I am aware that this proposal, while somewhat more acceptable than Jonathan Swift's "Modest Proposal" that citizens eat their babies as a solution to food supply and population problems, still will have its antagonists in two major groups—first, those child development specialist who operate in nonpublic school environments and, second, those persons who run the schools—or to be more fair, perhaps some substantial part of each group.

But the needs for coherent public policy must outweigh the provincial concerns of special-interest groups. If the school administrators or school boards are reluctant to take on this role, but we believe it to be in the public interest, this reluctance can be overcome. Recent examples that come to mind include providing educational opportunity for black and for handicapped children.

The fact is that there are many reasons for policymakers to consider the schools as the preferred service delivery mechanism. Without elaborating, let me name a few. There is a broad local and state fiscal base already extant that is designated for these basic purposes, i.e., the development and enhancement of the child's potential through the process we can define "broadly" as education. There are examples, already, of basing support for early childhood education on adaptations of state-aid formulas for education. There are buildings and the capacity for financing new construction or for remodeling exists. Further, the decline in birth rate is already reducing the crowding in many schools and this pattern seems likely to continue. Although many early childhood programs, such as home-based programs, would not need school building space, still others could use such facilities and are now housed in substandard facilities.

In addition, the public education system has the capacity to set standards, to certify, regulate, etc. While we are aware of the dangers of "over credentialing," appropriate standards will be desirable. The capacity to train educators and specialists is in place, and it, too, is seeking new avenues for development. I am not suggesting simply retraining "surplus" teachers, although many good early childhood specialists might be found in such populations; rather I am looking toward the capabilities of universities to develop new and effective early childhood education training programs to meet the changing demands of their students.

Finally, the schools are already moving in the direction of providing early childhood services, particularly in relation to services for handicapped children. Several states now mandate the provision of education, including compre-

hensive services, to handicapped children from age 3, and a number have provided what we call permissive legislation—that is, local districts may provide and be reimbursed for programs beginning as soon after birth as a child may be identified as handicapped.

These efforts are in the early stages, but they show a rapid growth rate. The evidence that effective programming can ameliorate or prevent later educational handicaps is such that we have made stimulating such programming a major priority of the U.S. Office of Education. In short, it seems likely that the public schools will offer preschool services to all handicapped children within the foreseeable future. Will some other agency provide parallel services to nonhandicapped children with all the attendent problems of continuity of programming when the youngsters reach school age? I hope not.

In identifying the schools as the prime service delivery agency, I recognize that many of the children we hope to serve will require what we have come to call "comprehensive" programs—that is, they will require special attention to their nutritional needs, health needs, etc. Further, a basic direction for such programming seems to require a major emphasis on strengthening the ability of the family to help meet the multiple needs of the child, rather than trying to replace the family with a social agency. I see none of this as inconsistent with the future role of schools as a total community resource. For example, the education system already has accepted the responsibility for responding to the nutritional needs of children, and there is increasing concern about improving the quality of the health-delivery system within the schools. I do not foresee the school system as necessarily having to supply all health and related services, but it can certainly take on the role of assisting and aiding parents in the location and receipt of needed services.

A recent study done by Rand for the U.S. Department of Health, Education and Welfare described the need for such "direction" centers, as they called them, as being a paramount concern if we are to respond appropriately to an estimated population of nine million children with various handicapping conditions, to say nothing of perhaps an equal number of nonhandicapped, economically disadvantaged youngsters with similar needs.

Among our objectives for improved services for handicapped children will be to encourage through model programs, and through the use of other federal funds, the development of identification and appraisal programs, direction centers and full educational programs for youngsters beginning as early in life as feasible. We have learned from many of our efforts for handicapped children that the tools and skills of the special education profession are most effective for dealing with nonhandicapped children as well.

In sum, we will be working to build comprehensive programs within the schools that will provide a basis for high-quality services for handicapped children beginning very early in life. I see no reason why these goals for the school system should be limited to services for handicapped children and should not be seen as the basis for similar programming for all children.

The "clear and present danger," to coin a phrase, is that those of us who see ourselves as the creators of public policy will continue a laissez-faire attitude, immobilized between various pressure groups and restrained by budgetary problems. This will lead us to all the problems in this area to which I have referred and to much rhetoric about wasteful duplication, overlap, etc. Study commissions will be appointed to see how to coordinate programs; new offices will be proposed, perhaps sitting right in the governor's anteroom to be sure they will have sufficient "clout," and so on.

In summary, then, while it may be fair enough to say to the public, "I never promised you a rose garden," I don't think we want to deliver them a Buddhist garden instead.

American Federation of Teachers

Chapter 5

Early Childhood Education: A Field in Search of Itself

Russell C. Doll and Beth Koelker*

I. Introduction

Early childhood education (ECE) today is an anomolistic mixture of many disciplines set in an equally anomolistic mixture of operational settings. At present, the early childhood educator can be a practitioner, theoretician, or policy maker from disciplines as wide ranging as physiology, psychology, nutrition, human development, sociology, family studies, and education. In its operation ECE includes a bewildering number of forms and settings such as day care centers, pre-schools, nursery schools, educational centers, Head start programs, experimental programs, all guided by an equally bewildering diversity of philosophies and goals. The term early childhood *education*, as it implies a formalized type of education, is probably a misnomer in many cases. It is a term used in conjunction with too many different programs, types of facilities and too many people doing various things to and with young children.

Distinctions which get at substantive differences between *simple, random experiences* per se and experiences structured towards *educational goals* are needed if ECE is to develop into a "field" which has its own identity. For example, it would be difficult to use the word education with "programs" which merely herd children together and let them fend for themselves under minimal guidance and which provide no meaning to the experiences. But programs offering experiences which are shared with other students and the teacher, often on a one to one basis, may justifiably use the word education, for it is here where the "experiences" have a greater chance to become "educational" for the child.

The situation is no different regarding the role of an early childhood educator. Despite attempts to bring order to the "field" through closer examination of what such a role entails and what kinds of training and skills are needed, the situation remains ambiguous. Some reasonable restrictions and enforcable standards are needed to ensure that qualified people deal with young children. In too many cases people having little but a willingness to interact with young children are considered capable of providing early childhood education and assume the role of early childhood educator in pre-schools, day care centers and educational centers.

The meaning of ECE, and the task of the early childhood educator, varies with the speaker or the article one is reading. It is a situation similar to Alice's when she spoke with Humpty Dumpty. If a word meant whatever Humpty wanted it to, then the practice of, ideas of, and goals of ECE often mean whatever the speaker, or designer of programs wants it to mean.

II. Common Settings for Early Childhood Education

Despite the many specific variations there are at least five "types" of settings in which ECE takes place, or is claimed to take place. Although each setting can be seen as unique there is some overlap in activities within some of the settings.

Kindergartens: Usually a school for children five years old. The age deadline is determined by the legal age legislated for entry into first grade minus one year. Sessions in most Kindergartens run three hours per day, five days per week. The teacher is usually licensed. Programs are generally formulated by individual teachers although many public schools now tend to begin the "3R's" in Kindergarten rather than in first grade.

Day Care Centers or Child Care Centers: These centers provide full day care (Approximately 7 a.m. to 6 p.m.) for children of working parents. Operating expenses are met through parental fees and/or government or philanthropic support. Some extended day care is available for school-aged children before and after school while parents work. The first priority of the day or child care center is to provide the child with a safe environment, nourishment and rest. The second priority (although not an element in many centers) is the education of the young child. These centers are often understaffed and unable to provide the educational program they wish to offer. The demand for full day care is constantly increasing as mothers seek to gain full-time employment.

Nursery Schools or Preschools: The children in the Nursery or Preschool programs range from ages 2-½ to 5.

*Dr. Russel Doll, Professor of Education, University of Missouri, Kansas City. Beth Koelker, Assistant professor of Education, University of Missouri, Kansas City.

The sessions extend for a morning or afternoon (about two to three hours per day). The number of days attended varies from two to five per week. Another term for these schools is Pre-Kindergarten. This term implies greater educational content as the priority in contrast to Day Care Centers where custodial care is the priority. The head teacher is usually licensed and the schools are typically private, running solely on fees paid by parents. Morrison, however, makes a distinction between nursery school and preschool with nursery school referring to an educational program for children 2-½ to 5-½ years which is operated as a service by public schools, or for profit by other agencies and individuals. Pre-school refers to any educational program prior to first grade. (Morrison, 1976)

Early Childhood Education Centers: These centers combine the services of the child care centers and the preschool. Additional staff and facilities are required to provide these educational services simultaneously with the necessary care services. Often these centers double as laboratory schools at universities and community colleges where teacher preparation programs and research can be performed. The teachers are usually licensed or in the training program. Fees are charged to parents in line with the typical day care rate for the area.

Model Centers: Model centers are funded by grants from various organizations to provide a testing ground for new programs. A particular researcher or program planner will conceive a specific model program he/she wishes to develop on a trial basis. Here innovative ideas and philosophies in ECE are born. Emphases vary among these programs (e.g. cognitively oriented, socially oriented) with teachers being specifically trained in the aspects of each project. Fees vary according to stipulations incorporated into each grant.

III. Specific Problems

A. Age

The major settings are rather clearly defined and provide a macro framework within which specific aspects of ECE may vary. One such specific is the minimum and maximum age levels at which a child enters ECE. Unlike the more clearly defined entry ages of the elementary and secondary schools, ECE varies as to age at "entrance" depending upon the definition of ECE chosen by each institution.

Usually most of the children addressed by ECE programs are under age eight. The maximum grade level is usually no higher than third. McClure and Pence think that ECE describes *formal* schooling under age six. (McClure, 1970) *The Encyclopedia of Education* has two to eight years as the range of ECE (Deighton, 1971) while the Educational Resources Information and Referral Center collects their ECE documents from birth through the primary grades. Morrison sees early childhood as the period from conception to age eight. (Morrison, 1976)

B. Multi-Perspective Influences

Age ambiguity is not a problem in and of itself. General agreement as to the age at which ECE begins will eventually develop as licensing requirements push for some kind of uniformity. Agreement will also develop as early childhood educators see the need for common definition simply to facilitate communication. The age discrepencies are important, however, as indicators of possible conflict among those interested in ECE as primarily a *human development* process (in a physiological sense) and those viewing ECE as primarily an educational process (in an instructive sense).

For example, the selection of birth as the minimum point for some settings and programs was influenced by those interested in human development. (Hess & Bear, 1968) Research in fields of nutrition, neuro-chemistry, neurology, bio-chemistry, and physiology are providing critical findings and arguments for including the development of physiological foundations for cognitive and emotional growth as part of ECE. (Essman & Nakajma, 1973; Lichtenbert & Norton, 1972; Nurnberger, 1973; Richardson, 1973) Such things as pre-natal care and the education of the mother-and-father-to-be are also beginning to be considered as a legitimate part of ECE. (Barratta-Lorton, 1975; Campbell & Everett, 1974; Evans, 1971; Seefeldt, 1974)

The total impact of this emphasis on human development will certainly benefit the child but such an eclectic approach pushes the idea of ECE beyond the five major settings mentioned earlier. It may also necessitate clearer distinctions being drawn between the "field" of ECE *as education* and ECE as *human development*. These distinctions are ultimately going to influence career patterns as well as programmatic concentration, curriculum and even future training requirements.

The human development/education differences will certainly surface in regard to funding of research and programs and has already caused some controversy between legislators and early childhood educators. This was evidenced in John Brademas's caustic reply to criticisms of the Comprehensive Child Development Bill and the Hewitt Report by some psychologists interested in early childhood education. Brademas stated that though a provision of the bill and report dealt with ECE the title of the bill included the word *Development* and the development provisions of the bill were not the provience of the critics so their criticisms were not appropriate. (Brademas, 1972; Moore, Moon & Moore, 1972)

C. Education/Experiences

Potential problems in the development of ECE as a "field" are found not only in the blurring between "education" and "human development" but between programs in ECE which emphasize *education* and those which offer primarily early childhood *experiences*. The distinctions are important.

The emphasis on education as the determinate word in a program tends to define a particular setting and process. Using the term education implies a kind of teaching/learning relationship developed through a variety of experiences. But these experiences have an ultimate goal such as a skill development or an outcome of some kind whether cognitive, social, or emotional, which was pre-determined by the educational experience. In these cases teachers are keenly aware that their job is to enhance and build upon the spontaneous chance learning in every child's choice of activity. Although these kinds of programs are not necessarily highly structured or strongly academically oriented, the goal is a definable and possibly measurable growth in skills or outcomes. In these settings and programs the word *"education"* in ECE is probably not a misnomer.

But there are hundreds, of settings and programs which, by self definition, are ECE but in which the emphasis is on a radomized variety of experiences, the experience being an end in itself. Any skills develop serindipitously. For example, a trip to the zoo may be taken as a "fun" trip but with no follow-up and no systematic attempt to develop general skills of contrast and differentiation through contrasting, let us say, the tiger and the leopard. In a setting which utilizes fun experiences as education and the children would have fun at the zoo but also be guided in the small and large discrimination tasks. In the "experience" settings the word "education" is probably a misnomer.

As ECE begins to define itself as a field it can no longer ignore what seems to be minor differences. These are differences which will inevitably enter into the question of "legitimacy" of practice which is always an issue as fields begin to develop. For example, in one directory there are 2,000 listings of ECE programs. Some of these programs are "educational", as defined above, others "experimental", others "experiential" and still others in which it is anyone's guess. There is a mind boggling array of philosophies, objectives, experiences, and curriculums. (LaCrosse, E. Robert, 1971) From this potpourri of programs it seems that the "field" of ECE becomes anything dealing with young children.

D. Custodial Care/Education

The development of ECE into a distinctive "field" necessitates the drawing of harder distinctions between programs which offer "custodial" care and those providing guided "education" of young children. For many, custodial care "means" education.

One writer, in all seriousness, makes the statement. . . "care is education," (Doherty, 1976) which is like saying that putting random letters on paper is writing. In a far fetched sense this is correct. But if writing is everything put to paper then the term "writing" as a discipline or field means nothing. So with ECE. If one accepts care, and caretaking situations, nursery schools or day care centers as early childhood education then the term education is devalued. If everything is ECE, then ECE is nothing.

The result of all this is a general tendency to accept *anything* as ECE as long as it deals with young children. The continuing tendency to accept almost anything dealing with young children as ECE will eventually make the development of a "field" of ECE impossible.

E. Problems in Priorities

Ironically early childhood educators themselves seem to be abetting the confusion. They not only seem willing to accept as ECE the widest possible diversity of settings and programs, but they seem confused as to priorities to be addressed in the development of a "field". In one State Report on ECE no less than 152 priorities were listed under major topic headings such as Standards and Certification, Programs, Professionals, Family and Health. (Doherty, 1976) Examinations of priorities from other states show a similar voluminous listing as does a listing of priorities by the Federal Government.

Today ECE seems to be at a point Elementary Education was at in the late 1800's and Secondary Education in the 1920's. Both were battling for public acceptance and funding and both were determining their common denominators. Only after a long period of internal struggle and external assistance by social and philosophical changes in labor and politics were the multitude of priorities consolidated into a general agreed upon form which defined the fields. Undoubtedly ECE will begin to evolve in the same fashion. The question is whether or not the social influences are such that they encourage the development of ECE into a "field" similar to elementary or secondary education.

IV. Social Influences

The changes in attitudes and social thought of the 1960's may hinder ECE from developing into as well defined a field as elementary or secondary education. These changes weakened the public's confidence in the "formal" school and encouraged the use of minimally trained volunteers and parents. (Friedenberg, 1967; Hentoff, 1966; Kozol, 1967) Further, the changing role of middle-income women has increased the need for custodial centers in which "education" plays a minor part (Rossi, 1971).

A Minimally Trained Adults

The acceptance by the public, and those in ECE, of day care centers, pre-schools, nursery schools, and programs providing "good" experiences for children is being influenced in great part, by the above social changes. One can offer children a roof over their heads, some fun and games, a cot to nap on, crackers, cheese, and juice and volunteer "teachers" and still be on the side of the angels. Just label it a Peoples Preschool, or Natures-Own-Day-Care, or Wee-Ones Playhouse, and the liberated mother, the blue collar working mother, the lazy mother, and other mothers, will leave their children in good faith.

Many of the facilities of the type mentioned above, as well as more formalized ECE programs, are moving toward volunteer assistance, a practical and valuable, but nevertheless chancy practice. It is based partly on the commonly held belief that any adult can teach or take care of a young child simply by virtue of the adult having gone through childhood.

A person can buy a book entitled *Day Care Do-It-Yourself-Staff Growth Program* which is a performance-oriented course designed by the General Learning Corporation for on-site training of day care, Head Start, pre-school, kindergarten, and open primary teacher assistants and volunteers. As of this writing there are five such manuals or handbooks available which, if followed, would provide "skills" for working with young children. There are available at least eight publications dealing with volunteer roles in day care centers or early "education".

The use of minimally trained volunteers and parents as "educators/caretakers" is probably a good idea when it comes to conserving funds and operating on limited budgets. But this trend decreases the need for extended training to produce a "professional" in ECE and slows the development of ECE as a field unto itself.

B. Changing Role of Women

The changing role of women, accelerated by the Women's Liberation movement, should be credited for being a major factor in the reawakening of the need for early childhood care facilities. However, the movement has shown minimal interest in the systematic development of an educational delivery system to compliment the interest in child care. Combined with the growing acceptance of minimally trained volunteers as early childhood educators and the acceptance of care and custody experiences in lieu of education, the women's movement will probably modify the importance of ECE as education and diminish the importance of the early childhood educator as "professional".

In an article, which was the clarion call from the woman's liberation movement, (Rossi, 1971) Ms. Alice S. Rossi sees "the question of child-care provision. . .of central importance in permitting women to enter and remain in the professional, technical and administrative occupations in which they are presently under represented." (pg. 150) The concentration on child care in Ms. Rossi's view is not on early *education* for the child but on early positive custodial

care. Experiences to develop readiness for cognitive skills or preparation for formal schooling are secondary considerations. Indeed, the main custodial care is to come from a "practical mother". These would be grandmothers, or (Rossi, 1971)

"older women who now work in factories or as cashiers or sales clerks, who would be more satisfied with child care jobs if the status and pay for such jobs were upgraded. . .if a reserve of trained practical mothers were available, a professional woman could return to her field a few months after the birth of a child, leaving the infant under the care of a practical mother until he or she reached the age of two years at about which age the child could enter a child care center for day time care. (pg. 149)

Ms. Rossi's idea of child care as a convience for self-fulfillment or achieving equality with men has since been echoed in one way or another by spokespersons for the women's liberation movement and has become a major concern of NOW, the political action group of the Women's Liberation Movement. If the change in the role of the middle income mother becomes permanent in our society, the use of minimally trained adults will accelerate as will custodial centers.

V. Conclusion

A very real possibility exists that ECE should never develop into a "field" unto itself. It may be that the ecology of early human development seems to require an eclectic approach which encompasses pre-natal education for parents, family and home intervention, early educational experiences, as well as general kinds of experiences. If this is so then the present potpourri of approaches is justified. What is not justified is the lack of adequate distinctions between the multitude of approaches and the lack of enforceable standards for ensuring the quality of education and of the general experiences.

Attempts such as Millie Almy's to develop an early childhood educator with competencies for handling children in a variety of settings is commendable. (Almy, 1975) If Almy and others are successful in their attempts to develop a new professional role recognized on a wide scale, this in itself will define ECE as a field.

Further, more and more states, are beginning to realize that tighter controls are needed and not everything dealing with young children should be legitimized with the label of ECE. This trend may also clarify the distinction among ECE approaches.

Finally, despite the need for eliminating the ambiguity surrounding ECE the danger of developing a specific field which becomes locked into "standards" exists. A more sophisticated model of ECE needs to be developed which would take into account what seems to be the three main thrusts dealt with in this chapter—human development/education/custodial care. If it can be kept in mind that the young child is a complex organism under the influence of, and responding to, many different influences and experiences presented in many different ways, then the present diversity might still exist within a clearer framework which ensures the best for the child.

BIBLIOGRAPHY

Almy, Millie. *The early childhood educator at work.* New York: McGraw Hill Book Company, 1975.

Brademas, John. When should schooling begin. *Phi Delta Kappan,* 1972, *10,* 612-13

Baratta-Lorton, Mary. *Workjobs for parents: Activity centered learning in the home.* California: Addison-Wesley, 1975.

Campbell, Sheila D. & Everett, Lorene M. *In-Home early childhood project.* University of Alberta: Department of elementary Education, 1974.

Deighton, Lee C. *Encyclopedia of education.* New York: Free Press, 1971.

Doherty, Joan. Points for consideration. *In Early childhood education regional report.* U.S. Office of Education, Region VII, Kansas City, Missouri, 1976.

Essman, Walter B. & Nakajima, Shinshu. *Current biological approaches to learning and memory.* New York: Spectrum Publications, 1973.

Evans, Elis D. *Contemporary influences in early childhood education.* New York: Holt, Rinehart & Winston, Inc., 1971.

Friedenberg, Edgar. Requiem for the urban school. *Saturday Review,* 1967, pg. 40.

Greenberg, Polly. *Day care do-it-yourself staff growth program.* Washington: General Learning Corporation, 1975.

Hentoff, Nat. *Our children are dying.* New York: Viking Press, 1966.

Hess, Robert D. & Bear, Roberta Meyed.(Ed.) *Early education.* Chicago: Aldine Publishing Co., 1968.

Hess, Robert D. & Croft, Doreen J. *Teachers of young children.* (2nd ed.) Boston: Houghton Mifflin Co., 1972.

Hildebrand, Verna. *Guiding young children.* New York: Macmillan Publishing Co., Inc., 1975.

Kozol, Jonathan. *Death at an early age.* Boston: Houghton Mifflin, 1967.

LaCrosse, E. Robert, Jr. *Early childhood education directory: A selected guide to 2,000 pre-school educational centers.* New York and London: R.R, Bowker Co., 1971.

Lichtenbert, Philip & Norton, Delores G. *Cognitive and mental development in the first five years of life.* Washington, D.C. National Institute of Mental Health, 1972.

Margolin, Edythe. *Young children: Their curriculum and learning processes.* New york: Macmillan Publishing Co., Inc., 1976.

McClure, William P. & Pence, Audra Mary. *Early childhood and basic elementary and secondary education; Needs, programs, demands, costs.* National Educational Finance Project No. 1, College of Education, University of Illinois, 1970.

Moore, Raymond S., Moon, Robert D. & Moore, Dennis R. *The California report: Early schooling for all.* Phi Delta Kappan, 1972, *10,* 615-21.

Morrison, George S. *Early childhood education today.* Columbus, Ohio: Charles E. Merrill, 1976.

Nurborger, John I. (Ed.). *Biological and environmental determinents of early development.* Baltimore: Williams & Wilkins Co., 1973.

Richardson, Frederick. *Brain and intelligence: The ecology of child development.* Maryland: National Educational Press, 1973.

Rossi, Alice S. Equality between the sexes: An immodest proposal. In M.H. Garskof (Ed.), *Roles women play.* Belmont, California: Brooks/Cole Pub. Co., 1971.

Seefeldt, Carol, et. al. *A guide for planning and operating home-based child development programs.* Washington, D.C.: Office of Child Development, HEW, 1974.

Chapter 6

Day Care: A Look at the Present . . A Hint of the Future

Paula Zajan*

Introduction

As America closes the final pages of its bicentennial and looks ahead to the next century, it is appropriate to assess some of the services offered to its youngest citizens—the children.

Although knowledge and understanding of how young children grow and develop and the awareness of their needs and those of their parents have come a long way since 1776, day-care facilities for children have not kept pace with the demand for readily available quality care for the preschool group. The purpose of this article is to define some of the day-care services that are presently available; to describe the qualities of a good day-care program; to give the rationale for expanding day-care facilities; and to acquaint the reader with some of the ideas which have been suggested for extending day-care services throughout the nation.

Day-Care Programs Offer a Variety of Services

Day-care is the name given to group care of young children and generally means all day care from early morning until late afternoon. Although day-care usually implies a program for children between the ages of three through six which is located in a center sponsored by a social service or government agency, there are many variations of this definition. There are, for example, centers which are open 24 hours a day or others which are available for infants and toddlers. Some may be sponsored by private businesses as a service to their employees while others operate as a business under a franchise arrangement. Still another variation is the Family Day-Care program in which five to six children are cared for in the home of a mother who is recognized by the sponsoring agency as providing an optimal physical and emotional environment for young children. Because the family day-care program offers a more intimate home environment for young children, it is often used as a transition from home to the child's first full group experience in a day-care center.

Essential Features of a Quality Day-Care Center

When children spend up to ten hours each day for five days each week, it is incumbent upon the center to provide the maximum quality environment for children who spend the largest percentage of their waking hours away from home.

Perhaps the most essential feature of a good day-care center, and the one most difficult to define, is the quality of life that exists within it. In such a center, the child's well-being, physical, social, emotional, and intellectual, takes top priority. All facets of the program focus on the child as an individual and as a member of the group. The staff, director, teachers, assistants, social worker, secretary, cook, and custodian all play important roles in determining whether the climate within that center is supportive and stimulating or whether it is passive, custodial, or even destructive. The feelings, attitudes, and communication among the staff members, among the staff members and children, and among the children themselves, give many clues to the quality of life within the center.

There is no question that a knowledgeable, harmonious staff deeply concerned with the needs of children make the difference between an adequate program and a good one. One of the main responsibilities of the center director is to hire competent staff and to continually upgrade their performance through on-the-job staff development. The director should have firsthand knowledge and experience in working with young children and their parents in addition to administrative and supervisory skills. The teachers and assistants must have, at the very minimum, the physical and emotional health as well as the skills necessary to work with young children in an all-day setting.

*Dr. Paula Zajan, Professor and Director of the Early Childhood Program, Hostos Community College, City University of New York.

Although the emotional climate takes top priority, the physical environment cannot be overlooked. A good day-care center should be a place that is safe, clean, and spacious. Classrooms should be bright and well-ventilated with sufficient storage and work space. Rooms should not be overcrowded. State or city health codes frequently determine the number of children in a classroom according to their age, the number of adults in the room, and the size of the facility. The three-year-old group usually has 8-10 children; the four-year-old group from 10-12; and the five-year-old group from 15-20. In addition to the classrooms, there may be a large free-activity room for children to use when inclement weather prohibits outdoor play.

Large muscle activity in an outdoor yard or on a rooftop is a "must" for young children. Whatever the arrangement, there should be sufficient protected space for children to move freely and to use outdoor equipment such as climbing apparatus, wheel toys, sandboxes, large hollow blocks, balls, and the like. In addition to "child space," there must be "adult space": offices for the director, secretary, nurse, and social worker as well as room for staff and parents' activities, a basically equipped kitchen and storage space.

Programs in day-care centers vary and they are generally influenced by the educational beliefs of the center director and teachers. In centers where there are advisory boards consisting of parents, community members, and professionals, input as to the educational content as well as operating procedures may be made by the advisory body.

Some center programs are very unstructured and free with little direction from the adults. Children in these programs are encouraged to choose their own activities within a flexible time schedule and great emphasis is placed on activities and experiences initiated by the children. Creativity and self-expression are highly valued in these centers and one would not be likely to see adult-directed art projects or large groups during story time or music. Children work at their own pace individually and in small groups and the adults take their cues from the spontaneous activities of the children.

At the other end of the spectrum, there are highly structured, adult-dominated programs. In these centers, children follow a tightly organized schedule and there may be little opportunity for flexibility and spontaneous activity. There are many adult initiated group activities such as in art, science, and language. Emphasis is placed on preparing children for subsequent schooling, and in such centers formal reading and mathematics readiness programs may be observed.

Falling in between, there is a broad range of programs that follow a middle road taking those facets which are compatible with the philosophy and beliefs of the staff and parents within that center. Although most center directors and teachers would "say" that they are concerned with the development of the whole child, physically, socially, emotionally, and intellectually, it is the underlying attitudes and beliefs of the adults and the pressures that are brought to bear that ultimately determine the type of program.

A developmental child-care center is not only concerned with the environmental and educational aspects of the program but also with the additional comprehensive services that are offered to the children and their families. These would include health services, counseling and guidance, social services, and the like. In many urban centers, men and women from the immediate community are hired to assist the professionals in providing these services. These assistants may be given the title of Family Assistant or Family Worker and while they may lack the formal educational credentials, they are knowledgeable about their communities and can speak to the families as neighbor to neighbor. When appropriate, these family workers may be bilingual and this brings an added dimension to the program. In some programs, family workers will pick up children in their homes, bring them to the center, and then escort them home in the evening. This practice is usually reserved for situations where parents are unable to bring their children because of severe handicaps, illness, or emergency situations.

In a comprehensive child development center, parents are encouraged to be active participants in the life of the center. They are urged to voice their opinions in the running of the center; to volunteer their time or skills whenever possible; and join in the parents' activities be they educational, social, or recreational. Staff members establish good relationships with the parents and work actively to keep them informed of their children's progress through individual and group meetings.

The Need for Day-Care Services

Group care for young children has existed whenever mothers have had to leave their children with other adults for varying periods of time. Such care may range from the informal minding of children by relatives or neighbors to highly organized educational facilities for larger groups.

The availability and quality of group care has differed from century to century and country to country and is influenced by cultural, economic, social, and political considerations. Countries such as Russia (Bronfenbrenner, 1973), China (Sidel, 1973), and Israel (Bettelheim, 1970), provide child-care facilities from infancy to school age.

In the United States child-care centers have been available but only on a limited basis. Some federally funded day-care centers were created as the result of the depression when in 1932 the Works Progress Administration sponsored nursery schools to feed children and provide jobs for unemployed public school teachers (Burgess, 1965). With the onset of World War II and the need for female defense workers, the Lanhan Act program absorbed the WPA nursery schools (Fleiss, 1962), but when the funds were terminated in 1946, these centers depended on state and local funds for survival.

With the exception of San Francisco and New York City most of these federally supported child-care programs closed when the war ended (Goldsmith, 1972).

Nevertheless programs for young children sponsored by local and state government agencies, philanthropic organizations and private enterprise continued to proliferate and flourish. One of the major reasons for this was the fact that more and more mothers with children under the age of six entered the work force. In 1950 for example, 14% of all married women with children up to age of 6 were employed. In 1973, the number rose to 34%. For children falling in the six and under age bracket, one out of three has a mother who works (U.S. Senate Committee on Finance, 1974).

Many reasons can be given for this increase in the female work force:

— The need for a second income to supplement for the ever-rising cost of living.
— Unemployment of the male head of the household may cause the mother to seek work.
— The one-parent family has increased due to such factors as the high divorce rate, abandonment by the father, or choice of the mother.
— The economic incentives for those who seek to raise their standard of living.
— The higher level of education of women.
— The increased desire of women to pursue their own career goals.

Another factor that enters into the need for increased day-care services for children is the difficulty of raising children in a complex, rapidly changing urban society. Family structure may be less secure and the quality of life more tenuous. The tensions and anxieties that result from living in a noisy, busy, crowded environment cannot but affect the development of the young child. And in the urban ghettos life is even more precarious, where hunger, cold, and fear may be the young child's daily reality.

It is not surprising therefore that there are increasing pressures from parents, community groups, civil rights organizations, women's liberation groups, and others who have joined with the traditional service professions of teaching, social work, public health, and the like, to demand readily available, quality care for young children. The need for these services has been so great and the availability of high quality programs has been so limited that there appears to be hope that federal funds will once again be made available, only this time on a much broader scale than in 1932.

The Years Ahead

In late 1969, the first of what were to be a series of child and family services bills sponsored by Senators Walter F. Mondale and John Brademas began hearings by the Senate and House Subcommittees. This bill, called the Child and Family Services Act, was passed by both houses of Congress in 1971 but was vetoed by the

then President, Richard Nixon. In August 1974, this comprehensive child development bill was again reintroduced by Senators Mondale and Brademas and was entitled the Child and Family Services Act of 1975. The fate of this bill is still unknown but there has been increasing interest generated by the hearings that took place during the winter and spring of 1975.

An awareness of the lowered birthrate and the increased unemployment of trained teachers has prompted several of the major teachers' organizations and unions to speak forcefully for the passage of this bill. The American Federation of Teachers (Kemble, March 1975) has taken a strong position that federally funded day care should have a strong educational component and would best serve the interests of young children and the teachers by being located in the public schools. Equally strong is the reaction of other groups who believe that the various organizations both public and private who now are responsible for day care should serve as the sponsoring agencies.

The danger in this division of opinion is that there is a sizable portion of the population who questions the value of day-care services to begin with. This group believes that such services are destructive to the concept of family life and would willingly see such legislation vetoed again.

Conclusion

For those who would question the concept of all-day care for young children, there are millions of others for whom day-care services fulfill a vital need. For children brought up in an urban society with all its attendant limitations and difficulties, day care can provide a far better alternative to some of the patterns of child care that exist.

It is of prime importance for all groups who believe that comprehensive day-care services should be available throughout the nation, to work together to support federal funding for such programs. But there is more than funding that must be kept in mind. Day-care facilities must reflect the best kind of care that can be offered families of all socioeconomic backgrounds. These centers must not provide minimum custodial care but maximal quality educational opportunity for our youngest citizens. For those who will make and write the history of this nation's tricentennial, it is the very least that we can do.

BIBLIOGRAPHY

Bettelheim, Bruno. *The Children of the Dream.* New York: Avon Books, 1970.
Bronfenbrenner, Uric. *Two Worlds of Childhood: U.S. and U.S.S.R.* New York: Pocket Books, 1973 (Paperback Edition).
Burgess, Evangeline. *Values in Early Childhood Education.* Department of Elementary-Kindergarten-Nursery Education, National Education Association. Washington, D.C.: 1201 Sixteenth Street, N.W., 1965.

Fleiss, Bernice H. "The Relationship of the Mayor's Committee on Wartime Care of Children to Day Care in New York City." Unpublished Doctor's thesis, New York University, 1962.

Goldsmith, Cornelia. *Better Day Care for the Young Child.* Washington, D.C.: National Association for the Education of Young Children, 1972.

Kemble, Eugenia. "Starting Off on the Right Foot: The Case for Putting Early Childhood Education into the Public Schools." *The American Teacher,* March 1975.

Sidel, Ruth. *Women and Child Care in China.* Baltimore, Maryland: Penguin Books, Inc., 1973 (Paperback Edition).

Committee on Finance, United States Senate. *Child Care: Data and Materials.* Washington, D.C.: U.S. Government Printing Office, 1974.

New York Teacher's Staff

B. Historical Perspectives

Introduction by Carol Harris*

The following section offers the reader an historical view of the early childhood movement in the United States from its beginnings as a recognized national need to its present status. Through the years, a wide variety of programs have been initiated. These programs, although all geared toward a similar age group, differ markedly in underlying philosophy, objectives, and sources of sponsorship. This lack of consistency has had both positive and negative effects on efforts to promote comprehensive care for the nation's young.

Marilyn Rauth views comprehensive child care as an "unresolved problem." She writes that some people face a problem only when it becomes a crisis, and that while arguments ensue over which solution is best, the crisis worsens, positions harden, and a solution becomes impossible. She documents the fact that our society's needs and attitudes reflect the state of the economy which, in turn, has a direct bearing upon the level of intervention by the private and public sectors in matters concerning program initiatives.

It is noted that there is presently an effort underway in Congress for passage of a new program to provide federal aid to early childhood education and day care. The question of prime sponsorship may dampen these efforts, however, What agency could best provide a universally accessible child-service system? Eugenia Kemble, in her article, presents the case for putting early childhood education into the public schools. With this matter still unresolved, no significant machinery has been put into operation to establish a network of progressive, economically feasible early childhood programs.

Joyce D. Miller stresses the urgency of such decisions in her historical review of child-care legislation. She also outlines the role that organized labor has played in bringing the child-care issue before the American public.

Much of the focus on child-care needs has been adult-centered—the working mother, the poverty-stricken head-of-household, the maladjusted family. Laura Ellis and Barbara Peltzman trace the origins of early childhood education in terms of its impact on the young child. The contributions of such famous psychologists as Comenius, Rousseau, Froebel, Piaget, and Dewey are examined as they relate to the teaching/learning processes during early years.

The influence of history upon the present and the future cannot be underestimated. The historical perspective provided by the following articles may help to give both meaning and direction to our ongoing efforts on behalf of our children.

*Carol Harris, Early Childhood Supervisor, Community School District #18, New York City.

Chapter 7
A Long Road to an Unresolved Problem: Comprehensive Child Care in the United States

Marilyn Rauth*

Problem, crisis, or resolution? Some say in the United States we face a problem only when it becomes a crisis, and while we argue over which solution is best, the crisis worsens, positions harden, and solution becomes impossible. Although the trend in our approach to child care appears to follow this route, it is hoped we will not see this prediction through to its ultimate outcome.

The federal government's unwillingness to provide services for the young children of this country is well documented. Despite the fact that recent years have seen record numbers of women entering the work force, its most recent comprehensive survey of child-care needs is based on 11-year-old data published in 1968.

The Bureau of Labor Statistics estimates that nearly 28 million children under 18 years of age had mothers who worked or were looking for work at the end of March, 1975. More than 6.5 million of these children were under age six. Obviously many of them are in need of care or supervision. A study conducted by the National Council of Jewish Women reveals that care is needed by an additional 2.5 million children whose mothers are not in the work force.

Yet the Child Welfare League of America estimates that there are, at most 4.3 million spaces available in child-care facilities. Many of these are unlicensed, and most—some 77 percent of them—are of such inferior quality that they should not be used.

The Child Welfare League, a national voluntary accrediting organization for child-welfare agencies in the U.S., and other sources have cited these shocking alternatives to adequate care:
- at least 10,000 children under six left alone during the day with no care or supervision while parents work;
- over 500,000 cared for by a sibling under 16;
- and 1.2 million at home with a parent too handicapped or sick to provide proper supervision.

There is ample research which underscores the importance of early learning experiences to optimal development of children. Yet a 1973 Census Bureau report reveals that only about 34 percent of four-year-olds and 14 percent of three-year-olds are enrolled in preschool programs, and of those; 70 percent attend nonpublic programs. In the majority of child-care arrangements, little progress has been made beyond the custodial care of the 1800s.

The most prevalent type of child care is in-home care with the "caregiver" (perhaps "caretaker" would be a better word) being a relative, friend, neighbor, or hired babysitter. Space and equipment are often limited, as are opportunities for social interaction. The next most popular facility is the family day-care home. It is widely estimated that more than half of all children taken out of the home for full-day care are in family day-care homes which serve five or six children. Smaller percentages of children are cared for in group day-care homes (extended or modified family residences which, if licensed, serve up to 12 children), day-care centers (serving 12 children or more), nursery schools, parent cooperatives, and the like.

Only about five percent of all family day-care homes are licensed. While most day-care centers are licensed, such licensing may mean little because of inadequate enforcement of regulations due to lack of staffing and/or negligence on the part of inspection agencies. Requirements, often minimal to begin with, do little more than set standards for scaled-down sanitation facilities, lighting, fireproofing, and so on (see box).

Looking Backward

A growing need for day nurseries first became evident just before the turn of this century. Rapid industrialization had lured thousands of uprooted rural families and even greater numbers of foreign immigrants into industrial urban areas. As the promise of affluence soon fell before the harsh reality of city life, it often became apparent that one breadwinner could not support the family's needs. Consequently, many mothers were forced to seek work, requiring long hours away from their children. A dilemma arose, for the mother who worked was considered derelict because she was not at home caring for her children; yet without the

*Marilyn Rauth is director of AFT's educational-issues department. She formerly was a classroom teacher in the Neshaminy school district in Pennsylvania.

additional income, she could not feed or clothe them. The problem was compounded for the many immigrant families who bore the burden of both survival and acculturation.

Working mothers, particularly those who were widowed or abandoned, were often forced to place their children in orphanages. As cautions increased that "the institutional child is not a normal child," alternatives were sought. Many children were placed in foster homes or sent to the country to live with farm families in an effort to provide family life, but none of these solutions proved practical on a large scale. Thus, day nurseries, based on the French model which attempted to simulate a loving home environment, came into being, as a reaction against the over-institutionalization of children. Funded principally by private philanthropy, they enjoyed great popularity from the 1870s to World War I. But history shows there was a shortage of concerned people, of money, and of knowledge about how to meet the needs of young children.

In her book, "Who's Minding the Children? The History and Politics of Day Care in America," Margaret O'Brien Steinfels reports:

The nurseries, usually converted houses or brownstones, were open six days a week, 12 hours a day. A great age span could be found in most nurseries: infants and children from the age of 2 weeks to 6 years—the addition of after-school programs brought that range to the elderly level of 8 and 9. Some day nurseries provided emergency night care when a mother was ill; others allowed a child to be dropped off for a few hours; some hired a visiting nurse to assist mothers when children were ill; others held classes for mothers in sewing, cooking, English, and child care.

Despite their ideals and good intentions, these nurseries fell far short of standards we would expect today. Their benefactors and personnel lacked the knowledge of how to transform good intentions into effective child-development programs. Overcrowding was commonplace; the quality of food extremely poor; and most of the personnel were untrained.

The criticisms of day nurseries in those days (some of which still are heard today) included: fears of weakening family ties; undermining the father's sense of responsibility for being the sole breadwinner; encouraging mothers to work, perhaps to provide only luxuries, thus causing them to neglect child-rearing responsibilities; and depressing male wages.

To counter these charges, philanthropists within the day-nursery movement reavowed their commitment to strengthen the family. Theirs was a charitable service to be used only on a temporary basis until the mother's "problem" could be remedied. They argued that not only could the mother learn how to discipline and care for her child from the nursery's example, but additionally, the child might be prevented from becoming a future welfare problem. It was their contention that as social and economic conditions improved, day nurseries would cease to exist, and mothers and children would return to their "rightful" place in the home.

Even at that time, the National Federation of Day Nurseries and many local associations recognized the variant causes of need for day nursery services and proposed they would not soon be alleviated. Theirs was a more practical view based upon the realities of single-parent homes, unemployment, poverty, and women's participation in the labor force.

Eventually, day-nursery federations and associations at the local and national levels began to promote upgraded standards in health, nutrition, record-keeping, adult/child ratios, and, to some extent, education. Compliance was voluntary and, in many cases, ignored. A degree of progress was made when, by the end of World War I, California had passed a state law governing day nurseries, and several cities had regulatory city ordinances.

Professionalization of Day Nurseries

The professionalization of day-nursery personnel occurred during the 20-year period following World War I. This resulted in major changes in entry age, program, and purpose. The practice of placing infants in day nurseries from the time they were several weeks old, where they were bottle-fed instead of at mother's breast, was challenged, and eventually the minimum entry age became three. Though some today regret the exclusion of infants, it should be remembered that the day-care associations of the time recommended an adult/child ratio of 1:8 for infants. In actual practice, the ratio was often much higher. Standard-setting organizations, such as the Child Welfare League, now recommend an adult/child ratio of 1:2 for infants, indicating that challenges to the day nurseries' infant care were quite justified. A second major change was replacement of nursery attendants with professional nursery-school teachers who changed education from secondary to primary importance.

The focus of day nurseries was further altered after 1919 by the new involvement of trained social wokers. Formerly a service to working mothers, day nurseries now became a form of social welfare. Admissions were thoroughly screened and were allowed only in cases of "social maladjustment" or "serious familial problems." Thus day care became further stigmatized. Steinfels points out that "poverty in the minds of the first day-nursery workers. . .was perceived to be the result of conditions external to the family—but having a strong effect on the family." The new view of "maladjustment" suggested "conditions internal to the family."

As a result of new quota restrictions in immigration and creation of widows' pensions in many states, large segments of the day nurseries' clientele were reduced. Ironically, passage of the 19th Amendment undercut the militant feminism movement and brought a renewed emphasis on the mother's responsibility in the home. Finally, economic expansion and the pursuant rise in the standard of living for some distracted attention from the plight of the poor. Though the need continued, day nurseries dwindled to those which provided only minimal custodial care. Privately run nursery schools catered to a limited number of middle- and upper-class children whose parents could afford such a program.

Federal Funds For Nursery Schools

Following the near demise of day nurseries, interest in child care continued alternately to wax and wane. The first public money for child-care programs was allocated in 1933 through the Federal Emergency Relief Administration and the Works Project Administration (WPA). Both were based primarily on an effort to create jobs, but to say there was no concern for the needs of children or working mothers would be to ignore a social awareness which did, in fact, exist at that time. Federal and state funds for child care during this period also were granted to alleviate the physical and mental handicaps imposed on young children because of economic and social difficulties of that period. All personnel—teachers, nurses, nutritionists, cooks, clerical workers, and janitors—were hired from relief rolls because of the government's concern with widespread unemployment. By 1937, some 40,000 children were served in 1,900 nurseries established within public schools. Pamela Roby in "Child Care—Who Cares?" cites a reference to the fact that those programs are "still considered by professionals to have provided excellent health and nutritional care as well as education."

Many of these nurseries ceased to exist as WPA programs were phased out. However, the day-care movement was soon revived when, during World War II, more and more women joined the labor force. In August, 1942, it was decided that the Lanham Act, authorizing the federal government to pay for half of the public-works programs in war-impacted areas, could be applied to day care. By the end of the war, almost $52 million had been spent by the federal government for 3,102 day-care centers serving 600,000 children. States contributed $26 million in matching funds.

The Federal Works Administration, authorized to administer the Lanham Act, channeled funds through state education departments. Most of these programs were placed in local school systems because of their existing facilities and trained child-oriented staff. However, because the federal government had not set any standards for these programs, quality varied from one locale to another.

After the war, most public funds for day care were shut off as, once again, it became the prevailing view that the mother belonged in the home (this attitude also made it easier for returning veterans to reassume their place in the labor force). Women using day care were again seen as neglectful mothers. This belief was reinforced by research in the 1940s describing damage done to institutionalized orphans and by John Bowlby's study in 1951 on maternal deprivation. Bowlby found that the institutionalized child's permanent separation from the mother resulted in abnormal development. Throughout the 1950s this was often cited as an argument against placing children in day-care settings. However, later research by Bloom, White, Caldwell, Mead, and others was to show that temporary separation under the proper conditions actually could be beneficial to the child.

The wars in Korea and Vietnam opened new employment opportunities for women. The "New Frontier" of the Kennedy era and the "Great Society" and "War Against Poverty" programs of the Johnson Administration (including the famous Head Start) brought heightened expectations in living standards, and more and more wives and mothers sought employment to supplement family incomes. The growth of inflation during the last several years has continued this trend. From 1950 to 1973, the number of working mothers doubled—from 22 to 44 percent. Approximately one-third of all preschool children now have mothers who are working or looking for work.

This rapid influx of women into the labor force was naturally accompanied by increasing demands for day care, as reflected in the legislation of the 1960s. At this point, the emphasis was primarily on needs of working mothers rather than on child development.

Child-welfare services, including day care, had been meagerly funded through the Social Security Act since 1935. Amendments to this Act in the late 1960s provided the first significant funds for day care, e.g. in Aid to Families with Dependent Children (AFDC) legislation, since passage of the Lanham Act during World War II; but the Revenue Sharing Act of 1971 placed limits on funding. There are now at least 60 different federally funded programs for child care and child development. The Senate Finance Committee reports that the federal government presently spends at least $1.3 billion in direct funds on child care.

Comprehensive Care?

Since the late 1960s, there has been a great flurry of legislative activity focusing on the child-care needs of this country. Much of this evolved out of former President Nixon's introduction of the Family Assistance Plan as part of a social-security and welfare-reform bill. Speaking to Congress in 1969, Nixon declared: "So crucial is the matter of early growth that we must make a national commitment to providing all American children an opportunity for healthful and stimulating development during the first years of life." The Administration's bill, in contrast to the rhetoric, was limited to day-care for children of welfare recipients who would agree to accept work, training, or vocational rehabilitation. Comprehensive developmental care was not required, and family payments were based on ability to pay.

In the first eight months of the 92nd Congress (1970–71), 10 proposals related to child-care programs were introduced. Sen. Russell Long (D-La.), for example, proposed a Federal Child Care Corporation supported by a $500-million Treasury loan to provide child care, first, for preschool and school-age children of welfare recipients who needed such services to work or to take employment training, and, secondly, for children of low-income working mothers not eligible for welfare. Federal funds would have covered all costs of child care for welfare mothers and subsidized the cost of services for other eligible working mothers.

It was, however, the Comprehensive Child Development Act of 1971 which ultimately garnered the largest Congressional and public support, finally passing as part of the Economic Opportunity Act on Dec. 6, 1971. This legislation would have created a nationally coordinated network of child-development programs for all children under 15, with priority given to those who were of preschool age or economically disadvantaged. Parental participation was assured through representation on elected councils and a wide range of services was to be offered—educational, nutritional, social, medical, dental, and psychological. Though many organizations, including the AFL-CIO, lobbied for this bill, former President Nixon vetoed the EOA on Dec. 9, 1971, alleging that, among other objections, the Act "would commit the vast moral authority of the national government to the side of communal approaches to child-rearing against the family-centered approach."

The attempt to override this veto was thwarted, ushering the first comprehensive child-development act to pass congress into the vast archives of legislative limbo. Sen. Walter Mondale (D-Minn.) and Rep. John Brademas (D-Ind.), chief sponsors of the Child Development Act, continued to submit child-care legislation to Congress in the following years, as did other Congressional leaders. Meanwhile, organizations which had worked diligently for passage of this legislation from 1969 to 1971 kept trying to build and strengthen their alliances to secure enactment of a comprehensive child-development bill.

By 1974, the prevailing social and political scenes appeared ripe for a second serious attempt at procuring comprehensive developmental programs and day-care services for all children of this nation, and the Child and Family

---

The Kindergarten Movement

An example of the flexibility of public education in the U.S. is the kindergarten movement, which evolved separately from day nurseries. First established in this country in 1856 by German immigrants, early kindergartens were devoted primarily to the education of the young German-speaking children. Philanthropist Elizabeth Peabody founded the first kindergarten for English-speaking children in Boston in 1860 to serve as a school for socialization of wealthy children. Her idea was replicated, providing the impetus for growth of a kindergarten movement. In 1873, the first kindergarten was established in a public school in St. Louis, Mo.

With massive immigration from Europe to this country in the 1880s, the focus of kindergarten was changed from the affluent to the poor. Many citizens saw this socialization process as a public responsibility and during the 1890s many kindergartens were incorporated into public schools. Today, while kindergarten attendance is not compulsory, 75 percent of all five-year olds attend and more than four-fifths are in the public schools.

Services Act of 1974 was introduced in both houses of Congress.

By this time, an impressive body of research existed, demonstrating the crucial nature of children's early years, from birth to age eight, in relation to their intellectual, social, emotional, and physical development. Burton White and others had shown that even as early as 10 months, a child's learning patterns are developing, and they therefore believed that child services could appropriately begin at the infant stage. Benjamin Bloom, in his well-known study, "Stability and Change in Human Characteristics," emphasized "the great importance of the first few years of school as well as the preschool period of the development of learning patterns and general achievement. These are the years in which general learning patterns develop most rapidly, and failure to develop appropriate achievement and learning in these years is likely to lead to continued failure throughout the remainder of the individual's school career."

In "Nursery Education: The Influence of Social Programming on Early Development," Martin Deutsch concluded from his research that higher group-intelligence-test scores were found among children who had preschool and kindergarten experience as compared to those whose initial contact with school was in first grade. Piaget explained further that "intelligence emerges as it is nurtured, it grows as the child has things to act upon," and J. McVicker Hunt wrote, "It now looks as though early experience may be even more important for the perceptual, cognitive, and intellectual functions than it is for the emotional and tempermental functions." Studies by Chittendon, Keister, Rice, Hood, and others found preschool programs to have a very positive effect on children's socialization skills and personality development. The research of Katrina De Hirsch and her associates demonstrated that many "intelligent but educationally disabled children . . . would not have required help had their difficulties been recognized at early ages. Early identification would have obviated the need for later remedial measures."

These and many other studies point to the fact that child development is a complex, continuous process enhanced by an environment conducive to learning and by skilled teachers who are knowledgeable about the child's intellectual, physical, social, and emotional growth.

Further agitation for child-care legislation was spawned by the problematic plight of poor and middle-class working parents.

In response to these needs, the Child and Family Services Act of 1975, proposed to establish an Office of Child and Family Services to oversee child-development, day-care, and family-services programs. Rather than being based on the child population in each state, the Senate bill's allocation formula continues the mixed formula approach: based on the number of economically disadvantaged children, the number of children under six, and the number of working mothers and single parents. Prime sponsors must establish Child and Family Service Policy Committees, one-half must be parents and one-third must be poor. The Secretary of HEW is authorized to develop new child-care standards based on the 1968 Federal Interagency Day Care Standards.

Many organizations differ in their outlook on these and other details of the bill, but prime sponsorship—the question of who shall manage funds and determine the nature of services to be offered and which agencies can best provide them—has become by far the most controversial aspect of this legislation. Presently designated in the bill as prime sponsors are states, localities, combinations of localities, or public and nonprofit organizations.

Controversy

The American Federation of Teachers, AFL-CIO, under the leadership of its president, Albert Shanker, is spearheading a drive to have public-school systems designated as presumed prime sponsors, allowing other public nonprofit organizations to assume this responsibility if a school system is unable or unwilling to accept it. Existing public nonprofit day-care operations which meet required standards might also be funded.

Shanker cites many reasons for AFT's position, among them the following:

1. Schools exist in every community throughout this country—urban, rural, small town, suburban—and therefore have the capacity to meet the goal of **universally accessible** early childhood education and day care for all on a voluntary basis.

2. The former shortage of school personnel and space no longer exists. Many unemployed early childhood teachers and paraprofessionals are available; many other unemployed teachers with suitable qualifications, as well as those in other occupations, might be retrained; and a portion of the vacant classrooms, already publicly owned, could be utilized for day care and early childhood programs, thereby decreasing some new construction and rental fees.

3. Schools have an established procedure for assuring that standards be met in terms of program, personnel qualifications, staffing ratios, and health and safety requirements. Enforcement efforts outside the public schools would require a large, new bureaucracy which would mean an unnecessary expenditure of millions of dollars of public monies and an extension of many years before an effective administrative procedure could be established.

A Crisis Stage

The United States is the only industrialized country in the world which does not provide basic child-care services for its citizenry. Our chaotic condition of demand far exceeding supply, and the absence of erosion of standards is further evidence of the lack of national commitment to providing services for children.

Traditionally child care in the U.S. has been available to the wealthy or, through private philanthropy or federal assistance, to the very poor. But the middle class, unable to pay for more than custodial child care or to qualify for assistance, has been left to contend with this dilemma on its own. As a result of government inaction, the U.S. has reached a crisis stage in terms of need for child care. The debate continues in Congress as to whether the federal government should fund comprehensive child-care programs, and if so, what the best delivery system would be.

AFT has been the vanguard in support of public-school prime sponsorship of comprehensive child-care programs. Many national organizations, including the AFL-CIO and a number of its affiliated international unions; educational organizations such as school administrators, school boards, PTA, and the National Education Association, have joined the AFT in endorsing the public schools as the most responsible means of delivering services to children.

4. A recent OCD study is typical of many reports showing that the lack of continuity between early childhood programs and primary grades causes preschool gains to diminish by the age of seven, eight, or nine. If there are innumerable sponsoring agencies, coordination between these two levels would be impossible.

5. Schools could quite logically become coordinators of screening procedures, in cooperation with public-health and social-services agencies. After needs are diagnosed through screening, the school system with parent's consent would provide services available and refer children whose needs it could not meet to other community agencies. Follow-through and maintenance of complete records would be important services within this program.

6. Placement of comprehensive child care in the public schools would necessarily increase parental involvement and contact, thus enhancing the school's position as a community center.

Opposition to presumed prime sponsorship by public schools, however, has arisen in several quarters. The National Association for Child Development and Education, representing the private for profit day-care interests, is lobbying against the exclusion of proprietary day-care centers from authorization for prime sponsorship. It argues that many centers already exist and that to deny them federal funds would be an insult to private enterprise, upon which our economy is based. The problem with proprietary centers grows out of their need to remain competitive with other forms of child care and still make a profit. In the absence of exorbitant fees, profit must come from adhering to a bottom line in one or a number of several categories: personnel, facilities, equipment, materials, food, and inservice training.

By far the majority of child-care advocates opposes their inclusion because of repeated studies showing the custodial nature of most operations and their failure to meet quality standards. The 1972 survey by the National Council of Jewish Women, for example, found that of 431 proprietary centers visited throughout the country, 49.5 percent were rated "poor," 14.5 percent rated "good," and only 1 percent "superior." Under the proposed legislation, prime sponsors may contract with proprietary centers for programs and services, a questionable arrangement.

Theodore Taylor of the Day Care and Child Development Council of America (DCCDCA) believes schools should not be presumed prime sponsors for two reasons: first, "even those teachers who would find day care a satisfying field in which to work . . . would have initial difficulties with adjusting themselves to an educational approach which is largely nonverbal," and second, that parents who seek day care" want, need, and deserve a closer connection with providers of day care than what the school systems feel necessary or desirable with the public schools."

Many educators retort that language development is an essential element in early childhood education programs and that school certification requirements would assure the use of only those teachers who are trained in all aspects of child development. They refute Taylor's second stated reason by pointing out that schools, being dependent for funds on voted bond issues or voted increases in property-tax millage, are responsive to the public's wishes and that responsibility for child development within the schools can only increase the desired parental involvement. It is likely that DCCDCA's position is influenced by the fact that proprietary centers constitute a sizeable proportion of its membership.

Of immediate concern to all in the labor movement were previous union efforts to establish child-care programs as a regular service to their members or as a benefit won through collective bargaining. Several unions such as the Communications Workers of America, the Amalgamated Clothing Workers of America, and others, developed and implemented day-care centers in several large cities. In 1968, the United Federation of Teachers, AFT Local 2, negotiated early childhood preschool programs in its contract with the New York City board of education. (These preschool centers have since been closed due to lack of funds.)

After much discussion, however, it became apparent that in the interest of making these programs available to all children for whom they were desired, public schools represented the only institution capable of providing the universal accessibility desired.

It was discovered that child care at the work site holds a number of problems, regardless of the sponsor:

• If a business or factory closes, the child-care center closes with it.

• It an employee is laid off or fired, child-care services are no longer available.

• It is more likely that a parent who is sick would take a child to a neighborhood school than to the work site; or that someone else in the neighborhood could perform this service.

• The working parent may not have sufficient time to investigate various child-care facilities in the area. The public schools, therefore, could better protect their interest.

On Oct. 7, 1975, the AFL-CIO convention adopted a resolution calling for a massive federal commitment for providing early childhood development and day-care services to all children who need them.

The Future

Only if the government is willing to make a major change in social policy will we avoid having inadequate and limited child care develop to a problem of catastrophic proportions. Yet we face a familiar political problem. Both the legislative and executive branches of the federal government

Poor Standards, Little Enforcement

The federal government has set a poor example in licensing, and establishing and enforcing standards in child care. A report compiled for the U.S. Senate Committee on Finance states that although the Federal Interagency Day-Care Requirements technically regulate nearly all child care provided under federal funds, "it is generally recognized that they are rarely monitored."

Licensing normally is contingent on meeting standards for health regulations and building and fire codes. Many states and localities are under pressure from proprietary day-care operators and others to relax even these minimal standards.

A report by the Auerbach Corporation in 1970 on the Federal Work Incentive Program found that the major problem cited by day-care operators "is in meeting the various local ordinances which, according to some staffs, are prohibitive. Some examples are: windows no more than 'x' feet from the floor; sanitation facilities appropriately scaled for children; sprinkler systems; fireproof construction; etc."

Another study, "Day Care Centers—The Case for Prompt Expansion," which examined the inability of New York City to meet the demand for day care, stated that insistence on strict adherence to the city's health code "severely handicaps the efforts of groups attempting to form centers in the substandard areas." The implication is that substandard child care is permissible in poverty areas.

Licensing laws rarely set standards for programming and curriculum; renewals are usually granted without an evaluation of program results and often without further inspection of the physical facilities. Some set minimum personnel qualifications, but the requirements are generally below those for administrators, teachers, health and social workers, and counselors working in all other levels of education. For example, many states require only that preschool "teachers" have a high-school education or its equivalent or make the vague stipulation that they be "equipped for work required."

hold out little hope for enactment of a comprehensive child-services act in the near future. They are content to ignore the desperate needs of individual citizens. They use the disagreement among various child-advocacy organizations over the best means of providing child care as a pretense to shirk their responsibility for assertive action. It is just this inertia, however, which has subjected the government to growing attacks. Our crisis in child care can no longer wait on the halting machinations of Congress.

The termination of overlapping, obscure, and diffuse programs is long overdue. Congress must be persuaded to take decisive action. And as in the one-time fight for public education, organized labor and its allies are leading the way in showing that only through the presumed prime sponsorship of public schools will it be possible to effectively coordinate quality child-development services for all children.

Public schools, under such a provision, would ultimately become a total community resource, seeing that the public's needs were met in regard to children's physical and emotional welfare, early childhood education, and extended day care.

Responsible critics have mistakenly overlooked an accessible compromise on prime sponsorship of children's services. Advocates of public-school sponsorship share many of their concerns and would be more than willing to join them in efforts to assure that legislation includes provisions for high standards, comprehensive services, and parental involvement.

With this type of unity, Congress would ill afford its complacency on child care. The result would be a universally accessible child-services system and even greater parental involvement in the public schools.

The alternatives portend further ineffective use of public monies. Right now, the federal government, through the Office of Child Development, has funded a project to promote greater coordination of child-development and education services between preschool programs outside the schools and the primary grades. This expenditure could be more efficiently made if preschool programs were coordinated through the public schools. Once most parties are willing to discuss continuity and when there is an effective way to begin bringing such continuity about, it will no longer seem an impossible feat. It is possible, for example, for New York City schools to coordinate their curricula, methodology, and classroom management with independent, nonprofit groups which meet standards throughout the city. It is true enough to say this would require a substantial amount of time and effort. It is a necessary venture.

While continuing diversity through various day-care programs, the public schools, as presumed prime sponsors, could act, as coordinators for all children's services, similar to the function of "direction centers" often used in special education. After needs are diagnosed through screening, the school system with parents' consent would provide services available and refer children whose needs it could not meet to other community agencies. This practice would lessen overlap of services and call attention to needs which are not being met.

Health services should include both preventive and remedial care. Among these services would be complete medical and dental examinations; immunization programs; speech, hearing, and vision tests; and assessment and treatment of any developmental, psychological, or physical disorders. Screening, diagnosis, and treatment should begin as early as possible since deficiencies in these areas are increasingly difficult to correct with each passing year of life.

Structure and content of early childhood programs must be based on goals determined by needs of individual children and their families in any given locale. Early childhood education should, however, encompass all aspects of child development—intellectual, social, emotional, and physical. For this reason, teacher training is essential, and preservice programs which do not address themselves to all of these criteria should be revised.

Although it would be inappropriate to endorse any one curriculum approach, certain elements are basic in any design. Play has been found to be an essential component of early childhood programs, valuable in development of socializing skills, motor coordination and concept development. The young child should be offered many opportunities for decision-making and problem-solving. Conceptual foundations should be laid in academic content areas with children free to progress at their own rate. As levels of maturity, which affect learning readiness, differ even among children of the same age, individualization is essential to a successful program.

The school environment, therefore, must offer a wide assortment of experiences suited to many developmental levels. Adult-child ratios required for such individualization are those recommended in the Federal Interagency Day Care Requirements:

1:10—Children six and over
1:7—five-year-olds
1:5—three and four-year-olds

When and if infant care is provided, organizations like the American Federation of Teachers, the Child Welfare League of America, and others recommend an adult-child ratio of 1:2.

Flexibility emerges as the key word in early childhood education. Public schools are well-equipped to administer alternative preschool and day-care programs based on goals and priorities established by parents. Accommodations can be made for variances in program approaches and philosophies; in length of programs—half-day, full-day, or 24-hour day-care services; and in program sites—in home, school, family day-care homes, day-care centers, and so forth.

Greatest caution must be given to maintenance of standards in staffing ratios, health and safety, program and personnel quality, and facilities and equipment. The public-school system represents the only institution with broad enforcement experience and capabilities. To ignore this fact would result in a poorly managed child-care program, the ramifications of which could be far worse than no program at all. □□□

REFERENCES

"Child Care Data and Materials," Committee on Finance, U.S. Senate, October, 1974.

"Early Childhood Education and Child Care Program," statement by AFL-CIO executive council, May 6, 1975.

"Federal Day Care Legislation," Inequality in Education, No. 12, July, 1972, Cambridge, Mass.: Harvard Center for Law and Education.

Fein, Greta C. and Alison Clarke-Stewart, "Day Care in Context," New York, N.Y.: John Wiley and Sons, 1973.

"Guidelines for Early Childhood Education," Maryland State Department of Education, Baltimore, 1972.

Mindess, Mary, and Alice V. Keliher, "Review of Research Related to the Advantages of Kindergarten," Washington, D.C.: Association for Childhood Education International.

O'Grady, Jane, "Child Care: A Growing Problem," AFL-CIO American Federationist, August, 1972.

Roby, Pamela, Ed., "Child Care—Who Cares?" New York, N.Y.: Basic Books, Inc., 1973.

Steinfels, Margaret O'Brien, "Who's Minding the Children? The History and Politics of Day Care in America," New York, N.Y.: Simon and Schuster, 1973.

"The Care and Education of Young Children," Massachusetts Early Education Project. Washington, D.C.: Day Care and Child Development Council of America, Inc., 1972.

"Toward Comprehensive Child Care," Day Care Consultation Service, Bank Street College of Education. Washington, D.C.: Day Care and Child Development Council of America, Inc., 1974.

Chapter 8

Starting off on The Right Foot: The Case for putting Early Childhood Education into Public Schools

Eugenia Kemble*

In August, 1974, Sen. Walter Mondale (D.-Minn.) and Rep. John Brademas (D-Ind.) introduced a comprehensive child-development bill into the Senate and House. It was re-introduced in the 1975 session of Congress. Their new program, entitled the Child and Family Services Act of 1975, is one in a long history of efforts to provide federal aid to early childhood education and day care. For the most part, such efforts have resulted in either small-scale, fragmentary funding or in legislation which failed passage or was killed by presidential veto.

Some seasoned observers have speculated that the unwillingness or inability of this country to establish a comprehenisve public program can be explained by the failure of a powerful unified constituency to emerge from the multiplicity of groups that now populate the day-care and early childhood field. Others say it is because of the conflicting social and political values which surround such issues as institutional care vs. home care; private vs. public sponsorship; the role of the family—particularly the mother—in raising children; the identification of day care with "welfare mothers" and work incentives; and the degree to which programs for young children should be considered "educational".

The American Federation of Teachers has entered this picture with a strong position that is taking the rest of the day-care community somewhat by surprise. By defining day care in educational terms, and by relating its expansion to current conditions in the public schools, the AFT has attempted to combine the interests of children with the interests of its members. A policy statement passed by the AFT executive council in December, 1974, describes the need for expanded early childhood education, and points to the educational crisis caused by high teacher "surplus," declining student enrollment, and underutilization of schools. The resolution proposed massive new funding reaching $2 billion a year for expanded day care and early childhood education to be administered by the public schools. Thus, not only does AFT emphasize the needs of children, but foresees a program to use vacant classrooms and employ jobless teachers.

AFT President Albert Shanker has called for amendments to the Mondale-Brademas bill which reflect these positions in his New York Times column, in letters to

Representatives and Senators, and in meetings with key legislators. As a result of the actions of the AFT council and president, the organization now is planning a major campaign for public-school sponsorship of expanded early childhood education and day care.

Early passage of this kind of comprehensive child-care and education program seems warranted by the combined impact of a number of social developments. To begin with, the teacher shortage of the 1960s has altered radically into the "surplus" of the seventies as the postwar-baby-boom children of the fifties have moved through and out of the public-school system. Declining student enrollment is leaving school district after school district across the country with the choice of cutting class size or firing teachers. The choice most often taken by budget-minded school boards is to cut staffs and leave classrooms empty. Some forecasters have estimated that by the end of this decade, there will be two teachers for every public-school job. The result already is the existence of a large pool of qualified teachers looking for employment alongside available but unused classrooms—even entire schools are being closed in some cases.

More Working Women

The second development favoring possible expansion of early childhood programs and day care is the growth in the number of working women who have children in need of such services. Whether for reasons of "women's liberation" or, as has been actually shown by a number of studies, the need for a second income, more women are working and consequently need child care and education for their children. The Women's Bureau of the U.S. Dept. of Labor estimates, for example, that "nearly 26 million children under 18 years old had mothers who were working or looking for work in March, 1972. More than 5.5 million of these children were under six years old. In 1960, 15.7 million children under 18 had working mothers, and about four million of these children were under age six." "Windows on Day Care," a report by Mary Dublin Keyserling based on findings of the National Council of Jewish Women, adds many other groups of children to its estimates of those in need of

*Eugenia Kemble chairs the AFT Task Force on Education Issues.

day care: 2½ million children under six whose mothers do not work but are from families in poverty; handicapped children; children of mothers who are students or are in work-training programs; and children of families who simply want sound, educational day care.

Fulfilling needs such as these with quality programs must take into account research findings about the importance of the early years to children's intellectual and social development. The most notable and frequently quoted of these experts is Benjamin Bloom, whose book "Stability and Change in Human Characteristics" reviewed a number of longitudinal studies and concluded that," . . . in terms of intelligence measured at age 17, about 50 percent of the development takes place between conception and age four, about 30 percent between ages four and eight, and about 20 percent between ages eight and 17." Bloom's belief in the developmental importance of the early years also is reflected in the work of J. McVicker Hunt, Jerome Bruner, Kenneth Wann, and Jean Piaget. A new interest in the work of these men began to emerge in the '50s and fully blossomed in the 1960s. The need to rethink the traditional custodial role of day care in light of their findings should be obvious.

The inauguration of Head Start with the passage of the Economic Opportunity Act in 1964 marked the beginning of a federal recognition that early services for children

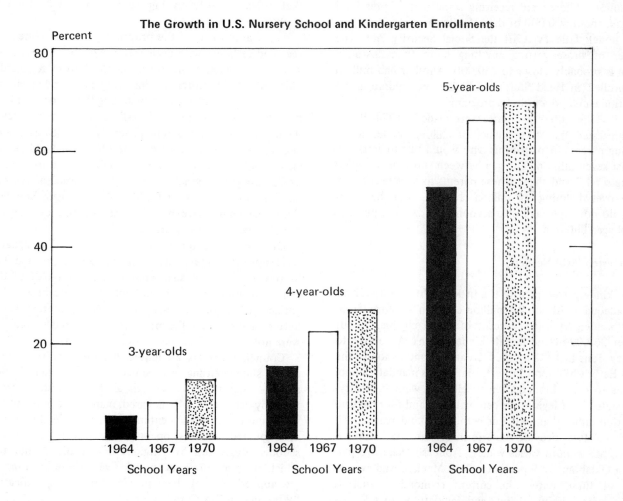

The Growth in U.S. Nursery School and Kindergarten Enrollments

Percent

3-year-olds

4-year-olds

5-year-olds

1964 1967 1970
School Years

1964 1967 1970
School Years

1964 1967 1970
School Years

Source: U.S. Office of Education, as reproduced in "Early Childhood Education," by Marlene Cotton, Croft Leadership Action Folio No. 39.

needed to be more than simple baby-sitting operations. With Head Start, compensatory education became an issue of concern to day-care providers. Head Start and its companion program, Fellow Through, reflected the first acknowledgement on the part of Congress and a presidential administration that early childhood preschool programs should have educational content. For the first time, the standard view that day care was something to use to get welfare mothers to work, had to share the public-policy arena with a new, education-oriented perspective. With Head Start and Follow Through came the recognition that developing quality preschool education for disadvantaged children might be a good idea.

Up until now, even the strengths of these developments have not turned enough political wheels to obtain adequate programs even of the traditional custodial type. William Pierce, director of policy development for the Child Welfare League of America, has estimated that even though the U.S. Dept. of Health, Education, and Welfare claims that about 1.3 million children are receiving some sort of preschool day care, about 600,000 of these "child care years" are provided under Title IV-A of the Social Security Act. The number of those getting anything more than custodial service is probably closer to 250,000. Another half million are enrolled in Head Start, which does incorporate some educational component in its programs.

At the time these estimates were made in 1974, Pierce also suggested that the number of children under six of working parents or of parents who would like to work was at least seven million. The gap between those preschoolers getting service and those whose parents may want it comes to an overwhelming six million children. And these estimates do not even take into account the day-care needs of school-aged children.

Kindergartens Still Needed

The kindergarten picture is a little brighter, but still far from adequate. About 2.1 million children are enrolled in public kindergarten—65 percent of those eligible. About another 360,00 attend private kindergartens. According to a survey done in 1972 by the Education Commission of the States Early Childhood Project, nine states mandate school districts to offer kindergarten to all who want it. Thirty-seven states have legislation permitting it, and four have no legislation either mandating or permitting kindergarten. Although 42 states provide some form of state aid to kindergartens, the amount varies widely—from as much as 75 percent in Oklahoma to 9 percent in New Mexico. And even in many of these states, the current economic crunch is causing state administrations and legislatures to take another look at their support for kindergarten. So, the subsidies we now see may be cut shortly.

As discouraging as these statistics are already, they speak nothing of the quality of services offered. In 1972, the National Council of Jewish Women published a comprehensive survey of 431 proprietary (for-profit) and nonprofit day-care centers which its members visited throughout the country (including Head Start centers, but excluding public kindergartens). What they found amounted to a devastating indictment of the quality of care offered, through the use of a scale of judgments termed "superior," "good," "fair," or "poor". In arriving at these judgments—which the Council says are necessarily somewhat impressionistic—its member-surveyors considered such characteristics as the size of the center, the buildings in which centers were housed, the degree of integration, qualifications of the staff, child-adult ratios, staff salaries, parental involvement, transportation, the educational program, supportive services, and equipment and facilities. The judgments also take into account the standards provided for in the Federal Interagency Day Care Requirements and those suggested by the Child Welfare League.

The Council's report "Windows on Day Care" concluded that private, profit-making centers provided the worst quality care:

". . . about half of the proprietary centers visited were regarded as 'poor' with respect to the quality of service rendered. Somewhat more than one-thrid were regarded as 'fair.' All of the centers in this category provided care that was essentially custodial. Even among the 15 percent of the proprietary centers in the 'good' category, only a few of them provided what is now generally regarded as comprehensive quality day care from the educational and developmental point of view. Fewer than half of the centers in this 'good' group had an adult-child ratio regarded as the minimum necessary to meet Child Welfare League Standards. Only one could have met Federal Interagency Day Care Requirements in this regard . . ."

Only one center qualified for the "superior" designation.

Nonprofit centers, including publicly supported Head Start centers, fared somewhat better. Over half of these centers qualified as "fair" and only 11.4 percent were categorized as "poor." Clearly the nonprofit centers were of better quality than the profit-makers, though even these were not as "good" as they could have been.

Council members attributed the low quality to inadequate state-licensing provisions and staff qualifications, among other things. Although all but two states require that day-care centers be licensed, many states exempt from this requirement those centers which are federally operated or regulated, centers operated by private or parochial schools, those run by religious organizations, and those which are primarily educational. Even where licensing laws are applied, few of them provide for staff qualifications. "Windows on Day Care" reports:

"In fact, a majority of states have no educational or training requirements for day-care-center teachers. Only 17 specify that the teacher must have some college education or its equivalent; nine that the teacher be a high-school graduate. The remaining states have no specifications. Even in the case of center directors, only about one-half of the states require that he or she have some college education or its equivalent; a few specify that the completion of high school is necessary, and the remaining states have no training requirements.

Since the Federal Interagency Day Care Requirements defer to the states in the licensing of centers and staff, there is very little to encourage the use of quality staff and program. To this grim picture, the council report adds the observation, "The fact that a center is licensed does not insure the continued maintenance of the prescribed standards. Most licensing offices are too understaffed to be able to monitor the centers they have approved.

Poor Quality Day Care

A more recent report published by HEW confirms this unhappy picture. The "Review of Child Care Services Provided Under Title IV, Social Security Act" found that of 552 centers and private homes in nine states, funded under Title IV of the Social Security Act to provide day care, 425 did not meet minimum health and safety requirements. More than a third did not meet child-staff-ratio requirements. Among the conditions noted were: poisons and medications stored in places accessible to children; inadequate kitchen facilities, fireproofing and outdoor play areas; and broken rusting equipment.

One of the conclusions of this report points to the problem of fragmentation that plagues the entire day-care and early childhood field. Authors of the report suggest that one of the reasons for poor administration of this program is the confusion over which agency directs its difference aspects—the Social and Rehabilitation Service or the Office of Child Development. Multiplied many times over, this kind of explanation of inadequacy pervades the field and accounts for many of the shortcomings. It may even explain why obtaining a comprehensive program with comprehensive standards has eluded the most ardent day-care and early childhood advocates.

The picture which now exists is loaded with ironies and contradictions. On the one hand are a whole list of powerful social circumstances pointing to expanded day care and early childhood education—the demands of working women; a large body of research showing the importance of the early years to intellectual development; and an extremely usable pool of qualified teachers and empty classrooms. On the other are the woeful inadequacies of early childhood and day-care services in terms of availability, standards, and staff qualifications. It would not seem to be an overwhelming intellectual task for social engineers and groups at interest to fit these two sets of conditions together. But it has not happened. The reasons probably have something to do with the structure of the early childhood and day-care field—the failure of a unified constituency to develop—and the organization of both the federal legislation subsidizing such programs and the federal bureaucracies which administer these subsidies. The picture can be described at best as chaotic.

Programs Overlap

Anyone trying to figure out what is going on in early childhood education and day care today is immediately impressed with the confusion of overlapping federal legislation, of state-federal jurisdictional lines, and of conflicting constituency interests—often of an extremely petty and

---

How Good Are Present Day Care Centers?

The following table is taken from "Windows on Day Care," by Mary Dublin Keyserling, a report based on findings of the National Council of Jewish Women, 1972, p. 120. It shows the number and percent distribution of nonprofit and proprietary centers by impression[1] of quality of care.

| Impression of Care[1] | Non-Profit Centers by Auspices | | | | | | | | | | | | | | Proprietary centers | |
	Head Start No.	%	Other Public No.	%	Philanthropic No.	%	Part Public Part Philan. No.	%	Hospital No.	%	Other No.	%	Total No.	%	No.	%
Superior	5	10.9	4	8.3	6	8.8	6	8.0	2	16.7	3	9.7	26	9.3	1	1.0
Good	15	32.6	15	31.2	23	33.8	21	28.0	4	33.3	1	3.2	79	28.2	15	14.5
Fair	22	47.8	26	54.2	30	44.1	44	58.7	4	33.3	17	54.8	143	51.1	36	35.0
Poor	4	8.7	3	6.3	9	13.3	4	5.3	2	16.7	10	32.3	32	11.4	51	49.5
Total	46	100.0	48	100.0	68	100.0	75	100.0	12	100.0	31	100.0	280	100.0	103	110.0
Inadequate Information	1	—			11		4		1		7		24		24	

[1] Impression of care is based on review of such factors as adult-child ratios, size of groups, services reported to be available, salaries reported paid, information on training, parental participation, hours open, observations of council survey participants on educational program, space, equipment, and other relevant aspects of care.

parochial nature. There are today some 60 or more federal programs that contribute to the funding of early childhood and day-care programs. The Women's Bureau of the U.S. Department of Labor has listed them all exhaustively in a 90-page pamphlet called "Federal Funds for Day Care Projects." They are administered by everything from the unlikely Department of Agriculture and Small Business Administration to the more obvious divisions of HEW—the Office of Child Development, the Social and Rehabilitation Service, and the Office of Education. The largest share of day care and early childhood education funds come under the legislative authorities of the Social Security Act, the Economic Opportunity Act, the Elementary and Secondary Education Act, and the Manpower Development and Training Act. (See Chart A for a summary breakdown of the main programs these acts authorize and the federal agencies which administer them.)

Not surprisingly, the various groups pressing for expansion of all these programs mirror the programs and legislation—and with equal complexity and confusion. Each group has its own axe to grind, often at the expense of the larger picture. As long as they fail to comprehend the structural failure of their lobbying efforts, day care and early childhood services probably will continue to be relegated to a legislative back seat.

Among the more powerful of the groups at interest are the AFL-CIO and the teachers' organizations. Of the teachers, the American Federation of Teachers is speaking on this particular issue with a louder voice—partly because the National Education Association suffers from some of the same organizational fragmentation as the day-care field.

In an excellent essay found in Pamela Roby's useful book "Child Care—Who cares?," Virginia Kerr comments perceptively on the meaning of the organizational maze surrounding early childhood education and day care:

...day care continues to suffer as an institution in search of a reliable professional constituency. One does not have to go far even today to find a social worker or an early childhood educator who will comment on the need for more and better day care, and at the same time deprecate the use of day care by women who do not have to work. Without such a constituency, the success of efforts to lobby for expansion of day care at local, state, and federal levels is contingent on the ability of its advocates to effect working coalitions among professionals and agencies competing for control of programs and among community and social-reform groups who often balk at any signs of compromise to their particular philosophies of care. . ."

But Kerr and others fail to take such observations one step further: If the legislation sponsoring day care and early childhood education was in one piece and provided a comprehensive program administered by a single agency and a single presumed* prime sponsor at the state and local level, would not this facilitate coalition-building among teachers

and other day-care advocates to further expand federal support—support which might eventually create the scope and variation in quality programs that all child advocates want?

The creation of the Office of Child Development in 1970 for the purpose of coordinating children's programs represented an unsuccessful gesture at making order out of chaos. To begin with, it could not even administer all the programs. The basic problems of fragmented constituency

CHART A

**Major Sources of
Federal Funding for Day Care**

SOCIAL SECURITY ACT

Program	Administering Agency
Aid to Dependent Children: grants-in-aid to state public-welfare agencies for day care	Social and Rehabilitation Service (HEW)
Work Incentive Program: job training and day-care services for welfare recipients	Social and Rehabilitation Service (HEW)
Child Welfare Service: day-care services, training and demonstration projects	Social and Rehabilitation Service (HEW)

ECONOMIC OPPORTUNITY ACT

Head Start: day care puls educational and other services	Office of Child Development (HEW)
Parent and Child Centers: comprehensive services to children under three	Office of Child Development (HEW)
Migrant and Seasonal Farm Workers: day-care services to migrant farm families	Community Services Administration (HEW)

ELEMENTARY AND SECONDARY EDUCATION ACT

Title I: public-school preschool programs; may coordinate with Head Start or AFDC to add educational component	Office of Education (HEW)
Migrant Program: education of migrant children	Office of Education (HEW)
Follow Through: follow-up educational, health, and social services to children completing Head Start	Office of Education (HEW)

MANPOWER DEVELOPMENT AND TRAINING ACT

Concentrated Employment Program: day-care services to facilitate employability	Prime Sponsor
New Careers: day-care services to those training for jobs	Manpower Administration
Neighborhood Youth Corps: assignment of youth as day-care aides	Manpower Administration, Bureau of Work Training

Sources: "Federally Sponsored Child Care," by Stevanne Auerbach "Child Care—Who Cares?," edited by Pamela Roby, Basic Books, 1973, and "Day Care Facts," Women's Bureau, U.S. Department of Labor, 1973.

remained to plague its efforts. And there was no administrative authority locally—such as the public-school system—to tie all of the funding strands together.

Day Care in Disarray

There are also serious substantive reasons why the day-care and early childhood field is in such disarray—reasons that have to be thrashed out before a real child-advocacy coalition can be built. It is not enough to simply suggest that everyone get together. There are disagreements related to the purpose and the quality of programs that are worth exposing and arguing about.

To begin with, the idea that day care should—or even could—be educational is relatively new, and is by no means universally accepted. Even those who recognize the potential of this idea may have vested interests in cheaper, custodial varieties of day care. The identification of day care as essentially a babysitting operation has a long history extending back to the early part of the 19th century in this country. Its most dramatic and telling expansion in recent history came during World War II, when federal financing under the Lanham, or Community Facilities Act, was freed for use in funding child-care centers. Forty-seven states established a total of 3,102 centers serving 600,000 children. When the war was over, federal funding ended and the centers closed down everywhere but in California and New York City. (Interestingly enough, Virginia Kerr attributes the continued public funding of day care in California and New York City to the existence of powerful, unified day-care constituencies there.)

What is interesting about the Lanham episode is the way it defined day care in terms that persist right up until today. The centers were created simply because mothers needed to get out and work to serve the defense needs of the country—not because children were thought to need the enriching experience of preschool or because women were insisting on more "liberated" lives. Day care was regarded as nothing more than a custodial operation that enabled women to work (women who—it was still felt—more appropriately belonged in the home with children who—it was still felt—needed their invided attention.

The postwar period was marked by strong sentiment against mothers working, reinforced by the publication of such books as John Bowlby's "Maternal Care and Mental Health," which argued that a continuous warm relationship with the mother was essential to a child's mental health. Day care and preschool—what little there was of it—were as unpopular and as out of tune with pervading social views as the working mothers who needed them, not to mention the many children who might have benefitted from good early childhood programs.

Day Care For The Poor

Since working, and therefore day care, were viewed as negative interferences with a healthy mother-child relationship then, curiously, the obverse situation also came to be regarded as true. If the mother-child relationship was "unhealthy," either for reasons of poverty or family breakdown, then day care was thought to be acceptable—it could even be used as a means of allowing welfare mothers to get out of the house and work. A double standard was being applied, of course—middle-class mothers should be home with their children, the reasoning went, but poor mothers should get out and work, particularly if they are on public welfare—but the definition of day care as an essentially custodial operation remained the same. Such notions exist even today. They are behind the Work Incentive Program funded by the Social Security Act, for example.

Even in the 1960s, when the work of Bloom and others began to point to the crucial importance of a child's early experience to his or her intellectual development, day care continued to be regarded in custodial terms. This is partly true, no doubt, because the first major breakthrough in federal funding for day care since the Lanham days came in the form of day care for welfare recipients under an amendment to the Social Security Act in 1962. (Underneath all the current debates about quality day care, there seems to exist an assumption that the children of welfare mothers do not deserve very much. Curiously, many organizations in early childhood and day care which claim to speak for the poor are doing their best to keep costs and standards down.) The bloom-type theories seemed reasonable to many parents and they enrolled their children in preschool programs. But day care remained in a category by itself. Virginia Kerr comments on this phenomenon as it emerged in the resolutions passed by the 1960 White House Conference on Children and Youth:

"The resolutions reflected the tradition of regarding the nursery school as a positive experience and day care as an unpleasant necessity and highlighted the ambivalence that accompanied attempts to merge the two services. In spite of the economic egalitarianism in the nursery-school recommendation, nurseries were clearly conceived as the only suitable type of service for upper-middle-income families, while their relative, day care, was endorsed with caution. Throughout the 1960s, federal spending for day care increased significantly but in a pattern calculated to reinforce an already segregated system of services—public day care for the poor, private nursery schools or child-care centers for the affluent, and potluck for those families who fell in neither category.

*(a) they meet the bill's standards, and (b) they wish to do so.

Head Start Begins

The one apparent exception to this pattern was Head Start, funded by the Elementary and Secondary Education Act in 1965. Head Start was created at a unique time when the ideas of the early childhood theorists were beginning to catch on and when the nation was willing to define special funding for the poor in educational terms. Though Head Start marks the beginning of a willingness to think about day care in terms of educational programs, the divided thinking which categorizes day care as custodial, and pre-school and kindergarten programs as educational still exists.

Perhaps the custodial and educational strands in the thinking of early childhood and day-care advocates were brought closer together during consideration of the Comprehensive Child Development Program in 1971.

This bill would have provided for a nationally coordinated network of child-development programs linked to federal resources through a single office within HEW. It would have incorporated existing programs like Head Start and added a wide range of other services. These services would have been universally available to children of working and nonworking mothers alike from all socio-economic strata. In doing this, the bill was acknowledging implicitly the value of quality day care as an educational experience for all children—not just those who were the offspring of career women or whose mothers were being prodded into working by the welfare system. This program—found in the child-development title of the Economic Opportunity Act (EOA)—was vetoed by President Nixon partly on the grounds that it had "family-weakening implications."

Even while Nixon was vetoing the EOA's child-development provisions out of concern for family solidarity, his administration was guiding the Family Assistance Plan through Congress. This plan provided day-care specifically to poor mothers and offered tax deductions to families when both parents were employed. Apparently the "family-weakening implications" of day care for the poor were perfectly acceptable in this legislation. In taking these steps on these two bills, the administration was reenforcing the entrenched notion that day care is a cheap custodial operation for the poor and not to be confused with education.

Universal Child Care Needed

The time has come for day care and preschool education to be combined and made universally available to all children. Women want it; research supports enriched early learning experiences for children; and the public schools, with the help of federal funding, now can offer the facilities and staff to make them a reality. Teachers are the most logical group to lead this fight as the core of a potentially unified early childhood constituency because they are organized and because they are connected to every public-school system in the country.

Unfortunately, this is a bad time for teachers to be urging a major expansion of public-school services. The public schools are under attack from a whole spectrum of critics, ranging from the "new left" deschoolers who claim that schools are like prisons and teachers are insensitive, to the more conservative budget-cutters who prefer to hang their hats on performance-oriented accountability plans and industrial models like Programming, Planning, and Budgeting Systems (PPBS) or performance contracting. In between are the voucher advocates and even the career-educationists, some of whom would like to turn as much of secondary education as possible over to private business.

Many of the groups now active in the early childhood and day-care field are sympathetic to one or the other of these camps and can be expected to oppose the AFT's support of public schools as presumed prime sponsors of programs funded under the new Child and Family Services Act. Already vocal in their opposition are such persons as Theodore Taylor, executive director of the Day Care and Child Development Council of America, Inc.; Jule Sugarman, chief administrative officer for the city of Atlanta and former acting chief of the old Children's Bureau; and

---

CHART B

Board Action Regarding Eligibility Requirements for the CDA Credential Application (Excerpted from minutes of the board of directors of the Child Development Associate Consortium, Dec. 7, 1974)

Eligibility Requirements Presented in Form of Motions	Board Action
1. For the purpose of assessment, proof of access to a child-development center.	Passed—unanimous.
2. Minimum age of 16 years.	Passed—unanimous.
3. Evidence of formal or informal child-development/early childhood education training.	Passed—unanimous.
4. Not less than 12 months full-time experience working with young children in a state-approved center.	Defer action for further study by staff and committee.
5. No conviction of any offense related to child abuse.	Approve inclusion of concept in eligibility requirements with further clarification brought to board for final decision on wording.
6. Ability to read and write English	Voted to delete from eligibility requirements.
In the near future, provision should be made for translation of all CDAC materials into needed languages.	Voted not be included as an eligibility requirement but supported as a separate policy decision. That in the near future provisions should be made for translation of all CDAC materials into needed languages.

Marion Wright Edelman, director of the Children's Defense Fund of the Washington Research Project Action Council. The National Association for Child Development and Education, which lobbies in behalf of profit-making day care, will probably join them, if it hasn't already.

In fact, virtually every group now involved in some aspect of federally funded preschool and day care—including the relevant offices in the various federal agencies that now administer those programs—can be expected to have some interest in the status quo and will probably criticize the AFT's position. Some Head Start directors and parents have recently questioned it, for example, preferring direction by local community-based boards and parent committees to public-school administration. Undoubtedly, the Child Development Associate Consortium, a group funded by the Office of Child Development to come up with "competency-based" definitions of early childhood and day-care professional qualifications, will have some problems with the certification and licensing standards of most school systems (see Chart B for its thinking on this subject as of December, 1974).

Despite these obstacles, the argument for public-school presumed prime sponsorship must be made. There are some likely allies on the scene, including U.S. Commissioner of Education Terrell Bell and Sen. Dale Bumpers (D-Ark.), Rep. William Lehman (D-Fla.) and Rep. Albert Quie (R-Minn.). They have expressed interest in expanding early childhood education programs within the public school system. Others can and must be found within the House and Senate.

Job For Public Schools

The value and legitimacy of using the public schools as a prime sponsor for early childhood and day-care programs should be clear. Current offerings are far from adequate—either in terms of numbers or quality. Existing programs are fragmented and incoherent—a situation which prevents the formation of a unified constituency to push for more and better programs. The facilities we have now do not provide enough in the way of educational program, nor are they qualified to do so. Using the public schools to administer

programs under the new bill would go far toward remedying all these ills.

It is fair and much more democratic for public money to be administered through public institutions. This is what makes public schools accountable for their use of funds. There is every reason why all federal funds likewise should be administered by publicly accountable bodies. Certification requirements and standards for the quality of facilities also should be set by elected officials or their designated agents. Schools are subject to democratic policy-making by elected bodies, unlike private, profit-making entities in the day-care business. State and local agencies should not delegate their public authority and responsibility in the administration of federal funds to private or unaccountable agencies.

For all these reasons, the American Federation of Teachers is convinced that the currently suggested legislation must be altered and urges that it be amended to provide for:

● A new federal funding commitment reaching $2 billion per year for early childhood education and day care.

● Universally available early childhood and day-care services offered on a voluntary basis through the public school system.

● The application of federal standards and program-licensing practices to all programs funded, and the requirements that all local school codes and laws be followed as well.

● Provision for the retraining of locally licensed personnel where necessary.

● Sufficient earmarking of funds to provide for extensive health, nutrition, counseling, and other necessary support services.

● Staffing ratios of one adult to 10 children for children six and over; 1:7 for five-year-olds; 1:5 for threes and fours; and 1:2 for infants.

● Provision for the training and use of paraprofessionals.

Should such a program gain support and eventually be enacted, day care and early childhood programs probably would become enduring components of the American public-school system which, with the help of a unified constituency of supporters, might even be expanded and improved from year to year.

Chapter 9

The Urgency of Child Care

Joyce D. Miller[*]

In this country, child care historically has been the family's job. Well into the 1900s, extended family groups that included grandparents, aunts and cousins often lived under one roof or near enough for frequent visits and family dinners. Several adults shared the responsibilities of child rearing and children were exposed to different people with different ideas, relationships, skills and competences.

Historically, facilities were set up to take care of children from poor families, or from families that could not adequately care for their children. For those who could afford them, educationally oriented nursery schools or private in-home arrangements were available. Alternative care was not available to those who could not pay the price except in desperate situations. When the first day care centers were established in New York City in the middle of the 19th century, it was for immigrant women, often separated from their families, who supported themselves and their children in the sweatshops of that time.

But the nation never has had a comprehensive philosophy of child care services, within which programs could have developed as a form of supplementary care, rather than as either a social work service to troubled families or a commercialized form of custodial care. This negative attitude toward child care has affected its desirability as well as its availability.

Over the course of this century, the percentage of fathers and mothers working outside the home has risen steadily. This has sometimes been a major factor in the increased demand for publicly supported child care. First fathers, then other male relatives left the household for a different workplace, sharply decreasing the care, training and supervision available to older children.

In the past 20 years, mothers, older daughters and other relatives have increasingly started working, thus decreasing the supply of both parents and relatives available for child care. An overlapping series of changes has had a cumulative effect on the family—the increased social acceptability and economic necessity for women to work outside the home; the desire of women with access to higher levels of education to use their training in a paying job: and the changing roles of women.

It is no longer relevant to talk about whether women with preschool or school-age children should work. They are already working, with women with children of all ages entering the labor force in ever increasing number.

In March 1974, almost 22 million women with husbands present and children under 18 were employed. Another 4.6 million women, heads of families with children under 18, also worked. These figures will continue to increase as rising prices and inflation require two incomes for basic family support. By 1985, the Department of Labor estimates that 6.6 million mothers aged 20 to 44 with children under five will be either working or looking for work. The number of children with working parents has continued to rise, even though the total population of children in the United States has declined substantially since 1970. A Special Labor Force Report indicated that by March 1973, there were 1.5 million fewer children in United States families, but 650,000 more had working mothers.

The 1973 figures present a startling picture of how the family has changed:

- Almost 45 percent of the nation's mothers were employed outside of the home.
- One in every 3 mothers with children under 6 was working.
- 10 percent of all children under 6, or 2.2 million, were living in single parent families with no father present.
- In a single parent family with the mother working, the average income was $4,200.
- Average income for a single parent family with children under 6 was $3,100.
- 1 million children under 6 with working mothers lived in families below the poverty level, defined by the government at $4,540 per year for a family of four.
- 1 million children of working mothers lived in families below the poverty level, defined by the government at $4,540 per year for a family of four.
- 1 million children of working mothers lived in families with incomes which are near-poverty—or $4,000 to $7,000 year for a family of four.
- As of 1972, the nation had licensed *child* care slots

*Joyce D. Miller is social services director and executive assistant to the general officers of the Amalgamated Clothing Workers of America. Reprinted with permission from The American Federationist, June 1975.

for 1,021,202 children, including full day care, half day care, licensed day care homes and Head Start.

Though a good deal of information is available on the economics and social characteristics of children with working parents, little is known about the current supply and demand for child care services and facilities. Most available information is either several years old or limited in scope. Earlier studies indicated that most pre-school children of working parents were cared for in the children's homes by older brothers and sisters, who often were forced to be absent or drop out of school; by grandmothers or other relatives; in the homes of neighbors, relatives or babysitters; or left without supervision.

The public response to the increased interest in and demand for children's services has been mixed: expectant, confused, impatient and contradictory. The growing effect, though slow, has been an increase in the pressure for improved services for children which has started to be reflected in the actions of government.

The reasons for the confusion are as diverse as the kinds of programs offered:

• Government continues to see child care as an agent for shifting mothers off the welfare rolls and into jobs.

• Industry sees child care as a fringe benefit to attract workers and stabilize the productivity of working parents.

• Women and minorities, in a press for equality of opportunity, have viewed child care as expanding options.

• Communities view child care in relation to federal dollars available.

• Universities see an additional source of training and research monies.

• Parents who don't need the service see it as threatening to take over a role that properly belongs to the family.

• Families who do need child care are concerned about the many aspects of providing quality care for their children and see child care as essential to their livelihood and entire way of life.

While the influx of women into the workforce has made the child care problem visible, it has not necessarily helped clarify what kind of child care the nation should be seeking. Analyzing the need for child care solely in terms of the increasing numbers of working mothers runs the risk of inadequate consideration of both the need and the potential range of solutions.

Resources, both private and public, leave a large gap between the very poor who are served by government programs and the more affluent who can pay for child care and nursery schools. In between are the families who have too much income to be eligible for most public programs and too little to afford good privately operated child care, even if they found it available.

To most people, the term child care means group day care centers or in its broadest sense, any situation where a child is cared for by someone other than a parent or guardian. This care takes many forms:

Baby-sitting for children in their own home can be provided by a live-in relative or housekeeper, a relative or friend coming each day or a sitter who is paid hourly.

Family day care is provided in the home of a relative, friend, neighbor or caregiver who is paid for the care. A caregiver or "provider" mother may be trained, licensed and supervised by a social agency, or may be unlicensed. These are frequently used for up to 6 children per home and offer flexible hours. Some family day care is also available for school age children in homes which offer mainly supervision.

Family day care systems link individual day care homes as satellites of a group child care center. In these instances the *centers will provide training for persons caring for children* in their own homes *or* if there is no center, the *sponsoring agency will do the training.*

Nursery schools or part-day programs under varying auspices may be free or may charge tuition. Most nursery schools are staffed by early childhood educators and see themselves as part of the educational system. These programs can operate for five days or a week or less.

Full-day group care can be operated under public, proprietary (for profit) or non-profit sponsorship. In most instances publicly funded programs are free to those who meet income-related eligibility. Proprietary centers base their fees on whatever margin of profit they hope to make. In non-profit programs, fees are determined by the sponsoring agency. Private, not-for-profit agencies usually subsidize part of the cost and often have a sliding fee scale. These centers usually serve children from 2½ or 3 years to 5 or 6 years. In a very few centers provisions are made for *infant care.* In both public and not-for-profit group care centers, there is a core of professionally trained staff. They supervise paraprofessionals and sometimes volunteers. The programs of the centers are usually very concerned with the child's development and work closely with the families of the children enrolled. Often, the centers will offer half-day as well as full-day care with flexible time for arrival and departure of the children within the hours of 6 or 7 a.m. to 6 p.m., five days a week. In most states the ratio of adults to children is prescribed by law.

Parent cooperative programs take on different forms. They may vary from full day care to informal play groups where toddlers meet once or twice a week under the direct supervision of some or all of the parents. Parents decide the *structure, including what the fees will be.* Parent cooperative programs must conform *to state licensing and other regulations.*

Head Start centers are pre-school education programs, mostly half-day, designed to prepare children in low-income areas for elementary school experience and learning.

Twenty-four hour care is available from some *religious groups.* In this type of situation the parent continues to have the main responsibility for decisions regarding the child's life, but the residential care is an extension of parental care and the lifestyle of that particular family.

These various options are often combined, based on the needs of the child, the parent and the resources of the community. The quality and comprehensiveness of the care which children receive depend primarily on the decisions made by those responsible. Who cooks, who purchases the supplies and who substitutes in the kitchen in an emergency can be as crucial to the quality of care of children as the more interesting decisions about curriculum and equipment.

These widely varied programs do not begin to add up to a national commitment to children. The infant mortality rate in the United States is higher than in 12 other major developed countries; 5 million children suffer from malnutrition; vast numbers of handicapped children receive no services; retarded children live in situations which amount to "institutionalized child abuse", child abuse and neglect is growing as a problem among all social and economic groups; teenage alcoholism is rising along with drug abuse; one of every nine children enters juvenile court before the 18th birthday; and suicide is the second leading cause of death for young Americans between ages of 15 and 24.

Unfortunately the momentum for a comprehensive federal involvement in child care services was broken, first by the 1971 veto of the Comprehensive Child Development Act and subsequently by the economic tailspin.

In December 1971, Congress passed the Comprehensive Child Development Act of 1971, making major child care available to all children as an extension of the Economic Opportunity Act. Authorization provided for up to $2 billion for its second year. But President Nixon vetoed the act, issuing an unusually strong statement of unwillingness to commit "the vast moral authority of the national government to the side of communal approaches to child rearing over against the family-centered approach." The bill was denounced for "fiscal irresponsibility, administrative unworkability and family-weakening implications." With the statement that "neither the need nor the desirability of a national child development program of this character has been demonstrated," three years of painstaking investigation by Congress were washed out—along with 1,715 pages of testimony by 166 experts and the recommendations of 4,000 participants of the White House Conference on Children, which the President had himself called in 1970.

Following the veto, the Administration's stiffened attitude toward all social programs often included bypassing Congress and accomplishing its aims by issuing departmental regulations. In February 1973, HEW issued the first of several sets of restrictions curtailing spending under Social Security, Title IV-A, the largest source of funding for programs that aid families and children.

When some people question the feasibility of establishing public child care centers on a large-scale basis in the United States, they are usually unaware that this country has earlier experienced one of the most massive, innovative and far-reaching child care programs ever attempted.

Until the Great Depression of the 1930s, the United States was the only major industrial country that did not provide some type of federally funded child care program. On October 23, 1933, the administrator of the Federal Emergency Relief Administration (FERA) authorized funds to provide wages for unemployed teachers and other workers on relief. Within three months, 30 states had organized a system of emergency nursery schools to make use of these funds. Some were open for five hours a day, some for nine hours and in several cases the schools functioned 24 hours around the clock.

From 1933 to 1940 the federal government spent $3.1 million on child care and provided services to 300,000 children. Three-quarters of these services were housed in public school buildings, which people felt were both desirable and possible, for provision of care and education of children under five years of age. The administrator of FERA supported the idea that the emergency nursery schools should become "a permanent and integral part of the regularly established public school programs." Today, there are state or locally supported kindergartens for five-year-olds, although in some states the programs are very limited—approximately 11 states mandate kindergartens for all who want them.

The second spurt of public child care began with the entry of the United States into World War II. Between January 1941 and January 1944, the number of employed women increased by 4 million. In August 1942, the War Manpower Commission ordered a program of federally supported child care centers for the children of working mothers in war-related industries. The President made available $400,000 from emergency funds. Almost at the same time, Congress passed a community facilities bill, the Lanham Act, which provided an initial $150 million for facilities including child care centers, to the same industrial area.

By June 1943, less than a year later, 39 states had fully operating, extended school services administered by state and local education authorities, and 30 states had similar services administered by welfare agencies. At the peak of July 1945, approximately 1.6 million children were enrolled in nursery schools and child care centers receiving federal funds.

The state response was also sizable. Within three years, 16 states lowered school age admission to provide for children below six years, 13 states passed laws for the establishment of nursery schools, 10 gave authority to local schools to use local funds for nursery schools and five states provided funds for emergency "child care programs for children 2–14 years old."

Besides the program for pre-school children, the centers

THE ONLY REAL ANSWER ... A FEDERAL COMMITMENT

The unmet need for child care is greater today than it has ever been because large and growing numbers of women have to work. They are being forced to leave their children without the care and attention they need. Other mothers, on public assistance, want jobs but cannot find adequate child care.

More mothers are constantly entering the labor force and many more need and want work. But lack of adequate child care poses a major problem to all of them.

By any measurement, the nation lacks a comprehensive system of quality child care services to meet these needs. Some local efforts in the child care field have been undertaken over the years with some success. Thousands of children have received beneficial, high-quality services from programs developed by trade unions, parent cooperatives, and local community organizations and church groups. Such programs fill an important need in the communities they serve. These programs, like the excellent centers operated by a number of AFL-CIO affiliates, should be encouraged and continued.

But these scattered efforts, however worthwhile are clearly far from enough. The only real answer is a massive federal commitment to the provision of early childhood development and day care.

Prime sponsors must be responsible elected officials. The AFL-CIO believes that there is great merit in giving the public school systems this prime sponsorship role.

In most communities, the school system would be the appropriate prime sponsor of the child care and early childhood development program, with the responsibility for planning programs, distributing funds and monitoring programs. Where the school system is unwilling or unable to undertake this responsibility in accordance with federal standards, some other appropriate public or non-profit community organization should be eligible.

Even where the public school systems are the prime sponsor, all of the services need not actually be offered in public school facilities. For instance, communities may want in-home childcare, family and group day care homes for children who are too young or not ready for large school facilities as well as special services for the emotionally and physically handicapped which may be offered outside the educational system.

Only public and non-profit groups should be permitted to participate in the program. There is no legitimate role for profit-making entrepreneurs in child care programs. The sorry record of profit-making organiza-

tions in the provision of human services, especially in the nursing home, health care and education fields, has led the AFL-CIO to strongly oppose any involvement of profit-makers in human services programs. Profit-makers were excluded from providing day care under Head Start. They should continue to be excluded in any new early childhood and day care programs.

To meet America's need for a high quality early childhood education and child care program, the AFL-CIO calls upon Congress to enact legislation that includes the following elements:

• Achievement as rapidly as possible of the goal of free, high-quality comprehensive early childhood education and child care services for all children who need them. Since the program will necessarily require a period of time to get fully under way, gradually increased funds should be provided toward earliest achievement of this goal.

• Coordination by the prime sponsor of a range of programs, including health, nutrition, counseling and other necessary support services and child care in a variety of settings, including family and group day care homes.

• Use of the public school systems as the presumed prime sponsors, wherever they are prepared to undertake quality programs meeting federal requirements.

• Insistence that all services must meet federal requirements and standards as well as all local school and facility codes and laws.

• Denying profit-making operators eligibility to receive federal funds.

• Declare existing public and private non-profit programs that meet federal requirements eligible to receive funds.

• Provide for effective parent involvement in these programs, since they are programs parents voluntarily choose.

• Require that all construction, renovation and repair undertaken under the program must conform to the prevailing wage standards of the Davis-Bacon Act.

• Provide for training, re-training and in-service training of professional and paraprofessional staff.

• Provide full protection of the job rights and employment conditions of workers in child care programs.

—Excerpted from statement on early childhood education and child care program adopted by the AFL-CIO Executive Council in May 1975.

were opened to older children after school, weekends, holidays, or whenever necessary; to non-enrolled children whose regular child care arrangements broke down; and to children who needed to stay on an extra shift because their parents were working overtime, attending union meetings or had recreational needs. Other extras included an infirmary, immunizations, home services food which could be picked up by parents after work, a mending service, a shopping service, barbers, a lending library of books and toys, booklets on child development and child care, a newsletter for parents and a store of necessities.

During both these periods, educators joined social welfare's early domination of child care services. Unfortunately, this liaison ended when, at the end of the war, centers were closed as quickly as they had opened. Within months, federal funds were withdrawn from all child care programs across the country. Although several states passed laws to provide state funding for child care, only California and New York City have retained public centers on a large-scale basis, largely for the disadvantaged poor.

When the government closed down the centers, many people struggled to keep the centers open, but their movement was not organized or powerful enough to change government policy.

In the mid-1960s, the federal government again began to increase its support for child care. Head Start began in 1965. In 1967, Title IV-A of the Social Security Act provided for an unlimited 75 percent federal reimbursement for costs for state investments in child care for welfare recipients, potential welfare recipients, and former welfare recipients. Its open-ended provision and broad coverage have been used by some states, such as Michigan and California, to broadly expand child care services.

Other states have held back from using Title IV-A extensively. Unwilling to provide the mandated 25 percent state support, lacking a clear public policy, incompletely understanding the issues, and fearing a massive, uncontrollable expansion of child care programs, some cautious politicians and administrators chose to wait until public demand was greater and the implications for government action more clear.

In 1968, Follow Through was developed to learn how to carry the gains of Head Start into primary schools. In early 1969 the Office of Child Development was established within the U.S. Department of Health, Education and Welfare as a major symbol of increased federal recognition of the importance of focusing on children.

In 1970 serious moves were made to bring reform in the welfare system and increasing pressure to improve child care and early education generated some movement. Major research projects were funded. The federal government commissioned studies to examine the issues, the costs and benefits of different kinds of services to children, the definition of "good" child care and how much it costs, the effectiveness of Head Start, Follow Through, Sesame Street and the delivery systems that should be developed to support children's services at the local level.

The White House Conference on Children in December 1970 increased the visibility of the needs of children and the pressure for government action to support expanded services. The stage was set for action when the Day Care Forum of the meeting stated that child care was a universal right and should be available to all children, regardless of race or social class.

In 1971 several bills were introduced in Congress to provide federal funds for child care. New bills and revisions of earlier ones appeared almost monthly. They slowly worked their way through Congress without a clear consensus on what approach or which bill should be supported. The debates echoed earlier issues of cost, eligibility, delivery systems, the role of the state governments, the effect on the welfare rolls and how much compensatory early education would really help disadvantaged children.

Several attempts have been made to revive the basic legislation. In 1972, a comprehensive Head Start, Child Development and Family Services Act passed the Senate by 72-13, but was never acted on in the House. The latest legislative attempt, the Child and Family Services Act of 1974, also re-introduced in January 1975, reflected the efforts of months of dialogue and the "national debate of child care" that was called for in the veto message of 1971.

Federal support for child care has risen from less than $10 million in the early 1960s to $1.03 billion affecting 1,338,080 children in 1973-74 (not including tax deductions for child care permitted under the Internal Revenue Act of 1971). Even so, Social Security money has gone unspent. The $2.5 billion in IV-A money attached to a revenue sharing bill has only been fully utilized in 13 states—including New York, Illinois, Washington and California. While advocates campaign to raise the ceiling on this money to $4 billion, $1.5 billion is being returned to the U.S. Treasury. General revenue sharing money has similarly gone unspent for services needs; an estimated 1 percent has gone to programs for children. Most communities have instead preferred visible, one-time efforts for these funds.

Changes continue constantly in the concept of federal support for the delivery of public services. Title XX of the Social Security Act was passed by the House and subsequently, at the last session of the 93rd Congress, by the Senate. This legislation replaced Title IV-A and will raise the eligibility requirements to a level where working people can gain access to many vital social services, including publicly supported child care. States will be required to hold public hearings on how this money will be spent.

The private sector also has become involved during this legislative stalemate. A number of new franchise operations were organized with the anticipation that with a major influx of federal funds, careful planning and economies of scale, child care could become a profitable business. Some industries experimented with child care to provide better working conditions for their employees and to reduce employee turnover. Some provided in-plant or nearby facilities, often operated through the private educational groups which have sprung up in the child care field. Most of these facilities required a payment by participating parents and were limited to the children of the plant workers.

But the Wall Street Journal reported in 1972 that fewer than two dozen industry sponsored programs were in operation around the country. Two centers which had closed gave the reason as lack of participation. Many parents find other types of care more convenient, or are distrustful of such group care operations. Recently, industry has instead moved to develop joint consortium programs in some urban centers with neighborhood-based programs.

In response to the enormous need for federal legislation, organized labor has continued as an active member of a coalition of private organizations formed prior to the Comprehensive Child Development Act veto. Prominent in this child care coalition were the AFL-CIO and numerous unions along with such other organizations as the League of Women Voters, the Leadership Conference on Civil Rights and the National Council of Churches.

The coalition viewed child care as providing children with a rich array of social experience with other children and adults, while pursuing basic physical, emotional and intellectual developmental objectives. Whether this environment was supplemental, complementary or a replacement to the child's home depends on the needs of individual families and children.

Unions have recognized that their commitment to a better standard of living and higher quality of life extends beyond the workplace to other needs of workers and their families. And union leaders have seen on trips to Italy or Scandinavia that virtually every European country has a more advanced policy than the United States toward services to children and families.

Union efforts in setting up child care programs have varied widely—from a Seafarers' program in Ponce, Puerto Rico, to a Newspaper Guild program in Vancouver-New Westminster, British Columbia.

One of the most active unions in setting up child care facilities has been the Clothing Workers, which has a large number of women members. Pilot centers sponsored by the ACWA Baltimore board first opened in September 1968 in Verona, Va. Five additional centers have been constructed since in Baltimore, in Chambersburg, Hanover and McConnellsburg, Pa., and Winchester, Va., providing child care for over 1,300 children. Approximately 75 area clothing manufacturers contribute a percentage of their total gross payrolls to a jointly operated health and welfare fund administered by seven trustees from labor and seven from management. Today this plan provides care for more children than any other private U.S. organization.

It costs the center $37 a week to care for each child; parents pay $1 per day per child. The six centers have a total staff of 150 and offer a complete range of developmental services. Each center offers a kindergarten program fully accredited by the respective states. A full-time nurse at each center coordinates the weekly visits of a pediatrician. About 90 percent of the child's nutritional needs are provided by the center in serving breakfast, lunch and an afternoon snack. The centers have a fully equipped institutional kitchen and can quickly deliver the family-style meals which provide a transition between morning activities and the afternoon rest period. The largest center, in downtown Baltimore, serves 300 children. The center's 20 classrooms are divided into four areas—art, block-building, science and housekeeping. It is also the office for the program's administrator and education director, responsible for much of the planning for the total program.

In Chicago, the Amalgamated Child Day Care and Health Center opened in March 1970 and serves 60 children. Under the direction of an early childhood educator, this center offers a complete range of educational, social, medical, dental and nutritional services without charge to participating families. To be eligible for the service, one parent must be a union member. The program is funded by the Amalgamated Social Benefits Association, a pre-Taft-Hartley fund, into which employers make contributions based on a percentage of payroll. The costs of providing quality day care are high, averaging $2,860 per year or $55 per week per child. The program has been used as a research and demonstration project by educational institutions and received a $60,000 demonstration grant from the Office of Economic Opportunity during the first and second year of its operation.

Subsequently, child care has gone beyond the center and continues to be expanded in several alternatives. Professional staff from the Amalgamated Chicago Center have been instrumental in developing and assisting the Harper Square Child Care Center, a 591-unit parent cooperative housing center which opened under union sponsorship in November 1973.

The ACWA Social Services Department in the union's headquarters is involved in helping to evaluate how family service needs might require a variety of child care arrangements in relation to other community resources. Program administrators must be sensitive to the cultural values and careful to supplement families rather than supplant them.

Union members whose children are receiving day care benefits are brought closer to the union as they bring and pick up their children. For example, in Chicago, parents learn from the day care staff about other services offered by the union, such as the professional social workers, the health center, the prepaid legal program, the retired members center, the supplementary insurance benefits program, and education and political action programs.

The ACWA's Montreal social services program includes information and referral to community agencies for child care and other needs. In addition, a unique feature is the use of retired members, coming to the union hall to provide after-school supervision and companionship to school age children. Social work students are included in the after-school program to provide assistance in personal counseling and problem-solving. Preliminary planning in another area is being done for a child care system which builds satellite family day care homes around center-based supportive services. In Nebraska, members are involved in a community-wide effort to provide training and upgrading for caregivers in family day care homes.

While the nation lacks a comprehensive system of developmental child care services, some local efforts in child care have provided beneficial services from church groups, parent cooperatives, local community organizations and business, in addition to labor groups. No systematic survey is available but services exist in communities all over the country.

All of these private efforts, including labor and management, fill an important community need. But while the creativity and resourcefulness of these private efforts may be commendable, they are not the entire answer, even under the best of circumstances.

The only answer to the broad problem of early childhood developmental care is a federal commitment to the provision of such services for all children. Individual efforts or private group efforts will always be too few, too costly, or too limited.

As the post-veto debate of child care continues, most Americans seem to support increased government services for children and families, but many are deeply worried about such development and some actively oppose them.

The circumstances of a rapidly changing society give a wider dimension beyond mere babysitting services while mothers are at work. It includes the profound changes in the American family and its pattern of living, about society's responsibilities to its citizens, down to the youngest child; and advances in educational theory that recog-

nize the importance of learning experiences of the early childhood years. Child care can play a significant social role in the well-being and healthy development of the nation's children.

These terms help to dictate the ingredients needed in child care services. While the home and family remain the central focus of the child's life, supplementary developmental services can contribute to the intellectual, social, emotional and physical growth needs of all children—from infants to teenagers. Such programs can have a constructive influence on children and their families, helping families to lead more satisfying lives and assisting children to become productive adults. A humane concern for the full development of the human potential is the reason for a national commitment to these needs.

In local unions, it may take time and patience to get child care near the top of the agenda. But discussions of child care among union members and surveys to assess the members' child care needs and preferences can be undertaken to assist in developing future programs appropriate to the local's needs, including home care, afterschool care, night care and infant care, in addition to full day care.

Although some complex and technical issues about child care and early education need research and professional advice which will hopefully provide more answers, basically most of the difficult issues are political: questions of value, priority and commitment.

Any attempt to conduct research in the context of social policy inevitably involves judgments about what is desirable for families and children.

Child care is in its growing phase. As a result, constructive contributions from individuals or groups are needed, particularly to help make public officials more aware of the needs of their constituencies. Programs and options through a national commitment to the needs of children and families is still as radical an idea today as when labor support for public education was challenged in the 1920s.

Organized labor can play as important a role in child care as it did in the public school struggle.

Chapter 10

Historical Origins of Early Childhood Education in the United States

Laura S. Ellis*

The field of modern early childhood education has come to be considered a coherent and unified area of study. A statement of purpose by the National Association for the Education of Young Children reads in part:

Today's concept of early childhood education now includes nursery, kindergarten, and primary years as a psychological entity requiring consistence in the child's development of concepts, relationships, and positive attitudes towards himself and his achievements. This is essential preparation for the more organized school life to follow (Nixon & Nixon, 1970, p. vii).

The acceptance of this concept has been formalized by agencies with the legal authority to issue credentials and by official college courses.

Since kindergarten and first grades are for the most part the young child's first introduction into the public educational system of most states, many schools consider this the period of early childhood education and plan for it as an entity. The idea of continuity in the young child's educational program resulted from the efforts of many prominent educators working separately and together during the first three or four decades of the twentieth century. They strived to achieve the unification of the two separate strands, kindergarten and primary grade education "as a means of achieving that continuity in a child's educational program which scientific findings lead one to believe is essential to optimum development (Langdon, 1933 p.1)."

Historical Context: Kindergarten

An historical review of events leading to our current conceptions of and practices in early childhood education will help to clarify its development. However, it is not within the scope of this review to present a detailed account of all the events and factors leading to the present. The purpose of the following review is to place present day kindergarten and primary grade education within its historical and conceptual context.

The early childhood education movement had its beginnings in the establishment of the first American kindergarten in Wisconsin in 1856. In 1873 the city of St. Louis opened the first public school kindergarten. Between 1856 and 1893 the kindergarten education movement expanded with the opening of many new kindergartens in cities of the East and Middle West (Lazerson, 1972).

The educational program of the kindergarten derived from the ideas of Friedrich Froebel (1889), a German idealist, who applied his philosophical and religious ideas to the education of young children. He believed that the first seven years of life were the most important ones for the young child's future development. The nature of the child was not merely that of a receptacle to be filled by the teacher. He conceived of the child as a dynamic being whose nature would unfold during the process of development. He believed that the curriculum should be child-centered; that young children were naturally active and that the educational environment should provide opportunities for physical activity. The kindergarten also required that the teachers be trained to work with young children. Teachers should display the qualities of warmth, affection, and tenderness (Froebel, 1895).

Play as the vehicle of the educational program was one of the most important contributions of kindergarten education. Through play the child learned what was required and was socialized into the adult and peer groups.

The kindergarten's emphasis upon development of the individual child's capacities through play activities, greater freedom of movement, and social attitudes of cooperation gradually helped to relieve the rigid discipline and formal atmosphere of the elementary school (Butts, 1955, p. 492).

Children were not to be subjected to long periods of sedentary activity requiring memorization and recitation. The kindergarten provided a place where love, warmth, and activity were part of teaching. Froebel believed that the

Adapted by the author from her unpublished doctoral dissertation entitled, *A Study of Kindergarten and Grade One Teachers As Managers of the Classroom*. New York: Teachers College, Columbia University, 1975.

*Dr. Laura S. Ellis, District Supervisor of Early Childhood Education, Community School District 12, Bronx, New York.

kindergarten should serve a happy group of children learning together in harmony. He stressed the importance of group activity for cooperative, not competitive purposes. Experiences planned for the children should be appropriate for each stage of their development (Weber, 1969).

With the great expansion of kindergarten the movement began to be professionalized. In 1884 the National Education Association established its Kindergarten Department. There emerged three national organizations whose main interest was the education of young children in kindergartens. The most important of these was the International Kindergarten Union, organized in 1892, whose members were kindergarten teachers, supervisors of public school kindergartens, and directors of kindergarten teacher training schools. By 1918 it was the third largest educational organization in the world (Lazerson, 1972).

During the period from 1900 to 1925 new people and new ideas entered the arena of early schooling. G. Stanley Hall introduced the "child study movement" through research into education. His concepts of child development had far reaching effects on the kindergarten curriculum. During the same period the kindergarten was influenced greatly by the scientific theories of Edward Thorndike's connectionism and John Watson's behaviorism, both of whom placed special emphasis on the learning process.

The work of John Dewey also had a great impact on kindergarten education. His was the most influential voice to reject the Froebelian kindergarten as too rigid and lacking in freedom and choice for the individual child. Dewey also disagreed with G. Stanley Hall who advocated a child-centered school. Child study could not be the source for determining the goals of education. Child study may posit what is possible and viable to do with children, but the political arena of the adult society would be the place where the goals of education were determined according to what the society believed to be the "good life."

Dewey (1966) believed that "learning in school should be continuous with that out of school (p. 358)." He proposed that the school be a model social community (Dewey, 1959).

To do this means to make each one of our schools an embryonic community life, active with types of occupations that reflect the life of the larger society, and permeated throughout with the spirit of art, history, and science. When the school introduces and trains each child of society into membership within such a little community, saturating him with the spirit of service, and providing him with the instruments of effective self-direction, we shall have the deepest and best guarantee of a larger society which is worthy, lovely, and harmonious (p. 49).

In essense, this was Dewey's concept of progressive educa-

tion. Progressive education should include the study of society, the study of the child, and the fostering of creativity.

Dewey brought together several recurring themes in education and gave them a contemporary interpretation. One of these was the emphasis on the needs and interests of the child, following the tradition of Rousseau, Pestalozzi, and Froebel, but now given a new perspective by the new science of psychology and child development. Another theme was the democratic faith in the public school, in the tradition of Jefferson and Mann, but now applied to the education and training of new urban and rural populations for industry and agriculture, and to do the Americanization of the new waves of immigrants (Dewey, 1959).

Patty Smith Hill (1923) introduced changes in materials and methods into kindergarten education. She endeavored to operationalize the ideas of John Dewey. Large blocks, which she designed, a variety of housekeeping toys and tools, a sandbox, and equipment for active physical play were brought into the kindergarten. New songs, which were more childlike, and creative rhythmic activities were also added. These new activities and materials were to be used in the application of democratic principles to classroom living. She believed that children should be trained in self-direction and given more opportunities for freedom and choice as well as for learning from each other. This would be possible if the children's experiences were initiated according to their own purposes and plans. To accomplish these goals, new methods of teaching would be necessary. The concept of the teacher as a guide rather than a dictator was developed by Patty Hill (1923).

To Patty Smith Hill goes the distinction of having developed curriculum for children from three to seven years of age, since her career included work in expanding nursery school education, revamping kindergarten education, and unifying kindergarten and first grade (Spitler, 1971, p. 245).

Historical Context: The Early Primary Grades

Quite apart from the movement discussed above, elementary school education had its beginnings in a much earlier period of our history. Schools were established during the colonial period to teach literacy and to provide religious training for selected segments of the population. Elementary education in the eighteenth century included in its curriculum reading, writing, spelling, arithmetic, and the rudiments of religious training. The vehicle for transmitting this knowledge was the textbook. The teaching method consisted of requiring the children to memorize letters, words, and passages from the book, and to recite them aloud to the teacher. The primer gained great acceptance during this period. There was little effort made to help children acquire new meanings or understand what they were learning. Drill was considered necessary and took the form of questions from the teacher answered by the children. Boys sat on benches separate from girls. Because school was extremely dull, discipline had to be maintained either by the force of superior authority or by means of the cane or the whip (Butts & Cremin, 1953).

The public school system as we know it today began to emerge in the nineteenth century. Horace Mann, the first Secretary of the Massachusetts Board of Education, successfully established the concept of the common school, a school common to all people. He educated a generation about the nature of educational issues in the new American society. In the 1830's and 1840's, in response to America's self-conscious awareness of its nationhood, schools began to take on the task of Americanizing the new immigrants. Education was considered necessary for all children in order to prepare them to function as good citizens. By 1860 a majority of the 33 states had adopted some form of public education. Teaching of the common branches was deemed necessary for the common school pupils so that they could discharge "the ordinary duties of life (Butts & Cremin, 1953, p. 118)." The common branches included reading, writing, common arithmetic, spelling, geography, history, and other subjects which were thought to prepare children for good citizenship.

Early in the nineteenth century the monitorial or Lancastrian system of instruction was imported from England. The teacher taught the younger children. The same methods of memorization and recitation were used. Around the middle of the nineteenth century, with the influx of large numbers of children into the common schools, the large cities began to introduce the Prussian system of separating children into classes or grades according to age. It was believed that this organization was more efficient since the teacher could then teach the same subject to all children in her charge, instead of dividing her time among the different age groups within one group or school. During the latter part of the nineteenth century first grade children spent the entire day having Reading, Writing, Spelling, and Numbers, each four times a day, nothing more. This "book-centered approach was supplemented by the rod of correction (Butts & Cremin, 1953, p. 220)."

Continuity Between Kindergarten and the Primary Grades

Between 1900 and 1929 many educators struggled with the issue of continuity and articulation between kindergarten and the primary grades. Dewey referred to it as the natural connection between the kindergarten and the primary school. In his view the presence of this natural connection provided articulation and organization. His definition of organization was "getting things in connection with one another, so that they work easily, flexibly, and fully (Dewey, 1959, p. 71)." In the absence of this natural connection he found isolation of various parts of the school system and "to the lack of coherence in its studies and methods (Dewey, 1959, p. 71)." Insofar as the primary school remained

foreign to the natural interests of the child, it was isolated from the kindergarten, so that it is a problem, at present, to introduce kindergarten methods into the primary school (Dewey, 1959, p. 73).

According to Dewey (1959), as long as the kindergarten and primary school remain isolated from each other, they would represent waste in education.

Patty Smith Hill at Teachers College, Columbia University, whose influence was widespread during the first quarter of the twentieth century, published, with others, a series of monographs on the education of young children. The *Conduct Curriculum* (Burke, 1923) described an expanded and continuous program for children in kindergarten and first grade. It was an effort to translate the work of Dewey, G. Stanley Hall, and Thorndike into a program for young children. It was also an attempt to bridge the gap of communication between kindergarten and primary teachers. During the same period Alice Temple was working at the University of Chicago toward the same goal of unifying kindergarten and primary grade education. Her book, *Unified Kindergarten and First Grade Teaching* (1925), written with Samuel Parker, was the culmination of her efforts to develop a program for kindergarten-primary education in the form of a curriculum for children in schools as well as a program for the professional education of teachers. During the latter part of her professional life Alice Temple was concerned mainly with the continuity of experience and education for young children. She worked diligently to persuade the teacher education institutions and the professional educators' organizations to incorporate kindergarten education into their primary education departments. *Childhood Education*, the journal of the International Kindergarten Union, carried articles relating to the education of children from two to twelve years of age.

Ella Victoria Dobbs was an important figure in the improvement of primary school education. Her great interest was manual and industrial arts for children in the early elementary grades. She proposed to give greater meaning to the curriculum through the industrial arts. Like Alice Temple and Patty Smith Hill, she was committed to the concepts of self-activity, continuity, and unity as basic educational principles.

In 1915 Dobbs became one of the founders of the National Council of Primary Education. The organization's aims were formulated at the first informal meeting at about 30 primary teachers who shared a similar point of view about

education in the primary grades (Snyder, 1972, p. 303):
1. Greater use of activities in the primary school.
2. Greater freedom of method for the teacher.
3. Greater continuity of effort through closer coopera-tion with the kindergarten and the grades above.

Thus there were educators at both the kindergarten and primary levels, although in separate professional groups, who were working toward similar goals. Members of both groups often held joint meetings, were involved in the same issues and causes, and served on joint committees. From 1929 until 1930 careful work and planning by committees in each organization finally culminated in the formal merger of the International Kindergarten Union and the Na-tional Council of Primary Education into a new group, henceforth to be known as the Association for Childhood Education. The bulletin reported the merger as follows (Snyder, 1972):

The year 1931 will stand as culmination of hopes for the unification of all interests of childhood education. At this time the International Kindergarten Union and the National Council of Primary Education united as the Association for Childhood Education (p. 373).

Educators in the field of kindergarten and primary edu-cation were finally successful in their efforts to unify them-selves as colleagues into one professional organization. Dewey's concepts of unity and continuity of growth would be the guiding principles of the new organization. These ideas were articulated by Dewey in his Lectures in Philoso-phy of Education (1899) as follows:

The child who leaves the kindergarten at five years and nine months and goes into the primary school at the end of the vacation at six years, has not undergone in his make-up any such complete revolution as he finds in the two environments that are about him. . . .Each phase of the kindergarten curriculum finds its counterpart in the curricula of our best primary grades, with reading and writing as additional forms of activity and expression. The work in each subject or type of activity common to the kindergarten and primary grades, therefore, should be so arranged that continuity is secured. . . .When this time comes, the teacher, whether her class is designated as kindergarten or first grade, should be prepared to teach these subjects according to the best known methods ((pp. 161-163).

The new organization, the Association for Childhood Education (which later became the Association for Child-hood Educational International), represented the

growing conviction that the period in a child's life be-tween the ages of four and eight was psychologically

one; therefore, no discontinuities in his educational experiences should be condoned (Weber, 1969, p. 119).

This period in the education of young children would now be the organization's main concern. One of its tasks would be to examine carefully the relationship of kindergarten to the primary grades and to ascertain the "contribution of each to the other (Langdon, 1933, p. 1)."

The unification of kindergarten and primary teachers also reflected the changes in the program for teacher prepa-ration that had been taking place betwwen 1915 and 1930. The professionalization of education during that period saw the takeover of training schools for teachers by normal schools, teachers colleges, and universities. Normal schools were changing into teachers colleges, and universities were adding schools of education. The great expansion of kinder-garten enrollments created a large demand for teachers trained to work with young children. Colleges and universi-ties added departments of kindergarten-primary education and set up requirements for the acquisition of a Kinergar-ten-Primary Certificate. During the 1920's educators believed that, as teachers did their theoretical and practical work in nursery schools, kindergartens, and primary grades, they would "recognize the contributions, requirements, and possible development of each level of maturity and this interchanging helps greatly to bring about a closer unity (Meek, 1929, p. 260)." By 1930 teachers were being train-ed to understand and work with kindergarten and primary grade children. The newly established departments of kin-dergarten-primary education became centers for the devel-opment of new curricula for this level of education (Weber, 1969).

Today teachers colleges and departments of education in colleges and universities offer separate sequences of study to future teachers preparing to work with children in early childhood education. In addition, certification and licensing procedures for teachers in New York City and elsewhere also have separated the early childhood period from the rest of the elementary school.

With the advent of the nursery school movement in the 1920's psychological, social, emotional, and physical nur-ture became the focus of educational programs for children below five years of age. Psychoanalytic concepts were also incorporated into the theoretical underpinnings of nursery school education. Leading teachers colleges and universities added nursery school classes to their research centers (Weber, 1969).

In 1962 the National Association for Nursery Education changed its name to the National Association for the Edu-cation of Young Children. Its area of concern became early childhood education, the period of development from two years to eight years of age. Recently both the National Association for the Education of Young Children and the Association for Childhood Education International agreed to work cooperatively to achieve their joint objectives (Childhood Education, 1972, p. 28C).

This historical review has endeavored to show how the period of childhood education came to be considered a distinct period of development, and how the educational programs for young children came to be thought of as having a coherent and definitive philosophy and style.

BIBLIOGRAPHY

Braun, S. J. & Edwards, E. P. *History and theory of early childhood education.* Worthington, Ohio: Charles A. Jones Publishing, 1972.

Burke, A., et al. *A conduct curriculum for the kindergarten and first grade.* New York: Charles Scribner's Sons, 1923.

Butts, R. F. *A cultural history of western education.* New York: Mc Graw-Hill, 1955.

Butt, R. F., & Cremin, L.A. *A history of education in American culture.* New York: Holt, Rinehart, & Winston, 1953.

Dewey, J. School and society. In M. Dworkin (Ed.), *Dewey on Education, Selections.* New York: Bureau of Publications, Teachers College, Columbia University, 1959.

Dewey, J. *Lectures in philosophy of education* (1899). Edited and with an Introduction by R.D. Archambault. New York: Random House, 1966.

Froebel, F. *The education of man.* Translated by W. Hailmann. New York: D. Appleton, 1889.

Froebel, F. *Pedagogics of the kindergarten.* Translated by J. Jarvis. New York: D. Appleton, 1895.

Hill, P.S. Introduction. In *A conduct curriculum for the kindergarten and first grade.* New York: Charles Scribner's & Sons, 1923.

Jammer, C. Patty Smith Hill and the reform of the American kindergarten. Unpublished doctoral dissertation, Teachers College, Columbia University, 1960.

Joint statement of Association for Childhood Education International, American Association for Elementary-Kindergarten-Nursery Educators and National Association for the Education of Young Children. *Childhood Education,* 1972, 49, 28C-28E.

Langdon, G. *Similarities and differences in teaching in nursery school, kindergarten and first grade.* New York: John Day, 1933.

Lazerson, M. *The historical antecedents of early childhood education.* Seventy-first yearbook of the National Society for the Study of Education. Chicago: The National Society for the Study of Education, 1972.

Meek, L.H. (Chm.) In G.M. Whipple (Ed.), *National Society for the Study of Education, twenty-eight yearbook.* Chicago: University of Chicago Press, 1929.

Meyer, A.E. *Grandmasters of educational thought.* New York: McGraw-Hill, 1975.

Nixon, R., & Nixon, C. *Introduction to early childhood education.* New York: Random House, 1970.

Parker, S.C., & Temple, A. *Unified kindergarten and first grade teaching.* Boston: Ginn, 1925.

Snyder, A. *Dauntless women in childhood education, 1856-1931.* Washington, D.C.: Association for Childhood Education International, 1972.

Spitler, J.A. *Changing views of play in the education of young children.* Unpublished doctoral dissertation, Teachers College, Columbia University, 1971.

Weber, E. *The kindergarten: Its encounter with educational thought in America.* New York: Teachers College Press, Teachers College, Columbia University, 1969.

Chapter 11

Origins of Early Childhood Education

Barbara Ruth Peltzman*

Recognition of the importance of the early years in the life of a child is not new. The principles and practices of modern early childhood education are the direct descendents of the work of Comenius, Rousseau, Pestalozzi, and Froebel.

John Amos Comenius (1592-1670) set down in the *Great Didactic,* "General Postulates of Teaching and Learning" which appear to be the first step toward a branch of education specifically designed for young children. Comenius discusses the path to knowledge, and compares the brain to pliable wax. In a translation of the *Great Didactic* by Keating (1921), Comenius stated:

This comparison throws remarkable light on the true nature of knowledge. Whatever makes an impression on my organ of sight, hearing, smell, taste, or touch, stands to me in the relation of a seal by which the image of an object is impressed upon my brain. (p. 44–45)

Thus, Comenius advocated learning through the senses which we interpret as learning through experience. Comenius further states that these sense impressions will be internalized for future interpretation through reason. Curtis and Boultwood (1961) state that Comenius believed "the acquisition of knowledge is essentially based on activity followed by reasoning. . .(p. 197)"

Modern principles of early childhood education stress the involvement of the child in an activity based curriculum through the use of the senses. Rudolph and Cohen (1964), in a discussion of kindergarten state that

. . .Only by building understanding of what his senses contact, will the child be ready for the symbolic learning that will come in time (p. 9–10)

In the above statement we see Comenius' ideas interpreted for application 300 years later. We find threads of his doctrine in the work of Dewey, Montessori, and Piaget.

In his book, Comenius further advocates different materials for children of different ages. He felt that nature establishes the order of development in the child step by step. Keating (1921) translates "all subjects that are to be learned should be arranged so as to suit the age of the stu-

dents, that nothing which is beyond their comprehension be given to them to learn. This process begins with the universal and ends with the particular. (p. 115–116)." Here we have the ancestor of Piaget's ideas about stages in cognitive development and sound principles of curriculum development for the early years of schooling. Comenius believed in giving the young child experiences and knowledge of the world through field trips, pictures, models, and real things. This background aids the child in future abstract learning.

Comenius suggested a system of education for all children, rich and poor, girls and boys. Pounds (1968) calls this the "ladder system" because all children would "take the same route and would merely stop at different levels. (p. 154)" Comenius comments on the individuality and differences among children. Keating (1921) translates "There is a great difference between the minds of men as exist between various kinds of plants, of trees, of animals; one must be treated in one way, and another in another, the same method cannot be applied to all alike. . . Each one will develop in the direction of his natural inclinations. (p. 181–182)."

In brief, Comenius' system of education consisted of four levels: 1) Infancy to age 6 - School of the Mother's Knee. This is similar to nursery and kindergarten games, music, sensory experiences, body movement, and manual work; 2) Age 6-12 - Vernacular School. The child is instructed in his native language. This was open to all children; 3) Age 12-18 - Latin School. This was similar to high school. Students learn the classic languages, logic, mathematics, and art; 4) Age 18-on - University and Travel. Comenius believed in equal education for girls because, according to Braun (1972), "girls are equipped with the same industriousness and capacity for wisdom. . .There can be no reason why females should be excluded from studying. (p. 32)."

Comenius was a man ahead of his time and the first to develop a special system of education for very young children. All those who followed him built their ideas around his work.

*Dr. Barbara Ruth Peltzman, Reading Consultant, New York City Public Schools, Adjunct Professor, St. John's University.

from

Jean Jacques Rousseau (1712–1778) rebelled against the formalism and artificiality of French society. He believed in naturalism in the education of children. His belief was, as stated in the Foxley (1911) translation, "Everything is good as it comes from the hands of the Creator of Nature; everything deteriorates in the hands of man. (p. 1)." To Rousseau, naturalism was the belief in the goodness of the child as he developed free from the evil effects of organized society. According to Bayles (1966), Rousseau's naturalism meant protecting the child from "his man-made surroundings—science and civilization—that his innate tendencies would have the opportunity to grow and unfold in accordance with his own nature. (p. 82)" The job of protector was assigned to education, but Rousseau believed that in order to be suited for this task, education had to be radically different from that of his generation.

In 1762 Rousseau's *Emile, Ou Traite de l'Education* was published. It was written as a novel and consisted of five books or parts. Each book deals with one of the developmental stages of the fictious child, Emile. Rousseau felt that since the child, in the natural state was good, all his impulses and actions were good, therefore, the child must be free to develop and learn naturally. Pounds (1968) states, "Rousseau emphasized the necessity for the child to be free to develop according to his own natural impulses. (p. 176)." Thus, to educate the child according to nature, Rousseau states, according to Duggan (1936), "we must study his nature and find out whether there are any laws discoverable in him comparable to the laws governing physical phenomena. (p. 207)." Here Rousseau is suggesting that child study, a radically new concept at the time, should be the basis of education.

Rousseau reports the several states of Emile's development as separate and distinct, in each state the child is different. These states correspond to the stages in the history of human progress from savage to civilized society. According to Bayles (1966), Pounds (1968), Curtis and Boultwood (1961), these stages are: 1) Infancy - birth to age 5. The child is a little animal not yet human. This is the period of body growth; 2) Childhood - age 6–11. The child is a human savage. This is the stage of social growth; 3) Adolescence - age 12–15. This is the Age of Reason when the child is civilized, but concerned only with himself. This is the period when the mind develops: 4) Youth - young adulthood. This is the period when the person becomes aware of and begins thinking of others. The youth is a social being. This is the period when the sex impulse arises, but reason takes over and morality governs life. This is the period of the development of the spirit. (Bayles, p. 83; Pounds, p. 177–178; Curtis and Boutlwood, p. 277).

Rousseau's theory is based upon the idea of unfoldment development from within the child. Bayles (1966) states that this theory is based upon the belief that "the child's innate destiny (is) enfolded within him at birth and destined to unfold in the stage - order predestined at birth . . . (p. 82)." This unfoldment concept is an important part of Rousseau's new education and from it Rousseau leads us toward a more important and lasting idea, that childhood is a special time. Rousseau stated a revolutionary idea for his time; children are different from adults. In the Foxley (1911) translation of *Emile* we find a plea for the rights of children to be children, not miniature adults. "Nature would have them children before they are men. If we try to invert this order we shall produce a forced fruit immature and flavorless, fruit which will be rotten before it is ripe; we shall have young doctors and old children. (p. 54)."

From Rousseau's plea for the respect of childhood grew the concept of readiness to learn. Comenius hinted at this idea in his early work, but Rousseau states it clearly. Rousseau suggested an atmosphere that was permissive in which the child would experience the education of things and social situations at his own pace. The teacher must not force new things and new social situations on the child. Rather, the teacher must wait as Thut (1957) states, "for signs of the internal strivings which signal the learners readiness to progress to new things and new social experiences before he is exposed to them. (p. 133)."

In the Foxley (1911) translation, Rousseau states that the "most useful rule of education . . . is do not save time, but lose it . . . The mind must be left undisturbed till its facilities are developed . . . Therefore the education of the earliest years should be merely negative. It consists not in teaching virtue or truth, but in preserving the heart from vice and from the spirit of error. (p. 57)." The heart of Rousseau's theory of education is let nature take its course, protect the child from well meaning adults and the vices of society.

Rousseau's *Emile* was a violent reaction against education that produced men of cold reason and made learning machines of children. Rousseau went to the other extreme making education a matter of nature only. His system was an education of the emotions, an education of the person. Duggan (1936) states that Rousseau changed education so that "the child replaced the subject matter as the central fact in education. (p. 214)." This was the beginning of a movement to teach children not subjects. Rousseau's classic performed the task of laying the groundwork for modern early childhood education to emerge. Duggan (1936) states, "the work of the *Emile* was by necessity primarily destructive, and it performed a great service in clearing the ground of much educational rubbish preparitory to laying a new foundation . . . It is so full of suggestiveness concerning the aims, content, and process of education as to be the starting point of a new education. (p. 214)."

Rousseau awakened Europe to the fact that a special type of education was needed for young children. Braun (1972) comments on Rousseau's impact on education, "The spirit of Rousseau may have been interpreted variously over the years, but certainly *Emile* has had an incalculable impact on education. In the move of teachers and students toward greater freedom and individuality, Rousseau's doctrine has taken root – though it has taken a multitude of different embodiments. No thinker after Rousseau could escape dealing with the ideas he set awing with a flurry of feeling . . . In harmony with Rousseau's belief in nature and the right of the child to grow untrammeled by society . . . Johann Heinrich Pestalozzi, was to express the counterpart of Rousseau's freshness of spirit in his own life a generation later . . . Rousseau's work prepared the mind of Europe to accept and to respect a man like Pestalozzi and Pestalozzi, in his turn, gave substance to what had been before him only hypothetical notions. (p. 43)."

Johann Heinrich Pestalozzi (1746-1827) unlike Rousseau was a teacher who put his theories into practice. Pestalozzi was one of the reformers upon whose work the movement to psychologize education was based. He initiated a movement which resulted in great changes in what Duggan (1936) calls "the aims, spirit, and methods of elementary education. (p. 222)." It is with Pestalozzi that a change in teaching methods and a formalization of teacher training begins.

Pestalozzi's life and work fall into three periods. According to Duggan (1936) these were: 1) 1774-1780, Experiment in industrial education for orphans; 2) 1780-1798, Writing for social and educational reform; 3) 1798-1827, Reform in teaching elementary school subjects.

Period one was a time of experimentation at a small farm called Neuhof where Pestalozzi attempted to prove that one's character is shaped by the environment. He believed that the more natural the environment, the better the child's character will develop. Pestalozzi found that Rousseau's ideas needed great modification and concluded that, according to Duggan (1936), "the most natural environment for a child was a home dominated by a spirit of strict, but loving discipline. (p. 226)." The orphanage experiment succeeded in helping the children, but failed financially in 1780.

In period two, Pestalozzi devoted himself to writing on educational and social reform. His works included pamphlets on the principles of the French Revoultion which emphasized educational reform. In 1781 Pestalozzi wrote *Leonard and Gertrude* in novel form. It was accepted by the intellectuals of Europe and won honors from the French National Assembly.

In period three, Pestalozzi worked at several schools for war orphans. Pestalozzi believed in working from hand to head. Bayles (1966) states the children learned that "by the work of their hands they would get sense impressions out of which ideas (head) would form. Ideas, the assumed precursor of actions, hence habits, would then coalesce into habit patterns – Pestalozzi seeing of course, that they were the right ones – thereby begatting character (heart) . . .

(p. 99)." Pestalozzi wanted to establish a school for poor children. Bayles (1966) states that in this school "love and kindness would reign and the intellectual powers of children would be fostered; beggers would grow into men and brutishness would give way to humanness. . .(p. 101)." Pestalozzi's chance came in 1798 at Stanz, a town ravaged by the French army. Pestalozzi set up an orphanage where he combined sense impressionism with kindness thereby modernizing teaching. At the Stanz school (1798-1799), later at the Burgdorf school (1799-1804), and at the Yverdon school (1805-1825) Pestalozzi further perfected his method.

Pestalozzi believed that educational reform would occur only when each child was allowed to develop his natural abilities to the fullest. This could not be accomplished without new methods and new materials of instruction. Duggan (1936) states "it was in this connection that Pestalozzi made his greatest contribution to educational reform . . . (p. 231)." Pestalozzi refused to believe that the only way to teach was to have children memorize material and then recite it. deGuimps (1890) states that Pestalozzi was convinced "that when the memory is applied to a series of psychologically graduated ideas, it brings all faculties into play. (p. 150)." Pestalozzi believed, as Comenius did, that sense perception was the basis for all knowledge and that observation was the basis for all instruction. He developed object lessons which emphasized oral teaching in order to put Rousseau's ideas into practice. Pestalozzi suggested according to Duggan (1936), that "teaching through the observation of objective material within the child's experience gave him clear ideas and trained him in oral expression; not to gain knowledge of the object studied. . . but to train the powers of the mind, of expression as well as impression. (p. 231)" Pestalozzi used music, art, spelling, geography, arithmetic, and a great many oral language activities in his teaching.

Pestalozzi went further using Rousseau's idea of readiness and Comenius' idea of graduated organization of knowledge to state, according to deGuimps (1890), that "in every branch teaching should begin with the simplest elements and proceed gradually according to the development of the child in psychologically connected order. (p. 155)." Here we have what Dewey and Piaget would later call cognitive development.

Braun (1972) states that Pestalozzi's "life was devoted to human relationships, a life of the mind, but more a life of feeling and of service. More than what he said, or wrote, what Pestalozzi *did* was his doctrine. His educational doctrine is not easy to follow for it must be followed with devotion, self-forgetfulness, deep loving concern for children and for the essence of childhood. (p. 60)."

Pestalozzi helped to humanize education. His schools were visited by scholars and statemen from all over Europe and America. His ideas were put into practice in various ways throughout the world. Braun (1972) states, "there is a strand that links the modern kindergarten to Pestalozzi . . . it is in the affection and concern for children and in the attempt to protect them as well as instruct them. (p. 61)."

Friedrich Wilhelm August Froebel (1782-1852) was the most influential of Pestalozzi's students. He studied Pestalozzi's method at Yverdon for two years. Froebel read the works of Comenius and Rousseau and he was greatly impressed by Comenius' description of the School of the Mother's Knee. Froebel decided to open a school for young children.

The *Education of Man*, (1826) contains an explanation of Froebel's educational theory, which, according to Weber (1969), reflects several streams of thought: the absolute idealism of his time, some of the naturalism of Rousseau, aspects of the sense realism of Pestalozzi, his own tendency toward mysticism, and his understanding of the child's nature viewed in the context of the other influences. (p. 1) Froebel developed the kindergarten as a garden rather than a school room in which young children could be free to learn about themselves and the world. He emphasized love and sympathy as the only relationship which should exist between teacher and pupil. Influenced by the desire for national unity in Germany, Froebel made the quest for unity part of his educational philosophy. Pounds (1968) states that Froebel developed his theory of unity from the idea that "the world is in a conscious cosmic evolution. God is the original, active source of all things and everyone and everything comes from this source. . . The essence of all things is found in God as his will is carried out on Earth. Froebel developed a theory . . . in which everything is a unity in and of itself, but is also part of a greater unity. This is a kind of part-whole theory. The unity of God's universe is best when all of its parts function together, but none of its parts would lose its identity within the larger whole. (p. 179-180)."

Froebel felt that if we study the changes in the evolution of nature we would see similar changes in the development of man since man and nature are one. He found hidden meanings in natural objects which he felt were valuable in revealing the world to a child. Froebel felt that humanity as a whole is revealed in each child in a unique way. Froebel (1899) states ". . . As the germ bears within itself the plant and the whole plant life, does not the child bear within himself the whole man and the whole life of humanity? (p. 622)." Froebel interpreted the unity of God and man to mean that the child is innately good and felt, as Rousseau did, that the child was not a learning animal. Froebel felt that the child is a behaving animal and the chief characteristic of the child was self-activity generated by the child's own interests and desires. Froebel (1899) states "all the child is ever to becomes lies—however slightly indicated—in the child, and can be attained only through the development from within outward. (p. 68)." This is the

aim of education according to Froebel about which Duggan (1936) states that "development of the inborn capacities of the child. . . hence education must provide for the development of the free personality of each child, it must guide but not restrict, it must not interfere with the devinity in each child. (p. 258)."

Froebel believed that the child should learn by doing and education should build upon the child's interests. Froebel saw motor-expression as the method of education for the young. Froebel made motor-expression a vital part of the school program. Duggan (1936) states "with Froebel motor-expression was not one step but all steps in the educative process . . . Motor-expression developed the powers of acquisition and accomplishment together, hence there was no break between thought and action. (p. 259)." Froebel is stating that the child's development comes from inner strivings and their connection with outward expressions of these strivings. The child's senses are involved. The child takes in stimuli through his sense and integrates the perceptions with activities he engages in. He internalizes events and the consequences of his actions in particular situations to form ideas and to help govern his actions. If a child is painting and accidently puts the brush with red paint on it into the white paint, he finds a new color. He sees this and is moved to ask "Did I do this? What did I do to get the new color?" He may ask his teacher what happened. He may return to the paint corner and try other ways of getting the new color. When he discovers that red and white makes pink he is able to reproduce the color anytime he paints. The child has learned that he can mix colors to get a new one.

Froebel felt that social cooperation was the means of kindergarten education. He believed in Aristotle's theory that man was a social animal who can realize his humanity only in cooperation with his fellow beings. Thus, Froebel felt that the child has instincts that made him engage in cooperative actions based upon his observation of children at play. Froebel felt that the spirit of cooperation should be cultivated from early infancy and the school should be a society in miniature.

Froebel believed that creativeness or rendering the inner outer was a vital part of the child's learning. Thus, the child fosters the unfolding process through his impulses for creative activity. By expressing the beginning ideas within him the child is led, according to Froebel (1899) to "produce outside of himself that which he conceives within himself. (p. 61)." Thus, the child's painting of a tree becomes important as a way of objectifying the vague idea of a tree. Froebel stated that the objects a child manipulates and handles awaken the inner world. Things help the child to imagine himself objectively and to be self-creative. Froebel suggested that children spend much of their time manipulating and constructing objects. Froebel was bold to suggest that children should play in school because play was a key factor in the development of the child. Through play the child achieves equilibrium between individuality and an organized curriculum designed to bring the child step by step through the subject matter of his education. Froebel (1899) states "play is the purest, most spiritual activity of man at this stage . . . it gives joy, freedom, contentment, inner and outer rest, and peace with the world . . . The plays of childhood are the germinal leaves of all later life; for the whole man is developed and shown in these, in his tenderest dispositions, in his innermost tendencies. (p. 55)."

Froebel used several means of expression in his child centered curriculum; music and songs, gestures, and construction with language development a vital part of all of these. He believed in the integration of all of these forms through the use of paper, clay, blocks and his famous Gifts, and Occupations. The Gifts were designed to be handled by the child to lead him to an orderly sense of reality. The Gifts were materials that did not change form: cube, cylinder, sticks, and tablets. The Occupations were used to train the hand, the eye and the mind. The Occupations consisted of materials that changed form through use: clay, sand, and paper. The *Mother Play and Nursery Songs* was Froebel's book of songs with pictures and notes explaining use. The songs described the work of people and notes explaining use. The songs described the work of people and simple games, rather like modern kindergarten activities. Modern materials such as crayons, paste, the doll corner and other activities greatly enrich the kindergarten program, but grew directly from Froebel's original materials.

Froebel's work remains a vital part of education today. His unique contributions have withstood the test of time. Modern open classroom techniques, day care centers, and nursery schools can be traced directly to Froebel's original kindergarten. Braun (1972) states, "with Froebel, preschool education as a planned, organized portion of the school system begins. With Froebel, modern teaching of young children becomes an entity in its own right . . . The result of his work was the kindergarten, the true beginning of modern preschool education, created out of love and concern for children. . . (p. 61)."

From the work of Comenius, Rousseau, Pestalozzi, and Froebel modern early childhood education has evolved. Each of these scholars drew upon the work of those who came before him, shaping the ideas and practices in light of his own beliefs and in the context of his own times. Their work has been modified and amplified by John Dewey, Maria Montessori, and the American Kindergarten Movement, but remains the foundation upon which early childhood education has been built.

REFERENCES

Bayles, Ernest E; and Hood, Bruce L. *Growth of American Educational Thought and Practice.* New York: Harper & Row, 1966.

Braun, Samuel J.; and Edwards, Esther P. *History and Theory of Early Childhood Education.* Worthington, Ohio: Charles A. Jones Pub. Co., 1972.

Curtis, S. J.: and Boutlwood, E.A. *A Short History of Educational Ideas.* London, England: University Tutorial Press Ltd., 1961.

deGuimps, Baron Roger. *Pestalozzi: His Life and Work.* Translated by J. Russell. New York: D. Appleton & Co., 1890.

Duggan, Stephen. *A Student's Textbook in the History of Education.* New York: Appleton-Century Co., 1936.

Foxley, Barbare. *Emile by Jean Jacque Rousseau.* New York: E. P. Dutton & Co., 1911.

Froebel, Friedrich. *The Education of Man.* Translated by William N. Hailmann. New York: D. Appleton & Co., 1889.

Froebel, Friedrich. *Autobiography of Friedrich Froebel.* Translated by Emilie Michaelis and H. Keatly Moore. Syracuse: C. W. Bardeen, 1889.

Froebel, Friedrich. *Education by Development.* Translated by Josephine Jarvis. New York: D. Appleton & Co., 1899.

Keating, M.W. *The Great Didactic of John Amos Comenium.* London, England: A & C Black, 1921.

Pounds, Ralph L. *The Development of Education in Western Culture.* New York: Appleton-Century-Crofts, 1968.

Rudolph, Margurita; and Cohen, Dorothy H. *Kindergarten: A Year of Learning.* New York: Appleton-Century-Crofts, 1964.

Thut, I. N. The *Story of Education: Philosophical and Historical Foundations.* New York: McGraw-Hill, 1957.

Weber, Evelyn. *The Kindergarten: Its Encounter with Educational Thought in America.* New York: Teachers College Press, 1969.

SUGGESTED READINGS

Aries, Philippe. *Centuries of Childhood.* New York: Vintage Books, 1962.

Frost, Joe L. *Early Childhood Education Rediscovered.* New York: Holt, Rinehart & Winston, 1968.

Forest, Ilse. *The School for the Child from Two to Eight.* Boston: Ginn & Co., 1935.

Lambert, Hazel. *Early Childhood Education.* Boston: Allyn & Bacon, 1960.

N.S.S.E. *Forty-sixth Yearbook – Early Childhood Education.* Chicago: University of Chicago Press, 1947.

Section II
Theoretical Bases

Introduction by Helen Robison *

Nine chapters in this section on theory indicate the broad range of topics which generate research on development and education of young children. Major theories dealt with in the following chapters concern socialization, psychosocial development and self-concept formation, role of early experiences in development, the dynamics of developmental change and growth, cognitive development and educational experiences which maximize cognitive potential.

Theory and research have been richly productive in recent decades in conceptualizing structure and process in early childhood development. Meaningful early childhood educational designs link structure and process in creative ways, to approach optimum learning environments.

Rogg's chapter on socialization emphasizes the four main agents of American enculturation as family, peer group, mass media, and schools. Sociological and psychological theories are identified which show how infants become functioning individual and group members in their culture. Nature-culture are contrasted to show how culture affects biological potential in life chances, sex role, self-concept, and coping skills.

Derevensky stresses a process objective, to heighten the child's self-esteem. Psychological theories of cognitive development, of perception, and of interpersonal communication are outlined as the basis for a Ginott-type of "Childrenese" interaction in classrooms. Since positive attitudes toward self, learning, and school are more easily developed than redeveloped to displace negative attitudes, early childhood educators welcome the theory base to support good practice.

A continual controversy over home-rearing vs. day-care center experiences for young children receives objective data from Kagan's studies, in his chapter on effect of day care on early development. Kagan reviews his own and other researchers' data, to show that intact and psychologically supporting families do not damage their children by enrolling them in day-care centers. Here again psychosocial theories of development generate research which sheds light on urgent contemporary questions. Since Kagan's data deals with cognitive, social, and emotional development, it constitutes broad support for what has been intuitive wisdom, that is, that the family's press is primary and basic, and not easily diluted.

Humanistic theories of parenting and teaching are described by Rapp in his chapter on developmental humanism. Rapp emphasizes three child development concepts—freedom within limits, simple to complex, and individualization—integration. He outlines process theories further in identifying five elements or tenets of humanistic development—centered responsibility for one's own life, mutuality or relationship, here and now perspective, acceptance of the non-Hedonic emotions, and growth-oriented experimenting. Rapp's objective is a school curriculum oriented to positive self-concept development.

The other chapters feature cognitive development. Weybright, in his chapter on the development of thought in the young child, stresses action and interaction. Logically developed from Piagetian concepts of the active process required to develop intelligence, the stages of development, and the social interactions which are necessary to the construction of intelligence.

Nevius, in his chapter, identifies the kinds of experiences which are important to the cognitive growth of young children. Basing his curriculum suggestions on Piagetian theory, and citing research findings based on this theory, Nevius emphasizes productive learning possibilities which closely parallel and support children's spontaneous desires to explore, manipulate and discover. As Nevius points out, pleasure in learning results from appropriate cognitive challenge. It is "horizontal development," or application of current skills and knowledge to related areas, which are especially important to early cognitive development at home and at school.

*Dr. Helen Robison, Professor of Education, Baruch College, City University of New York.

Chapter 12

The Effect of Day Care on Early Development

Jerome Kagan*

Do infants attending a nurturant, responsibly administered group care center five days a week for a little over 100 weeks display different patterns of psychological development during or at the end of that period compared with children of the same sex and family background who are being reared in a typical nuclear family in the northeastern United States? Why would two child psychologists and a pediatrician* and several federal and private funding agencies be interested in that question? An answer to this second inquiry requires a deep examination of some of the unstated premises that form the foundation of a major segment of psychological research. The fundamental premise behind much developmental investigation is that experience exerts a primary force on the young child's development and the earlier the experience the more profound the effect. The basis for that assumption lies everywhere, in our history as well as our contemporary literature. Over two centuries ago post-revolutionary journalists regularly affirmed the critical importance of the early years and urged mothers to stay home with their infants and young children and treat them tenderly while political leaders worked for the establishment of public schools to insure that the child was exposed as early as possible to responsible models who would guarantee the proper sculpting of the child's character.

There are at least four seemingly independent sources for the supposition that variation in early encounter contributes to psychological variation in later childhood. One of the first is John Locke's metaphor of the *tabula rasa* and the desire of many 17th century intellectuals to make experience primary in the shaping of man's mind. A second historical force comes, oddly enough, from Protestantism in the form of a maxim that one must prepare for the future. Good deeds are tallied and influence one's state of virtue. As with the Hindu view of karma they constitute a kind of tote board that summarizes each person's moral posture. If a person's next life is determined by virtue displayed in the present then the future is knowable, to some degree, and the child can attain salvation if parents are careful in socializing proper values and actions. Colonial America's intellectuals, influenced strongly by Protestants with an egalitarian ideal, repeatedly urged mothers to care for the young children, implying that concern for their future was

not likely gathering wood in August to prepare for December's wintry winds.

The remarkable discoveries of the neurosciences during the last two decades have reinforced the old view that it is potentially possible to translate psychological experience into sentences with physiological content. Many citizens award allegiance to the notion that experience is translated into material changes in the neurons, like marks on a tablet that are fixed rather than transient. This view of the relation of brain to psychological experience evokes the metaphor of a tape and a tape recorder. The iron filings on the tape are permanently altered by experience and if no one erases the tape they will preserve their information with fidelity for an indefinite period of time.

A final reason for maintaining a strong belief in the staying power of early experience is a logical derivative of entrenched social practices in our society, especially the tendency to rank children on valued traits both in and out of school. This practice sensitizes every parent of a young child to the fact that inevitably rankings will be made during the elementary school years which will influence the quality of education the child receives throughout elementary and high school and the probability of his gaining entrance into a quality college and a dignified vocation. From the perspective of parent and child, the goal is to be ahead early in the race—to be as high in the rank order as possible when the competition begins at 6 years of age. And proper early experience is the best guarantee of a fast start.

The premises, some metaphysical and some rooted in social reality, contributed to the intellectual foundations of the research to be reported.

The subjects in our study were over 100 Chinese and Caucasian children, from both working and middle class homes, living in the Boston area. The 32 experimental children attended a research administered day care center from 3 or 5 to 29 months of age, while the primary control group consisted of infants from the same ethnic and social class groups who lived at home. The children were enrolled

*This work was a collaborative effort among the author and Richard B. Kearsley, M.D., Ph.D., and Philip R. Zelazo, Ph.D. of the Tufts-New England Medical Center, Boston, Massachusetts.

**Jerome Kagan, Professor of Psychology, Harvard University.

in the experiment when they were between 3½ and 5½ months of age. The day care children were in residence at the center five days a week from 8:30 in the morning until about 4:00 in the afternoon. Each infant was assigned a primary caretaker and in most cases the caretaker was of the same ethnicity as the child. The curriculum had a middle class American bias for it encouraged cognitive development, a one-to-one affective interaction between adult caretaker and child, and tried to maximize the opportunities for successful mastery experiences.

Each child was assessed by a research staff not involved in any aspect of caretaking at 3½, 5½, 7½, 9½, 11½, 13½, 20 and 29 months of age. This report is concerned only with the information gathered at 20 and 29 months. The assessment procedures involved aspects of cognitive, social, and emotional development. The cognitive battery included a vocabulary recognition test, an index of the child's familiarity with particular concepts (a test originally developed by Dr. Francis Palmer of the State University of New York), items from the Bayley Scale of Infant Development, an embedded figures task, and a test of short term memory for locations. In addition, degree of apprehension with an unfamiliar peer was assessed by comparing the child's play when he was alone with his mother with his play when an unfamiliar child of the same age and sex was introduced. The child's tendency to approach his mother when distressed—which some regard as an index of attachment—was assessed in a 45 minute session in which the child played in a room with his mother, an unfamiliar woman, and his primary caretaker (if he was from the day care group), or a familiar adult (if he was in the control group). Additionally, we assessed the child's tendency to protest following departure of his mother. Finally, the child was observed in an unfamiliar day care center.

Generally, there was very little difference between the day care and home control children on these procedures. There were no differences between the two rearing groups on any of the cognitive tests, even though the expected effects of social class on linguistic and conceptual knowledge were in accord with previous research. Middle class children attained higher scores than working class children, whether they came from the day care or home control groups.

During the 45 minute attachment session all children showed an overwhelming preference for their mothers when they were bored, tired or apprehensive. The ratio of time spent proximal to mother vs. the familiar adult or day care teacher was about 7 to .1. The day care children seemed no less attached to their mothers than the home controls. This conclusion was corroborated by the fact that there was no difference between day care and home control children in the tendency to protest maternal departure from 3½ through 29 months of age. The growth function for separation protest seemed to be monitored primarily by cognitive

maturation, for protest was low prior to 9 months, rose dramatically from 9 to 20 months, and then declines.

Both groups of children showed obvious inhibition and apprehension to the unfamiliar peer. The child approached his mother and decreased his play and maximal inhibition occurred at 20 months. However, the children reared at home were slightly more apprehensive than those attending the day care center. Hence prior experience with the child seemed to buffer the uncertainty generated by the unfamiliar child at 20 months. But this difference was temporary and had vanished by 29 months when all the children had matured to a point where they were able to resolve the uncertainty generated by the unfamiliar child. The children in day care played a little bit longer than the home controls in the unfamiliar day care center but the difference was not very dramatic. The majority of children made few social overtures toward other children and the similarity between the two groups was more striking than the differences.

It appears that attendance at a day care center staffed by conscientious and nurturant adults during the first 2½ years of life does not sculpt a psychological profile very much different from the one created by total home rearing. This generalization is based not only on our formal assessments but on our informal observations of the children over the 2½ years. Some have argued that the day care experience promotes an insecurity in children which makes them prone to seek their mother when frightened or bored. But all children were disposed to approach their mother when they became uncertain and the reaction to maternal departure revealed a remarkably similar growth function for all children. Some investigators have suggested multiple caretaking by several adults dilutes the child's emotional bond to his mother. But we found that the day care and home control children were equally likely to choose the mother as a target for solace and attentive nurturance when they were bored, tired, or afraid.

The entire corpus of data supports the view that day care, when responsibly and conscientiously implemented, does not seem to have hidden psychological dangers.

Since that conclusion flies in the face of popular belief it is both useful and reasonable to maintain a skeptical attitude toward that generalization for it is possible that our methods were not sufficiently sensitive. But if our methods are sensitive and there are few important differences in cognitive, social, and affective development between the two groups we should ask how that is possible, considering the fact that the day care children spent as much time in the center as they did at home.

One interpretation assumes that the psychological experiences at home have a priority; they are more salient and more affectively charged than those at the center. The mother's psychological impact on her child may be greater than that of the caretakers in the group care environment because the mother is more unpredictable than the day care teacher. Hence she is a more salient object in the infant's psychological space. A conscientious and nurturant caretaker in a group setting is aware of the psychological diversity among the children in the setting and sensitive to the differences in standards and values between each parent and herself. She is less likely to hold rigid standards of behavior for all children or expectations as to when particular developmental milestones should appear. She is likely to be more relaxed about these standards than the parents and she is less strongly identified with the children in her care. This tolerant attitude toward diversity would lead her to give each child considerable license to behave in accord with his temperamental disposition and level of maturity. With the exception of extremely destructive or regressed children, the hired caretaker would not impose restraints on children when they seem occupied and happy and as a result the child would not generate serious uncertainties about the caretaker's actions when he is exploring the environment. The mother, on the other hand, diagnoses deviations between her child's developing profile and her standards. When these deviations are too large she intrudes into the child's life space and attempts to shape his behavior so that it is in closer conformity with her understanding of the appropriate growth curve. Each intrusion creates a temporary node of uncertainty which alerts the child to the mother and to the action just issued. As a result the mother is less predictable than the caretaker, and more difficult to understand. In the language of psychoanalytic theory, the mother is more highly cathected than the caretaker; in the more modern language of information processing theory, the mother is a more salient event. Of course, if the caretaker behaved like our caricature of a mother then the caretaker would also become highly salient and affectively charged.

It is interesting to note that a recent study of kibbutz reared children, who spent most of every day in an infant house with a metapelet, also reported that the mother was the more salient figure. Infants during the second year were more likely to approach their mother than their metapelet when an unfamiliar woman was in the room with both caretakers, and the children were less apprehensive when with their mother and the unfamiliar woman than when they were with the metapelet and the same stranger. It appears that the amount of time a child spends with a caretaker is not as important as the details of the psychological interaction.

The data from this project, which are in accord with at least half a dozen similar studies published during the last five years, imply that children from intact and psychologically supporting families who experience surrogate care during infancy and early childhood resemble home reared children from their own social and ethnic group to a greater degree than they resemble children of different ethnic and class backgrounds in the same extrafamilial environment. The effects of the home have a significance that is not easily altered by group care. The family appears to have a mysterious power, which is perhaps one reason why it has been the basic and most stable social unit in this and other societies for so long a time.

Carroll Goldstein

Chapter 13
Socialization and Early Childhood Education

Eleanor Meyer Rogg*

Every year millions of infants are born whom scientists classify as homo sapiens. These infants are born naked and helpless, dependant in large part for what they become on the adults around them. For some time sociologists have been interested in whether all homo sapiens are human beings. Park & Burgess (1921) concluded that homo sapiens are not born human but become human slowly by acquiring culture from those around them. Culture includes everything that human beings think, have and do as members of a society. (Bierstedt, 1974)

How then does a small infant acquire culture? Culture is acquired through a process called socialization. Light and Keller (1975) define socialization as "the process of acquiring the physical, mental and social skills that a person needs to survive and to become both an individual and a member of society (p. 94)". While socialization is a process through which infants acquire culture and become human, socialization is also a way that culture continues to exist and is passed on through the generations. A number of terms have been used to describe the process of socialization. Anthropologists prefer the terms enculturation, culturation and child-rearing, for example.

We can distinguish two parts which occur simultaneously in the socialization process. First, the infant develops a self-identity. McGinnis and Finnegan (1976) apply the formal term "self-system" to this part of the socialization process. The child's "internal functioning" reflects a unique combination of thoughts, feelings, experiences and actions.

The second part of this process involves the infant becoming a member of society. Each child must learn to play certain required and specified roles provided by the society. McGinnis and Finnegan (1976) refer to this part of the socialization process as a person's "life-style." Life-style refers to a person's "observable network of consistent interpersonal patterns, which determine the ways in which a person functions (thinks, feels and acts) in the interpersonal sphere (p. 102)." Life-style deals with a person's external functioning, the outside behavior.

To conclude, socialization is a life-long learning process that turns a barely human, helpless homo sapien into a functioning group member and an individual.

Biology vs. Environment

The socialization process begins with naked biological specimens and potentials. Biological differences exist which may effect infants' life chances. These differences include, sex, race, size, and strength as well as any aberrations which may improve or impair the infants' ability to function as biological specimens and as members of society. For example, the life chances of males giving birth to infants are infinitesimally small.

However, what is often critical in determining individuals' life chances is not biological differences but the way cultures react to these differences. For example, in our society, many Americans would acknowledge that while males can still not give birth to babies, males may be able to play the role of mothers very well. In some other societies, if you were born male, no matter how inclined you were to be a mother you would not be allowed to play the role. Oppositely, if you were born female in some cultures, no matter how intelligent or strong you were, you would not be able to become a priest or a witch doctor.

Not only do cultures limit the roles people play according to biological differences between their members, but despite biological potential, if the cultures does not include certain roles then the potential will never be realized. For example, no matter how biologically inclined any of us are to become witch doctors, as long as we live in the United States, we will not play this role. If you were born in a primitive culture and were a potential genius in nuclear physics, this potential would also not be realized.

For generations, sociologists have debated the question of which factor is more important in determining what an individual becomes, the person's heredity (inherent biological potential) or the person's environment (external cultural factors). Vander Zanden (1970) concludes the question is spurious. Scientists keep debating it, but in reality the two factors operate simultaneously and in combination and should not be treated separately. Kenkel and Voland (1975) feel the question is so important in a society like

*Dr. Eleanor Rogg, Chairperson, Department of Sociology & Anthropology, Wagner College, Staten Island, New York.

ours that is based on the presumed equality of all people, that it will continue to rage hotly. Are there any true biological differences in ability between the different sexes or races, or are all the observed differences due to cultural and socialization factors? The answer to this question might profoundly influence our society. Bierstedt (1974) believes that sociologists will continue to consider both heredity and environment because both are obviously necessary to create a human being.

Social Interaction and the Child

Infants react to their physical feelings of comfort and discomfort. Infants do not know the boundary of their own bodies. When the infants are uncomfortable, they may cry but they do not know that they are crying. Parents react to infants in terms of the infants biological needs. Babies must be fed and cleaned. When and how parents will do these jobs depends upon the culture in which the family is found. Much of the early interaction of infants with others is in terms of physical touching. As time goes on, babies begin to develop feelings about these encounters. Babies begin to recognize the person who is primarily responsible for their care. They slowly recognize other members of the family. Not only is a physical interaction developed but an emotional interaction as well.

Broom and Selnick (1970) point out that parents are both a source of satisfaction and frustration to infants. Babies experience feelings of rage and hostility when confronted with deprivation. One task children must learn during the socialization process is to control and manage these feelings.

An even more difficult emotion that children face is anxiety. Since anxiety is a diffuse emotion arising from inner conflict, and vague threat, children cannot dispel the feeling easily by striking out at the source of the problem, since the source is often unrecognized. Broom and Selznick (1970) believe that (in the United States) this anxiety may be the result of the dependence of human infants for such a long period of time on small group of people. As children mature and enter school, further anxiety is introduced by the competitive society in which they are expected to compete. Feelings of inability to stand on their own and to compete successfully are always creating nagging self-doubts.

Studies have shown that children appear to need close physical contact and repeated interaction with significant adults in their lives. Without this contact, socialization often fails. (Broom and Selznick, 1970).

Developing The Self and Learning Roles

In the process of interaction with others, infants slowly develop a sense of self. First infants become aware of their own bodies. Slowly children are able to distinguish themselves from others, as they gradually learn language. As one part of the socialization process, babies learn not only rules, values, and beliefs but also how to apply them to themselves.

Charles Horton Cooley is famous for his theory – The Looking Glass Self. Bierstedt (1974) summarizes this theory in the statement "I am what I think you think I am (p. 197)." There are three parts to this theory. (1) In the first step I imagine what I appear like to you. In a sense, you become a mirror in which I see myself. I imagine what I look like in that mirror. (your eyes). For example, lets pretend you are my teacher and I notice you looking at me. I might say to myself that "she sees me working at my desk."

(2) I then imagine how you judge what you see in me. I look for clues to confirm this judgment. For example, I look at you, and if you smile at me, I might say to myself that you like me because I am working at my desk. (3) I now have some sort of feeling toward myself dependant upon how I think you have seen and judged me. For example, I feel I am a good diligent student because I was seen working at my desk when my teacher smiles at me.

Closely related to this concept is Merton's famous concept of the self-fulfilling prophecy. He points out that what people think about themselves will come true. For example, if a student believes he will fail an exam, he will fail that exam because the student will bring about the conditions that will cause the failure. If this student feels he will fail, then he will probably not study because that studying won't help. Of course, if our student does not study, then his chances of passing will diminish and the prophecy will come true.

Similarly, teachers can create self-fulfilling prophecies. If a teacher believes a student is incapable of doing better, then the teacher will often not try to help the student do better, and when the student doesn't do better, the teacher's original prophecy will have come true.

Children begin to develop looking-glass selves by the time they are two or three and these selves are gradually built up and reinforced throughout their lives. Early childhood education is critical in the development of these looking-glass selves.

While Cooley has demonstrated that the self is created in social interaction, George Herbert Mead shows how the self develops in various stages of social interaction. Mead stresses the need for language, playing at a role and games in the socialization process. For Mead the development of a vocabulary, including the words "I" and "me", are critical for the development of a self-concept. At first children refer to themselves in the third person, perhaps by their own names, but as they reach two or three years of age they are able to refer to themselves as "I" or "me". They begin to distinguish themselves from other children. "I" is the active, creative part of the self, while "me" is the passive part, being acted upon. Once children have language they are able to think about what "I" want to do, or what is expected of "me" and how people are reacting to "me". Once they are able to imagine how other people are thinking about them, they are also able to think about how to get people to react to them the way they want. Children begin to play at certain roles, the role of a good girl the role of a pupil, the role of a mother, the role of a teacher. Children begin to imagine what is expected of a person occupying that role.

The final stage that Mead discusses is the game stage. When children play at a single role like mother, they imagine how their behavior appears to one other person. By age 8 or 9, in the game stage, children begin to play with several other children and have to consider how they appear to all of these other people simultaneously. Thus, children develop a sense of the group, the generalized other. Children begin to be concerned with the question of how "they feel". As people mature, the idea of the generalized other gradually expands until they develop the concept of society.

While Cooley and Mead stress the development of human rationality and creativity in the socialization process, Sigmund Freud emphasizes the repressive influences of society. Broom and Selznick (1970) see Freud and Mead's view as not totally incompatible. Freud and Mead divide the self into two parts. Freud sees the passive conventional part of the self (that Mead calls the "me") as the superego. Freud sees the "id" as the part of the self that society will never totally dominate. The "id" is the part that consists essentially of the biological drives and desires. The ego tries to mediate between the id and the superego, between the drives and the demands of society.

Erik H. Erikson, a leading student of Sigmund Freud, is famous for describing stages of human development. The first four stages which concern early childhood education, deal with the problem of children from infancy up to adolescence. The first stage occurs in infancy. Babies must confront the problem of trust or mistrust. When parents treat their infants' needs consistently and warmly, babies begin to trust the world as a reliable, dependable and accepting place. If treated erratically by parents, children begin to fear their environment. The second stage of development occurs during early childhood from about 2 to 4 years of age. Children must confront the problem of autonomy vs. shame and doubt. During this stage children learn to control the muscles of and nerves of their body. This time can be very satisfying and can build self-confidence when children are able to do things for themselves but it can be very frightening when children lose control. Erickson suggests that parents and teachers should provide atmospheres where children are encouraged to try things for themselves but are protected from self-doubt and being shamed.

The third stage occurs from about ages four to five. Children must confront the problems of initiative vs. guilt. Instead of simply passively imitating others, children begin to create and initiate projects of their own. If their attempts are disparaged feelings of guilt may arise.

The final stage of childhood occurs from about ages six to twelve. For many children it is the first time that they must deal with a group other than their family. They enter a world of secondary relationships, formal and impersonal. They are not supposed to be valued for whose child they are, but for what work they are able to do. If children feel that their background is not acceptable to the group around them, they may develop feelings of inferiority. Some children may attempt to overcompensate for these feelings by being extremely industrious.

Acquiring Culture Through Agents of Socialization

As part of the socialization process, children internalize the ideas and norms of their culture. American society is sometimes called culturally plural, that is within the dominant American culture there are many subcultures, many variations on the main stream. Which aspects of American culture children will internalize depend upon the agents of socialization through whom the culture is mediated to the children. There are four main agents of socialization that filter the culture to American children. They are (1) the family (2) the peer group (3) the mass media and (4) the schools. Let us examine the influence of each of these groups.

The Family

For the first few years of life, the family is the whole world of the small child. The only people who matter to small children are the ones who are raising them. These people are their significant others, their looking glasses. The view children have of themselves and of the world are first formed here. Reiss (1976) points out that parents and their offspring form a primary group in the full sense that Cooley meant when he coined the term. "Cooley means a group which was primary in the sense of influencing the individual first and having an impact of first importance (p. 345)."

Even when children come in contact with other socialization agents like teachers, friends and movie stars, the family will remain primary because it has the most continuous and longest lasting interaction with the children of any of these people (Vander Zanden, 1970).

Elkin and Handel (1972) show that the family is an "interaction structure" in which children establish the first intimate and personal relationships with others. The capacity for developing relationships with others is formed here.

The family is a model for patterning later interaction with others. Ideas about the roles of females and males, husband and wives, and friends emerge.

The family "places" the child in the larger society. How the child will be treated by others during childhood as well as the child's life chances are determined in part by the social class, race, ethnic and religious groups of which his family are members. The family's position will determine how the culture is mediated to the child. What activities the family engages in as well as the attitudes and feelings expressed by family members about other groups and subcultures will mold the child into a particular kind of American. (Elkin and Handel, 1972).

Philipe Aries (1962) in his book *Centuries of Childhood* theorizes that conscious socialization of children is a relatively recent phenomenon in Western Culture. During the middle ages, children were simply considered little adults, and were dressed and treated as such. The concept of a childhood without responsibilities took a few more centuries to emerge. By the early twentieth century, parents had become aware of their role in socializing children, and their responsibility for the behavior of their children, Vander Zanden (1970) sees three ways in which parents socialize children. One method is didactic teaching, where children are instructed formally in some skill. A second method is imitation, where children mold their behavior after that of their adult caretakers. And the third is reward and punishment for conformity or nonconformity to the wishes of the parents.

When parents (particularly middle class parents) are in doubt today as to how to properly socialize their children, they no longer turn to members of the extended family. They tend to turn to a group of "experts" who have gained increasing popularity throughout the twentieth century. Dr. Benjamin Spock has been one of the most well known of these experts. Some confusion results for parents who conscientiously read a number of these experts, since the experts don't always agree.

Traditionally the role of the mother has been considered the most influential one in socializing the child. The literature abounds with the importance of the mother, as the primary caretaker of the infant, and as the first person with whom the infant has a relationship and from whom the infant develops the first sense of self. (Bierstedt, 1974) Increasingly, we have greater numbers of single parent families developing in our society, and whether the single parent is a male or female, the role of the primary caretaker of the infant becomes even more important.

When a second parent is present, or perhaps an older sibling, some important socialization functions may be performed. This second individual may help lessen the dependancy of the child on the primary caretaker and may help the child develop a sense of the larger group.

In many ways, siblings may act similarly to members of

the child's peer group in the socialization process.

The Peer Group

Until they reach school age the most important playmates or friends of small children may be their older siblings and friends of their siblings. As more children attend nursery schools and day care centers, the role of the peer group in the socialization process begins to play a part at earlier and earlier ages. By the time children reach adolescence, the peer group becomes a more significant socializing agent than the family. Indeed children begin to reject parental influence and increasingly conform to the standards of the peer group. Light and Keller (1975) point out that the child learns to form egalitarian relationships with people of the same age, sex and student status in the peer group. Relationships with parents and teachers are between unequals, with parents and teachers holding the power.

Vander Zanden (1974) points out that a second function of the peer group is to transmit certain cultural patterns including fads, customs and forbidden knowledge that the child will not learn from other authority figures. For example, peer groups are important disseminators of sexual information. Some sociologists believe that sexual education programs in schools approach the question so clinically, that the most important emotional questions as to how to handle sexual relationships are never even discussed.

Broom and Selznick (1970) note that the peer group introduces children to impersonal authority. Children have to learn to play by the rules of the game and to develop a sense of fairness.

Children are also able to challenge the adult world and its values when in the peer group with less fear of parental punishment. Groups of children will feel freer to cut up in the classroom, than when they must individually approach their teachers.

Finally, Elkin and Handel (1972) point out that peer groups afford children the opportunity to develop friendships with others based on individual needs and interests, not simply on the basis of being children.

Schools

A third important socializing agent for American children is the school system. The school system functions to formally transmit the culture of a society to its children. This aspect of socialization is better known as education.

Children are expected to acquire a significant amount of the culture's knowledge in school. In this way, the society assures that its culture will be transmitted to the next generation (Bierstedt, 1972). Not only does the school help to preserve our cultural heritage, but also, it reinforces the norms and values of the dominant groups in the society.

Generations of immigrant children were expected to learn to become like their Anglo-Saxon forefathers. More recently, advocates of cultural pluralism stress that early teaching methods imposed middle class WASP values on children from varied backgrounds thus robbing both the children and the society of a rich ethnic heritage. (Perry and Perry, 1976)

Schools also socialize children by preparing them for adult roles, both socially and occupationally. Increasing emphasis is being placed on career education from the earliest years in school.

Elkin and Handel (1972) point out that the school system functions to lessen children's emotional dependence on home. It is perhaps the first institution with which children come into extended formal contact outside of the family. The school is a conservative reinforcing agency of the society passing on its major values and attitudes.

The classroom provides children with the experience of adapting to a large group of peers and strangers. Children must learn to share, take their turn and not be distracted by neighbors. Children learn to become a member of society.

The class and teacher provide children with a new looking glass. Children are being constantly evaluated in this setting by teacher judgments and peer comments as well as report cards, marks and comments on papers. Traditionally, children have slowly developed a reputation that follows them on their record cards throughout the school system. Vander Zanden (1970) sees this sorting and sifting as a way of selecting out children for upward mobility. The numbers and remarks on this card will effect the kind of future classroom experiences the child will have. Will the child be put in a fast, average or slow class? Will the child be admitted to an academic sequence in high school? Will the child be able to get into college? Note that the school sequence can potentially lock a child into certain programs which limit the kinds of adult roles, the child will eventually be able to play.

Mass Media

Typical American children spend about one sixth of their waking hours in front of a television. Along with T.V. viewing, however, children also read comic books, newspapers and go to the movies. The mass media can be a great potential socializing agent. (De Fleur et. al. 1972). How much of a socializing agent the media actually are is a matter of great debate within the social sciences. Some critics of the mass media contend that the media influence children profoundly and often negatively. For example, violence on television is believed to create a very violent population. This type of theory, DeFleur refers to as the cultural norm theory of media influence. This theory states that when the media consistently use certain violent themes "the media

may create the distorted impression that their "definition of the situation"—or set of norms—is a reflection of the real society p. 166f." In other words, if one sees a great deal of violence on TV then one believes that is how people are supposed to act in the real world. Both Elkin and Handel (1972) as well as DeFleur (1972) believe that there is no real hard data to prove this position. More research is required.

Other sociologists believe that the media are not primary socializers of children or adults. Instead the media are simply reflections of the changing norms values and attitudes of Americans. If American society is growing increasingly violent, then the media will reflect this situation by showing more violent programs. A number of thinkers would accept the position that a good deal of "incidental learning, an unplanned by-product of entertainment" takes place by default. (DeFleur, p. 166). That is, if children watch a great deal of television, and it is their only source of information about some subject, then children will pick up their ideas from this source.

However, Elkin and Handel (1972) point out the mass media rarely influence the child in isolation. The television programs a child watches and the interpretation of these programs generally depends upon the groups of which a child is a member. Much television watching is done with other members of the family or peer group present. These groups have a considerable influence in determining what is watched and in defining what is valuable.

Indeed children's reaction to all of the agents of socialization, their family, peer group, school and the mass media are very often guided by value systems which develop from experiences common to their (1) ethnic, racial and religious background (2) social class background and (3) neighborhood whether urban, rural or suburban. Let us consider these special experiences of children.

Ethnic, Racial and Religious Influences on Socialization

At the core of an individual's self-concept is an identification with an ethnic, racial and religious group. Even children whose families have been in this country for generations and whose families have intermarried are able to rattle off their ethnic ancestry. Thus, Americans don't think of themselves as simply American but precede the term with an ethnic label. Shibutani and Kwan, (1965) define an ethnic group as consisting of "people who conceive of themselves as being alike by virtue of common ancestry, real or fictitious, and are so regarded by others (p. 572)."

Traditionally, certain ethnic groups have been considered superior to others in our society. At the top of this stratification system have been WASPs (White Anglo-Saxon Protestants.) Traditionally to be the best kind of American has meant to be as much like a WASP as possible. Generations of immigrant children learned this lesson in classrooms across the United States. The ways of immigrant parents were inferior. Conflict was produced in the homes of many immigrant families when the values and ideas taught in the schools conflicted with the values and ideas of immigrant parents. Some children resolved this conflict by dropping out of school. Others broke away from their families. Many tried to live in two worlds and to have two identities.

Many Americans have discovered that they cannot melt into main stream America. No matter how hard they try their skin color will always remain different. Others have felt that they have been robbed of their own immigrant heritage. Michael Novak in his book *The Rise of the Unmeltable Ethnics* (1972) expresses the feelings of many of these people. Today, many groups are fighting back and there is a movement known as 'the new ethnicity.' Novak (1974) describes the new ethnicity as:

first, a growing sense of discomfort with the sense of identity one is supposed to have—universalist, "melted", "like everyone else", then a growing appreciation for the potential wisdom of one's own gut reactions (especially on moral matters) and their historical roots; a sense of being discriminated against, condescended to, or carelessly misapprehended; a growing disaffection regarding those to whom one has always been taught to defer; and a sense of injustice regarding the response of liberal spokesmen to conflicts between various ethnic groups, especially between "legitimate" minorities and "illegitimate ones." There is, in a word, an inner conflict between one's felt personal power and one's ascribed public power; a sense of outraged truth, justice and equity. (p. 262.)

The new movement is pressuring school systems across the country to acknowledge that American society is a culturally and structurally plural society. New ethnic heritage programs are developing to help children identify with their own backgrounds and be able to take pride in their respective heritages. It is theorized that as schools encourage positive self-images among children from ethnic backgrounds which have been less favored that these children's attitudes toward the school system may improve as they are able to identify with a multi-cultural system.

Milton Gordon (1964) has pointed out that stratifying every group are social class levels. Within each ethnic group, people identify most with other members who are on the same social class level. Indeed, he suggests that for white ethnics, social class is a more important indicator of the way a person thinks, feels and behaves than ethnic group membership.

Social Class

Children are born into families that differ in the amounts of wealth, influence, prestige and life chances they can offer their children. In terms of socialization of these children; the most important differences between socio economic strata in the United States are the different ways of life, or subcultures each class reflects.

Social class effects the life expectancy, health, food, leisure activities, residence, clothing and other consumer goods, religious participation, and education that children will receive. Class effects almost every area of the children's lives.

Child-rearing patterns differ between social classes. Discipline techniques differ. Middle class parents use the threat of withdrawal of love and guilt feelings, whereas lower class parents rely more on physical punishment. (Walters and Stinnert, 1971, Kerckhoff, 1972)

Swinehart (1963) found that as socio economic status increased, maternal stress on satisfying a child's social and emotional needs increased, while stress on satisfying a child's physical needs decreased.

Melvin Kohn (1974) studies the relationship between parents occupations and their child-rearing values. He believes that the characteristics the children's parents find valuable on their own jobs, will be the characteristics that the parents will try to instill in their children. Working-class fathers who have to follow orders from their foremen will stress obedience to authority in their children. Middle-class parents who need initiative and self-discipline to succeed in their professions will stress these values. Thus Kohn (1974) contends that working-class parents

value obedience, neatness and cleanliness more highly than do middle-class parents and that middle-class parents in turn value curiosity, happiness, consideration and—most importantly—self-control more highly than do working-class parents . . . To working-class parents it is the overt act that matters; the child should not transgress externally imposed rules; to middle-class parents, it is the child's motives and feelings, that matter; the child should govern himself. (p. 283).

Kohn (1969) recognizes that different life experiences cause members of different social classes to see the world differently—"to develop different conceptions of social reality, different aspirations and hopes and fear, different "conceptions of the desirable" (p. 7)

We have already noted in this article that middle-class children tend to perform better in school and reach higher educational levels than do lower-class children.

Vander Zanden (1970) advances three hypotheses. (1) He suggests that middle and lower class subcultures may not offer children the same skills and attitudes for academic success. Middle class children have better verbal skills and larger vocabularies when they begin school. Since many schools teach with standard English, those children whose first language is not standard English are further disadvantaged. Middle class children tend to be more familiar with books, crayons, pencils and paper by the time they begin school.

(2) A second hypothesis that Vander Zanden advances is that "lower class children are victims of educational self-fulfilling prophecies (p. 445)." We have already discussed this idea under Cooley's looking-glass theory.

(3) The final hypothesis Vander Zanden advances is that lower class children are alienated from school by its middle class value system. The sociologist defines the "lower class" as the members of the society with the least power, privileges, resources, and rights. The term "lower class" has many other connotations for middle class individuals.

Elkin and Handel (1972) feel that it is used to refer unfavorably to the way of life followed by people so situated. Thus, lower class implies ignorance, instability of employment and family life; 'premature' initiation of heterosexual activity and subsequent promiscuity; 'low standards' of personal grooming, housekeeping and language usage; in short, a wide array of behavior that is unacceptable to middle-class people. (p. 79)." These two sociologists question whether the use of the term lower class should be continued, it may be so destructive.

Urban Influences

The residential setting for many poor in our society is the inner city. Suzanne Keller (1963) studied "The Social World of the Urban Slum Child" among 46 children in an elementary school in one of the poorer sections of New York City. She found that 55% of the first grade and 65% of fifth grade children expressed low self-esteem. When these children compared themselves with their school mates, they described themselves unfavorably. By the time these children reach adolescence they are very conscious of social class differences and the advantages enjoyed by others.

Large cities in the United States are characterized by many groups and subcultures coexisting in densely populated neighborhoods. Herbert Gans (1962) identifies five urban life-styles. (1) The "cosmopolites," characterized by high socio-economic status, mostly professionals and intellectuals who enjoy the city's cultural facilities (2) the "unmarried or childless" who also live in the city by choice and enjoy its social life (3) the "ethnic villagers", who except at work generally associate only with other members of their ethnic background. They tend to develop strong kinship and in-group ties, with other ethnics, overcoming a sense of anomie in the city. (4) "the deprived," who comprise a large proportion of the inner city's population and

who stay in the city because they can find work more easily, and pay less rent. Welfare payments also tend to be higher in the city. They tend to live in deteriorating housing in aging slum neighborhoods. The families tend to be poor, non-white, and many are single-parent homes. Children in this group are often socialized more by their peer group than by their family. With mothers working and fathers out of the house, these children become "street wise" at very early ages. They learn to survive in their neighborhoods and often know more about traveling around the city alone than do children from higher social classes. Since they are not sheltered from the "street scene", they learn to defend themselves physically at early ages and try to act tough. Many of these children have a sense of isolation, from the larger city and tend to stay within the smaller neighborhood they know and feel safer in. (Duberman, 1976) (5) The fifth and last lifestyle is "the trapped". This group is made up of the elderly on small fixed incomes who remain because they cannot afford to move.

Middle-class suburban images of the city tend to stereotype urban areas as corrupt, dirty and evil, while rural areas are seen as beautiful, pure and good. (Vidich and Bensman, 1958) These images have been most destructive in attempts to solve urban problems. Suburbanites have not been willing to recognize the part they have played in the creation of these urban problems. Many middle class individuals earn their livings in the city and use its free facilities, but return to their suburban homes at night and don't want to pay taxes to the city. Rural and suburban legislators are unwilling to allow the cities power to govern themselves and solve their own problems.

De Fluer (1972) believes that:

Urbanism, as we have seen, does not necessarily breed alienation and discontent. The crisis of today's central city has deep-seated roots in the past. It seems to be less a product of "size, density, and heterogeneity: than it is of the passive or overt opposition of a predominantly white, middle-class society to the integration of its black population. The lack of structural relationship between the slums and the rest of the city now makes it unlikely that the slum dweller will learn the norms and roles that could make such integration possible. (p. 298)

Summary:

Helpless infants become human by acquiring culture from their adult caretakers. These infants are products of both their heredity and environment. They acquire self-images and learn to play roles in social interaction with significant others around them.

Four main agents of socialization filter the culture to American children. These agents are (1) the family, (2) the peer group, (3) the mass media and (4) the schools.

Children's reactions to these agents are guided by value systems which develop from experiences common to their (1) ethnic, racial and religious backgrounds (2) social class background and (3) neighborhood, whether urban, rural or suburban.

BIBLIOGRAPHY

Aries, Philipe. *Centuries of Childhood.* New York: Vintage Books, 1962.

Bierstedt, Robert. *The Social Order, 4th edition.* New York: McGraw Hill Inc., 1974.

Broom, Leonard; and Selznick, Philip. *Principles of Sociology.* New York: Harper and Row, Co., 1970.

DeFleur, Melvin; D'Antonio, Wm., and DeFleur, Lois. *Sociology: Man in Society, Brief Edition.* Illinois: Scott, Foresman & Co., 1972.

Duberman, Luccile. *Social Inequality: Class and Caste in America.* Philadelphia: J.B. Lippincott, Co., 1976.

Elkin, Frederick and Handel, Gerald. *The Child and Society: The Process of Socialization, second edition.* New York: Random House, 1972.

Erikson, Erik H. *Childhood and Society.* New York: Norton, 1950.

Gans, Herbert J. "Urbanism and Suburbanism as Ways of Life: A Re-evaluation of Definition." *In Human Behavior and Social Processes,* edited by Arnold M. Rose. Boston: Houghton Miffling, 1962.

Gordon, Milton M. *Assimilation in American Life.* New York: Oxford University Press, 1964.

Jackson, Philip. *Life in Classrooms.* New York: Holt, Rinehart and Winston, 1968.

Keller, Suzanne. "The Social World of the Urban Slum Child. *American Journal of Orthopsychiatry,* 1963, 33: 823-831.

Kenkel, William and Voland, Ellen. *Society in Action.* San Francisco: Canfield Press, 1975.

Kerckhoff, A.C. *Socialization and Social Class.* Englewood Cliffs, N.J.: Prentice Hall, 1972.

Kohn, Melvin L. "Social Class and Parental Values." *American Journal of Sociology,* 1959, 64: 337-351.

"Social Class and Parent-Child Relationships: An Interpretation." In *Selected Studies in Marriage and the Family,* edited by Winch and Spanier. New York: Holt, Rinehart and Winston, 1974.

Class and Conformity: A Study of Values. Homewood, Ill.: Dorsey Press, 1969.

Light, Jr., Donald and Keller, Suzanne. *Sociology.* New York: Alfred A. Knopf, 1975.

McGinis, Thomas and Finnegan, Dana. *Open Family and Marriage: A Guide to Personal Growth.* St. Louis: C.V. Mosby, Co., 1976.

Merton, Robert K. *Social Theory and Social Structure, enlarged edition.* New York: Free Press, 1968.

Novak, Michael. "The New Ethnicity." *In The Social Web,* edited by Perry and Perry. San Francisco: Canfield Press, 1976.

Park, Robert E. and Burgess, Ernest W. *Introduction to the Science of Sociology.* Chicago: The University of Chicago Press, 1921.

Perry, John and Perry, Erna. *The Social Web: An Introduction to Sociology, second edition.* San Francisco: Canfield Press, 1976.

Reiss, Ira L. *Family Systems in America, second edition.* Illinois: Dryden Press, 1976.

Rosenthal, Robert and Jacobsen, Lenore. *Pygmalian in the Classroom: Teacher Expectation and Pupils' Intellectual Development.* New York: Holt, Rinehart and Winston, 1968.

Shibutani, Tamotsu and Kwan, Kian M. *Ethnic Stratification.* New York; MacMillan, Co., 1965.

Swinehart, James. "Socio-Economic Level, Status Aspiration and Maternal Role." *American Sociological Review,* 1963, 28: 391-399.

Vander Zanden, James. *Sociology, A Systematic Approach, 2nd edition.* New York: The Ronald Press, 1970.

Vidich, Arthur J. and Bensman, Joseph. *Small Town in Mass Society.* Princeton, N.J.: Princeton University Press, 1958.

Walters, James and Stinnett, Nick. "Parent-Child Relationships: A Decade Review of Research." *Journal of Marriage and the Family,* 1971, 33: 95-96.

Chapter 14
Dimensions of Right and Left Brain Learning in Early Childhood

Rosemarie Harter Kraft and
Marlin L. Languis*

Research beginning in the late sixties to the present time has given us extensive advances in the understanding of underlying neural mechanisms of thought and learning. Perhasp the most dramatic advance is the discovery that man has two interacting thinking systems, housed in the left and right hemisphere of the brain, each complete with its own memories, cognitive mode and learning style.

The left hemisphere is the linear, analytic specialist which stores its memories in words, learns best by the sequential building of constructs and is an expert at analyzing the parts of a whole, propositional thinking and the temporal structuring of the world. Whereas the right hemisphere is the gestalt, synthetic specialist which stores its memories in images, learns best by the holistic synthesizing of constructs and is an expert at filling in missing pieces to understand the whole picture and the spatial structuring of the world.[1] For instances, when the young child verbally names and classifies objects into categories, left brain learning is probably taking place and when he constructs a topological picture of the world through spatial exploration, right brain learning is probably taking place.

Right Brain: The Dominant Thinking System in Early Life?

Although evidence suggests that structural[2] and functional[3] differences between the two hemispheres are present at birth, the brain of the young infant appears to be flexible.[4] Development of brain function and perhaps brain structure is probably an interaction of genetic propensities, chemical interactions in the body due to factors such as nutrition and hormonal levels at critical periods in neural development and early experience. (Harris, in press; Wiesel, 1976, duBois, 1976). However, there is reason to postulate that the right brain system is the dominant mode of thinking and learning in the very young child, particularly in the first two years of life. Harris (1975) presents a convincing argument for this position. Citing research indicating that 1) the visual cortex of the right hemisphere matures faster than the left, 2) high fevers which produce greater brain damage in the most active hemisphere causes more right hemisphere damage in infants before the age of two, and 3) newborn infants tend to lie in a position which will enable most of the incoming sensory information to be processed by the right hemisphere,[5] he postulates that the cognitive development of the right hemisphere precedes that of the left. This learning is evidenced by the early ability to recognize and discriminate between faces,[6] and the synthesizing of a multi-modality space in early infancy.[7] By eighteen months the infant knows that permanent objects exist in the multi-modality space, and by the age of two is constructing topological space (Piaget, 1973). As language is acquired and spatial concepts are compacted into a single symbol (word) which stands for the entire concept/process, the left hemisphere becomes the dominant thinking system. However, the propensity for spatial exploration throughout childhood clearly suggests evidence of the right hemisphere's synthetical learning modality beyond language acquisition.[8]

Functional Split Personality Throughout Infancy and Early Childhood

There is also reason to suspect that infants and young children may be developing the two thinking systems independently; that they are functional split personalities. Research involving adults which have had the fibres connecting the left and right hemisphere surgically severed has demonstrated that it is possible to disconnect the two thinking systems resulting in two people in one head. Although the styles of learning and thinking in the two are remarkably different, each of the disconnected hemispheres have memories of the past and are capable of being simultaneously conscious.[9] (Also, see Footnote 1). Gazzaniga (1974) and Galin (1976a) suggest that because this connecting fibre system slowly matures throughout infancy and childhood[10] the young child may be a functional split brain, developing each thinking system independently (functional split personalities). The maturation of these connecting fibres closely parallels Piaget's development stages (Kraft, 1976; Kraft and Languis, in press: Galin, 1976a). This suggests that the cognitive development which

*Rosemarie Harter Kraft, Assistant Professor of Education, Ohio State University. Marlin L. Languis, Professor of Education, Ohio State University.

Piaget has charted may be the ontogeny of fibre systems in the brain which increasingly permit the two systems to communicate, integrate knowledge and work together efficiently to solve problems.

Differences in Neural Organization

There appears to be individual and group differences in neural organization. Three organization patterns have been defined: 1) lateralized functioning (those individuals having most of their language functioning housed in one hemisphere and most of their spatial functioning in the other hemisphere), 2) diffuse language functioning (those individuals having language representation in both hemispheres, which results in spatial deficits), and 3) diffuse spatial functioning (those individuals having spatial representation in both hemispheres, which results in language deficits).

Current research findings suggest that males tend to have lateralized functioning, while females tend to have diffuse language representation in both hemispheres.[11] (Summarized in Harris, in press) These findings may partially explain the well documented differences between the sexes in spatial and language tasks. (Buffery and Gray, 1972; Maccoby, 1974) Other groups having diffuse neural organization are the left handers and individuals which mixed hand-eye dominance.[12] On the basis of these findings it is postulated that genetic factors predispose certain individuals for adequate performance on spatial-synthetical and verbal-analytical skills or superior performance in one with deficiencies in the other.[13]

There is also evidence that early experience which is influenced by cultural preference in cognitive mode[14] may further reinforce or deter these predispositions. However, the influence of environmental factors should decrease with age as neural structures develop and mature and become increasingly less flexible.

Designing an Optimum Learning Curriculum

McVicker Hunt (1961, 1966) suggests that the most facilitating match for learning is one which has "an optimum of incongruity" (i.e., just a little beyond the present cognitive development) for each child at each point in his development. Therefore, knowing the cognitive developmental level and neural organization of a given child may give educators a powerful tool for facilitating learning by constructing an appropriate learning environment and planning effective teaching strategies which match the child's level of neural development.

Juxtaposing McVicker Hunt's observations and the recent discovery that the child is developing not one but two cognitive systems reveals that the optimum learning environment must challenge each of these systems. Furthermore, if these two systems gradually develop the ability to communicate, to function integratively and selectively,

then, a third match is suggested. A match which challenges the spatial synthetical specialist and the verbal analytical specialist to work together in a complementary fashion. There is evidence that a curriculum designed to encourage integrative hemispheric functioning increases verbal memory and learning[15] and may be a necessary condition for creative thinking and problem solving (Bogan and Bogan, 1969; Bogan, 1976; Languis and Kraft, 1976).

Wittrock (1976) further suggests that complementary functioning can be best facilitated by challenging the dominant modality first while supplementing this instruction with secondary instructional techniques which encourage the other hemisphere to participate in the activity. Whereas, Hunter (1976) pragmatically concludes that prior knowledge of the child's dominant modality is not necessary. She encourages educators of young children to vary instructional techniques until the correct match for a given child is found. However, if neural organization can be predicted by factors such as sex and hand-eye dominance as well as early reinforcement patterns (parental and cultural) prior determination of the dominant modality should be predictable. Future research in this arena should advance diagnostic techniques and perhaps lead to prevention rather than remediation of a variety of learning problems.

FOOTNOTES

[1] As early as 1861, Paul Broca, a French pathologist and pioneer in neurosurgery, reported functional asymmetry between the two cerebral hemispheres. Citing the behavior of patients with lesions of the left frontal lobe, Broca (cited in Milner, 1974) postulated that articulated speech was a function of the left cerebral hemisphere. Broca's statement precipitated numerous other reports of patients suffering from loss of language functions in association with damage in the left cerebral hemisphere (Harris, 1975).

In 1874, Hughlings Jackson (cited in Benton, 1972) a British neurologist, reported that damage in the right cerebral hemisphere was associated with loss in visuo-spatial recognition and memory resulting in visuo-spatial disorientation, failure to recognize faces and inability to dress. Following Jackson's observation were other reports of spatial disorders associated with lesions of the right cerebral hemisphere, such as loss of geographic memory and inability to locate objects and self in space.

In the years that have followed, these reports have been confirmed and extended. Observations of patients with hemispheric lesions have indicated an association of the left hemisphere with reading, writing, speaking, understanding the spoken word, calculation and analytical tasks and an association of the right hemisphere with visuo-spatial performance such as visual pattern identification, visual closure, spatial orientation, musical pattern and Gestalt, synthetic tasks (Benton, 1972; Corkin, 1965; Milner, 1965,

1969, 1974). However, the significance of this functional asymmetry was not understood until the later 1960's when R. W. Sperry and his associates began publishing the results of tests performed by "split brain" patients. These patients have undergone surgical sectioning of the major commissures connecting the two cerebral hemispheres in order to prevent the interhemispheric spread of epileptic seisures (Bogan and Vogel, 1962; Bogan, Fisher and Vogel, 1965).

The hemispheres in these "split-brain" patients functioned independently, yet had specialization of function. The right hemisphere had few words but had little or no impairment in visual discrimination tasks and spatial impairment but scored well on the verbal subtests of the Weschler and was able to calculate (Sperry, 1969, 1974; Gazzaniga and Sperry, 1967; Bogan, 1969; Bogan and Gazzaniga, 1965; Sperry, Gazzaniga and Bogan, 1969; Levy, 1974).

Thus began the theory of two states of consciousness, two personalities within one brain. Each was conceived as having its own system of processing sensory information as well as its own cognitive mode. The role of the commissures then was viewed as that of unifying the two into a single personality, the self. (Kraft, 1976, p. 14)

Following Sperry's discovery a growing body of literature has been accumulating which confirms that the functional asymmetry reported in lesion and split-brain patients is also evident in "normal" people who have intact commissures and no history of brain damage or neurosurgery. Comprehensive reviews of this research and its implications are found in Wittrock (1975), Kraft (1976), Languis and Kraft (1976), Berluchhi (1974), Galin (1974), Ornstein (1972), Levy (1972), Dimond and Beaumont (1974), and Lee, *et al* (1974).

[2] Geschwind and Levitsky (1968) in a postmortem study of one hundred adult brains, which had no significant pathology, found the temporal plane to be approximately one third longer in the left cerebral hemisphere than the right in about 65 per cent of the brains, equal in 24 per cent and larger on the right in 11 percent. This part of the brain is in the temporal speech cortex and has been identified with higher analysis of speech sounds (Harris, 1975). These findings have been confirmed by other researchers in fetal, infant, and adult brains (Witelson and Pallie, 1973; Witelson, 1976; Wada, 1969, Lemay and Culegras, 1972; and Geschwind, 1974).

Although less conclusive than the evidence of a longer left temporal plane, Harris (1975) cites research suggesting that the parietal occipital area is larger in the right hemisphere of right-handed subjects. This area is associated with visuo-spatial perception.

[3] Molfese (1972) found asymmetrical electrical activity to verbal (greater left hemispheric activity) and nonverbal (greater right hemispheric activity) in subjects as young as one week of age. These results have been confirmed by Gardiner, Schulman and Walter (1973).

[4] Case histories have shown that very early brain damage usually results in functional recovery. The degree of recovery usually depends on the locus of the brain injury and the age of the patient indicating functional plasticity of the brain in infancy. There is often a better chance for recovery when the injured area is removed suggesting that the injured brain structure which subserves a function competes with the uninjured structures which can take over that function (Rassmussen and Milner, 1976). Based on case histories indicating full recovery of language facilities in infancy and early childhood, some researchers are speculating that adult lateralization of function occurs between the ages of five to twelve (Krashen and Harshman, 1972; Dorman and Geffner, 1974, and Berlin *et al*, 1973); while Brown and Jaffee (1975) present a convincing theory of lateralizaton which extends into senescence.

[5] The incoming sensory information from left side of the body primarily goes to the right cerebral hemisphere and vice versa (Teyler, 1976; Thomas, 1975).

[6] Facial recognition requires configurational spatial discrimination and has been consistently shown to be a task which the right hemisphere is superior (Levy, *et al*, 1972; Yin, 1970; De Renzi and Spinnler, 1966; Gloning, *et al*, 1967; Hecaen and Angelergues, 1972). Infants have been shown to discriminate between individual faces (familiar and unfamiliar) as early as twenty weeks of age (Kagan, 1965; Ambrose, 1961, 1963, Fitzgerald, 1968).

[7] Aronson and Rosenbloom (1971) have reported that infants as young as thirty days of age have a stress response when mother's face and mother's voice do not appear to be located in the same space.

[8] An excellent example of synthetical hemispheric functioning is Einstein's "Theory of Relativity", which was first formulated in images (right hemispheric modality), later refined and extended by the sequential modality (mathematical symbols), and finally, translated into words (Clark, 1971).

[9] The role of the commissure fibres between the two hemispheres is that of a communication system for the incoming information and the subsequent processing of information between the hemispheres. This communication role may involve both facilitation of information to be shared and inhibition of information. The role of the fibres from the reticular formation is to inhibit and/or facilitate functioning of the hemispheres, or subparts of the hemispheres (Thompson, 1975; Holmes and Sharp; Schulte, 1969).

Yakolev and Lecours (1967) report that the maturation of these two fibre systems is barely apparent until two years of age. The commissures between the two hemispheres myelinize rapidly from two until seven, while those fibres passing to the hemispheres from the reticular formation myelinize rapidly from two until twelve and continue into senility.

[10]Sperry (1969) states that ". . . the two hemispheres (in the split-brain subjects) appear to be independently and often simultaneously conscious, each quite oblivious of the mental experiences of the opposite hemisphere, and also of the incompleteness of its own awareness."

[11]Research involving children as young as six years of age by Kraft (1976) revealed evidence of diffuse language functioning in girls and lateralized functioning in boys.

[12]Left handers often have a greater discrepancy between language and spatial skills than right-handers (Levy, 1972, 1974; Miller, 1971). Levy and Reid (1976) found that the left-handers with inverted hand posturing (i.e., write back-handed or in a hooked position) have either a diffuse language functioning, resulting in either superior language performance and poor spatial performance or diffuse spatial functioning, resulting in superior spatial, but inferior language performance. They further suggest that right-handers which exhibit inverted hand posturing also have diffuse neural organizational patterns. Furthermore, Kirshner (1974) citing research on men and women with mixed hand-eye dominance states that mixed dominance patterns might be a function of diffuse organization.

[13]Levy (cited in Harris, in press, p. 76) suggested that "during pre and postnatal development, genetic factors will predispose each neural blueprint—language for the left hemisphere, spatial for the right—to seek control of the organization not only for its designated hemisphere but for the other as well. 'If the verbal blueprint wins, then the language hemisphere is fully appropriately organized for verbal function, but the nondominant hemisphere also is partially organized for verbal functions, so that this hemisphere's organization is, to some extent misappropriately designed for spatial functions. Such people will manifest perceptual-spatial defects. . . because the neural organization within this hemisphere is incompletely developed to serve spatial functions.'"

[14]Studies by Cohen (1969) and Marsh (1970) have indicated that subcultures may be characterized by emphasis on a predominant cognitive mode: the middle class employ a verbal-analytical mode and the urban poor are more likely to utilize a spatial synthetic mode (Galin, 1976a; Bogan, 1969).

[15]The superiority of the right hemisphere's visual memory system (i.e., imagery) has been demonstrated by Haber (1970) by presenting subjects with 2,560 photographs at the rate of one every 10 seconds finding an 85 to 95 per cent recall several days later. Dimond and Beaumont (1974) report that the right hemisphere not only has the capacity to remember more material for a longer time, but does not tire out as quickly as the left hemisphere. Seamon (1974) has also demonstrated that the verbal memory system of the left hemisphere can be enhanced by actively eliciting the right hemisphere's imaginal memory.

REFERENCES

Ambrose, J.A. The development of the smiling response in early infancy. In B. M. Foss (ed.) Determinants of *Infant Behavior.* New York: J. W. Wiley & Sons, 1961.

Ambrose, J.A. The concept of a critical period of the development of social responsiveness in early human infancy. In B. M. Foss (ed.) *Determinants of Infant Behavior,* II. New York: J. W. Wiley & Sons, 1963.

Aronson, J. and Rosenbloom. Space perception in early infancy: Perception with a common auditory-visual space. *Science,* 1971, *172,* 1161–1163.

Benton, A.L. The 'minor' hemisphere. *Journal of History of Medicine and Allied Sciences,* 1972, *27,* 5–14.

Berlin, C., Hughes L., Lowe-Bell, S. and Berlin, H. Dichotoc Right-Ear Advantage in Children 5 to 13. *Cortex,* 1973, *9,* 393–402.

Berluchhi, G. Cerebral dominance and interhemispheric communication in normal man. In E. O. Schmitt and F. Worden (eds.) *The Neurosciences: Third Study Program.* Cambridge, Mass.: MIT Press, 1974.

Bogan, J. E. The other side of the brain I: Dysgraphia and dyscopia following cerebral commissurotomy. *Bulletin of the Los Angeles Neurological Societies,* 1969, *34,* 73–105.

Bogan, J. E. Final Panel IV. In W. L. Smith (ed.) *Drugs and Cerebral Function.* Springfield, Illinois: Charles C. Thomas, 1971.

Bogan, J. E. The A-P Hypothesis and Neurosociology. Presentation at *Conference for Educating Both Halves of the Brain.* UC, Berkeley, California, February, 1976.

Bogan, J. E. and Bogan, G. M. The other side of the brain III: The corpus callosum and creativity. *Bulletin of Los Angeles Neurological Society,* 1969, *34,* 191-220.

Bogan, J. E., Fisher, B. and Vogel, P. J. Cerebral commissurotomy. *Journal of the American Medical Association,* 1965, *194,* 1328–1329.

Bogan, J. E. and Gazzaniga, M. S. Cerebral commissurotomy in man: Minor hemisphere dominance for certain visuo-spatial functions. *Journal of Neurosurgery,* 1965, 23, 394–399.

Brown, J. and Jaffee, J. Hypothesis on Cerebral Dominance. *Neuropsychologia*, 1975, *13*, 262-266.

Buffery, A. W. and Gray, J. A. Sex differences in the development of spatial and linguistic skills. In C. Ounsted and D. C. Taylor (eds.) *Gender Differences: Their Ontogeny and Significance.* London: Churchill Livingston, 1972.

Clark, R. W. *Einstein: The Life and Times.* New York: The World Publishing Co., 1971.

Cohen, R. A. Conceptual styles, culture conflict and nonverbal tests of intelligence, *American Anthropologist,* 1969, *71*, 326-256.

Corkin, S. Tactfully-guided maze learning in man: Effects of unilateral cortical excisions and bilateral hippocampal lesions. *Neuropsychologia*, 1965, *3*, 339-351.

DeRenzri, E. and Spinnler, Influence of verbal and nonverbal defects on visual memory. *Cortex,* 1966, *2*, 332-336.

Dimond, S. J. and Beaumont, J. G. (eds.) *Hemisphere Function in the Human Brain.* New York: John Wiley & Sons, 1974.

Dorman, M. F. and Geffner, D. S. Hemispheric specialization for speech perception in six-year-old black and white children from low and middle socioeconomic classes. *Cortex,* 1974, *10*, 171-176.

du Bois, R. Biological individuality. In *Readings in Human Development 1976/1977: Annual Editions.* Guilford, Connecticut: Dushkin Publishing Group, Inc., 1976.

Fitzgerald, H. E. Autonomic pupillary reflex activity during early infancy and its relation to social and nonsocial visual stimuli *Journal of Experimental Child Psychology,* 1968, *6*, 470-482.

Flavell, J. H. Concept development. In P. H. Mussen (ed.) *Carmichael's Manual of Child Psychology.* New York: John Wiley & Sons, 1970.

Galin, D. Implications for Psychiatry of left and right cerebral specialization. *Archives of General Psychiatry,* 1974, *31*, 572-583.

Galin, D. Lateralized function and psychiatric condition in man. Presentation to the *New York Academy of Sciences: Conference on Evolution and Lateralization of the Brain.* New York, October, 1976(a).

Galin, D. Educating both halves of the brain. *Childhood Education* October, 1976, pp. 17-20(b).

Galin, D. and Ornstein, R. E. Hemispheric specialization and the duality of consciousness. In W. J. Widroe (ed.) *Human Behavior and Brain Function.* Springfield, Illinois: Charles C. Thomas, 1975.

Gardiner, M., Schulman, C. and Walter, D. Facultative EEG Asymmetries in Babies and Adults. *UCLA BIS Report #34*, 1973, 34-40.

Gazzaniga, M. S. *The Bisected Brain.* New York: Appleton-Century-Crofts, 1970.

Gazzaniga, M. S. Cerebral dominance viewed as a decision system. Bimond, S. J. and Beaumont, J.G. (eds.) *Hemisphere Function in the Human Brain.* New York: Wiley and Sons, 1974.

Gazzaniga, M. S. and Sperry, R. W. Language after section of the cerebral commissures. *Brain,* 1967, *90*, 131-148.

Geschwind, N. The anatonical basis of hemispheric differentiation. In Dimond, S. J. and Beaumont, J. G. (eds.) *Hemisphere function in the Human Brain.* New York: John Wiley & Sons, 1974.

Geschwind, N. and Livitsky, W. Human brain: Left-right asymmetries in temporal speech region. *Science,* 1968, *161*, 186-187.

Gloning, K., Harb, G. and Quatember, R. Standardislevung einer untersuchungsmethode der sogenannten 'prosopagnosie'. *Neurospychologia,* 1967, 5, 99-101.

Haber, R. N. How we remember what we see. *Scientific American,* 1970, *222*, 104-112.

Harris, L. J. Neurophysiological factors in the development of spatial skills. In Eliot, J. and Salkind, N. J. (eds.) *Children's Spatial Development.* Springfield, Illinois: Charles C. Thomas, 1975.

Harris, L. J. Sex differences in spatial ability: Possible environmental genetic, and neurological factors. In Kinsbourne, M. (ed.) *Hemispheric Asymmetries of Function.* Cambridge, England: Cambridge University Press, In press.

Hecaen, H. and Angerlergues, R. Agnosia for faces (prosopagnosie) *AMA Archives of Neurology,* 1962, 7: 92-100.

Holmes, R. L. and Sharp, J. A. *The Human Nervous System: A Developmental Approach.* London: Churchill, Ltd., 1969.

Hunt McViker, *Intelligence and Experience.* New York: Ronald Press, 1971.

Hunt, McVicker. Toward a theory of guided learning in development. In R. H. Ojemann and K. Pritchett (eds.) *Giving Emphasis to Guided Learning.* Cleveland, Ohio: Educational Research Council, 1966.

Hunter, M. Right brained kids in left brained schools. *Today's Education.* November, 1976.

Kagan, J. Growth of the 'face' schema: theoretical significance and methodological issues. Paper read at American Psychological Association Convention, 1965.

Kirschner, J. R. Occular-manual laterality and dual hemisphere specialization, *Cortex,* 1974, *10*, 293-302.

Kraft, R. H. *An EEG Study: Hemispheric Brain Functioning of Six to Eight Year Old Children during Piagetian and Curriculum Tasks with Variation in Presentation Mode.* Unpublished doctoral dissertation. The Ohio State University, 1976.

Kraft, R. H. and Languis, M. Hypothesis of Ontological Parallelism between Piagetian theory and asymmetrical brain functioning theory. Submitted to *Child Development.*

Languis, M. and Kraft, R. H. An educational perspective on the hemispheric process of the brain. In Williams, C. R. (ed.) *EMCE Occasional Paper.* The Ohio State University, February, 1976, 1-19.

Lee, R. L., Ornstein, R. E., Galin, D., Deikman, A., and Tart, C. T. *Symposium on Consciousness.* New York: Viking Press, 1974.

Lemay, J and Culebras, L. Human Brain. *The New England Journal of Medicine,* 1972, *287,* 168-170.

Levy, J. Lateral specialization of the human brain; behavior manifestations and possible evolutionary basis. In Kiger, J. A. (ed.) *Biology of Behavior.* Oregon State University Press, 1972.

Levy, J. and Reid, M. Variations in writing posture and cerebral organization, *Science,* October, 1976, 337-339.

Levy, J., Trevarthen, C. and Sperry, R. W. Perception of Bilateral Chimeric Figures Following Hemispheric Deconnection. *Cortex,* 1972, *95,* 61-78.

Maccoby, E. E. & Jacklin, C. N., *The Psychology of Sex Differences.* Stanford, California: Stanford University Press, 1974.

Miller, E. Handedness and the patterns of human ability. *British Journal of Psychology,* 1971, *62,* 111-112.

Milner, B. Visually-guided maze learning in man: Effects of bilateral hippocampal, bilateral frontal and unilateral cerebral lesions. *Neuropsychologia,* 1965, *3,* 317-338.

Milner, B. Residual intellectual and memory deficits after head injury In E. Walker, W. Caveness, and M. Critchley (eds.) *The Late Effects of Head Injury.* Springfield, Ill.: Charles C. Thomas, 1969.

Milner, B. Hemispheric specialization. In F. O. Schmitt and F. G. Worden (eds.) *The Neurosciences: Third Study Program.* Cambridge, Mass.: MIT Press, 1974.

Molfese, D. Cerebral asymmetry in infants, children and adults, *Journal of the Acoustical Society of America,* 1973, *53,* 363.

Ornstein, R. E. *The Psychology of Consciousness.* San Francisco: W. H. Freeman, 1972.

Piaget, J. Piaget's theory. In O. H. Mussen (ed.) *Carmichael's Manual of Child Psychology.* New York: John Wiley & Sons, 1970.

Piaget, J. *Psychology of Intelligence.* Totowa, New Jersey: Littlefield Adams and Company, 1973.

Rasmussen, T. and Milner, B. The role of early brain injury in determining lateralization of cerebral speech functions. Paper presented at the *New York Academy of Sciences: Conference on Evolution and Lateralization of the Brain.* New York, October, 1976.

Seamon, J. G. Coding and Retrieval processes. In Dmind, S. and Beaumont, J. G. *Hemisphere Function in the Human Brain.* New York: Wiley & Sons, 1974.

Schulte, F. J. Structure-function relationships in the spinal cord. In R. J. Robinson (ed.) *Brain and Early Behavior.* New York: Academic Press, 1969.

Sperry, R. W. A modified concept of consciousness. *Psychological Review,* 1969, *76,* 532-536.

Sperry, R. W. Lateral specialization of cerebral function in the surgically separated hemispheres. In F. O. Schmitt and F. G. Worden (eds.) *The Neurosciences: Third Study Program.* Cambridge, Mass.: MIT Press, 1974.

Sperry, R. W., Gazzaniga, M. S., and Bogan, J. E. Interhemispheric relationships, the neocortical commissures: Syndromes of hemispheric disconnection. In P. J. Vinkin and G. W. Bruyn (eds.) *Handbook of Clinical Neurology,* Vol IV. Amsterdam: North Holland Publishing Co., 1969.

Teyler, T. *Primer of Psychobiology.* San Francisco: W. H. Freeman, 1975.

Thompson, R. F. *Introduction to Physiological Psychology.* New York: Harper and Row, 1975.

Wada, J. A. Pre-language and fundamental asymmetry of the infant brain. Paper presented to the *New York Academy of Sciences: Conference on Evolution and Lateralization of the Brain.* New York, October, 1976.

Wiesel, T. N. The development of the nervous system: Genetic and environmental influences in society for neuroscience, 5th annual meeting. *Summaries of Symposia (BIS CONFERENCE REPORT # 43).* UCLA, Brain Information Service, 1976.

Witelson, S. F. Asymmetry in anatomy of the brain. Paper presented to the *New York Academy of Sciences: Conference on Evolution and Lateralization of the Brain.* New York: October, 1976.

Witelson, S. F. and Pallie, W. Left hemisphere specialization for language in the newborn: Neuroanatomical evidence for asymmetry. *Brain Research,* 1973, *96,* 641-646.

Wittrock, M. C. (ed.) Education and the Hemispheric Process of the Brain. *UCLA Educator,* 1975, *17* (2).

Yakolev, P. and Lecours, A. R. The myelogenetic cycles of regional development of the brain. In A. Minkowski (ed.) *Regional Development of the Brain in Early Life: Symposium.* Philadelphia: F. N. Davis, 1967.

Yin, R. K. Face recognition by brain injured patients: a dissociable ability. *Neuropsychologia, 1970, 8,* 395-402.

Chapter 15

Effective Communication with Children: Movement toward a More Positive Self Concept

Jeffrey L. Derevensky*

Early childhood educators, maybe more than other educators, have begun a careful examination of the goals of their educational curriculum. While few educators would oppose the statement that the aim of any educational program should be the development of the individual's maximum potential, the method by which this aim is achieved is highly controversial. In the past decade there has been a considerable shift away from the notion that education is the mere transmission of information, and a movement toward a more conceptual and cognitive approach (e.g. Bereiter & Englemann, 1966; Kamii & DeVries, 1974; Kamii & Radin, 1970; Lavatelli, 1970; McClelland, 1970; Weikart, 1969). In addition, a great deal of emphasis in the early childhood curriculum has focused upon the child's social, emotional, and moral development (e.g. Brophy, Good & Nedler, 1975; Frost & Kissinger, 1976; Hess & Croft, 1975). Thus, the modern "enlightened" curriculum has as its goal the development of both affective and cognitive skills.

It is not the intent of this article to systematically deliniate the specific goals of various early childhood education programs nor their respective underlying theories since this has been well documented in many introductory texts (e.g. Brophy et al., 1975; Evans, 1975; Hess & Croft, 1975), nor is it the intent to provide a specific methodology designed to facilitate the achievement of a particular set of goals given a particular theoretical and/or practical model. Rather, this article is intended to provide an indepth examination of methods for more effective communication with young children. The underlying premise being that effective communication with the youhg child fosters a more positive self concept and heightened self esteem, both of which results in a more positive attitude toward self, the school environment and learning in general.

The development of self concept and self esteem is acquired in much the same way as the young child forms concepts of his physical environment. From a great deal of information processed through a variety of experiences the young child begins to generalize and form concepts–in one instance he derives a concept based upon his perception of an object, in the other about himself, his behavior, feelings, attitudes, and emotions. It would appear that there are predominately four major sources by which self concept and self esteem originate: 1) the impressions the child receives from others; 2) the child's experiences; 3) the child's ability to achieve and internalize the goals set for him by "significant others"; and 4) the child's ability to evaluate his performance based upon his own standards (Coopersmith, 1967). The information the child receives from significant others is essential in the formation of his self concept. Their comments about him, their concern for his welfare, their approval or disapproval, their inclusion or exclusion from their activities, their attitudes, their facial expressions, their intonations, all influence the manner in which the child perceives and values himself (Hess & Croft, 1975).

The development of the self concept is thus dependent upon the child's perception and interpretation of an event in any given situation. However, quite often children's and adult's perceptions are not congruent, this being true even on a very basic level. One need only to look at the Piagetian research to suggest that the processing of visual information without the more sophisticated and elaborate cognitive constructs often produces a distorted and inaccurate picture in the child's mind. For example, it is only by the age of six that the child's cognitive structures are sufficiently developed with respect to conservation of quantity (solids) so that he no longer merely relies upon his visual perception of the objects (Beard, 1963). In Piagetian terms the young child is "perceptually bound" and very egocentric. Elkind (1967) has hypothesized that egocentrism continues from early childhood through adolescence but takes on a continually changing form based upon the acquisition of newly acquired cognitive constructs. I would like to suggest that this process of egocentrism continues throughout ones lifetime. As a result adults often have difficulty in viewing the young child's world as he perceives it. I am reminded of a school which decided to convert an extra grade two classroom into a pre-kindergarten classroom. With great excitement and zeal the kindergarten consultant, the early childhood consultant, the principal, and several teachers began to make a detailed sketch of the classroom and eagerly ordered the necessary and appropriate material and equipment. All the traditional materials and equipment were

*Dr. Jeffrey Derevensky, assistant Professor, Dept. of Educational Psychology McGill University, Montreal, Quebec.

purchased (see Mixon & Nixon, 1970) and finally after several months of carefully planning and designing a child centered curriculum the center opened its doors to 15 four year old children. It only took one day to realize that these adult educators had made several errors. The preschoolers were unable to open the classroom door as the handle was too high, the water fountain and sink were out of the child's reach, and the doors on the bathroom were much too heavy. Had they overlooked the obvious or did they have difficulty in perceiving the "child's world?" Again I remember an instance in a well designed and decorated kindergarten classroom where I was sitting on the floor observing several children attempting to solve some mathematical problems when the teacher asked the children to stay where they were but to look at the picture she was holding. Since I was sitting on the floor and the teacher had some paper lanterns strung across the classroom, I was unable to see the picture. Furthermore, neither could the children see the picture since my height sitting was the same as their's standing. The teacher was proceeding under the premise that an adult when standing could see this picture. The recent television program 'Land of the Giants' had adults trying to cope in a foreign situation where everything was magnified. Weekly shows were based upon "unexpected" events. While the physical relationship in this series was somewhat overly exaggerated compared to the world in which the child lives, nevertheless, the young child lives in an adult world. I have often observed teachers telling young children to walk more quickly when going up a staircase. A close examination of the young child's physiological development would indicate that each of the steps in a staircase for a young child would be equivalent to two or three steps for the adult. Yet without taking this into account, the teacher expects the young child to be able to climb the stairs at the same rate as an adult. These examples illustrate the necessity for a conscientous understanding of the child's world. Educators of young children should be able to look introspectively at the child and to perceive the child's world from his point of view. While incongruity exists between the adult's and child's perceptions it becomes the child's perceptions and interpretation of particular events which becomes crucial in understanding his behavior.

Since verbal and nonverbal interactions between the child and the teacher are most important in the development of the child's self concept, a closer examination of these interactions is warranted. It is only through the comments direction toward the child that he perceives of himself as shy, noisy, good or naughty, pretty, nice, careful, neat or sloppy. The young child lacks the sophisticated cognitive structures for self analysis thus his attainment of a negative or positive self concept is externally produced through the interactions with significant others. For example, Tommy a kindergarten student accidentally spills a jar of paint while painting a picture on an easel. Teacher A replies "Why are you so sloppy? Nobody else in the class spills their paint! Can't you be like everyone else?" Unfortunately for Tommy, in his haste to clean up the paint he inadvertantly knocks down a small bookcase containing the class library. Teacher A responds by saying "You'll always be a. . . , Why are you so. . . . Why can't you ever. . .What's the matter with you? Don't you. . . ." To make matters worse Teacher A brings her class to the library and tells Teacher B (with the entire class present), "Watch out for Tommy, he has been disruptive and a nuisance all morning. He knocked over the paint and the class library. He is such a. ." From this conversation it is apparent that Teacher A is displeased with Tommy's behavior independent of whether or not his behavior was intentional. Tommy is not only subjected to these derogatory remarks but is also cognizant that Teacher A doesn't care whether he and his classmates hear this criticism. Situations such as these do little to enhance a positive self concept in children.

Are there alternative approaches to that adopted by Teacher A? In order to alter the previous vignette, one must be cognizant of the child's feelings. Therefore there exists a presupposition that even a young child, has feelings, an ego, and a sense of self pride. Too often adults either ignore the child's feeling or assign to it a nonmeaningful and/or nonrelevant value. We continually hear statements such as: "What is the matter with that child; you would think someone was killing her?" "He is only a child, what does he know?" or "he cries over such silly matters." I once observed a teacher holding auditions within her grade 3 class for the play "Snow White and the Seven Dwarfs". Naturally every girl in the class desired to be Snow White. Since the teacher was only able to select one child for that part and this production was to be performed before the entire school, the administration, the teacher's colleagues and the children's parents, the teacher proceeded to select the child in her class who appeared to be most talented. One of the other girls in the class who just missed being selected (first runner-up) proceeded to burst out in hysteria (obviously shaken about missing the lead role). The teacher empathetically ran over to the girls and said, "Now, now, don't worry maybe next year you'll get the lead role." Sympathetically the teacher told me—"she will get over it." This is quite a difference from Teacher A, however here again the teacher failed to look introspectively, that is, to put herself in the position of the child. The girl who just missed the lead role would probably not ever get it. The fact is this same child missed the lead role in a production in grade 2 and subsequently lost it again to the same girl in grades 4, 5 and 6. Her dismissal of the child's hysteria as merely childish and nonsignificant did little to help the child deal with her feelings.

Communication—effective communication[1]—becomes

---

[1] Much of the idea and principles are based upon the psychological, philosophical and educational ideas of Dr. Haim Ginott (Ginott, 1961, 1965, 1972, 1973; Faber and Mazlish, 1974).

the mechanism by which teachers can encourage a strong self concept and heighten self esteem in the young child. Let no adult ever underestimate the significant power of his words for through verbal interactions teachers can strengthen an ego or destroy a self image, have the power to humiliate, humour, hurt or heal; and have the ability to make a child's life miserable or joyous. This language of communication is based upon a mutual respect between adult and child and an understanding of the significance and importance of the "hidden" messages in both verbal and noverbal interactions. An essential component for effective communication lies in the ability for the educator to "talk to the situation and not to the personality and character." The elimination of phrases such as "Why can't you ever. . Why are you so. . .You're nothing but a. . .You never. . .You'll always be a. . .What's the matter with you? Don't you. . . How many times. . .", is a necessary prerequisite for the acquisition of "childrenese." The acquisition of this new language inherently involves changing a teacher's expressions of anger, the tenor of directions, the method of criticism and style of praise. Similarly the methods of evaluating progress, and grading practices, the manner of comforting and reassuring and particularly the method and manner of speaking with children must be re-evaluated. (Ginott, 1972).

The acquisition of "childrenese" for teachers is not a simple task, however, the results are most advantageous and rewarding for it fosters a sense of self pride, confidence and allows the child to have a clearer and better understanding of himself. As a result, the child will feel better about himself and will begin to rely on his own resources with greater self confidence. He will search and find constructive outlets for his emotions, and will be able to face failure without collapsing (Ginott, 1972; Faber & Mazlish, 1974). Helping children overcome feelings of a deprecatory self-image, implanting hope where there is hopelessness, producing rewarding experiences which accentuates the positive, and instilling a feeling of self worth can be achieved through the medium of introspection and this 'new' language of communication.

Several concrete examples which utilize the principle of talking to the situation and not the personality and character should help clarify what is meant by "childrenese." In a grade one classroom during the children's snack period two boys were found to be engaged in a contest to see who could throw more cookies out of the window with several cookies missing the window and smashing on the floor. The teacher replies with "I get very angry and I am most displeased when I see food being wasted and thrown. Cookies are not for throwing, I think the area near the window needs immediate cleaning." This verbal interaction clearly stated the teacher's philosophy about throwing food without any verbal abuse or insults. No comments were made concerning the children involved in this episode nor about their personal characteristics. Furthermore, no derogatory

attack was made upon either child. An alternative approach could have been "You two irresponsible young troublemakers! Who do you think you are? I demand this mess be cleaned up immediately! Where were you brought up in a barn? Don't you know how many hungry children there are in the world? If I see this disgusting behavior again, the principal and your parents will be notified immediately!" Both statements most probably accomplish the same immediate and long range goal, that is, the remaining cookies would be picked up and this type of behavior would not be repeated.

I am reminded of another situation in a grade one classroom where Gail brought home her mathematics workbook to complete an assignment and failed to bring it back with her to school the next day. Without asking for an explanation from the child the teacher responded, "Gail, you always forget everything! Why can't you be like everyone else in the class? You would lose your head if it weren't attached. Now you can't do your math with us. Sit in your seat and be quiet." Not only were the remarks derogatory, selfdefacing, humiliating and represented a personal attack upon this young child but she was denied a valuable educational experience. Furthermore, at least some of the comments would not be true, that is, she was most certainly similar to the other children in many ways. An alternative approach might have been "It is difficult to do our mathematics without our workbooks. It would be very helpful if everyone brought in their mathematics book each day. Those children who forgot their books today, please sit with a friend so that we may go over the lesson." Again, both interactions indicate the necessity for bringing in the child's workbook, the latter in a more humane way without depriving the child of an educational experience.

In incorporating "childrenese" in our daily interactions with children several phrases must be stricken from daily usage. These include such phrases as:

Why can't you ever. . .
Why are you so. . .
Who did that. . .
You're nothing but. . .
You'll always be a. . .
You are. . .
What's the matter with you? Don't you. . .
You never. . .

Rather, an adoption of new phrases would more likely achieve the same results and allow the child to maintain his self esteem, integrity and dignity. These new phrases include statements such as:

You wish. . .
I have confidence that you'll. . .
I am annoyed. . .
It would be helpful if. . .
To see you. . .would make me happy.
Then you really feel that. . .
I would appreciate. . .

A dramatic change in the manner in which we speak with children can result in substantial changes in behavior. If teachers effectively communicate with young children, these very same children will feel better about themselves as individuals and will begin to adopt these sample principles of communication with their parents, siblings and friends (Faber & Mazlish, 1974).

One further comment about communicating with children is essential before adopting this new approach in daily interactions. Children do not necessarily interpret our communication in the manner in which we intend. I remember telling children in my grade three class on one particular occasion that I was not feeling well, and would be most appreciative if they would do their work and refrain from talking. No sooner had I issued my plea when I observed two children begin a lengthly conversation. After 5 minutes I interrupted their conversation and repeated my request for "no talking." As their conversation quickly resumed I found myself getting considerably frustrated and angry and asked the children if they had heard what I said. They responded in the affirmative. I then proceeded to ask them why they were talking. One of the little boys responded by saying, "Sir, we were not talking, we were practicing our spelling." It then became obvious to me, that for those children "talking" was equivalent to having fun and *not* schoolwork. Their interepretation of the word "talking" was quite different from mine. Is it a case of semantics or perception? I am inclined to think the latter. Another bad habit teachers (and parents) often perpetrate is that of 'name calling'. Sometimes in jest a few teachers refer to children as 'feather brained', 'noodle-head', 'shorty', 'fatty', and on occasion I have heard children called 'dummy', 'stupid', and 'idiot'. While these names are referred to in jest, they might be misconstrued as in this conversation between two children:

"My friends and me call each other stupid all the time, and its just a joke. But when your mother or father call you stupid or your teacher then you think its true because they ought to know (Faber & Mazlish, p. 54).

While I am reminded of the cliché 'sticks and stones will break your bones but names will never harm me', I would like to suggest that the language we use in the classroom can be a powerful tool in the development of the child's self concept. However, this same tool can be a devastating weapon if inappropriately used. To look through the child's eyes, to see his perspective, to see the world as he sees it, is a most enlightening experience. Because our cognitive constructs are considerably different from the child's, this process does not come easily nor naturally and involves a great deal of deep thought, time and effort. Introspectively looking at the child's world yields a greater understanding of the young child's behavior and actions in a multitude of settings and situations.

There still remains some disagreement among professional educators as to whether self-esteem contributes to successful performance or follows from it. One view maintains that children need to feel good about themselves and their abilities and that this self confidence and self esteem will enable the child to seek and achieve academic success. The other view hypothesizes that a heightened self concept only results from a clear demonstration of skills and competencies. Without the ability to master a particular task, the child can only "hope" to do so (Hess & Croft, 1975). There is little doubt that the child's personal experiences is a significant determinant in the development of the child's self concept. Furthermore, if we are going to improve our communication, then not only must we examine our verbal interactions with young children but we need to re-examine our concept of academic success.

Early in the primary grades children come to view themselves as successful or unsuccessful based upon their academic experiences. The traditional techniques of dividing children into ability groups provides a clear indication to the young child of his level of success. Since educators have long known the potential significance of this grouping technique on the child's self esteem, various measures have been implemented to disguise the ability level of the group. Thus, there exists a tendency to refrain from labelling groups as top, middle, bottom; rather progressive educators tend to assign some arbitrary name such as 'Blue Jay', 'Black Hawks', and 'Yellow Eagles'. If you were to ask the children which group had the smartest children (best readers, spelling, etc.), I contend that the children's and teacher's responses would correlate very highly. Regardless of the label, children can accurately perceive whether or not they are successful according to a previously established criterion.

Masking techniques for ability grouping by grade level has similarly undergone some radical changes in the past decade since we no longer desire to 'intentionally' label or stigmatize young children. Ten years ago the classification system was such that class 3-1 was the brightest, 3-2 next, etc. Each child desired to be in class 3-1 or 3-2 but if you were in class 3-9 or 3-10 you must be pretty 'dumb'. In an effort to raise the self concept and image of these downtrodden students in classes 3-9 and 3-10, educators in their wisdom changed the order such that class 3-10 was the brightest and 3-1 the slowest class. That new classification failed to hide the child's ability. Today in many schools we have completely eliminated the numerical allocation based upon ability and have succumbed to a more humane way of classification such that we have classes labelled 3-201, 3-206, and 3-209; the first number indicating the grade level and the second series of numbers referring to the room designation. Yet, one can still enter any school and ask the children which is the brightest grade 3 class and most (if not all) children will tell you Mr. X's class. Has anything really changed?

Publishers of children's classroom readers have traditionally labelled books in order to suggest their appropriate readability level. Here again we witness a progression from numerical symbols (e.g. 2^1, 2^2, 3^1, 3^2) to pictorial symbols (e.g. : : : :) and finally readers no longer have any labels, this being done so that the child having difficulty in reading in a grade 4 class will not be aware that he is reading a book designated for a grade 2 child. The elimination of visible labels has admirably succeeded in achieving its desired goal yet an unexpected consequence is that it has thoroughly confused teachers, such that many teachers are unaware of the readability levels of the various texts in their classroom.

I have argued that it is extremely difficult to disguise a child's ability from himself. The answer may lie in trying to devise appropriate methods and tasks that will ensure that each child can be successful and that each child is reinforced for these successes rather than attempting to hide a child's ability from himself. On a theoretical level, few if any educators and psychologists would argue against the idea that each child is a unique individual with different abilities and interests. Yet, this often fails to get translated into a meaningful educational experience as most children are encouraged to achieve very similar goals. Every parent wants his child's report card to be filled with 'excellents' and every teacher demands a 90% criterion rate of success on spelling tests. To establish individual goals and acceptable criterion levels is a most admirable aim.

How can we incorporate introspection and childrenese into the principles of reinforcing academic success? Behavioral psychologists have long argued (i.e. Skinner, 1968) that there exists a greater need for positive reinforcement in the classroom as a means by which stated objectives can be achieved. Too often a teachers' behavior is not consistent with her objectives as in the following situation: Teacher B has taught a math lesson and asks the class "Can anyone tell me the answer?" Most of the children respond by raising their hand. Mary does not know the answer and the teacher responds with "Weren't you paying attention? Why don't you ever listen?" The next time the teacher asks a question Mary raises her hand. Unexpectedly the teacher calls upon Mary and she responds in a timid voice "Hmm. .hmm, I'm, Uh, I'm not sure." Teacher B replies "Well why did you raise your hand?" It is extremely likely that in this particular situation there was less probability of being called upon if Mary raised her hand than if she hadn't. Had the teacher look introspectively she might have realized why Mary raised her hand. Children, even very young children learn very quickly that if you avoid eye contact with the teacher then the likelihood of being called upon is less than when eye contact is established.

I have often contemplated whether the curriculum places an inordinately large emphasis on achievement, whether motivation for achievement is precipitated by teachers or whether parents instill this 'virtue' before school entry. The educational system as it presently exists continually reinforces these children who succeed based upon a predetermined criterion level. I would like to suggest that a child who goes from a grade of 20 percent to 50 percent in a traditional spelling test (20 words has made greater improvement than a child who goes from 90 to 95 percent. I am not suggesting that we do not reinforce (praise, stars, verbal approval, placing the child's work on a bulletin board, etc) the child who has achieved a 'high' grade, yet I am suggesting that we should also reinforce the child who demonstrates sufficient *progress.* We would not expect the child who consistently achieves at a low level to achieve an excellent grade in a very short period. Although a child may demonstrate progress in a particular subject if he has not reached a particular criterion level (this being arbitrarily set) the child's work may still receive a grade of 'F'. The emphasis on perfection, that is, a universal criterion for all must be discontinued. Rather, educators must begin to set reasonable goals and standards for individuals and use the knowledge derived from learning theory to reinforce improvement in general. Since very young children are unable to set appropriate goals, educators must continually assist these students in establishing suitable goals and continuously reassuring and reinforcing improvement in academic tasks. Continuous failure in school will result in a deprecatory self image and a lack of motivation toward academic tasks. One of the lessions learned from Sesame Street is that television doesn't punish children thereby greatly relieving the continuous pressure for the child to succeed. "A child can flunk school, neighborhood, family, friends and a host of other things, but he can't flunk television" (Warren, 1976).

Educational theory and practice is continually undergoing revisions. The focus of this paper has been on 'how' we teach rather than 'what' we teach. Effective communication and an understanding of the child's world as he perceives it can facilitate our producing more humane, independent, rational and educated citizens. The development of a strong self concept will allow the child to become more introspective of himself, enhance his understanding of others and provide the child with more acceptable methods of expressing his feelings and emotions. The adoption of some of the ideas discussed in this article may lead to an elimination of a statement once expressed by a teacher "I taught then but they didn't learn" (Postman & Weingartner, 1969). Brigg (1970) has suggested that the development of the self concept should be the aim of every teacher. She states, "How to create strong feelings of self worth is the central challenge for every parent and teacher". The adoption of 'childrenese' and the ability to look introspectively at the young child's world seeks to provide a method by which this challenge can be met.

REFERENCES

Beard, R.M. The order of concept development studies in

two fields *Educational Review*, 1963, *15*, 228–237.

Bereiter, C. and Engelmann, S. *Teaching Disadvantaged children in the Preschool.* New Jersey: Prentice Hall, 1966.

Briggs, D.C. *Your Child's Self Esteem.* New York: Doubleday & Co., 1970.

Brophy, J.E., Good, T.L. and Nedler, S.E. *Teaching in the Preschool.* New York: Harper & Row, 1975.

Coopersmith, S. *The Antecedents of Self Esteem.* San Francisco: W.H. Freeman & Co., 1967.

Elkind, D. Egocentrism in adolescence. *Child Development*, 1967, *38*, 1025–1034.

Evans, E.D. *Contemporary Influences in Early Childhood Education.* New York: Holt, Rinehart & Winston, 1975.

Faber, A. and Mazlish, E. *Liberated Parents, Liberated Children.* New York: Avon Books, 1974.

Frost, J.L. and Kissinger, J.B. *The Young Child and the Educative Process.* New York: Holt, Rinehart & Winston, 1976.

Ginott, H. *Group Psychotherapy with Children.* New York: McGraw Hill, 1961.

Ginott, H. *Between Parent and Child.* New York: MacMillan Co., 1965.

Ginott, H. *Teacher and Child.* New York: MacMillan Co., 1972.

Ginott, H. Driving Children sane. *Today's Education*, 1973, *62* (7), 20–25.

Hess, R. and Croft, D.J. *Teachers of Young Children.* Boston: Houghton Mifflin, 1975.

Kamii, C.K. and DeVries, R. *Piaget for Early Education.* New York: Prentice Hall, 1974.

Kamii, C.D. and Radin, N.A. A framework for preschool curriculum based upon some Piagetian concepts. In I.J. Athey and D.O. Rubadean (Eds.), *Educational Implications of Piaget's Theory. Mass: Ginn-Blaisdell,* 1970.

Lavatelli, C.S. *Piaget's Theory Applied to An Early Education Curriculum.* New York: Learning Research Associates, 1970.

McClelland, D. *Ypsilanti preschool curriculum demonstration project: The cognitive curriculum.* Mich: High/Scope Educational Research Foundation, 1970.

Nixon, R.H. and Nixon, C.L. *Introduction to Early Childhood Education.* New York: Random House, 1970.

Postman, N. and Weingartner, C. *Teaching as a Subversive Activity.* New York: Dell, 1969.

Skinner, B.F. *The Technology of Teaching.* New York: Appleton-Century Crofts, 1968.

Warren, J. Children's Television Workshop: The researcher is part of the crew. *Educational Researcher*, 1976, *5* (8), 6–8.

Weikart, D.P. *Ypsilanti Preschool Curriculum Demonstration Project.* Michigan: High/Scope Educational Research Foundation, 1969.

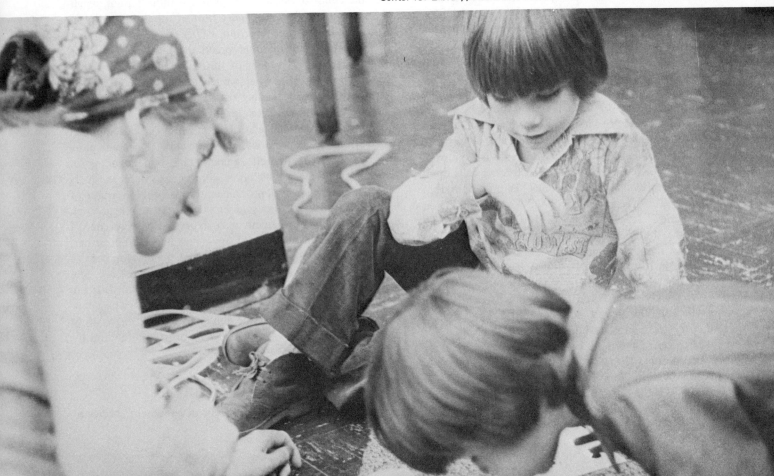

Chapter 16

Philosophies of Early Childhood Education

Lillian Oxtoby[*]

Introduction

Since the beginning of the 19th century, different theories of how one does or does not learn, and what does or does not determine intelligence, have appeared in literature, films and other meida and have affected and influenced the field of early childhood education.

Several theories have advocated and expounded the genetic theory of learning and intelligence. This is based on the fact that one is born and endowed with certain genes and these genes determine one's learning ability and intelligence. Others have advocated the theory of environment and its effect on learning and intelligence. These two are sometimes referred to as the "nature" and "nurture" theories of approaches to learning.

Today it is recognized that the relation between learning and intelligence is a combination of these two elements or factors which are interrelated and which affect the growing child.

These two themes have been the foundation for the current theories of learning such as those that deal with cognition and behavior modification.

This chapter will describe some of these learning theories and those who have developed them, as well as some of the early childhood education programs which have resulted from the application of these theories.

Friedrich Froebel (1782-1852), a German philosopher and educator, is often referred to as the "father of the kindergarten movement." His philosophy stated that there should be a program of education specifically designed for young children. In his kindergarten he provided many opportunities for the children to live comfortably and fully, both indoors and outdoors. He also believed that children developed knowledge by being encouraged to explore, to express themselves, and to learn by doing. Froebel observed children in their play and as he did so he became increasingly aware of two points: The significance of play in learning and the fact that young children's learning seems to proceed naturally from the concrete to the abstract.[1]

For this reason Froebel felt that children's learning could profit by being guided by a series of organized "experiences." Froebel devised a set of educational materials and experiences which came to be known as the "Froeblian Gifts and Occupations."

As an outgrowth of his concern for the development of the whole child, he wrote textbooks and set up training centers for those who wished to prepare themselves to be kindergarten teachers. The training courses were designed to help teachers learn how to help children to live fully and by so living to build for themselves good foundations for the more disciplined system of education which was to follow.

Froebel's greatest contribution to the field of early childhood education stressed the following: He emphasized working closely with either the mother or mother substitute; he stressed the fact that the kindergarten should *not* be a break with the home, but rather an *extension* of the home. The homelike atmosphere of today's kindergarten is a reflection of his concern that the classroom should resemble as far as possible a pleasant family situation. Lastly, his concern for the child's doing and discovering for his/herself is reflected in the wide variety of materials available to children both in work and play.

Dr. Maria Montessori (1870-1952), the first women to break the sex barrier in the field of medicine in Italy, contributed immeasurably to the field of early childhood education.

As a young physician, she became director of a new Orthrophrenic school, which was responsible for the education of mentally retarded and disturbed children. Because of her contact and interest in the problems of these children, she studied the works of O. Edouard Seguin, a 19th century French psychiatrist who worked with, and developed materials to assist, mentally retarded children. She also studied Jean Itard, an earlier pioneer than Seguin, who worked with disturbed and retarded children. Itard influenced Montessori with his emphasis on clinical observation of the child, whereas Seguin's influence was the stress

---

[1] In order to help others become aware of the significance of play in learning, Froebel wrote, among other books, a book titled *Mutter Und Kose Leider* (Mother Play and Children's Songs). This was a book of songs and games for mothers to use with young children.

*Dr. Lillian Oxtoby Assistant Professor, Chairperson of the Child Care/Early Childhood Education Program, New York City Community College, CUNY.

on prepared materials.

The influence of these individuals can readily be discerned in Montessori's book. (1964). She worked in the school for retarded children for several years, but soon realized that it was necessary for her to pursue exposure to normal children. This opportunity occurred when she was approached by a real estate developer who had built housing projects in the slums of Rome, but found that the buildings were being vandalized and defaced by young children who were left alone while their parents went to work. The developer agreed to give Dr. Montessori a room in the housing development so that the children would receive some semblence of supervision. In 1907 Maria Montessori opened her first "Casa Dei Bambini" or Children's House for 60 children who ranged in age from 3 to 7 years in the poorest neighborhood of the city of Rome.

Montessori utilized her prior experiences of working with retarded children and used the prepared materials that had proven so successful with former pupils. She found that the prepared environment of organized and coordinated materials were used differently by normal healthy youngsters. She also realized that she had to adjust her philosophy, routines and program because of the physical environment as well as the fact that these youngsters were not disturbed or retarded.

Montessori based her educational theories and methods on readings, observations and practical experiences. The theories include the following: The teacher is a directoress who supervises children in their school environment; she is an enabler and guide; she is there to help the child become independent in thinking and solving problems. The child should learn to read, write and be knowledgeable about arithmetic. The teaching of the academic subjects are presented to the children with the prepared educational materials that Maria Montessori developed. Each child is expected to develop at his/her rate of capacity and will seek aid from the Directoress when a difficult or incomprehensive problem arises. Montessori believed that the materials that she designed which foster the use of the tactile, auditory, visual, olfactory, gustatory and baric senses (the word baric refers to ability to discern weight) would develop the child's independence and persistence in solving problems. She also advocated the knowledge of knowing the rules of courtesy and good conduct. She believed that a child should have full command of his/her body and be graceful in movement. Basically Maria Montessori wanted her students to be powerful in concentration and independence and persistent in pursuit of academic subjects. She believed in the fostering of a prepared environment with specific educational materials (with the concept that things are the best teacher). She viewed the teacher as a guide, supervisor or consultant who is there to provide support and bodies of knowledge when needed.

Montessori's influence can be readily seen throughout the U.S. The materials she developed are being utilized extensively as well as being adapted and copied. Since the 1950's a great many Montessori schools have opened and flourished. Many of these Montessori schools are not totally Montessorian as prescribed by Maria Montessori, but some are. The interest in the Montessori method stems from several factors: The prepared environment or structure of its program; allowance for individual learning capacity; stress on independence and persistance as well as courtesy and good conduct.

Another contributor to the field of early childhood education is Jean Piaget (1896,-), a swiss psychologist. He is the person most identified with and most influential as regards the great impact of the cognitive process as learning theory.

Piaget actually received his training in Zoology and later switched to psychology. Piaget observed and studied his three children, Lauren, Lucienne and Jacqueline; from these observations he made certain hypothesis about learning and intelligence. Piaget describes learning as a continuous process with four stages. (Ginsburg and Opper, 1969). He describes these stages as sequential rather than chronological or maturational as did Arnold Gessell.

The most important aspect of Piaget's theory of sequence of development is emphasis on the building process of learning skills. The child first learns by doing (sensori motor) and conceptualizes (symbolic) at a later time. The child must go through the four stages as specified by Piaget, but the chronological age may not always be the age stipulated by Piaget, the child may be either older or younger in his/her sequence of development. For example, Janie may be 28 months chronologically, still in the sensori motor stage according to Piaget's sequence of development, but this does not mean that Janie cannot go through the other stages of development later on. The ages as described by Piaget are actually guidelines that one can refer to as a frame of reference to use with judgment and experience.

Piaget views cognition as the growing and building process. Another way to view Piaget's theory is to watch a house or an office building being constructed. One would then see that a foundation would have to be laid. The next step would be the frame, then the body and finally all the finer parts such as floors, plumbing, electrical outlets etc. The analogy of the house being built and Piaget's concept of learning is one and the same, inasmuch as there is a building process and one part is contingent and dependent upon the others.

While Piaget's advocates have been expounding the importance of the cognitive process, another psychologist, B. F. Skinner has been stressing the importance of stimulus and conditioning upon one's learning ability, but utilizes these factors in what is referred to as behavior modification. Skinner was influenced by such psychologists as Pavlov, E. L. Thorndike and C. L. Hull. These men were the pioneers of behavior theory in the field of psychology.

These men believed that behavior could be controlled

and predicted. They utilized the tools of Stimulus-Response or what is commonly known as the S-R factor. The most famous conditioning experiment known is the one that Pavlov describes of the connection between the presence of food, the dog's automatic salivary response and a bell that is rung at about the time the food is presented to the dog. Pavlov observed the phenomena of the dog's reaction to food, the bell and also the experimenter who fed the dog. This study also led Pavlov to introduce other stimuli so that he was able to observe that behavior could be changed by introduction of different stimuli.

Skinner borrowed these principles of classical conditioning and even went a step further by working with and studying pigeons and rats. He and his followers stated that human behavior can be changed, adjusted or modified through an external stimulus. Skinner refers to his type of conditioning as *operant conditioning.*

Operant Conditioning entails a building process of reinforcing the behavior desired. For example, Skinner and his associates were able to make pigeons turn their heads by offering a food reinforcement for the desired turn. The food was withdrawn after the elicited turn was demonstrated. In order to have a greater head turn, the pigeon was given the same or additional stimuli to increase the turn. Once this elicited behavior was accomplished, the stimulus was again withdrawn. Thus Skinner was able to demonstrate that desired behavior can be modified successfully by taking segments of behavior patterns and changing them bit by bit. Several early childhood programs have adopted the behavior modification method as a means of improving learning for the young child.

A good example of how different learning theories can be incorporated and applied in practice is the Florida Parent Educator Model which is designed to integrate the role of the parent and professional as a team in order that the young child in a home environment can profit from this joint effort intellectually, emotionally, socially and physically.

This model was developed by Ira J. Gordon and his associates at the University of Florida. Gordon describes his specific aims as follows:

The overall aim was to investigate the effectiveness and praticability of a home centered technique for cognitive,

language and personality development of mother and child, based upon the use of parent and child educators who are themselves members of the population to be served. It represents an innovation in family services which, if effective, extends the reach of the professional, upgrades the competance and importance of the non professional and in the long run reduces the needs for such services as participants become more capable of meeting their own needs. (Frost, 1973).

The emphasis of this model is to have educators who work with mothers to teach intellectual stimulation as well as to stimulate social and personality development of the child under three years of age. The parent educators are untrained community persons who are trained by teachers and other professionals from such disciplines as psychology, nursing and nutrition to teach these community persons to be trainers of parents in the home. The parent educator is a link between the home environment and the academic environment. The parent educator is there to bridge the gap between the austere atmosphere of the classroom environment versus the physical inability of the parent to leave the home environment for many and various reasons.

The curriculum is based upon Piagetian and non Piagetian principles as Gordon refers to it. The parent educators are taught activities and given toys to work with in order that they will be able to visit the assigned homes and teach the parents in their own home environment. The parent educators are also asked to observe the parent as they teach the children these activities and use of toys. This is done in order to evaluate whether or not the parent understands what is being taught. The parents are also taught how to use equipment to stimulate learning activities. The basic thrust of the Florida or Gordon model is the utilization of community persons who are trained as parent educators to go out in the community, visit assigned families and then train these families to stimulate their children's developmental processes. These parent educators make use of Piagetian and non Piagetian learning theories in their work with these families.

The following is a list of some of the programs that have utilized the concepts of the philosophies described in this chapter.

DESCRIPTIONS OF EARLY CHILDHOOD EDUCATION PROGRAMS

Program	Philosophy	Objectives
1. Bereiter—Engelmann	structured program; behavior modification plus Piagetian influence	— stress of academic skills (reading, writing, mathematics) — utilization of sensory skills (tactile, auditory, visual) shouting, clapping, stamping — utilization of a reward system using raisins and hugs.

DESCRIPTION OF EARLY CHILDHOOD EDUCATION PROGRAMS

Program	Philosophy	Objectives
2. Behavior modification, U. of Kansas	based upon B.F. Skinner's theory of behavior modification	— utilization of re-enforcement such as snacks, story time recess, as well as token system — teacher must be attentive to child's level of learning. — parents are trained to learn techniques of behavior modification
3. Ypsidanti-Michigan Project	Piagetian approach	— the development of social knowledge, logical knowledge and representation — program builds upon a sequential learning process, rather than pure memmorization — teacher must prepare tasks and materials so that the child has developed learning capabilities
4. Montessori program	prepared environment; self discipline; individual learning	— teacher is a supervisor — stress on academic skills, reading and writing also knowledgeable about math. — stress on good manners and courtesy — child should have full command of one's own body and graceful in movement
5. Bank Street	concerned with the total child (intellectual, social, physical and emotional development	— teacher's role is very critical, because the program is individualized — teacher is a model — the child is viewed as a total human being focusing upon the total development
6. Responsive Model	enriched environment; draws upon child's sensory perception; "autotelic"–self rewarding activities, child learns because he/she wants to learn and is not given an external reward	— the child is viewed as an individual — teacher is trained to be responsive to child's needs, but *only helps* child resolve problems — enrichment is structured, but enriched with many activities — draws upon the tactile, auditory, and visual senses.
7. Tuscon Early Education Model TEEM	developmental approach plus an enriched environment	— the teacher is there to give direction and help — program assistant who works with teacher to provide new techniques and approaches to teaching — language development — stress on other academic skills as well as social skills
8. Educational Development Center	based upon British Infant School	— child viewed as an individual, and is child oriented — teacher is a resource person — advisory teams to help teachers — develop activities and areas of interest from children in the group — classroom is informal, but organized — there is a stress on mutual respect between teacher and children
9. Florida Parent Educator Model	integration of parent and professional as a team to develop the child's cognitive development in a home environment	— parent educators who are trained by professionals — parent educators visit the home, and train parents to stimulate intellectual personality and social development of the child under 3 years of age — curriculum based upon Piagetian and neo-Piagetian principles — makes extensive use of toys and activities that can be implemented in the home

SUMMARY

In this chapter the importance of such persons as Friedrich Froebel, Maria Montessori, Jean Piaget, B. F. Skinner and Ira Gordon, as well as their influence in the field of early childhood has been described.

Although a great deal of factual knowledge of how children grow, develop and learn has been made available to the practitioner through research and experience, there is no single theory that has yet emerged which is the final answer.

Just because there is no *one* answer it is incumbent upon the teacher or assistant to be as knowledgeable and open to learning as he/she can possibly be. The greater the knowledge and the deeper the perception of the needs of children on the part of those who work closely with them, the closer the gap between the aims of preschool education and the programs which exist for young children.

BIBLIOGRAPHY AND SUGGESTED READINGS

Bereiter, Carol and Engelman, Siegfried. *Teaching the Disadvantaged Child.* Englewood Cliffs, New Jersey: Prentice Hall, Inc., 1966

Bloom, Benjamin S. *Stability and Change in Human Characteristics.* New York: John Wiley and Sons, Inc., 1964.

Braun, Samuel J. and Edwards, Esther P. *History and Theory of Early Childhood Education.* Worthington, Ohio: Charles A. Jones Publishing Co., 1972.

Evans, Ellis D. *Contemporary Influences in Early Childhood Education.* New York: Holt, Rinehart & Winston, 1971.

Frost, Joe. L. *Revisiting Early Childhood Education: Readings.* New York: Holt, Rinehart & Winston, Inc., 1973.

Gesell, Arnold *et al. The First Five Years of Life.* New York: Harper and Brothers, 1940.

Gesell, Arnold and Ilg, Frances L. *Infant and Child in the Culture of Today.* New York: Harper and Brothers, 1943.

Ginsburg, Herbert and Opper, Sylvia. *Piaget's Theory of Intellectual Development: An Introduction.* Englewood Cliffs, New Jersey: Prentice Hall, Inc., 1969.

Gordon, Ira J. *Parent Involvement in Compensatory Education.* Published for the Eric Clearinghouse on Early Childhood Education. University of Illinois Press, 1968.

Gordon, Ira J. "A Home Learning Center Approach to Early Stimulation," in Revisiting *Early Childhood Education: Readings* by Joe L. Frost. New York: Holt, Rinehart & Winston, Inc., 1973.

Hechinger, Fred M., ed. *Pre-School Education Today.* Garden City, New York Doubleday and Co., 1966.

Kamii, Constance. "A Sketch of the Piaget derived Pre-School Curriculum Developed by the ypsilanti Early Education Program" in *Revisiting Early Childhood Education: Readings* by Joe L. Frost, pp. 150-165. New York: Holt, Rinehart & Winston Inc., 1973.

Maccoby, Eleanor E. and Zellner, Miriam. *Experiments in Primary Education Aspects of Project Follow Through.* New York: Harcourt, Brace and Jovanovich, Inc. 1970.

Montessori, Maria. *The Montessori Method.* trans. from the Italian by Anne E. George. New York: Schocken Books, 1964.

Piaget, Jean. *The Language and Thought of the Child.* The World Publishing Co., 1955.

Piaget, Jean. *Play, Dreams and Imitation in Childhood.* trans. by C. Cattegno and Film Hodgson. New York: W.W. Norton and Co., 1962.

Weber, Evelyn. *Early Childhood Education Perspectives on Change.* Worthington, Ohio: Charles A. Jones Publishing Co., 1970.

Chapter 17

Action and Interaction in the Development of Thought in the Young Child

Loren D. Weybright*

The development of intelligence in the young child, according to the Swiss psychologist and philosopher, Jean Piaget, is based upon action and interaction. The activity of the child or adult is expressed through two types of action: first, as external, sensory-motor investigations of the child's surroundings, such as exploring the texture of clay or the feel of water; and second, as internal, thinking actions, such as comparing (sand and water), counting (the blocks), or matching (apples with children).

Piaget's conception of intelligence as an active process is a central notion in his theory, and is related to several other developmental themes, all of which have direct implications for the early childhood educator. A second theme is that children's thinking is qualitatively different from adult's thinking. The differences are expressed in terms of successive stages of development. The third theme describes the importance of observing children's development. These three themes provide the basis for understanding the fundamental relationship between development and education, between activity and schooling.

The theme of action and interaction is reflected throughout Piaget's investigations into the origins of knowledge. He focused, not on static elements or isolated actions, but upon discovering the rules that actively coordinate behavior. These investigations suggest that the only way for a child to develop intelligence is to construct it for herself or himself. This active, knowing behavior may be seen in the infant as he or she begins to establish that important concept of object permanence, the idea that a rattle, for example, still exists even though it may be out of sight. He or she needs to physically manipulate the rattle, to practice grasping and shaking it. He simply cannot be shown that it is still there, but out of sight; he needs to act upon it. The infant's first actions are external, sensory and motor activities on things or with people. These actions serve to develop later, internal ideas about the permanent nature of objects, or mothers, or fathers.

The child and the adult develop intelligence through action and interaction in several other ways. The most fundamental form is the internal, logical, and mathematical knowing, as observed in the actions of classifying, or adding and subtracting. Logical thought also develops through external actions on objects or with people. Social interaction, in Piaget's view, is a principal formative agent in the

development of logical thought, and in the development of social rules and morality. (See Brearly, 1970, on the importance of social interaction.)

Operations, which include the logical actions of calssifying or adding, are fundamental to the theme of action and interaction. An operation is an internal, mental action which cannot be observed directly, but inferred by observation of the child's behavior.

While an operation is an internalized action upon the child's view of the world, it is not merely a mental copy of that environment. It modifies, it transforms the object under examination, evolving an understanding of how the object is constructed. The child's understanding, however, is limited by his or her point of view or level of development. In art, for example, the young child draws what he knows of the world, not what he sees. An operation is reversible. By turning in an inverse direction it can negate its own action, as in adding, then subtracting. An operation never exists in isolation. It is dependent upon other operational structures which are combined or integrated to make a larger whole. For Piaget, operations constitute the framework of mature intelligence.

Operations may also be described in terms of children's responses to Piaget's experiments. The conversation of quantity problem, using two balls of clay is appropriately administered to children from about 4 through 8 or 9 years of age. (For other Piagetian interviews similar to this one, see Copeland, 1974, and Sime, 1973.) The interviewer shows the child two small clay balls, exactly the same size. The examiner first establishes equality. He makes certain that the child understands that the balls are the same size and weight, letting the child play with the clay a bit. The child is then asked to take a ball and roll it into a long hot dog or snake. Soon, the interviewer asks if there is the same amount of clay in each piece (ball and hot dog shape). Alternately, the interviewer may ask the child to imagine that the clay was candy, saying, "Would there still be the same amount to eat in both pieces?" A young child, characteristic of irreversible thinking, would firmly declare that one piece (usually the hot dog) is now bigger. When asked why

*Dr. Loren D. Weybright, Professor, Department of Elementary Education, The City College of New York, CUNY.

so, he might respond "Because its longer," not noticing that the hot dog was also thinner. Older children will just as convincingly affirm that there was still the same amount of clay in each case. They may even wonder aloud as to why you asked such a silly question.

These different, age-related explanations for transformations in the ball of clay are based on different points of view, different structures of thought. The preschooler focuses on only one aspect of the object at a time, reflecting his or her one-dimensional, irreversible point of view. The older child (6–8 years of age) is able to account for several dimensions at once in his or her explanation of equality. The older child knows the quantity of clay remained unchanged, answering, "There still is the same amount of clay. (How do you know?) You can just put it back the way it was before." His response was one definition of reversibility, being able to logically construct an image of the way it was before or to think your way back to the beginning condition.

The teacher's support for an active conception of intelligence depends upon a classroom organization which allows children to act directly upon meaningful materials and to interact closely with other children and adults.

If the children are to construct their own ideas about their physical and social world, they (and their teachers) must develop a familiarity with that world. Familiarity means, as Duckworth (1972) explains, feeling at home with the materials (clay or blocks, for example), knowing what to expect of it, exploring what are the limits of the thing.

The adults in the classroom, it is clearly implied, must also work directly with the materials, and become familiar with them, if they are to provide support for the children's investigations. The adult's involvement is on two levels, understanding the worth of ideas and interests of their own, and of the children. As Duckworth (1972, p. 225) concludes, it is important to allow the children to know their own work, and themselves, so they may have the courage and the understanding to go on by themselves.

The second theme, proposed early in Piaget's work, is that children's thinking is qualitatively different from adult's thinking, and that these qualitative differences can be expressed in terms of developmental stages. Contrary to what was once assumed, Piaget discovered that children don't just know less, quantitatively, than adults, but that these are fundamental differences in the form and pattern of thought, roughly defined according to age. The very framework, or what Piaget calls "structure", of children's ideas about their world differs in essential, often dramatic ways from adult's ideas.

The preschooler's egocentric point of view, as mentioned in the clay example, is also illustrated by a three-year-old's remark, to his father, who was in another room, "See the picture I made, Daddy!" The child can see it, so he thought that others should also see it.

Another example of egocentric thinking reveals the child's ideas about the cause of natural events; rain, in this case. A six year old, when asked where rain came from, responded, "Oh, that's easy. It's like when my mother has the kettle on the stove. The steam comes out and it rains." When asked why it wasn't raining all the time, she thought a moment, and then said, "Because my mother isn't cooking all the time." (Weybright, Adams, Voyat, 1975).

The qualatatively different points of view expressed in these examples characterize one of four stages within Piaget's developmental stage theory. Before describing the differences between stages, several common characteristics of all stages will be identified.

First, the stages develop in a constant order, a higher stage appearing after, but never before an earlier stage. While the sequence remains invariant, even across cultures. Piaget often cautions that the age of attainment varies among individuals. Each stage prepares for the one to follow. In turn, each stage results from the preceding one, integrating earlier forms of thinking (operations) into a higher level.

Second, the unified character of each stage makes it possible to define basic patterns within the overall structure. There are, for example, general patterns of sensory-motor actions in the infancy stage.

Later, these actions develop into the symbolic representations (e.g. language) of the preschooler, distinctively separate in pattern and form from the first.

Third, each stage has a period of formation (genesis) and a period of attainment; a period of disequilibrium, alternating with a period of equilibrium. The child, during the period of formation, first develops conservation of mass (as shown in the reversibility of thinking about the clay problem), then conserves weight, and finally conserves volume. During the period of attainment he is able to conserve across many areas of development (Piaget & Inhelder, 1969, P. 153–154).

The sequence of stages, and their characteristic patterns provide a framework for those who work with young children. Implicit in this framework is the idea that the teacher seeks to understand how individual modes of thinking are related to the general developmental sequence, and to provide support for growth by actively involving the child with meaningful materials. Piaget suggests, however, that the concept of stage and sequence does not imply that one should immediately attempt to accelerate children's development through those stages.

The alternating periods of formation and attainment within stages are related to the vertical (formation) and horizontal (attainment) dimensions of development between stages. For the educator, the vertical dimension suggests a long-range point of view, encompassing several years and several stages. On this dimension the teacher seeks to support children in their growth towards the next higher level of development. The teacher has the advantage of observing children's development for nearly a year, and sometimes over several years in integrated-age classrooms. Within this perspective, the expectation is for a broad range of individual differences in developmental patterns. Learning to read, like learning to speak may be several years in developing; and perhaps not within the particular year determined by some external criteria (Weybright, 1976a).

The horizontal dimension emphasizes social and cognitive growth within the context of a particular developmental stage. There is a strong theoretical connection between the two dimensions, each depending upon interaction with the other for growth and change. The teacher has the greatest opportunity to support development through horizontal enrichment and change in patterns of thinking within one developmental period.

The sequence of stages leading to the final, formal stage follows: The sensory-motor stage of infancy, from birth to about 1½–2 years; the preoperational stage of the preschool child, extending from about 2 through 5 or 7 years; the concrete operational stage of the elementary years, ranging from 5–7 through 10 or 12 years of age; and the formal operational stage of adolescence and adulthood, extending from 10 to 12 years onward.

The sensory-motor stage of infancy is characterized by the child's practical (or external), perceptual, and motor actions upon things and people. One remarkable achievement of this stage is the development of object permanence. This scheme enables the infant to develop the emotional attachments to the people important in his or her life, attachments that are so essential to later development.

Piaget (1963) describes the end of the sensory-motor stage and the beginning of the preoperational stage, as a period of transition where the child invents new means of acting and understanding through mental combinations, new means to fit old situations.

The preoperational stage of the preschooler begins with the development of symbolic thinking, expressed through imaginative play, language, and through physical and social action and interaction (e.g. counting or grouping objects, and in role play). The object/symbol relationships found in the young child's actions is essential to all later development, and to learning skills such as reading and mathematics. The symbol first appears to the child as part of the object it represents. The young child's natural interest in the use and the origin of names is a case in point.

Piaget (1960) recorded the spontaneous remarks of two children (6½ years old) during their play with building blocks. One child remarked, "And when there weren't any names. . ." The other child replied, "If there weren't any words it would be very awkward. You couldn't make any thing. How could things have been made? (p. 62)." The implication was that if there were no names, the objects themselves would not exist. The name of things, at this stage, appears to be the essence of things.

Piaget's (1951) investigations into the symbolic function of play, imitation, and dreams, focused on the crucial role of play in the development of thinking. The young child at play creates his or her own environment, untroubled by objective, external "reality." A box may be brought in to play as a ferry boat, for example (Weybright, 1976b).

The developmental innovation in the discovery of symbol is that the preoperational child may now represent something else, such as ferry boat, through a medium or pivotal object that has some resemblance to the original construction, such as the box. In the prior, sensory-motor stage the child was unable to separate the symbolic meaning from the real object. As Furth (1969) explains, it is the preoperational child's double knowledge—he knows what a box is and he knows what a boat is—that enables him to use one scheme of knowing for another purpose. The preoperational child remains unable, however, to consciously distinguish between symbol and object, between make-believe and reality. This awareness only appears, Piaget proposes, through the development of concrete operations.

The development of symbolic thought provides the framework for language development, not the inverse. Piaget views language, instead, as one way to symbolize thinking, but symbolic thinking is not just verbal expression. To summarize, the preoperational stage is characterized by the acquisition of symbols and signs, and the ability to begin to separate things from their names or symbols. As the child begins to develop towards true operational thought, there remains several limitations. The preoperational child is egocentric, "centering" on his own view much as he centers or focuses on one dimension of the clay hot dog. He depends upon concrete, sensory and motor actions, making his thinking somewhat rigid and immobile. He lacks reversibility and does not conserve.

The concrete operational child is characterized by his growth out of egocentrism towards sociocentric thinking. He decenters, no longer focusing on his own view, but understands other perspectives. He is able to serialize items, arranging them from the largest to the smallest, for example. He can conserve mass, weight, and (eventually) volume. And he can classify objects into groups.

One of Piaget's experiments designed to illustrate classification is the problem of class composition, or the ability to deal with part-to-whole relations. This problem uses colored beads, and is appropriate for children from about 4 to 8 years of age. A child is presented with a box of wooden (or plastic) beads, with 3 blue beads and 12 or 15 white beads. After the child examines them and understands that all the beads are wooden, only a few are blue, and most are white, he or she is asked several questions (sequence not being important): "Are there more wooden beads, or are there more white beads?" "Why?" "Let's take all the white beads out of the box." "Will there be any beads left?"

The younger, preoperational child invariably answers,

"There's more white ones." An older concrete operational child thought it was a foolish question, responding, "Of course! There's more wooden ones. The white ones and the blue ones are both made of wood."

The same problem, put another way is stated: "I'm stringing a long necklace with these beads. Should I use all the white ones or all the wooden ones?" The younger child, again, would likely respond: "Use the white ones." The older child insisting you need to use the wooden ones. "They're *all* wood!"

From an adult point of view, the preoperational child's response may seem surprising. While the adult easily accounts for two or more dimensions at once, the preschool child can see only one dimension or one class of objects. The young child considers only the color or the woodenness, one class of beads at a time. The concrete operational child, like the adult, understands (but may not easily explain) that the class of wooden beads includes the sub-class of blue and of white beads. Reversible thinking among the older children is apparent when they realize, intuitively at first, that if the colored beads (a subclass) were all wooden (the larger class), that's what they remained, regardless of how you changed them from box to box, or onto a long necklace.

An interesting variation of this problem uses children instead of beads. Ask eight or ten children to stand in a row, making certain there are more of one group, using for example, eight girls and two boys. After establishing that all in the group are children, and there are more girls than boys, ask: "Are there more children or more girls?" "Which makes the longest line (hand-to-hand), all the girls or all the children?" (Demonstrate, but only after they have had an opportunity to respond). Because of the difference in the problem content, some children may classify in one case (the children problem), and not in another (the beads problem).

Individual differences may appear in these problems because one child may be more familiar with the content, than another child. The basic operation required, classification in this example, remains the same however. The son of a potter will very likely conserve a quantity of clay earlier than his peers, but his "early" start may disappear by the time he conserves volume.

The concrete operational child, in summary, is able to classify, order, and serialize objects or people, but he or she is confined to concrete, perceptual data. The child at this level is able to operate on real objects, but not yet able to test hypotheses on data which are not directly observable. He has reversibility of thought, distinguishing him from the preoperational child. He cannot, however, organize the subsystems of reversibility, which include inversion ("It's the same, because you can put it back the way it was before.") and negation ("You didn't add anything, and you didn't take anything away.") into a unitary whole.

The final stage of development, the formal operational

stage of adolescence and adulthood, is the period when the child can follow the form of the argument while disregarding its concrete contents. The "concrete" and "formal" stage designations, Flavel (1963) contends, fit Piaget's ideas of operational intelligence better than the more common "concrete-abstract" distinction.

The third theme is about observing children. Piaget observed children, using the clinical interview, with several aims in mind: First, he established an inventory of the child's beliefs and explanations through a partially structured interview. The child's own statements served as guide to the interviewer's next question. Second, he evaluated the authenticity of the explanations, looking for internal consistency in their statements. Third, he attempted to establish trends in development by looking for patterns in the child's entire inventory of explanations.

The direct implication for those who wish to relate the active development of intelligence to their work with children is to conduct a careful observation and on-going analysis of children, both in partially structured problem settings, and in the unstructured settings of the classroom. However, the early childhood educator will soon discover that, in order to establish an inventory of the child's belief system, and to determine overall patterns in development, he or she must know more about the child than his or her stage of development.

The practitioner can go beyond a determination of stage by comparing a child's "stage of development" with the dynamics of the child's ordinary behavior in the classroom. One design for relating development to ordinary behavior is to observe children during their imaginative play (Weybright, 1976a). Piaget suggests that the action and social interaction of play provides fundamental support for the child's overall development. The format of the observation was based upon Piaget's (1932) interviews of children's ideas about the rules in organized (marble) games. The interview was adapted for the imaginative play settings, including, but not limited to the block area or the housekeeping area of the early childhood classroom. The questions of the observer focus on the origins, maintenance, extensions and/or termination of the children's ideas about their procedures or rules for their imaginative play.

Observations and discussions with children about the rules for their play could provide the basic data base for going beyond stage-of-development interviews. Play is central to uncovering the "trend of the child's mind," and represents the essential relationship between everyday experience and the development of intelligence.

SUMMARY

Piaget's theory on the development of intelligence may be characterized by several themes. The first theme is Piaget's notion of intelligence as an active process, which develops through the action and interaction of childhood. The child and the adult must construct intelligence, not through passive, didactic instruction, but through personal action on his or her surroundings, and through social interaction and cooperation with others.

Piaget (1932) speaks directly to those who work with children as he describes the importance of individual action and social cooperation: "Let us therefore try to create in the school a place where individual experimentation and reflection carried out in common come to each other's aid and balance one another (p. 404)."

The second theme demonstrates that children's thinking is different from adult's thinking in terms of its structure or framework. Piaget proposed that these structures (e.g. symbolic thought, classification, reversibility) develop through a sequence of stages, a sequence found to be invariant across cultures.

The third theme of observing children draws upon the clinical interview and the questions concerning the development of children's ideas about rules in their play. Observing and questioning children in an unstructured, developmental context allows (classroom) practice to illuminate theory.

SELECTED BIBLIOGRAPHY

Bearly, M. (ed.) *The Teaching of Young Children: Some Application of Piaget's Learning Theory.* New York: Schocken Books, 1970.

Copeland, R. *Diagnostic and Learning Activities in Mathematics for Children.* New York: Macmillan, 1974.

Duckworth, E. The having of wonderful ideas. *Harvard Education Review.* May, 1972, *42* (2), 217-233.

Flavell, J. *The Developmental Psychology of Jean Piaget.* New York: Van Nostrand Co., 1963.

Furth, H. *Piaget and Knowledge.* Englewood Cliffs, N.J.: Prentice-Hall, 1969.

Ginsburg, H.; and Opper, S. *Piaget's Theory of Intellectual Development: An Introduction.* Englewood Cliffs, N.J.: Prentice-Hall, 1969.

Piaget, J. *The Moral Judgment of the Child.* New York: Harcourt, Brace & World, 1932.

Piaget, J. *Play, Dreams and Imitation in Childhood.* New York: Norton, 1951. (Original French edition, 1945.)

Piaget, J. *The Child's Conception of the World.* Totowa, N.J.: Littlefield, Adams & Co., 1960. (Original French edition, 1924.)

Piaget, J. *The Origins of Intelligence in Children.* New York: Norton, 1963. (Original French edition, 1936.)

Piaget, J. *Six Psychological Studies.* New York: Random House, 1967.

Piaget, J. *To Understand is to Invent: The Future of Education.* New York: Viking, 1973.

Piaget, J.; and Inhelder, B. *The Psychology of the Child. New York: Basic* Books, 1969.

Sime, M. *A child's Eye View: Piaget for Young Parents and Teachers.* New York: Harper & Row, 1973.

Weybright, L. "A Comparison of Cognitive and Social Development in Free Play and Interview Settings." A paper presented at *The Fifth Annual Symposium of the Jean Piaget Society.* Philadelphia, Pa., 1975.

Weybright, L. "The Teacher's Role in the Development of Play and Logical Thinking." *The Urban Review,* Summer, 1976a.

Weybright, L. *Piaget and Children's Play.* Fairlawn, N.J.: JAB Press, 1976b, (Audio recording, 40 minutes.)

Weybright, L., Adams, R., & Voyat, G. *Piaget and reading.* Fairlawn, N.J.: JAB Press, 1975. (Audio cassette tape recording, 85 minutes.)

Chapter 18

Piaget, Parents, and Young Children: Some Ideas that Work with Youngsters

Thomas D. Yawkey and Ann M. BurkeMerkle[*]

Does my child fully benefit from school?

Why does my child say those things?

My child can count but she still says one has less! Why?

Why doesn't he do what I tell him to do?

Some answers to these questions and many others can be found in the work of a Swiss child psychologist named Jean Piaget. Piaget started his career in biology, but became very interested in how his own children were learning. A lot of things Piaget says may seem familiar to many parents but the way he explains them adds depth and breadth to our understanding of children.

About the most important thing Piaget is saying is that all children, all over the world, go through four basic stages in the way they think. Children go through these stages at different ages, but the stages and their order are always the same.

The first stage of thinking goes from birth until the child begins to talk. Children at this age learn by watching and imitating. Try making funny noises to a very young child, and he will probably imitate the sound right back. At first, an infant can only repeat his own actions. For example, a six month old baby might see that when he kicks his foot the mobile over his crib moves, and since he likes to see it move, he repeats his action again and again. From 12 to 18 months he might be able to predict in his mind what will happen if he does something. For example, he might go up to a strange object and touch it because it looks soft, and he likes soft things. During this young age, it is important for the child to have toys around which he can look at, and touch, and observe how they move. Toys which will respond to his action with movement or sounds will motivate him to experiment again, to repeat his actions and slowly modify them through repetition. The baby is not "just playing." He is beginning to think about his environment and his actions and how the two things work together.

The beginning of speech is very important to both the child and his parents, and the child has a long way to go before he can understand all the words that adults say and use. From the time children begin to talk, until about age six or seven, they are playing games which help them find out what life is all about and just what people are really doing. Very often when a child uses words at this stage, he means something entirely different from what an adult

would mean if he were using them. This is one reason a child's speech or answers to adult questions may seem absurd. The child has answered "correctly" for the way he perceives the question. The problem is that he perceives it very differently from the adult. Parents can help their child's self-confidence by accepting these absurd answers as having real meaning for the child.

Children can be helped toward more realistic answers by parents providing them with concrete experiences, assisting them in exploring all aspects of their environments. Instead of giving children answers, parents can ask open-ended questions which motivate children to think. Questions which begin with..."What would happen if...?" and "I wonder if...?" or "Can you find another way to...?" or even the statement "Let's find out!" will encourage children to look further and find alternatives.

At this and other stages parents can help their children. Children can watch how Mommy and Daddy do things. For example, by watching Mommy comb her hair a little girl will learn how to comb her own hair. How many times have we seen small children "reading" a book! The book may be upside down, and the words only meaningless squiggles on the page but to the child this is real reading. Young children should be encouraged to talk about their experences and act them out. If a child goes with Daddy to the office, he may delight in telling Mommy what Daddy does there. The young child should be encouraged to show his parents what happens at Daddy's job. Children playing house or doctor or being animals is not just a way to pass the time: they are learning.

Children in the stage from 2 through 7 years, also are learning to use symbols for things. This first step can again be seen through play. The child might take a block of wood and move it around the floor pretending it is a car and making sounds as it moves. This pretending is very important according to Piaget. The young child has the idea of a car in his head and can think of the way it looks, sounds, and moves even when there is no car around. In

Dr. Thomas D. Yawkey, Assistant Professor of Early Childhood Education and Director. Dr. Ann M. Burke-Merkle, Candidate and Staff Member, Wisconsin Early Childhood Study Center, University of Wisconsin, Madison. Reprinted with permission from CONTEMPORARY EDUCATION, Summer, 1974.

the same way, the child who is beginning to talk may say the word "Mommy," have an image of her in mind, and also recognize her name when written.

Children in ages 2 through 7 years are just forming the concepts basic to mathematics, reading, science, etc. They are learning about what Piaget calls conservation—that equal things remain equal regardless of outward appearances. Strings of the same length remain equal in length even when one is curled like a snake and the other is straight (conservation of length). Equal amounts of liquids remain equal regardless of the shape of the containers (conservation of volume). The same number of objects remain the same regardless of arrangement (conservation of number). Equal amounts of clay are equal even when one is put into a different shape (conservation of substance). These are all things that parents understand and accept, but children must be given many chances to develop the basic understandings. Without conservation of length, volume, number, and substance, no child can really understand mathematics, science, or for that matter reading. Conservation is also basic to other school subjects.

There are three levels in acquiring the concepts of conservation. Parents may want to try a few games with their young children to find out where their children are in sequence of development. In the first level, children cannot conserve at all. When equal amounts of something are shown, a child will generally acknowledge that they are the same in amount. If an outward change occurs in the object, the nonconserving child will insist that the amounts are no longer equal. No amount of arguing will talk him out of it. To him things are only equal if they look alike in every way. He does not take more than one dimension into account at one time.

The second level can be very frustrating to children. In this level they know that equal amounts must remain equal. However, they want to trust their eyes and say that an outward change has made them unequal. The child will change his mind in his answers, never sure what is really right. He will usually be deceived by perceptual changes in volume, or number or length and mass.

At the third level children know that equal amounts remain equal regardless of outward appearance. This level is usually reached around age 7. Experiences which involve a lot of manipulating of real objects and the sharing of the experience with other children and adults will enhance the growth in these thought processes. If your child has not reached the conservation level at age 7, he needs a little more time and good, solid, manipulative experiences.

Some Conservation Games:

Try Them, You'll Like Them!

Length. Parents with 2 through 7 year olds might try the following to find out if measurement principles are under-stood. Take two pieces of string of equal lengths. Stretch out the pieces of string and place them on the floor or table, putting one piece right below the other piece. Have the child determine they are of equal length. Then bend one of the pieces in and out like a snake. Ask the child if the strings are still the same length. To get an idea of how he is thinking, ask him why he gave the answer he did.

In the first level of length conservation, the child may say the strings are the same length. If the snake-shaped string is then stretched out, the child can tell that both strings are equal in length. However, when put back into a snake a child at the first level may or may not say that the two strings are equal.

A child in the second level can run his fingers along the strings and say that the snake string is just as long as the other string. He will say, however, with some uncertainty that the two strings are or are not the same length.

At the third level, the child says immediately that the snake-shaped string is just as long as the other string.

Volume. Parents might try this little game the next time their youngster has a friend over for a snack. Take two identical measuring cups and fill each one to the ½ cup line while the children watch. Ask the children if both have the same amount of liquid or drink. Children at almost any age will see that the two cups have equal amounts. Now set out two glasses. Make sure one glass is tall and thin and the other short and fat. Pour one of the ½ cups of drink into the tall thin glass. Pour the other of the ½ cups of drink into the short fat glass. Ask the children which glass has more drink in it.

The kinds of answers to this question will depend again on those three levels of conservation. In the first level of volume conservation, the child will say that one of the glasses has more drink and, of course, he wants the glass with more drink. At this point he can only look at one dimension at a time. The glass either has more because it is taller or because it is fatter.

The second level child will say that one has more than the other, but he will not seem convinced that this is the right answer. At this point he has a problem. He knows that one ½ cup is the same as the other ½ cup, but he will trust his eyes and say that one glass looks as if it has more.

In the third level, the child will say that the two glasses each have the same amount of drink. If asked why, he will say this glass is taller but the other is fatter, and ½ cup is always ½ cup.

Number. During the same snack time, try something else. Give each child five cookies. Now, put one set of five cookies in a row and another set of five cookies in a row beneath the first. Have the children determine that both rows have the same number of cookies. Spread out one of these rows so that one row is longer than the other. Ask which row has the most cookies in it.

A child in the first level of number conservation will say that the longer row has more cookies. He does not understand that five cookies are always the same number of cookies. To him more cookies is determined by the length of the row and not the number. He is deceived by the amount of space the rows of cookies occupy.

In the second level the child will say that the longer row has more cookies. Ask him to count each row. He will say that each row has five cookies. At this point he will be very confused because he wants to trust his eyes and say that the longer row has more cookies, and yet counting he sees that each row contains the same number.

In the third level this conflict is resolved and the child can look at the rows and say that they contain the same number of cookies. When asked why, he will tell you that five cookies is always five cookies or that you can count them and see that they are the same. It is not until this point that a child can understand the concept matching and counting.

Substance. Parents might want to try one more type of game based on Piaget's work. This involves conservation of substance and can be played with a ball of clay or playdough. Give the child two balls of clay of identical size and mass. Most children will say that the balls each contain the same amount of clay. If not, let the child adjust the balls until he is satisfied they are of equal size.

Now, take one ball and flatten it to a pancake. Ask the child which piece of clay has more. A child in the first level of conservation will say that the pancake has more, because it is all spread out. He cannot compare things in two dimensions at the same time. He sees that the pancake takes up more space so he believes it to have more dough.

The second level child will say that the pancake has more, because it looks like more. He will not seem very sure of his answer because he just saw that the two balls had equal amounts. He may change his answer back and forth and never be quite sure which answer is right.

The third level child knows that the two pieces of clay have equal amounts. It does not matter what shape they are in. He understands that if the two balls had equal mass to begin with and no clay is added or taken away, they remain equal in mass, regardless of shape.

Parents need to realize that no child can add and subtract with real understanding until he has mastered conservation of mass.

Understanding The Games

These games do not teach number or volume or mass, but may help parents to estimate where their child is in conservation sequencing. Young children need to have a great deal of experience from which number and reading concepts can be formed. The children are actively handling materials and observing changes in shape and arrangement all the time. They are continually contrasting, comparing, accumulating and organizing things—the basic stuff from which mental operations can be formed when the time comes for more formal instruction. As children accumulate more and more experiences, the forms of their answers to the questions in the games will change. Children will not conserve in all areas at once, but the underlying reasoning involved in conservation will gradually generalize to take into account more and more types of changes in matter as well as in social-emotional situations.

Parents can help children learn basic understandings by providing the variety of materials and experiences children need. It is a wise parent who exhibits an accepting attitude towards answers children give which appear to be wrong. This will add to the child's confidence in seeking out other experiences and sharing them with the parent. It is these further experiences and communications with others which will shed the light of new perspectives on the activities and enable the child to give the "right" answer. Young children need to manipulate, order, count, compare, contrast, construct, and reorganize. Children will profit from experiences playing with such things as cups and saucers which they can match, blocks which can be put in order of shape or size, or pebbles and stones which they can order by size, weight, or color. Experiences with fitting objects or themselves into something and with repeating stories or experiences will help children learn about space and the sequencing of time. Educational toys and experiences are often found in the most familiar settings of the home and yard rather than in the local store.

Young children need other kinds of help from parents as well. Children can only see things from their own perspective and do not take into account feelings or perspectives of others. Young children always believe they understand what is being said and always believe they are understood by others. Piaget calls this egocentrism. For example, young children ask many questions of adults. If mother has a headache and explains this to her child, asking him to stop bothering her with questions, the child may stop for a second but will almost immediately begin with a string of questions again. The child is not trying to make mother's headache worse, he just has no conception of what she feels like and how this relates to his questions. The repetition of questions can also mean that what the child believes to be reality is inconsistent with how his question was answered. Therefore, he is motivated to continually repeat the question to be sure he heard the answer correctly. He again is not being perverse but is really learning new things and gaining experiences.

Another example of this egocentricity is seen in trying to teach a young child the difference between left and right. Stand opposite the child and raise your right hand saying, "This is your right hand!" The child cannot turn things around and see from another person's point of view. Thus, if you really want to teach left and right to a child, stand beside or in front of him.

Still another example can be observed when 2 through 6 year old children are talking together. They really have, as yet, no conception of what a conversation is. They both talk, but neither child listens. One child might say, "My cat had seven kittens last night!" and the other, "Daddy planted seeds and they will grow to be big pumpkins at Halloween." They are not being purposely rude to each other by not listening. At this point each child is only concerned with his own thoughts and does not need the response from the other child to keep talking. As children become less egocentric they learn to accommodate to the needs and interests of others and their conversations become more adult-like.

Another thing that young children must learn is to internalize rules. Parents might tell a child not to run in the driveway because a car might be driving in. Parents are very surprised when the child runs after a ball that goes into the street. Perhaps he just wasn't thinking! Piaget says that it takes a while for a child to gerneralize and see the way "the-no-running-in-the-driveway rule" applies to "the-no-running-in-the-street" for the very same reason of the presence of a moving car. Another example of the rule problem can be seen when parents constantly remind their children to say the magic words "please" and "thank you." Again, perhaps parents think the children sometimes forget, but it is more probable that "please" and "thank you" have little personal meaning for the child so take time to generalize across different situations.

These problems begin to be resolved between the ages of 7 and 12. The child begins to think and communicate in a more adult manner. He knows that equal things remain equal in spite of perceptual changes. The child also slowly realizes that his perspective of the world is not all there is. Much to the parents' pleasure, the child begins to generalize rules and incorporate them into his life. By the age of 12 the child moves into the stage of reasoning and logical thinking. Strong groundwork must be laid during the child's first several years to enable him to enter this stage and become a mature reasoning adult.

REFERENCES

Baldwin, A.L. **Theories of Child Development**. New York: Wiley & Sons, 1967.

Brearly, M. & Hitchfield, L. **A Guide to Reading Piaget**. New York: Schocken Books, 1966.

Copeland, R. **How Children Learn Mathematics**. New York: Macmillan, 1970.

Flavell, J.H. **The Developmental Psychology of Jean Piaget**. New York: D. Van Nostrand, 1963.

Furth, H. **Piaget and Knowledge, Theoretical Foundations**. Englewood Cliffs, N.J.: Prentice-Hall, 1969.

Mussen, P. Conger, J. & Kagan, J. **Child Development and Personality**. New York: Harper and Row, 1969.

Piaget, J. & Inhelder, B. **The Psychology of the Child**. New York: Basic Books, 1969.

Piaget, J. **The Language and Thought of the Child**. New York: World Publishing, 1971.

Richmond, P.G. **An Introduction to Piaget**, New York: Basic Books, 1971.

Bill Wallace, NYC Board of Education

Chapter 19

Some Experiences Important in the Cognitive Growth of Young Children

John R. Nevius[*]

Is there a relationship between experience and logical thinking in young children? An important point emerges immediately from the examination of this question: whatever experience undergirds such development, it is in all probability very broad, nonspecific, and unstructured in nature. The development of logical thinking seems to be a universal happening. However, even though it may be relied upon to take place, the quality of development will be influenced by a variety of factors. For example, ones intellectual ability is determined by hereditary potential (Anastasi, 1958). On the other hand, appropriate experience is a factor of an individual's developmental level, for the developmental level determines the effect of the experience.

Young children require experience with which they can work in a sensori-motor and perceptual way. They discover that when a ball is rolled against a wall, fence, or step, its angle or reflection equals the angle of incidence. The learning occurs because they are able to work on the problem through many experiences consistent with their sensorimotor, perceptual manner of thinking. For young children, they are allowed to experiment with and manipulate materials, than whey they are taught by mother, father, or teacher in a directed manner. Hunt (1961) asserts that the need to work actively on the environment is common to all young children. Activities such as cooking, woodworking, clay modeling, experimenting with sand and running water, patterning, comparing, categorizing, and predicting are some experiences that let the child be involved with learning by observing the transformations that can take place in the materials. It is through situations such as these or similar ones that the great conceptual learning of young children takes place. As Piaget describes it, the child creates this learning through the force of his own logic (1951). One need only observe children for a short period time, and it becomes apparent that the learning of social and physical concepts is the child's primary curriculum during his first six to seven years of life.

So we find that children are prime candidates to learn about the reality of the physical and social world through concepts, but that for this learning to take place the environment must provide for experimentation and manipulation of materials.

As the child pursues the experience made available to him he discovers the incongruity that occurs in the mismatch between old learning and new learning. When the incongruity matches the knowledge the child has available and the experience being provided, learning becomes both highly motivational and pleasureful.

As a child works within the environment of his everyday world, he does not repeat endlessly an already-mastered experience, although he may practice that experience, thus recreating an already familiar success. Nor does he leap to the other extreme and attempt to conquer experience that is highly incongruous with his current capability. Neither of these experiences will remain fully satisfying for long. Motivation occurs when there is a new success, a reward that generates good feeling about the activity. The outcome, a pleasureful learning experience, occurs because the child is challenged to think, and extend his cognitive powers or other capability at the point of congruity with old learning and the slight incongruity with new learning.

Proof of this may be obtained through both observation and research. All teachers of young children are aware of the delight their pupils take in new activities that are challenging at an appropriate level—and the learning that results. Given a proper environment, children search out their own level of learning—the point of slight incongruity, thus making learning highly pleasureful. For example, young children may learn the basis for arithmetic in preschool or kindergarten. Their method of learning is by playing games consisting of blocks, cuisenaire rods, cubes, and other materials in building, sorting, stacking, and arranging in rows, creating volume and area out of various three-dimensional structures. The learning experience is similar to the description provided by children who define prenumber area or volume as: "area is when you put four blocks this way, and five blocks this way, and then fill them all in and count them." or: "volume (or building) is when you put blocks on top and more blocks on top of them."

*Dr. John R. Nevius, Jr., Associate Professor, College of Education, Texas Tech University, Lubbock, Texas.

All teachers observe examples such as these in which motivation is high. Hunt validates this from a research viewpoint when he refers to Hebb (1947) and Piaget (1928) who suggest that the basis for pleasure and motivation is the effort required to close the gap between existing knowledge and skill, and the new knowledge or skill being learned. Hunt, Hebb and Piaget all agree that pleasure in learning occurs when knowledge can operate upon experience. They also see the difference as a potential basis for fear and distress when the discrepancy is too great or incongruous, to be understood by the child (Nevius and Murphy, in press).

As an illustration of children's motivation in learning and their ability to acquire knowledge, consider their use of concept terms such as in front, behind, frontwards, backwards, beside, under, above, and a whole host of others These labels define a conceptual meaning. Who is the teacher for this? Does one generally sit down with a child and teach the specifics of a concept such as high up? Usually not for we do not need to. This knowledge and almost all other knowledge the young child learns is acquired through a process of sensing, manipulating and perceiving, and effective process, because it is the child's own mode of thinking and solving problems-it is based on the horizontal transfer of problem solving skills rather than the vertical acquisition of new knowledge (Nevius and Murphy, 1976).

The research of Wohwill (1970) identifies horizontal transfer of knowledge as a major component in the environmental facilitating concept learning. Elkind (1974) verifies the same idea, although he labels it horizontal elaboration.

The Function of Transfer

To increase or enhance a child's cognitive thinking ability, and thus his capability with logical thought, a teacher must realize all educational practice, independent of acceptance or level of concern, has its inception in theory. Concept learning is predicated upon the transferability of information, but not in a single vertical strand as though one were teaching a specific concept, as for example the many attempts at teaching children to conserve. Instead it depends upon broad ranges of horizontal transfer. The parent or educator should strive to facilitate "horizontal development," that is, to develop learning opportunities that cause the child to use his current skill and knowledge in many related but different areas (Nevius and Murphy, 1976).

Siegel's (1972) investigation of learning classification skills supports the function of horizontal transfer. He taught young children the related skills of grouping, application of verbal labels for grouping, and wider basis for groupings and for relational responses. By increasing practice with these skills he was able to improve horizontal transfer in problem solving situations. The outcome was an increase in knowledge about higher levels of classification.

Siegel hypothesizes that classification is an important antecedent of logical thought. Ultimately as explained by Wohwill (1970), it is the increasing complexity of horizontal transfer that promotes or accelerates vertical levels of thinking. Wohwill's (1970) experiments involve the function of measurement in a variety of forms such as length, area, distance, and vertical height as contributors to the learning of conservation. While the data for any single testing of any one of these forms of measurement show only a marginal correlation between measurement and conservation, a much stronger relationship exists when all four forms of measurement are taken into account on a pretest, intervention (teaching for measurement), posttest design. The research lends support for the hypothesis that vertical acceleration or learning of aspecific concept, such as conservation, is generalized from the learning of many less difficult concepts, and skills like the various forms of measurement. The mastery of complexity that transfers horizontally, provides a foundation for the mastery of difficulty that transfers vertically. Slowly knowledge develops on a broad but narrowing base, similar to a pyramid, until the understanding of a new and more difficult concept is achieved.

Research indicates that complementary activities in a horizontal arrangement provide the transfer necessary to move to higher levels of cognitive thinking. It is also apparent that the difference in what children can learn at varying stages of development is not content amount *per se*, but the extent of horizontal transfer applying knowledge from one idea to another similar idea. The curricular implication is that logical thinking is not developed in situation-specific conditions, but instead when children have many broad experiences that provide opportunities for the transfer of information and problem-solving skills.

An Example:

One of the complex concepts which young children learn through interaction with their natural environment is multiple categorization (Lavatelli, 1970). Children learn this concept through experiences with many materials in problem solving situations. Multiple categorization provides a good example of how a teacher or parent can create an environment to support the learning of difficult concepts. To create a multiple categorization a child must identify and categorize an object or symbol on two or more properties. Current research and theory suggest teaching for horizontal transfer will facilitate the learning or understanding of higher level concepts. Therefore, an environment for young children should provide: 1.) many experiences that allow for transfer of information; 2.) experiences that are truly experiential in nature; and 3.) experiences that require the transfer or use of similar problem solving skills.

Environments which fulfill the requirements mentioned above may clearly be designed through the unique opportunities provided by learning activities that allow children to work with an array of materials and strive for new learning through the congruent—incongruent level of the task. However, to facilitate transfer, the center must not be a simple, single activity. Many activities are required, all complementary to the desired outcome, with each activity having its own clear and inherent objective. For example, the following five classes of concepts provide an illustration of how an environment can be structured to produce the horizontal transfer required to learn the concept multiple categorization. The classes of concepts are: 1.) patterning—the discovery of a repetative system, from which the child develops appropriate responses; 2.) comparison (including sorting and grouping)—discovery of differences and similarities among classes of objects, based on physical properties; 3.) categorization—discovery of inference based on comparison; 4.) prediction—discovery of implications of previous experience; 5.) hypothesis formation—discovery of propositions leading to new concept investigation. These concepts relate to multiple categorization in a manner that is similar to the way measurement relates to conservation in Wohwill's experiment, and grouping skills relate to classification in Siegel's research.

We do not suggest the concepts referred to in the example are the only ones useful for teaching the transfer of problem-solving skills. Instead, we believe it is teachers' familiarity with them that makes them useful as an example. It is important to note that concepts are not learned only in science or mathematics centers, but also in music, art, language, physical activity, block building, and dramatic play centers or activities as well. The desired intent of the teacher should be to provide young children with experience that is highly structured but that appears to be very broad, nonspecific and unstructured.

A look at some practical features in each of the five concept classes may be helpful in facilitating environments that provide mechanisms for the development of logical thinking. It is important to realize that the mentioned activities are not single, concerted endeavors, but that all must be considered in order to provide maximal horizontal transfer value and thus generate knowledge and skill with multiple categorization.

Activities to Promote Patterning

1. *Patterning* is designed to help children observe and become aware of repetition. This may be facilitated through the use of auditory, visual and tactile discrimination.
   In a group activity awareness of patterns might be created through clapping a sequence in cadence, drawing attention to patterns of color, and texture in clothing.
2. *Comparison* builds upon skills of observation as children create distinctions between or similarities to ob-

jects, materials, and ideas.
   Comparison tasks are not only prereading, but prenumber as well. Their direct transfer value is found with categorization and patterning.
3. *Classification* may be promoted through tasks which require children to make decisions by creating two or more groups with any variety of materials or ideas. Through classification children may create inferences which lead to predication or back to comparison.
4. *Predictions* are made on the basis of prior learning and experience. Prediction is significant in that it teaches children how to pose questions before assigning answers.
5. *Hypotheses* are formed by making statements and conclusions through investigations of many materials and forms of similar objects. Ultimately the child determines logical consequences from predetermined clues.

The classroom environment would provide several centers for learning activities related to the six areas in the example. Since young children learn by active manipulation and experience with materials, sufficient range from simple to complex should be provided at each center, so children can find their level of work. Some center activities are:

Center for Patterning—Activities

1. Copy the colored pattern in crayon on a 1 inch x 10 inch grid.
2. Repeat the patterns on the peg borad with colored pegs.
3. Make an original pattern by glueing macaroni on construction paper.
4. Create a pattern through repetition of numerals.
5. Create a pattern on a 2 inch x 24 inch strip of paper by glueing on object (paper) with two properties—such as shape and color.

Center for Comparison—Activities

One of the most difficult skills for a young child to learn is observation of the environment, both patterning and comparison help develop this skill.
1. Children can learn distinctions between or similarities to: size, texture, shape, and color.
2. Compare the growth rate of plants, animals and seedling.
3. Weigh or measure objects and materials for mass length, size, number.
4. Compare degrees of cold or heat.
5. Count objects (beads or small cubes) to determine amount compared to appearance of volume.
6. Compare, match and group or sort objects and materials on the basis of self chosen or designated features (properties).

Center for Classification—Activities

1. Classify by color, shape, structure.
2. Classify by use or other relationship.
3. Classify and arrange in three or more groups by some ascending or descending order.
4. Create multiple categorizations that relate objects by two or more properties.
5. Group by alike and not alike.
6. Group by properties like soft vs. hard, round vs. flat and thin vs. fat.

Center for Prediction—Activities

1. Test the effect of prediction through use of magnets, scales, balances, water and volume measurement.
2. Use charts which inquire as to how many_____ can you pick up in one hand.
3. How many cotton balls fit in jar #1, in jar #2 and in jar #3.
4. Predict how long (length) the sweet potato will grow.

Center for Hypotheses—Activities

1. Make statements and draw conclusions concerning: water, ice, steam, cooking, materials whose shape may be altered, sand, and dry tempera powder.
2. Work with batteries. lights, buzzers and switches.
3. Make statements about salted, spiced and untreated meat products with respect to preservation properties.
4. Investigate the tactile qualities of sticky substances—how can the sticky property be changed?
5. Investigate the effect of heat, flame and cold on various objects or substances.

Based on prior knowledge, the child seeks to test his or her environment, determining the logical consequences of action and thought, (Nevius and Murphy, 1976).

By no means should the above list be considered all-inclusive. It is merely a representative model that may provide some directional clues. Many parents, teachers, and other adults can attest to the success of such measures based upon the child's interaction in his or her natural involvement. Therefore, these proposed activities should not be considered new or radical. In fact, careful observation would indicate that such activities as these are common to all young children, and do indeed generate very productive learning.

From Piaget's (1952) work comes support for the idea that a young child's learning style requires him to experience the environment by sensory motor manipulation and also by actually perceiving what is happening. This is what Piaget (1967) refers to as operating upon the environment to bring about change. The young child views the world in a subjective, egocentric manner; he is not yet fully aware of physical laws of logical consequences. However, he slowly acquires such knowledge when provided experiences that permit him to act on materials and ideas. Preschool children learn many concepts through active involvement with the environment, always generating problems to be solved. Therefore it is crucial for the young child to be involved in experience through which his or her thinking and learning style is given full range of expression. The major concluding point is, that there exists today a body of knowledge supported by research that indicates thinking skills can be taught when the situation exphasizes horizontal transfer.

Adults who work with children should be open and receptive to the learning styles of young people, therefore capitalizing upon the child's motivation to explore, manipulate and discover. Activities that closely parallel a child's natural inclinations toward learning afford the greatest opportunity to maximize his potential for logical thinking. When this maximization occurs early it can help insure higher probability of school success.

REFERENCES

Anastasi, A. *Differential Psychology* (3rd ed.) Macmillan, New York, 1958.

Elkin, David, "Piagentian and Psychometric Conceptions of Intelligence." *Harvard Educational Review*, 39, 1969.

Lavatelli, Celia S., Piaget's Theory Applied to an Early Childhood Curriculum. Boston: Center for Media Development, 1970.

Hebb, D. O., "The Effects of Early Experience on Problem-Solving at Maturity." *American Psychologist*, 2. (Fall 1947), 3-6 308.

Hunt, J. McVicker. *Intelligence and Experience*, New York: Ronald, 1961.

Nevius, J. "Teaching for Logical Thinking is a Prereading Activity" *International Reading Association* (in press).

Nevius, J. and Murphy, J.T. "Individualizing Instruction: Striking the Right Match." *Texas Tech Journal of Education.* (in press)

Nevius, J. and Murphy J.T. "Experience and Transfer: Steps to Cognitive Thinking in Young Children." (manuscript-Texas Tech University). 1976

Piaget, J. *Judgment and Reasoning in the Child*, London: Routledge and Kegan, Letd., 1951.

Piaget, J. *The Origins of Intelligence in Children.* New York: Int. University Press, 1952.

Piaget, J. *Judgment and Reasoning in the Child,* New York: Harcourt, Brace and World, 1928.

Piaget, J. *Six Psychological Studies.* New York: Random House, 1967.

Siegel, I. "The Development of Classificatory Skills in

Young Children: A Training Program." *The Young Child,* Washington, D.C.: NAEYC, 1972.
Wohwill, Joachim. "The Place of Structured Experience in Early Cognitive Development." In Joe L. Frost (Ed.) *Revisiting Early Childhood Education,* New York: Holt, Rinehart and Winston, 1973.

American Federation of Teachers

Chapter 20

Developmental Humanism: A Growth Approach to the Basics

Don W. Rapp*

The search for the basics in Home-School Education in the United States is complicated by our pluralistic, interdependent industrialized world society. This article will highlight a synthesis approach to finding those basics which are common to all education on all developmental levels. The approach is called Developmental Humanism.

Human behavior, like a fever, is only a symptom of other underlying physiological and psychological processes. What we think of as educationally basic is often a quite superficial cultural invention. In my opinion, the three Rs as such have been educationally exaggerated beyond reason. The usual meaning of the "back to basics movement" is pointed minute by minute unrelenting emphasis on "readin', writin', and rithmetic." Agreed, the three Rs are necessary and vital tools to the control and maintenance of our industrialized society. But the three Rs and their preschool readiness counterparts are not necessarily educationally basic. To repeat, they are tools, marvelous ones.

Frederick Froebel (1824) and Marie Montessori (1962), both admired educational innovators, were not great because of his sequential gifts or her systematic use of toys and equipment. These two educators invented new "styles" of looking at children, styles very different from the orthodox ways of the Germany and Italy of their day. Both Froebel and Montessori respected children; they thought of them as persons in their own right; and they related to them as if they were present and not just bodies and minds waiting to become adults. A. Maslow (1962), styled his psychology to do much the same, concentrating on health rather than pathology. C. Roger's (1967), epitomized this when speaking of his counseling relationship as requiring, "genuineness, empathy, and unconditional positive regard." From this positive health orientation, modern humanism was born. Froebel's and Montessori's systems eventually taught the three Rs, but did so with a "style" that generated deeper growth of the more basic parts of man's nature.

Developmental Humanism blends Maslow's human potential view with the time-growth philosophy of Child Development. This chapter will discuss concepts that have come out of both of these traditions. Further, it will attempt to synthesize them into a home-school curriculum that costs nothing to adopt, except an understanding on the part of the child guider that new ways of teaching and parenting are possible and even mandatory.

THREE CHILD DEVELOPMENT CONCEPTS

I. Freedom Within Limits

Structure exists in all that we perceive. Freedom has a structure of a very different sort.

An elementary physical example of the concept of freedom within limits is the bullet and shell placed within the chamber of a gun. The triggered explosion forces the bullet to move in the only way it can go, out the narrowly directed barrel. The bullet has much freedom to go as far and as fast as it will, but it is limited to barrel directional orientation.

Children experience narrow limits at birth. Mothers push hard to birth them, and the baby struggles to "get out" of the limited space. A neonate can't do much. But what they do, they do marvelously. They live, i.e., they demonstrate life as a baby. They know a great deal without ever being taught. Babies seem to have great knowledge within great ignorance, (a paradox, if I ever saw one!!). Babies are free to survive, but only when the limits of their environments are in line with what the babies are programmed to be.

The funny thing about limits, be they limits of the universe or of a parents guidance technique, or a classroom, is that absolutely no one, has ever found all the free usable space for movement under any given limit. There is always room for new reinterpretations and explorations.

All of us abhor limits and fight against them. We should. But, at the same time, we find great joy in the challenge of searching and researching for spaces that are real to us within the limits. Thus, children require teachers and parents as necessary limit makers. And as limit makers, teacher-parents are merely extensions of the universe that is structured, in part, according to this concept.

One of the growth oriented attributes of this concept is that the proper setting of limits encourages the child toward the outward search of testing limits, as well as the inward search of discovering new freedoms within the limits set. As a group of young people during the 60's were told, "I applaud your push of the limits you find and feel, but I will equally applaud your push toward the freedoms that are yet undiscovered within limits of your perception."

*Dr. Don W. Rapp, Associate Professor, Home and Family Life, Florida State University, Tallahassee, Florida 32306.

II. Simple To Complex

On a very superficial level this concept is gentle and true, but it can quickly roll beyond its own complexity.

One cell is simpler than 10,000 cells. Thus, the one cell fusion of the sperm and ovum is simpler than the baby formed nine months later. Fewer is quantitatively simpler than many. With the aid of the electron microscope and other scientific techniques, we find that even that first human cell being has within it the blueprint of all that is to follow. Is the blueprint simpler than the actual building? Yes, because it is just a blueprint and not the finished product. But as far as information is concerned, the blueprint has it all. The one cell has the potential of all the later actual complexities manifested in the baby.

Once the baby is born and growing, we see this even more clearly. For example, placing too many toys in front of a child makes some children tense rather than promoting growthful attention. Children's progressive ability to choose comes from practicing simple choices first. Then, as brain complexity grows, choice making complexity grows. And too much is too much, even for many adults. The nouveaux riches have the same troubles in choice making as the deprived child who experiences for the first time a "rich in toys" nursery school. Practice makes perfect. Thus, parents and teachers are required to construct safe environments where children may exercise their growing abilities.

A good rule of thumb in teaching-parenting: Start with the simple, both qualitatively and quantitatively. In other words, first, calibrate the complexity of the lesson or situation while you simultaneously judge your child's ability to handle complexity. If the situations' complexity level is commensurate with the complexity (developmental) level of the child, let them at each other. The child will learn under these harmonious circumstances.

We are talking not so much about chronological age but about qualitative abilities to learn. Some cultures are childlike, primitive and uncomplicated. And some others are so complex and stressful, that many babies respond to the stress with ulcers before the first year of life. Proper parental application of this concept is predicated on knowing the child's developmental level in relation to the level of simplicity-complexity of the situation.

III. Individualization-Integration

Separateness is a fact, but so is association. Our earth is a separate physical reality in the universe, very different from our moon. There is distinct separateness, but both moon and earth jointly interact through mass attraction, giving rise to a predictable rhythmic system.

At the beginning of our acquaintance, I differentiate myself from you, by simply knowing we occupy different spaces. Then later, I begin to find my attention drawn to this or that about you and you discover my interesting side. We begin to find an integration knowing, enhanced by our differences.

Segregation is perfectly normal and necessary, but integration is also essential. How can children play bat and ball unless the ball and bat are separate in physical reality and function, but at the same time associated in one place at one time? How can separate men and women (individualized anatomy and character) produce children unless they interact through sexual intercourse?

Individuality (difference, uniqueness, separateness) is a structural reality. Integration, (articulation, similarity, association) is also a structural reality. Together, as in Werner's Orthogenic theory of growth states, they foster hierarchial integration, one way to define life.

One inoperative organ in the body will deny life to the total body. One inoperative part of the nervous and/or blood system equally denies life to the total body. The paradox is that both functions, individualization and integration, are simultaneously occuring. Each does its own thing, but both are essential parts of a living system.

This seemingly bipolar, but interacting concept underscores the point of uniqueness as a rule of the universe. There would be no continuation of uniqueness unless two uniques were continually coming together to form new and unique relationships. Galaxy-wide separateness is a fact, but so are dramatic and constant interrelations of every bit of universe with every other bit of universe.

A non-exhaustive synonym-antonym list is given below to assist in the definition of Individualization-Integration.

INDIVIDUALIZATION	INTEGRATION
separation	synthesis
dissociation	melding
operative	co-operation
energetic	synergetic
bifurcation	blending
mix	intermix
divergence	convergence
differentiation	articulation

Children and adults live in separate bodies and worlds. However, through memory, empathy, and knowledge of growth, adults know the necessity of proper care for children's survival and optimum development. Children go to their own world of school; parents live their own lives; then hopefully at supper time, the gathering of the clan allows sharing of facts and feelings, plans, and memories. The separateness of individualized bodies are enhanced by the rhythmic joining, and the integrative interactiveness of the whole of the family life is enhanced by periodic separation.

The interactive growth concept of Individualization-Integration occurs on the individual level as well as on the family and the community level. The universality of this concept is obvious although a seeming paradox. The essential joining of opposites seems to be a large part of what life is. However, paradoxes drop from view when we come to a deeper understanding level.

The author has placed these three growth concepts in one integrative model. First, growth begins as simple and limited. As greater structural complexity develops, great freedoms are made possible. Second, as complexity and freedom become more mature, the individuality and closely related synthesis capability are advanced. And third, each healthy bit of growth adds to the total system, and the growth of the total system fuels the continued growth of each part. The model is three dimensional and dynamic. It has relevence for parenting-teaching, psychotherapy and for self-help growth at any age.

FIVE TENENTS OF THE HUMANISTIC ETHIC

R.J. Bugental's (1971) five Tenents of the Humanistic Ethic are a most succinct short hand description of modern Humanism. I shall attempt to be even more succinct than Bugental in this discussion.

I. Centered Responsibility For One's Own Life

Rollo May (1959) suggests the word "centeredness" to mean each person's ability to demiate the outside forces that enter their life. The word responsibility written response-ability (ability to respond) suggests that it is each of us, in the final analysis, who determines just how we react to outside forces.

There is no one to delegate this responsibility to, because this centeredness is the foci of what we humanly are. Thus, we have choice to abdicate or to use our lives to further our own human potential.

Your life belongs to you, if you believe that it belongs to you. A person who believes this point finds himself capable of creating and sustaining sufficient inner will to make the decisions to take even greater healthful centered responsibility for his own life. There is no end to this growth response-ability process.

Erikson's seventh component of a healthy personality is "generative vs self absorption". Bugental's first tenent of Centered Responsibility for Ones Own Life is very much a generative endeavor. One generation of responsible thought and behavior leads to another generation of quality. This is true on more than one level. Responsibility is its own quality control.

Although we cannot control all that happens to us, we can control how we respond to it. We are, as Bugental writes, the most and often the only "responsible agent" for our own lives. Admit it and, immediately, you are in greater control.

II. Mutuality of Relationship

This tenent is the center of Buber's (1953) I-thou relationship. It is one of reciprocal interdependence. No one member of the relationship is owned by another. No double standard exists. The focus is more on the relationship than on the individuals. Although the individuals do retain their healthful and rightful autonomy, they are connected with the other in an attachment of mutual concern. Neither person becomes an object to be manipulated by the other. Relationship authenticity is the prime goal.

Teachers with two year olds exhibit this type of relationship, first by getting on the eye level of the children. But this is only superficial physical mutuality. Teachers must deeply know that the similarities between them and the children are more important to their mutual growth than their differences. The basics of humanity are present in all people. To relate to this humanity in a two year old is difficult for many adults, but when it happens it is mutually rewarding.

III. Here and Now Perspective

The concept of time in this perspective is moment by moment, rather than linear. There seems to be only one time, *now*, with a mute but influencial past and an unknown but projectionable future. People who live in this perspective are valued for their presence not their presents. They are valued for what they are and not what they have been or will be. However it should be added that what you were and what you presently are will influence what you become. But the most important of these is your presence here, right now.

The word *play* is vital to this concept and to Early Childhood Education. Young children learn greatly when allowed to play. In free play they can attend for long spans of time and foxus with remarkable concentration. Their flighty behavior is most evident when they perform to the distates of others. The here and now perspective is enhanced by teachers who consider equipment and schedules as secondary to the child's practice of being fully present and accountable within their own bodies and minds. Teachers must become a "Helpful Let Be" as Maslow (1962) defines his ultimate teacher.

A bumper sticker once said, PLAY SCHOOL AND LEARN. Paraphrased, your full mind-body presence is required for full learning; play-practice will move you to that important place in the here and now.

IV. Acceptance of the Non-Hedonic Emotions

Simply, this means acceptance of our own humanity. The Non-Hedonic emotions of anger, fear, conflict, grief, guilt, pain, and so on, are often treated as "Unfortunate defects" in our human characters. But they are real, and when accepted as real, we better know ourselves and our kind.

Our culture strongly surpresses the so called negative emotions. We tell boys it's unmanly to cry, or we say love your neighbor when your neighbor is unlovable, and we elevate optimists over the pessimists who rightfully may have data for our general concern. Be helpful and supporting in times of emotional stress, but let reality be recognized.

Children must understand that pain is a normal part of skinned knees, and that grief is OK when a friend leaves school, never to be seen again. Our constitution says we may pursue happiness. It does not promise it. We might also allow the pursuit of the understanding of pain or fear. Repression of pain takes more energy than feeling the pain. General acceptance of the Non-Hedonic emotions would greatly heighten human functioning.

V. Growth Oriented Experimenting

This fifth tenent of the Humanistic ethic is an honest and intimate desire to become the best possible person within the time constraints of one's life. It suggests that human potential is always greater than any one now sees. Inherent in this tenent is the willingness to risk the effort of learning, to risk the fear of the unknown, to risk social ridicule against a searching attitude, and to risk failure.

Children do this all the time, naturally. They seek out the sound and emotion of ugly words and see how others respond; they discover how muddy they can get. Simply, they test limits. They purposely place themselves, mentally and physically, socially and emotionally, in positions to learn. Children are learning when they respond to new sensations and situations and when the outside world responds to them. Those few children who fully retain this growth orientation into adult life, are the discoverers of newness where others only see the orthodox. Growth oriented experiencing is a way to vibrant awareness of all perceived reality.

DEVELOPMENTAL HUMANISTIC CURRICULUM CRITERIA AND FIVE AREAS OF EMPHASIS

Good curriculums primarily stem from good human beings who fully interact as the result of their growth orientation. These teachers promote lifelong continued growth in their own lives wich directly sustain and rejuvenate immediate and continued life-long growth in children.

Acquisition of facts, concepts, and skills are learning-growing fuel. To learn is to grow; to grow is to learn. Developmental Humanism suggests that learning to read is an aftermath of a body-mind attitude that is willing and able to handle the complexity which reading demands.

Without this willingness and ableness, nothing. You can't get blood from a turnip!!

So then what are basics to education and parenting. Following are eight priority suggesting statements that flow out of the three Child Development concepts and the five tenents of the Humanistic Ethic.

1. Learning how to learn by learning is more properly stimulating than learning how others learn. Learning about others can't hurt, unless you believe them to be your boss.

2. People related matters are more important to learning how to learn than thing related matters.

3. Reality is more exciting than vicarious talking about reality or viewing of shadows, even in color.

4. Full sense involvement heightens learning more than concentration on just one or two senses.

5. Child oriented *doing* is more productive than adult imposed or even self imposed paper assignments. Although paper is OK when you have momentarily run out of your own things to do.

6. Discovery of self is more enriching in the long run than discovery of and adherance to cultural authority.

7. Playing and coordinating with peers demonstrates more humanity than individualized instruction, which might be critized as education for the hermit.

8. A trial and error classroom climate allows more creative learning possibilities than one working for first run-through perfection.

Please quickly recognize that whatever is educationally done well in today's schools, could be continued in this self-concept oriented curriculum. Self-concept could be studied through anatomy, through parents' occupations, through historical events, through language interpretations, ad infinitum. The three Rs would not be left out. However, there would be five elements added and infused into the minute by minute classroom action. These five elements are: 1. Patience, 2. Empathy, 3. Decision Making, 4. Curiosity-Experimentation, 5. Acceptance of feelings as human.

I. Patience-Impatience

I was a long time into my college teaching before I realized that the concept of growth and development was essentially a time concept. It takes time to grow bigger; it takes time to develop from the simple to the complex; it takes time to progress from the rudimentary state to human consciousness. Without the understanding of the time-body time, astronomic time, atomic time, philogenetic time, emotional time, biological time, and man-made watch time, a person is imprisoned in any one or all of the historic myths of time. Time is pervasive in the universe. The understanding of patience is one way to grow more at home in a time pervasive universe.

It takes time to become. Nothing grows in an instant. Like the phrase, "come and go" or "ebb and flow", time is really a verb. Time is an essential part of man, thus man is a verb (as R.B. Fuller (1970) has often said). Man is in process, man is ongoing. And that takes time. Even light is finite, precisely 186,000 miles per second. Evolution is a time concept. Because of our brief time perspective, about 70 years, man sees infinite time boxed in a finite frame. The essential building principle of the universe is time. We must learn all we can about it and its earthly human representative which is patience.

Patience has to do with timing, and timing is rhythm, which is the understanding of proper sequencing. Patience is basic to tasks which require time to learn what to do first and then doing the right thing next, etc. Also timing has to do with knowing how much time is needed between each doing. And this is patience; the waiting between a doing. Patience is the opposite of impatience. In this curriculum proper impatience would also be taught by plan. It is culturally correct to be impatient, under certain conditions; and it is also correct to be patient, when that is right. Children would very soon begin to ask, "How do we know when to be patient or impatient?" And there is the question that begs to open the door of wisdom. To know when to do or when not to do....is wisdom. And very practically, (and a little sarcastically) with patience as part of a curriculum, children would, at least, know a reason why they are made to wait in lines.

II. Empathy

Empathy is cognitive; we need to know facts and perceptions. Empathy is social; we need other people to empathize with. Empathy is emotional; we need to know and feel on a deep affective level. And empathy is physical; we need our bodies and sensitive minds to empathize with other body-mind sensitivities. Empathy is full perceptions. By helping others become more empathetic, we spread human learning around like light from well placed mirrors.

Hilda Taba spoke of empathy with the phrase "discentric action."* She wished to convey the reverse of egocentricity. Empathy is getting outside one's self and becoming (more than learning), the perception of another. Each person is a point of view. The more points of view we become, the broader we are. As viewpoints multiply, we grow as a human brush stroke, we flow to form a picture of something more than just ourselves. And in the growth process we never lose our original viewpoint, for it is still intact, reminding us of what we were.

III. Decision Making

At some point, each self has to decide it is a self and that others also have selves. Continual progression toward full humanness is the result of an extraordinary decision.

Decision making is one of the most complex behaviors that we are asked to perform as human beings. Seemingly, it takes billions of "lessons" to become a decision maker who can vote intelligently or run a business properly, or, on the four year old level, pick strawberry over vanilla.

Decisions have to be made at two years of age on a two year old level, then at three at a three year old level, etc. Home practice must be managed by parents who have made the decision to permit, encourage, and plan for their child to become a good decision maker. They must allow the maximum practice possible. Of course, this takes parents and later teachers who are often willing to shut their mouths and allow their children to learn through their own decisions. This kind of home and school is very different from the setting that does all the thinking for the child.

A little poem by Petre Hein says:

> The noble art of losing face
> May some times save the human race.
> And turn into eternal grace
> What weaker minds would call disgrace.

One does not learn this kind of wisdom in a minute. This type of decision making takes patience with self and others; it takes an empathetic knowing of more than one viewpoint; and it takes a decision to work for the greater good.

Like the practice of medicine, decision making is always in the state of revision and perfection. To give up the practice is defacto suicide, both personal and group.

IV. Curiosity-Experimentation

A major life sustaining trait is curiosity. Babies and young children learn more per minute than the usual less healthy adult. Over the years, scientists have invented sequential steps to make discovery more likely. But without the basic child-like curiosity, no one would bother learning any experimental method for future knowing.

True genius is found where a person has retained the basic elements of curiosity bubbling forth in spontaneity, zest, flexibility, and vivaciousness, all well integrated with the hard nosed experimental techniques, the analytical mind, the compulsion of preparation and a dogged ability to verify beyond doubt.

Imagination exercises would be part of this curriculum, but it would never omit the tried and true tools that connect the student to academic knowledge. Curiosity-Experimentation channels the energies of want and desire into action. I see Curiosity-Experimentation as a two-headed tool working as a unit through man for his survival.

V. Acceptance of Feelings as Human

Human feelings have been long ignored, feared, and repressed. These actions are often taken because human feelings are known to many as "ugly". And the only reason they are called ugly is that they are not accepted as human.

Acceptance of all human feelings allows and even promotes the full humanness, which is Maslow's other term for self actualization. Acceptance of self, as an element of self concept, is vital to the changing of self behaviors. Full perception of self is only possible when acceptance of self is full.

Dreams are often laden with emotions you don't want to acknowledge. Your bad, immoral, frightening, disheartening, murderous, disparing, sinful dreams are the product of no one else but you; just as your human, loving, helping, fostering, generous, altruistic dreams are also personal products. They are parts of the self popping through the screen between no man's land and consciousness. Acceptance of self, even of those "naughty" dreams, makes dreaming ever more imaginative and more enjoyable to "witness". And interestingly enough, accepting the reality of this total array of feelings is a true source of energy. Acceptance of reality turns fear to understanding.

Feelings are powerful happenings. Often good feelings overwhelm us, and we say nothing good can come from feeling *that* good. So we "cool it" by not feeling the true goodness of our feelings. And the bad feelings really make us miserable because we have bought the myth that says nothing should ever be *that* bad. So most of us become middle of the road, not making waves, being monotone personalities. To accept ourselves as having a full range of ups and downs in many emotional dimensions is common sense, which is far too uncommon.

The human mind is designed for learning. It takes real effort to stop it, but stop it we do with inaccurately calibrated programs and inane parenting and teaching.

Children living this developmentally humanistic curriculum with growing accepting adults would surely better see more of life and feel their own dynamic self-forces within it. Good parenting-teaching stresses these five elements today. But too infrequently. More parents and teachers

must be motivated toward the demonstration of a full life and have a dedication to healthful growth.

Developmental Humanism is a synthesis approach toward a future of positive growth and development. Developmental Humanism* is time oriented, gentle, and a very human course for pre-service and in-service teacher education. It insists that parents take proper responsibility for their children as family-community members.

REFERENCES

Baldwin, Alfred L. "Heinz Werner's Theory of Child Development". *Theories of Child Development,* New York: John Wiley & Sons, Inc., 1967.

Buber, Martin. *I and Thou,* Edinburg, T&T Clark, 1953.

Bugental, James F. T. "The Humanistic Ethic-The Individual In Psycholotherapy As A Societal Change Agent". *The Journal of Humanistic Psychology,* San Francisco: Association for Humanistic Psychology, 1971.

Erickson, Erik. *Childhood and Society,* New York: Norton, 1963.

Froebel, Frederick. *The Education of Man,* Appleton & Comp., 1903.

Fuller, Buckminster, *I Seem To Be A Verb.* New York, Bantam Books, 1970.

May, R. Toward the Ontological Basis of Psychotherapy. *Existential Inquiries,* 1959, 1 (1), 5-7.

Maslow, Abraham. *Toward a Psychology of Being,* Princeton, N.J., Van Nostrand, 1962.

Rapp, Don W. *The Developmental Nature of Self-Concept,* Bureau of Educational Research, University of Southern Mississippi, Harriesburg, Miss., 1974.

Rogers, Carl R.; & Stevens, Barry. *Person to Person: The Problem of Being Human.* Lafayette, California, Real People Press, 1967.

Standing, E. M. *Maria Montessori–Her Life and Work.* New York: New American Library of World Literature, Inc., 1962.

Section III

Learning Environments

Introduction by Antonio Bilbao*

Experimentation has been the significant ingredient in early childhood education for more than a decade. The consequence of this period of experimentation, however, has not been the formulation of a new, innovative, integrated curriculum upon which to evolve a comprehensive early childhood program. Instead, the product of experimentation has been the promotion of further experimentation. Thus, the field of early childhood education exists in a state of "limbo" as if waiting for an external force to cause a coming together into a structured plan.

The major sources of a majority of these experiments relate to varied forms of activity-oriented approaches to learning. These methods are a drastic diversion from the traditional techniques of the past. This traditional curriculum followed a pattern which had pupils at desks with a textbook-instructional approach centered around the teacher. This method utilized varied types of educational materials, but with a concept of teacher-directed status. The curriculum had built, over a period of several decades, within the program structure time schedules that enabled activity experiences. However, these usually related to physical and humanity activities which emphasized recreational goals rather than learning objectives. In fact, the entire thrust of activity, in terms of the curriculum of early childhood education in traditional systems, was significantly integrated with recreation and had almost no relation to learning in the academic skills area.

The past decade has lead to a conversion of this idea to the point where activity-orientated programs are specifically related to learning in the academic levels and the term recreation has become less significant in the curriculum. This process of activity-orientated learning has evolved from the creation of materials that have the child learn by being involved in the completion of a task under the instruction and demonstration of the teacher. These tasks when formulated in a planned structure, which is sequential, become a cohesive program for the learning of a specific area. This task approach to learning has progressed from traditional type materials to the more sophisticated multi-media structured, educational materials. With the advent of instructional mechanical materials, which provide individual and small group instruction under the direction of the teacher, activity-oriented learning programs have expanded to change the structure of the classroom. These changes first began as activity centers within the traditional classroom and then progressed to independent learning centers which were used in small group instruction situations. This finally led to the development of the open classroom concept which is a classroom designed for a complete activity-orientated learning program.

The direction toward activity-orientated learning programs have evolved through the process of experimentation without the conformity to one specific plan. Consequently, educators have as many forms of these programs as their inventive capacities permit. Thus, controversy as to method, purpose and results has developed throughout the educational community. The end product of these endeavors has been that more questions than answers have been formulated as to the direction and merit of our early childhood eudcational programs. A definitive evaluation of these new approaches has not emerged because experimentation has developed as an end in itself. All too, often, then, early childhood programs exist in our schools that are as varied as the personalities of the children which they are teaching.

It is hoped that the following articles will shed some insights into the problems confronting the current status of our early childhood education programs, and that from this confused present a comprehensive structured future will evolve.

*Antonio V. Bilbao, Principal, New York City, New York.

Chapter 21

Helping Young Children to Cope with School

Josephine S. Gemake and Teresa A. Trimarco*

In this chapter is discussed the problems of a young child's adjustment to the school environment. After a presentation of the fundamentals of this question, a number of specific techniques are considered which a teacher might employ to help a child make a smooth and pleasant transition to the "world of the school" from that of the home.

When young children enter school, they begin formal participation in the larger aspect of society. Many children approach school with excitement, aroused by the challenge of learning, and the expectation of spending work and playtime with peers. Others approach school with fear, apprehension about separation from parents and uncertainty about interaction with strangers. However, all children expect to succeed. No child enters school with the intention of failing.

Young children are very special people. Between birth and age six, physical, intellectual, social, and emotional gains are rapid, significant, and irregular. Children at this time are developing large and fine muscles, and gaining mastery over their bodies. More than half of their measurable intelligence develops. They have in their speech repertory the basic phonetic, syntactic and semantic constructions that they will use throughout their adult life.

They are learning to relate emotionally to persons outside their families, and through these interactions, are developing concepts of right and wrong behavior. A child of five may have the verbal ability of a six year old, the motor coordination of a four year old, and the emotional stability of a three year old. It is the task of the teacher to recognize these commonalities of development among children and identify those unique and specific patterns of development peculiar to each individual. Children who are recognized as individuals, and who receive instruction and support on their levels will cope positively with learning, and begin a successful school experience.

The problem of helping the child to cope with the school situation begins with parent information and involvement. Parents do not surrender their rights when they enroll their child in a school. It is up to the school to clarify the roles that teacher and mother play in the development of the child. Parents of children entering school should be invited to an orientation meeting. At this time, objectives and curriculum should be discussed without jargon. Parents should know what will be taught in each subject area so that they can support learning goals. If any new methods of instruction are to be implemented, these should be demonstrated, and the reasons for the innovations should be presented. When the parent enters the school, the physical aspect of the classrooms should be designed to display the work of the children and reflect the daily routines of the classroom. At this orientation meeting, the teacher must actively involve the parent in the child's world of work. Parents should be divided into small groups, and instructed and encouraged to paint a picture, accompany a tune with rhythm instruments, solve a work job, build a city of the future with blocks, or create a clay sculpture. By accomplishing the tasks of childhood, parents gain an insight into the development of the skills of childhood. Parents as well as children learn by doing, and build an understanding of the problems with which children must cope in learning.

Many teachers enter communities where problems in communication may arise because of differences in ethnic and cultural backgrounds, and educational and socioeconomic levels. Stereotypes will exist among the attitudes of teachers and poverty parents. The teacher comes from a middle-class background which may be alien to the poverty parent. The poverty parent may represent the negative aspects of society to the teacher. Not all teachers can overcome a prejudiced and frequently fearful view of a different culture. There is no novelty, spontaneity, freedom or redeeming quality in the child who represents an alternative approach to study, routine, and discipline. These teachers have problems coping, and can do very little to assist the child to cope. Teachers must make an honest appraisal of their prejudices and tolerances, and decide if a teaching situation in a poverty area will be challenging and comfortable for them, and be a positive educational experience for the children.

In order to ease the transition from home to school, it is vital that teachers plan, in detail, their first few weeks of

*Dr. Josephine S. Gemake, Assistant Professor, Division of Education, St. John's University, Staten Island Campus.

Dr. Teresa A. Trimarco, Acting Chairperson, Division of Education, St. John's University, Staten Island Campus.

school. Lessons should be short and interesting, and involve the children in manipulation and movement. Routines must be established with the children. An explanation for a routine gives the child a reason for cooperation. Rules for behavior should be generated and explained at a class meeting. The child must verbalize the purpose for compliance. Once the child understands the expected behavior, the teacher can correct misbehavior simply by asking, "Why must we listen now?" At this age, demands for routines and standards of behavior may conflict with the egocentric drive present in young children. If the child has participated in making the routines and rules, and has defined the purpose for the routines and rules, the child will better be able to cope with the necessary demands made by the teacher for order.

Contracts are a simple technique which can be used to help children cope with their responsibilities toward work and behavior. The contract becomes a language experience. Each child can develop an individual contract to accomplish a simple task. Cookies, candies, toys, tokens, or playtime can be used as a reward and reinforce for the completion of the task.

In order to enable children to cope with the curriculum, the first activities in learning should enlarge upon everyday experiences. (Rogers, Vin, 1976).

An attempt should be made to help children view familiar ideas and materials in new and different ways. Most children know that a dead flower is thrown away. Few will know that the dead flower represents seed development, and that these seeds can be gathered and planted. Most children recognize a rock. However, a novel approach to these familiar items can be developed through a work job that asks children to classify them into big or little, flat or round, or shiny or dull. The teacher should be on the alert for experiences with familiar materials which will help children to develop a spirit of inquiry toward their environment.

Children respond to models. Literature can provide examples of models who have coped successfully with problems and challenges. Recently, Bettleheim (1976) evaluated the worth of fairy tales. He feels that the child in modern society no longer grows within the security of the extended family or of a well-integrated community. The modern child needs images of heroes who have gone out into the world and secured places by following the right way with deep inner conviction and confidence. Fairy tales communicate the idea that struggle in life is unavoidable, that one can meet hardships, master obstacles, and emerge victorious. The mystery, action, and romance of fairy tales have made them favorites of children for centuries. That these marvelous pieces of literature can

be used to provide coping models is another reason for their inclusion in the curriculum.

Older children provide another available resource to the teacher who is interested in helping the child to cope. The older child provides a model for the younger child, and in the course of working with the younger child for a period of time, becomes friend and partner as an affectionate relationship develops. Older children experience a sense of being needed, and generally show responsibility in attending to their young charges. In addition to the support provided by this interaction, the teacher is freed so that individual attention can be given to that special child who requires an extra measure of help and direction.

The degree of difficulty experienced by a child just entering a new school situation will, of course, vary with the youngster. However, a basic core of common problems will, in general, exist. We feel that teacher awareness of the hurdles to be expected and the use of appropriate methods such as those discussed, can go a long way toward helping children to cope with their new situation.

BIBLIOGRAPHY

I.   Books

Bettleheim, Bruno, *The Uses of Enchantment: The Meaning and Importance of Fairy Tales.* Alfred A. Knopf., Inc. 1976

Winnicott, D.W. *The Child, the Family and the Outside World.* England: Penguin Books, 1964. pp. 189–198.

II.   Journal

Coleman, James S. "Methods and Results in the IEA Studies of Effects of School on Learning." *Review of Educational Research,* Summer 1975, Vol. 45, No. 3, pp. 355–386.

Rogers, V., *Instructor,* "Crank up your Curriculum", Aug.-Sept., 1976.

III.   Magazines

Kiester, Edwin Jr. "School Discipline." *Better Homes and Gardens,* September 1976, p. 8.

Needham, Dorothy. "The Learning Connection: Teacher, Student Teacher, Child." *Teacher,* September 1976, pp. 80–83.

Rasmussen, Margaret. "Mr. Gibbons must be doing something right." *Instructor,* August-September 1976, p. 42.

IV.   Newspaper

Flaste, Richard. "Sad Songs of a Child's Private World." *New York Times,* Tuesday, August 31, 1976, p. 22.

Chapter 22

Learning Centers in the Early Childhood Classroom

Mary Elizabeth York*

A practice which has been traditional in nursery schools, is often found in kindergartens, and seldom seen in primary classrooms is that of providing centers in which the children may choose to participate. These centers are variously called interest centers, activity centers, or learning centers. I prefer to call them learning centers, for while these centers are designed to appeal to children's interest and to elicit their active involvement, it is in these centers that learning occurs.

Piaget (1973) tells us that knowledge is built through a process of assimilation and accomodation. This process of acquiring knowledge occurs as the result of (1) physical action upon materials or involvement with others, (2) logical-mathematical reasoning, (3) social contacts whereby one acquires verbal knowledge from others, and (4) equilibration which is a self-regulator similar to homeostasis.(pp. 71-93). It is through equilibration that a new experience encountered by the child is either rejected as too discrepant from what he already knows or is fitted into his mental structures (assimilated and accomodated) thus becoming part of his body of knowledge. If we consider that the acquiring of new knowledge is an individual experience which takes time and occurs through the four means outlined above, then the real learning takes place as the child is actively engaged in the teaching-learning process. And this may well be when he has chosen an activity and is engaged in it independently of the teacher.

A learning center, then, is a clearly defined area of the classroom containing materials selected by the teacher to facilitate the teaching-learning process in which a small group of children, generally from one to six in number may work independently.

Learning Centers as Part of Classroom Structure

Classroom structure is the result of the amount and type of planning by the teacher for what is to happen in the classroom. It is erroneous to talk about "structured" and "unstructured" classrooms for all classrooms have structure. The question is the amount and type of the structure, for the structure of the classroom affects the learning and behavior of the children.

In classroom structure, there are two forces: dynamic and static. Dynamic forces include all the social aspects of the classroom: grouping, interaction between peers, interaction between teacher and children, means used to establish discipline, scheduling, and techniques of guidance. The static forces include the inanimate aspects of the classroom: space, furniture, materials, and the ways these are arranged.

If the teacher recognizes the power of these two forces and plans so that these forces work together, the probability of children's meeting expectations is much greater; If, for example, the teacher expects children to work independently with materials and put them away when finished, then the materials must be readily accessible to the chidren and the shelf and containers where they belong clearly marked. If only three children are to be in a center at once, only three chairs and three sets of materials should be provided. If children are expected to walk, not run, in the classroom, then space must be so broken up that there are no long empty spaces which invite running. If tools are to be used safely, the appropriate way to use them must be demonstrated, and the workbench of such size that children can easily use them in recommended ways. It is also important that there be continuing guidance and follow-through, but this will be discussed later.

Setting Up Learning Centers

What centers shall be included and what materials shall be placed in those centers? The reader is referred to the end of this article for suggestions, but to answer this question, one must consider the goals of the program, the number, ages, abilities, and interests of the children, and the size and shape of the room.

The goals of the program will determine priorities for the inclusion or exclusion of specific learning centers.If

*Dr. Mary Elizabeth York, Assistant Professor of Education, Co-ordinator of Early Childhood Studies.

program goals put a high emphasis on academic skills, then language, mathematics, and science centers receive top priority. If social skills are highly prized, then dramatic play, building and construction which require cooperation, and projects which require team-work would have high priority.

In planning learning centers, the number of children in the class, the size of the room, and the length of time children will be there should be considered together for these factors have interactive effects.

In a small room with a fairly large number of children, there will need to be enough centers and materials provided that all children may be kept busy but not so much that children are falling over each other and the materials. If it is a long day, more choices will need to be provided than if there is a short day. Remembering that we need to consider these aspects in an interactive way, let us consider each one separately.

When there are fewer children in a class, the centers may be fewer in number but will need to be changed frequently as the children appear to lose interest and are ready for new experiences. For a large class, more centers will need to be provided, but change may not need to be as frequent since not every child will have had an opportunity to work in each center as often.

The number of centers depends to a large degree on the physical characteristics of the room in which the class is held-size, shape, location of doors, built-in furniture, and windows. In a small room or one in which doors, built-ins, and windows take up much space, one should avoid a too-crowded, cluttered appearance and choose a few well-equipped centers, changing materials as interest wanes. A crowded, cluttered room with many attractions tends to be confusing and overly-stimulating and may result in unde-sirable behavior.

The length of the school day needs to be considered, for a longer time in school means more opportunity to choose more different kinds of activity.

The age, abilities and interests of children will determine not only the centers to be set up but also the materials to be placed in the center. A language center which includes writing materials, tape recorders, and alphabet letters would be inappropriate for most groups of three-year-olds, for example. Not that they do not need to develop language skills, but that for this age group, skills related to language are more appropriately developed in dramatic play centers where they will engage in conversation, manipulative mater-ial centers where they will practice perceptual-motor skills, and the art centers where they will learn to handle imple-ments similar to writing materials. Looking at picture books and having an adult read to them leads to the three-year-olds appreciation of books also.

On the other hand, a dramatic play area which includes toy housekeeping materials and dolls, may well be inappro-priate for seven-to-eight-year-olds who are ready for real cooking experiences and are beginning to grow out of doll play. Setting up a store which involves buying and selling, making change, communicative skills, and recording trans-actions would be appropriate for these older young child-ren.

In planning the placement of the centers, traffic pat-terns, proximity to needed sources of water, light, and elec-tricity, interference between activities in adjoining centers, and aesthetic appeal need to be considered. Art activities, particularly painting and papier-mache, require water and should be located near a source of water. Science activities, particularly those involving growing plants and prisms need to be next to the windows for the sunlight. A car-pentry center placed next to a reading or other center where quiet concentration is expected would tend to destroy the atmosphere of quiet. A block area located in the pathway to toilet facilities would result in block struc-tures accidentally knocked over by children on their way to the bathroom.

Over and above these practical considerations is that of aesthetic appeal. The centers should be attractive in the literal sense of the word; that is, children should be drawn to them both by nature of the materials in the center and the way they are arranged. In effect, the center should, by its appearance, say to the child, "Come, play, explore, dis-cover!" Each center should provide a variety of related materials displayed in a manner which is neither cluttered nor barren. The materials should provide a range of difficul-ty from those which are simple enough for the youngest child to use successfully to those complex enough to challenge the most mature.

Guiding The Teaching-Learning Process

The use of learning centers in the educative program is at one and the same time an easier and a more difficult way of teaching. It is easier because children become more self-directive, self-sufficient, and more interested in learning. The teacher, then, finds that less time need be spend in telling children to be quiet and pay attention. It is more difficult because it requires the teacher to be aware of what each child is doing in order to insure that the child makes progress in each area of learning deemed important. It also requires the teacher to be creative and analytical. "Going by the book" is simply not part of this kind of teaching.

The following diagram may be helpful in understanding the teacher's role in this style of teaching.

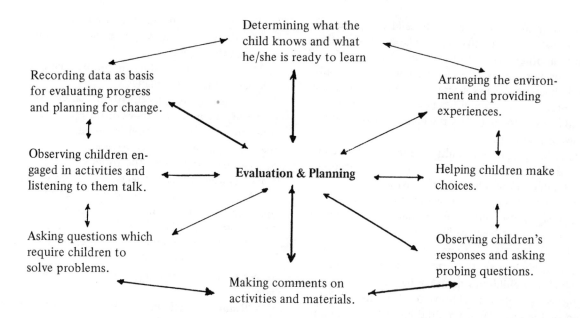

Determining what the child knows and what he/she is ready to learn

Recording data as basis for evaluating progress and planning for change.

Arranging the environment and providing experiences.

Observing children engaged in activities and listening to them talk.

Evaluation & Planning

Helping children make choices.

Asking questions which require children to solve problems.

Observing children's responses and asking probing questions.

Making comments on activities and materials.

There is no one place where a teacher should start on this circle nor does any one of the activities suggested necessarily follow or precede any other activity. The successful teacher is constantly doing any or all of these.

Centers are set up originally based on what the teacher expects children of the age of the class to know and to be able to do. When they arrive, they are introduced to the centers and to the procedures of the classroom. Then they are allowed to choose the center in which they wish to work. Once children are active in the centers, the role of the teacher becomes one of the keen observer who listens, watches, and learns about the abilities and interests of the children.

The teacher intervenes when a child is having a difficult time making a choice, when a child is interfering with another child's activity and that child cannot deal with the intruder, when it appears that a child needs encouragement or a suggestion for using materials in a different way, when a careful question will help a child discover a new concept, or when the child appears to be ready to verbalize what has been learned.

Through this process of listening, watching, and questioning, the teacher ascertains what new materials should be added and what materials have grown stale and should be put away.

A record-keeping system will be needed to insure that each child has a well-rounded learning experience and progresses at a reasonable rate.

Evaluating Learning

It has been shown that when goals and objectives are clearly stated, children's learning is increased. (Weikart,

1970). The successful teacher using a learning center approach has broad general goals which usually reflect a minimum standard which she expects all, or nearly all, children to reach. For example, a kindergarten teacher may expect that by the end of the year the children will be able to count objects up to ten, initiate and complete a project without assistance, recognize and name the letters of the alphabet and so forth.

For individuals in her class she has specific goals related to their own needs and abilities. Overly dependent Suzy can count twenty objects with ease. For her is the goal of initiating and completing a project without the need for frequent approval. Socially skilled Sam has difficulty counting past five. For him the goal is to extend his numerical ability.

What means can be utilized to insure these multiple goals are reached? There are two parts to this question. The first is "how can one be sure that each child participated in goal-related activities?" and the second is "how can one be sure that satisfactory progress is being made?"

The centers having been set up so that they provide activities which are related to the goals of the class, it is important to see that children do not avoid some centers and spend excessive amounts of time in others. Each teacher will need to devise a method with which he/she feels comfortable. Some suggestions follow.

One teacher allows children to choose freely at the first of the year and then introduces a double laminated tagboard wheel. On the inside wheel are pictured the various centers in pie-shaped wedges. On the outside wheel, extending about an inch and a half beyond the edge of the inside wheel, are clothespins in groups of three on which are printed the children's names. Each day the clothespin wheel is turned so that the names of three children appear opposite a different section of the learning wheel. Each child is expected to start in the assigned center and complete one project, after which she/he may trade places with another child or go to another center if there is room.

Another teacher allows free choice, but makes a daily record on a checklist she has devised of which children are in which centers. When a center has been avoided for a long time, she takes steps to encourage the child to participate in the activities of that center.

For evaluating progress, a multiple approach is recommended. This consists of checklists of objectives, anecdotal records, and dated samples of children's work.

Another teacher asks children, as they meet together for a planning session, to choose a center and directs them to centers which may have been avoided.

A checklist of objectives may be devised. There may be a checklist for each child or the teacher may prefer a large chart on which the children's names appear across the top and the objectives written in abbreviated form listed in the left column of the chart. When a child has achieved an objective, the date is written opposite that objective. Knowledge of this achievement may come either through observation of the child or through a one-to-one test situation set up by the teacher.

Specific goals for individuals might not appear on the checklist described above or the teacher might want to record intermediary progress toward an objective. An anecdotal record is useful in these cases. For example, the teacher overhears Suzy ask Sam for eight blocks and observes that Sam counted out and handed her precisely eight blocks. She makes an abbreviated note of the event and later records for Suzy that she had started a block structure without prompting and, without approaching the teacher, asked Sam for needed blocks. She dates this recorded event and then turns to Sam's folder and records that he accurately counted out eight blocks, a stepping stone on the way to counting ten objects.

Gathering and keeping samples of children's work graphically illustrates progress which has been made. From time to time, children's drawing and written work may be collected, dated, and put into a folder. For three-dimensional structures—blocks, sculpture, or carpentry—polaroid pictures could be taken and filed. This helps the child evaluate his own progress and is invaluable in parent conferences.

Older children should be encouraged to keep records of their own work and to select samples of their work for their files.

GUIDELINES FOR LEARNING CENTERS

(A Summary)

1. Centers and materials to be used in centers should be selected on the basis of class goals and objectives; number, ages, abilities, and interests of children; physical characteristics of the classroom, and the length of day.

2. In each center there should be a variety of materials in-

cluding those which are simple enough to be successfully accomplished by the youngest and complex enough to challenge the oldest.

3. Materials in the centers should be changed as children's abilities and interests change.

4. In planning the placement of centers, traffic patterns, proximity to needed sources of water, light, and electricity, interference between activities in adjacent centers and aesthetic appeal need to be considered.

5. Inanimate aspects of the room will affect children's behavior as well as social aspects.

- Materials are more apt to be put away if storage places are clearly marked and teachers remind children before they leave the center.

- The desired number of children in any one center is more easily maintained if the furnishings and materials provided are the same in number as that which the teacher announces.

- Running is eliminated when spaces which invite running are eliminated.

- Climbing on furniture is eliminated when children can see and obtain materials without climbing.

- Children will be more deeply involved in activities when there is not interference from adjacent centers or traffic.

- Children will choose activities when materials are well-displayed and the way they are to be used apparent.

6. When children are engaged in activities, the active roles of the teacher continues.

- The teacher is a keen observer, listening and watching for behaviors which indicate the abilities and interests of children.

- The teacher is a guide, asking children questions and making suggestions which will further their learning.

- The teacher is an evaluator, checking completed work and watching for evidence of concepts or skills learned.

- The teacher is a mediator, helping children to settle disputes.

- The teacher is an encourager, commenting appreciatively on children's work.

- The teacher is a planner and provisioner, deciding on new materials to be added and old ones to be retired.

7. Evaluating learning includes insuring that each child participates in a wide variety of activities and ascertaining when goals and objectives have been reached.

- A system for checking on individuals' participation in the various centers should be devised.

- A checklist of objectives and dates when they are achieved by a child may be used to record progress.

- An anecdotal record of behavioral events which indicate progress toward objectives may be used to record progress.

- Samples of children's work, dated, and filed illustrates progress to the children themselves and their parents as well as to the teacher.

Suggested Centers

Center	Variations	Materials	Possible learning or benefits
Dramatic Play	Housekeeping	dolls, doll furniture, dress-up clothes, dishes, cutlery, cleaning implements, telephone. Add food, flowers, etc. as play develops.	Self-expression, language for communication, social roles, one-to-one correspondence, belonging identity.
	Store	play money, shelves, empty cans and cartons, purses, hats	Names of coins, one-to-one correspondence, buying and selling, social exchange, language.
	Doctor's office or clinic	uniforms, play thermometer, stethoscope, flashlight, spoons, used pill boxes, sugar pills, or M & M's, throw-away syringes (minus the needles), bandages.	Reduction of fear of doctors, social roles, health care. Language for communication.
	Post office	Play money, used stamps and envelopes, paper and pencils, scales, caps.	Transporting messages, buying and selling, communication forms (symbols).
	Restaurant	tables and chairs, cutlery, dishes, aprons, paper napkins, simple foods (apples, crackers, lemonade), play money.	Social exchange, language for communication, one-to-one correspondence, self-expression.
	Puppets	stage hand puppets.	Self-expression, language, sequence.
Building and Construction	Blocks	blocks of various sizes and shapes, toy animals and people, cars and trucks.	Cooperation, observations, mathematics (more, less, higher, shorter, number), self-expression, geography (farms, zoos, towns, houses), classification.
	Carpentry	scrap lumber, nails, hammer, saw, drill.	Cooperation, care of materials, safety, balance, self-expression.
	Pipes	scraps of threaded pipes from plumber, elbows, wrench.	Self-expression, physical properties of metals, mathematics (shorter, longer).
Manipulative Materials	Puzzles	inset puzzles.	Whole-part concepts, likenesses and differences, manual dexterity, care of materials.
	Beads	Long strings with metal tips, large wooden or plastic beads of different colors and shapes	Color and shape discrimination, mathematics (number, longer, shorter) manual dexterity.
	Pegboards	Various types of perforated boards with pegs or tiles, cards with printed numbers.	Color discrimination, number relations, patterns, manual dexterity.
	Matching games	Lotto or Bingo type games (commercial), matching shapes or colors, matching numbers and quantities.	Likenesses and differences, language for communication, names of shapes, colors, objects, social skill of game playing—taking turns, etc.

Center	Variations	Materials	Possible learning or benefits
	Parquetry or small table blocks	Blocks of different colors that can be fitted into a pattern.	Discrimination of color and shape, relative sizes and shapes, manual dexterity, balance, care of materials, counting.
	Cuisenaire rods, stern rods, etc.	Materials of precise mathematical proportions.	Number relationships.
Art	Painting	Water mixed tempera paints, brushes, old shirts for smocks, paper sponges and water, table or easel.	Discrimination of colors, properties of paints, expression of feelings and concepts, care of materials.
	Clay	Modeling or salt-and-flour clay, sticks, rolling pin, table knives.	Expression of feelings and concepts development of imagination.
	Crayons	Crayons and paper, flat materials of different textures for rubbings.	Expression of feelings and concepts, development of imagination, colors, textures.
	Scissors and paste	Scissors, paste or glue, paper, catalogs and magazines.	Likenesses and differences, expansion of vocabulary, matching, self-expression, color discriminations.
	Collage	Paper or paper plates, variety of scrap materials (may be collected on nature walk).	Textures, self-expression, observation, esthetic appreciation.
Music	Rhythm instruments	Drums, rattles, sandpaper blocks, rhythm sticks, tambourines, bells.	Esthetic appreciation, self-expression, rhythms, movement, sound discrimination.
	Listening I	Record player, records, scarves, streamers	Esthetic appreciation, rhythm, sound discrimination, self-expression, movement.
	Listening II	Television, rug, cushions for watching Sesame Street, Mr. Roger's Neighborhood (should be used with discretion and not as substitute for active involvement).	Concepts presented on these programs.
Language	Books	Shelves, books, rug, cushions, rocking chair, display rack, pictures	Association of written words (symbols) with spoken Appreciation of stories, sequence of events, communication of ideas, socializing influence.
	Alphabet	cut-out plastic letters	Letter recognition, alphabetical sequence.
	Communication	Tape recorder, cassettes	Practice in communication and use of oral language, imagination, self-expression, sequence, verbalization of feelings and impression.
	Writing	Paper (lined and plain), pencils, stapler, crayons models of letters and words	Writing, reading.

Center	Variations	Materials	Possible learning or benefits
Science and Math	Plants	Paper or styrofoam cups, earth, seeds, water, sweet potato, etc.	Plant needs for growth, germination.
	Aquarium	Tank, water, sand, filter, fish, plants, magnifying glass	Aquatic life forms, release of tension, curiosity and wonder.
	Magnets	Magnets of different sizes, objects of various materials (metal and non-metal)	Attraction and repulsion, properties of magnets.
	Balance	A balance rod, cups to hang on it, jars of beans, stones, marbles, etc.	Equilibrium, discrimination of weights.
	Counters	Objects in cans: beans, nuts, macaroni, stones, poker chips, plastic straws, abacus	Classification, grouping, comparing: likenesses and differences, counting, one to one correspondence.
	Sand and water	Sand in a box, water, pitchers, measuring cups, spoons, cans, basin, objects that will float or sink.	Release of tension, comparison of amounts, conservation of volume, absorption, buoyancy, displacement.
	Light, Magnification, Color	Magnifying glass, kaleidascope, colored plastic sheets, mirrors.	Esthetic appreciation, colors, mixing colors, reflections.
	Soap bubbles	Several cans, soap chips, glycerine, water, plastic straws, wire hoops.	Breath control, duration, refraction.
	Nesting or graduated objects	Nesting materials, materials that can be arranged in progressively larger sizes	Larger and smaller, classification, seriation.

REFERENCES

Busis, Anne and Chittenden, Edward. *Analysis of an open classroom.* Princeton, N.J.: Educational Testing Service, 1970.

Furth, Hans G. and Wachs, Harry. *Thinking Goes to School.* London: Oxford University Press, 1974.

Kamii, Constance and DeVries, Rheta. *Piaget, Children and Number.* Washington, D.C.: National Association for the Education of Young Children, 1976.

Kritchevsky, Sybil and Prescott, Elizabeth. *Planning environments for young children: physical space.* Washington, D.C.: National Association for the Education of Young Children, 1969.

Piaget, Jean. The Development of intelligence in the child: heredity, environment, and self-organization. In Frederick Richardson (Ed.), *Brain and intelligence.* Hyattsville, Md.: National Education Press, 1973.

Schickedanz, Judith, York, Mary Elizabeth, Steward, Ida Santos, and White, Doris. *Strategies for teaching young children.* Englewood Cliffs, N.J.: Prentice-Hall, 1977.

Spodek, Bernard. *Early childhood education.* Englewood Cliffs, N.J.: Prentice-Hall, 1973.

Spodek, Bernard. *Teaching in the early years.* Englewood Cliffs, N.J.: Prentice-Hall, 1972.

Weikart, D.P. A Comparative study of three preschool curricula. In J.E. Frost and G.R. Hawkes (Eds.), *The disadvantaged child.* Boston: Houghton-Mifflin, 1970.

Yardley, Alice. *The teacher of young children.* New York: Citation Press, 1973.

Chapter 23

Children, Materials, and Adults in Early Learning Settings

David S. Kuschner and Peter Y. Clark*

One of the major characteristics of early childhood education programs is the use of materials to promote and foster children's learning and development. Virtually all types of programs, be it Head Start, university-affiliated laboratory school, nursery school, or day care center, provide children with a variety of toys and manipulable materials. Goodlad, Klein, and Novotney (1973) surveyed over 200 early childhood programs in this country, and their data suggests a great deal of similarity in terms of materials provided for children's activity. Such items as blocks, art media, books, and puzzles can be found in almost any program. In fact, if an observer did not find those materials, that particular program might be considered lacking.

The educational materials in a program often serve as the basis for arranging physical space and organizing the daily routine. Many early childhood programs arrange space according to activity centers: the block corner, the housekeeping area, the art area, and the language corner, to name a few. In addition, a program's daily activities are often scheduled according to when children can play with tabletop toys, such as puzzles and science materials; when they can be involved with large motor activities, such as blocks and transportation toys; and when they can play out of doors.

Historical Influences

An emphasis on children's activities with materials has a long tradition in early childhood education. Beginning with Friedrich Froebel (1782-1852), known as the father of the kindergarten, a great deal of importance has been placed on children's play. Froebel created a variety of toys, or gifts as he called them, designed to help the child learn about the world and about himself (Froebel, 1902). During the late 1800's, kindergartens in this country were greatly influenced by Froebel's ideas, especially his emphasis on children's play with materials. It is interesting to note that the Milton Bradley Company first produced and sold Froebel's toys during that period.

Maria Montessori (1870-1952) also designed an elaborate set of materials, and her influence is still acknowledged within the field of early childhood education, both in terms of schools bearing her name and other programs as well.

Stressing the importance of sensory education, Montessori developed methods and materials to increase children's abilities to discriminate among stimuli and to order stimuli along various dimensions, such as height, weight, and color (Montessori, 1965). In the Montessori system, "the critical relationship is that between the child and his learning materials" (Evans, 1971, p. 42).

John Dewey, (1859-1952) in his writings, emphasizes the importance of experience. Although his interests were not primarily the education of young children, his ideas certainly do pertain to early childhood education. According to Dewey, thinking is best promoted by allowing children the opportunity to engage in experiences which suggest problems to be solved. These experiences should be guided by the children's own interests, and should also allow children to test out solutions for the problem (Dewey, 1938). Most interpretations of this position suggest that those experiences, expecially for young children, need to be concrete in nature.

There is perhaps no single contemporary influence on the curricula of early education greater than that of Jean Piaget (1896-   ). Studying for over fifty years the ways in which children come to understand their world, Piaget has concluded that early sensori-motor experience with concrete objects plays a crucial role in the development of thought (Piaget, 1973). That, coupled with his use of concrete tasks to probe the minds of young children, suggests that children below the age of five or six need to have a variety of experiences with concrete manipulables, such as blocks, sand, and science-oriented, table-top toys. As Ginsburg and Opper (1969) write:

Perhaps the most important single proposition that the educator can derive from Piaget's work ... is that children, especially young ones, learn best from concrete activities. (p. 221)

*David S. Kuschner is an Assistant Professor and Chairperson of the Early Childhood Education Program at the Center for Teaching and Learning, University of North Dakota. Peter Y. Clark is a Teaching Assistant with the Early Childhood Education Program, at the Center for Teaching and Learning, University of North Dakota.

Typical Functions of Materials

If one is to investigate the typical materials found in early learning settings, a high level of consistency is apparent. By providing an array of materials, the child is afforded a range of opportunities to develop and elaborate a repertoire of skills and concepts. The child is encouraged to manipulate and explore these materials in a variety of ways, and it is often assumed that he or she will learn as a result of this interaction. In most cases, specific materials are viewed as having uses or learning potentials that correspond to certain areas of concept development and/or subject matter.

Blocks are a standard item found in early education programs. They are viewed as useful and important because they provide the child with opportunities to do things that promote the acquisition of certain skills. Those most frequently mentioned are mathematics, spatial relationships, and motor coordination. In addition, block play is viewed favorably because the child has a high degree of freedom to define and structure his own activities with the blocks.

Books and other language-stimulating materials are useful because the child is given opportunities to develop further linguistic and pre-reading skills. Language-experience materials serve to stimulate visual and auditory discrimination, receptive and expressive language, and communication skills. Although books are the most common materials found in a language center, such items as felt boards, tape recorders, alphabet blocks, and puppets are often provided and used in a variety of ways. Language materials of this sort can be used effectively in child-directed or teacher-directed activities. In addition, they are of value in both formal and informal learning sessions.

Table-top manipulable materials such as puzzles, sorting boxes, parquetry blocks, jars and lids, etc., serve several important functions. First, they provide the child with many opportunities to develop and elaborate such concepts as color, shape, size, pattern, and order. They necessitate the use of perceptual-motor skills, such as eye-hand coordination, visual discrimination, and tactile sensitivity. Frequently, children will engage in quiet, self-directed learning activities that are either self-correcting or open-ended in nature. Manipulable materials are also valued because they involve the child in the kinds of skills and thinking that provide the foundation for the development of reading, writing, and mathematical operations, as well as providing the child with gratifying, successful experiences.

Art and modeling materials lend themselves to psycho-sensory experiences, self-expressive activities, and representational thinking. Such materials as crayons, tempera paint, finger-paint, clays and doughs, and a variety of collage materials are standard items found in most early education environments. They are important, not only because of their aesthetic qualities, but also because they provide mediums within which many concepts can be explored. In using art materials, a child often deals with color, shape,

and cleaning utensils, and clothing, provides the child with the implements needed to engage in imitative and symbolic play, individually or collectively. Because these materials are familiar to every child, they provide even the reluctant child with a sense of the familiar. A variety of roles and behaviors can be experienced by the child in using these materials, thus expanding the individual's understanding of self and others. Exploration of such concepts as social roles, family roles, and sex roles are naturally encouraged by providing house-keeping materials. In addition, language, motor skills, and cooperation often become an integrated part of activities involving these props and materials.
tactility, smell, and visual discrimination, to name a few. In addition, by using art materials, a child is given opportunities to engage in a process which results in a unique product that becomes a mode of self-expression to be shared with others.

A house-keeping corner or center, which generally contains a variety of household items such as furniture, eating and cleaning ustensils, and clothing, provides the child with the implements needed to engage in imitative and symbolic play, individually or collectively. Because these materials are familiar to every child, they provide even the reluctant child with a sense of the familiar. A variety of roles and behaviors can be experienced by the child in using these materials, thus expanding the individual's understanding of self and others. Exploration of such concepts as social roles, family roles, and sex roles are naturally encouraged by providing house-keeping materials. In addition, language, motor skills, and cooperation often become an integrated part of activities involving these props and materials.

The provision of sand and water as learning materials has a wide-spread backing and use in early education settings. The free-flowing qualities of sand and water seem to catch and hold the attention of most young children. Both types of materials encourage the child to explore and think about physical qualities and concepts. As the child manipulates sand or water, he can be engaged in basic scientific processes or the elaboration of dreams and fantasies. The calming and soothing qualities of sand and water are often attractive to children and teachers alike. It is not uncommon for the sand or water table to be the most extensively-used resource in the entire learning environment.

There are a number of materials that have not been discussed but are of equal importance. Music materials which include records, instruments, and songs are very worthwhile. Science materials, including living and non-living things, can be the basis of a host of learning activities involving manipulation, observation, and record-keeping. Cooking and nutrition-oriented activities can also be a basis for science projects as well as relating to the daily activities of cooking and eating. The final group of materials that generally enjoys widespread recognition and use are the motor-skill materials or equipment. A variety of apparatuses that encourage the child to use all parts of his body in developing strength, coordination, and body awareness should be a major part of any early childhood education program.

The role of the teacher

In stating that there is a high level of consistency in the array of materials found in early learning settings, it is not implied that the role of the teacher and the sanctioned uses of the materials are equally consistent amont these settings. To the contrary, the role of the teacher and the approved uses of materials does vary from setting to setting. In many ways, these differences can be accounted for by examining the philosophical and pedagogical positions held by early childhood educators.

The teacher in all cases is given the task of insuring that a well-thought out, prepared environment is developed and maintained. It is the teacher who usually makes decisions about where materials will be located and what modifications in their arrangement will take place. Because young children learn as a result of interactions with concrete materials in their environment, the teacher has the responsibility for providing these materials and the space within which children can expand their understanding of the world by acting upon it.

A second role the teacher has is to sanction, moderate, and, in many cases, control what interactions and behaviors take place. The teacher brings a philosophical and pedagogical valuing system into the environment, which serves as the basis for the teacher's interactions with the materials and the children. The range of views on teaching and learning can be put on a continuum whose endpoints are represented by teacher-centered prescriptive learning and child-centered, self-directed learning.

This spectrum of teaching styles can be understood by viewing a few historical antecedents to contemporary early childhood practices. As noted before, Friedrich Froebel developed the notion that the focus of early childhood education should be on the child's manipulations of concrete materials. Most interpretations of Froebellian pedagogy, however, have emphasized the prescriptive aspect of the teacher's role in terms of the objects presented to children, as well as what children actually do with the objects (Fein and Clarke-Stewart, 1973). From this perspective, for example, teachers would not only provide blocks for children to play with but would also prescribe certain activities for the children to engage in, such as constructing specific patterns.

Maria Montessori has also had a substantial influence on contemporary views of the role of early childhood teachers. For Montessori, the two main aspects of a teacher's responsibility were the preparation of the environment, and the close observation of the children as they interacted with the environment. Active involvement, on the part of the teacher, in the children's interaction with materials was considered, by Montessori, to be interfering with children's natural learning. In preparing the environment, the teacher identifies particular materials from which children can choose and, in addition, specifies ways in which they may and may not be used. Children are not encouraged to use the materials in novel ways, but rather in prescribed ways.

Educational practices, following from the ideas of Rousseau, stress the importance of establishing a safe and nurturing environment for young children. Within this view, teachers are responsible for providing time and materials for children to pursue their own ideas and natural inclinations—what children want to do, is what they should be doing (Kohlberg and Mayer, 1972). From this perspective, what is often called a laissez-faire attitude is adopted. Teachers are to do nothing more, in terms of children's activity, than maintain an atmosphere which allows children's development to unfold in its natural direction, without external pressures.

Historically, then, there has been the view that children's interactions with materials is important. The foregoing discussion suggests, however, that there exists, for the early childhood educator, a wide range of teaching modes and styles from which to choose. Some are highly directive, either by teacher prescription or selection of materials, while others are relatively non-directive and child centered. The teacher's role vis-a-vis these interactions has reflected a range of approaches based on differing philosophical assumptions and pedagogical practices. The remainder of this article presents a framework from which teachers can analyze children's interactions with materials. Based upon such analyses, teachers can make decisions that can enrich these interactions.

Children's Interactions With Materials

In order to provide the best educational environment possible for young children, it is necessary that one takes seriously the concept of *interaction* as it relates to children and materials. As Dewey and Piaget both have written, development and learning come about as a result of the interactions children have with their environment (Dewey, 1938; Piaget and Inhelder, 1969). By focusing on interactions, teachers of young children are able to understand, plan for, and facilitate children's use of materials. This is most effectively accomplished by taking into consideration what the child brings to the interaction in terms of knowledge, skills, and experience; understanding what particular materials ask or require of children; and finally, being able to decide what to do in order to enrich children's experience with materials.

Children and materials

Children interact with the environment based upon what they have done before. They put to use skills acquired, concepts developed, and emotions felt. These skills, concepts, and emotions are often indicators of the particular stage of development at which a child is performing and thinking. Piaget, in elaborating his theory of developmental stages, maintains that children, at different times in life, possess qualitatively different conceptions of how the world operates (Ginsburg and Opper, 1969). This conception, to some extent, affects how and what children do with specific materials. For example, a four-year-old might think that a ball of clay rolled into the shape of a sausage contains more clay than when it was ball-like, because it looks like more. A seven-year-old, on the other hand, understands that no clay was added or taken away: therefore, the sausage has the same amount of clay. The younger child relies on perceptual appearances to decide on questions of amount, whereas the older child takes into consideration the changes undergone by the object.

As Piaget has emphasized, observing children closely provides the teacher with valuable information as to the understandings a child may be bringing to his play with materials (Piaget, 1973). A child who puts a policeman's cap on his head and proceeds to arrest people over and over again may be exhibiting a limited conception of a policeman's role. Watching a child go back to the end of the line at the slide on the playground, when there are no other children waiting, suggests that this child has a ritualized notion of what "taking turns" means. Listening to a first-grade child say that children cannot go down into sewers through a manhole, "because they're not kidholes," indicates that this child has some sense of the creative nature of language.

Each of the foregoing examples, observed by the authors, demonstrates that by watching and listening to children it becomes readily apparent that rarely do they enter into play with materials randomly or "empty-headedly." Children have a tremendous desire to organize their environment and to act on it based upon rules and understandings which they have constructed. The stages which Piaget has elaborated often are used as a means of gauging a child's readiness for some particular learning. From that perspective, it is usually concluded that a child can or cannot do a specific task or understand a specific concept. It is also true, however, that stages describe the major characteristics of a child's thought, the thought that the child is using to make decisions in his world. The child who does not take into consideration the changes applied to the ball of clay is still making a judgment, a judgment based upon his understanding of what determines quantity.

Children also bring past feelings to a particular interaction; for example, feelings of success or failure. In addition, a child brings attitudes and behaviors which have been shaped by experiences at home. If a child, for example, is discouraged from talking loudly or making loud noises at home, it may be difficult for that child to become fully involved with certain large group activities in the early childhood program. A child whose parents encourage explora-

tion and experimentation and who sanction the disorder which may accompany such behavior, is likely to benefit a great deal from activities like finger-painting and water play, which require the willingness to get "messy."

Children, therefore, interact with materials in ways that make sense to them. Their attitudes toward particular materials is a product of previous interactions or lack of interaction with the materials. How a child understands his actions and their results depends upon his level of thinking. What a child does with materials is also based upon the prior acquisition of certain skills, in addition to his attitude and level of development.

Materials and children.

On the other side of the interaction coin are the materials themselves. Each type of manipulable material requires a slightly different combination of skills, competencies, etc. In addition, they ask different questions of the child. It is interesting to wonder about the traditional diversity of materials found in early childhood education programs. What do materials such as blocks ask of children that puzzles do not, or vice versa? It seems safe to assume that there are differences, otherwise why not have a program consisting of block play only? As trivial as these questions may seem, the analysis needed to answer them is vital if one is to help make full use of the materials as mediums or catalysts in children's thinking and learning. A few examples will help to illustrate that point.

Blocks are one of the most frequently-found materials in early childhood programs (Goodlad, et. al., 1973). As previously mentioned, they are said to aid in the development of spatial and mathematical concepts. What then do blocks ask of children? To begin with, children early in their experiences with blocks need to grapple with the problem of gravity. When building towers, children have to place blocks in such a way that balance is achieved. In addition, two blocks positioned against one another do not adhere, therefore, support has to be taken into consideration. Another constraint blocks place on children's play is their rigidity, a characteristic which certainly distinguishes blocks from materials such as modeling clay. A child who wants to build a curvy road with blocks will need to work out the engineering problems based upon the specific set of blocks he has available. He obviously cannot change the shape of a particular block in order to fit his needs.

Modelling clay, on the other hand, has some very different properties than blocks. It is moldable so, if a section of curvy road is needed, all the child has to do is shape a section of road. Building three-dimensional structures, however, poses some problems that block-building does not. The lack of rigidity makes it difficult to build too high in a vertical direction. The child's building must counteract gravity in a very different way compared with block-building.

Puzzles ask very different questions of children than do blocks or clay. In order to solve a puzzle, a child needs to successfully fit the pieces together both in terms of how they interlock with each other and how they form a picture. Puzzles provide feedback to the child as to whether or not she has completed the task correctly, whereas blocks leave that decision to the child herself. In other words, a puzzle directs a child's behavior, while blocks and clay elicit more self-directed play.

The materials of language experience differ from both blocks, clay, and puzzles. The most obvious difference is that the materials of language—sounds, meaning, syntax, etc.—are intangible. Even though a child manipulates these materials as he manipulates blocks and puzzle pieces, his actions do not produce concrete results. This is one reason why language is at times a difficult process to discuss and examine. In addition, to some extent a child is free to use language in conjunction with other activities. This cannot be said of certain other materials when there are programmatic concerns involved; for example, mixing paint into the sand in the sand table.

Even though all materials ask certain similar questions of children, each material has its own special nature. It is true that in block play, the child *relates* a block to a construction; in working with a puzzle, the child *relates* a puzzle piece to the picture being formed; and in using language the child *relates* one word to other words in constructing a sentence. As noted above, however, the special nature of each material makes the child's interactions with the various materials appreciably different.

Children, Materials, and Adults

Once a teacher has analyzed materials and observed children using them, he/she has valuable information concerning ways to promote learning and development. If he/she sees a child continually placing blocks so that they do not balance, he/she might conclude that the child's understandings of the effects of gravity are not complete. In a similar manner, hearing a child talk about "kid-holes" might suggest to a teacher that the child is aware that language is comprised of elements which can be combined and re-combined in order to construct new words. A framework, as illustrated below, may be a helpful tool with which teachers can analyze such interactions between children and materials.

Material	Nature of Material	Nature of child's actions
ex: BLOCKS	rigid 3-dimensional non-adhering	balancing combining putting into part/whole relationships

This chart can be used in one of two ways. The staff of an early childhood program can use it as a way of discussing general principles of child/material interactions. If this were the case, then the child in question is a hypothesized child. On the other hand, a specific child could be observed and his actions with blocks, for example, could be charted. Having such information about children over a period of months

could be instrumental in terms of promoting children's learning and development.

Another very important use of such a chart centers on the suggestions for facilitating a broad variety of experiences for children. A fourth column, then, should be added to the chart labeled, "Suggestions for Adult." This column itself is divided into two categories; suggestions for materials and suggestions for actions.

Material	Nature of Material	Nature of Child's actions	Suggestions for Adult
ex: BLOCKS	rigid 3-dimensional non-adhering	balancing combining putting into part/whole relationships	(a) Suggestive materials– —irregular shaped —blocks of different weights —non-rigid materials (b) Suggestive actions– —place blocks in vertical orientation if child is using them only in horizontal orientations

The suggestions for adults noted above are basically those of broadening the possibilities for children in terms of their interactions with materials. If a child only arrests people while wearing a policeman's cap, a teacher can suggest an expanded role by donning a hat herself and performing different actions, such as helping people. A teacher's behavior such as that falls under the category of "suggestive actions." A teacher could provide "suggestive materials" by making sure that the set of blocks the children play with includes blocks of different weights and shapes, some irregular, thus insuring a variety of experiences involving gravity and balance.

The concepts of suggestive actions and suggestive materials also relate to the question of what children bring to their interactions with materials. A child was observed working on a puzzle, with the formboard in an upside-down position in front of her. For this child, the way in which the pieces interlocked with each other was possibly the basis for putting the puzzle together. The picture being made was unimportant. After watching the child put a number of puzzles together in this same fashion, the teacher proceeded to work on a puzzle herself, all the while verbally noting different parts of the picture being formed. In this way, the teacher was suggesting that information concerning the completion of the puzzle was also available from the conceptual image being pieced together. We should not worry about the question of modeling behaviors for children as something to be avoided, as long as through our modeling, we are suggesting alternatives and, as Hawkins writes, "sanctioning variety" (Hawkins, 1974, p. 26). Knowing what alternatives might be appropriate, however, is only possible if the analysis of what materials ask of children is coupled with the close observation of children using the materials.

Conclusions

As noted in the beginning of this article, the use of concrete materials in early childhood education has a long tradition, and a good tradition it is. However, it is not a tradition which should be taken for granted. Children and standard materials should not be, in effect, placed together in a room with the assumption that the best possible experiences will occur. Adults are a crucial part of the mixture. That is certainly not to say that teachers should prescribe what children do with materials. On the contrary, to the greatest degree possible, children need to determine what tasks they want to pursue while playing with materials. Teachers should be suggesters, modelers, and prodders. To be effective, they need knowledge, skills, and experiences in three basic areas. The first is the area of child development, including the cognitive, physical, and socio-emotional domains. With that background, teachers can observe children's activity from the perspective of developmental continuua. This means that children's behavior indicates not only where they are in terms of a specific concept, but where they are going as well.

The second competency is that of familiarity with the materials themselves. A teacher cannot really understand the child/materials interaction unless she herself has had experience playing with the materials. Any staff training program in early childhood should include "Hands-on" experiences with the materials provided for children's play. Such experiences go a long way in encouraging teachers to enter the child's world as a "co-player." In effect, a wide array of materials is only a learning tool for the teacher to the extent that the teacher understands the potential utility of the materials in a broad sense.

The final competency is that of observation. Teachers need a great deal of experience with different techniques of observing children at play. Videotape is very useful in this regard because it can freeze time and allow teachers to view a particular episode of children's play as often as needed. Teachers have to have experience and training in going beyond surface analyses of what children are doing and begin to focus on the specific actions children perform with specific materials.

Obviously the three areas of competency—child development, use of materials, and observation of children—are closely related. To the extent that a teacher understands various developmental concepts and understands the potential of various materials, she can closely observe children at play. In a very real sense, these areas of competency do not exist in isolation. What does exist, however, are degrees of competency. The tremendous importance of children's interactions with materials demands that teachers be prepared to as high a level of competency in all three areas as possible. As knowledge of child development, materials, and observation techniques are inextricably intertwined, so should be children, materials, and adults in the early childhood program.

REFERENCES

Dewey, J. *Experience and education.* New York: Collier Books, 1938.

Evans, E. D. *Contemporary influences in early childhood education.* New York: Holt, Rinehart and Winston, Inc., 1971.

Fein, G. G., & Clarke-Stewart, A. *Day care in context.* New York: John Wiley & Sons, 1973.

Froebel, F. *Pedagogics of the kindergarten.* Translated by Josephine Jarvis. New York: D. Appleton and Company, 1902.

Ginsburg, H., & Opper, S. *Piaget's theory of intellectual development: An introduction.* Englewood Cliffs, N.J.: Prencitice-Hall, Inc., 1969.

Goodlad, J. I., Klein, M. F., & Novotney, J. M. *Early schooling in the United States.* New York: McGraw-Hill Book Company, 1973.

Hawkins, F. P. *The logic of action: Young children at work.* New York: Pantheon Books, 1974.

Kohlberg, L. & Mayer, R. Development as the aim of education. *Harvard Educational Review,* 1972, *42*(4), 449–496.

Montessori, M. *Dr. Montessori's own handbook.* New York: Schocken Books, Inc., 1965.

Piaget, J. *To understand is to invent.* New York: Viking Press, Inc., 1973.

Piaget, J., & Inhelder, B. *The psychology of the child.* New York: Basic Books, Inc., 1969.

SUGGESTIONS FOR FURTHER READING

Barnes D. *From communication to curriculum.* Harmondsworth, Middlesex, England: Penguin Books, Ltd., 1975.

Hawkins, D. The triangular relationship of teacher, student, and materials. In C. E. Silberman (Ed.), *The open classroom reader.* New York: Vintage Books, 1973.

Hirsch, E. S. (Ed.). *The block book.* Washington, D.C.: National Association for the Education of Young Children, 1974.

Lindberg, L., & Swedlow, R. *Early childhood education: A guide for observation and participation.* Boston: Allyn and Bacon, Inc., 1976.

Smilansky, S. Can adults facilitate play in children?: Theoretical and practical considerations. In G. Engstrom (Ed.), *Play: The child strives towards self-realization.* Washington, D.C.: National Association for the Education of Young Children, 1971.

Chapter 24
Alternate Valuing Strategies for Young Children

Jesse S. Liles*

The interest of American educators in the open school concept has created a demand for teachers with skills for dealing with concepts in the affective domain. The particular teaching situations which arise in an open classroom almost demand attention to value-laden problems. This is because pupils entering the open classroom typically lack certain affective skills necessary for their full participation in the cognitive domain lessons and learning centers prepared by an instructional team. As an example let us examine the problems which tend to arise when pupils lack two specific affective skills. An examination of these problems will lead to the description and evaluation of alternative valuing strategies available to teachers of young children.

One of the affective skills necessary in the open classroom is pupil willingness to engage in solo work or small-group work independent of close teacher supervision. Unless pupils possess this ability teachers are placed in a double jeopardy situation. They have to design and produce independent learning centers, and they have to supervise pupil participation in the activities of these centers. Such a sequence of events tends to be defeating of the purpose of open classroom arrangements. These arrangements are intended to make it possible to instruct some pupils individually or in small groups while other pupils engage in independent learning activities.

Another of the affective skills necessary in the open classroom is pupil ability to distinguish between community and personal property. In an open classroom materials of all types are spread around a large area. Usually pupils have a small space, often called a tote tray, in which to keep their personal belongings. If pupils put community materials in this tote tray, or remove personal belongings from other pupils' trays and use these materials on community projects, conflicts tend to arise. Valuable time needed for cognitive instruction can be wasted.

Given that such problems tend to arise one assumes that instructional teams in open schools would give specific attention to instilling the necessary affective skills for pupil participation. This means planning instructional sequences and individual lessons with affective domain goals. One obvious goal would be to produce a willingness on the part of pupils to participate in unsupervised learning experiences. As pupils mature we begin to regard this willingness as a

character trait. We call this trait "responsibility." Another obvious goal is to have all pupils come to understand and respect the differences between community and personal property. As pupils mature we regard this ability as another character trait. We call this one "honesty." We may now conclude that affective education in the open school must include specific attention to instilling responsibility and honesty. We can conclude this not only because our society regards honesty and responsibility as good traits but also because we have seen that pupils must possess such traits if they are to perform effectively in open classrooms.

Given that open schools have good reasons for devoting special attention to instilling affective domain skills such as honesty and responsibility it would appear that the next relevant question is: "How should one instill such values?" A meaningful discussion of this question requires that we note certain salient features of our society. We must also remind ourselves, as teachers, of some of the characteristics of schools. We know that our society expects children to be honest and responsible long before they are capable of understanding the rational reasons for so doing. It follows that parents and other adults must use nonrational means for conditioning children to be honest and responsible. A simple illustration would be the parent who conditions a three-year old to get a thrill from paying at the check-out counter for the candy the child may casually pick up in almost any store.

As teachers we must constantly remind ourselves about the nature of our goals. In the area of moral values we aspire to help our pupils become self-disciplined adults. What is self-discipline? It consists of rational assent to the norms of society. It also consists of that type of understanding of moral principles which guides a person in the humane practice of a principle such as the moral requirement for honesty or truthfulness. Psychologists (Glasser, 1969) tell us that it is impossible to use conditioning strategies to develop norm-assent based on understanding. Simple logic tells us that it is unlikely that we can produce rational assent to values like honesty and responsibility when we

*Dr. Jesse Liles, Associate Professor of Education, Secondary Education Dept., Madison College, Harrisonburg, Virginia.

utilize only the types of non-rational, conditioning strategies to which many parents resort when they begin the process of instilling the values of our society into their young children. We know that while conditioning strategies can be used to train children not to take candy without paying, conditioning alone can never result in adults who refrain from stealing because they understand the rational reason why society prohibits theft.

We are now prepared to state a major dilemma which arises when teachers of young children attempt to answer the question: "How should one go about teaching values like honesty and responsibility?" If one uses only non-rational strategies like conditioning and modeling one may not be contributing to the attainment of the ultimate social goal. We have defined this goal as self-discipline or the humane application of social rules to the unique situations of daily life. Yet teachers know that the age at which our society expects honest and responsible conduct from pupils is so early that at this maturity level only strategies which the pupils experience as non-rational are likely to influence their conduct. Logically there are two solutions to the dilemma. One is to refrain from teaching values until pupils reach a maturity level such that rational strategies may be successfully employed. This would mean waiting until pupil's cognitive development was well into the stage of abstract operations. (Phillips, 1969) The other logical solution is to abandon the ultimate goal of producing rational assent to social norms and attempt to condition pupils so thoroughly that as adults it would never occur to them to ignore a social norm. The first logical solution is obviously impractical. It would mean that teachers could not consciously strive to influence pupil's normative behavior until after the primary years. Such refraining would be self-defeating, especially in an open school situation. The second logical alternative is obviously incongruent with the fact that we strive to have the values we teach in our schools contribute to the maintenance of a democratic society. If we condition future citizens in the manner suggested by the second logical alternative then as adults they would be ineffective participants in the democratic process. What then are we to do? Can teachers resolve this dilemma?

Any solution to the dilemma must satisfy two criteria. First, the solution must permit teachers to utilize those non-rational affective domain strategies such as conditioning and modeling which are affective with young pupils. Second, the use of whatever valuing technique is selected must enhance or at least not damage the subsequent ability of the pupil to achieve rational understanding of and assent to the value system he acquired as a youngster. What sorts of valuing strategies satisfy these criteria?

In a real sense this is the type of tough question for which professional teachers must work out their own unique responses. Indeed this is the type of decision that requires professional, rather than technical, expertise. However, it is possible to suggest two lines of approach which have proven fruitful. Teachers can design and utilize value clarification strategies. (Simon, Howe, and Kirschenbaum, (1972) Teachers can conduct with groups of pupils cognitive moral dilemmas (Kohlberg and Selman, 1972).

Several interesting pupil outcomes are produced when teachers use value clarification strategies. One outcome is that pupils acquire, through practice, skill in making value-laden choices. A second outcome is that pupils are provided an opportunity to conclude that successful group work depends on the effective utilization of human relations skills. A third outcome is that pupils have experiences which causes them to recognize the worth of other persons' opinions, feelings, and possessions.

Exactly what type of value clarification strategy would begin to accomplish these goals? Let us suppose a teacher has a class of twenty to twenty-five youngsters. One simple value clarification strategy may be called "the picture lesson." The teacher must acquire eight cheap water-colors or prints of a size small enough to be handled by the pupils. Divide the eight pictures into pairs and place them on viewing stations around the room. Write the words "group" and "cooperation" on the chalkboard. Brainstorm what these two words mean to the class. Record the individual responses on the chalkboard. Then divide the class into four roughly equal groups assigning each group to a viewing station with a pair of pictures. Tell each group that its task is to pick one of the pictures as the winner of an art competition. Be sure each group understands its task but do not offer assistance. Carefully observe the interaction in each group. As the groups make their choices encourage them to explain how they produced their consensus. After sufficient time, regardless of whether all groups have completed the task, call the class together again. Lead a discussion which encourages each group to explain how they made their choice. If one or more groups were unable to agree examine the problems which caused the disagreement. Encourage the pupils to compare what actually happened with the ideas about "groups" and "cooperation" which the class verbalized in the earlier brainstorming session. Encourage the pupils to draw their own conclusions about why there are differences between what they thought about group cooperation and how they actually behaved when faced with a task successful completion of which required a group decision. Ask the class if they would like to try another group task sometime soon.

The author's experience with this and similar value clarification lessons has indicated that pupils enjoy and benefit from the choice making, the analysis of the group interaction, and the opportunity to share their opinions and values with their peers. A continuous stream of short lessons of this type will soon begin to elicit from a class the type of responsible, unsupervised group work so necessary to the successful implementation of the open school concept.

Since most value clarification strategies involve open-ended choice-making on the part of pupils it seems unlikely that this approach to teaching values will result in a youngster conditioned for life to obey without understanding the rules which express the norms of his society. More likely this value clarification approach will result in a pupil who, as he enters the stage of abstract operations, will seek to acquire a rational understanding of the necessity for the human relations skills he has already learned to practice.

Cognitive moral dilemmas of the type suggested by research (Kohlberg, 1963) into the nature of how individuals acquire their moral reasoning abilities are just as easy to conduct, but they are somewhat more difficult to explain. Kohlberg discovered that all individuals acquire their ability to engage in moral reasoning by passing through all or a portion of six stages arranged in an ascending heirarchy. Only the first two of these stages need concern us here. Immature individuals—not confined to young children—respond to the threat of punishment when they are resolving moral dilemmas. This "stage one" reasoning is typified by the child who tells his father not to exceed the speed limit because if he does the policeman will stop him. Slightly more mature individuals—not necessarily older—respond to the hope of reward when they are resolving moral dilemmas. This "stage two" reasoning is typified by the child who tells his father not to exceed the speed limit because we want to keep "Mom", who is riding in the car with us, in a good mood. Although these stages of moral development are not associated with any particular chronological age it would be appropriate to assume that teachers of young children are working with individuals who are just beginning to move from "stage one" reasoning into "stage two" reasoning.

Exactly what kind of valuing exercise would begin to accomplish the goal of leading pupils to acquire a more mature level of moral reasoning. To be developmental in nature and meaningful to young children any cognitive moral dilemma must meet two criterion; one theoretical, the other practical. The theoretical criteria is drawn from the idea of stages of moral development. If one is teaching a group which is a mixture of stage one—stage two pupils then successful resolution of the dilemma by the pupils must "call" for stage two reasoning. As pupils respond to the dilemma a mixed bag of reasoning including some stage two reasoning must occur. This in turn makes it possible for the stage one pupils to move toward the more mature reasoning of their stage two peers. Stage one pupils recognize the greater power of the "anticipation of reward" type reasoning used by their classmates who are operating at the stage two level.

The practical criterion which a cognitive moral dilemma must meet is that all pupils must identify with the dilemma as it is posed. The dilemma must not be an "adult" type problem requiring mature reasoning for its resolution.

Neither can it be posed in an "adult" manner. It must be posed using a medium which has the power to engage the pupils' attention. Storytelling is an excellent format. The story may be about real people—children, not adults— or it may be about imaginary, cartoon-type characters. With very young pupils pantomine and/or hand puppets are helpful. In order to conduct a cognitive moral dilemma with an "honesty" theme the teacher may tell a story about some children the same age and social class as the group hearing the story. The story must be about a character who has an opportunity to decide whether or not to be honest about a matter significant to children in a situation where apprehension and punishment of a dishonest act is a fairly remote possibility. At the same time the events in the story must be arranged so that a reward for an honest act is almost a certainty. The teacher must stop the story at the point where the central character must decide whether to be honest or dishonest. Then ask the listening pupils to indicate privately what they would do in such a situation and why. Have the pupils make as permanent as possible a record of their choice and reason; using physical symbols if pupils cannot write. Lead a discussion which highlights not the choices—many children will say that they would be honest in such a situation—but the reasons. In the discussion some reasons will be essentially fear of punishment, but some will be anticipation of reward type reasons. Encourage the pupils to compare and evaluate one another's reasons. It is when the reasons are evaluated publicly by the pupils in the discussion that moral maturity will be developing.

If the theory of moral development (Kohlberg, 1970) underlying cognitive dilemmas is valid then the teacher who uses such strategies with young pupils will have created a classroom setting which encourages the development of moral maturity. Teachers can expect that in such a climate the pupils will develop a desire to experience justice or "fairness." Pupils will come to expect that there be powerful reasons which guide the acts of other pupils and teachers. Once individual pupils begin to expect "fairness" in the manner in which they are treated by others, teachers can begin to work to have individual pupils apply the "fairness" standard to the manner in which they choose to treat others.

We may now compare and contrast the cognitive moral dilemma (story-telling) type valuing strategy with the value clarification (picture-lesson) type of valuing strategy. The strategies are similar in that they provide for choicemaking by the pupils. This pupil choosing occurs in a setting where peer and teacher evaluation of it may be structured toward the achievement of definite purposes. With the value clarification "picture-lesson" pupils get a chance to face the dichotomy between what they say and what they do. Becoming more consistent will be encouraged, but no "right" answer to a value-laden question wll be identified. With the moral dilemma "story-telling" the pupil choosing leads to an evaluation of the cognitive worthwhileness of the reasons or justification for a particular choice. Since some reasons are better than others it will be obvious that some acts are regarded as being more worthy than others. A desire to perform the right act for the right reason will be encouraged by this type of valuing strategy. The basic differences between the strategies may now be stated. Value clarifications rest on the fundamental presupposition that values are relative, matters of individual choice governed by time and circumstance. Cognitive moral dilemmas rest on the presupposition that values—at least moral values as distinguished from aesthetic values—are universal, remaining constant regardless of time or circumstance. Moral values are seen as enduring because the "right" choice in the face of a moral dilemma can be identified by anyone—regardless of age or social class—if that person uses mature cognitive processes to identify the most convincing reason why a given act should be performed in a given set of circumstances. As these convincing reasons become progressively more rational in nature moral maturity increases.

The practical import of this key difference between the strategies is clear. Young children exposed to a steady diet of value clarifications may develop an awareness of the need for consistency between what one says and what one does. They will also come to share the relative assumption about the nature of values which lies behind the value clarification strategies. In a pluralistic society where aesthetic and political values manifest rapid change children who internalize such an assumption probably will adjust well to adult responsibility. Young children exposed to a steady diet of cognitive moral dilemmas eventually will be able to apply reason and rational procedures to the resolution of moral dilemmas. They may also come to share the universialist assumption about the nature of moral values which lies behind the cognitive moral dilemmas. Surely such persons will be needed by a society struggling to find some set of unifying principles.

REFERENCES

Glasser, William, *Schools Without Failure.* New York: Harper and Row Publishers, 1969.

Kohlberg, Lawrence, "The Development of Children's Orientation Toward A Moral Order: Sequence in the Development of Moral Thought." *Vita Humana 6,* 1963.

Kohlberg, Lawrence, "The Development of Children's Orientation Toward A Moral Order: Social Experience, Social Conduct, and the Development of Moral Thought." *Vita Humana 9,* 1963.

Kohlberg, Lawrence, "Education for Justice: A Modern Statement of the Platonic View." In *Moral Education: Five Lectures* edited by Nancy F. and Theodore R. Sizer, Harvard University Press, 1970.

Kohlberg, Lawrence and Robert Selman, "First Things: Values; A Strategy for Teaching Values." Guidance Associates, 1972. Filmstrip kit.

Phillips, John L., *The Origins of Intellect: Piaget's Theory.* San Francisco: W. H. Freeman, 1969.

Simon, Sidney B., Leland W. Howe, and Howard Kirschenbaum, *Values Clarification: A Handbook of Practical Strategies for Teachers and Students.* New York: Hart Publishing Co., Inc., 1972.

SUGGESTED READINGS

A. Cognitive Moral Dilemmas

Hare, R.M., *The Language of Morals* (New York: Oxford, 1952).

Kolhberg, Lawrence, "The Child As A Moral Philosopher," *Psychology Today,* September 1968, pp. 24–30.

Kohlberg, Lawrence, "A Cognitive-Developmental Approach to Moral Education," *The Humanist 32,* no. 6 (November/December 1972), pp. 13–16.

Kohlberg, Lawrence and R. Kramer, "Continuities and Discontinuities in Childhood and Adult Moral Development," *Human Development 12* (1969), pp. 93–120.

Kohlberg, Lawrence, "The Development of Children's Orientation Toward a Moral Order":
I. "Sequence in the Development of Moral Thought," *Vita Humana 6* (1963).
II. "Social Experience, Social Conduct, and the Development of Moral Thought," *Vita Humana 9* (1963).

Kohlberg, Lawrence, "Development of Moral Character and Ideology," in *Review of Child Development Research,* ed. by Martin L. and Lois W. Hoffman (New York: Russel Sage, 1964).

Kohlberg, Lawrence, "Education for Justice: A Modern Statement of the Platonic View," in *Moral Education: Five Lectures* (Cambridge: Harvard University Press, 1970).

Kohlberg, Lawrence and M. Blatt, "The Effects of Classroom Discussion on Level of Moral Judgment," in *Moral Development,* ed. by Lawrence Kohlberg and Elliot Turiel (New York: Holt, Rinehart & Winston, forthcoming).

Kohlberg, Lawrence, "Moral Education in the School," *School Review 74* (1966), pp. 1–30.

Kohlberg, Lawrence, "Stages of Moral Development as a Basis for Moral Education," in *Moral Education: Interdisciplinary Approaches,* ed. by C. M. Beck, et al. (Toronto: University of Toronto Press, 1971).

Piaget, Jean, *The Moral Judgment of the Child* (New York: The Free Press, 1965).

B. Values Clarification

Allport, Gordon, *Becoming: Basic Considerations for a*

Psychology of Personality (New Haven: Yale University Press, 1955).

Baier, Kurt, and Nicholas Rescher, *Values and the Future* (New York: The Free Press, 1969).

Harmin, Merrill, Howard Kirschenbaum and Sidney B. Simon, *Teaching Subject Matter With A Focus on Values* (Ohio: Charles E. Merrill, 1966).

Maslow, Abraham A., *New Knowledge in Human Values* (New York: Harper and Row, 1959).

Raths, Louis, Merrill Harmin, and Sidney B. Simon, *Values and Teaching* (Ohio: Charles E. Merrill, 1966).

Rich, John Martin, *Education and Human Values* (Mass.: Addison-Wesley Publishing Co., 1968).

Rogers, Carl R., *Freedom to Learn* (Ohio: Charles E. Merrill, 1969).

Rogers, Carl R., *On Becoming a Person* (Boston: Houghton Mifflin, 1961).

Simon, Sidney B., Leland W. Howe, and Howard Kirschenbaum, *New Strategies for Value Clarification* (Ohio: Charles E. Merrill).

Jack L. Mahan

Chapter 25

The Importance of Play

Allen Sher*

Play is the spontaneous or organized recreational activity of children. It is pleasureful and absorbing and it has been considered the crux of the preschool experience. Play is serious business and the opportunity to play freely is vital to the healthy development of our girls and boys. Children do play for pleasure but play is not recreation for them as it is for adults. Play is necessary for children to function properly and it lies at the heart of the nursery school curriculum.

Play fulfills a wide variety of purposes in the life of a child. It develops physical skills by helping children to develop their large muscles. They do this when they pull a wagon, lift blocks, dig with a shovel, climb on a jungle gym or throw beanbags. In addition, children develop small muscles by using a paintbrush, crayons, and scissors, handling manipulative toys like cars, trucks, and puzzles, by doing finger plays, and by having activities in connection with dressing, buttoning, and lacing shoes.

It develops intellectual skills. Children learn through the use of blocks, e.g., concepts of size (smaller, larger, equal). By pouring water, children learn liquid measure and volume. Through imagination, children are helped to distinguish between reality and fantasy. When they make believe, young people become masters of the environment. They are in command, they establish the conditions of the moment and they make choices and decisions as the action progresses.

It develops social skills. Whenever one child is involved with other children, he learns how to enter a group and be accepted, how to get along with others so that everyone has satisfaction from the play, how to take turns, and the give and take that is the key to successful group interaction.

Play provides emotional values. Children express negative and positive feelings as they react to the activities in which they are involved. They release their tensions, frustrations, and fears as well as their joys and hopes.

Developmental Stages of Play

Children's play progresses through a series of three developmental stages. Very young children tend to be self-absorbed and to indulge in solitary play. Then, they become involved in parallel activities. They play side by side with other youngsters often using the same materials but largely without social interchange. Finally, children become involved in social play. There, the activity occurs between two or more children.

When children play, they acquire concepts, skills, understandings and attitudes. Since these learnings happen simultaneously, the children draw relationships among these concepts. Many activities in play require observation, inquiry and problem solving, all of which lead to a high level of thinking. For example, when a child is building with blocks, she is concerned with shapes, sizes,, and relationships. She measures, matches, and classifies. She faces problems of construction. She shares materials and communicates her ideas and feelings. When a child learns through play, the learning becomes internalized and becomes part of her being.

Play occurs in the lives of young children whenever they are able to be active and have some degree of freedom. A teacher should, therefore, plan to structure some of the play activities that are made available to her children. At the same time, she should provide that children have opportunities for spontaneous play. Imagination flourishes when children play. It is equally valuable for social, emotional, mental, and physical development. As children play, they find different ways of dealing with social situations. They learn about their environment and the roles people have. As they interact with others, they strike a balance between dependent and independent behaviors. In this interaction, children deal with successes and frustrations and learn the very important discipline of self-control. A child who plays hard is assuredly learning to work hard.

A teacher of preschool children should arrange for four kinds of educative play: manipulative play, physical play, dramatic play, and games. Manipulative play involves a child's handling equipment with small pieces: puzzles, peg sets, cuisenaire rods, color cones, beads. The manipulations are self-contained and the values come directly through the child's handling of the material. Physical play involves the use of large muscles. Activities like running, climbing, jumping, or riding a tricycle help children increase their physical skills or learn to use them in different situations. Dramatic play enables a person to assume a

*Dr, Allen Sher, Professor of Education, College of St. Joseph the Provider, Rutland, Vermont.

role and act it out in informal situations. In the housekeeping corner, children take the roles of family members in actions representing home situations. Putting on a piece of clothing like a fireman's hat or a nurse's cap enables a child to make believe he is a fireman or nurse. Games for young children are a form of play activity but they should be easy, uncomplicated, and quickly learned. The rules must be simple and at this level should be designed to include everyone and not eliminate children. Circle games, with or without music, can be used very effectively with young children.

Outdoor Play Activities

In the nursery school and kindergarten, outdoor activities are an essential part of the educational environment. Children need fresh air, physical exercise, a change of pace, and reorientation in space just as much as they need indoor activities. They welcome the general stimulation and different kinds of play possible outdoors. In addition, the child's individual observation of his surroundings and of nature are sharpened by going outdoors. Boys and girls should go out-of-doors some time every day if the weather permits. Much of the outdoor play is spontaneous and young children often play alone as they run on the playground, climb, crawl, dig, swing, or slide.

Outdoor play provides many opportunities for children to be creative. Youngsters are able to use their imaginations and their abilities to think in divergent ways. To some children, adventure is being up high: at the top of a hill, or on a slide, swing, jungle gym, or tree house. Privacy is being inside something, out of sight, in the child's thinking, from other children and the teacher. He can hide or rest in a playhouse, a tent, a packing case, or a tunnel. Concentration is adapting to achieve a purpose: movable ramps, a hose that unhooks and stretches, a fallen tree to climb on, or blocks to make a bridge. The following are suggested ideas for improvised outdoor equipment:

concrete pipes or barrels make tunnels to crawl through

large rocks or tree stumps are stepping stones when placed in certain patterns

tires can be used for swings

an inner tube is good for rolling

large cardboard cartons or wooden packing cases are props for children to make believe

a raised platform built around a tree makes a fine tree house

gardening tools have multiple uses in dirt and sand.

Preschool children are permitted and encouraged to have a wide variety of play activities. Concomitant with play are experiences that are part of regular curriculum. Science is one area where formal and informal learning can take place outside of the classroom. Each year, children should be taught about the seasons in succession. A teacher who takes children on nature walks is having fun in the outdoors and is having children observe the characteristics of the four

seasons. Especially in the autumn, children should be helped to observe caterpillars on the ground, changes in the color of leaves, seed pods, birds flying and feeding, and the harvest of foods. Other experiences that children have during a nature walk include:

collecting insects, shells, stones and leaves

a treasure hunt looking for the largest leaf, the smallest cone, the smoothest stone, etc.

observing a bird nest

studying cloud formations and describing the shapes

examining the topography of the play area (flatness, depression or rise in earth surface)

investigating the surface of the yard (cement, stones, soil).

For additional outdoor play activities, a teacher on a windy day should have the children run about, feeling the wind on their faces or play with kites and pinwheels. They may take a walk to the supermarket, florist, or pet shop. Activity in the sandbox is popular and for variety, kitchen utensils should be provided for straining and sifting. Water play should be brought outdoors with children using a hose or sprinkling cans or making bubbles with plastic rings. An old tire, cut lengthwise to form two halves, and filled with water, becomes two canals for sailing boats. Balls of different sizes are a must for a kindergarten playground. Children may use a ball for rolling, twirling, bouncing, kicking, and catching. Games with balls may be individual or group.

Just being outdoors supports growth, as a child learns about wind, shadows, rain, ice, and snow. For some youngsters, the outdoor playground offers stimulation that no indoor playroom can give.

Indoor Play Activities

Children's play embraces an extensive repertory of activities and the wide use of toys, play materials, and games. Each child spontaneously learns what is truly relevant and meaningful for him, always with feelings that will persist in his subsequent learning. When a child makes discoveries through his play, it is his personal involvement that adds intensity to the experience. Through play, a child learns what no one can teach him.

Play in school is consequently planned with definite purposes. Through play, children learn to get along with one another, develop good habits, and learn about the world around them. Listening to stories, looking at pictures, talking about interesting happenings, playing word games, acting out favorite stories, and looking at books are fun. All of these help to develop a feeling for language and are important experiences in reading readiness. Children are not and need not be aware that when they are playing with blocks, they are learning to count, to compare sizes and shapes, to add and take away. Play is a child's business but it is also his fun.

The arrangement of the room in centers of interest and the choice of equipment and materials permits children to engage in many experiences simultaneously. The following indoor play activities suggest the variety that is available for young children. It is essential for a nursery school teacher to do short-range and long-range planning in order for her pupils to have as many of these activities as possible:

> blockbuilding.
> dramatic play,
> art experiences,
> waterplay,
> sandbox,
> games.

Playing with blocks offers numerous opportunities for growth. Among these are the development of: desirable social habits, cooperative activity, responsibility, effective work habits, accurate observations, carry-over interest, mathematical concepts, geographical relationships, science learnings, physical skills, and creativity. Stacking, reaching, grasping, lifting, shoving, carrying, and balancing are some of the motor skills that are practiced in block play. As for creative play, blocks by nature, are unstructured and may be used to build anything that suits the child's fancy. Older children enjoy planning such structures in advance, but younger ones will content themselves with the experience of stacking and balancing for its own sake and perhaps assign a useful function to the construction at a later point in the building.

Dramatic play is play in which a child usually assumes a role. It can take many forms and can arise from almost any classroom or home situation. It may be the play in the housekeeping corner, the reliving of a story, or the rhythms accompanying a chant or musical selection. These dramatic play activities reflect family background and social experiences as the children make believe they are driving a car, shopping for groceries, preparing meals, or cleaning house. Teachers can demonstrate respect and heightened appreciation for the adults who perform services at school and in the community when children are encouraged to take the role of the plumber, carpenter, custodian, nurse, or letter carrier. In the early part of the school year, much of the play is self-centered. It takes time and experience for children to invent plots and play roles. As the year progresses, they play less as soloists and more in groups of three and four, with increasingly complex plots and sophisticated oral expression. The dramatic play may then become more structured so that the teacher needs to assume more leadership.

The dramatic play or housekeeping area may be equipped with tools for make-believe: tables and chairs for eating; stove, cupboard, sink, dishes, silverware, and pots; beds, carriage, doll clothes, dress-up clothes; accessories for playing the roles of father, grandmother, policeman, doctor; cleaning tools such as mops, dust pans, brooms, and what-

ever odds and ends a teacher can assemble that add detail to the imagining and acting.

The young child is by nature an explorer and an inventor and this characteristic is nourished and satisfied through creative art experiences. With the slighest encouragement and given the opportunity, youngsters can carry their play impulses into activities involving art media. At this age of development, children use art materials for the pleasure of the manipulative experience and the excitement derived from the process rather than from the resulting product. The finished piece of work reveals only a part of the worthwhile experience the child has had in the art of creating. In addition, art experiences, even at the very early levels, give the child a sense of expressing something that she feels within herself. The results of her efforts provide her with a feeling of satisfaction and of self-reliance on her own choice and judgment. In early childhood education, a teacher should plan art experiences that include: painting on an easel, finger painting, drawing, modeling with play dough and clay, papercraft, puppetry, woodworking, and art appreciation.

Water play is one of the freest play activities we can provide for children. Some teachers hesitate to include it because they think that youngsters will become uncontrolled or overstimulated. The opposite is usually the case. Water play is absorbing and soothing; children will stay with it a long time and come away refreshed and relaxed. It provides relief from pressures, tensions, and it stimulates social play.

There are bound to be spills, but sensible rules, good protective aprons, and handy sponges give double service in the areas of education and sanitation. The teacher must establish clear guidelines for the protection of the children's health and safety. As they use different learning tools with water, children receive pleasure, gain knowledge, and learn responsibility.

Pouring and measuring develop eye-hand coordination at the same time that they teach the mathematical concepts of estimating and liquid measure. Water can be offered in dishpans, sinks, galvanized laundry tubs, or even plastic wading pools. Variations in water play can be provided through different kinds of water (clear, soapy, colored, hot or cold). In addition, water can be used in experiments that show floating and sinking. Unbreakable bottles and funnels of various sizes should be available, together with spoons, ladles, pots and pans and sprinkling cans. Washing of dolls, doll clothes, scrubbing vegetables, and watering the plants have the added appeal of participating in meaningful work.

A child learns many lessons at the sand box. Properties of sand can be explored by running it through fingers, a sieve, sifter, or a screen. Sand, like other unstructured material, takes on different meanings with different accessories. Again, there must be sensible limitations and ground rules in using sand: what goes or does not go into the sandbox; sand cannot be used to throw on the floor or at others or on the walls. Children working as a team, often use the whole sandbox to make a display of parks and housing units. By adding miniature objects such as trees, vehicles, animals, and people, they create a community. The outdoor sand pit is only usable during part of the year but the indoor sandbox can be used daily.

The teacher of young children should plan indoor games that give children the exercise they need for building large muscles. Ball handling can be used indoors if it is limited to catching and rolling the ball. Children form a circle, sit down on the floor and spread their legs so that the ball will stay inside the circle. The teacher starts the ball rolling by sending it to one child who returns it to her. With experience in handling and controlling a ball, children will be able to send it back and forth to one another.

Games that are played in the classroom should be simple ones with few rules and directions. The teacher should explain the whole game quickly and then give directions for the various parts of the game. Many games can be accompanied by music, providing additional enjoyment. Six categories of games are: singing games, activity games, bean bag games, sense games, ball games, and quiet games. In some circle games, only one player is active. A teacher can hold the interest of more children by starting with two or three players inside the circle doing the required action. Since children do not enjoy waiting to have a turn or watching others play, several small groups working simultaneously keep the entire class actively involved.

Formal classes for preschoolers vary greatly in their size, location and setting. Regardless of whether children gather in a home, a day care center, a nursery school, or a kindergarten, the teacher must work with the children and their parents. The parents are the single most significant factor influencing the lives of young children. Teachers and child care workers supplement the important tasks and roles of caring for children. Parents, too, have the obligation of arranging that their children have the varieties of play that have been mentioned. Mothers and fathers can provide additional play for their children by having fun: around the house, on the outside, at the supermarket, at the library, at the playground, and at the zoo. Finger plays were once called "Mother Play" because they were used by mothers to amuse and comfort their children.

It is the combined effort of parents and teachers that develops skills and abilities in young children. Parents have a right to expect their children to learn in school, even at the nursery school and kindergarten level. The school is likewise obligated to inform parents concerning the concepts that their children are learning through play. It is an important responsibility of the teacher to provide the experiences for play, to observe the children at play, and to interpret the values of play to parents.

BIBLIOGRAPHY

Braun, Samuel J.; and Edwards, Esther P. *History and Theory of Early Childhood Education.* Worthington, Ohio: Charles A. Jones Publishing Company, 1972.

Draper, Mary Wanda; and Draper, Henry E. *Caring For Children.* Peoria, Illinois: Chas. A. Bennett Co., Inc., 1975.

Frank, Lawrence K. "Play and Child Development." in *Play – Children's Business,* edited by Margaret Rasmussen. Washington, D.C.: Association for Childhood Education International, 1962.

Hendrick, Joanne. *The Whole Child: New Trends In Education.* Saint Louis: The C.V. Mosby Company, 1975.

Hurd, Helen Bartelt. *Teaching in the Kindergarten.* Minneapolis, Minnesota: Burgess Publishing Company, 1965.

Lindberg, Lucile; and Swedlow, Rita. *Early Childhood Education.* Boston: Allyn and Bacon, Inc., 1976.

Read, Katherine H. *The Nursery School: A Human Relationships Laboratory.* Philadelphia: W.B. Saunders Company, 1971.

Spodek, Bernard. *Teaching in the Early Years.* Englewood Cliffs, New Jersey, Prentice-Hall, Inc., 1972.

Starks, Esther B. *Blockbuilding.* Washington, D.C.: National Education Association, 1960.

Todd, Vivian Edmiston; and Heffernan, Helen. *The Years Before School: Guiding Preschool Children.* New York.: The Macmillan Company, 1970.

Chapter 26

Outdoor Learning Environments and Playgrounds

Jack L. Mahan, Jr.*

As with adults, the young child discovers truly meaningful and significant learnings not primarily through formal instruction but rather through creative commerce with the complexities of its various environments. From each challenge posed by the realities of its environments, the child creates alternative feelings, acts, solutions, and self-attitudes. Wisdom, knowledge, self-respect and creativity, therefore, are products of environmental challenge—the consequences of each act re-create both the environment and the child.

This discussion is concerned with maximizing the development of the young child by utilizing the outdoor area of a school, nursery school, or day-care facility as a learning environment. Since much classroom instruction emphasizes cognitive aspects of the young child, early childhood educators have frequently associated learning with the "inside." That is, learning has often been limited not only to inside the child's head, but also to inside the classroom. This situation has frequently generalized to the idea that learning and play are somehow unassociated. As a consequence, "free-play" becomes the time of lesser learning, while "circle-time" is the serious business of instruction. In response to a feeling that something more is happening during play, many early childhood educators are once again looking into the learning value of play. Results of this renewed interest suggest that many traditional distinctions between classroom and playground may be artificial ones. That is, since play is a form of learning, then the outdoors offers many learning experiences absent from indoor programs. Moreover, the outdoor learnings may be both supplementary and complementary to those in the motor, cognitive, and social skills learned outdoors may lead to greater confidence and to more effective classroom learning. In addition, many early childhood educators are re-discovering the outdoors as an exceptional laboratory, not only for learnings relative to play, but also for learning about the natural environment, ecology, math, science, and many other classroom programs and subjects.

Playgrounds And Learning Environments

Three categories tend to describe the basic types of playgrounds today: (1) traditional, (2) creative, and (3) adventure of "junk" playgrounds. The *traditional play-ground* is generally characterized by ambiguous, open spaces and unrelated equipment such as swings, slides, seesaws, climbing bars, domes, etc. Play in these playgrounds tends to be fragmented (a child plays on one piece of equipment, bores with it, and then moves on to another) and time spent on them tends to be short—particularly when the child has a choice. More frequently than not, these playgrounds are blessed with an overabundance of blacktop or asphalt surfaces that do little to stimulate the child to learn. The barrenness and lack of stimulation encourages little learning beyond that experienced as exercise. Moreover, as suggested in a study by Rohe and Patterson (1974, p. 169), the lack of resources in this type of an environment may tend to stimulate negative behavior in children.

Creative playgrounds tend to "emphasize novel forms, textures, and different heights in esthetically pleasing arrangements. Generally, these playgrounds are somewhat sculptured, frequently based on sand or concrete forms and may include...mounds to which slides are attached, tunnels under walls or mounds, and a tree house or platforms above the ground. They may also contain some traditional equipment (Rothenberg, Hayward and Beasley, 1974, p. 123)." These playgrounds tend to supply complexity and variety, with children's activities reflecting more cooperative role playing and creative use of the forms. Activity on such forms tends to be high initially, but as the novelty of the forms decreases over time, so too may the children's exploratory behavior (Derman, 1974, p. 364). The advantage of this playground type is the forms tend to generate cooperative role playing activities (i.e., socio-dramatic play). This activity stimulates the child to utilize the environment in various roles, thereby dealing with environmental challenges at all levels of development. Another advantage tends to be that it provides an interesting background for the child to utilize when creating the environment into what imagination demands. This would tend to meet one criterion for a learning environment. For example, Ellis (1974, p. 306)

*Dr. Jack Mahan, Child Development Department, Palomar College, San Marcos, California 92069.

suggests: "One essential characteristic for a playground is that it should elicit new responses from the child as he plays, and that these responses increase in complexity as play proceeds."

The *adventure playground*—sometimes called "workyards" (Rudolph, 1974)—was adapted from the Scandinavian and British adventure playgrounds (see Lady Allen of Hurtwood, 1968). A play supervisor is available, often on a vacant lot, to assist children create, play, and build with found and discarded materials. Used wood, tires, pipes, dirt, fire, bricks, rope, boxes, water and almost any other cast-off material form the elements with which children build and develop their basic skills. The edifices created then become "clubhouses" requiring social organization, maintenance work, remodeling, and frequently demolishing to make room for some new creation. The environment of an adventure playground is indeed complex, varied and stimulating. Rothenberg, Hayward, and Beasley (1974) indicated children stayed longer at the adventure playground. Also "...most children made the decision to be there, they came almost every day, and named this playground as their favorite one (p. 128)." Because complex constructions are the rule, many skills required of a child in an adventure playground are beyond the capabilities of the young child. The Rothenberg, Hayward, and Beasley study found only 1.74% of the users of this type of playground to be of preschool age, while 44.58% were school-aged, and 32.16% were teenaged—the remainder were adult (p. 125).

It would seem, then, that one might combine the nature of the creative playground with that of the adventure playground in such a way as to yield a maximumly effective learning environment for the young child. This might produce a good environment for development by providing integrated structures and forms linked with channels for movement (which variations in space, height, complexity, etc.) combined with resources available (i.e., loose parts) for the child to participate in construction, manipulation, experimentation, investigative exploration and change. With each of these resources scaled to the behavior of the young child, the environment would state challenges and stimulate construction activities. Enhancement of the playground with items to make it a learning laboratory for study of ecology, math, science, movement, and other subjects would create an outdoor learning environment. The playground would yield experiences for development, as well as experiences encouraging investigation, exploration, and creativity. When this is a social situation, additional learnings will be provided by peers and friends—both lessons in social interaction and lessons in awareness of new discoveries.

An outdoor learning environment is one enhanced and structured for learning, containing items and experiences which would lead the child to discover, in the real outdoor world, concepts generally instructed about indoors. The learning environment would be a place for manipulation,

testing, evaluating, creating and making mistakes. Challenges in the real world would encourage the child to practice to mastery. Social skills could be fine-tuned and—if the teacher recognizes that each time the child is rescued from slight danger or some social conflict (within limits of safety) that this is thwarting the child's progress to another level of development—social and personal conflicts can be resolved without teacher intervention. Confidence could result from such commerce with the real environment, and this confidence is necessary for future risk taking behavior both in the classroom and out. Fears could be experienced, dealt with, and mastered.

Some criteria for an outdoor learning environment are given by Ellis (1974) in the form of questions to be asked about items placed in the outdoor play areas:

Which manipulates the child in the greater variety of ways?
Which allows the child to manipulate it in the greater variety?
Which preempts the behavior of the child least?
Which allows for cooperation between children?
Which seems to be capable of teaching most, or which seems likely to teach what you want the children to learn?
Which combination of items maximizes the variability of behavior exhibited?
Which set or combination will allow rearrangement of the setting to extend the possibilities for play either by the introduction of change, or by increasing its complexity through a season (p. 306–307)?

Additional learning environment criteria would relate to the presence of: (1) loose parts, (2) safety, (3) openendedness, (5) graduated challenges, and (6) connectedness. *Loose parts* are those small manipulatable objects in the environment (often cast-off wood, tires, sand toys, etc.) which allow the child to build and create. Nicholson (1974) states the theory of loose parts as follows:

In any environment, both the degree of inventiveness and creativity, and the possibility of discovery, are directly proportional to the number and kind of variables in it (p. 223).

The theory suggests the addition of "adventure playground" style activities scaled to the capabilities of young children.

Safety is the underlying criterion for all items in the environment. When the preschool child climbs so high as to be dangerous—often five feet or so—there should be a railing to keep accidental and inadvertent mishaps from occuring. The environment should be challenging with minor scratches, bruises and splinters tolerated—these are important learning experiences—but the child should be protected from undue hazard.

Openendedness is the quality of the environment to stimulate inquiry and construction. It encourages choice among activities and it facilitates problem solving by posing questions to be answered. *Abstractness* means a bold generalized statement of objects so as to provide the child with some general raw materials for fantasy and imagination. An abstract enclosure can be fantasized into any number of makebelieve settings (e.g., houses, fire stations, boats, cars, airplanes, etc.), but if the object is built to look like a house in fine detail, most play will be limited to "house" type activities. The less recognizable the object may be, the greater the chance that a variety of role playing activities will be stimulated.

A *challenge* can be defined as that requirement by the environment which encourages the child to participate in activities just one step beyond its current capabilities. The challenge engages the child in practice behavior and as a result pulls the child from a lower level of development to a higher one. The concept of *graduated challenge,* as described by Datner (1969), is stated as follows:

A playground...should present a series of challenges, ranging from simple things that toddlers can master to ones that challenge older and more experienced children. There should be continuity, so that each child always has the dual experience of having mastered some aspects of his environment while knowing there are other aspects that he may still aspire to master (p. 47).

Connectedness is that quality of the environment which makes it a coherent setting for behavior. By providing channels of movement from one behavioral setting to another, the child is lead to utilize each of the various experiences in its play activities. If a climbing structure is connected to a tropical island by a bridge, cooperative role playing may fantasize the pirates as climbing on-board ship (i.e., the climbing structure) and crossing the bridge to dig for treasure near the compost pile. The pirates might then climb the rocks and jump into the ocean of sand to fight the pelagic sharks, and so on. By providing areas that are unique but connected in some abstract or apparent way, the child is drawn through participation in various perceptual-motor, gross-motor, fine-motor, social, sensory, and other experiences by the natural course of its cooperative role playing. One of the most apparent deficiences in most early childhood, preschool, and day-care facility playgrounds is that there is little connectedness—a pipe climber at one corner, a swing over there, a sandbox here, and a great mass of barren space in between. Frequently the equipment is all lined up against the fence with a large open space in the middle—a situation that does not frequently lead to interest or excitement. When the children bore of these independent units, they often get into trouble by creating social conflict.

A Laboratory For The Study Of Nature And Ecology

Jean Kluge (1971) has suggested that "through observation and first-hand experiences, children will become sensitive to their environment; and as they mature, their awareness will form the basis for intelligent action necessary to protect our natural resources (p. 260)." As suggested in the discussion to this point, the child's discovery and personal experience with concrete objects in the environment lead to the development of concepts and the ability to use these in future contexts. With this in mind, the playground becomes a most appropriate place to experience the various ecological cycles, the relationships, interactions, inter-dependencies among living things, and most of all mankind's place in nature. Kluge writes:

Help them see how things are similar, how things change, how objects and systems depend on or help each other, and also how things live in and adapt to their environment. Even big cities have trees. Help the children to really look at one by touching it, by making crayon rubbings of the bark, by feeling the leaves that grow on it, or just by trying to put their arms around it. How is it like other plants—perhaps a dandelion or a bush nearby? How is it helpful to us,.....The leaves or rocks a teacher places on a "nature table" inside of the classroom without the outdoor experience will not be as meaningful as those found by the child in their natural setting (p. 262).

Rocks, dirt, water, leaves, trees (both deciduous and evergreen), twigs, grass, birds, plants, local animals, ants, insects, squirrels, snakes, etc. all become discoveries in the playground. The more one looks, the more one sees. And, the more one sees, the more one wants to look.

With these items in the playground the teacher can then facilitate discoveries. One way of doing this is to have the teacher available as a reference person to help the children label their discoveries with names of plants, bugs, animals, etc. Another way is to have the teacher assist the child in discovering the underlying relationships in nature. The National Education Association (1970) has described an approach called the "strand approach" which provides an investigative, completely openended method of environmental study. "The strand approach uses five broad, universal concepts as a way of drawing the environment under a total integrated 'umbrella.' The concepts or strands are five: Variety and similarities, patterns, interaction and interdependence, continuity and change, and evolution and adaptation. For example, patterns can be applied to the arrangements of beach fauna (biology), mountain ecology (natural history), or people living in an urban area (social sciences) (p. 22)." So too, each of the five categories could be applied within a playground.

In addition to the playground being a laboratory for learning about ecology, it can serve to provide real life examples of other subjects. For example, the playground is a perfect place to exhibit the basic machines of natural science, namely, the wheel and axle, the screw, the inclined plane (or wedge), the lever and fulcrum, and the pulley. The concept of mechanical advantage can be learned by hanging a pulley from a rope over the sand area. The children will experience mechanical advantage while participating in fantasy or other manipulative play in the sand area. Levers, for example on toy steamshovels and other items, provide insight into how machines work. The shadows of the sun as they move, the wind, the barometric pressure; all can be experienced in the playground. The list of possibilities is limitless.

Designing The Outdoor Environment

When considering the types of items to place in the outdoor learning environment, one needs to evaluate how the outdoor environment will relate to the indoor environment. For example, some early childhood education programs use the indoors for free-play, choice activities, "circle times," and tend to conduct most of the learning activities inside. Other programs use the inside for quiet type learning activities or interest centers, while an "outdoor classroom" or patio serves as an area for crafts, art activities and other traditionally indoor learnings. Yet other programs have no distinction between indoors and outdoors and conduct learning activities in all areas of the facility. No matter which division of labor is shared between the indoors and the outdoors, an enhanced playground can be used to support curriculum objectives.

A popular rationale for designing the playground is that one should put examples or symbols in the playground that represent real life. As a consequence of participating in these playground experiences, the child is better prepared for the real world. Another way of generating ideas for the playground is to start with the needs of the preschool aged child, use these as a checklist, and include playground items to facilitate each of the needs. Example needs might be: physical, sensory, emotional, intellectual, social, cultural, and natural (i.e., the need to experience the natural world). The approach would be to ask what experience would facilitate the development of children in each category and provide these experiences in the outdoor environment. The ideal approach to generating items for the playground would be similar to one suggested by Studer (described in Derman, 1974, p. 343): (1) Definition of those behaviors that are to be supported, facilitated, or managed, (2) specification of the physical form or configurations that might facilitate the defined behaviors, (3) execution of plans for the physical facility, and (4) verification that the desired results have been achieved by observational evaluation.

One approach by Burnette (1972) suggests that for an infant environment, elements should represent classes of symbols in the real world; for example: Countryside and

recreation, council chamber or sacred place, work or factory, highway and other social environments (e.g., eating area and place of meeting). Another approach would suggest that one start with a large major area where a particular kind of activity is to be supported (e.g.. a sand area, a climbing structure, a tropical island, a highway, etc.) and then develop sub-areas or micro-environments within each of the larger environments. For example, if the macro-environment (i.e., the large area) is a sand area, perhaps it should consist of two micro-environments, one small one for private activity, the other one larger for social sand activities or water play. If a climbing structure were the macro-environment, then perhaps micro-environments might include strength areas, social and private areas, agility areas, balance areas, coordination areas, fearful areas, safe areas, etc. The macro environment vs. micro-environment distinction helps one see what specific activities should be included within larger environments.

The following checklist of macro-environments has been used successfully by the author for several preschool playgrounds. Ten basic environments are suggested (although others could be added) with at least one private and one social space provided in each environment. *Self-discovery* environments are comprised of areas for climbing, moving, manipulating, crawling, etc. Frequently this area includes climbing structures, tunnels, bridges, climbing trees, etc.— see Gail Ellison (1974). An *outdoor classroom environment* should provide open grass space or patio space for outdoor learning activities. A *sand environment* should be provided with "sand toys," shovels, cups, pulleys, levers for sand manipulation and possible water play in the sand area. Rocks and boulders help define places in the sand area and lead the child to understand soil generations. Sand tables or places for the children to work should be provided in the sand area. An *urban living environment* may comprise a series of enclosures symbolic of community stores with streets (often tricycle paths), vehicles, street signs, etc. *Geology and soil environments* may show rocks and the hard rocks weather to hard dirt; hard dirt weathers to soft dirt with pebbles. Leaves fall from trees to combine with the sand from rocks. This combination is worked by insects and decay processes to produce soil. Some rocks under trees near a compost pile provide great insight into the way soil is built. Moreover, the scraps from indoor cooking projects can be added to the compost pile teaching recycling of organic materials.

A *water resources environment* might include a pond, fountain, wading pool, or drainage ditch. A piece of plexiglass suspended over the water could show evaporation as the first step in the hydrologic cycle. Fish, frogs, and insects in the pond show the water food-chain and tadpoles provide a good example of transformation and metamorphosis—look at the water under a microscope. This area could also be used for water play and learning other things about water and liquids. A *forest and plant environment* would include items such as a log pile, dead climbing tree, live climbing tree, pine forest, christmas tree grove, tropical island, local flora, etc. A mixture of evergreen and deciduous trees will provide experiences related to the seasons. When the summer is hot the deciduous trees will provide shade; with winter cold, the bare trees will permit the sun to warm the area.

A *wildlife environment* (or animal care environment) comprising a corral for larger animals and a bounded space for smaller animals and children should be provided for experiences related to animal husbandry, conservation, and the nature of living things. Also, local animals such as birds, rabbits, or squirrels might be attracted to bird feeders (e.g., wildbird seed feeders, suet feeders, and hummingbird feeders). A birdbath and a feeding station for local animals could help the children in the playground experience various wildlife activities. For example, a wildbird feeder becomes the center of activity depicting the food-chain. Air birds eat the wildbird seed, but drop some to the ground. On the ground, the seed either germinates, grows, and produces the same seed in the feeder, or is eaten by ground birds (such as morning doves) or squirrels and other small rodents. With the birds or small animals on the ground, preditors (frequently cats, or other local predators) come to feed on them. Thus, the food-chain becomes evident. In the air, the presence of a concentration of flying birds may attract predators from the air (often hawks) to feed on the air birds. An aware teacher can provide many hours of quality experiences for the child by helping it become aware of activities related to the natural food-chain in the playground.

A *cultivation environment* consisting of an area for children to plant a garden or grow flowers and crops is desirable. Leaves and debris from the garden can be plowed under or placed in the compost pile completing the growth cycle. The *weather environment* would have items in it for the children to explore the various cycles of weather. Flags, streamers and pennants give indications of wind speed and direction. Homemade barometers (e.g., sometimes an 18 inch striped branch of a balsam fir tree, or a coke bottle filled with colored water hung upside down corked with a U-shaped glass tube) or professional equipment can be made to show barometric pressure, while sundials present the suns various travels. Thermometers and rain gauges are also helpful. A most exciting and unique experience for the children comes from large curved triangular prisms. Hung in the sun outdoors, the sun light becomes a rainbow of pure color projected on nearby surfaces.

One of the most useful ways of looking at designing the outdoor learning environment was suggested by Lynch (1960) relative to cities, Burnette (1974), and later by this author. The approach taken by Mahan (1974) suggests looking at the playground in terms of elements which characterize both the natural and man-made environments and how these affect the perception, symbolization, orientation, privacy, performance, territoriality, and other abilities of the young child. When a person places structures or boundaries in the playground, one is limiting a child's time and space. Time is frequently limited by creating movement experiences; Space is limited in both horizontal and vertical dimensions by the way boundaries are placed in the environment. One way to look at the playground, is to imagine it as a room with a floor, a ceiling, and walls. The walls give dimension to the space; the ceiling (i.e., trees, or shade screens, etc.) provides a feeling of placeness and protectedness, while the floor provides an area for behavior. Time and space are experienced by the child moving through the "room". Within the "room," furniture gives it interest and provides settings for activity. This furniture makes boundaries of various heights which encourages some behavior and discourages other;

The following items make up the "furniture" of the playground. First, we limit horizontal space by a *boundary*. A boundary separates an inside from an outside. Second, we limit vertical space with *edges*. Edges are at various heights; and to get to one edge from another the child must use perceptual-motor skills, often by climbing or jumping. Boundaries are often used as *walls* in various ways; namely, to mark-off a space, to retain one from moving from one space to another, or by screening one completely from another space. *Retaining walls* are protective in nature; they allow the child to experience both inside and outside but protect it from the outside—often retaining walls are railings on climbing structures or around high places. *Screening walls* function to keep the child from perceiving the outside, while focusing the child's attention on activities inside the screening wall. The walls of a room screen-out one's perception of the outside; so too, trees or plantings or structures screen one's perception. Trees, plants and the walls of enclosures or playhouses act in this way. When walls form an enclosure, this frequently is associated with role playing situations involving houses, stores, fire-stations, etc. A *permeated wall* is a special type of retaining or screening wall which retains the child but is not solid, so the child in its imagination can either close-in the wall to make it solid or open the wall as if it was not there. In this case the solid wall is permeated; it is a wall with open spaces between solid spaces (e.g., often a surface made of slats, or netting). The old picket fence is a permeated wall. Permeated walls are frequently used in towers to allow the child to experience openness yet remain safe.

Space can be limited by boundaries, edges, and walls to create a *behavioral setting*. A behavioral setting is a place for behavior to happen—a sand area, a portion of a climbing structure, an enclosure, or a grass place for romping and rolling. When two or more behavioral settings occur in some connected fashion, it can be referred to as a *district* of behavioral settings. A district can be a complete climbing structure. It can be a connected and integrated play area consisting of various settings, such as a sand area, discovery area, tropical island, etc. The district is used by children to support their role playing activities (e.g., the pirates go from the ship to the tropical island and then to the pirate cave—three behavioral settings). A district is a series of behavioral settings connected by channels of movement. *Channels of movement* are paths, routes, or traffic patterns that show a child the way to go from one behavioral setting to another. They could be stepping stones, a path in the grass, or a traffic pattern through a climbing structure. Channels of movement are important to the child because they tell the child: "how to get from one place to another."

Another item which gives dimension to the child's environment (as well as the adults) is a landmark. *Landmarks* are prominent items, generally tall, which can be seen from a long distance. They tell the child "where it is," "who it is," and its relative significance, competence, importance, and scale (i.e., I am taller than the rock, but not as tall as the tower). Landmarks can be trees, buildings, mountains, or other tall objects such as climbing structures or towers. In the playground, a tower, as part of the climbing structure, not only tells the child where it is and something about its self-concept; it also affords the child an opportunity to experience the environment from an eye level above that normally experienced. This experience is grand, compared to the perception on the ground, and it serves to expand the child's awareness.

Enclosures are experienced by the child as a space separated from the outside. Enclosures (i.e., at least two walls and a ceiling) are frequently private places when small in size and social places when large. Since enclosures symbolize the concept of a building, they often stimulate both social and private role playing. They do so by providing a setting for the child's role behavior.

By understanding some of the perceptual and motor effects of boundaries, edges, and walls, one can use these to create places and behavioral settings within the playground. Since cooperative role play stimulates the use of the playground, it is important to understand that cooperative role play is facilitated by providing channels of movement to connect the various behavioral settings. With this "connectedness," the environment generates play which then takes the child through the various learning experiences provided by the playground. When discovery structures (characterized by the above elements) are combined with "loose parts" plus macro-environments and micro-environments for personal and environmental learnings, one creates the variety, complexity and stimulation necessary for investigative exploration, problem solving, role playing, emotional response and creativity. That is to say, one creates an outdoor learning environment.

A Low Cost Approach To The Playground

When funds are unlimited, it is relatively easy to hire a professional to design your playground (assuming the designer is familiar with children) and a builder to build it. However, most schools are not blessed with large budgets, especially for the outdoors. The situation calls for most early childhood educators to maximize learning in the playground while minimizing cost. Labor from the school, community parents or friends can be used to build the playground for free. The approach is frequently time consuming and often frustrating, but those who have used it are generally gratified by the results. Power poles, telephone poles, cable spools, railroad ties, planks, used bricks, peeler core logs, rope, tires, and other items can be utilized for the structures.

With this low budget approach , it is recommended that attention be given to: (1) identifying resources, both labor and materials, and (2) master planning the complete environment (this can often be a sketch or a model). The priority would be: materials, master plan, labor and implementation, and construction. Once the materials are found or donated, the design stage and master plan stage are of utmost importance. A master plan of the entire playground is necessary to understand the inter-relationships among items to be included. One need not build everything at once, but it is important to have the proper connectedness and relatedness established in the master plan. The design can be completed by teachers, or with help of parents and children. Jeremy Joan Hewes (1975) provides an excellent description of this process. The master plan is emphasized because a "hit and miss" "start on any structure" approach will most likely end in the usual uninteresting, non-teaching playground. Once the master plan is complete, the items can be completed all at once or in phases. The following checklist might be helpful:

1. Get preliminary excitement generated among:
   a. children, parents, teachers, owners, administrators, etc.
   b. potential labor and material donators (a social occasion where intentions are presented with pictures of ideas about the playground is helpful)
2. Present preliminary planning ideas to above.
3. Establish what resources are available.
4. Prepare master site-plan and sketches (or model).
5. Acquire materials.
6. Construct the environment (in phases if necessary) coordinating the volunteer resources:
   a. choose a simple, quickly completed, but impressive structure or macro-environment first.
   b. use it and the master plan excitement to motivate volunteer resources toward completion.

In summary, it has been suggested that the playground be considered as a learning environment. One which challenges the child to discover itself, its abilities, concepts and ideas, the outdoor world, and the place of mankind in nature. When classroom concepts and programs are brought outdoors, they become more meaningful. The playground is a learning environment because it challenges the child's physcial, psychological, and social abilities and encourages the child to become skillful at living.

SELECTED BIBLIOGRAPHY

Lady Allen of Hurtwood. *Planning For Play*. Cambridge, Mass.: The Mit Press, 1968.

Burnette, Charles. "Designing to Reinforce the Mental Image, an Infant Learning Environment." In *Proceedings of the Environmental Design Research Association, EDRA 2*, edited by John Archea and Charles Eastman. Stroudsburg, Pa.: Dowden, Hutchinson & Ross, 1972.

Burnette, Charles. "The Mental Image and Design." In *Designing For Human Behavior*, edited by Jon Lang, Charles Burnette, Walter Moleski, David Vachon. Stroudsburg, Pa.: Dowden, Hutchinson & Ross, 1974.

Dattner, Richard. *Design For Play*. New York: Van Nostrand Reinhold, 1969.

Derman, Asher. "Children's Play: Design Approaches and Theoretical Issues." *In Alternative Learning Environments*, edited by Gary Coates, Stroudsburg, Pa.: Dowden, Hutchinson & Ross, 1974.

Ellis, Michael, J. "Play: Theory and Research." In *Alternative Learning Environments*, edited by Gary Coates. Stroudsburg, Pa.: Dowden, Hutchinson & Ross, 1974.

Ellison, Gail. *Play Structures*. Pasadena, Ca. 91105: Pacific Oaks College and Children's School (714 West California Boulevard), 1974.

Hewes, Jeremy Joan. *Build Your Own Playground*. Boston, Mass.: Houghton Mifflin, 1975.

Kluge, Jean. "What the World Needs Now: Environmental Education for Young Children." *Young Children,* 1971, 26: 260–263.

Lynch, Kevin. *The Image Of The City*. Cambridge, Mass.: The MIT Press, 1960.

Mahan, Jack. L., Jr. "Creative Movement Environments." Unpublished presentation to Early Childhood Movement Conference, September 21–22, Ohlone College, Fremont, California, 1974.

National Education Association, Association of Classroom Teachers. *Man and His Environment*. Washington, D.C. 20036: National Education Association (1201 16th Street, N.W.), 1970.

Nicholson, Simon. "The Theory of Loose Parts." In *Alternative Learning Environments,* edited by Gary Coates. Stroudsburg, Pa.: Dowden, Hutchinson & Ross, 1974.

Rohe, William; and Patterson, Arthur H. "The Effects of Varied Levels of Resources and Density on Behavior in a Day Care Center." In *Proceedings of the Environmental Design Research Association, EDRA 5; Man-Environment Interactions: Evaluations and Applications, 12: Childhood City,* edited by Daniel H. Carson. Milwaukee, Wisc.: Environmental Design Research Association, Inc., 1974.

Rothenberg, Marilyn; Hayward, D. Geoffrey; Beasley, Robert R. "Playgrounds: For Whom?" In *Proceedings of the Environmental Design Research Association, EDRA 5; Man-Environment Interactions: Evaluations and Applications, 12: Childhood City,* edited by Daniel H. Carson. Milwaukee, Wisc.: Environmental Design Research Association, Inc., 1974.

Rudolph, Nancy. *Workyards: Playgrounds Planned for Adventure*. New York: Teachers College Press, 1974.

Chapter 27

BEEP: A Radical Experiment in Early Childhood Education

Arnold J. Keller*

You don't have to ponder it very long to begin to suspect that all too many school children are being labeled as educationally handicapped or as "underachievers" these days. Perhaps 10 to 20% of our nation's children and youth are now classified by school authorities under those rubrics. The reasons cited for these developmental maladies usually include our children's addiction to television, the disintegration of family life, malnutrition, and neurological or physical impairments. Some psychologists now even contend that food additives have had a detrimental effect on learning. Yet seldom is the single most important factor mentioned, namely,that we as a society wait too long before systematically educating the nation's most precious resource, our children.

Times are changing, however, as a quiet but significant revolution is underway. It concerns early childhood education. Not education for three or four year olds as is the case in the many head start programs across the country. Nor in the early childhood education program recently initiated in California, nor even in the renascence of interest in nursery schools or day care centers, all of which are figuring more prominently in the educational plans of parents. It is education commencing at birth about which I speak.

The pioneer program was begun in 1972 when the public schools of Brookline, Mass., launched BEEP— short for the Brookline Early Education Project. Since that date, the school district has served as surrogate parents for nearly three hundred babies during the critical period of infancy and beyond. It is a radical experiment in which a public school system and parents—for the first time in the United States (and maybe the world) have become partners in raising hundreds of babies.

Since BEEP's inception, considerable interest in infant/toddler education has been created, the result being that an increasing number of communities across the country are generating similar programs. And with federal monies beginning to flow for such projects, there is no telling how rapidly other school systems might leap on to the BEEP-like bandwagon. The fledgling movement could be the broadest reform in public education—there are 25 million preschoolers in the country—since the introduction of the comprehensive high school seventy-five years ago. And it

will probably transform American education so that ultimately its present recognizable features may be difficult to discern.

BEEP represents an unusual collaborative effort among the Brookline Schools, the Harvard Graduate School of Education, and the Children's Medical Hospital of Boston. A policy committee with members from the above groups as well as other community organizations meets regularly to discuss the program and plot its direction. BEEP presently costs parents nothing. Funding has been provided by the Robert Wood Johnson Foundation, the Carnegie Corporation, and the Brookline Schools. Over the years,the cost including planning and research has amounted roughly to two million dollars.

The beginnings of BEEP came about innocently enough. Dr. Robert Sperber, Brookline's superintendent of schools was troubled by the inability of his community's schools to have a significant impact on children with educational deficiencies, even with generous expenditures in regular as well as remedial programs. If affluent Brookline, considered by prominent educators to be a "lighthouse" school district with optimal learning conditions, could not help students overcome their educational deficits, Sperber thought, then what is probably happening nationally, given the growing number of students who require remediation in basic skills areas, is a massive waste of time and money. If the schools could reach the students sooner, he believed, educational benefits to the child and perhaps financial savings to the district could result. As a staunch advocate of early childhood education, Sperber considered earlier admission to schooling a positive step in the right direction.

Yet the superintendent had no intention of starting anything as unique as BEEP until he received a rude awakening in a conversation with Dr. Burton White, a psychologist and the director of the Harvard Graduate School of Education's Pre-School Project. Sperber was told in no uncertain terms that his plan was a "dumb idea," for school admission at age three was even too late to be of compensatory value for most children. The superintendent was a rapt listener for

*Dr. Arnold J. Keller, Assistant Professor of Education, St. John's University, New York, N.Y.

the Harvard psychologist's expertise was the result of nearly two decades of intensive research on early childhood development by himself and a revolving cadre of graduate students.

According to White, there are four fundamental learning topics that all children cope with before their third birthdays: language development, curiosity, social development, and foundations of cognitive intelligence. His extensive research has revealed that children, in terms of any of these facets of their development, succeed, fail, or are partially crippled, depending upon what their parents do with them, especially between the ages of eight months and eighteen months. Over the years, White found that the mothers of the most competent children clearly demonstrated superior performance in three key roles during the eight to eighteen month span: (1) as designers and organizers of their children's physical environment; (2) as authorities who limited potentially dangerous behavior; and (3) as consultants to children in brief episodes when needed. (White, 1974, pp. 2-5).

Of particular consequence is the finding that lasting educational deficits do not manifest themselves (for most children who will do poorly later in life) until some time during the second year of life, and become quite substantial by three years of age. Thus if a child is six months or more behind in language and problem solving skills at age three, he is not likely to be successful in his educational career. And rarely, White concluded, does the cause of a developmental deficiency reside in the child himself. Given a healthy youngster, external factors play a much more significant role in his growth and development.[2](White, 1976).

White's position was clear and concise. If children were to develop to their maximum potential, the schools, by simply lowering the age of admission a year or two, would be spending good money for marginal benefits. To do it properly, White contended, the schools should try to help parents do a more thorough job during all the pre-school years, in effect, from birth. There was, he said, sufficient evidence to indicate that children are far more intellectually precocious than we give them credit for.[3](Pines, 1976).

In effect, the Harvard academician summed up for Sperber what developmental psychologists have been saying for nearly two decades. A mounting body of evidence has confirmed that the first 45 months—from the moment of conception until three years of age—largely determine whether or not a child will be able to live up to his genetic potential. By that time a child is set on a developmental track for life. He proceeds inexorably along the growth channel now established and how well he does, how far he goes toward reaching his inborn potential, depends to a large extent on how he has been handled during his first 45 months of life. These early years are exceptionally crucial, for although growth is a lifelong process, the sheer velocity of development of the prenatal stage and the earliest years is never

again matched.[4](Wyden, 1976).

Obviously, such conclusions make parenting an even more vital experience than we have generally thought and instantly elevates programs such as BEEP to the status of an educational imperative. And so, enrolling babies (and parents) in public school is not as absurd as some might think at first glance. However, the school is not the traditional one with which we are familiar. Rather BEEP is designed as comprehensive home-based diagnostic and educational program geared to assist families to provide for each child's optimal health and environmental conditions in which he may grow toward the full realization of his abilities by identifying and treating potential educational problems in their incipient stages. BEEP underscores the concept that educating a child is a shared responsibility between the family and the professional educator with the family as the paramount partner.

Unlike many early childhood programs of past years, BEEP's clientele comes from diverse racial, economic, and social strata. In 1972, all expectant parents who resided in Brookline were invited to partake in the program, provided they had no plans to relocate in the near future. Since most of the community's participants were from white, middle class families, the program's administrators recruited black, Chinese, and Spanish children from the nearby Bosston area. Currently, these latter groups are approximately one-third of BEEP's students. At last count, about 300 children were enrolled in BEEP. Less than ten families have dropped out of the program, most of whom moved from the area. Therefore, a significant number remains as an experimental group which will be closely monitored during its school career and compared with other children the same age.[5](Pierson, 1975).

BEEP'S program for child and parent includes on-going medical screening and developmental evaluation of the children, regular home visits by teachers who work with the infants and parents, and small group seminars at the program's base of operations where the infants' development is discussed by parents and staff. The doors of the BEEP Family Center are always open to parents and their children at any time during the day; in certain instances, free child care is provided to give harried mothers some respite. The center also houses an array of resources such as toys, books, and films, and assistance is always available by phone, where any questions are readily answered. To counter the isolation peculiar to motherhood, parents have started special interest groups, such as the one in which the special problems of raising a black child in America are discussed. Furthermore, there are frequent meetings at night to hear speakers on various facets of child development.

BEEP becomes operational for parents soon after the mother arrives home from the hospital with her baby. This is usually a difficult time for many parents. Even though many BEEP parents are relatively wealthy and possess advanced degrees, all too many would readily admit they are terribly ignorant of what it takes to effectively raise their children in the first few years of their lives. There are all sorts of questions to be answered about feeding habits, sleeping patterns, etc., and so the first visit by a specially-trained BEEP teacher is most welcome. And although BEEP teachers may not have all the answers—who does when it comes to raising children—enough information and support is given to the parent to cushion the emotional shocks of the first several months.

BEEP teachers are trained to act as resources and not as quasi-parents. As such, their main task is to assist parents in analyzing why their child behaves as he does and to provide parents with techniques which would prove salutary in their daily contacts with their child. When parents understand the underlying motives for their child's behavior, they can take advantage of those "teachable moments," as Piaget calls them. In essence, fathers and mothers are alerted to seize upon teaching opportunities which can stimulate learning by their child.

Consistent with Burton White's research, particular attention is devoted to the child between eight and eighteen months for this period is the time of rapid social and intellectual development. The infant roams the house more, recognizes adults with whom he has had previous contact, gets into those fixes so typical of the age group, and acquires a grasp of language. It is also a dangerous time for the child; more accidental deaths, poisoning, beatings by others, maimings by animals happen during this period. Yet the mother cannot simply imprison her youngster out of fear. To do so would no doubt stunt the child's instincts for curiosity and exploration and probably affect his intellectual development adversely. Mothers are shown how to prevent many of these tragic occurrences by being alert to the physical environs of the child, thus enabling the child to freely explore the unknown and stimulate his curiosity. (Pierson, 1974).

Both Sperber and White realized during BEEP's planning stage that parent training needed to be complemented by monitoring the babies' health and development. Through foundation support, BEEP is able to provide the most intensive series of diagnostic medical and psychological examinations yet devised, tracking a child through the first five years of life. These evaluations provide the staff with a developmental profile for each child. Physical, neurologic, vision, hearing, and developmental assessments are conducted periodically in order to detect conditions predictive of later learning problems. And early detection of abnormalities enables treatment to begin at a time when it can be most effective.

The diagnostic services continue to expand. In April, 1975, BEEP incorporated into its services a routine lead and anemia screening for all BEEP children and siblings between the ages of twelve months and six years. In September, 1975, a program of dental screening and education

was begun.

BEEP also maintains a social service component. The social worker and teacher work closely in preventing or assisting in family crisis situations. They may confer about an assortment of problems including a particular family's need for counseling or psychiatric care, a sibling with a behavior problem, welfare matters, or assistance in locating more suitable housing. The support of the BEEP social worker assists families over difficult times and no doubt means much to those in dire straits.

A central concept in the BEEP diagnostic strategy is that the total picture of the child is best captured in the melding of medical and developmental information. The pediatrician and developmental psychologist work closely together in observing the child and sharing insights. Important contributions are made to this team by the BEEP teacher, social worker, and staff nurse, who are assigned to each family.

At the periodic evaluations, the mother is questioned at length by the staff nurse about her child so as to pick up any indications of problems not revealed by the diagnostic tests. Details are sought regarding such items as infections, rashes, medications, sleeping patterns, falls, erratic behavior. When all the information is finally collated, the child's home teacher joins the BEEP team for a "feedback" session and to give the mother the chance to ask about anything that might be of concern to her.

The thoroughness of the diagnostic tests have revealed physical and psychological problems not identified by the child's own family doctor. For example, since the program's beginnings several babies were found to be suffering from hearing defects, four were discovered to have poor vision, three were mentally retarded, several were backward in speech development or had delayed motor coordination, and a number appeared hyperactive. These physical or neurologic problems, left untended, can grow in severity and interfere with learning. Although BEEP does not provide free medical care, it does refer parents to specialists who can give the best possible treatment.

Since the oldest children in the BEEP program are only three, it is much too soon to assess the program's value. Indications of the program's worth will become more evident as the children reach the age of four, though it won't be until age seven, or at the end of the second grade of school, that a fairly accurate assessment of BEEP can be made. Nonetheless during the summer and fall of 1975, an interim evaluation was made in which 100 BEEP parents were interviewed. Care was taken to assure parents that only the program was being evaluated and not the parents, that candor was essential, and that their anonymity would be protected.

The results were most heartening. Parents reported the primary impact of the program to be in developing in them a keener awareness about their child, a better understanding of their role as parent/mother, and the emotional lift in knowing that the BEEP staff stands ready to assist them whenever necessary. In a few cases, parents reported that BEEP had no impact on the parent. Where it did, the impact varied from family to family. Some found the resource materials available to be exceptionally fine, while others possessed a pervasive feeling that BEEP was the most significant event to happen to them as parents.[8] (Pierson, 1975).

As one might expect, the home visits by the BEEP teacher was considered the most vital aspect of the program. Parents view the home visitor in exceptionally positive terms: sensitive, warm, helpful, pleasant, good with children, communicative, understanding. In virtually all cases, the home visitor's role is perceived as totally positive, a great source of reassurance and moral support.

The diagnostic team was accorded a high rating as well. Its members are seen as truly interested practitioners, whose thoroughness and consideration are greatly appreciated. Parents felt that sessions with the diagnostic team generally result in a further educational experience for them as questions are fully answered and the "why" of what is happening is fully explored. Interestingly, a good number of parents found that the BEEP staff has developed better rapport with their child than their own family physician.

If BEEP's rationale proves itself to be essentially correct, then our traditional early childhood programs really come too late to seriously affect a child's development. Most of the nation's early childhood ventures have been geared to three and four year olds in head start programs, nursery schools, day care centers and kindergartens. And the chances that an early childhood program has been carefully conceived, much less carried out by qualified personnel, is slim. These initial experiences away from home have generally been little more than opportunities for socialization and custodual care. Thus, few children benefit as things now stand.

BEEP's lasting success could result in a complete reassessment of our present educational priorities. If White's research is essentially correct, and there is a growing body of evidence to confirm that position, expanding educational opportunity primarily at the upper end of the spectrum as we have done for the past 200 years is not as practical or egalitarian as has been thought. Our policy has been based on tradition rather than our growing knowledge of human development. Obviously, there should have been a greater effort to educate the very young. As a nation, we have spent next to nothing on the most important years, those when a child's capacity to learn is being laid.

The timing of this reassessment is propitious. Sagging enrollments, surplus teachers, and empty buildings are just the right combination of factors to give impetus to new programs such as BEEP. And, if it is argued that the cost may border on the prohibitive, it can be just as congently put that substantial longrun savings can be realized by eliminating costly remedial programs for many students.

No one really knows for sure whether education beginning in infancy will mean anything in the long run. Nonetheless, if BEEP and similar programs prove successful, and first signs are encouraging, our nation is headed for a radically different structured educational system that we have now—for children and their parents. In the process, society will have taken one more step toward the goal of equality of educational opportunity.

BIBLIOGRAPHY

Maeroff, Gene. "Educators Ask How Young Is Too Young?" *New York Times,* Sept. 7, 1975, 125:18.

Pierson, Donald E. *The Second Year of the Brookline Early Education Project.* Winchester, Mass.: MASBO Cooperative Corporation, 1974.

Pierson, Donald E. *The Third Year of the Brookline Early Education Project.* Winchester, Mass.: MASBO Cooperative Corporation, 1975.

Pines, Maya. "Head Head Start." In *Readings in Human Development,* edited by Anne Kilbride et al. Guilford, Conn.: Dushkin Publishing Group, 1976.

"School District, Seeking 'No Fail,' to Enroll Babies." *New York Times,* July 23, 1975, 125:32.

White, Burton, L. *Reassessing Our Educational Priorities.* Unpublished transcript of presentation to the Education Commission of the States, Early Childhood Education Symposium, Boston, Mass., Aug. 3, 1974.

White, Burton, L. *The First Three Years of Life,* Englewood Cliffs, N.J.: Prentice-Hall, Inc., 1975.

White, Burton, L. et al. "Competence and Experience." In *The Structuring of Experience,* edited by I.C. Uzgiris and F. Weizmann. New York: Plenum Press, 1977.

Wyden, Barbara. "Growth: 45 Crucial Months." In *Readings in Human Development,* edited by Anne Kilbride et al. Guilford, Conn.: Dushkin Publishing Group, 1976.

Chapter 28
Behavior Modification in Early Childhood Classrooms

Shirley Moore*

Behavior modification in the classroom means different things to different teachers. To some, it calls to mind a "token economy" in which children are given tangible rewards for having completed a task, participated in an activity for a specified period of time, or demonstrated learning to criterion. To other teachers, behavior modification is a research strategy used by psychologists to demonstrate the malleability of human behavior. To still others, it is a clinical tool to be used in the management of children with severe behavior or learning problems.

Behavior modification, in fact, is all of these things and more. Techniques to change child behavior are used by teachers from the time their children enter the classroom in the morning until they leave for home. Some teachers are deliberate and analytical about their attempts to influence child behavior while others function intuitively in their classrooms without making their goals and strategies explicit.

Many preschool and day care teachers are "turned off" by a behavior modification classroom approach in which child behavior is managed through the use of extrinsic rewards for learning (such as tokens to be exchanged for trinkets, food or free time). Good teachers at all educational levels prefer to feel that the children in their classrooms participate eagerly in their school programs because they like school and find school tasks intrinsically rewarding. The attraction that school has for the child has been particularly important to nursery school teachers. Preschool children, after all, are not required by law to attend school; if school is an unpleasant experience for them, their parents simple withdraw them.

Teachers should, indeed, be concerned about the extent to which schools are intrinsically satisfying to children. In a token-economy early childhood classroom the curriculum is relieved of much of the burden that it must bear in other classrooms in which children are free during much of their school day to participate in activities or not as a function of their interest in the activities. Young children have been known to suffer through some very dull and pedantic school tasks for the sake of contingent external rewards that are delivered at intervals along the way. A child whose participation in a lackluster school program is maintained by external rewards may very well master the materials

and even take satisfaction in his accomplishments, but find the learning process itself boring and tedious. If this is the case, we will not have served him well. Even when participation in school activities is to be rewarded extrinsically, it is a good rule of thumb to submit curriculum for young children to the test of a setting in which children can come and go from activities as a function of their interest in the materials and tasks. The ultimate balance in any classroom should be heavily weighted in favor of learning experiences that are intrinsically satisfying to the children as well as academically beneficial. The movement toward open school planning at the elementary level is undoubtedly an attempt on the part of teachers and parents to make schools for older children a more intrinsically rewarding experience; early childhood educators should not abandon their own traditional emphasis on "user satisfaction."

Rapport and the Use of Social Reinforcement

Young children usually come to their preschools or Head Start programs directly from the family fold and are having their first experience at functioning in the peer group; consequently, teaching strategies in early childhood programs are oriented toward helping the children to learn to feel secure and to function effectively in an unfamiliar and complex social environment away from home. Teachers of young children typically go to considerable lengths to establish and maintain good rapport with their charges. They are friendly, considerate and affectionate with the children and are willing to perform many of the supportive care functions of a parent as well as the instructional functions of a teacher. Because the children are socially inexperienced and cognitively immature, teachers feel that they must be patient; in fact, patience has been one of the most valued characteristics of the traditional early childhood educator; not endless patience, but more than an ordinary amount of patience. Gentle persuasion is the rule and punishment is used sparingly. Teachers reason that children do not change their behavior patterns overnight. A child who is used to

*Shirley Moore, Professor of Child Psychology and Director of the Laboratory Nursery School, Institute of Child Development, University of Minnesota, Minneapolis. Reprinted with permission of CONTEMPORARY EDUCATION, Summer 1974.

grabbing toys, interfering with the activities of other children, responding to frustration with explosive anger, or expecting more than a reasonable amount of help and attention from adults, is likely to continue these behaviors in school, gradually replacing them with more adaptive, appropriate behaviors. This development takes time. The adults in the classroom start with the assumption that the children are both willing and able to adapt to the new situation if they are given appropriate feedback and time to learn. Consequently, the teacher's first job in modifying behavior is to give the children the information they need. Teachers take pains to explain to the children what is expected of them and to remind them when they forget or ignore the school "ground rules" about sharing or caring for school materials or equipment.They may appeal to a child's sense of fairness or obligation and help the children to understand the consequences of their misbehavior. Whenever possible, the teachers provide a reasonable alternative for something that a child wants to do but is not permitted to do because of the consequences for him or for others. Given time, the children will be expected to accept the constraints on their behavior that are deemed necessary for the group to function cooperatively and constructively.

Most young children come to their schools expecting to have to conform to adult requests even though they may procrastinate a bit and test the limits of the situation. They are prepared to "like" their teachers. They are quick to sense an atmosphere of caring and ocnsideration when it exists between teachers and children and generally return the good will. Social approval from a warm and friendly adult is an important commodity to the young child and most are willing to modify their behavior in response to adult approval. In fact, the young child's sensitivity to positive feedback from adults is clearly the most powerful single tool a teacher has in the service of classroom management. Even children who stubbornly ignore teacher **disapproval** show behavior changes in response to persistent teacher **approval**.

One misconception that has been conveyed to teachers by psychologists involved in early childhood classroom management is the impression that any attention, approval or disapproval, for a particular behavior, tends to increase the occurence of that behavior; consequently teachers are told to ignore instances of misbehavior as much as possible. While it is true that some children are insensitive to disapproval and may even take delight in eliciting disapproval from their teacher, this is not true generally of children in early childhood classrooms. Most young children respond differentially to attention that implies criticism and disapproval: they seek praise and try to avoid criticism. The exceptions stand out in the minds of teachers and psychologists because they are difficult to manage in the normal course of classroom events. In any group of twenty children, there will probably be a few children—perhaps two of

three—who are insensitive to mild criticism and disapproval from adults. The teacher may, indeed, decide to ignore the misbehavior of these children as much as possible (since disapproval has not been effective) while the child is given regular doses of praise and approval for good behavior when it occurs. Misbehavior that cannot be ignored, such as excessive aggression or destructiveness, should be handled promptly and consistently. The consequences for these behaviors should be made clear to the child and they should be imposed consistently from one time to another and from one adult to another.But always the heaviest burden for behavior change should be invested in the use of positive feedback for good behavior when it occurs. Teachers sometimes have the impression that the problem children never do show the acceptable target behaviors so that being alert to their occurrence is a thankless job! Observations suggest that this simply is not true. Aggressive children do use non-aggressive means at times to accomplish their purposes, impulsive children do concentrate and persevere at times, unfriendly children do show fleeting instances of friendly behavior, and uncooperative children do cooperate. Teachers who are oriented toward watching for these behaviors will see several instances of them in any school day. If these instances are reinforced with praise and approval, behavior change will amonst certainly occur.

Classroom observations indicate wide variation in teacher sensitivity to good behavior. Almost all teachers are sensitive to misbehavior and most teachers feel an obligation to attend it in some way, but in the busy hubbub of classroom life, good behavior often goes unnoticed and unrewarded despite the fact that it is blatantly clear from both research and casual observation that positive attention for good behavior increases its occurrence. Psychologists from the University of Kansas and other centers, working in early childhood classrooms, have demonsttated again and again that systematic attention in the form of smiles, a kind word, an affectionate pat or a compliment given to a child directly following a particular behavior—such as a friendly act or participation in a school activity—will increase the instances of these behaviors. The Kansas investigators have also brought about reductions in the occurrence of temper tantrums, destructiveness, unfriendliness, and over-dependence in a matter of a week or two exclusively through the use of teacher approval for mature behaviors and the withdrawal of teacher attention for immature behaviors (Harris, Wolf, & Baer, 1967). The children involved in these demonstrations were never criticized or punished for their immature behavior.

Punishment in the Classroom

Through positive sanctions take precedence over negative sanctions in the classroom, mild forms of punishment for misbehavior, such as withdrawal of privileges and brief social isolation, are used at times by teachers of young children. Harsher punishments involving humiliation, ridicule, and shaming through public criticism are not used by most early childhood teachers. Though these forms of psychological punishment may be effective in repressing misbehavior, they may be damaging to a child's self-image or arouse fear and hostility. Also, most teachers of young children feel that physical punishment should not be used in the school setting. While there is no evidence to suggest that mild forms of physical punishment (such as spanking) are more harmful to children than non-physical forms of punishment, many teachers feel that administering physical punishment is the prerogative of parents, not teachers.

When negative consequences for misbehavior are imposed on children in early childhood classrooms, teachers usually prefer consequences that bear a logical relation to the misbehavior. If a child persists in misusing a particular toy or piece of equipment after reasonable reminders and warnings, the teacher may refuse to allow the child to use the equipment until the child appears to be sufficiently impressed with the need to use it properly. If a child is overly aggressive in his interactions with peers, he may have to leave the group and play alone for a time.

A rational connection between a punishment and an offense has several advantages for the child and the teacher. It appears to be less arbitrary on the teacher's part since it can be presented to the child as a necessary step that must be taken to protect the materials or the other children (which, indeed, it is). A reasonable connection between a misbehavior and its punishment also focuses the child's attention on the behavior to be changed. Not being allowed to go for a neighborhood walk with the group following some teasing episodes of running away from the group is likely to impress the child with his "walk behavior" more than would a punishment that is unrelated (such as being deprived of a snack for that day). Also, the child may be more likely to interpret the misbehavior as the "cause" of the punishment. If he feels that he has caused the punishment, he may also feel that he can rectify the situation if he convinces his teacher that he can manage walks in the future. A strategy of this kind for determining negative consequences hopefully will help children to learn to take more responsibility for their own destiny in the school environment.

Consistency is an important characteristic of effective classroom discipline that can reduce the occurrence of misbehavior and thus the need for punishment. Fortunately for all concerned, **complete** consistency is not necessary for effective learning, but an "on again, off again" appraoch to classroom rules and regulations will almost certainly lead to chaos and confusion. Teachers work and plan together in deciding which behaviors will be permitted or encouraged and which will be discouraged in the classroom. Each adult must then do his part to help the children to learn what is expected. In the interest of feasibility and fairness, there should be no constraints placed on the behavior of children that are not necessary for effective classroom functioning. Every rule or regulation should be examined for its relevance and importance. Only the necessary ones should survive this scrutiny. The children then should be expected to comply with the classroom protocol.

In early childhood classrooms in which misbehavior is a very common occurrence, one must suspect multiple causes. Factors that are likely to lead to pervasive misbehavior are too few adults for adequate supervision, too many children for the available space, inappropriate expectations given the developmental level of the children, not enough interesting and challenging handling of misbehavior when it occurs, and poor general rapport between the children and the adults. Ironically, through rapport between children and adults is essential if low-key discipline is to be effective, rapport is probably determined more by the things that teachers do when children are **not** misbehaving than by the things they do when children **are** misbehaving. A child's feeling of compatibility and good will toward his teacher is probably determined more by the number of pleasant experiences he has with his teacher than by the teacher's handling of misbehavior. When a teacher is a very salient person to a young child, a little disapproval goes a long way since the child has much to lose if he loses the good will—even temporarily, of a supportive, nurturant adult.

The Use of Reasons and Explanations

Teachers of young children vary in the extent to which they justify the demands and restrictions that they impose on children. Some teachers supply reasons and explanations as a common courtesy to their children so that discipline does not seem to be so arbitrary and inconsiderate. Other teachers feel that talk and reason only complicate the picture and accomplish little. While undoubtedly there are times when a teacher's talk accomplished little, giving children reasons and explanations probably does help them to learn the general rules that govern social behavior in a classroom or a society. If a child is told not only **what** is forbidden but **why**, he has a better chance of using that information to avoid disapproval or punishment in similar situations another time. Even children as young as three or four are expected to learn very complicated rules to govern their behavior. Aggression, for example, is not just permitted or forbidden! It is permitted—provided that the child aggresses only upon reasonable provocation, provided that he does not use the more bloodthirsty forms of aggression, and provided that he does not aggress against babies, parents, visiting guests in the school or teachers. The child will almost certainly be aided in learning this complicated protocol if his teacher explains, if not on every occasion, at least on many, specifically why he may not be aggressive on a particular occasion or in a particular way.

Needless to say, explanations will not assure a child's compliance but it may lesson the time it will take him finally to grasp the rules he is being asked to observe. While there is some risk of teacher-child discussions of misbehavior placing undue emphasis on the behavior or becoming the focal point for classroom tension, discussion has the advantage of giving the child both the opportunity and the responsibility for examining his own behavior in terms of its justness and reasonableness. If his teacher is sincerely interested in helping him to manage the constraints placed upon his behavior within the social context of the school, discussion can lead to more effective solutions to classroom problems. There is evidence, from the child-rearing literature to suggest that giving children reasons and explanations facilitates the early attainment of self-control in young children (Becker, 1964; Sears, Macoby & Levin, 1957). Since this is one of the major goals of discipline, the regular use of reasons and explanations should be given serious consideration by teachers.

Even the most skillful early childhood teacher will not be totally effective in the management of classroom behaviors. Fortunately, in most early childhood classrooms the teachers and the children are resilient enough to survive each other's blunders so that a classroom atmosphere of contentment and enthusiasm can prevail.

REFERENCES

Becker, W.C. Consequences of different kinds of parental discipline. In Hoffman and Hoffman (Eds.), **Review of child development research, I.** New York: Russell Sage Foundation, 1964.

Harris, R.R., Wolf, M.M. & Baer, D.M. Effects of adult social reinforcement on child behavior. In Hartup and Smothergill (Eds.), **The young child: Reviews of research.** Washington, D.C.: National Association for the Education of Young Children, 1967.

Sears, R.R., Macoby, R. & Levin, H. **Patterns of child rearing.** Evanston, Illinois: Peterson and Co., 1957.

New York Teacher's Staff

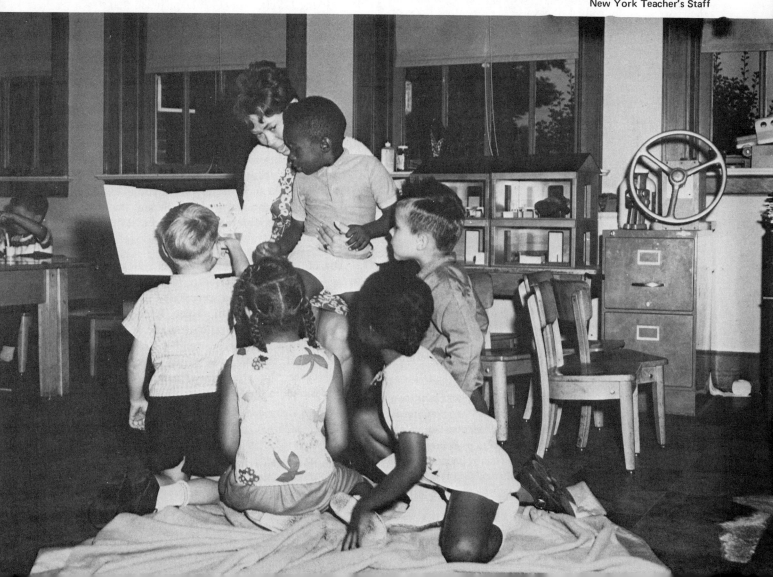

Chapter 29

Open Education vs. Traditional: Round Two

Barbara Ruth Peltzman*

"The conflict between advocates of traditional and progressive (open) education has flared anew here (England) with the publication of a new study praising old-fashioned methods. (*New York Times*, May 8, 1976, p. 12)."

The conflict described by the *Times* was originally touched off in 1967 by the publication of the massive Plowden Report on children and primary schools. The Plowden Report was a three year study of the nature of Primary education in Great Britain. The Plowden Report became the bible in Britain and America for those who favored, what the *N.Y. Times* (1967) called "the introduction, and proliferation of progressive teaching and methods, and their stress on individual discovery, opportunities for creative work, and a general reduction of teacher directed activity...(p. 12)."

The late 1960's saw a rush by many American educators toward adoption of the New British system called the Open classroom, integrated day, child-centered education, and the open space approach. Educators such as Lillian Weber of the City College of New York visited Great Britain to learn the new way to teach and returned to write a book for classroom teachers and parents. Harold W. Sobel (1975) states "There is no question that open education has generated much excitement...Lillian Weber (who helped bring open education to these shores from England in 1976) became a household word as rapidly as Spiro Agnew, at least among educators, on the basis of her pioneering efforts (p. 551)." There were also those experts who had never set foot outside the United States who wrote books on the open classroom. A great many books and articles were imported from Britain and all over America school systems and individual teachers were converting to the open classroom. Special buildings without interior walls were constructed for the new method. However, each interpretation of the British method turned out to be different.

Irving J. Spitzbert (1973) states "Every summer hundreds of American teachers invade England to participate in workshops on Britain's famous 'open classroom'...and are looking for a model to solve the problems of primary education in the United States. But there is no single model of the open classroom; the label, as advocates are generally careful to stress is used to cover a wide range of teaching styles and techniques. Consequently, each group returns to the United States with a different picture of what an open classroom is depending upon the particular school-indeed, the particular classroom—it observed...(p. 5)."

Thus, we see that there is not one open classroom model, but many according to the way each administrator and teacher interprets the theory. This has resulted in a variety of teaching styles and interpretations of the open classroom on both sides of the Atlantic.

In his study of five classrooms in different parts of England, Irving J. Spitzberg (1973) concluded that "each teacher has developed for himself a subtly different open classroom from all others...representing the efforts...to cope with the learning problems their pupils bring them...(p. 12)."

The implementation of the theory of open education varies. The central core of the theory has been pulled out into many branches. In a review of research literature on open education, Lyn S. Martin and Barbara N. Pavan (1976) state " in most of the literature, open space refers to an architectural arrangement which may or may not be conducive to open education. Generally, the open space concept evolved out of a recognition that a young child's need to move about and interact with people and the environment is strong. It offers a more natural way for children to learn... (p. 310)."

The underlying principles of open education theory are to be found in all the literature reviewed. Every researcher found that the programs were based upon the idea of a child-centered, freedom of choice, freedom of movement, teacher as guide not dictator, and the learn by discovery philosophy. Each researcher implies that the program was individualized, flexible, and suited to the needs of each child. It was the arrangement and conceptualization of these Basic philosophical tenants that made each classroom different.

*Dr. Barbara Ruth Peltzman, Reading Consultant, New York City Public Schools, Adjunct Professor, St. John's University.

Stanley G. Sanders and Jean O. Wren (1976) state that:

...There is no unanimity on the definition of
openness. Some schools are called "Open" because
they have movable walls to allow flexibility of
grouping students...Some new schools have no
interior walls to allow free-flowing adjustment
of programs and groups of students. In some
schools openness implies a philosophy that
embraces nonstructures and permissive programs...
(p. 57).

Part of the problem in England is that there is no cen-
tralization of Primary Education. Each Head Teacher, who
has a position similar to the American Principal but with
more authority, sets the curriculum and no two schools are
alike. Thus, we have a variety of interpretations of the
theory of Open Education along with a lack of standardized
goals and curricula. However, efforts to measure the success
or failure of open education in Britain have been undertaken.

In an attempt to study pupil progress in Britain's open
education classroom, Dr. Neville Bennett of Lancaster University engaged in a research project. Dr. Bennett studied
400 children in Lancashire and Cumbria. John Mansfield of
the British Broadcasting Corporation states "all the children
were about 11 years old from classes in the last year of primary school. They were tested in June 1973 and again the
following June...(p. 524)." *The New York Times (1976) review of Dr. Bennett's rese*arch states "thirty-seven classrooms across the spectrum of teaching styles were chosen,
and the chidren's progress was charted by comparing their
performance in tests in reading, writing and arithmetic...
(p. 12)." Dr. Bennett was interested in teaching styles and
how they effect pupil learning. He identified several teaching styles ranging from, according to the *New York Times*
(1976). "the totally progressive (learning by discovery, integration of subjects, no attempt to curb talking or movement among children, no tests or grading) to totally traditional (teacher dominated classrooms, subjects taught individually, no free movement or talking, regular testing, corporal punishment for misbehaving). He found that about
one in four was taught in a strictly traditional fashion,
about one in five on a progressive model, and the rest—by
far the majority—somewhere in between...(p. 12)."

The research done by Dr. Bennett has provided fuel for
the fires of controversy. His study "Teaching Styles and
Pupil Progress" published in April 1976 renewed the conflict between traditionalists and open education advocates.
According to the *New York Times* (1976) "with the issuance
of the Lancaster report, which was a front-page story in
Britain, the battle cries of both camps was being heard...
(p. 12)."

What did Dr. Bennett's research uncover? Why did his

findings cause the second round in the fight between open
education advocates and traditionalists to begin? What effect
will this renewed battle have on the future of open education? In order to answer these questions we must look at
Dr. Bennett's research findings.

In an interview with Dr. Bennett, John M. Mansfield of
the B.B.C. reported that Dr. Bennett stated:

...The Plowden Report makes many assertions about
progressive education, but nowhere in that report will
you find any research evidence on which to base
those assertions...The conclusion to that report
claims that 'finding out' has proved to be better than
'being told' and yet I have been through the whole report and found no research evidence whatsoever on
which to base such statements. So it was obviously
necessary to test some of the assertions included
there (p. 524).

Dr. Bennett set out to back up the assertions in the
Plowden Report with empirical research. Dr. Bennett is a
trained open education teacher. With questions about the
validity of the assertions of the Plowden Report in his mind
Dr. Bennett undertook the present project. The data from
400 children in thirty-seven classrooms in two geographic
areas were fed into a computer to analyze achievement,
according to the B,B,C, interview, " over one year for every
child and about the teaching style they had experienced,
and some of our results were very unexpected...(p. 525)."

The *New York Times* (1976) reported that "within the
course of the year, formally taught pupils achieved higher
test scores in all academic spheres...The study also found
that anxious or insecure pupils seemed to perform better in
more structured environments, while extroverted children
seemed to deal more easily with less structured situations...
(p. 12)." In the B.B.C. interview Dr. Bennett reported that:

Somewhat contrary to our expectations, the findings
clearly favored formal schools. On the reading scores,
we chose a test that was specially devised for a wide
range of classrooms, and on this we found that the
mixed and formal children were at the same level: the
latter progressed more than we had expected, whereas
the informal children had progressed less than we expected. The difference between the mixed and formal
children and the informal children was something in
the order of three to four months in reading age. On
the arithmetic, the gap was a bit wider and the pattern somewhat different, in that formal schools again
came out well above what we had expected, whereas
mixed and informal schools were somewhat similar
and below expectations, and the gap between the
formal and the mixed and the informal was something in the order of four to five months...On the
English...the formal above expectations, the mixed as

one would have expected and the informal again below expectations, and the difference between the formal and informal was in the order of three to four months...(p. 524-525).

From the interview with Dr. Bennett, we can see that he did not start out to destroy informal or open education and that his findings correlate with studies done in the United States. J.B. Warner (1970) found no significant difference between open space children and traditional classroom children, but J.W. Sackett (1971) and J.W. Townsend (1971) found lower achievement gains for open space children on standardized achievement tests. Sackett (1971) also found that the self-concept of open classroom children was significantly lower than children in self contained or departmental situations.

One of the major claims that open education advocates ascribe to their type of education is that creativity is stimulated and self-expression thrives. In his B.B.C. interview Dr. Bennett stated:

Creative art is one of those areas which...critics alleged...could not (be) measured, but greater opportunity for self-expression is one of the proudest boasts of the new progressive styles of teaching. Here again...findings may cause at least some extremists to have second thoughts.

Creative art is very difficult to evaluate, as researchers who have attempted to do this have shown...so we decided to concentrate on creative writing...(p. 525).

Dr. Bennett stated that the creative writing exercises were graded by three teachers, one progressive, one mixed, and one formal. The results revealed that there was no difference across the different types of classrooms. A second writing exercise, a descriptive story called "What I Did at School Yesterday" was analyzed for spelling and punctuation errors by a special category system. The results revealed that there were, according to Dr. Bennett's remarks in a B.B.C. interview, "no difference in spelling across classrooms, there was quite a difference in punctuation, in that the formal and mixed children had far fewer errors than those in progressive classrooms...(p. 525)."

Dr. Bennett's study looked at other aspects of classroom life. The open classroom advocated make claims about aspects which are difficult to measure and evaluate and criticize Dr. Bennett for attempting to measure them, but Dr. Bennett stated in the B.B.C. interview that:

There are a number of aspects that educators would tell us are incapable of evaluation. But my reply to this is: 'If *you* can't evaluate them, and *we* can't evaluate them, how do either of us know whether they have been achieved or not?' It strikes me as odd that

you are basing an educational system on aims that can never be evaluated...(p. 526).

Dr. Bennett is attempting to make the open education advocates focus in on all aspects of education not just the elusive and difficult to pin down aspects which open education claims to make the most progress in, but measurable aspects—can the children read, write, spell, punctuate and know how to complete a task. Dr. Bennett further states that he did not start out to overthrow open education. In the B.B.C. interview Dr. Bennett states:

We are not saying go back to formal teaching. What we are trying to do is isolate those elements of formal teaching which we now know lead to greater achievement gains, so that they can be incorporated into a progressive teacher's classroom but without destroying the environment that the teacher provides... (p. 526).

Dr. Bennett revealed that one striking thing about the research was that in one informal classroom very high progress in reading, and mathematics and English was found. After analysis Dr. Bennett stated that:

...Although the classroom was organized as an informal classroom...the differences we noted were in relation to the curriculum, and the way that she (the teacher) was putting over the curriculum...She had a stress on English and mathematics, and she was putting this over in a very carefully structured and sequenced way, and we have taken from this that it is the sequencing and structuring of the curriculum that is perhaps more important than the organization of the classroom (p. 526).

The *New York Times* (1976) reported about this significant findings and quoted Dr. Bennett's statement "it is... easier for a child to be attentive and task-oriented in a classroom in which the curriculum is more teacher-directed than in a classroom where less direction is imposed...(p. 12).:: Commenting on this finding further the *New York Times* (1976) quoted Dr. Bennett as stating:

"...It would seem that a structured cognitively oriented curriculum, operating within an informal classroom environment, provides the necessary context for pupil progress...Within the context of the basic skills—reading, writing, and particularly mathematics—there are certain concepts that children have to have before the next logical step...It seems to work better if the teacher decides on how the material will be presented...If the children decide what to do and when to do it there is a danger that these basic steps may not be gained at the right time...(p. 12)."

Thus we have fuel for the fires of controversy. Immediately after the publication of Dr. Bennett's study, according to the *New York Times* (1976) "virtually all the leading newspapers (in England) commented in editorials that addressed themselves to the underlying fear that children simply may not be learning as much in an open classroom as they would in a formal one...(p. 12)." Critics were quick to respond to Dr. Bennett's findings saying that his population was too small, he had not considered socioeconomic factors in his study, that Dr. Bennett is confusing two factors and neglected to acknowledge that there is good teaching and bad teaching. Feelings ran high as reports from British newspapers stirred up parents and teachers.

Dr. Bennett upheld his belief in his research findings by stating, according to the *New York Times* (1976) "...We do not have to have children in rows with the teacher talking to them all day. We can still build in pupil choice in other areas...We are not calling for a return to form teaching...If you can get a structured curriculum within the informal classroom that would be the ideal to strive for...(p. 12)."

The publication of the Bennett report has caused Educators to take a second look at Britain's infant schools. The *New York Times* (1976) states "...The criticism inherent in Dr. Bennett's report...strike a responsive chord even among committed observers of Britain's progressive infant schools...Educators interviewed agreed that the atmosphere of the infant school classroom...has to be thought out carefully to be successful...(p. 12)."

The controversy stirred up by Dr. Bennett's report has led to questions by parents on both sides of the Atlantic. The *New York Times* (1976) states "the debate has significance to parents trying to choose the proper schools for their children both here and in the United States, because Britain's primary school system...has had significant influence over American educational practices...(p. 12)." *The Daily Mail* (1976), a British newspaper, published "How to Pick Your Children's School" soon after Dr. Bennett's report appeared. The article quotes Dr. Bennett's advice to parents "...Dr. Bennett said that parents should not despair if their child's school was organized on partly progressive lines. The vital thing was whether the teacher understood the need for systematic teaching of the three R's...Yesterday parents were promised a new Black Paper of education following Dr. Bennett's report. Rhodes Boyson, Member of Parliament, for Brent and chairman of the National Council for the Preservation of Educational Standards, said: "We need a new Black Paper setting out what we have achieved so far. We have said there is something wrong with the schools, but now the progressive army is in retreat, and now we need to spell out what we need in our schools. The first Black Paper (1968) launched a bitter attack on progressive primary schools but the criticisms were condemned as rubbish by the Labour Government at the time...(p. 7)."

Dr. Bennett's report now provides additional information and ammunition for those who wish to launch a new attack through a Black Paper on Education. His report also stimulated new research. The *Times (London) Educational Supplement* (1976) reported new research at Leicester University which will compare "styles of primary teaching (and) will cover the same ground as Dr. Neville Bennett's controversial "Teaching Styles and Pupil Progress" But the Leicester work will attempt to go beyond Dr. Bennett's results...The team will repeat Dr. Bennett's comparison of formal and informal styles...The Leicester program will last longer and cover a wider age range. One of its objectives is to discover how learning is affected by the different teaching styles...(p. 15)."

Thus, we see that Dr. Bennett has reawakened the controversy and debate on open education. His work has stimulated questioning and research and forced a reexamination of both types of classroom organization under a new light. We can speculate that both the British and American's will engage in new research and write new books and articles. This author hopes that Dr. Bennett's and other's findings will help educators learn that they do not have to take sides in armed camps, but that peaceful coexistence can be a reality. It is also speculated that new research will look into teachers as individuals who, like children, can work in different situations according to their temperament and personality. It is hoped that research will reveal that not every teacher and not every child works well in a totally open situation. Perhaps the fear of being eclectic will be overcome and education can take the best from traditional education and the best from open education to create a child-centered-back to basics curriculum which will benefit all children. Only time and research will tell the outcome, but the situation is hopeful thanks to Dr. Bennett's new findings.

REFERENCES

Bryant, R.V. Doubts About the Open Plan System. *Times* (LONDON) *Educational Supplement,* April 18, 1972, pp. 4-5.

Doe, Bob. After Prof. Bennett. . .It's Prof. Simon's 'Glass Box'. Times Educational Supplement, May 14, 1976, pp. 15.

Johnson, T.D. A Comparison of British and American Reading Instruction. *Phi Delta Kappa*, 55(10) June 1974, 678-679.

Maeroff, Gene L. Liberals Defend Open Classroom Against Back-to Basics Forces. *New York Times,* April 20, 1975, pp. 40.

Mansfield, John M. How Many R's in Education?—the new report on primary schools. The Listener, April 29, 1976, pp. 524-526.

Martin, Lyn S., & Pavan, Barbara N. Current Research on Open Space, Non-Grading, Vertical Grouping, and Team Teaching. *Phi Delta Kappa,* 57 (5), January 1976, 310-315.

Sackett, J.W. A Comparison of Self-Concept and Achievement of Sixth Grade Students in an Open Space School. (Doctoral dissertation, University of Iowa, 1971) *Dissertation Abstracts International*, 1971, 32, 2372A.

Sanders, S.G., & Wren, J.P. The Open-Space School—How Effective? *The Elementary School Journal*, 77(1), September, 1976, 57-62.

Sobel, H.W. Is Open Education a Fad? *Phi Delta Kappa*, 56(8), April, 1975, 551-553.

Spitzberg, I.J., Jr. Visiting Britain's Open Classrooms: A Look at Five Alternative Teaching Styles. *New Leader*, March 5, 1973, pp. 5-12.

Townsend, J.W. A Comparison of Teaching Style and Pupil Attitude and Achievement in Contrasting Schools: Open Space, Departmentalized, and Self-Contained. (Doctoral dissertation, University of Kansas, 1972) *Dissertation Abstracts International*, 1972, 32, 5679A.

Warner, J.B. A Comparison of Student's and Teacher's Performance in an Open Area Facility and in Self-Contained Classrooms. (Doctoral Dissertation, University of Houston, 1971), *Dissertation Abstracts International*, 1971, 31, 3815A.

Weinraub, Judith. New British Study on Education Says Old Way is Best. *New York Times*, May 8, 1976, pp. 12.

Wilkinson, M. From the Man Who Challenged 'Progressiveness:' How to Pick Your Children's School. *London Daily Mail*, April 27, 1976, pp. 7.

SUGGESTED READINGS

Blackie, John. *Inside the Primary School*. New York: Schocken Books, 1971.

Nyquist, E.B. & Hawes, G.R. *Open Education: A Sourcebook for Parents and Teachers*. New York: Bantam Books, 1972.

Rogers, V.R. *Teaching in the British Primary School*. New York: Macmillan, 1972.

Stephens, Lillian. *The Teacher's Guide to Open Education*. New York: Holt, Rinehart & Winston, 1974.

Weber, Lillian. *The English Infant School and Informal Education*. New Jersey: Prentice-Hall, 1971.

Chapter 30

New Worlds: Experiences for the Young at Science and Technology Centers

Joan Munzer and John Holst*

A unique type of institution, the science and technology center is becoming a popular place to visit and an important science education facility. The impact of such centers on visitors' science learning has yet to be measured and evaluated effectively. However, the importance of these centers is recognized. Experience in these centers create positive learning situations for children using participatory exhibits and science courses as a basis. Curiosity and problem solving are the unique qualities that these centers encourage in youngsters.

To be a science and technology center a museum must have exhibits and programs designed to further public understanding of these two disciplines. Other requirements are the utilization of visitor participation techniques and involvement in educational activities. The Lawrence Hall of Science in Berkeley, California has in addition to a public center, a teacher training facility and a research and development center. Similar institutions are contributing important scientific research to specialized areas of science.

Young visitors arrive at centers for many personal reasons which include sightseeing, school trips and reservations for special activities. Whatever the initial reason, there is generally more interest and motivation for a visit than there is for spending the day in school or at home. The visitor is there by choice. This stimulation creates an unusually positive learning environment. The choice of learning is an individual one, but there is interest in the environment and the museum takes advantage of this. Presentation of exciting exhibits, live demonstrations, special group programs and science courses are the methods used to captivate the youngsters and encourage creative thought.

There is great variety in the programs available at science and technology centers. Dramatic demonstrations that illustrate basic laws of science and applied techniques are scheduled at specified times. The "Lightning Demonstration" at the Franklin Institute in Philadelphia and the operation of the full sized coal mine at the Museum of Science and Industry in Chicago are fine examples of this. Special mini-theater or classroom programs are offered that consist of simple talks explaining an exhibit or a topic with an audio-visual presentation and perhaps an experiment demonstration. Visiting school groups may be scheduled for a series of in-depth lessons on topics such as energy, pollution, weather and oceanography. The Little Red School House

Program at the Hall of Science in Flushing, New York offers a 'hands-on' approach to science learning for visiting groups in grades K-5. Topics in this program include magnetism, light, sound, animals and plants which supplement school curriculum and enable the students to explore by using equipment not readily available in many individual school classrooms. Special activities and events are scheduled at science centers that are of value to family and community groups. A film/lecture series on the topic of "Space Exploration" which includes a visit with an astronaut at the Pacific Science Center in Seattle is a memorable experience for such audiences. Making science and technology understandable through exhibits on the principles of science and the application of technology is the major purpose of such centers.

Science and technology centers could perhaps more accurately be called "discovery and learning centers." Visitor participation is the key to the philosophy of these institutions. Unlike traditional museums these centers are designed for the public to interact with the exhibit components so that the basic science principles may be clarified and more thoroughly understood. In not attempting to exhibit collections in the traditional manner, exhibit designers at science and technology centers are challenged to develop unique ways to demonstrate scientific concepts that will allow the visitors to touch, manipulate and seek solutions in order for them to become active learners. The how and why of technology must also be presented to offer the visitors experiences that are not readily available outside the center. Through this deeper personal involvement visitors tend to find these experiences rewarding and more meaningful than the viewing of glass cased exhibits.

The reason for this approach can be explained through an example given by the Boston science center in a recent report (Educational Facilities Laboratories, 1975):

> A simple pair of Eskimo snow goggles can tell us volumes about the harsh demands of the artic, of relief from squinting at ice floes in the glare of the low spring sun, the craftsmanship of the Eskimo and even

*Joan Munzer, Director of Education, Hall of Science of the City of New York; John Holst, Supervisor, New York City Board of Education, Education Consultant, Hall of Science of the City of New York, President, Elementary School Science Association.

the shape of his face, but the goggles will not tell their story while locked inside a glass case, even when 'explained' by a neatly typed label. Snow goggles are not to look at...they are to look through (p. 5).

For the young these institutions are fantastic learning adventures. Where else can one stand next to a Tyrannosaurus Rex, walk through a beating heart, listen to a lecture on care of teeth while sitting on a molar inside a gigantic mouth, ride a spacecraft, watch a traffic light work, observe and help skilled craftsmen at work, operate a king sized math puzzle, push a pendulum, manipulate a lazer beam, become master of an optical illusion, operate a ham radio, challenge a computer, pet an owl, climb aboard an old train, walk through a plane, spend time thinking why a weather balloon rises, marvel at the beauty of birth...? No child visiting the Hall of Science Chick Hatchery makes an error in contemplating the size of a new born chick. They see it for themselves. They have stored an experience on the book shelves of their minds. An experience they can draw on and use to make conceptual connections while they are reading, writing and learning throughout their lives. In the 1976 Association of Science-Technology Centers publication, "Survey of Education Programs at Science-Technology Centers, (p. 7)" Dr. Laetsch, director of the Lawrence Hall of Science indicates informal education that permits youngsters to bring their own agendas to the learning environment allows different channels for learning and this is essential because of the variety of ways students learn.

The science and technology center is also affecting the lives of the young learner in two other dramatic ways. Most centers offer courses for the young learner in science and math, and use their own exhibits as the focus or reinforcement for the courses. In this manner a child in New York learns about rocketry by visiting the "Rendezvous in Space" show at the Hall of Science with its three dimensional models, and a child in Boston learns about the stars in the planetarium at the Museum of Science. These youngsters get turned on to learning as never before, because it is real, relevant and dramatic. The third way these centers affect the young learner is through the growing influence on teachers. Many teachers seeing their students interacting and working with an exhibit come to realize the importance of active learning. This experience influences teachers to become innovative in their classroom techniques. Centers also offer programs for teachers in order to share with them successful methods and curriculum innovations. Thus, many more children are being reached because teachers are being trained in participatory methods.

The courses and exhibits offered to young learners vary according to the institution, the influence of public requests and the physical limitations of the centers. The teaching approach that is basic to all includes active individual participation in utilizing apparatus to explore the topic at a level that is personally determined by the youngsters' interest and abilities.

The modern child through the constant exposure to mass media tends to learn in a very static mode. The classroom follows this non-participatory approach: The teacher explains, the text describes and the filmstrip shows. Yet, learning theorists, such as Piaget (Inhelder and Piaget, 1958) have demonstrated quite forcefully, that manipulative experiences with concrete objects is one of four critical interrelated factors that influence mental development of the young learner. As these skills are increased the thinking through processes involving them are also heightened. Their and Linn (1975) state, "experimental science programs are better than traditional book oriented programs at fostering scientific reasoning and logical thinking (p. 3)."

Parents and educators have always known as stated in the Educational Facilities Laboratories report, "the typical classroom experience is cut off from the real world (p. 5). In seeking solutions to their children's learning problems outside the confines of the classroom, they are using this new type of institution as a learning center because these centers are pertinent to today's world.

The ultimate goal of all education is to foster in children the ability to be independent learners. Can the child gain confidence in his own abilities if he is never allowed to experiment? The exhibits and courses at the science and technology centers allow the young child freedom to think and to experiment. Does the child like this independence and responsibility? The enthusiasm generated within the class indicates the affirmative, as does the fact that many of the children return to attend classes regularly throughout the year. Informal survey evaluations and letters from parents indicate that students and parents are enormously pleased with the type of programs offered. Courses are over subscribed and parents continually request that additional programs be established.

Parents who enroll their youngsters in various courses have stated that their children's science learning has increased, but more importantly their children's attitude towards learning has drastically changed. Positive affects can be described through the typical remarks that instructors hear: "Cartoons don't compete with Saturday Science classes;" "My child wants books from the library on last week's lessons;" "He hasn't tried to read before."

Science and technology centers will be involved to a greater degree in nurturing the educational development of young children for numerous reasons. This type of institution is gaining in public acceptance. There has been a noticeable increase in the number of centers. The most recent study (ASTC, "Survey of Education Programs at Science-Technology Centers," 1976, p. 8) states that there are 54 member ASTC centers in North America (p. 8). Twenty-four percent of them have opened within the last ten years. (ASTC, "Profile of Science-Technology Centers, "1975, p. 9) The same survey notes that in more than ten cities in the United States various stages of planning and construction of science and technology centers is taking place (p. 22). Most of its members are also planning expansion because of public demand. Young children are visiting these institutions in constantly growing numbers. In 1975 preschool and elementary school age visitors comprised 39% of the total number of visitors as noted in "Survey of Education Programs at Science Technology Centers (ASTC, 1976, p. 24). Total attendence at science centers increased from 15 million in 1973 (ASTC, 1973) to 20 million in 1974 (ASTC, "Exploring the World of Science," 1975) and 34 million in 1975 (ASTC, "Discover and Learn," 1975).

The reality that science and technology centers virtually destroy themselves because of their insistence in using participatory exhibits implies that the centers are very dynamic and ever changing. Exhibits require regular service and most wear out completely and must be replaced every two to five years. Education departments are constantly changing their programs to integrate the best of the institution's changing exhibits. Centers are at the forefront in acquiring the newest information on scientific and technological advances. They have a philosophy and obligation that requires this to be presented to their visitiors. This is accomplished through the exhibits and more immediately through their education programs and courses. This vitality and dynamism leads to outstanding methods and curriculum developments which are transmitted to the public.

The Ontario Centennial Centre for Science and Technology in Canada quotes William Blake in its visitors' guide. Written in 1803 this idea describes the experience they hope their visitors have. It captures the philosophy that the science and technology centers are attempting to bring to the early childhood learner.

> To see a World in a Grain of Sand
> And a Heaven in a Wild Flower,
> Hold Infinity in the palm of your hand
> And Eternity in an hour.

BIBLIOGRAPHY

Association of Science-Technology Centers. *Making Science* _____*Understandable,* Washington, D.C., 1973.

_____*A Profile of Science-Technology Centers* 1975.

_____*Exploring the Wrold of Science,* 1975.

_____*Discover and Learn at Science and Technology Centers,* 1976.

Centennial Centre of Science and Technology. "Visitor's Guide," Canada, 1969.

Educational Facilities Laboratories. *Hands-On Museums: partners in learning,* New York, 1975.

Inhelder, B. and Paiget, J. *The Growth of Logical Thinking from Childhood to Adolescence,* New York: Basic Books, 1958.

Linn, M.C. and Thier, H.D. "The Value of Interactive Learning." Unpublished paper presented at the Education and Science Centers Workshop, Association of Science-Technology Centers, Boston, Massachusetts, 1975.

Science Curriculum Improvement Study. *SCIS teacher's handbook.* Berkeley: University of California, 1974.

Section IV
Curriculum Methods

Introduction by Frank Scalzo*

Young children enter school with a great deal of curiosity, interest, and natural ability. The classroom teacher must be aware of these traits and make a conscientious endeavor to build upon them.

The curriculum of early childhood is in a state of constant change. Many new and exciting methods are being implemented in the primary classroom. This section explores some of these new approaches in the following subject areas:

1. Mathematics. Preschool experiences extend a young child's mathematical thinking and limitations. A review of the current research and mathematical abilities of children entering kindergarten and first grade will be explored. Activities related to the world of a young child as vehicles for teaching mathematics are also considered.

2. Reading and Language. A presentation of how to gear reading towards the native language of the pupil without the use of any commerical program is discussed as well as the "problem" of a nonstandard dialect.

3. History. The concepts of time, change, the continuity of human life, and the past are identified as appropriate topics to introduce to young children. It is noted that nearly all teachers have heard children plead for "just one more story about the olden days when you were little."

4. Dramatics. The "seeds" of the beginnings of creative dramatics abound in every early childhood classroom. It is suggested that a creative dramatics program should be developed from elements that exist in the curriculum and the children themselves.

5. Art and Music. After offering insights into the art and thought of the young child, this section examines two orientations for the use of art in early childhood education. Literature, painting, and film are used to trace the origins of process and product art.

A specific program of musical expression is offered as the means of encouraging creative improvization in young children.

*Dr. Frank Scalzo, Assistant Professor, Queensborough Community College City University of New York.

Chapter 31

Beginning Reading and the Goal of Literacy

Jeanette Veatch[*]

In view of the continuing failure of traditional commercial reading programs to provide durable and significant improvement in reading achievement, it is wise to develop schemes and approaches not dependent upon such mass produced, profit-oriented material. To this end, the names of Sylvia Ashton Warner, Roach Van Allen, Dorris May Lee and others come into their own. Progress towards a systematic, yet humanistic, organized, non-commercial approach is needed. It should be geared towards the native language of the child pupil and should involve the best that can be found in past writings on the language Experience approach.

As spoken language is the source of literacy, we feel there are five elements in getting started. These permit the most advantageous use of the spoken language of the child in the classroom setting. They are:

I   TEACHER-PUPIL DICTATION (group of class)
II   KEY VOCABULARY (one to one)
III THE ALPHABET (individual group of class)
IV   WRITING INDEPENDENTLY (individual)
V   THE USE OF GOOD LITERATURE (group or class)

These five elements do not have a particular order, although many teachers find it easier to help pupils "catch on" to what reading and writing is all about by starting with the famed "Key Vocabulary" of Sylvia Ashton-Warner (1962). This paper is about literacy, for when reading excludes writing, as is so often found in commercial programs, the proper connection between the two is hard to make. Literacy, of course, is the heart of the matter and the goal of teaching. Whatever program, approach or scheme a teacher uses, every single child must—sooner or later—realize the greatest miracle of all literate societies is that of "I got words in my head!" There is no faster way to this essential realization than by seeing one's own words written down.

So let us take each element and describe it briefly.

I. TEACHER-PUPIL DICTATION

This is also called the "language experience approach," as the process involved when teachers take dictation from a pupil. Our term is more precise, we feel, as it describes the actual action during the instructional process, i.e., the teacher takes dictation from the pupil. But, on the other hand, the other term is quite acceptable as it means that the language used is that which comes from the experience of the child. This is how it works:

Usually a teacher gathers the class around her/him in front of an easel or blackboard. It is nicer and more produtive if children are sitting cross-legged on the floor rather than more formally in seats. Then the teacher faces the biggest challenge in all teaching.

"Conversation must be got." (Ashton-Warner, 1962, p. 35). Talking must be encouraged, yet waited for. Ways and methods of managing the talking are developed, so that all who so desire have their turns. In this way, the teacher finds several topics are prime for that morning or that day. "What has happened since last night that should go into our news?" is a marvelous way to begin such a session.

As topics become apparent, the teacher repeats them and identifies the pupil from whence each idea came. A decision is made as to which one should be the FIRST one in the news.

The child retells the idea with the teacher listening closely and mentally editing the words into a usable form WITHOUT destroying the idea itself. The teacher writes on the easel or chalk board, saying the words as they appear on the paper or board.

One by one each idea is transcribed by the teacher while the class watches. Usually about four or five ideas make up the "news" and use about 50 to 70 words in six or seven lines. When this first rough draft—albeit readable!—is done the teacher then goes back and rereads the entire chart or news with a "talking" voice as contrasted to the halting, word-by-word reading when she/he was writing the ideas down.

Children take turns reading their's and others' lines. Practice takes place with good oral reading styles. All sorts of words are found, such as: words that begin like someone's name. Words that rhyme, words that being alike. Words that have long vowels in them or whatever. It can be a challenging, sparkling teaching session if the teacher so chooses. And that is the point. Doing these kinds of things with the children's own words is basically interesting simply because they ARE their own words. But, some teachers

---

*Dr. Jeannette Veatch, Professor Emeritus, Arizona State University, Tempe, Arizona.

make anything dull. Alas, from these valuable daily dictation exercises, the most potent material possible is available for reading—and writing instruction.

In the early grades these daily "news" should be hung on the wall for all to see *and refer to*, for spelling, for ways to write letters or words, or what have you. Thus on the wall will be MONDAY, TUESDAY, WEDNESDAY, THURSDAY, FRIDAY charts or news sheets. The next week new Monday goes over the old Monday, the new Tuesday over the old one, and so forth. At the end of each week the news can be dittoed off, stapled together and taken home to show the folks "how well I can read." Truly these charts are exceedingly useful, if only to show parents teachers know what they are doing.

But let us go on to the other elements in beginning reading.

II. KEY VOCABULARY

While the preceding element is usually (although not necessarily) done with the whole class, the key vocabulary activity is best done with a single child at a time, even though about eight are sitting in a semi-circle. Again the teacher faces the great challenge of helping children to know that their thoughts and ideas are wise, wonderful, helpful and useful. "What is the BEST word—in all the words in the world that you know—TODAY?" In the beginning children come and whisper their special word, their "magic" word in the teachers ear. For some reason this juices up the whole activity and incites children to exceptional heights of interest. They can hardly wait to give their word to their teacher—or to hear those of their classmates. It is, indeed, as Sylvia Ashton Warner has so eloquently written, an exciting, pregnant time.

Standing beside the teacher the child calls out the letters of the word as the teacher prints them on a large tough card with a thick, black, and preferably juicy, marker. As each letter is identified, the teacher refers the child to that letter in the alphabet which should be near by on the wall at eye level.

Letter identification is crucial to acquiring the skill of one-to-one correspondence of the alphabet. Most children can sing-song the alphabet before they arrive in school, but to recognize each letter out of sequence is necessary if literacy is to be achieved.

After the word is printed on the card, and "read" aloud by the child, the teacher then asks that the letters be traced. This begins the critical habit of left-to-right, top-to-bottom directional writing patterns. Side by side—and VERY close—to the teacher provides a warm and positive setting for learning those writing skills necessary for later legible penmanship.

As each word is given and recorded in this fashion the session is closed by the teacher helping the child to "do

something" with his word. He may copy it a number of times. He may draw a picture about it. He may use the word as a "story starter" or whatever. But it is his word. He knows it. He will probably never forget it.

The Key Vocabulary, and Teacher-Pupil dictation, then become the most efficient means to make the child's language *accessible to him* so that he can write it. The process begins first thru the initial phoneme by use of labial, or bilabial, sounds. This is one way it can be taught.

As pupil after pupil gives his Key Word to his teacher, there will come, sooner rather than later, a word that begins with a lip sound, a labial. Lip sounds are wonderful because, as every teacher of the deaf has known for years, the letter is visible on the lips. The pupil can FEEL a "B." The teacher can see it as the child starts to say it. This kind of a dialog is helpful:

Child: My word is "BIKE."
Teacher: Fine. (and records it while child calls out the letters) Now, girls and boys, listen to Mary's word.
Mary: "BIKE"
Teacher: Every one say it LOUD!
All children present: "BIKE"!
Teacher: Now, START to say it but don't make a sound. I want to see what your mouth looks like. (all children frame their lips to make the word "BIKE", and incidentally the letter.) Good, now stir up the words in your head and give me another word that FEELS (NOTE!!!!) FEELS the same way.
Children: "Boo", "Ball", "Baby, "etc.etc.

In this way the teacher has worked to make each child aware that ANY word beginning with that particular mouth formation begins with a "B". Done right, never again will such a child need to be taught how to start a word beginning with that letter. So it goes for "F", "V", "M", "P". To this extent the child is resourceful enough to be independent of the teacher, certainly a desireable outcome for kindergarten or first grade.

A word of caution is needed so that the teacher not spoil the unique excitement inherent in Key Words. Using them only for initial phonemes sets in motion an awareness of the connection of "words in my head" and written language. Other aspects of phonics can be taught with other activities, notably the experience charts and similar teacher-pupil dictation.

He has realized that the basic act of reading and writing is to gain meaning from those hen tracks we adults call letters and words. But literacy requires more than just word recognition, even if the words involved are the most personal and important to the learner. Thus, we come to the Alphabet, not as something separate, but as a part of the language experience approach, charts, Key Words, whole process.

The Alphabet is foundation of our culture, of our civilization. No society is literate without one, or something that serves as such, as is found in the Orient. As we could not exclude the use of the Alphabet from the preceding elements of beginning reading, so we cannot exclude words from this section on the Alphabet.

III. THE ALPHABET

The Alphabet must be learned, as are numbers, in two ways, by rote, and by individual, one-to-one correspondence. To understand this, pupils must learn how letters work to make words. Part of the problem is the decades old "Alphabet Song" still popular, which contains the phrase "L,M,N,O." As sung, these letters become slurred together and to become the "ellemeno" problem. That is, the children are not aware that the letters in the song are separate in themselves.

The fastest way we have found to resolve this, is identifying letters in Key Words as the teacher writes each on those cards.

The alphabet must become a useful, helpful resource, rather than a matter for endless drill and repetitive sing song activity. As we said above, other phonics can be taught thru the experience charts described in the first section, I, TEACH - PUPIL DICTATION.

The physical display of the letter cards is crucial. They should be put on the wall at eye level and *within reach* of all children. This is important for children to go and match words, letter by letter, to reinforce their recognition of how their own words are spelled, i.e. letter by letter.

Each card should be large enough to be seen across the room, so no child need get up unnecessarily and go over to it to make sure of a letter. Each picture should be of an article that begins with the appropriate letter. as "A", "a", "ANGEL", "B", "b", "BALL", "C", "c", CELERY' etc. (Veatch, 1973, p. 151).

They can be hand made but there are several commercial alphabets that meet certain standards, not the least of which that no blends be pictured (as "TREE" for "T", for example.) All initial phonemes must be single consonants. But most important of all, perhaps, is for the child to realize that most of the letters in the alphabet sound enough like their names to be recognizable. Those letters that have other sounds (such as all short vowels, "H", "X", "Y", and hard "G") simply need to be learned by heart.

As most letters in the alphabet sound enough like their name to be recognized, and there are just those few that have other sounds, the learning of letter sounds becomes a matter of SAYING a word and then realizing how it starts, how it ends, and what is that vowel sound in the middle. For example:

Child: How do you spell 'most'?

Teacher: Say it again.

Child: Most.

Teacher: What is the first letter? How is your mouth

fixed? What letter makes your mouth like that? Look down the alphabet. (She tries to help him find his letter without telling him.)

Child: (With mouth pressed to say the word 'most'.) It is like "M".

Teacher: Right. Now say the word slowly—stretch it out—don't weck the word—just stretch it out. What do you hear?

In this way the teacher develops the ability of the child to say the word he wants to know (to read or to write) slowly enough to recognize the sounds. Of course, this will not work if the child articulates the letters in a separate fashion.

The Bullock Report (1975) says it very well by stating, "To teach a child that "kuh-a-tuh" says 'cat' is to teach him something that is incorrect." (p. 88). Stretching out a word is not isolating letter sounds.

Labials and bi-labiels are the easiest letters to learn, as are the long vowels which sound exactly like their name. Letters of differing types, as sibilants as "S" in "sun", or "Z" in "zoo" and the like come more easily when the child understands the basic process thru the most easily acquired letter sounds. He comes into his own when he has no problems with "L" in "lady", recognizing that even the "L" is pronounced "ell", it is not "ellady" but "lady", he is off and running with phonics.

As pupils daily are identifying letters and reinforcing each act thru the wall pictures of the letters, they learn to by the power and potency of the Key Words themselves. To learn that "GHOST" has the letters "G" etc, is to learn it faster and more permanently because it IS such a personal, and scary, word. The connection between the words "in my brain", as many a child states, and the writing or print before him is so obvious that the basic act of reading and writing becomes a logical, rational, utterly sensible human act. Not a meaningless jumbo of isolated letter sounds, the child learns words in order to read. His *words* teach him his letters, not the other way around, i.e. to teach pupils letters in order to learn words. That is what is wrong with most commercial reading programs on the market.

Nor are we talking about "look-say" either. We are talking about living language being turned into print. Once this realization dawns on the child, he is over the major hump of learning to read and write. Literacy can hardly be kept from him, and if so, at high cost of bitterness and frustration.

These are the ways in which a child gains "ready access" (Bullock, p. 111) to any word in his speaking vocabulary. The long process of discovering, on his own and thru instruction as described, that his own language can be written down, helps the child find the best tool possible to record his thoughts, ideas, pains, and pleasures. Of such stuff is civilization made. For communication between human beings is essential. One cannot talk to every one save thru the written work, the only way such is possible.

With these tools of inner recognition and discovery, the child, or illiterate adult, for that matter, is ready to write. And that is where we go next.

IV. WRITING INDEPENDENTLY

The flow of events, as can be seen from what has preceded, is that spoken language gets written down, as the classic sequence Van Allen (1963) recorded years ago. By such writing, then, reading takes place and the printed word becomes the means by which children can extend their ability to read and write.

Once a child has a pile of words of his own that he clutches possessively, and has the chart news in plain sight for reference, and a teacher who knows how to stir the latent ideas in his head, he lacks not for content of original writing.

A la Robert Louis Stevenson, "Life is so full of a number of things" etc. "How can a person NOT know what to write! How disadvantaged the teacher who feels the need to lay awake nights to think up topics for the next day's compositions. How pleasant the class where children are lost to their world while transcribing an inner important thought.

Some classes start writing by setting up cassette tape recorders (Smith & Morgan, 1972) in a private place, and as children learn the simple way to run the machine, they can record thoughts, ideas, and experiences. A later typed return of those tapings again reinforces the crucial realization of "I have words in my head."

But writing can come from outside as well as inside, from pictures, not one, but dozens!. From music, from poetry, and of course, from literature, as we will describe next.

The mechanics of writing though, do not come accidentally. There is much instruction needed with these original spontaneous outpourings. Let us see. Whether or not a teacher uses a formalized program modified spelling, or, as it is sometimes known "phonetic spelling" has a necessary place.

There is a stage, not widely enough recognized among educators, called a phonetic spelling stage. That is, a child in recording his thoughts and ideas, writes those letters he thinks he hears. "Give" becomes "gv" for example. "Dark" becomes "drk". "From" becomes "Frm", and so on. Teachers should welcome these signs of auditory discrimination rather, than as is so often the case, view them with alarm. Seeing such a phonetic spelling, a teacher should say something like this to that author:

"You are really hearing very well. You put down letters that you heard. That is good. As you get older you will remember, tho, that 'give' is spelled 'g-i-v-e'. See it has more letters than you heard."

Thus a teacher can set the child's feet on the path to writing what he hears. He has that "ready access" to his own speech. Memorizing what is not heard then becomes a much simpler matter than the common test-drill-test and meaningless exercises of the ineffective and inefficient spelling texts on the market. Quite obviously no speller can be printed with words misspelled. But a child writing what he hears is half way to learning CORRECT spelling, and the "hiss, spit, and chug" method of phonics goes to its just reward of oblivion.

On the way to this state of excellence, tho, the child is acquiring the ability to be resourceful and self-reliant in finding out how to spell words he wants to write. He can, in short, make up stories of his own. He can write letters to someone ALIVE some where who wants to get a letter from him. He can record the results of his science observations—what DID happen to that pollywog, or that butterfly. He can make up his own math problems to stump his classmates. He is released from the drudgery of endless filling out of exercises and drill that kills the time of the school day but teaches very little.

Those teachers who have found out how to help children write their own ideas report that quantities of writing result. Children write PAGES when they have something to say. And who doesn't when one explores ones fears, fun and frolics, and follies? We all do.

Thus writing takes its place in the melange of beginning of literacy. We next move into one of the finest products of a civilized world, the tradebooks. Exploring good literature with a teacher who loves it, is a privilege and the good fortune of some children. May these guidelines expand the activity to all.

V. THE USE OF GOOD LITERATURE

Story telling is common with small children as it should be with any age group. Unfortunately as the grade levels advance, teachers, mistakenly, we feel, worry about "not having enough time." But in the early grades story telling, or more frequently, story *reading* is frequent. While there are some pit falls that must be guarded against, it is well that good literature is not a stranger to the kindergarten and first grade. Since the days of MC Guffey, no less, readers given to little children have not been spectacular for their fine prose. Of late, the programmed readers, the inaccurately called "linguistic readers," and even the much maligned "look-say" variety of "Run, Spot, run." readers are appalingly badly written. The demands of controlled vocabulary by the authors have seemed to bring about excruciatingly inept, unnatural, vapid, and markedly unchildlike material. This is the stuff that comprises too many children's reading diets. The only antidote now on the horizon, outside of the language-experience approach, is that of teachers reading from books written by true artists with illustrations to match. Good literature is to be welcomed at all levels of education. It should be read aloud lovingly, to the enjoyment of both the reader and the audience. How does this come about?

There are several guidelines. Perhaps the first one is a teacher who loves good literature and chooses to read aloud only those books that he/she finds personally enjoyable. A second guideline would be that these books be of the sort that the children would not, perhaps, pick up themselves. For example, it is the rare child that would not pick up Dr. Suess on his own. Thus Dr. Suess might not be the kind of book that a teacher would chose to read aloud. Better one that has a dramatic quality that NEEDS a skilled reader to enhance the story. The Story of Ping (Flack, 1935), for example.

Thus we come to a third guideline. Teachers should be the best oral readers in the class. Whether or not they are is a moot question. They should practice to be a dramatic, spellbinding reader. This implies that books should not be used as rewards. "If you are good in the auditorium, I will read you a story" etc., etc. Also, sometimes teachers use a book for disciplinary purposes, as, "I am *waiting* for the back row to get quiet," etc.etc.etc. If the teacher is that poor a reader the cause is hopeless. Values coming from hearing good literature will not be realized.

For values that are, aside from enjoying beauty, and learning about the worlds unknown. For hearing the best of English prose will go—in effect—inside the brain and come out at a later time. Better English does result from the listening to perfect English from a trade book. Some children bring those dialects to school that require English be taught as a second language. There is no better way than to hear the best available language read enchantingly aloud. It gets *absorbed* in the mind. It will find expression later—somehow—somewhere. Usually in speech and writing, and thus is available to the teacher that knows how to use the good language for instruction.

Not to be ignored is the fact that just hearing good books read aloud literally improves reading achievement (Cohen, 1966) itself. A mighty goal, indeed.

Thus the teacher that inserts much good literature in the daily cognitive—and effective—domain of a class will reap rewards in many ways. All of them aimed at producing a citizenry that loves the printed word. Children will learn to read and write, and the world will benefit.

PUTTING IT ALL TOGETHER

So we come to the end of our five elements that comprise early reading instruction. Is it necessary again to repeat that reading alone is a starvation diet? The term reading must be interpreted to mean literacy, that makes for a literate society. For Jefferson noted long ago that education is the hope of humanity. There is no education without reading.

Civilization is not a group of people. Civilization becomes more than a collection of human beings when communication between individuals is enhanced. That, then, is the role of literacy. It makes people civilized.

SELECTED BIBLIOGRAPHY

1. Allen, Roach Van. *Language Experiences in Communication.* Boston: Houghton Mifflin, 1976.
2. Ashton-Warner, Sylvia; *Spinster.* New York: Simon & Schuster, 1959.
3. Ashton-Warner, Sylvia: *Teacher,* New York: Simon and Schuster, 1962.
4. Bullock, Sir Alan, Chair, Committee on Inquiry; *Language for Life.* London. Her Majesty's Stationery Office. *1975.*
5. *Bur*rows, Alvina. *They All Want to Write.* (4th ed.) New York: Holt, Rinehart Winston 1970.
6. Lee, D.M. and Allen, R.V. *Learning to Read Thru Experiences;* (2nd ed.) New York: Appleton-Century-C Crofts 1963.
7. Smith, Lewis and Morgan, Glenn. *Communication Skills Thru Authorship* Title III E.S.E.A. Right to Read Office. Dept. of H.E.W. Washington, D.C. 1972.
8. Stauffer, Russell G. *The Language Experience Approach to the Teaching of Reading.* New York; harper & Row. 1970.
9. Veatch, J. *Reading in the Elementary School (2nd ed.) New York.* Ronald Press 1976 Chapter 9.
10. Veatch, J. Sawicki, F., Elliott, G., Barnette, E., Blakey, J. *Key Words to Reading,* Columbus, Ohio 1973.
11. Yardley, Alice: *Young Children Learning: Exploration and Language,* New York: Citation Press 1970.

Chapter 32

Language Arts in the Primary Grades

Jane Hornburger[*]

We often consider the experiences of primary children to be quite different from those of preschoolers since our goals and expectations for them change dramatically after they enter first grade. While the primary language arts program may be a continuation of the language learning activities of the earlier years, it is specifically designed to provide more skill and assurance in communication. It is expected that language arts activities in the primary grades will develop a sufficient background for the advanced skills instruction these children will receive in the later grades.

Everyone will agree upon the importance of language to *all* children but "nowhere is this fact more evident than in the primary grades" (Greene & Petty, 1971, p. 121). A child who fails to achieve competence in language in the early grades is certain to face problems in the later grades. Language arts are the core of the curriculum, and even though reading, English, spelling, and writing may be taught separately, they are still parts of the language arts program. It is not possible to teach the language arts in distinct, self-contained parts since the communicative skills very rarely function individually.

Each skill is related to the others and each involves thinking, which is sometimes called the fifth language art. There would be no reason for speaking if there were no one to listen, and the mental processes necessary for understanding and evaluating the printed page are very similar to those used when listening to ideas which are presented orally. The skills of listening, speaking, reading, and writing are grouped together as the tools of communication. Whether they are referred to as English, the English language arts, the communicative arts, or language arts, they comprise that portion of the curriculum devoted to the teaching of language communication skills.

In the recent past, there have been many attempts to redefine the language arts, establish limits and seek direction in order to set priorities on teaching the communicative skills. Greene and Petty (1971) have said that "an effective language arts program is built into a framework of communication for genuine purposes. It is a continuing process of receiving ideas and information, and expressing thoughts generated by them" (p. 122). It is generally agreed among educators that language arts is the basic ingredient for all living and learning in the primary grades since it is the major means by which ideas are shared.

Objectives of the Language Arts Program

What things do children need to help them develop fully and individually?

● What kinds of classroom situations are conducive to this development?

● What are the most effective ways of helping children to express themselves freely and exercise the different functions of language?

● How may I utilize, to best advantage, the children's own incentives for developing greater language facility?

These are questions which many teachers must have pondered at one time or another while planning for their primary classes. Because it is clear tht adequate language control is the basis for success in our society, the alert teacher is aware of the importance of providing the kinds of life-like experiences which he/she believes will contribute most effectively to the development of language arts skills. Likewise, the alert teacher realizes that any group of children may reflect distinctive experiential backgrounds, various levels of vocabulary development, different stages of maturity and varying capacity levels. Since children do not perform at the same academic level, they cannot be expected to speak with the same verbal facility, nor can they be expected to exhibit the same level of vocabulary development. The spoken language of children usually reflects that which is used by their parents and playmates. Some children may still be using "baby words" when they enter the primary grades. This kind of language could have been ignored at home or reinforced by those who considered it to be "cute", in which case there was no incentive to speak differently. However, this kind of speech often becomes a source of embarrassment as the children grow older, and effort should be made to correct it. "Baby talk" can soon be overcome with some genuine language exchange with the teacher.

Other children might speak a nonstandard dialect which some teachers may consider to be a handicap but, as yet, there is no research evidence to support the notion that dia-

*Dr. Jane Hornburger, Assistant Professor, Boston University.

lect interferes with learning to read or academic achievement. In recent years, there has been a trend toward greater understanding and acceptance with regard to speakers of nonstandard English. Petty, Petty, and Becking (1973) have described this trend in the following manner:

While many persons think only the people in the South or Brooklyn or Boston as speaking dialects, increasingly teachers and others are aware that everyone speaks a dialect, that a dialect should not be equated with "bad" or "incorrect" language, and that we all speak in different ways as we engage in different social activities. This latter fact is a most important understanding for teachers concerned with the education of the disadvantaged. That is, every teacher needs to understand that not only do well-educated, partially educated, and uneducated people speak the dialects of their geographical regions and societal settings, but they all speak different varieties of those dialects. (p. 468)

Many informed teachers today do not attempt to eradicate the nonstandard dialect but, instead, help children to maintain it while learning "standard" speech. At the same time, they encourage the youngsters to switch dialects as the language setting changes. Early (1971) offers some guidelines which primary teachers may utilize in their work with speakers of nonstandard dialect.

In the beginning, teachers should use the language children bring to school. That means using the children's grammar in experience charts, at first retaining, however, standard spelling. Gradually, the teacher introduces standard plurals, possessives, and verb tenses in dictated stories and, as soon as possible, introduces children to the standard dialect in preprimers and picture books. Of course, she speaks and writes her own version of the standard dialect, but she can role-play in other dialects. The important point is that she *accepts* the child's home dialect and admires his proficiency in it. (p. 89)

The emerging trend is encouraging because it prevents children from being singled out as "different" and bearing the stigma of speaking an unacceptable language. It is possible that this acceptance by teachers could raise the self esteem of nonstandard speakers and thereby enhance their progress in learning "acceptable" speech. It is evident, however, that persons who are able to use the standard dialect successfully have greater opportunities for academic achievement and social mobility in our society.

Every teacher who is concerned with language learning will support the view that a firm foundation in the language arts is essential if primary children are to function effectively in the later grades. Likewise, every teacher concerned with language learning is conscientious about creating and maintaining the kind of rich, language-learning environment that will most effectively contribute to the optimal development of every child.

In teaching we try to give direction to our work by determining objectives. Experience has taught us that the only safe way to assure success is to plan for it. What kinds of objectives, then, do we plan in order to meet the different needs reflected in a class? In determining the goals and setting priorities for primary children, the teacher might be guided by a question such as this: What instructional goals are essential to the most effective development of the communicative arts in the primary grades? The answer to this question might find expression in the following widely accepted instructional dimensions. Primary children should demonstrate ability to:

● Express themselves freely and easily in spontaneous situations.
● Share description through pantomime.
● Listen effectively.
● Present ideas which reflect feeling and thought through pictorial and other informal sharing.
● Speak freely and easily using clear speech and voice control.
● Organize ideas for expression in oral and written form.
● Read in a way that indicates growing vocabulary and skills development.

Language arts skills grow best in a setting that fosters an appreciation of language as it is used in a variety of situations. The most essential ingredients are the teacher and the objectives which she/he sets for the children.

Integrating the Language Arts

The language arts are intrinsically interrelated and this is due to the fact that language is involved in each form, whether it is receptive or expressive. For this reason, growth in one area will affect growth in another; consequently, when we are helping children with reading we must consider the important role that listening and speaking play in the process. Oral expression is based on organizational skills, an understanding of vocabulary is needed for effective listening and speaking, and spelling and penmanship are necessary components of good writing.

The fact that all the language arts go hand-in-hand provides justification for the modern programs which include the teaching of the other language arts with reading. An integrated approach to language offers many possibilities for learning activities in reading, writing, listening and speaking. Of course some rescheduling of time periods might be necessary, but it should be possible to combine two short periods into a long language arts period. This kind of arrangement would allow the teacher to plan experiences which focus upon the relationships between the language arts. This could be done with a short story which is either read, listened to, written about, or told. In this way children could see that the story can be enjoyed by using either of the four areas of language arts. The method may also be used to demonstrate the recurrence of certain story words in these areas and, thereby, function as vocabulary exercises.

Telling, or voluntary reading of parts of the story, would provide practice in speaking and listening. An activity in sequencing may be designed by printing the story on oak tag, cutting it into strips in the correct order. Acting out parts of the story (without learning lines) will deepen understandings, aid in voice control, extend concepts and heighten enjoyment for the total group. Of course, children may write their own stories to be shared with others and this is another good way to integrate the language arts. Writing stories to share with others helps children to realize the need for clarity and they will be inspired to improve their writing.

Language arts are best taught in a life-like setting where learning is accomplished through activities which help children to communicate with others rather than through skill drills. "Concentration on skills draws attention away from the normal and self reinforcing uses of language, and instruction often unnecessarily makes a natural, everyday activity seem foreign and stilted" (Pinnell, p. 318).

This writer believes that language skills will be learned as children feel the need to communicate definite messages, obtain information, have needs met and establish certain relationships. In a rich language learning environment where children are encouraged to explain things in written and spoken forms, find solutions to problems and make decisions, skill drills do not seem to be needed. Early (1971) believes that:

Skills such as punctuation, plurals, and possessives, forming tenses, and achieving sentence variety are best taught incidentally in connection with reading and writing. Any good basal series calls attention to the way writers punctuate and why they use paragraphs. Every good teacher helps children to use the conventions of written language as they need them...I see no reason for formal study of syntax or parts of speech in primary grades. (p. 89)

In a classroom where children feel accepted and experience freedom to speak in ways that are comfortable for them, language learning will thrive. "A school atmosphere in which children talk freely with others and receive immediate feedback from their peers and from their teachers helps to build the language skills necessary for functioning in society..." (Pinnel, p. 325).

Creative Activities in the Language Arts Program

One of the best ways to provide an effective language arts program is through the use of flexible creative activities. However, for one reason or another, many teachers are unwilling to utilize the approach. Darkatch (1972) expressed surprise at the reluctance:

I am amazed with the repeated statements concerning what is taught in language arts. Spelling from a workbook, grammar from a text, capitalization and punctua-

tion from a course of study, are taught without hesitance; but the creative aspects of the language arts are seldom tried, with the reason given that little is known about how to proceed. This is a serious loss and often causes the all-too-frequent conditions of sterile teaching to result. (p. 120)

In spite of the reluctance of some teachers, creative teaching can bring excitement and success to them and their pupils. From the skills development aspect, the creative way of teaching the language arts may prove to be even more efficacious than the practice of teaching the components separately because children will find more joy in learning.

If there are any doubts concerning the free expression and unstationary bodies, if you are concerned about the quality of planning and teaching, Early (1971) offers this bit of encouragement:

The more fluid and flexible the language arts program is on the surface the more firm it must be at its foundations. Essential to the structure is the teacher's ability to language skills. What kinds of questions does a child have ready answers for? Do his errors in oral reading show that he is not paying attention to the content? Does he consistently confuse certain vowel diagraphs; Does he skip strange words or miss syllables when he tries to identify long words? ...What reasons lie behind the performance? (p. 86)

Creativity has been defined as a new way of looking at an old problem or situation, a process that results in something new, different, or imaginative. The creative product may be an idea rather than a physical object. It may even have been considered by someone else, but as long as it is new to the creator, it is a creative product. What are the creative aspects of the language arts program made of? Poetry, storytelling, choral speaking, dramatics and creative writing—that's what they are made of. On these bases, then, children's literature is the very essence of the creative program in language arts. Early (1971) puts it this way:

It should be clear by now that the major components of the language arts program are children and teacher—and books. Trade books matched to the range of children's reading abilities; works of contemporary and classic literature for the teacher to read aloud; picture books to be poured over by the younger. read, admired, and imitated by older children; all kinds of references texts and fact-finding books for children; lots of non-fiction tradebooks and textbooks, including basal series. (p. 87)

Indeed, literature can be the teacher's greatest ally in meeting the needs of *all* children regardless of their reading levels or speech patterns. "With a little teacher ingenuity, literature can provide a fountainhead of activities capable of meeting the intellectual-emotional needs of every student in a class" (Hornburger, 1975, p. 22).

Perhaps the most rewarding thought about integrating language arts through the use of literature is the fact that it helps the teacher to provide balance in the program. Traditionally, major emphasis has been placed on reading and this has sometimes caused the other language arts to be neglected. Evanechko (1975) explains the situation:

For as long as there has been public education both professional educators and their clients have focused on inculcating the most readily developed of the language skills, reading. Every person concerned with language learning will admit reading is only one of the language skills which must be mastered by functioning members of any literate society. (p. 839)

Research has shown that there is a high correlation among all the language skills, receptive and expressive. Nevertheless, this knowledge has not changed our way of teaching. Evanechko (1975) says:

As language teachers we have focused too much attention on one aspect of language learning. We appear to have assumed that developing the ability to read is more important than developing any other language ability... Faculties of education offer several courses in reading and school administrators turn to rigorous programs of skill building in reading whenever the question of language inadequacy in children is raised. Publishers produce a dozen times as much material for "reading" instruction as they do for instruction in the other language skills. (p. 840)

No educator would encourage teachers to neglect reading instruction, but many would agree with the idea of giving more consideration to the other three language arts.

There are those who believe that writing and oral communication also fail to receive their fair share of attention in the primary curriculum. Since about 80 per cent of our working day is spent in verbal communication and listening, it would seem that these two skills should also have a special place in the curriculum.

Through the use of literature and other creative activities, children may receive practice in all of the language arts skills. Young children especially enjoy acting out Mother Goose Rhymes and fairy tales. *Little Miss Muffet, Little Jack Horner, The Three Billy Goats Gruff* and scenes from *Peter Rabbit* are fun to use. Those who choose may act and the class could guess the title of the book or story.

Storytelling is always good to use with children. They enjoy hearing stories read by the teacher who serves as a model and, then, this can also be the starting point for children to give their creative versions of the story. They might add different endings or provide different and more satisfactory solutions to problems. The stories children write themselves are most important to the language arts program. The first story may be a total group endeavor with teacher doing all of the writing. This shared experience will provide encouragement for individual attempts.

Stories such as *Little Red Riding Hood, Where the Wild Things Are,* and *Blueberries for Sal* are good to read aloud because they are popular with children.

Creative Writing can also be used in the primary grades with some help from the teacher. Seasonal poetry is especially effective because most of it provides sensory images. To get them started, the teacher might ask, What sounds can you hear at Christmas time? Children will probably say sleigh bells, church bells, bells on fire trucks, etc. The teacher might also read some familiar poems and omit the endings or certain other words and have children supply the missing endings. She/he might also print on the board these beginnings for children to write about: "I Like _____ ," "I wish I had _____." Children who wish to share their creations should be encouraged to do so for this provides practice in oral expression and listening skills.

Listening skills may also be strengthened through games involving children's books. For example, "Who Am I?" would need three or four questions about a familiar book character with the hardest question coming first and the last one giving a big clue to the title. The questions might be similar to these: I was sent to Grandmother's to take a package. Who am I? I stopped in the woods to pick flowers. Who am I. I was wearing my red cape when a big bad wolf appeared. Who am I? This activity can be used with several book titles as well.

There are many book activities which can be used effectively to enhance the teaching of language arts skills. The variety and scope are almost limitless and by participating in them, children will soon realize that learning really can be fun.

REFERENCES

Chomsky, C. Language development after six. In J. Destefano & E. Fox (Eds.), *Language and the language arts.* Boston: Little Brown, 1974.

Darkatch, M. Creative avenues for the language arts. *Education,* 1972, *92,* 120-127.

Early, M. Components of a language arts program in the primary grades. *International Reading Association Conference Papers,* 1971, *16,* 79-90.

Evanechko, P.O. Reading is only one of the language arts. *Language Arts,* 1975, *52,* 839-840+.

Greene, H.A., & Petty, W.T. *Development language skills in the elementary schools* (4th ed.). Boston: Allyn & Bacon, 1971.

Hornburger, J.M. Teaching reading by way of literature. In L. Golubchick & B. Persky (Eds.), *Innovations in Education.* Dubuque, Iowa: Kendall/Hunt, 1975.

Johnson, K. R. Teacher's attitude toward the nonstandard

negro dialect: let's change it. In S. Destefano & E. Fox (Eds.), *Language and the language arts.* Boston: Little Brown, 1974.

Petty, W., Petty, D., & Becking, M. *Experiences in language: tools and techniques for language arts methods.* Boston: Allyn & Bacon, 1973.

Pinnel, G.S. Language in primary classrooms. *Theory into practice,* 1975, *14,* 318–327.

Ruddell, R. Encounter to expresssion: language as experience. *Reading-language instruction: innovative practices* (Chap. 6). Englewood Cliffs, New Jersey: Prentice-Hall, 1974.

Association of Science Technology Centers

Chapter 33

Science in Early Childhood: Some Whys and Hows

Mary Ann Porcher*

Why Don't Teachers Teach Science?

Many teachers of young children have a misunderstanding of what science really is, which keeps them from making science part of the curriculum. They remember formulas they had to parrot back and experiments that did not seem to be connected with anything that interested them, so they mistakenly see science as a subject full of meaningless facts and hard-to-understand explanations. They see it as having only vague interest for non-scientists. How unfortunate! Because these teachers were cheated, young children are being cheated of a chance to study something they are very interested in, something that is well suited to their way of learning.

What is Science?

When children watch the class guinea pig eat and sleep and grow and eliminate and do all the things that living things do—that's science. When teachers won't let children go into the wet school-yard wearing sneakers, but insist on rubbers or boots—that's science. Even matching yourself against your best friend to see who is taller is science. It's science when hot, clear water and red powder change first to a red liquid and then to a red gelatin dessert after being refrigerated. Noticing that empty containers float, but filled containers sink, is also science. Going for a walk around the block to gather tree seeds, see the change in the leaves, compare the materials people build with, or look for ways that people have polluted the environment are all science for young children. But then so are discussions about why children have begun to wear sweaters or jackets in the Fall. Science can be found in almost every experience people have in their daily lives. Living things, the weather, the earth, the way things work—and how any of these affect people and how people affect them—are all sources for science content. In other words, science includes a body of knowledge about the natural and the man-made worlds and about their relation to people.

But science also includes the methods or processes through which people acquire this knowledge. Observing the guinea pig, comparing its appearance from one time to another, measuring its weight or its length or its girth at various times, are all activities which can raise questions, but which also help to answer questions. Sharing observations and conclusions, comparing them with those of other children, then pooling all the information, also help children answer questions and gain knowledge.

Children generalize that water behaves differently with different materials by having experiences with sneakers and rubbers, with umbrellas and without, with raincoats, without raincoats. If they hold these materials up to a light or look at them through magnifying glasses, children discover that some materials are "holey" and others are not. Children who classify materials as "holey" and "not holey" may realize that it is the "not holey" ones that are used to make raincoats and umbrellas and rubbers and tablecloths and shower curtains. They may then be able to predict whether a new kind of material will make a good smock for the water play area.

In other words, children find out about science by using "the methods of the scientist: exploring, observing, discovering, collecting evidence, recognizing problems, planning, testing, inquiring, experimenting, summarizing, reporting, evaluating...the processes essential in a world of expanding knowledge" (Heffernan, 1967, p. 78). Significantly, these are the same skills used not only by scientists, but by all problem solvers. When people solve problems—regardless of how small and ordinary, or how large and world-shaking—they solve them by using the same methods and processes. When children acquire knowledge by using science processes, they are learning and refining skills that they can apply to any other area of the curriculum or to any other part of their lives.

Science knowledge and the way science is learned just can't be separated. Science is not only knowledge about the natural and man-made worlds and about their relationship to people. Nor is it only the method of the scientist. It is both. Together they make up science.

How Are Children Like Scientists?

One of the characteristics that endear young children to

*Mary Ann Porcher, Brooklyn College, School of Education, City University of New York.

171

teachers is their curiosity about the world and their eagerness to investigate. This tendency to wonder and explore has led several authors to compare the thought and work of the scientist with those of the young child and to find a strong similarity (Brearley, 1970; Isaacs, 1974; Lawrence, Isaacs and Rawson, Rudolph and Cohen, 1964). This similarity between children and scientists in their approach to the world not only makes it "absurd to question the place of science in the primary classroom" (Weber, 1973); it also means that teachers can't keep children from learning some science, even if science isn't part of the curriculum. How do you keep young children from learning science when activities typical of Early Childhood classrooms provide so many opportunities for it?

What Is Science in Early Childhood Classrooms?

Teachers of young children are quick to mention classroom pets, keeping plants, growing seeds and marking the weather chart as examples of science. If the class has a water table, teachers may realize that children can learn about sinking and floating, or about how water affects different things. Children are often taken to gather Fall leaves or tree seeds. But many teachers do not look beyond such obvious sources of science content.

When children work in the art areas, not only do they learn about color, form, size and texture in an natural way, but they can learn about many other things. They can learn about the different ways that things either mix or dissolve (or don't) through such common experiences as mixing powdered paints, blending colors, making papier mache, concocting "homemade" fingerpaints, softening hard clay and using wax resist. Children learn these things by using their senses to observe the characteristics of the materials they work with; comparing the original materials with their changed state; commenting on them; and perhaps classifying them according to how they mix or dissolve.

Collage gives children repeated opportunities to investigate the characteristics of different materials when they look at, touch, feel and smell them in order to choose the pieces they consider "right" for their own collage. When they do this, they refine their skills of observing comparing, and classifying. Making mobiles and stabiles also helps children with these skills while also giving them experience with weight and balance.

When children prepare food, they have experiences that are enjoyable for their own sake, but which also let children become involved with everyday changes in matter. They see butter, and margarine, and ice and ice cream melt when exposed to heat, but eggs, pancake batter and cake batter become more solid under the same conditions. Cooking rice and noodles and vegetables shows children that still other things soften when they're heated, rather than hardening or melting. Making lemonade for snack time and preparing soup, dough or batter extend experiences with mixtures

and solutions into contexts other than art and lead children to generalize about them.

Children in Early Childhood classes are not too young to learn about work and about the fact that simple machines make some work possible and other work easier. Cutting, beating, grating and scraping food teach them that in one context. Hammering, pulling out nails, putting in screws and sanding rough wood teach it in another. Ramps, pulleys and toy cars in the block corner give children still another context and another opportunity for observing, comparing and generalizing about the kinds of work that need to be done and the kinds of machines that help people do it.

Children who build with blocks are faced with countless problems to be solved. As children's block constructions develop, remain standing (or don't), problems are involved, and children have to use what was referred to above as the processes of science in solving them. Blocks can inform children about size and shape and texture, as do art activities, but they also have the attribute of weight which children can experience when they build. At the same time they learn about balance and stability and horizontal and vertical space.

These examples are a few of the almost endless possibilities for science learning in the Early Childhood classroom. Anyone who works with young children regularly can find more.

What Is Thinking?

A look at the nature of young children's thinking is needed in order to understand why science is a highly appropriate learning experience for them. The outstanding influence on recent views of the way thinking develops is the Swiss psychologist Jean Piaget. By carefully observing and recording the behavior of his own and other children, Piaget developed some theories about thinking and how it develops.

A good place to begin is with a simplified version of a common experience. For example, many very young children at first call all small four-legged animals "doggie." Each time they see that sort of animal, they classify it as a "doggie." Eventually, a child has enough experience with small four-legged animals to begin to realize that they are not all the same: some say "bow wow," some say "meow," they use their tails differently, and so on. Finally, the child recognizes too many differences to be able to call all new four-legged animals "doggie," and begins to call some of them "kitty."

This is an example of what Piaget meant when he said that thinking was an active process. In his view, people create catagories in their minds to help them organize new information. These categories are built through repeated experience. The more experieces people have, the more categories they form. When a person has a new experience, he takes in new information and matches it against one of his existing categories. (in the example above, "doggie" was the category.)

When a young child sees a new four-legged animal and calls it "doggie," he is, according to Piaget, *assimilating* the new information, That is, when he matches what he has just seen (this particular new four-legged animal) against his category called "doggie," for him it fits. But after more experieces,the child finally realizes that there are differences among four-legged animals. The first idea of "doggie" is no longer good enough--it is too broad a category. It includes too many different things. The information won't fit any more and *assimilation* is no longer possible. What happens? The child has to change the old category to allow the new information to fit more exactly. He has to *accomodate.* That's exactly what happened in this example. With accomodation the large, very general category "doggie"—which at first meant all small four-legged animals—was broken up into two, more precise categories: "doggie," which now includes only those animals which say "bow wow" and wag their tails; and "kitty," the category which includes animals that say "meow" and sometimes purr. Refinement and clarification result every time *accomodation* takes place.

This example also shows that thinking is not a matter of only *assimilation* or *accomodation.* It involves both. First, *accomodation* resulted in two new categories. And then the new information was *assimilated* into the new category named "kitty."

How Do Young Children Think?

Human beings grow and change with maturity. Piaget believes that the way the human mind organizes information also changes with maturity. All human beings think, but how they think depends on their level of development. Infants and toddlers think differently from children or preprimary or early primary age. Those children are different from children in the upper elementary years. And children in that group think differently from the way adults do.

Most young children fall into what Piaget has called the Pre-Operational Stage. Anyone who has observed children of approximately 2½-7 will not be surprised to be told that these children depend on their senses to bring in new information. When they are allowed to, they will approach something new by observing it with as many senses as possible. They will touch, feel, look, smell, and perhaps even listen and taste. They will manipulate, explore, compare, and use the processes of science. Because their way of learning uses many of the same methods scientists use, young children and science make an appropriate combination.

Young children have no choice. At this stage of mental development, they characteristically approach new things in this active way. They cannot think abstractly. They cannot think logically. They have to have actual experiences--con-

crete experiences--in order to figure things out.

Even children at the older end of what we call the Early Childhood years depend on concrete experiences. Unlike those in the Pre-Operational Stage, these older children are capable of logical thinking--but only if they have concrete things to work with. Piaget made that point clear when he called this stage of mental development the Concrete Operational Stage.

Seeing the guinea pig do all the things living things do is a concrete experience, which means more than reading about the characteristics of living things. Getting caught in an unexpected shower without an umbrella and getting wet, or testing different materials in water are concrete experiences which teach more than watching any teacher demonstration. Smelling Spring odors tells more than the most beautiful picture of a Spring flower. In other words, children have concrete experiences whenever they come into direct contact with their environment by using any of their senses. These contacts arouse curiosity in children about the nature of their world and their relation to it. This in turn is closely connected with the content of science. That is another reason science is an appropriate area of study for young children.

What Does All This Mean For Teachers?

An understanding of *assimilation* and *accomodation* suggests that if children learn by comparing the new with the familiar, they can understand something new more easily if it is not too unfamiliar. Good teachers have always known that it is best to begin with what children know, with "where the child is."

Piaget's theory also suggests that the more experiences children have, the more precise and refined their categories for thinking will be, and the better they will be able to think. These ideas agree completely with what good Early Childhood teachers have known for a long time—if you want children to be thinkers, give them lots of experiences to draw on.

But not all experiences are equally useful for young children. Successful Early Childhood teachers have always known that young children need to have concrete experiences, opportunities to use their senses, to manipulate, investigate and explore as scientists do.

To summarize, for young children to learn science or anything else successfully, teachers must provide them with lots of first-hand experiences built on previous familiar ones.

Why Else Teach Science?

There is still another reason science belongs in an Early Childhood program—a reason that also has to do with how appropriate science is for young children. For a long time, people who work in Early Childhood have accepted the idea that the different areas of the curriculum should be integrated—as life is integrated. Science integrates extremely well!

Activities which give children opportunities for exploration and investigation are exactly the kind that will stimulate children to write and to speak. Young children deeply involved in what they are doing are more easily motivated to tell others about it. About what they have observed. What they think might happen and why they think it might. Even children reluctant to participate in "Show and Tell," or other commonly used "communication" activities are more likely to communicate if the circumstances are more exciting. They are also more likely to make a contribution to an experience chart or a class book, or dictate a story of their own if it is about something they are interested in.

These may be labeled Language Arts activities or thought of as using the process of communicating. It doesn't really matter, if they offer a more meaningful alternative or addition to the more usual ways of getting children to share ideas.

Young children's science explorations can also lead them to read and use books more. Occasionally a childs's interest and curiosity cannot be satisfied by exploration alone. Sometimes a piece of information is needed before the investigation can go on: What do we feed a guinea pig? What kind of animal would be right for our classroom? What else can I find out about the dinosaurs we saw at the museum? Whether the teacher reads a related book to children or they read it to themselves, there is a relevance in books like these which gives real importance to the words on the page, and a significance often missing in a basal reader.

Many science experiences can also be expressed in nonverbal ways. Young children who cannot read or write, or who cannot yet do either very well, can often express what they have learned through music or movement or one of the visual arts. For example, take young children pretending to be a variety of objects caught in a breeze. They can express more clearly and correctly then they could in words that the shape and density of an object affect the way it floats in a current of air.

A group of four-year-olds communicated their observations of their Guinea Pig, Milky, by making up words and setting them to the tune of the folk song "Aiken Drum." Five of the verses were built around things they had observed about him: He's growing because he eats a lot; His color is fur-white; His eyes are red as raspberries; His ears they are real pink; and His squeak sounds like this _____ . The chorus interspersed between the verses informed everyone that "He eats carrots and apples, and he eats paper, too."

A mural made by a group of children following a class walk answers more personally and exactly the common question "What did you see?" or "What did you like best?" Better yet, for children who cannot read yet, works of art

hanging in a room are meaningful reminders that can be "read" without the aid of a teacher. People in pre-literate societies have always communicated in such ways with success and satisfaction.

It is almost impossible for young children to do anything in science without comparing and classifying. Matching height; seeing if the guinea pig has grown; observing what happens when a plant isn't watered; measuring shadows early in the school day and again closer to noon; looking for the puddles that were in the school yard earlier in the day; choosing blocks, colors, or items for a collage: testing to see what a magnet will attract or which things will float and which things will sink—all these are examples of ways in which children compare and classify. When they do that, they are also having math experiences otherwise called measuring and forming sets, even if blocks—not gram counter-weights—are used to weigh the guinea pigs, and if lengths of string or tongue depressors—not rulers—are used to measure the lengths of the shadows or the children.

Children of this age are intensely interested in how anything is connected to them personally. What is their impact on the world? How does the world affect them? What are the effects of littering and polluting and what can we do about it? Can you separate those questions? What are the buildings in the neighborhood built of? Why? Where does the food at the supermarket come from? How did it get there? How is it kept? Why? Questions such as these show that there is such a close relationship between science and social studies that it is often almost impossible not to integrate the two.

What Should Be Taught?

This article has stressed that science appropriate for young children should be based on the commonplace in their everyday lives. This does not mean that science curriculum should be developed only from what children bring to a teacher's attention. While it is very important for teachers to help children pursue their interests, this by itself results in too many missed opportunities and a disconnected quality to the curriculum.

The same is true of Early Childhood science that is no more than science tables that are never changed, and perhaps a few routine activities. Common examples of such activities are making daily weather charts, taking care of the class pets, and going for a walk to look for signs of Spring.

One way teachers can plan science for children is by organizing it around major ideas or concepts. This provides a framework for connecting many ordinary experiences in a meaningful way. Concepts such as Variations are broad enough to help children learn about many of the characteristics of things in the world, whether living or non-living—their variety, their similarities and their differences. Such an approach encompasses all the fields or areas of science, a more traditional way of planning curriculum. Another organizing idea might be that of Change—which could include experiences as diverse as making gelatin, observing the birth and growth of the class guinea pig, watching the changes in the local park throughout the year, and recording the effects of temperature change on water. Still another might weave connections among experiences with the common thread of Interrelationships. Curriculum built around broad concepts such as these gives meaning to ordinary experiences by repeating them in many different contexts, and by showing relationships among them. Such large concepts also allow for the fact that learning usually takes time, because they discourage the tendency among some teachers to teach science by condensing the breadth of experiences leading to a broad understanding into one or two crammed and rushed lessons. Children rarely learn under these circumstances in the fullest sense of the world "learn."

In short, a full and meaningful Early Childhood program should be built on young children's interests, and organized around ordinary experiences. It is an active program, consistent with the way young children learn. It is integrated—always intentionally, sometimes unavoidably—with the rest of the curriculum. Unlike the science that so many teachers remember unhappily, a program like this is what science is really about.

REFERENCES

Bearley, Molly et al, "Science: Expectations, Conjectures and Validations," in *Teaching Young Children: Some Applications of Piaget's Learning Theory,* Edited by Molly Brearley, New York: Schocken Books, 1970, 17-33.

Chittenden, Edward A., "What Is Learned and What Is Taught," *Young Children,* October 1969, 25:12-19.

Heffernan, Helen, "They Grow Nine Feet High," *Childhood Education,* October 1967, 44:75-78.

Isaacs, Nathan, "Early Scientific Trends in Children," in *Children's Ways of Knowing,* edited by Mildred Hardeman, New York: Teachers College Press, 1974, 81-97.

Lawrence, Evelyn, Isaacs, Nathan and Rawson, Wyatt, "The Common Roots of Science," in *Science in the Open Classroom,* Edited by Ruth Dropkin, New York: Workship Center for Open Education, The City College of New York, November 1973, 11-15.

Kohlberg, Lawrence, "Early Education: A Cognitive-Developmental View, *Child Development,* 1968, 39: 1013-1062.

Piaget, Jean. *The Origins of Intelligence in the Child.* New York: International Universities Press, 1956.

Piaget, Jean, "Cognitive Development in Children: Development and Learning," *Journal of Research in Science Teaching,* September, 1964, 2:176-186.

Rudolph, Marguerita and Cohen, Dorothy H. *Kindergarten: A Year of Learning.* New York: Appleton-Century-Crofts, 1964.

Weber, Lillian, "But Is It Science?" in *Science in the Open Classroom,* Edited by Ruth Dropkin, New York: Workshop Center for Open Education, The City College of New York, November 1973, 3-10.

SELECTED BIBLIOGRAPHY OF ADDITIONAL READINGS

Almy, Millie with Chittenden and Miller Paula. *Young Children's Thinking.* New York: Teachers College Press, 1966.

Blough, Glenn O. and Schwartz, Julius. *Elementary School Science and How to Teach It,* 5th Edition. New York: Holt, Rinehart and Winston, 1974.

Bush, Phyllis S. *The Urban Environment.* Chicago: J.G. Ferguson Publishing Co., 1974.

Chittenden, Edward A. "Piaget and Elementary Science," *Science and Children,* December 1970, 8:9-15.

Ferreira, Nancy. *The Mother-Child Cook Book.* Menlo Park, California: Pacific Coast Publishers, 1973.

Hawkins, David, "Messing About in Science," *Science and Children,* February 1965, 3:5-9.

Moffitt, Mary, "Children Learn About Science Through Block Building," in *The Block Book,* Edited by Elizabeth S. Hirsch, Washington, D.C.: National Association for the Education of Young Children, 1974.

Neuman, Donald, "Sciencing for Young Children," *Young Children,* April 1972, 27: 215-225.

Pulaski, Mary Ann. *Understanding Piaget.* New York: Harper and Row, 1965.

Russell, Helen Ross. *Ten Minute Field Trips.* Chicago: J.G. Ferguson Publication Co., 1973.

Wadsworth, Barry. *Piaget's Theory of Cognitive Development.* New York: David McKay Co., 1971.

Yardley, Alice. *Discovering the Physical World.* New York: Citation Press, 1973.

Chapter 34

The Mathematical Knowledge of the Entering School Child

Rowland Hughes*

It is a great mistake to suppose that a child acquires the notion of number and other mathematical concepts just from teaching. On the contrary, to a remarkable degree he develops them himself, independently and spontaneously.... True understanding of them comes only with his mental growth.

Jean Piaget (1953)

The world of mathematics is one of abstractions mainly concerned with symbols. This world seems utterly remote from the small world of the pre-school child—the world of home, family, and neighborhood; the world of things that can be seen, touched, tasted, heard, and smelled. Yet if we are to consider the developmental pattern within which a child begins to perceive the relationships of mathematics we cannot ignore the early years.

EARLY PRE-SCHOOL EXPERIENCES

Four distinct kinds of pre-school experiences which extend a young child's mathematical thinking have been outlined by authors (1967) of the Nuffield Mathematical Project in England. This contemporary discovery approach to learning mathematics has emphasized that these early experiences can and should lead to the all-important growth of language.

Throughout their education children draw upon resources gained through previous experience to enable them to cope with a new problem or assess a new situation. The roots from which language will grow lie in the child's early environment, and we are beginning to realize more fully the relationship between the language of the child's early environment and his intellectual growth and development.

A. Experience with Materials-Continuous and Discontinuous.

The colored beads on elastic thread stretched across baby Linda's carriage offer endless possibilities for experience. The beads feel hard and they move. They can be pushed along or turned around, and they don't all do it at once. The beads in contact with Linda's hand can be moved about, while the others remain in the same position. The string of beads is composed of *separate* or *discontinuous* items.

When Tom is two, three, and four years old, he will come in contact with different materials throughout his waking day. He will learn to discriminate between them with different frames of reference—for example, how the material *feels* or "what I can do with it." Tom can empty his box of building blocks onto the floor and see them as *separate items,* or he can build a vertical tower with his blocks. It soon becomes too tall and topples to the ground. Again Tom sees his blocks clearly as separate items. He may refer to a *lot of blocks* and in this instance he is manifestly dealing with *discontinuous* materials. When Tom takes a bath, the bath water makes a splash when he hits it. Although Tom may refer to a *lot of water* in the tub, the content of the water is not separate items but a *continuous stream.*

B. Experience of Space, Shape, and Size. The key to the child's awareness of space is *movement.* As baby Linda becomes more mobile, the world enlarges. She cannot yet crawl but will nevertheless try to move if placed on the floor. Linda will have plenty of experience of being enclosed within a confined space—a crib, a carriage, a playpen, a room, or even a house.

Linda's early experiences of *shape* arise in a variety of situations. When she places a building block on the floor, it stays put. When she puts her ball down, it usually rolls away. She can pile building blocks on top of each other, but she cannot reflect this action with the balls. When Linda helps mother to unpack the shopping bag, she will see and handle many different shapes, a large number of them cylindrical and rectangular. And Linda's crayons fit into the box only if they are put in the right way.

To gain any understanding of what *size* means to young Tom or Linda, we have to imagine the appearance of, say, a room from the eye-level of a three-year-old. Chairs and tables are comparatively enormous. The situation is further complicated by the fact that Tom and Linda are growing. Shoes that Tom once called too *big* soon become described as *too small.*

*Rowland Hughes is an Associate Professor of Mathematics Education, Fordham University, Lincoln Center, New York City.

C. Experience of Containing, Matching, and Measuring.

The young child confronts situations concerning containers almost every day. If Tom knocks the box containing a jigsaw puzzle off the table, he can easily pick up the pieces and put them in the box. The milk that Linda drinks for lunch has to be contained in a glass or cup.

Laying the table for a meal provides experience with *matching.* Linda learns that a cup goes on a saucer, a knife is placed with a fork. Tom places "a plate for mommy—one for daddy—and one for me."

When mother takes Tom to buy some new clothes, they are matched against him for *size.* When she knits Linda a sweater, she holds it against the child to see if it is long enough. Tom and Linda may watch daddy matching wallpaper to the wall or mommy matching curtains to the window. These young children are having valuable *pre-measuring experience.*

D. Experience of Number Words and Symbols.

1. Vocabulary. Long before children go to school they come in contact with *numbers as names*—that is, they see and may recognize numerals or number symbols as names. The words one, five, three, etc. form a part of Tom's vocabulary almost as soon as he learns to talk. In a store he hears "*Two* dollars and *four* cents, please." Linda's daddy tells her, "We'll go on a *twenty-six* bus today." To Linda, this reference is the *name* of the bus. In some strange way these words seem to identify or describe the objects to which they refer. Similarly they seem to be used to describe the child himself. "Yes, hasn't Tom grown, he's *five* now." Quite soon Tom and Linda will learn to recite these words in a particular order—"one, two, three, four"—and so on.

2. Folk Tales and Nursery Rhymes. As soon as Tom and Linda are old enough to enjoy traditional nursery rhymes and stories, they will meet number words in the world of fantasy, nonsense, and magic. To Linda some words, such as *three* and *seven* may appear frequently, as in "the *three* little pigs," "the *three* bears," "Snow White and the *seven* dwarfs." Tom likes to recite this popular rhyme with its sequence of number words:

One, two, buckle my shoe,
Three, four, knock at the door,
Five, six, pick up sticks,
Seven, eight, lay them straight,
Nine, ten, a big fat hen.

Both Linda and Tom, however, are a long way from establishing the notion of number, which will make these words meaningful.

3. Number Symbols. At the very early age some children are able to identify the symbol on the front door of their home. Home is obviously an important place to a young child, and this symbol on the mailbox or door identifies this place as "mine." If the symbol is a simple shape such as the "seven" on Linda's front door, the young child may even be able to reproduce it. Number symbols or numerals are all around Tom—on birthday cards, clocks, buses, telephones, price tags—so it would be a mistake to suppose that he first meets them in school. We must not also assume that these symbols are as yet meaningful to a child in a mathematical sense. Essentially they are concerned with *naming* and *belonging.*

Nuffield Mathematics Project teachers (1970) have aptly stressed the importance of pre-school experience:

The background of experience of the child determines the starting point when he comes to school. If he has not been fortunate enough to have enjoyed a rich and varied set of activities in these early years—if he has not been able to discuss these with someone who uses language with flexibility and imagination, then these opportunities must be made available in school as a first priority, for on such a foundation does his future development depend (p. 5).

Learning language by imitation tends to cause confusion in the young child's mind. Frequently using "big" and "little," young Tom may describe his environment with such statements as these: "The house we live in is big." "Mama and daddy are big." "I am little." Notice that the people and the object concerned are all big in relation to the child himself, who, of course, is the central character in his own life during these early years. However, at the same time Tom hears "You ate a big dinner." "Linda is growing big." "You have a big bruise on your knee."

The eventual arrangement Tom makes in his own mind about these two sets of statements is going to determine whether he understands that the words "big" and "little" are used *relatively* and are not absolutes. The relative use of words will also apply to the whole range of language which has been referred to as *number vocabulary*—although it is not concerned *only* with numbers—including such words as *many, few, tall, short, wide, deep, low, high,* etc. When Tom and Linda come to school, their teachers should provide them with many varied experiences so that these young children realize that these words describe *relatively* quantity, size, place, and proportion. Linda's teacher will have to accept the child's statement that "My puppy is smaller than I am because it is little." The teacher knows that the statement is not wrong but represents a stage of Linda's thinking. The child's ideas of relative size and command of language have not yet become aligned.

RESEARCH ON THE ENTERING SCHOOL CHILD

Rea and Reys (1970) have noted the lack of research on the mathematical abilities of kindergarteners:

The teacher of young children who turns to the literature of research for a description of the mathematics abilities of five-or six-year-old kindergarteners finds little information for planning instruction. Research in this area is sparse in quantity, narrow in scope, and largely dated by having been carried out prior to the many developments which have greatly expanded the experiences of today's young children. (p. 66).

Callahan and Glennon (1975) have provided a current review of research related to mathematics concepts by youngsters entering school. Although the frequently cited study by Brownell (1941) is discussed, it should be indicated that this research was based on youngsters in first and second grades rather than entering kindergarteners. Brownell concluded that the following skills and concepts seem to be well developed by the time most children started the second grade: rote counting by ones through 20; enumeration through 20; identification of number through ten; with objects, the concepts "shortest," "longest," "tallest," "widest," "middle;" exact comparison or matching through five; number combinations with objects to sums of 10; in verbal problems adding 1 and 2, and probably most facts with sums to 6 and 7; unit fractions through halves and fourths as applied to single objects; ordinals through "sixth"; geometric figures "circle" and "square"; telling time to the hour; recognition of all times to the half hour.

More recently, many studies have concentrated on the concepts and skills possessed by the five-year-old when entering kindergarten. Investigations by Bjonerod (1960), Sussman (1962), Dutton (1964), and Williams (1965) suggested that those kindergarteners knew as much about arithmetic as first-grade children did a few decades ago. Unfortunately, according to Suydam and Weaver (1975, p. 49) the generalizations that can be made from such studies are limited because of relatively small group size; the implementation of one point in time, as well as only one locality, by most investigators; and the use of a variety of methods of collecting information—individual interviews, group tests, and single or multiple questions.

Suydam and Weaver (1975) have emphasized the fact that what teachers really need to know is not what *other* children know, but what *their* children know. As Brownell reported, "Research findings tell the teacher...little about the class as a whole, but they tell much less about the number abilities of particular children" (1941, p. 6). No research study can replace the teacher's careful assessment of the concepts and skills of each child.

The development of instruments for assessment of the mathematical knowledge of young children has been a more recent evaluative contribution. Tests devised by Schwartz (1969) and Rea and Reys (1970) were implemented to assess the mathematical concepts of five-year-old children.

Using their *Comprehensive Mathematics Inventory*

(CMI) Rea and Reys (1970, 1971) examined the competencies of 727 entering kindergarteners in the areas of number, money, measurement, and geometry. Some of their reported findings are as follows:

NUMBER

Numeral Identification - More than 75 percent could identify one-digit numerals; 10-13 were more difficult; less than 25 percent could identify two-digit numerals 14-21.

Sequences - More than 75 percent were able to continue the count when the cues 1, 2, 3 and 5, 6, 7 were provided. Fewer were able to respond correctly when only one number cue was given, and they were asked what came before or after. Generally, they were more competent in responding to what comes "after" than what comes "before."

Cardinal Number - Skills in counting and recognition of small groups were well developed by over 75 percent of all kindergarten entrants.

Ordinal Number - Ordinal skills seemed less developed. Less than 50 percent responded correctly to tasks requiring concepts of second, third, and fourth.

Comparisons - The majority of entrants were able to make small group comparisons.

MONEY

Identify - Over 75 percent could identify a penny, nickel, and dime. Quarter and half-dollar were more difficult. Over 50 percent identified $1.00, $5.00, and $10.00 bills.

Making Change - This was more difficult, and less than 25 percent were able to respond accurately.

MEASUREMENT

Weight - Over 75 percent were able to discriminate between size and weight.

Time - All were able to identify a clock. About 25 percent could identify 12:00 and 3:00 o'clock setting on a clock. Few could identify half-hour settings. Only about 25 percent knew the name for a calendar, but over 50 percent knew its use. Less than 25 percent knew neither day of the week and month of the year they were being tested, nor their birthday.

Linear - About 50 percent were able to identify a ruler and know its use. About 20 percent were able to use a ruler to measure the side of a card.

Temperature - Less than 25 percent could name a thermometer, but over 25 percent knew what it was used for.

GEOMETRY

Shape Matching - Over 90 percent of the children could match a shape with its illustration on paper.

Vocabulary - Over 50 percent correctly labeled square and circle. Triangle, rectangle, and diamond were less frequently labeled correctly. Correct identification of "sides" and "corners" was made by over 75 percent.

Spatial Relations - Determining number of sides or number of corners was more difficult than just identifying them. Over 75 percent could reproduce various lines in given relationship.

The doctoral investigations of Richard (1964) and Heimgartner (1968) verify that children have acquired many mathematical skills and concepts before they begin formal school instruction. Moreover, evidence suggests that a great deal of variability exists within a group of typical kindergarten entrants. Callahan and Glennon have cautioned that "the kindergarten teacher must also be aware of the distinction between verbalization of mathematical concepts and performances which demonstrate the stability of these concepts" (1975, pp. 52-53).

Suydam and Weaver have concluded that "the variability of the methods of assessing the knowledge of children entering kindergarten makes it difficult to affirm precisely what children in general know" (1975, p. 49). They have reported the following summary of the data on five-year-olds without prior schooling:

1. Many children can count and find the number of objects to ten, and some are able to count to at least twenty.

2. Some can say the number names for tens in order (that is, ten, twenty, thirty...) but far fewer can say the names when counting by twos and fives.

3. Most know the meaning of "first" and many can identify ordinal positions through "fifth."

4. Many can recognize the numerals from 1 to 10, and some can write them.

5. Most can give correct answers to simple addition and subtraction combinations presented verbally either with or without manipulative materials.

6. Most have some knowledge about coins, time, and other measures; about simple fractional concepts; and about geometric shapes (1975, p. 49).

REFERENCES

Bjonerod, Corwin E. "Arithmetic Concepts Possessed by the Preschool Child," *Arithmetic Teacher,* 7:347-50, November, 1960.

Brownell, William A. *Arithmetic in Grades I and II: A Critical Summary of New and Previously Reported Research.* Duke University Research Studies in Education, No. 6., Durham, N.C.: Duke University Press, 1941.

Callahan, Leroy G. and Vincent J. Glennon. *Elementary School Mathematics: A Guide to Current Research.* Fourth edition. Washington, D.C.: Association for Supervision and Curriculum Development, 1975.

Dutton, Wilbur H. *Evaluating Pupil's Understanding of Arithmetic.* Englewood Cliffs, N.J.: Prentice-Hall, Inc., 1964.

Heimgartner, Norman L. "Selected Mathematical Abilities of Beginning Kindergarten Children," Unpublished Doctoral dissertation, Colorado State College, Greeley, Col., 1968.

Nuffield Mathematics Project. *Mathematics Begins.* New York: John Wiley and Sons, 1970.

Piaget, Jean. "How Children Form Mathematical Concepts," *Scientific American,* 189:74-79, November 1953.

Rea, Robert E. and Robert E. Reys. "Competencies of Entering Kindergarteners in Geometry, Number, Money, and Measurement," *School Science and Mathematics,* 71:389-402, May, 1971.

"Mathematical Competencies of Entering Kindergarteners," *Arithmetic Teacher,* 17:65-74, January 1970.

Richard, Esther E.S. "An Inventory of the Number Knowledge of Beginning First Grade Children Based on the Performance of Selected Number Tasks," Unpublished Doctoral dissertation, Indiana University, Bloomington, Ind., 1964.

Schwartz, Anthony N. "Assessment of Mathematical Concepts of Five-Year-Old Children," *Journal of Experimental Psychology,* 37:67-74, Spring, 1969.

Sussman, David. "Arithmetic Readiness of Children Entering Kindergarten," Unpublished Doctoral dissertation, University of California, Berkeley, 1962.

Suydam, Marilyn and Fred Weaver. "Research on Mathematics Learning." In *Mathematics Learning in Early Childhood.* Thirty-seventh Yearbook of National Council of Teachers of Mathematics. Reston, Va.: N.C.T.M., 1975.

Williams, Alfred H. "Mathematical Concepts, Skills, and Abilities of Kindergarten Entrants," *Arithmetic Teacher,* 12:261-268, April, 1965.

Chapter 35

Beyond the Workbook: Mathematics and the Young Child

Helene Silverman*

Open a kindergarten mathematics workbook! They are all similar in content - comparing sets to determine which has more or less, identifying the cardinal number of a set by matching a numeral to a corresponding set of pictured objects, writing numerals, finding plane figures, and learning to use some of the language of measurement and position.

Consider a broader curriculum. One that concerns itself with the child in his environment and is based upon the following natural inclinations of the child:

1. Using the senses as a means of collecting information
2. Developing an interest in making and arranging collections.
3. Making comparisons
4. Observing spatial aspects of our environment
5. Observing numerical aspects of our environment
6. Finding appropriate language to describe experiences

This can seem overwhelming. However the opportunities are there in the traditional centers in the kindergarten room—blocks, water and sand, dramatic play, art and music, woodworking, mobile food unit, and outdoor activities as well as in a special mathematics and science area.

Blocks

Playing with blocks offers children the opportunity to engage in physical activity, dramatic play and creative expression while developing kinesthetic and visual perception of solidarity, size, shape, weight, and spatial relations. Carrying, piling, fitting, and balancing—all early activities with blocks can provide the basis for concepts about weight, length, solid shapes, structure and symmetry. Structures with broad heavy bases seem to support higher piles of blocks. Cylinders can be stacked in a row on their circular bases, but will roll away when piled on their sides; structures become taller with less unit blocks than half-unit blocks; circular curves can be used to help turn a corner but make poor foundations for buildings. The child experiences these ideas and can be helped to develop appropriate language to describe these situations.

Class trips, small vehicles, wooden or plastic figures, or stories can stimulate thinking about situations which stimulate creative "building". The teacher interacting with the child, can stimulate thinking about proportion, balance and symmetry as the size of a garge for a toy car is decided, a roof for a house is selected, or pillars for a bridge are placed.

Large hollow blocks also provide the opportunity for dealing with space on a larger scale and for creating environments in which the child can relate his own physical space to the world in which he lives by creating structures on which he can climb, into which he can crawl, and in which he can enclose himself.

Sand and Water

The sand and water areas in the classroom may be two separate areas or two adjacent areas since similar materials can be used in each area. In addition to a basic trough or water table, pouring equipment should be available—bowls, teapot, watering can, tubes, strainers, funnels, squirt bottles. spoons, cups and plastic bottles. Ideas about filling and containing, volume and weight are easily developed as the children pour the water from one container to another.

Dry sand has similar properties to water as a material for filling and pouring. In addition it can be used for modeling. The joy of making "pies" with cups and pails also provides a foundation for ideas about solid shapes and volume. Similarities and differences between sand structures when compared and discussed can provide a basic foundation for discovering properties of geometric solids.

Dramatic Play

Many dramatic play areas include basic activities for housekeeping. A set of dishes and utensils easily stimulates setting of a table. As the children distribute the materials, they have practice with one-to-one correspondence. The role playing of the distribution of food also provides practice as the frequently overheard phrase "and one for you, and one for you, and one for you, and one for me" is repeated.

---

*Dr. Helene Silverman, Assistant Professor, Lehman College, City University of New York.

Playing roles of shopper and storekeeper stimulate ideas about money, weighing, surface area, and one-to-one or one-to-many correspondence as objects are selected, contained, wrapped and bartered or "paid for."

Role playing may also stimulate arranging and making collections as objects are sought to establish a post office, meal service, doctor's office, or grocery store. The opportunities are unlimited.

Art and Music

Clay is a marvelous medium in which to explore conservation of material, to manipulate shapes, and to duplicate solid objects. While modeling, chopping, and rolling the children learn about texture, shape, tensile strength, and mass. How much meaning the properties of a sphere take on after rolling "dough balls," how much experience with conservation of material is provided as the children roll small balls from the one large mass and recombine them to form a large clay ball!

The rhythms of line in finger painting and the various imprints which can be made by fingers can provide basic language for the exploration of patterns and space. Printing, paper folding, creating structures from junk material, cutting and recombining shapes—these all form a foundation for work with symmetry, structure, spatial relations, and shape recognition, and classification.

The various rhythms in music help to develop auditory perception of number quantities and provide an experience with a variety of tempos in a time span. Continuity and discontinuity are intuitively explored as musical patterns repeat and suddenly disappear or fade. Additional experience can be provided with patterns and symmetry using auditory perception.

Woodworking

The excitement of attaching shapes to create new forms combined with creative play and the sense of power derived from the ability to split larger parts into smaller ones or rearranging objects to form new wholes are very important to young children. The various weights, thicknesses, lengths and textures also provide additional experience with comparisons and beginning ideas about measurement. The complete involvement which most children have with woodworking projects provides an ideal setting for developing rich mathematical language as appropriate.

Mobile Food Unit

A baker-oven or hotplate, some disposable tins, measuring equipment and basic ingredients can easily form a mobile cooking center if placed on a cart which can be set up as it is used. What an ideal place for developing basic ideas about measurement, matching, ordering, one-to-one corres-

pondence, and counting as children follow simple recipes under the guidance of the teacher, observe changes in the combined ingredients, and distribute the product of their work to classmates.

Outdoor Activities

The child looking down at his surroundings and classmates from the top of a jungle gym can easily learn the concept above and below because now it has meaning. Going up the ladder of the slide and feeling the rapid decent down give meaning to the words, up and down when they follow the kinetic experience.

The school building is *near* the outdoor play area, but it is *far* to the post office. Going *around* all the obstacles is difficult. What fun it is to crawl *through* the barrel and to curl up *inside* the carton. These words take on meaning following the experience if an adult is around to help the child to apply the right vocabulary.

Relative position takes on meaning as games are learned where children have to deal with people to the left or to the right of them, behind them, in front of them, next to them, etc.

Concepts of distance are learned as the children learn to throw a ball and to move in the space allocated.

The rhythm of a jumprope or the bounce of a ball, provide good opportunity for counting in rote as familiar chants are learned.

Math and Science Area

The math and science area may also have collections of objects for children to sort—leaves, rocks, shells, nuts, seeds, etc. The children can be encouraged to organize and arrange their collections in a variety of ways. In addition, commercial sorting materials should be available.

The children can be taught to keep records of the changes in natural phenomena and to collect data in the classroom.

Table games and activities can be available both commercial and teacher-made-which help to teach one-to-one correspondence, cardinality, ordering and number relationships. In addition geometric materials should be made available for children to explore shape and size relations. Simple measuring devices should also be a part of the center. Children can then learn the function of various tools of measure and learn to explore a variety of standard and non-standard measures.

The Formal Lesson

In addition to informal work in each of these areas in the kindergarten, the teacher may wish to work with a child, a small group, or the class. Sometimes the workbook may be appropriate to practice a skill. At other times an experience which occurred in one of the centers or outside of school may become the focal point for the introduction of a new concept. The main difference is that the progression of these lessons are planned and can often be highly structured. However, it is important to note that these lessons are richer because of the experiential work in all the other areas.

SELECTED BIBLIOGRAPHY

Biggs, Edith. *Mathematics for Younger Children.* New York: Citation Press, 1971.

Frobisher, Beryl and Susan Gloyn. *Infants Learn Mathematics.* London: Ward Lock Educational, 1971.

Hirsch, Elisabeth S. (ed.). *The Block Book.* Washington, D.C.: National Association for the Education of Young Children, 1974.

Nuffield Foundation. *Beginnings.* New York: John Wiley, 1971.

Nuffield Foundation. *The First Three Years.* New York: John Wiley, 1970.

Nuffield Foundation. *Mathematics Begins.* New York: John Wiley, 1967.

Nuffield Foundation. *Pictorial Representation.* New York: John Wiley, 1967.

Parry, Marianne and Hilda Archer. *Two to Five: A Handbook for Students and Teachers.* London: Macmillan Education for the Schools Council, 1975.

Payne, Joseph N. (ed.) *Mathematics Learning in Early Childhood.* Washington, D.C.: National Council of Teachers of Mathematics, 1975.

Pickering, Dorothy and John M. Pickering. *Pre-School Activities.* London: Anchor Press, 1974.

Schools Council. *Early Explorations.* Book 1 in the Using the Environment Series. London: Macdonald Educational for the Schools Council, 1974.

Yardley, Alice. *Discovering the Physical World.* London: Evans, 1970.

Chapter 36

"Is Today Tomorrow?" History for Young Children

Carol Seefeldt*

"Is today tomorrow?" asked Alethea as she bounded into the kindergarten room. For Alethea's teacher had told her over and over the day before, in answer to her eager and continuous questions, that "tomorrow is the day we will go to the zoo."

Young children who have little concept of time, and even less understanding of the events of the past, have generally been given limited exposure to the concepts of history. Yet, as early as 1921 Margaret McMillan wrote that preschool children can start the study of history "as long as it is approached from a point of view suggested to the teacher, not by learned professors, but by the bright eyed children themselves...." (McMillan, 1921, p. 215). Children are highly interested in the past. Who has not heard a young child beg for "just one more story about the olden days when you were little?" Furthermore, many of the concepts associated with the study of history are familiar to young children, and other concepts can be easily managed and enjoyed by them when presented in meaningful, active ways.

The study of history has been defined as a time oriented study that refers to what we do know about the past. History deals with the concepts of change, the continuity of human life, and includes knowledge gained from a critical and systematic investigation of the past. (Senn, 1971, p. 74). Using this definition, the concepts of time, change, the continuity of human life, and the past can be identified as appropriate to introduce to young children.

The Concept of Time

An understanding of time is necessary for the study of history.

What notion of TIME has our Tommy got? As he flattens his small palms and nose on the bathroom window and gazes out dreamily at the terrace and the mulberry tree? Does yesterday exist for him, save as something very distant, vague and separate as were, a little while ago, his own toes and feet? (McMillan, p. 235).

Research would seem to indicate that young children, as Tommy in Margaret McMillan's London nursery school of the early 1900's, have very few concepts of time. And yet even the youngest baby, crying from hunger or discomfort, experiences time as he waits for someone to care for him. These daily experiences of being hungry and fed, being cared for, gradually develop in the child the differences between day and night, morning and afternoon.

In the preschool, routines, the things that happen in a predictable order, an order the children can count on and depend on, help the children to develop an understanding of time. "I don't know what time it is," said three-year-old Sarah in a child care center, "but I know my daddy will come and get me because he always comes to take me home after my nap." Flexible as they might be, the regular routines of washing before lunch, playing outside after nap, or reading a story before going home convey ideas about time to children.

Young children, even though they cannot tell time by the clock, are intrigued with measures of time. As they become familiar with the things that measure time, children are experiencing concepts of duration, the sequence of events, and temporal order.

Children can use:

...a stop watch to see how long it takes them to..put the blocks away..hang up their coats..hop across the room.

...an hour glass to turn over and watch the sand trickle into the bottom glass or use the hour glass to see if they can..wash the tables..pick up the scraps..get ready to go home before the sand empties into the other half of the glass.

...a cooking timer that buzzes when set to remind them to..take the cookies from the oven..to come in from play..or to get up from rest.

...an old alarm clock to play with..to turn the hands..to take apart..to set the alarm.

Learning about history, dealing with the events of the past also requires that children develop a sense of the passage of time. "What did you do today?" the teacher of the two-year-old asks as she helps her into her coat before going home. "What did we have for lunch yesterday?" "What did we do last week?" "What did you like best about the

*Dr. Carol Seefeldt, Assistant Professor of Education, University of Maryland. Reprinted with permission from Young Children, January 1975.

year in kindergarten?" are all questions that help children to recall the passage of time.

The Concept of Change

With the passage of time comes change. History, in many respects, is the study of change. The record of man's existence is a record of change. Some changes represent progress, others do not. Nevertheless, change is a part of living and being able to adapt to change is critical. Change is not valued for bringing something new and different or innovative, nor is it feared for the differences it brings. Rather the value of accepting the inevitability of change, and methods for adapting to change are taught to the children.

Change surrounds the children. Whether a child care center, kindergarten, or primary classroom, things are constantly changing. Children's observations can be focused on the changes that occur in the pets, seeds, bulbs, and plants in the classroom. The children themselves change. They grow, learn new skills, lose teeth, get their hair cut, and make new friends. Children can discover all of the ways they have changed. They might:

...find out how much they weighed at birth, go outside and fill a plastic bag with enough sand to equal their birth weight. A bathroom scale is usually adequate to weigh the bags of sand. Actually holding 6 pounds of sand in their hands, children gain some understanding of exactly how much they have changed since their birth.

...taste a bit of strained baby food, perhaps string beans, and then taste the string beans they now eat. Why did they need the strained food when they were babies? What can they eat now that they could not eat then? How have they changed?

...examine items of clothing they wore when they were much younger. Many children may be able to bring in some item, a bonnet, baby shoes, christening dress, or old diaper, to compare with the clothing they now wear.

...begin a history book of their year in the preschool. Snap shots, taken throughout the year, pieces of work the children have completed, records of weight and height, some of the interesting things they might have said can be recorded in the history book. At the end of the year each child will have a booklet of her own life, a booklet that will give her a meaningful understanding of change.

The Concept of the Continuity of Human Life

Although life is continually changing, there is a continuity to human experiences. Exploring the children's family history provides a sense of the continuity of human experiences. Not every family will be able to give their children a complete family history, yet each family has something unique and of worth to give their children from the past. McMillan, who taught children of working class families wrote:

What is it to belong to an old family? Just this. It is belonging to people who are worth thinking about and being remembered for a long time, at least by their own children. At the bottom of all this is a dim consciousness that life is not a trivial thing, not a scurrying across a stage and ending in utter darkness, but a play with some kind of relating and meaning to the acts. (p. 239).

For many parents who are faced with the struggles of day to day living, the questions their children ask about the past may seem rude, prying, or strange. Teachers might help these parents to see the value of talking to their children about their own past as they interest the children in their family's history.

Every parent, no matter what they remember of their past, can talk to their children about the games they liked to play, the things they liked to do, how they used to do their hair, catch a cricket, fold sheets, or play in puddles.

The Concept of the Past

Children are intensely interested in the past, both the immediate past and the very long ago. Helping children to understand and explore the past does not mean that a true historic sense of time can be developed. In helping children to gain a concept of the past, Wann stated that "Adults must shuttle back and forth with children from the past to the present as they react to the ever present urge to understand what has gone before. This dipping into the past without concern for a logical development of chronology from the past to the present does not violate basic principles of learning." (Wann and Dorn, 1962, p. 53).

Even though the past is untouchable and far away, experiences with the past are possible for young children. Many resources are available to help young children understand the past.

...people as resources

Their own parents, grandparents, the school staff, the neighbors, are all resources for helping children to understand the past. The grandfather who can tell about hitching up his horse to go to church, a grandmother who shows the children how she used to wash clothes on a scrub board, or the mother who tells the children about listening to the radio before the advent of television all give the children a vicarious sense of the past.

...objects as resources

Tools, kitchen utensils, rolling pins, old wooden cookie cutters, kettles, eggbeaters, are all excellent resources. As the children wonder over the marvels of a coal oil lamp or a hand eggbeater, they can compare these objects from the past to the ones in use today.

Other antiques, those that cannot be handled by the

children, can still be shared in the classroom. Children seem to understand that something very old is very valuable.

Nearly every community has some type of museum to preserve the traces of the past. The local library, fire station, or church may house relics for the children to observe. If only large museums are available in the community, the teacher could select one room for the children to visit or just one section of the museum for a field trip. Older homes, buildings, mansions that have been renovated and restored can also be visited by the children.

Toys and models that depict things from the past are enjoyed. Cars, boats, and planes that are modeled after those no longer in use, give the children an opportunity to make comparisons between the things they know and use today and things from the past. With any object from the past teachers initiate discussions to help extend and clarrify children's concepts. "Why do you think the train was made this way?" "Who do you think used this?" "How do you know it was used a long time ago?" "How is it just like the ones we use today?" are questions that might stimulate children's thinking.

The Methods of the Historian

Preschool children are not being prepared to become historians, but there is much in the historic method that can be of value to them. The historian uses the methods of science in order to interpret and understand the past. Historians, as scientists, formulate problems, gather information and data, observe the data, analyze, infer, and reach conclusions based on their data. These processes, the same ones that are involved in problem solving and the scientific method, can be developed in young children.

...identifying a problem

Children must be able to identify their own problems, at least they should perceive the problem as their own. When a problem is determined by the teacher and presented to the children for solving, it may be an exercise for the children rather than a problem to solve. Problems that arise in the classroom, school, home, or immediate community have elements of being "real" to the children.

...gathering information

In order to solve a problem, information must be gathered. Historians gather traces of the past as they attempt to solve problems. Children might examine traces of the past—books, relics, objects—or they might interview older people to obtain information.

...observing data

After the information has been collected, careful observation takes place. Children's skills in learning to observe

are fostered continually as they are asked to describe what they see, feel, taste, touch, and hear throughout the day.

...analyzing information

Once gathered and observed, information is analyzed and inferences are made. Children, as historians, based on their observations of the traces of the past, make inferences as to what life was like, how people lived, what they did, and what they believed in a long time ago.

...drawing conclusions

In problem solving, children may, because their data is incomplete or their inferences are less than accurate, draw conclusions that are also incomplete and inaccurate. Rather than correcting the children's conclusions, the teacher concerned about the process of problem solving, and not a correct answer, accepts the children's judgements. Activities that will clarify the children's conclusions could be planned for the future.

The Role of Play

Just as the teacher structures and plans experiences and activities designed to foster children's understanding of history and build concepts of time, change, continuity of human life, and the past, she provides opportunities for children to play.

Fostering children's play, props suggestive of some period in the past that is of interest to the children, can be added to the dramatic play area. A sunbonnet, cowboy hat, long dress, old lunch bucket, tools, boots might stimulate children's play. Historic films, stories, slides are shared to give children additional information as a base for their play. Large blocks of time and as much space as possible, both indoors and out, are set aside for play.

Together, a program rich with play and experiences planned to foster concepts associated with the study of history can develop the preschool child's understanding of history. This understanding will not be complete or final, it may even be vague, on the order of a precept rather than a concept, and yet however incomplete, this understanding will form the foundation on which all future learnings will be built.

BIBLIOGRAPHY

Margaret McMillan, *The Nursery School*, New: J.M. Dent and Sons, 1921.

Peter R. Senn, *Social Science and Its Methods*, Boston: Holbrook Press, 1971.

Kenneth D. Wann, Miriam Selchem Dorn, and Elizabeth Ann Liddle, *Fostering Intellectual Development in Young Children*, New York: Bureau of Publications, Teachers College, Columbia University, 1962).

Chapter 37

Creative dramatics in Early Childhood

Jean Mandelbaum*

The "seeds" or simple beginnings of creative dramatics abound in every nursery, kindergarten, and primary classroom. They can be observed in children's experiments with music and movement, in their responses to favorite songs and stories, in their spontaneous dramatic play, in their own "made-up" material, and in connection with shared events, such as trips or the arrival of a new pet.

A teacher who is aware of the dramatic possibilities in these everyday classroom experiences, and is also sensitive to the needs and interests of young children, can help the members of her group develop their own dramatic sequences and in that way intensify and deepen their experiences and concepts. As the children shape their dramatizations and make decisions as to form, content, and characterization, they participate in the challenge and excitement of the creative process, and in addition, develop a familiarity with some of the concerns of drama as an art form.

The attention span and intellectual scope of the young child will limit the complexity of the work, but there is no reason to believe that the three-to seven-year-old cannot actively participate in creative dramatics or benefit as much from the process as the older child. I would like to offer some suggestions as to how teachers of nursery through second grade children might develop a creative dramatics program from elements that are already in the curriculum and, more important, in the children themselves. As Brian Way (1966) has put it; "The problem of starting, with any age group, is reduced to the minimum if we keep in mind the fact that we are not attempting to add something new and strange—we are simply taking what already exists and working outwards from there." (p. 43)

Music and Movement Can Lead to Drama

The young child comes to movement experiences at school with his own movement "vocabulary," style, and tempo. By asking motivating questions, offering additional materials, and providing an atmosphere of acceptance and respect for the child, the teacher encourages creative exploration, discovery, and problem solving. For example, a simple walk can be the basis for stimulating movement experiences. The group might start by walking to a steady, even drum beat. As they move, the teacher helps them explore a variety of different walks by suggesting images, moods, and characterizations. Now walk as if it is freezing out—The streets are ice.—The ice melts and there are enormous puddles all around.—You suddenly realize that you are lost. Show how you feel by the way you walk.—Oh! There is your street! Your body shows how you feel."

A small dramatization might develop as a result of this simple movement experience. But this time, the teacher will hope to elicit more from the group. Now *they* determine the action and provide ideas for movement. The teacher helps by asking questions. "Who is it who is walking? Where is she? Is it day or night? Whom does she meet? Where is she going?" etc. When this kind of prethinking and planning occurs and when the teacher uses the children's ideas, she helps them to see their contributions as important parts of a successful collaboration.

Since it is very difficult for young children to invent dialogue and concentrate on movement at the same time, the teacher serves as narrator, while the children use pantomime or other expressive body movement to tell their story. A drum or other simple instrument might be used as accompaniment. Sometimes another group of children can support the action with instruments, and vocalizing of all sorts. "To help this, the teacher can say,'We will try to make sounds that belong to the way you are moving. We will watch you move, so try to be clear!' These comments help both the (actors) and musicians to become more focused." (Stecher and McElheny, 1972, p. 84).

Young children identify with animals easily, and they are able to capture the movement quality of familiar animals with remarkable ease. Of course, if the child has not had firsthand experience with a particular creature, his characterizations will tend to be more stereotyped or limited. Many teachers draw on this interest to stimulate various movement experiences. These can be extended and enhanced by developing a dramatic theme or incident in which the animals become part of a larger idea as they move in their own distinctive way.

*Dr. Jean Mandelbaum, Instructor in Early Childhood Education, City College of New York. Reprinted with permission from YOUNG CHILDREN, January, 1975.

One group of four-year-olds* became particularly interested in dramatizing the life cycle of moths, frogs, birds of all kinds, and the most satisfying of all—the human baby. A simple story of growth and change can be very dramatic for a young child and offer a great many opportunities for movement exploration and identification with a role. The children in this group moved with complete absorption from the teacher's first line; "When you were just born, you lay in a basket sleepy and small"* The story took the children through the discovery of fingers, toes, learning to turn over, stretch and crawl, until the exciting end when the teacher proudly announced, "Now you can do anything! You can jump!—You can run!—You can even hop on one foot!—You can walk backwards! And you can fall to the floor without hurting yourselves, relaxed, calm, and still."

It is important to end dramatic sequences at a place of rest and resolution both physically and mentally. The child needs a moment to savor the experience as a whole and to move from the excitement of his artistic and emotional release to the less intense emotional climate of reality.

Dramatizations of Songs, Stories, and Poems

Children's favorite songs, stories, and poems provide excellent material for creative dramatics. As the children improvise dialogue and movement, and create characterizations, they become more familiar with the literature and increase their appreciation of it. It also helps them to understand more fully and with greater depth, the universalities that the piece deals with. (Heathcote) Even with the youngest child, another dimension is added when a story, song, or poem is acted out.

A group of three-year-olds were delighted with a dramatization of the familiar fingerplay "The Eensy, Weensy Spider." In this group, the teacher asked the children to decide whether they wanted to be a spider, the rain, or the sun. They were divided according to their choices into three groups, and each group was given time to find a way to express its part. The spiders developed a special walk and a rolling movement for getting "washed out." Those who played the rain practiced "coming down" and "drying up," and the sun children found a variety of ways to radiate. After a while, they put their dramatization together while the teacher sang the song at a pace which allowed each sequence to be fully realized.

Five- and six-year-olds love to dramatize "The Fox Went Out on a Chilly Night." (Landeck, 1950, p. 46). This song has interesting characters, a dramatic plot, and a chance to see "right and wrong" from a different point of view—the fox's.

Songs may simply set the scene for a dramatization or provide a theme which the children develop. The song "John the Rabbit" (Seeger, 1948, p. 100), is about a farmer who is very angry because his crops are devoured by the rabbit. This theme and solutions to the farmer's problem have been explored and dramatized many different ways by interested four- and five-year-olds.

Stories for young children are particularly fine sources for dramatizations. These can be played as pantomimes with a narrator, with improvised dialogue, or with a combination of both. When young children begin to create dialogue, it "will be scanty, despite the most careful planning. It is an early stage in the development of the group, and may, at that point, indicate real progress." (McCaslin, 1974, p. 95) Acceptance, encouragement, and practice will help children to become more fluent. Nellie McCaslin mentions *Caps for Sale* as a good story for young children to dramatize. (p. 96) Some others for the nursery through second grade are:

The Little Fisherman (Gruenberg, p. 108) by Margaret Wise Brown. In this simple story, contrast between big and little is explored. Rhythm and repetition help the story unfold.

A Fly Went By by Mike McClintock. This is an amusing, "add on" story with a large cast of different animals and a mystery to be solved.

Ask Mr. Bear by Marjorie Flack is a lovely story for three to five-year-olds. A boy and his animal friends are looking for the best birthday present for his mother.

Swimmy By Leo Lionni is a wonderful under the sea drama about a little fish who uses his special qualities to solve a big problem.

In the Forest by Marie Hall Ets. A small boy takes a walk in the forest and meets many animals who join him. This story was done as a shadow play by a group of five year-olds with considerable success.

The teacher helps children develop these dramas by posing questions, such as: "What scene shall we begin with? Where does the play take place? Who are the characters in the story? How do they walk, talk, move, grimace and react to the various situations presented in the story?" (Hopkins, 1969, p. 153).

Of course there are many other fine stories for dramatization.* Those that lend themselves best have several characters with distinctive styles, and move the story forward through the action rather than the dialogue.

Some poems that have worked well with young children also provide opportunity for movement and characterization. Here is a very simple one which has been interpreted in many different ways.

---

*All anecdotal materials refer to groups of children at the Horace Mann School for Nursery Years, N.Y., and the Marble Hill Nursery, N.Y.

*Adapted from, Betty Miles, "When You Were Very Little," *Let's Hear a Story*, ed. Gruenberg (New York: Doubleday & Co., 1961), p. 27.

*See Lease and Siks, *Creative Dramatics for Home, School, and Community* (New York: Harper and Row, 1953) Appendix A, p. 241, for additional suggestions.

Like Leaves in Windy Weather

Dance and twirl together
Like leaves in windy weather.
Puff! Puff! Puff!
All fall down.

by Bernice Carlson (1965, p. 50).

The next poem helps children reach further into their experience in order to portray a cat rather than settle for a first , less thoughtful characterization.

Cat

The black cat yawns
Opens her jaws,
Stretches her legs,
And shows her claws.

She shows her sharp teeth,
She stretches her lip,
Her slice of a tongue
Turns up at the tip.

Lifting herself
On her delicate toes,
She arches her back
As high as it goes.

She lets herself down
With particular care,
And pads away
With her tail in the air.

by Mary Britton Miller (Arbuthnot, 1971, p. 54).

Dramatizations of nursery rhymes are often successful with young children because they know them well enough to speak the lines or improvise on them as they play out the action. "Little Miss Muffett, "Simple Simon," "Sing 'Song of Sixpence," "The Old Woman in the Shoe," and "Mary Had a Little Lamb" are all small stories with action and a satisfying conclusion.

Dramatic Play and Original Stories
Lead to Creative Drama

In her book *Creative Dramatics in the Classroom*, Nellie McCaslin distinguishes between dramatic play and creative dramatics. Dramatic play "is the free play of the very young child in which he explores his universe, imitating the actions and character traits of those around him....It has no beginning and no end and no development in the dramatic

sense...." (p.5). Whereas creative dramatics has form. It makes use of a story "with a beginning, a middle and an end." (p. 7). Both dramatic play and creative dramatics involve the child in improvised dialogue, identification with a role, and minimal use of props. The most important similarity is that the process is guided by the child's interests and serves his artistic, emotional, and intellectual needs.

A sensitive teacher will not interfere with a child's dramatic play when she sees that its content and intensity are deeply personal and gratifying to the child. However, there are many times in an early childhood classroom when a teacher's questions can extend the play, deepen the participant's involvement, and perhaps help structure it so that it does indeed result in a creative dramatic experience.

C, and B., two five-year-old boys, had finished building a large boat in the block corner. They were sitting in it and were pretending to be sailors. C. put a captain's hat on, and B. was looking through a mailing tube "telescope" at some imagined distance. Soon, other children came to play, and it looked to the teacher as if C. and B. were able to incorporate the new players or improvise on their theme any more. She approached the group with some questions. "What kind of a boat is this?" C. and B. answered together, "A big ship." "Where is it going?" the teacher asked. A good deal of discussion and arguing led to the consensus, "Puerto Rico." Further questioning clarified the situation. A large family is going to Puerto Rico to visit a grandma whom they haven't seen in a long time. The ship has a captain and a helper, and there is going to be a storm before they get to Puerto Rico. Before very long, a plan emerged and the children were ready to play it. They knew who they were and what was going to happen. Some of them had hastily put together some props and dress-up items to help them in their improvisation. The first time through was hesitant, and the teacher was needed to guide the action and remind the small players of their plan. The storm involved a great deal of movement, and someone brought cymbals and drums from the music area to help create the mood. At last, there was calm; the boat arrived at Puerto Rico, and a scene of happy reunion with the grandmother took place.

This became a favorite play which was replayed in this classroom with variations and additions many times.

Sometimes a favorite class drama comes from a "made-up" story offered to the group at circle time or told to the teacher in a quiet moment. Here is one that a four-year-old told.

There was once a little swan who had a mother and a father. One day, the mother said, "You can go play by yourself today." He went so far away, he didn't know what to play and he got lost. That is why his mother and father were never happy again.

The class was very eager to act it out. All the children

who wanted to be the little swan were asked to form one group; the mothers and fathers formed another group. After they acted it out, they asked to do it again. It was surprising to the teacher that they enjoyed this play so much. When she asked the "little swans" if they wanted to be found next time, they all said "No!"

Important Events in a Classroom
May Lead to Creative Dramatics

In much the same way as adults enjoy reliving the highlights of a vacation by telling anecdotes and showing photos, children want opportunities to review, savor, and clarify pleasurable events. By eliminating the mundane and unimportant aspects of an experience and emphasizing the significant and exciting elements, a bit of reality can be transformed into art, and in the process become more real or more deeply felt and understood than it was at the time it took place.

Trips to the firehouse, the river, the gas station, and the zoo are all extensions of the early childhood curriculum. Teachers want to use this kind of trip to help motivate interest in classroom work. However, the usual experience charts, art work, and thank you letters would be more meaningful if the children were able to dramatize the most interesting aspects of these trips, and in that way share responses, insights, and recollections. Often this playback of a trip reveals to the teacher that *her* highpoints were not at all the same as her class's, and sometimes what is most significant to the group is an accidental encounter, rather than the planned main event.

A group of five-year-olds were enjoying a variety of cooking experiences in their class. This led the teacher to plan a trip to a nearby bakery. After arrangements were made, the group excitedly left the school to walk several blocks to the shop. On the way they had to pass a construction site where a new apartment house was being built. After a brief stop to look at the machines and workers, the children went on their way. The owner of the bakery was expecting the group. He welcomed them warmly and led them to the kitchen where they observed the swift and elegant movements of the master baker. Treats and samples of raw dough for each child brought the visit to a pleasant conclusion.

The next day, the teacher asked if they would like to do a play about "our trip to the bakery." All agreed so she asked, "What parts will we need for the play?"

"A bulldozer," said one child.
"The baker," said another.
"A steamshovel."
"A great big dough mixer."
"A cement mixer."

It was clear that for some, the building site was the exciting place, and for others it was the bakery. The play that resulted had two very different scenes, and a new avenue for further exploration and experience was opened.

The teacher's role in guiding work in creative dramatics is clearly another facet of her overall concern for the intellectual, social, and emotional growth of her children. Dramatics offers a media which encompasses many other aspects of the curriculum and invites the child's full participation and involvement.

A special benefit is gained by the child who is usually typecast in the same sort of role in spontaneous dramatic play by his peers or predisposition. For him, creative dramatics offers an opportunity to play a role that explores a less dominant part of his personality. "As a child participates in many creative dramatic experiences and becomes many different characters, he gains a better understanding not only of others but also of himself." (Lease and Siks, 1952, p. 14).

A teacher who values the ideas, concerns, and natural abilities of young children, and who becomes aware of some of the possibilities for developing everyday classroom happenings into creative dramatics, will find the early childhood classroom particularly conducive to his work. Activities in music and movement, songs and stories, dramatic play, science and social studies can be a constant source of inspiration. And the relaxed and individualized approach to learning that exists in good early childhood classrooms helps to provide an atmosphere of acceptance and encouragement which is so important in the nurturing of creative beginnings. As for where the teacher should begin, Brian Way suggests, "Start from where you yourself are happiest and most confident...." (p. 8). Once the program is underway, its continuance is assured.

REFERENCES

Arbuthnot, May Hill. *The Arbuthnot Anthology of Children's Literature.* Chicago: Scott, Foresman & Co., 1971.

Carlson, Bernice Wells. *Listen! And Help Tell the Story.* New York: Abingdon Press, 1965.

Ets, Marie Hall. *In the Forest.* New York: Viking Press, 1944.

Flack, Marjorie. *Ask Mr. Bear.* New York: Macmillan Co., 1932.

Gruenberg, Sidonie Matsner. *Let's Hear a Story.* New York: Doubleday & Co., 1961.

Hopkins, Lee Bennett. *Let Them Be Themselves.* New York: Citation Press, 1969.

Landeck, Beatrice. *Songs To Grow On.* New York: William Sloane Associates, 1950.

Lease, Ruth and Siks, Geraldine Brain. *Creative Dramatics for Home, School and Community.* New York: Harper and Row, 1952.

Lionni, Leo. *Swimmy.* New York: Random House, 1963.

McCaslin, Nellie. *Creative Dramatics in the Classroom.* New York: David McKay Co., 1974.

McClintock, Mike. *A Fly Went By.* New York: Random House, 1955.

Seeger, Ruth. *American Folk Songs for Children.* New York: Doubleday & Co., 1948.

Stecher, Mariam and McElheny, Hugh. *Music and Movement Improvisations.* New York: Macmillan Co., 1972.

Way, Brian. *Development Through Drama.* New York: Humanities Press, 1966.

American Federation of Teachers

Chapter 38

Genesis: The Art of the Young Child

Olive R. Francks*

In the beginning, the young child drew a mark, and the mark became a scribble. With this as his first statement, the child said a great deal more about himself than the things of this world, as we know them. Those grownups and near-grownups who live and work with younger children, tend to look upon the art of the scribble with a variety of expectations. Some expect and make too much of the event, while others belittle it as quite perfunctory. Neither is correct.

In general, the adult tends to be caught in an ambivalent situation to which he feels he must react and respond. The purpose of this chapter is to provide a few insights into the art and thought of the young child. If this view seems to cast off some popularly held myths concerning the art of the young child, it may also add to the knowledge of the caring adult regarding the importance of art in the life of children.

The life cycle of a scribble

Rhoda Kellogg (1967) believes that children universally proceed through the same series of stages in their early art development. She has discovered that at first, the child deals with scribble and chance forms, and soon moves on toward controlled marks and basic forms. At this stage, art may be seen simply as the placement of marks on a surface by the use of a tool. For example, the use of a pencil or paint or crayon or even the child's own finger on paper, wood, cloth, or any available material. This act is a visible one and can be observed and analyzed. Then, too, young children often create and draw nonvisibly, as in the case of "painting" in water or in the air. As we shall discover, this fluidity actually helps to explain the true purpose of young children's art work.

By the ages of two and three years, children have begun to scribble in earnest. They are often deeply involved in intensive activity which, if it were not so beloved to them, could be called "work" by our standards. If paper is near-by, the child scribbles on paper; if he is at the beach, he scribbles on sand; in the city, on concrete, buildings, tile, furniture--in fact, on anything and everything in his pathway, including himself. This early, innocent, free-flowing activity is very much like graffiti, for it is a way by which the child affirms for himself and the world, who he really is.

As adults, we should look upon these early scribbles with interest rather than dismay. The key to the tangle seems to be in freeing oneself of preconceived notions and judgments about art: to revisit one's own early years, and to begin to see life through different lenses. Many adults have, indeed, rediscovered the beauty in childhood scribble. Led by such artists as Kandinsky, Chagall, and Miro who returned to the sources of child art for their own study and inspiration, we realize that art need not be pictorial in order to be aesthetically pleasing.

Scribbling, like the babbling of early speech, is a form of "making" activity for the young child which soon begins to acquire symbolic overtones (Gardner, 1973). Kellogg and O'Dell describe scribbles as "the building blocks of children's art." In the eyes of many adults, a scribble is a scribble is a scribble. This, however, is not the case at all. There are at least twenty basic scribbles used by young children, including lines that are vertical, horizontal, diagonal, circular, curved, and waving, as well as several patterns of dots (Kellogg, 1967). Scribbles can also be found in different patterns of placement. For example, a child may scribble in the left-half, right-half, or in the center of the space or surface. Seventeen such placement patterns have been identified by Kellogg and substantiated by other researchers. These patterns are utilized by the child who is doing his scribble art, each one discovered in its own time. It is also important that we understand that once the child has found and developed these patterns, they become part of his art repertoire and continue to reappear throughout the years of his artistic development.

Shape and design: self taught

Soon after the placement stage, the child begins to deal with shape (Kellogg, 1967). This occurs so close in time to the earlier stage, that only the alert observer will notice the subtle change. At first, the child begins to make his scribbles with several strokes of his crayon, pencil, or brush.

*Dr. Olive R. Francks, Assistant Professor, Fordham University. Division of Curriculum and Teaching.

The first shapes are implied, rather than overtly stated, and are not contained within a boundary line or outline. Later, as he continues to experiment with shape, he also begins to outline the shape. He may then draw such familiar shapes as circles, ovals, squares, rectangles, triangles, and crosses, all of which are part of a broad repertoire which is already assimilated. Each has been self-taught and mastered through endless scribbling exercises which the child has devised for himself. They should never be directly taught or shown to the child by the adult. Whether or not the child wishes to talk about what he is drawing or has drawn is of far less importance than the fact that he set them down in the first place. This fact is indicative of his growing ability to organize and order his universe in his own fashion.

The shape stage seems to melt into one leading to design, in which the child uses the shapes he has discovered, practiced, expressed earlier. He now puts these into structured forms, such as a cross inside a square, or a smaller circle within a large circle. At this special moment in time, the child has entered into the design stage (Kellogg, 1967). He has learned for himself that shapes can be juxtaposed, moved about, placed near or far from one another. In so doing, he may also discover that he can play with ideas in the same way. Because the act is pleasing and meaningful to the child, he repeats it over and over, without being told to do so. He is still too young to provide us with "pictures" we can understand and relate to, but then, this is not the purpose of his design at all. It is, after all, his purpose, not ours, which must be served.

Toward realism: uniting inner/outer visions

The pictorial stage, as we know it, flows directly from the design stage (Kellogg and O'Dell, 1967). Usually between the ages of four and five years, the child begins to set down structured designs which are clear enough for the adult to recognize and name. This stage represents a dramatic breakthrough for the child. Now, he can actually put together his scribbles, placement patterns, shapes, and designs into pictorial art work -- in the direction of realism. Still, at this stage, the child is seldom concerned about drawing objects or scenes as the adult would like to see them, but draws them according to his own particular perceptions and visions.

There is still much about the young child's art that is hidden and unknown to us. We must remind ourselves that the child as fetus, before his birth, has had an existence in space and time, and that traces of this life stage are still quite real to him (Grozinger, 1955). Thus, he is far more delighted in describing *his* picture of the world than in trying to satisfy others. He has not yet reached the stage in his development when he perceives as the adult does.

In drawing a house, for instance, he may wish to add wiggly lines and loopy loops around it. The adult may interpret these decorations as real smoke from a real chimney, because this is the way the adult responds to the world. For the young child, these may just as likely be wiggling strings or floating tracks as "smoke", and their meaning may be closer to Zen than to any reality we know. When asked what he is making, the child may shrug his shoulders, or explain simply, "How do I know until I have finished?" (Kellogg and O'Dell, 1967). And this is so. The child's pictorial world is filled with objects which change shape and form even as they are being created. His drawings are molded in the same way as his clay sculptures: over and over, continually rearranged to fit the meaning of the moment. This is the fluidity of which we spoke earlier. There may be no answer to the adult's question, but if the child chooses, he may concoct an answer to please the observer, or perhaps, to startle him!

Underlying the child's pictorial efforts is a visual order which develops gradually, until with greater security in utilizing his scribbles and outlines, the four-to-five year old reaches the point where he can put it all together. Suddenly, or so it seems, he creates all sorts of shapes and figures which are familiar and recognizable. Schaefer-Simmern (1973) sees this move toward figure-ground relationship as important to the child's mental growth "because by its formative quality the significance of an experience is mentally fixed (page 29)." The circle or circular figures become starting points for still-to-be-discovered relationships in art. Now, for example, he may draw lines which radiate out from the center of a circle, looking like the customary sun-with-rays, or perhaps, a modified centipede. In truth, they may be neither.

This particular type of formative artistic effort has its own unified structure which is "the outcome of an intuitive process of pure vision, a nonreflective activity independent of conceptual thinking and rationalization" (Schaefer-Simmern, page 30). The unified structure—the sunburst or centipede, for instance—is an organized visual formation which hangs together as an entity. It is, for all intent and purpose, a work of art, a formative activity which *is* mental activity. Art, described in this way, is a visual means by which the child learns to structure his thinking. Through his work in art, the child practices visual thinking, a creative process which continues throughout childhood. At the same time, he gains competence in the symbol system of his culture, which as Gardner (1973) states, "is a necessary antecedent for creative efforts in the arts (page 160)."

As the child matures, he comes to terms more and more with his external world. In so doing, he uses and sharpens his powers of observation, bringing back to his art work greater visual awareness of the world as he sees and knows it. As far as the child is concerned, he understands his visual statement. If we are unable to decipher its meaning, that may be a disappointment to us, but is of little concern to him. This is as it should be.

The process: meaning and message

In most of our daily adult endeavors, we tend to look for products, rather than process. We have become conditioned by our training, to evaluate along a good-better-best type of continuum, rather than through quiet observation and analysis. Whether or not we realize it, our critical judgment is generally directed toward the outcome: the finished art product. This is at best, a limited way of enjoying and experiencing any art form. There is, however, a world of difference between the art work done by young children and that of mature artists.

The young child's art work is really not created for the purpose of becoming a work of art in itself. It exists solely for its own sale—as a record of the child's exploration of his world—a time when new skills are continuously being acquired and practiced. His marks and scribbles reveal something about his inner drama, as well. This may not be fully conscious on his part, but he still finds it important to make a visual statement about it.

The young child is not at all ready to step aside, to detach himself from what he is scribbling or drawing, in order to distinguish between inner feeling and outer reality. This more complex act belongs to the role of the mature adult, the skilled artist who has consciously studied and practiced his art to such an extent that detachment has become second-nature to him. For the young child, however, there is no difference between inner and outer reality because "everything *is* and nothing merely *seems*."(Lindstrom, page 10) His art work, as all his activity, acts as a bridge between the two, engrossing and satisfying to him, for he is fully engaged in the physical and mental activity of *doing*.

For each child, the process *is* the message which contains meaning for him. The making and doing of art are important to his learning. Through the visual statement he makes—as in his crayon scribbles or his red-smeared and scrabbled painting—he is better able to resolve some of life's mysteries for himself, to gain control thereby over what may have perceived as overpowering, unmanageable "things" (Lindstrom). Such phenomena are dealt with naturally and with immediacy through art. They need not be understood to be valid. The child's art work validates itself by the very fact that it has come into existence.

The role of quiet observer

Because of its process orientation, it is wiser for adults to observe and enjoy the art experience along with the child, rather than interrupting the flow of his thinking. If you must know about the image he has created, simply ask the child to tell you about it, if he is willing. But, restrain yourself from such statements as, "That's very good," or "I like John's best because it is a real train," or the myriad of unnecessary expressions which leap so easily to mind and tongue. It is far better to maintain a friendly silence, or merely to sit quietly and mind one's own affairs, as it were.

A nursery school teacher responded to one parent's reaction to her child's art work:

I gave a water painting back today. The water had dried, so basically what Adam proudly presented to his mother was a wrinkled piece of white paper. She asked him what it was. When she received no answer, she said, 'Adam, there's nothing there at all, so let's throw it out and take home one that has a pretty picture on it. Can you make me a pretty picture for tomorrow? (Eileen Eisenstadt).

Later, the same teacher reflected upon her experience in watching well-intentioned parents question their children about their art work, compare this with another child's, then try to suggest ways to improve the work. "It has been my experience that, in no way does a young child need *help* in expressing himself better than the way he chooses to do it for himself." (E. Eisenstadt)

The great variety of scribbles available for the young child's use makes it quite tempting to help the child along, to speed up the process. This is not only unwise, it is unkind. Teachers, parents, and all who work with young children should accept the fact that we are not there to "teach" scribbling or drawing or art in any form. We are simply there as observers and lovers of young children, privileged to share in an act of creation with them.

Summary

We have noted that the young child encounters his new world by exploring, experimenting, testing, sensing, generalizing on his own. His discoveries in art, as in all his inquiries, help him to define this universe and to structure his own thinking in a visual way. The young child's art is important, not as a finished art product but for the mediation it provides between his inner and outer worlds. It also acts as a means of self-affirmation. Art is, therefore, a very valuable vehicle in the child's development. There are several stages associated with mental and artistic growth, but from the very moment that the child discovers what it looks and feels like to set down his scribble marks, he has once and for all time, found art.

The adult is cautioned to tread carefully within the realm of art, so that the child may work out his own thoughts and feelings without the constraint of evaluation. What we *can* do is to provide time, space, place, materials for the child, and then, allow him the dignity of "doing his own thing." Be patient, learn to wait, and be prepared for just about anything. Above all, be happy for the child creator, even if he does not create what we would like him to (Grozinger, 1955).

Some "do nots" include: do not ask "What is it?" when the child shows you his thoughts on paper. Let him talk or not talk about his work, as he chooses. Do not "teach" scribbling or art to the young child, but let him go about his own discoveries in peace. Do not compare him or correct him or project yourself into his art work. Remember that he is, above all else, a child, not an artist, and love him deeply for himself alone.

Before our very eyes, we can see the young child give his own personal statement, a map of the mental strides he has already taken. Out of "blooming, buzzing confusion," not far in time from his emergence into a brand-new world, he has established a degree of visual order, sense, and beauty. From the nothingness of blank paper, he has begun to create something which for him, never before existed anywhere, or at any other time. This visual statement is his story, his genesis, from which may be revealed a new earth and heaven, according to his own visions. It is our great responsibility and privilege as caring adults, to encourage such creation to evolve spontaneously and joyfully throughout the years of childhood.

SELECTED BIBLIOGRAPHY

Arnheim, Rudolph. *Visual Thinking*. London: Faber & Faber, 1969.

Gardner, Howard. *The Arts and Human Development*. New York: Wiley, 1973.

Grozinger, Wolfgang. *Scribbling, Drawing, Painting*. New York: Praeger, 1955.

Kellogg, Rhoda. "Understanding Children's Art." *Psychology Today*, Vol. 1, no. 1, May 1967.

Kellogg, Rhoda with Scoot O'Dell. *The Psychology of Children's Art*. New York: Random House, 1967.

Lewis, Hilda P. (ed.). *Child Art*. Berkeley: Diablo Press, 1973.

Lindstrom, Miriam. *Children's Art*. Berkeley: University of California Press, 1957.

Schaefer-Simmern, Henry. "The Mental Foundations of Art Education in Childhood." In *Child Art*, edited by Hilda P. Lewis. Berkeley: Diablo Press, 1973.

Source

Eileen Eisenstadt, a nursery school teacher, New York City, who shared her thoughts with the writer.

Center for Library, Media and Telecommunications NYC Board of Education

Chapter 39

Process and Product Art: New Implications for Education

Margot Kaplan-Sanoff[*]

Writing of a "recurrent opposition of two views of literature," Northrup Frye (1956) claims that "These two views are the Aristotelian and the Longinian, the aesthetic and the psychological, the view of literature as product and the view of literature as process (p.144)". While Frye concedes that all works of literature are ultimately products, his distinction between literature as process and product helps to clarify the two different ways that authors involve readers in their work. In literature, as in product, readers are forced to see the work as teleological, continually pushing towards some inevitable end. In a work of product art like Fielding's *Tom Jones*, events and circumstances are not seen individually or by themselves; rather, readers are constantly asking where those events and circumstances will finally lead. While we may enjoy,for example, Mrs. Water's skill in seducing Tom, we must also ask ourselves how this transgression will effect Tom's relationship with Sophia. Literature as process, on the other hand, demands that readers involve themselves directly and often emotionally in each circumstance or event without considering how it will effect the ending. In Lawrence Sterne's *Sentimental Journey*, the concept of a journey without any predetermind destination informs the plot and action of the novel and suggests how completely *The Sentimental Journey* is literature of process. The reader of Sterne's novel, like Yorick, the "Sentimental Traveller", travels through Europe, observing local customs and characters, while commenting upon them. Since the journey and the plot have no preconceived destination or end, the reader is involved directly in each individual scene: what we get out of Sterne's work is not a sense of closure, an action completed, but rather we learn Yorick's particular emotional way of viewing events.

Before examining how this bifurcation between process and product art affects the teaching of art, it might be helpful to view this distinction as it can be seen within other fields of artistic expression. The radically different landscapes of Constable and Turner offer an excellent example of this dichotomy. Constable's art is essentially product-oriented. He strives to recreate on canvas exactly what he sees before him. Such art lies within the static domain, focusing attention on external reality, the observable behaviors of life. Constable's landscapes rarely embody fluid movements; trees stand still, even the oxen in the fields seem frozen in time. Confronted by such paintings, the observer can only stand back and measure how accurately the artist has copied the scene depicted. Turner on the other hand, involves the viewer directly in his picture. Faced with Turner's swirling depth of color, the viewer first experiences a sense of urgency and threat within the images and forms. This initial sense of urgency is further developed by the gradual realization that Turner has depicted the rages of a seastorm. While the reds and pinks of Turner's storm are hardly realistic, Turner's concern is with the psycological impact of the painting. In other words, Turner's art involves the viewer in the process of experiencing a world filled with intense energy and emotion. His goal is not to produce a mimetically accurate product.

Perhaps a more pedestrian example emerges from film. The action of *The Sting* is clearly focused on an end result-- will their confidence game succeed? Although the observer enjoys the excitement of the pace, his attention is directed toward how things will end, not to the individual events themselves. While his surprise at the intricate ending has been anticipated only by the producer, the viewer is nevertheless satisfied by the sense of closure at the movie's end. However, in *I am Curious Yellow* the viewer literally watches a film crew make a film. Becoming a part of the process, he cuts scenes, directs action, interviews actors. Action is focused on the present with little consideration for future events or the end result. Involvement in the process of creating a work of art, particularly a pornographic work, takes precedence over the concern for the finished product. Both films present the viewer with something of a puzzle; *The Sting* requires the viewer to piece together the parts of its puzzle in their exact chronological order so that he may understand the significance of the whole. *I am Curious Yellow* offers divergent ways to put together various scenes that comprise its puzzle, Only experience will determine if the puzzle fits. If the former dictates that there is only one right answer to the puzzle, the latter emphasizes the process of how the pieces may be put together in different configurations.

[*]Margot Kaplan-Sanoff, Instructor and former Head Teacher, Child Development Center of Virginia.

A review of the literature on art education presents two basic views on the teaching of art to young children. These two strategies, directive and developmental, closely correspond to the product-process dichotomy. However, the directive strategy does not require a finished product but rather emphasizes a structured approach to achieving an end, e.g. specific steps to pasting. In the directive approach the teacher determines what project is to be done and how the child is to do it. She chooses the type of activity, provides the specific materials needed, and expects a finished product which conforms to her perceptions and demands. She dictates that today the class will all make bunnies to celebrate Easter. She provides paper, scissors, paste, and crayons; she proceeds to direct the children in how to cut the ears from pink paper, attach them to the head, and so forth. She then encourages them to watch what she has done and responds to their art according to their attempts at reproduction. Just as the observer of a Constable painting judges the artist's accuracy of detail, so the teacher gives approval to imitative representation in the children's work. Her concern is with the finished product and the correct sequence of steps to achieve that end. Art educators tend to become quite emotional on this issue of directive art activities:

> Let's be honest and clear the air...where exciting, colorful, and dynamic elementary art practices exist, the teacher of art is on the job—guiding, challenging, suggesting, approving, prompting, planning....when teachers of art are truly concerned about the expressive growth of the children not always approve. They could take the easy way out by letting the youngsters do what they please in art but, being concerned and conscientious, they continue to set the highest creative challenges for their students.
>
> (Wachowiak, 1971, p. 19)

For Wachowiak, the teacher's perceptions of the end product are the keystone to teaching art.

Developmental strategies for teaching art also provide the child with motivation, encouragement and guidance. However, the concern centers on the process of creating, not on the final product. As Henri Matisse writes,

> I put down my tones without preconceived ideas...the expressive qualities of colours impress me purely instinctively. To paint an autumn landscape, I should not try to remember what colours are proper to that season, I should only be inspired by the sensation they gave me: the icy purity of the sky, which is an acid blue, would express the season just as well as the colours of the leaves.   (Linderman and Herberholz, 1964, p. 5)

The teacher becomes a facilitator, creating an atmosphere and environment for children in which to pursue their individual ideas. There is no set time for everyone to "do art", nor is it necessary or beneficial for all children to work in the same medium towards the same goal. How the child approaches material is more important than what he creates with that material. "The child does not regard what he has made as a painting or piece of sculpture. He lives through a series of experiences as he paints or models (Bland, 1968, p. 9)."

These two strategies of art education are not mutually exclusive. As we will see, both have a place in teaching young children. However, we must first identify how children's artistic growth develops and what children are capable of accomplishing at each stage of their development, before we can evaluate which type of experience, directive or developmental, best fits the needs of young children.

I

While there is no precise pattern of development for each child at each age, there are certain characteristics that serve to identify stages in children's growth. Children's artistic expressions vary according to individual experience, perception, and maturity, yet there is an evident and gradual growth process which almost every child goes through beginning with tentative exploration and evolving through stages of greater sureness in control of material and expression. Physically, the child develops in a cephalocaudel direction, from the center of the body outwards. Infants thus gain control over head movements long before they can control their lower limbs; shoulder control develops prior to hand control. Similarly, when planning art activities for young children, we must consider their individual growth sequences: a child just developing wrist control will not have the fine motor dexterity in his fingers to cut paper successfully.

The first identifiable stage of artistic development is the scribbling (Lowenfeld, 1975) or sensori-motor stage (Piaget, 1952). Scribblers begin at about 12-16 months to draw random marks on paper, uneven lines which are vertical if drawn on a vertical surface and horizontal if the child works on a horizontal surface. These disordered scribbles reflect the physical ability of the toddler, his use of whole arm movements to produce large scribbles, holding the marker between clenched fingers or tight fist. For him scribbling represents a physical and psychological exercise, not an attempt at representation. As the child develops control over his elbow, his lines begin to curve; by two years of age he has the necessary wrist control to make circles, radials, and mandalas. He then begins to name his scribbles, retaining a mental image that can be translated into shape. Circles are generalized in the child's mind to "a dog", "my daddy", and finally the whole human race. The child has produced a symbol for man. (See Fig. 1, p. 198).

Gradually the symbol for man becomes more elaborated—a big head with two vertical lines for feet. Yet, this first drawing should not be regarded as an immature representation, but as an abstraction or schema derived from a large array of complex stimuli. As such, it demonstrates the beginning of pre-operational thought (Piaget, 1952) and represents the preschematic stage of artistic development.

At this stage a child's art can be seen as a direct reflection of the child himself—his perceptions of self and his understanding of his relationship to his environment. He conceives of space as being primarily related to his own body, an egocentric conception of body space. Visual correlations between reality and artwork are unimportant to the child. His observations are based on experiences within his world and colored by his emotional responses. Often the scale of an object or person will be enlarged or distorted, giving prominence to those parts which most impress the child. (See Fig. 2, p. 198).

Through continuous experimentation, the school-age child begins to discover the relationship between reality and the drawn object, and his own ability to produce likeness. As the child's cognitive ability to conceive of himself and his environment in specific schemata develops, he creates his own highly individualized schemata which undergo change and deviation as the child's concept of his world enlarges and becomes more differentiated. Base line and sky strip, symbolic devices which place all objects in common space relationships, begin to appear in his pictures, clearly delineating the random space of the preschematic stage from the abstracted space of the present schematic stage (Lowenfeld, 1975). (See Fig. 3, p. 198).

II

The developmental stages of artistic growth highlight two major concerns—cognitive level of understanding and muscular ability. Children at each stage have different levels of functioning, and therefore their art experiences should match their developmental capabilities. Product-oriented educators stress direct instruction in technique as a method of overcoming the child's inability to handle materials in an appropriate manner. They advocate step by step group instruction on how to assemble a collage, how to draw a body, how to paste eyes on a pumpkin. The child's work is then evaluated for its realistic attempt at reproduction and imitative detail. Yet it has been clearly established that young children cannot decode their environment by adult standards; a preschematic child cannot process the accurate vertical sequence of eyes, nose, mouth, nor can the scribbling child control his visual perceptual skills to the degree needed to draw a body; "Projects planned for the scribbling child occasionally undercut his confidence—projects that are too difficult for a young child to accomplish by himself, projects that are conceived by and for adults (Lowenfeld, 1975)." The product model of art education offers an extremely limited conception for an art program. Trying to

compensate for the child's lack of ability, rather than building on his strengths and capabilities, product art can at times denigrate a child's growing concept of self-worth, while also stifling his creativity.

The process model offers five fundamental principles of guidance for teachers of young children:
1) provide the child with the opportunity and encouragement to express freely his ideas and feelings;
2) offer acceptance and respect for what the child has created;
3) advance suggestions as alternative possibilities, not as correct techniques;
4) do not regard time spent in experimentation as time wasted because no finished product has been created;
5) do not measure the quality of the experience in terms of the amount of time spent on the experience.

Process-oriented teachers conceive of art as a vehicle for growth. Art does not have to result in a finished product for the experience to be considered valid. Using materials to express his ideas and feelings in concrete form helps the child to understand what is happening to him in his environment. Art provides an expressive outlet, while strengthening the child's power to weigh choices and to face the consequences of his decisions. With tempera paint he can change his mind and try new forms and colors; with clay he can repound and start again. Art gives him the opportunity to discriminate among materials, to explore cognitive relationships of space, size, and color, to exercise developing muscular skills. And perhaps most importantly, process art helps the child to become independent and self-reliant, relying less on help from adults, forming his own aesthetic standards rather than judging his work by the artificial standards of others. If, as Piaget says, the goal of education is to create men capable of doing new things, then process art should be given a much greater emphasis in the teaching of art to young children.

Obviously, within the process model there is room for directive teaching strategies. Techniques seem to have no value in themselves, but when a child wants to learn how to cut with scissors, then direct instruction is appropriate. But again, if direct guidance does not help the child to achieve his goal, then the teaching should be stopped. A child without the proper maturational readiness or cognitive schema will not benefit from tedious, repetitive teaching of art technique.

The stages of artistic development follow an invariant, hierarchical order; each child advances through this sequence at his own pace, dependent on his past experiences and maturational level. As in other areas of education, attempts to accelerate a child's developmental growth or to increase a particular skill have not met with much success (Kohlberg, 1972). The erroneous assumption that practice on a task will improve one's skill in accomplishing that task has lead to much direct instruction on how to draw in perspective, how to shade still lifes, and so on. But this assumption ignores the fundamental consideration that prerequisite experiences cannot be overlooked. Maturational readiness, cognitive concepts, and past experiences must be developed before a complex artistic task can become meninful to the child. The child who encounters paste for the first time will need to explore its consistency before he can understand the admonition not to put too much paste on his paper. Similarly the schematic child uses repetition of form and color to create spatial design. This repetition seems to be a natural part of the child's development, occurring spontaneously and unconsciously. Teaching the design fundamentals of balance and rhythm would be detrimental to this spontaneity, interfering with the innate urge for expression.

At each stage of development the child encounters new problems to explore; he must solve these problems before he can advance to the next developmental stage. Adult solutions do not substitute for the knowledge gained by the child working out his ideas for himself. There appears to be experimental data showing that children subjected to a dictatorial type of art education could not rely upon their own powers of thinking in art when the opportunity for free choice was made available.

> Young children who are asked to copy adult symbols appear to be retarded, at least for the length of time they used the symbols (over two years in some cases) in comparison with children who devise their own. (Gaitskell, 1952)

We cannot positively affect a child's behavior by providing him with patterns and procedures to follow in order to achieve a better looking product. Change in the product itself should come about through changes in the child's thinking, feeling, and perceiving. It is through process art that changes in behavior and growth patterns develop; it is through this type of art that meaningful changes take place in the product.

SELECTED BIBLIOGRAPHY

Bland, Jane Cooper. *Art of the Young Child.* New York: Graphic Society, Ltd., 1968.

Burns, Sylvia. "Children's Art: A Vehicle for Learning". *Young Children*, 1975, 30: 193-204.

Cherry, Clare. *Creative Art for the Developing Child.* California: Fearon Publishers, 1972.

Cohen, Elaine. "Does Art Matter in the Education of the Black Ghetto Child?". *Young Children*, 1974, 29: 170-181.

Croft, D.; and Hess, R. *An Activities Handbook for Teachers of Young Children.* New York: Houghton-Mifflin, 1972.

Herberholz, Barbara. *Early Childhood Art.* Dubuque, Iowa: Wm. C. Brown Company, 1974.

Jameson, K. *Art and the Young Child.* New York: Viking Press, 1968.

Lewis, Hilda. *Art for the Preprimary Child.* Washington, D.C.: National Art Education Association, 1972.

Linderman, E.; and Herberholz, D. *Developing Artistic and Perceptual Awareness.* New York: Wm. C. Brown Company, 1964.

Lowenfeld, V; and Brittain, W. *Creative and Mental Growth.* (6th ed.) New York: Macmillan, 1975.

Sparling, Joseph; and Sparling, Marilyn. "How to Talk to a Scribbler." *Young Children*, 1973, 28: 333-341.

Wankelman, W; Wigg, P.; and Wigg, M. *A Handbook of Arts and Crafts.* Dubuque, Iowa: Wm. C. Brown Company, 1961.

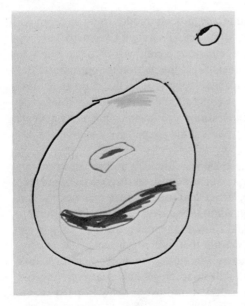

Figure 1

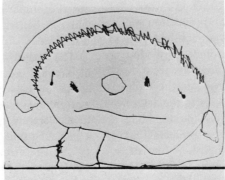

Figure 2

Figure 3

Chapter 40

Musical Expression and the Young Child

Roberta Frankfort*

All too often one's music experiences in school are remembered as distasteful or just simply boring. Who hasn't heard about the child who was considered "tone deaf" and was told by the teacher to mouthe the words to the songs during the special assembly presentation; And the hours of monotonous preparation that went into the program to make it exactly perfect seemed endless! For some of us looking back, the only occasional music time was spent with a special teacher who, if she succeeded in quieting the class, might have the group sing a few familiar songs. Percussion instruments hanging in the back of the room or stored in a closet could not be touched except when passed out to the whole group. Some records might then be played and the class could beat time to the music. Spontaneous singing and chanting were often stopped abruptly.

It is of course apparent that such experiences not only prohibit freedom of expression but can force an association of music with rigidity and joylessness. Music should be a vehicle for developing children's creative potential; music should enable children to release emotional and physical energies. Yet it would be a mistake to view music solely as a means for releasing tensions, particularly those tensions accumulated after hours of reading and math.

Music has an intellectual content of its own, and becoming familiar with musical concepts which include melody, rhythm, harmony, tempo, dynamics, and form will enable children to identify and appreciate the qualities of the music that they are creating or listening to. This awareness increases enjoyment. Therefore, neither the cognitive nor the affective aspect of music can be ignored. The teacher must know and understand these concepts in order to help children add to the richness of their musical moments.

According to Stecher, McElheny, and Greenwood in their book *Music and Movement Improvisations* (1972), music "is most effectively approached not as a subject to be taught but as experience to be lived—part of a life style (p. 9)." The intellectual content of music cannot be separated from the creative expression. The teacher should not proceed to teach musical concepts in a vacuum. She must integrate any discussions about these concepts with the children's actual experiences.

Starting with Sound

Classroom teachers—indeed, many adults,—are often self conscious about their musical skills. Unfortunately, some teachers feel so strongly about their lack of musical talent that they do not generally incorporate music into their classrooms. It is of course foolish to feel that one must be a virtuoso or even a musical talent to encourage young children to enjoy rich and diverse musical experiences. Approaching music through sound can be very rewarding for the teacher who is uncomfortable with her musical abilities. Emma Sheehy writes in *Children Discover Music and Dance* (1959): "Music is sounds put together (p. 5)." And she goes on to talk about the tremendous interest that children have in sounds and sound-making which all of us who have observed children at play can confirm. We must use this spontaneity to begin to develop children's enjoyment and appreciation of music.

Instead of quieting the clucking noises that some of the five-year-olds are making after they have finished their snack, why not join in on every other beat, varying the rhythm of the sound? Or make the sound higher or lower than the children's sounds. They will very likely be excited by the teacher's participation and a discussion about the different types of sounds should be lively. Talk to children about the sounds they heard on the way to school and then read *The Listening Walk* by Paul Showers or *Do You Hear What I Hear?* by Helen Borten. Better still, take your own listening walk with the children. When you return to the classroom, the children will be eager to recall the sounds that they heard. Use some of the musical concepts to organize the data that they have collected. For example, children might remember sounds that were especially loud (dynamics): the sound of construction, children playing in the schoolyard, or a horn honking: some children might have heard some soft sounds such as leaves rustling or an airplane high overhead or birds chirping amidst the din of the street sounds. It is important to remember that the high-low sounds are relative to each other and that children must learn to appreciate that the horn honking may sound high when compared with the construction sound but low when compared with the birds chirping. After listening to various

*Dr. Roberta Frankfort, Assistant Professor, Brooklyn College.

sounds and categorizing them in different ways, some children might want to collect various materials that make interesting sounds. They can begin to explore properties of materials that cause different sounds to occur: Does the larger metal bowl make a different sound when struck with a spoon than the smaller one? Why? Individually or in groups the children might enjoy making "sound poems" with the materials they have collected, testing out, in the process, ways of combining such musical elements as form, rhythm, and dynamics in order to create pleasing sets of sounds. The teacher should certainly encourage these early attempts at musical compositions. She might, too, bring in recordings of unusual sounds (Folkways has a good collection) and familiarize children with some of the wonderful collections of nonsense literature where sounds are put together in ingenious combinations of form and rhythm. Children will already be familiar with some nonsense verses and phrases, for the poems from children's games and nursery rhymes are strewn with nonsense words: hickory, dickory, dock; eeny, meeny, miney, mo. The following verse is an old "counting-out" rhyme:

> Intery, mintery, cutery, corn,
> Apple seed and apple thorn,
> Wire, briar, limber lock,
> Three geese in a flock.
> One flew east, one flew west
> And one flew over the cuckoo's nest.
> O-U-T spells out goes he.
> (Allyn & Bacon, *This Is Music* K&N, p. 55)

Children's sound making, then, should not be squelched. Rather, the teacher must recognize that the children's spontaneous and natural interest in sound can be the raw material for rich explorations into music making.

Percussion Sounds: Using Instruments

Children who are interested in sound-making will naturally want to use percussion instruments. Indeed, most children seem to light up at the sight of the drums, triangles. tambourines and other percussion instruments. All too often they are reserved only for large group use, and children never get the opportunity to experiment with the variety of sounds that they can make with these instruments. Many times children are told how to play them "correctly" (as if they were such inhibiting regulations!). There must be opportunities for children to *individually* explore the sound-making potentials of these instruments. Stecher, McElheny and Greenwood write: "As in all the arts, creativity grows best when the individual is permitted a wide degree of self-direction and control of materials. These controls develop out of a growing awareness of possible structures with these materials. These controls develop out of a growing aware-

ness of possible structures with these materials. Awareness, however, is gained initially through many unstructured experiences (p. 9)."

Growing awareness of the ways in which these instruments can be used is essential particularly for nursery and kindergarten children who have not had much experience with percussion instruments. In order to facilitate this, the teacher must permit children to have easy access to the materials during play time: instruments should be available in the same way taht art materials, blocks, games, etc. are accessible. It will be necessary, of course, to establish rules for the use of these materials just as rules are set up in the block corner or at the easel. For example, the teacher would want to prohibit the throwing of any instruments and might want to limit the number of children using the instruments at once. But the teacher's role should involve more than setting limits on their use. She can play an important part in the child's discovery process by asking leading questions... What happens when you rest your hand on the triangle when you strike it? Where else can you strike the drum other than the top? Does the large drum sound the same as the smaller drum? How softly can you play those maracas? How loudly? Can you play the tambourine very slowly and then play quickly? Frances Aronoff writes in *Music and Young Children* (1969) that "classroom instruments can be used to encourage the discovery of distinctive tone-qualities and their expressive potential as well as to introduce some cause-and-effect science phenomena to children. They may also present and secure such concepts as pitch, duration, and dynamics (p. 45)." These discoveries and learnings cannot occur without individual experimentation and the teacher's sensitive guidance.

Children who have gained some control and appreciation of the instruments may wish to use them in groups. Small groups of children amy spontaneously begin to combine instrument sounds in different ways. The teacher might sense that children are ready for some larger group experiences and might plan activities that will enable children to share some of their discoveries with the larger group and will also permit new explorations into sound combinations and musical concepts. Of course planning must be flexible enough to allow children's spontaneous, creative responses to guide some of the group's experiences. There are many types of activities that a teacher could think about. Children might share with the group new methods of playing the various instruments: children with the same instrument could group together, each playing a different way. Rhythmic games with instruments could involve one child playing a simple rhythm and the group repeating the pattern: the next child would think of a new one and so on around the circle. Simple jingles (TV and radio commercials, for example) as well as nursery rhymes are almost always very rhythmic, and children might enjoy having the group guess which jingle they are beating out. Smaller groups could form and half of the smaller group could beat out the rhythm of a nursery rhyme while the other half dramatizes it in time to the beat. Familiar songs could be sung and accompanied: some children might be ready to beat out the rhythm while another group beats out the melody line. A few members of the group would welcome the opportunity to conduct, and they might devise signals for changes in tempo and dynamics. Classification of instruments according to the primary type of material that they are made of—or how they are played can spark lively discussions. A song could be chosen with repetition of lines (such as *Skip to My Lou*) so that each group of instruments might have a different line to play. Sounds of the world around us can be imitated on instruments: sounds in such familiar songs as *Wheels on the Bus* or *Old MacDonald* can be played on various appropriate instruments instead of spoken. There are endless ways of using these instruments and not all of them need revolve around a musical session. They make wonderful sound effects during creative drama sessions; they can be used, too, for counting and number games.

Children enjoy making their own percussion instruments. The process integrates different curriculum areas: older children might read "recipes" from charts, science discoveries occur when children experiment with sound properties of different materials or the same materials of different sizes, materials for instruments will have to be painted, sawed, glued, etc. And of course they should be made to be used. Indeed, it is sometimes easier for a child to experiment with different ways of playing a home-made instrument because he probably will not even consider that there is a "right" way of playing his wood block tambourine or his papier mache maracas.

It is clear that children derive enormous satisfaction from using instruments. They should never be stored in a closet or hung to gather dust in the back of a classroom.

Exploring Melody and Harmony

Some instruments such as the piano and xylophone are categorized as percussion but can also, of course, be used to play melody. The piano, in particular, is an instrument that is often found in classrooms but rarely used by children. It is feared that "banging" will result if they are allowed access to it. But the piano is fascinating to children and, with some teacher guidance (including a rule not to "bang" but to use it with care) children can discover all kinds of tonal combinations. Some children will be able to pick out familiar melodies; others will just enjoy experimenting with combinations of sounds, hearing them with and without the pedal, loudly and softly, high and low. Open the piano and let children strum the strings: Why are the strings different lengths? What happens to the strings when the pedal is pushed down?

Tonal blocks, resonator bells, and xylophones are also instruments which allow children the opportunity to discover pitch variation and combinations of tones. Again, the teacher's leading questions are important: While playing a note on the piano, the teacher might ask a child working with the tonal blocks: Can you find a tone that sounds the same as this one? Can you start with the highest tone on your bells and go down to the lowest? Can you use more than one bell to go from the lowest to the highest? What tones are in the middle? Children will like using the tonal blocks and resonator bells in groups of two, finding pleasing. harmonic combinations. Older children can make their own tonal instruments by using glasses and varying amounts of water. They might use any of the melodic instruments to tune them.

Through the use of melodic instruments and the singing of songs particularly those which have wide melodic ranges, most children will become aware of the changes in pitch and will be able to identify the directions that simple melodies take. This awareness is a prerequisite to learning to read music (notation), but it is unwise to try to teach formal notation to young children. Beginning steps which follow naturally from a discussion of the directions of a melody can be undertaken, however. Young children might enjoy drawing a picture of a simple melody which goes up and down (in this case, *Jack and Jill* from Allyn and Bacon's *This is Music* K&N, p. 154):

Or, try making a diagram on the floor so that children can walk up and down the tones as they sing them.

Autoharps, guitars, and ukeleles are other instruments which children like to play especially because of their interesting sound combinations. They are also excellent accompaniment instruments and can be easily learned and used by the teacher during singing times. The piano, when used for accompaniment, tends to isolate the teacher from the group; these smaller instruments allow for closeness. Since most children's songs have very simple melodies, two or three chords on these instruments can go a long way. Adults are often surprised at how quickly they feel comfortable playing them.

Songs and Singing

Singing should be fun for both the children and the teacher. Preoccupation with beautifully sounding voices ruins the enjoyment. There is an enormous range of children's songs to fit every occasion and mood. Try to become familiar with a variety of songs, but don't forget that children like to sing the songs they know again and again, If the teacher becomes too bored with a song, children sense it; it is best, then, to satisfy yourself also. Don't force a new song on children by tediously teaching it line by line. Sing it through a few times at different periods of the day as well as during a group sing, and let children catch the rhythm, moving their bodies to the song. They'll soon join in the singing.

Some people think that young children's voices are very high and consequently end up screeching along with the children. Find a medium pitch that's comfortable; it will likely be comfortable for the children as well. Children who do not wish to sing or join in on any musical activity should never be forced. Sometimes, instead of singing they prefer to clap, swing their feet—or just listen.

Singing does not have to occur only at designated times. Some of the most enthusiastic singing occurs spontaneously during play or snack or right before going home. Improvising words to familiar melodies is fun, too. Some teachers enjoy using simple melodies to sing directions to children or to announce a change in activity. The following jingle was adopted from the Campbell Soup commercial:

Time for rest,
Time for rest,
That's what the clock says;
Time for rest.
(Stecher, McElheny, Greenwood, p. 17)

Songs with finger play and those that lend themselves to whole body movement and dramatization can be especially pleasurable. Children will be enthusiastic about singing; join in joyfully.

Quieter Times....

The variety of music that children enjoy listening to is endless. Teachers should provide listening times as often as possible and introduce different pieces of music. Trying to compete with children's voices by putting on recordings during play time can only add a frenetic quality to the classroom; perhaps several children might want to listen to a recording in a quiet corner. At times when the group is calm and children are together, they might like to listen to an old favorite like the *Sorcerer's Apprentice* or they might enjoy a recording of folk music or calypso music.

Recordings often spark children's movement, and these reactions should be encouraged. Teachers can provide art materials at times so that children can visually express their feelings about the music.

There are, then, great varieties of musical activities. Music should be experienced in all of its facets, individually and in groups of all sizes. It is a curriculum area with its own intellectual and affective aspects. Yet it also can be a rich supplement to other subject areas such as math, social studies, and science. A teacher's uneasiness about her musical ability should not be an impediment to children's enjoyment. This feeling can be combated with an open mind: try, as a first step, experimenting with percussion instruments. Slide your fingers down the piano, try single notes and combinations in a marching tempo, take a tambourine and shake it, beat it, and run your finger tips around the surface. You should have a sense of discovery and might even feel the excitement that children often exhibit in their musical experiences.

SELECTED BIBLIOGRAPHY

Aronoff, Frances Webber. *Music and Young Children.* New York: Holt, Rinehart and Winston, 1969.

Bailey, Eunice. *Discovering Music with Young Children.* New York: Philosophical Library, 1958.

Jones, Elizabeth. *What Is Music for Young Children?* National Association for the Education of Young Children pamphlet, 1958.

Mandell, Muriel and Wood, Robert E. *Make Your Own Musical Instruments.* New York: Sterling Publishing Co., Inc., 1957.

Sheehy, Emma. *Children Discover Music and Dance.* New York: Holt, Rinehart and Winston, 1959.

Stecher, Miriam B., McElheny, High, and Marion Greenwood. *Music and Movement Improvisations.* New York: Macmillan Company, 1972.

Chapter 41

Reinforcing Bilingual-Bicultural Early Childhood Instruction With Music and Movement Activities

Minerva Benitez Rosario*

Introduction

In recent years there has been a trend towards the creation of educational programs that take into consideration the diverse ethnic make up of the various groups within this society. The language culture and distinct identity of these groups should be maintained. The existence of bilingual-bicultural programs is a step forward in recognizing the needs of different ethnic groups.

These programs recognize the fact that non English speaking children do have a language in which they may continue learning. The culture and language of the child are used to strengthen learning. Bilingual education gives "children the opportunity to become fully articulate and literate and broadly educated in two languages and sensitive to two cultures". (Andersson, 1970) Bilingual education programs allow the children to feel pride in their culture and heritage and in being able to communicate in two languages. This in turn helps the development of a positive self image in a child.

Children coming to bilingual classes may do so with quite diverse language and cultural backgrounds. There may be varying levels of bilingualism as well as differing abilities and backgrounds amongst the children attending bilingual programs. The teacher must consider all of this when planning curriculum and when searching for suitable materials to reinforce language learning and cognitive skills. Hence, the consideration of music and movement activities as a means to convey and strengthen learning in a bilingual *education classroom.*

The education of young children through music and movement is not often thought to be particularly related to bilingual education instruction. However, through music and movement activities, exciting and most challenging teaching experiences may be provided that will help children acquire skills necessary to learning in all curriculum areas. Not only are so many skills reinforced through this medium but the teacher may accomplish what is an essential part of bilingual-bicultural education, the development of pride in oneself and a positive self image.

Following is an attempt to show how music and movement, with their universal qualities, would be excellent, enjoyable vehicles for teaching children of different language backgrounds. A description will follow showing how music and movement activities not only reinforce language and learning skills that may be transferable to other curriculum areas, but with them the teacher may provide a program that will help the development of the "whole" child, physically, emotionally, socially, and intellectually.

Physical Growth and Development

Whether monolingual, bilingual or multilingual, children are naturally active and full of energy. Sitting still is indeed a very difficult task for them. This energy and spontaneity can be channelled to more creative directions in an educational program that makes use of music and movement. Most children living in the cities receive exercise while playing in the streets. Working parents have few opportunities to take their children to parks or places where they can run and play freely. The dangers of the streets stop many parents from allowing their children to play outdoors without their supervision, so these children receive little, if any, exercise and physical activity. It is therefore up to the school to provide a program giving enough opportunities for children to exercise and develop physically.

A movement program may provide activities that will help the development of large and small muscles. Activities involving locomotor and nonlocomotor movements will allow the children to develop better body coordination while moving through space. Children will not feel as restricted when provided with opportunities to move about freely and explore space with their bodies. Body movement is a most important language of expression for the young child. Children use their bodies to communicate their thoughts, feelings, moods, and experiences. The child who is non English speaking is encouraged to participate through music and movement activities. Singing games, finger plays, playing rhythm instruments, all provide a means of helping a child develop physically since they exercise their small and large muscles and develop manipulative skills when performing these exercises.

*Minerva Rosario, Assistant Professor, Early Childhood Education Program, Hostos Community College, City University of New York.

Emotional and Social Development

Emotionally, these activities help to free children of tensions and worries and provide a natural, healthier outlet for aggressive feelings. As a child gains control of his body he also gains self confidence and respect for his achievement. A child entering a bilingual classroom may need even more encouragement than most. This is especially true if the child is not truly bilingual but is learning English as a second language and may have recently arrived in this country. The teacher must provide encouragement and help develop in him the feeling of achievement so important to his emotional development. A child's ability to conquer a particular motor task, to play games and sing songs that are part of his culture, to play an instrument, to create a dance, gives him feelings of accomplishment or achievement that are important in the development of a positive self concept. This is vital in the learning process since it may lead to more confidence when attacking problems or participating in activities in other areas. The child's learning accomplishments help develop in him a self confidence that may be transferred to other classroom activities. Among the many benefits to children attending bilingual programs is the development of a better self concept, being proud and positive about oneself and one's abilities. A child's feeling of success in these activities fosters this essential part of a bilingual program.

Not only do these activities help a child feel comfortable, relaxed and welcome in the classroom, but they help him relate to others and socialize. Children are encouraged to participate and their attitudes towards each other greatly improve when they share enjoyable experiences. Singing, dancing and moving together gives children opportunities to partake in group activities. They work together, relate to each other, learn to lead, to follow and take turns. This is all essential to their social development.

Intellectual Development

Cognitive skills may be reinforced or developed through these activities. Instruction given in both languages will not only develop positive attitudes in children about speaking both languages but will facilitate the learning of both. Children will participate successfully because they understand and are able to follow the instructions given. Verbal comprehension is enhanced, new vocabulary may be developed for both languages being taught as well as problem-solving and decision making skills.

The Curriculum

Bilingual teachers should use music and movement in their classrooms. Teaching in two languages will be enhanced when the lessons include such enjoyable experiences and a great deal can be learned about different cultures through their music and dances. No special training or large amounts of money are needed. The teacher can make use of the child's experiences to create activities. The teacher should base selection of the activities upon the needs, characteristics, abilities, levels, and interests of the children. Preplanning must take place so the teacher may examine how the class will benefit from the activities. How these activities will be incorporated into the program and how instruction in both languages is to be given is up to the individual teacher. Special time may be set aside for everyday activities in music and movement of these could very well be integrated with the rest of the curriculum to make learning more pleasurable and enjoyable in these areas.

Music and movement activities provide an exciting way of making concepts and words become a part of the child. Interpreting words, phonics lessons, dramatizing stories and rhymes through movement can help the child to better understand and adds another dimension to the Language Arts program. Singing can be a most enjoyable way of learning another language. The rhythm and flow in a song make the pronunciation of unfamiliar words a much easier task. Children become more conscious of numbers and mathematics lessons are strengthened when they keep time and count beats in dance movement. Finger plays and songs may reinforce math skills like counting, subtracting, adding. Spatial awareness is gained through movement, horizontal and vertical space may be explored. The Social Studies area can be made more interesting and exciting when children study the music, instruments and dances of the different cultures. They may learn new songs and act out scenes from each culture they are studying and in the different languages they are learning. Different countries have their own birthday songs, holiday songs, folk songs, that may contribute to study about particular cultures and languages. The child may participate in specific activities that will help reinforce science concepts, such as interpreting natural phenomena through movement. Snow falling, lightning striking, the wind, the rain cycle, all lend themselves to dramatization through movement. These are only a few examples of how music and physical activities may be used to reinforce learning in the different curriculum areas.

Suggestions for Activities

Directions for the following activities may be given in either language being studied; The teacher may evaluate the child's understanding of the language by observing if he or she was able to perform the particular tasks required.

1. To help children relax and make free movements with their bodies, let them dance to a fast, exciting record. This activity will allow exposure to music from many cultures, for example, African, Latin, Oriental.

2. To have the children exercise their body parts, the teacher may play a record and have the children isolate parts of their body (for example, the hips, head, shoulders,

etc.) moving these parts in as many ways as possible while keeping time to the music.

3. Moving to the beat of rhythm instruments (drum, tone block, guiro, bongoes) may provide a way for the teacher to introduce various instruments from different cultures to the class. As the instrument is played, the player may increase or decrease the tempo and the children match the tempo with locomotor and body movements.

4. Pantomiming or acting out words and stories with action and no words. A child may choose a word or story and try to act it out through movements. The others try to guess. Feelings (sad, angry, happy, afraid, hurt, pain), animal movements (elephant, lion, snake, monkey, bird, turtle), and games (hop scotch, jacks, baseball, basketball, football) easily lend themselves to interpretation through movement.

5. In group pantomime the child may work together with the group as well as individually. Groups may dramatize scenes with movement and no speech. Playground, family, school, beach scenes may all be used for gorup pantomime.

6. Stories and rhymes from various cultures may be acted out through movement and speech.

7. Finger plays and songs may be taught. These reinforce language, math, and other skills.

8. The teacher may provide experiences with action songs or singing games.

9. Making up songs or adding own verses to familiar tunes allows for creativity and language development through music.

10. Dancing with scarves, balls, sticks, hoops, balloons, and ropes, the children will respond creatively to rhythm.

11. Have the children create and record their own dances. They may combine body and locomotore movements counting the beats necessary for each and creating a definite sequence of movements.

12. Have the children perform simple dances typical to a specific culture.

Conclusion

Creativity on the teacher's part may lead him or her to think of many different ways music and movement activities may be used to bring about a better understanding and appreciation of both cultures and both languages in a bilingual program as well as providing more exciting lessons in all areas of the curriculum.

BIBLIOGRAPHY

Bilingual Education

Andersson, Theodore and Boyer, Mildred, *Bilingual Schooling in the United States*, Volumes I and II. Southwest Educational Development Laboratory, Austin, Texas, January 1970.

Saville, Muriel and Troike, Rudolph, *A Handbook of Bilingual Education*, Teachers of English to Speakers of Other Languages, Washington, D.C., 1974.

Saville-Troike, Muriel, *Bilingual Children: A Resource Document*, Center for Applied Linguistics, Arlington, Virginia. August 1973.

Music and Movement

Andrews, Gladys, *Creative Rhythmic Movement for Children* Prentice-Hall, Inc. Englewood Cliffs, New Jersey, 1954.

Bentley, William G., *Learning to Move and Moving to Learn* Citation Press, New York, 1970.

Dauer, Victor P., *Essential Movement Experiences for Preschool and Primary Children*, Burgess Publishing Co., Minnesota, 1970.

McCall, Adeline, *This is Music*, (For Kindergarten and Nursery School), Allyn and Bacon, Inc., 1966.

Miller, Mary and Zajan, Paula, *Finger Play*, G. Schirmer. New York 1955.

Murray, Ruth Lovell, *Dance in Elementary Education*, Harper and Row Publishers. New York, 1975.

Sheehy, Emma, *Children Discover Music and Dance*, Teachers College Press. New York 1968.

Section V
Exceptional Children

Introduction by James J. Shields, Jr.*

An important outcome of the civil rights movement of the 1960's was the interest it stimulated in the widespread discrimination against handicapped children. As a result, programs aimed at bringing early and equal educational opportunities to all children, including the handicapped, are now a matter of national policy.

As more and more educational programs for children classified as physically, emotionally, or mentally retarded are developed, the evidence grows to support the belief that handicapped children can be helped considerably if intervention is begun early. Some researchers estimate that as many as fifty percent of handicapped children can have their handicap alleviated or cured if medical and educational services are provided early enough. These claims appear to be supported for genetically retarded children as well as for those for whom the origin is primarily environmental.

The proliferation of special education programs has generated numerous questions which strike at the very heart of the fundamental purposes and functions of American public education. These questions include matters related to the definition and identification of the handicapped as well as the tracking of the handicapped into separate facilities as opposed to their integration with other children, a procedure known as mainstreaming.

Some critics claim that all too often special education programs are used to exile troublesome and racially and culturally different pupils from the regular classroom. Certainly, the large percentage of minority group children identified as handicapped and placed in special education programs requires closer public scrutiny of these programs.

The essays in this chapter provide a basis for exploring these and related questions and for placing them in the wider international perspective of educational practice in Western Europe, the Soviet Union, Israel, and the People's Republic of China.

*Dr. James J. Shields, Professor of Education, City College, City University of New York.

Chapter 42

An Examination of Early Identification Procedures

Richard A. Schere and Adrienne Schere[*]

The purpose of this chapter is to examine some of the measures available for identifying early the problems of young children. Research has well established that handicapped children can be helped considerably if intervention is begun early. Such special education experts as Kirk (1958), Gallegher, (1968), and Hammer (1971) have estimated that reduction of difficulties and sometimes even cure is possible in more than 50% of the cases if programs are provided children in their preschool years. However, before children can be placed in appropriate programs, they must be first identified.

Mauser (1976) identified and described three hundred separate instruments used to assess the learning disabled. Of these, one hundred forty were indicated appropriate for preschoolers. The instruments were classified under the categories of (1) intelligence tests, (2) preschool readiness tests, (3) motor, sensory, and language tests, (4) reading readiness tests, (5) diagnostic reading tests, (6) survey reading tests, (7) oral reading tests, (8) diagnostic tests of math ability, (9) creativity tests, and (10) vocational tests. One hundred fifteen of the tests indicated appropriate for preschoolers fell under the categories of either intelligence tests, preschool readiness tests, and motor, sensory, and language tests. Sixty-two were classified as motor, sensory and language tests.

Buros (1972) lists sixteen tests undet the category of learning disabilities tests. Of these, nine were appropriate for preschoolers. Six of the instruments cited were also listed in the Mauser volume. However, the Buros compilation is quite comprehensive and many of the tests described by Mauser were listed by Buros under other classifications.

In surveying the tests available and the research that has been conducted to evaluate their effectiveness, it appears possible to reduce the tests to four classifications that reflect the approach taken to identify young children who well may be "at risk." These four classifications are: (1) Developmental Screening Tests, (2) Traditional Intelligence Tests, (3) Tests That Directly Measure Learning Skills and (4) Predictive Tests for Specified Populations. In contrasting this approach to Mauser's, we find that (1) many of his ten classifications are subsumed under these four, and (2) other classifications given by Mauser are not appropriate for the early identification of young children which is the concern of this chapter. We shall now consider the general orientation of each of these four test-types to early identification and discuss in greater depth one particular test representative of its type.

1. Developmental Screening Tests

Developmental screening tests attempt to identify the pattern of a given child's developmental history. There has been much research on the normal development of children. From many various perspectives, researchers such as Gessell (1947), Piaget (1952), Wechsler (1949), and Vallett (1966) have established norms for physical, cognitive, social, and emotional behavior which can serve as a frame of reference for comparing the development of any particular child. Indeed, certain specific patterns of development are clinically significant. For example, slow, even development, in general, is their limitations. Much information is indirect and dependent upon the accurate recollection of parents and guardians who may have difficulty recalling precise behavior from years past and differentiating the specifics one of their children as compared to others. Furthermore, scales that request only information about present functioning for purposes of normative comparison may not yield sufficient data for determining significant patterns such as those described earlier. Finally, developmental scales are descriptive, and often significant qualitative variables (nuances of behavioral *manner*) are lost.

One of the developmental scales used frequently with young children is the Denver Developmental Screening Test. It is used for children form the ages of birth to six years, takes about twenty minutes to administer, and covers the four functions of gross-motor, language, fine motor-adaptive, and personal-social- development. Its purpose is to detect children with serious developmental delays. By and large, although doubt has been raised about the applications of the Denver's norms to children, from lower socioeconomic groups, research results have been favorable. Nelson, (1967) reports high validity and reliability in study involving over one thousand children. Furthermore, Denver results

*Dr. Richard Schere, Program Head, Training Teachers for the Learning Disabled, School of Education, Brooklyn College, City University of New York. Adrienne Schere, Director, The Kennedy Learning Clinic, Brooklyn, New York.

correlate highly to other developmental measures especially the Yale Developmental Examination and the Developmental Screening Inventory.

2. Traditional Intelligence Tests

Ever since Benet developed his classic test to identify French children who would not profit from traditional instruction, the Stanford Binet and the Wechsler scales that were developed later have been essential tools used by psychologists with children. Despite recent criticism about labeling, these tests still remain among the most valid and reliable for identifying children with potential learning difficulty, a fact reestablished by Sattler, (1974). These tests sample children's performances on a variety of verbal (auditory-vocal) and performance (visual-motor) tasks and compare performance to normative data collected from a national sample.

The Wechsler scales are perhaps the most widely used tests of intelligence. For preschoolers, the appropriate Wechsler version is the Wechsler Preschool and Primary Scale of Intelligence (WPPSI). It requires approximately one hour for administration and yields a performance I.Q., a verbal I.Q., and a composite I.Q. Six sub-tests constitute each of the two phases. The verbal I.Q. taps general information, social comprehension, vocabulary, arithmetic (mental calculation), similarities (reasoning as to how two concepts are alike) and sentences (repeating sentences exactly as they were verbally given). The performance I.Q. taps picture completion (identifying the detail missing in a picture), animal house (placing colored pegs under pictures of animals according to a code) geometric design (drawing), block design (placing blocks of color and half colors so that they are exactly like the demonstration), and mazes.

The test yields rich data, but the interpretation must be made not only on the basis of the different I.Q.s, but also on the basis of the score pattern of the sub-tests and the manner in which the child works at the task. For these reasons, only a psychologist can administer and interpret the scores which many consider a weakness of I.Q. tests. A well known text describing Wechsler interpretation is authored by Glasser and Zimmerman (1969).

Other I.Q. tests have been designed for non-psychologists. Of these, the most well known include the Peabody Picture Vocabulary Test and the Slosson Intelligence Test. Although I.Q. estimates obtained form these measures correlate adequately to Wechsler and Stanford-Binet I.Q.'s, qualitative data is not as rich and thus these alternative intelligence tests have positive but limited value.

Intelligence tests have been criticized by many. In 1975, the State Department of Education held a conference to discuss the problems of psychoeducational evaluation in New York State. From this conference a number of important principles were established. Those pertaining to intelligence tests include (1) selecting formal tests standardized in a population of which the child to be tested is representative, (2) utilization of informal procedures to probe more specifically the trends suggested by the formal tests, (3) greater emphasis upon effect of etiology on learning skill strengths and weaknesses and less emphasis on etiology and classification, (4) comprehensive evaluation to guarantee recurring themes and the ability to predict from one test to another so as to increase accuracy and objectivity, (5) emphasis on the recommendations, and (6) follow up. Schere and others (1975).

3. Tests That Directly Measure Learning Skills

A variety of tests directly measure skills established by research to be crucially pertinent to successful learning. Such skills include skills of acuity, perception, memory, assoication, problem-solving, and visual-motor integration. Some tests such as the Developmental Test of Visual-Motor Integration tap one skill specifically. In this test, a child is asked to copy a printed design in the space provided below. A handbook allows the examiner to score the drawing and determine a visual-motor age to compare to the child's chronological age. The test is brief and requires no more than ten minutes. Such tests of specific skills are useful in focusing in on a suspected area of difficulty. However, more widely used are tests that attempt to measure directly a variety of specific skills. Of these, the Illinois Test of Psycholinguistic abilities is the most well-known. The test enables the examiner to identify a child's strength and weaknesses with regard to (a) phases of learning-receptive, organizational, and expressive, (b) modes of learning-auditory, visual (in the receptive and organizational phases), and vocal, manual (in the expressive phase) (c) specific areas of skill-reception, sequential memory association, closure, expression, and sound blending, and (d) levels of organization-automatic processes versus representational (symbolic, reflective) processes. The test requires about one and one quarter hours for administration and is designed for children from 3-10 years old.

Although research has found the test to be fairly valid and reliable (see critical review of research, Hallahan and Cruckshank, 1972) there aremany problems with the test. Schere, (1974) outlined some of these difficulties and recommended ways of compensating for them. Some of the issues discussed included: (1) sub-tests whose titles are misleading, (2) contaminating variables in the test procedures and (3) the lack of guidelines to denote the child's test behavior.

4. Predictive Tests for Specified Populations

A number of tests have been developed with a specific population in mind. Search, for example, was developed by

Hagin and Silver (1975) to identify New York City kindergarten children who are vulnerable to learning failure. The test predicts which children will most probably read below grade level at the end of first grade, and Search scores within different ranges even correlate to certain etiological variables (neurological problems, developmental problems, and emotional problems). The test is very well designed and is the culmination of twenty-five years of research. Directions for administering the test are modified to accomodate some of the sub-culture factors so common among New York City Children. The test taps underlying skills that provide a profile helpful in planning remediation. These skills include (1) discriminating and matching asymmetric figures, (2) observing and recalling immediately the orientation of asymmetric figures, (3) copying a series of designs of graduated difficulty, (4) remembering commonly heard rote sequences and ordering elements within the sequences as according to positional or temporal concepts, (5) detecting similarities and differences between orally presented meaningful and non-meaningful words or syllables which are either identical or which vary by one phoneme, (6) reproducing the sounds of common words, (7) writing the first letter of names received auditorially, (8) demonstrating stable concepts of spatial orientation by motorically following directions given orally, (9) perceiving and localizing tactile stimuli and conceptualizing finger schema, (10) demonstrating appropriate finger grip. Search has yielded high validity and reliability estimates, in much of the research conducted primarily by the authors. One of the advantages of a test designed for a specific population is that validity and reliability are more probably high because the subject is truly representative of the population against whom the test was standardized. Many tests that have been constructed for wider use have been justly criticized as not always being appropriate for a given child.

It is important to emphasize that most agencies and professionals who test young children utilize a battery of measures. However, it is hoped that this brief survey has helped the reader gain some insight into some of the issues and orientations related to the early identification of children with learning difficulties.

Identification Measures Cited

Denver Developmental Screening Test - Denver, Colorado: Ladoca

Project and Publishing Foundation, Inc.

Developmental Test of Visual-Motor Integration - Chicago, Illinois: Follett Educational Corp.

Illinois Test of Psycholinguistic Abilities - Urbana, Illinois: University of Illinois Press

Peabody Picture Vocabulary Test. - Circle Pines, Minnesota: American Guidance Service, Inc.

Search - New York, New York: New York University - Bellvue Medical Centre, Learning Disorders Unit

Slosson Intelligence Test - East Aurora, New York: Slosson Educational Publications

Stanford-Binet Intelligence Test - Boston, Massachusetts: Houghton- Mifflen Co.

Wechsler Preschool and Primary Scale of Intelligence - New York, New York: The Psychological Corporation

REFERENCES CITED

Buros, O.K. *The seventh mental measurements yearbook* Highland Park, New Jersey: The Gryphon Press, 1972

Davie, R. Butler, N. and Goldstein, H. *From four to seven: a report of the national child development study* London: Cloves, 1972

Gallagher, J. J. Preschool and early education programs needed for handicapped children. Statement before the Select Subcommittee on Education of the Committee on Education and Labor, House of Representatives, July 19, 1968.

Gessell, A. and Amatriuda, C. S. *Developmental diagnosis* (2nd ed.) New York: Paul B. Doeber, 1947.

Glasser, A. and Zimmerman, I. *Clinical interpretation of the Wechsler Intelligence Scale for Children.* New York: Grune and Stratoon, 1969.

Hallahan, D. and Cruickshank, W. *Psychoeducational foundation of learning disabilities.* Englewood Cliffs, New Jersey: Prentice-Hall, 1972.

Hammer, E. *Review of the literature in early childhood education with emphasis upon early education of handicapped children: A staff training manual.* 1 (8) Austin: Texax U, 1971.

Kirk, S. A. *Early education of the mentally retarded.* Urbana: University of Illinois Press, 1958.

Mauser, A.J., *Assessing the learning disabled: Selected instruments.* San Rafael, California: Academic Therapy Publications, 1976.

Piaget, J., *The origins of intelligence in children,* New York: International Universities Pres,, 1952.

Sattler, J. M., *Assessment of Children's intelligence,* Philadelphia: W. B. Saunders, 1974.

Schere, R. A., Guidelines for the psychoeducational assessment of retarded children. A position paper prepared at the request of the New York State Department of Education, Albany, 1975.

Schere, R. A., Clinical utilization of the I. T. P. A., *Psychoeducational Journal for the Treatment of Children,* 1975, 2 (2), 15-24.

Silver, A., Hagin, R. and others. A search battery for scanning kindergarten children for potential learning disability. *Journal of Child Psychiatry,* 1976, 15 (2), 224-239.

Vallett, R. E., *Vallett developmental survey of basic learning abilities.* Palo Alto, California: Consulting Psychologists Press, 1966.

Wechsler, D., *Manual for the WISC.* New York: Psychological Corp., 1949.

Samuel Teicher

Chapter 43

Early Intervention: Its Potential for Reducing the Problems of Special Children

Richard A. Schere and Rosalind I. Reiss*

Special education experts such as Kirk (1958), Gallagher (1968) and Hammer (1971) have estimated that more than 50% of handicapped children can have their handicap alleviated or sometimes even cured if medical and educational services can be provided early enough. This estimate is based upon the results of longitudinal research studies, perhaps the most significant of which is the Milwaukee Project (Garber & Heber, 1973; Heber & Garber, 1974). According to Gallagher (1968), "There is probably no sounder proposition in education than 'the earlier the child is educated, the greater the return for energy spent.' This is particularly true of the handicapped child whose problems in early development can multiply upon one another and create even more serious problems before the youngster is ready to enter the traditional school program."

While special educators agree that early intervention is advisable, if not essential, its widespread implementation and acceptance has hardly begun. In 1967 the Office of Economic Opportunity provided seven million dollars to establish some thirty-five Parent and Child Centers throughout the country. These programs were to mobilize community resources to aid the families of children, younger than three, with the expectation that both the children and the families would benefit (Caldwell, Bradley & Elardo, 1975). This was followed by the Handicapped Children's Act, as ammended by Public Law 91-230 which calls for the establishment of preschool and early childhood programs for high risk handicapped children beginning at birth. This legislation provides monies to service children and their families and (2) assists in the dissemination of information. More recent Federal legislation grants appropriate public education to all handicapped children, which establishes that, at least in policy, intervention will be enacted from the time of birth.

It appears then, that a major objective of the Bureau for the Education of the Handicapped has been to provide equal educational opportunity for every handicapped child, with special emphasis especially in preschool and early childhood programs. (Martin, 1971).

A major concern among special educators has been the question of when to provide separate facilities or the handicapped and when to integrate them with non-handicapped children, a procedure known as mainstreaming. Traditionally, programming for the children with handicapping conditions has been to segregate them during the formative years of birth through nursery school (Hammer, 1971). Negative effects of segregated special class placements, especially for mildly handicapped children, have been described by Schere (1974) as reflecting more a subtle social control, as being relatively non-effective as measured by research studies, and as focusing on etiological variables rather than educational variables. Support for integrated or mainstreamed education for handicapped children has also stemmed from normalization principles (Wolfensberger, 1972) which have helped establish the civil rights of handicapped children to be part of the community rather than excluded from it.

There seems to be the need for community based, mainstream oriented programs which focus on the very youngest handicapped children. Day Care Centers and Head Start Programs would seem to be ideal facilities to help the handicapped since they meet these criteria. Also, they have a history of successful intervention with the disadvantaged (Lilleskov, 1974; Silverman & Wolfson, 1970). Various kinds of early intervention programs, which can be applied to the Day Care structure, are important to consider. Caldwell (1971) identified early stimulation programs as being either (1) omnibus models, (2) parent-oriented models, (3) child-oriented models, or (4) some combination of these. The term early stimulation generally refers to the provision of a quality environment for children below the age of three, an environment which will facilitate optimal child development. Omnibus model programs were described as attempting to provide more than one pattern of service to children and families and to aim enrichment effort simultaneously (not necessarily with the same intensity) to the infants and parents. In such models, health and social and vocational service components were often as important in the total program as were the educational activities. Parent oriented programs were described as offering some kind of tutorial or group experience for parents with the clear in-

*Dr. Richard A. Schere, Program Head, Special Education, Brooklyn College, CUNY. Dr. Rosalind I. Reiss, Lecturer in Special Education, Brooklyn College, CUNY.

tent of having this effort produce an impact on the child by virtue of changed behavior of the parents. Child-oriented programs were described as offering enrichment programs almost exclusively to the child. The parent was not necessarily expected to observe or to carry out any continuing activities with the child.

Other kinds of programs involving children older than three emphasize systematic exposure to varied experiences, the development of socialization skills, vocabulary and language activities, and deficit perceptual and perceptual-motor training. These educational interventions seem to be quite productive especially if aspects of the omnibus and parent-oriented models are included. Bronfenbrenner (1974) cites studies which indicate that rises in I.Q. occur if living conditions, and sequential strategy for continuous intervention. Caldwell, Bradley and Elardo (1975) describe nine experimental early intervention programs reported between the years 1968 and 1974, designed to prevent mental retardation. All but one reported significant improvement in children receiving early intervention. A distinction is made between programs aimed at alleviating retardation which is primarily organic in origin and programs aimed at alleviating retardation which is primarily organic in origin and programs aimed at ameliorating retardation which is primarily environmental in origin. What is important is that although improvement in children who are retarded primarily because of environment exceeds, as one would expect, the improvement of children retarded primarily because of organicity, there is improvement in both groups as compared to control populations not receiving the benefit of early intervention. Beilen (1972) discusses how slow and gradual improvement of retarded children through early intervention must statistically in time make a major and worthwhile contribution to society. Wexley and his associates (1974) in their evaluation of Montessori and Day Care programs for disadvantaged children, found that both early intervention programs had equal and positive effects as compared to nonintervention.

Neisworth and Madle (1975) present a model for normalizing Day Care programs for handicapped and normal children. Basic to this model is programming for developmentally retarded children. Six steps are recommended: (1) the assessment of developmental level through informal assessment, developmental checklists, or professional evaluation, (2) the selection of developmental materials which are the same as those typically used for a normal child of the same approximate age and skill level, (3) the modification of materials and methods which require analysis of the materials themselves (stimuli), the actions required of the child (responses). and the outcomes of a child's responses (consequences), (4) a systematic procedure for evaluating the child's progress, and (5) revision of materials and methods.

In their discussion of modifying methods and materials, Neisworth and Madle (1975) made several suggestions. With regard to the presentation of materials, they advise (1) that materials be as concrete and tangible as possible, (2) that the intended stimulation be exaggerated such as in discrimination learning, (3) that stimulation be repeated, and (4) that several senses be involved. With regard to children's responses, they suggest that (1) responding should be made easier (e.g. if a child cannot speak well, allow him to gesture), and (2) provide for response alternatives so that many routes to expression are encouraged. With regard to responding to a child's responses (consequences): (1) respond as immediately as is possible, and (2) remember that retarded children are developmentally younger and require less mature forms of feedback (e.g. a hug as compared to saying "good").

The majority of early intervention programs seem to be based on generalizations of children demonstrating specific problems, and not on findings established from individual assessments of children. Part of the reason for this seems to be related to both political and professional concern about the labelling of children. Mendelson and Atlas (1973) discuss the limitations of grouping young children on the basis of standardized testing. Their list of limitations include (1) tests may assess a very restricted range of information, (2) a child's physical and internal state at the time of taking a specific test may adversely affect his performance on it, and (3) tests show a child's final answer, but not how he arrived at it. Levine (1973) discusses how early labelling can lead to the degrading of social identity that can result in rejection and ostracization of a child and his family. Yet, Nagera (1975) argues that the impact of poorly designed Day Care centers on the intellectual, emotional, and psychological development of children can be disastrous and can result in a mass production of children with psychopathology. It would seem as argued by Schere (1975) that testing and evaluation, in order to develop appropriately structured programs, are necessary but must be done carefully. In a position paper prepared for the New York State Education Department, he outlined suggestions for the psychoeducational assessment of retarded children. These include: (1) selecting formal tests standardized on a population of which the child to be tested is representative, (2) utilization of informal procedures to probe more specifically the trends suggested by formal tests, (3) greater emphasis upon effect of etiology on learning skill strength and weaknesses and less emphasis on etiology and classification, (4) use of diagnostic achievement tests to help specify strengths and weaknesses according to modes, levels of presentation, and specific skills, (5) comprehensive evaluation to guarantee recurring themes and the ability to predict from one test to another so as to increase accuracy and objectivity, and (6) emphasis on recommendations which are the only justification for having conducted an evaluation to begin with, and (7) follow-up.

Mainstreaming seems to be another controversial issue influencing the development of early intervention programs for special children. On the one hand, legislation guaranteeing equal educational opportunity for all children realistically mandates the mainstreaming of at least mildly handicapped children (Reiss and Schere, 1975). Yet, the application of the mainstream concept does not mean that all handicapped children have to be placed in classes with nonhandicapped students. The principles of mainstreaming include not categorizing a child on a label reflecting a gross diagnostic category. Rather, mainstreaming advocates the grouping of all children, handicapped or not on the basis of defined educational needs (Reager, 1974).

Neisworth and Madle (1975) review the numerous advantages of mainstreaming Day Care, which they perceive as a normalization process:

1. Children with developmental delay benefit from models provided by their normal peers. Instead of being surrounded only by other abnormal children, they are mingled with children who show more advanced behavior that can be imitated (Baer, Peterson, and Sherman, 1967).

2. Members of the general communtiy, for example, parents of normal children begin to learn tolerance for those with deviations and learn of the uniqueness and contributions that each child can make.

3. Many unwanted and troublesome traits of children are produced when children are treated as being "different" (Goffman, 1963). Lowered or peculiar expectations of children contribute to creating abnormal behavior (Mercer, 1970). Integration has great developmental advantages because of the important function it serves in preventing, and sometimes reversing abnormal characteristics that result from physical and social isolation (Bijou, 1966).

4. Normalization in day care reduces the possibility that the handicapped will be blamed for his problems by correctly placing responsibility for enhancing development on programming and on society generally.

5. The wide array of capabilities presented by a mixed group of children converts lip service about "individualization" into action.

6. Integration is not only developmentally efficient, it has multiple advantages from a cost-benefit point of view. (Wolfensberger, 1972). It is far cheaper in money and time to work with handicapped children in the same setting with normal children.

However, many fear for the prognosis of handicapped children struggling in the mainstream without guarantee of needed support services.

The effect of nutrition is being increasingly viewed as a subtle, yet major factor in reducing the problems of handicapped children. Malnutrition occuring during a critical developmental period is one agent which can cause retardation in brain growth and ultimately hinder brain function (Winick, 1970). A study by Cravioto and his associates (1966) found that children exposed to early malnutrition show perceptual deficits, and, indeed, the earlier the malnutrition, the more profound the psychological retardation. Studies of children from around the world strongly suggest

that early malnutrition stunts physical growth and that, if malnutrition occurs during a critical growth period later nourishment will not reverse the earlier insult (Stoch and Smythe, 1963). These and many other studies support the principle that early intervention programs, in order to be effective, must be concerned with the analysis and provision of adequate diet.

Although progress has begun in initiating integrative early childhood programs for the handicapped, the old fears and prejudices against special children as well as the difficulty of people to adjust to change have limited their success. Personnel have demonstrated resistance to the sudden and dramatic changes occuring in early childhood education. Bloom has advocated in-service training of personnel designed to help bridge the transition of handicapped children into the mainstream (1975).

The Bureau for Education of the Handicapped is mandating a master plan by region for training programs hoping to receive government funding. The need for retraining especially with regard to the attitudes of teachers toward handicapped children is highlighted in a personal article by Gorelick (1973).

Despite the 1972 legislative mandate to enroll handicapped children in Head Start programs, there is an apparent discrepancy between the number of handicapped children who are reportedly enrolled and those actually observed during site visits. Nazzaro (1974) reports that although 10% of the children in Day Care and Head Start Programs receiving federal funding were supposed to be handicapped, the De Howe Report accused HEW of over reporting by improperly labelling children with conditions such as minor ear loss as handicapped. Furthermore, she continues, the Syracuse Report indicated a discrepancy between the number of handicapped children reported to be in Head Start Programs and the number actually observed during site visits.

The possibility exists, that children with more minimal handicapping conditions are being maintained, without label, within existing regular Day Care facilities. However, at this point in time, while earlier intervention holds potential for reducing the problems of special children and while the Federal Government has enacted legislation and funding patterns for these purposes, judgment must await as to whether that potential will be realized.

Summary

Early intervention holds great promise for reducing the problems of special children. Studies continue to demonstrate the positive increments gained by handicapped children able to take advantage of such programs. Indeed, some studies, such as the Milwaukee Project, suggest that environmentally induced mental retardation may be curable if intervention is initiated from time of birth. Recent legislation has established that early and equal education for all children including the handicapped, is now a matter of national policy. Unfortunately, fears and prejudices against special children combined with resistance to change has impeded the implementation of this new national policy.

There are various kinds of programs advocated for early intervention. Early stimulation, designed to provide a quality environment for children below the age of three, is described in depth. Programs stressing varied experience, language and vocabulary, socialization and deficit perceptual and perceptual-motor training are also discussed. It would appear that all programs have potential for success providing they emphasize family involvement, adequate living conditions, and sequential strategy for continuous intervention.

A number of issues are discussed that reflect importantly upon early intervention programs for the handicapped. They include (1) assessment and the labelling of children, (2) problems inherent in mainstreaming, (3) the importance of nutrition in fostering healthy development, and (4) the need to retrain personnel especially with regard to their attitudes toward special children.

BIBLIOGRAPHY

Baer, D., Peterson, R. & Sherman, J. The development of imitation by reinforcing behavioral similarity to a model. Journal of the Experimental Analysis of Behavior. 1967, *10*, 405-416.

Beilen, H. The status and future of preschool compensatory education. In J. Stanley (Ed.) *Preschool programs for the disadvantaged: five experimental approaches to early childhood education*. Baltimore, Maryland: The John Hopkins University Press, 1972.

Bijou, S. A functional analysis of retarded development. In N. Ellis (Ed.), *International review of research in mental retardation Vol. I)*, New York: Academic Press, 1966.

Bloom, B. Normalizing the education experience. *Deficience Mentale/Mental Retardation, 1975, 25* (1), 2-7.

Bronfenbrenner, U. Is early intervention effective? *Day Care and Early Education*, 1974, *2* (2), 14-18.

Caldwell, B., Bradley, R.H., & Elardo, R. Early stimulation. In J. Wortis (Ed.) *Annual Review of mental retardation and developmental disabilities* (Vol. VII) New York: Bruner Mazel, 152-194, 1975.

Cravioto, J. Nutrition growth and neurointegrative development—an experimental and ecologic study. *Pediatrics*, 1966, *38* (Suppl.) 2.

Gallagher, J.J. *Preschool and early education programs needed for handicapped children*. Statement before the select subcommittee on Education of the Committee on Education and Labor (Howe of Representatives, July 19, 1968).

Garber, H. & Heber, R. *The Milwaukee Project: Early intervention as a technique to prevent mental retardation.*

National Leadership Institute Teacher Education/ Early Childhood. The University of Connecticut Technical Paper, 1973.

Goffman, E. *Stigma: Notes in the management of spoiled identity*. Englewood Cliffs, N.J.: Prentice-Hall, 1963.

Gorelick, M.C. *What's in a label: careers in integrated early childhood programs*. Paper presented at teacher training sessions. Preschool Laboratory Home Economics Dept. California State University., Northrudge, 1973.

Hammer, E. Review of the literature in early childhood education, with emphasis upon early education of handicapped children. *A staff training manual*. 1 (8), 1971 (Texas U., Austin).

Heber, R. & Garber, H. The Milwaukee Project: A study of the use of the family intervention to prevent cultural-family retardation. In B.Z. Friedlander, G.M. Sterritt & G.E. Kirk (Eds.) *Exceptional Infant*, Vol. III, New York: Brunner (Mazel, 1975).

Kirk, S.A. *Early education of the mentally retarded. Ursana:* University of Illinois Press, 1958.

Levine, D. The dangers of early identification. *Child Care Quarterly*, 1973, *2* (4), 251-255.

Lilleskou, R.K. Experiences with early intervention. *Psychosocial Process*, 1974, *3* (1), 14-27.

Martin, E.W. Bureau of Education for the Handicapped commitment and program in early childhood education. *Exceptional Children*, 1971, *37* (9), 661-663.

Mendelson, A. & Atlas, R. Early childhood assessment: paper & pencil for whom? *Childhood Education*, 1973, April, 357-361.

Mercer, J. Sociological perspectives on mild mental retardation. In H.C. Haywood (Ed.) *Sociocultural aspects of mental retardation*. New York: Appelton-Century-Crafts, 1970, 378-391.

Nagera, H. Day-care centers: red light, green light or amber light. *International Review of Psycho-analysis*, 1975, *2* (1), 121-137.

Nazzaro, J. Head Start for the handicapped—what's been accomplished? Exceptional Children, 1974, *41* (2), 103-6.

Neisworth, J.T. & Madle, R.A. Normalized day care: a philosophy and approach to integrating exceptional and normal children. *Child Case Quarterly*, 1975 *4* (3), 163-172.

Roger, R. What does mainstreaming mean? *Journal of Learning Disabilities*, 1974, *7* (8), 513-515.

Reiss, P. & Schere, R. Movement in special education. In: L. Goldbchick and B. Persky (Eds). *Innovations in Education*. Dubuque, Iowa: Kendall-Hunt, 1975.

Schere, R. "Social Control and its Double-Bind Effect on the Education of the Exceptional" Paper read at the 51st Annual Meeting of the American Orthopsychiatric Association. San Francisco, 1974.

Schere, R. "Guidelines for the Psychoeducational Assessment of Retarded Children." A position paper prepared at the request of the New York State Department of Education. Albany, 1975.

Silverman, M. & Wolfson, E. The use of small educational-therapeutic groups in a program for disadvantaged preschoolers. *Psychosocial Process*, 1970, *1* (2), 47-59.

Wexley, K. & others. An evaluation of Montessori and Day Care programs for disadvantaged children. *Journal of Educational Research*, 1974, *68* (3), 95-99.

Stoch, M.B. & Smythe, P.M. Does undernutrition during in-

fancy inhibit brain growth and subsequent intellectual development. *Archives of Disease in Childhood*, 1963, *38*, 546.

Winick, M. Nutrition and mental development. *Medical Clinics of North America*, 1970, *54*, 1413-1429.

Wolfensberger, W. *The Principle of Normalization in Human Services*. Toronto: National Institute on Mental Retardation, 1972.

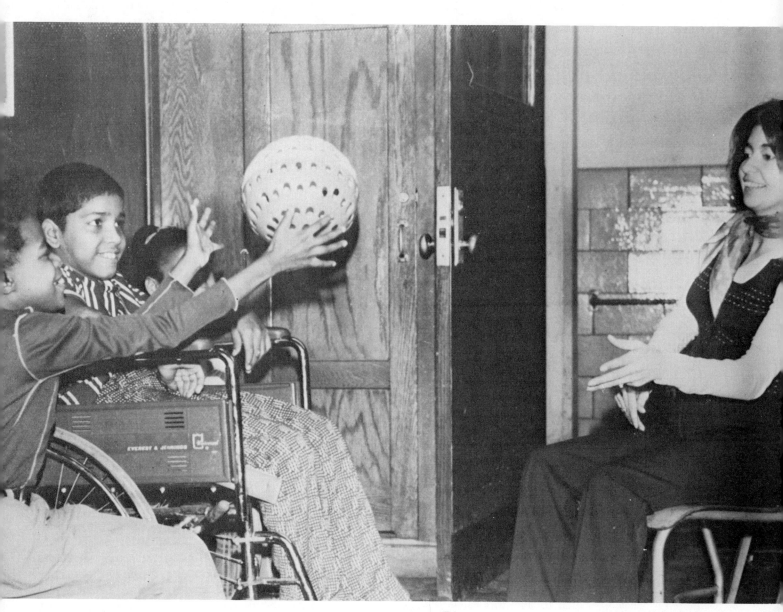

Samuel Teicher

Chapter 44

Mainstreaming Aggressive and Passive Preschoolers through Play

Charles H. Wolfgang*

Armed with a large block, four-year-old Tommy stands over a fellow preschooler ready to strike. Potentially dangerous, such behavior along with lesser forms, punctuate the preschool teacher's day. Seemingly, in nearly every preschool classroom, especially those which attempt to mainstream children with special needs, there are one or two of these children who endanger others and disrupt the play environment. How shall we view this aggression? And what can we as teachers do in an open, child-centered environment to help these children integrate themselves into the productive stream of activities?

We may say that at birth, the infant, in the widest sense, is aggressive. A minor frustration caused either by the external world full of objects and others or the child's internal physical world, will produce a screaming infant who will fling himself about until his caregivers help satisfy his need. With gradual maturity on all fronts the child will learn to delay this immediate gratification and gain ascendency over his own impulses and behavior. This is a long, difficult process which is not well completed until near the beginning of middle childhood. The preschool years are, therefore, a transitional period requiring us as teachers to learn techniques or methods to assist their development.

We may, for the purpose of discussion, view the young child as a balloon full of water. With any mild frustration the pressure builds up inside until a "crack" occurs allowing this inner pressure to spill out as a violent stream of aggresion such as hitting, kicking, spitting, or even biting. When we observe such behavior as adults we are understandably fearful and we quickly act to keep everyone safe. The form of this intervention and our view of such behavior is critical. If we saw the same negative behaviors in adults we would be shocked, but as teachers dealing with young children who are still far from adulthood and the attainment of mature self control, it might be more helpful to view "difficult" children's behavior as that of an entity along a growth continuum toward the attainment of self control, and, through intervention, support this growth.

Hypothetically we may view this impulse control on a continuum which ranges from passivity to physical aggresion, to verbal aggression, and finally, through the use of language, to the attainment of one's goal in a controlled, acceptable manner. (Spitz, 1957) The young toddler, because of the new ability to walk, moves rapidly into a dangerous world and is quickly trained by adults through the use of the work, "no." "No, you may not play with the bread knife, daddy's stereo set, or the wall plugs." The toddler's first response to such limits is one of simple surprise and passive behavior. This quickly changes from helpless passivity to physical aggression. Now when he is faced with the frustrating limit of being told "no," the child strikes out with all of the many violent acts described above.

Still later, with increased maturity, we begin to see the behavior that we might call the child's verbally aggressive "No." When the child is discovered by his parents doing something "naughty" the child will shout, "No! No!" at his parents before they are able to chastize him. In fact, the toddler passes through a global "No" phase wherein he says "No" to nearly every request. This "no" response signals that the child is intelligently beginning to remember those things which he is not permitted to do, and once this remembering it beforehand occurs, the child can maintain self control. (Fraiberg, 1959)

Now, there are many children who, for a whole host of reasons, (Sapir, 1973) may have difficulty moving through these phases. In fact, the "difficult" child's general mode of responding to the daily classroom frustrations produced by peers or in trying to use preschool equipment, is to generally react in a defensive manner by being passive, aggressive or verbally aggressive.

If we return to the hypothetical model of a balloon full of water, and respond to that stream of released aggressive impulsive behavior by punishment, thus shutting off the child's outlet, this pressure builds up inside the child as he attempts to maintain himself passively. In turn, we see the pressure erupt through *many* "cracks", with behaviors that are not productive and at times harmful to the child, such as excessive thumb sucking, head banging, or rocking, masturbation or other forms of passive stimulation, or self inflicted pain. Contradictory as it may seem, if we accept

From the book *HELPING* aggressive and passive *PRESCHOOLERS* through *PLAY* copyright 1977 by Charles H. Wolfgang. Published by Chalres E. Merrill.

*Dr. Charles Wolfgang, Professor, Ohio State University.

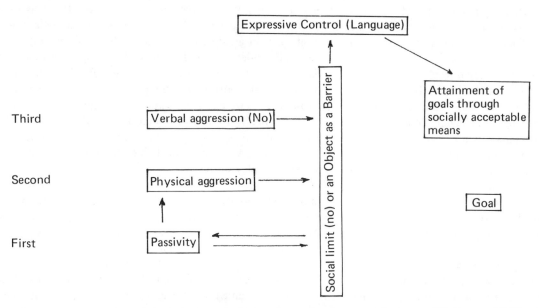

Figure 1. Impulse control as a developmental process (Wolfgang, 1977)

the passive, physically aggressive, and verbal aggressive continuum toward impulse control we must value aggression and understand that the aggressive child is still desperately trying to master this world even though his acts are far from being socially acceptable.

In dealing as a teacher with violent, or near violent, acts it might be helpful to pass our form of intervention on a contunuum with regard to the degree of intrusion that we use. The most intrusive from of intervention is physical intervention. We actually physically need to restrain Tommy form striking with the block to keep others physically safe.

AMPLIFIED TEACHER BEHAVIOR CONTINUUM

OPEN . . . . STRUCTURED

1. Visual looking	3. Verbal questions	4. Verbal directions
	2. Non-directive	5. Physical help or modelling Teacher
1. (Visual looking on)		Moves physically close
2. (Non-directive statements)		"Some puzzles are hard to do."
3. (Verbal questions)		"What could you do or say?"
4. (Verbal direction)		TELL HIM EXACTLY WHAT TO DO (not what *not* to do)
5. (phys		
5. (physical intervention)		Channel from the Body to the Toy, Toy to Play

Figure 2

Becoming less intrusive, we may place verbal directions next on our continuum. When Susie is beginning to get overly excited with her easel painting and begins to paint herself or others, we simply give verbal direction stating, "You need to keep the paint on the paper." What is impor-

tant in such a response is not to tell Susie what she is not to do, but to tell her what she is to do, which in her excitement she has forgotten.

Becoming still less intrusive on the Teacher Behavior Continuum we may use verbal questions. For example, we may say to two children who are about to get into conflict over a possession, "I see one of you wants some of the clay that the other has! What could you say to him to tell him you want some clay?"

Moving up this continuum we may now place non-directive statements as even being less intrusive. These are the Rodgerian statements that we may make to children which verbally "mirror" their feelings or behavior. To a child who is becoming frustrated by a puzzle that he cannot complete, "Some puzzles are very hard to do, and after a while they make us angry. I'll stay and watch you complete it and if you need my help you can tell me."

Finally, the least form of teacher intrusion or control may be classified as "visually looking on." For example, we find Karen has just "snatched" a toy from a peer. We simply move physically close, make our appearance known, and look on, giving the children time to resolve the confrontation on their own. If this does not work, we may need to become increasingly intrusive, and begin to move up the continuum in the opposite direction, i.e., non-verbal statements, verbal questions, etc. The general rule is to use the least form of intrusion needed, so the children will be able to self-regulate. (Wolfgang, 1977)

The Teacher Behavioral Continuum is simply a chart by which we may direct our own behavior. Holding the belief that self control is a developmental process which grows within the child aiding him to become less dependent on us as adults to resolve his problem, we may employ this TBC to offer any necessary help by moving from visually looking on to physical intervention, or from physical intervention to visually looking on as the case might require.

Finally, how can we handle the physical intervention necessary when we are dealing with a violent child? What do we do with the child who is kicking and throwing himself about, who is attempting and at times succeeding to hurt us? The teacher must be aware of her own feelings at this critical point in the interaction. We are responsible for the safety of all our children, and such a child frightens us with the potential danger he may cause. It is this very moment when the child is flooded with his own inner fears, that he is in greatest need of our help. If we cannot intellectually understand and emotionally accept that this child is growing and moving up this passive-aggressive continuum towards self control, we are powerless to help the child grow. But, if we can accept this strong expression of feeling with its manifestations of immature behavior, and not take the child's actions as a personal affront to our "authority" as a teacher, we may channel this aggression into a socially acceptable play outlet.

First, while physically restraining the preschooler, we move him (bodily, if necessary) to an enclosed space where we can screen out the rest of the classroom activities. We may line up three or four chairs around one corner of the room or use an area that is enclosed by shelves within, not outside, the room. We place the child within this semi-enclosed space where we join him, as we state, "I can't let you hurt me and I am not going to hurt you. This is a safe place, I'm here to help you get control and when you are ready, you may go back to play." It is helpful to place a full upright mirror and a variety of miniature-life hand toys in this "time-out" space.

The child who is flooded by his own fear and anger has totally lost a sense of control and self awareness. We re-establish this awareness of self by showing him his image in the mirror. "See, Tommy, there you are, you're all right, I'm here to keep you safe." Most children, after repeated experiences with mirrors will, during a tantrum, see themselves and gain self control. Once they quiet, especially after a violent act, they might begin to retreat back into passive thumbsucking or masturbation, while some children will actually fall asleep. If this occurs we try to re-engage the child to come back to the outside world through "mirroring," by doing different body referencing games, such as "This is Thumbkin," or by stating, "Tommy, look into the mirror and show me your nose, show me my nose. Show me my eyes, show me your eyes," etc.

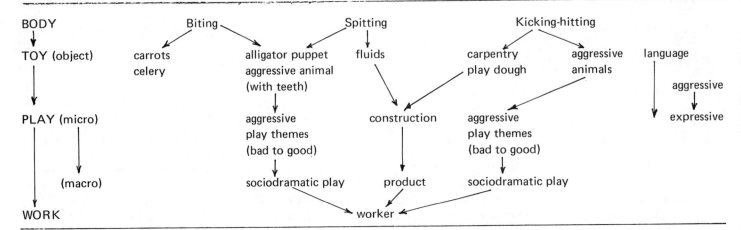

Figure 3. Channeling Aggression (Wolfgang, 1977)

Finally, we wish to move the aggressive act from the body to the toy. For the child who is biting, we place (either in the "time-out" space or back in the full classroom space) an alligator puppet with fierce teeth on his hand, or aggressive miniature toy such as a lion, and encourage him to bite in play. Using the model of the child as a balloon full of water, we accept the physical expression and find an acceptable outlet for it in play.

In dealing with a child who is spitting, we might use an alligator puppet with a mouth, or play with water play or finger paints. The child might move kicking and hitting behaviors into play with carpentry and play dough or aggressive miniature animals.

Finally, we encourage the child with the miniature life toys to elaborate a story-like play theme with the toys or create symbolic products with art material as construction. (Wolfgang, 1977)

In fantasy, the child can safely express the behavior that is unacceptable in reality. During the playing out of themes the child will become the aggressor himself. (Peller, 1954) The child who had become aggressive when he was told by the teacher that there were no more cookies, can, with the teacher's encouragement, make hundreds of "cookies" in the clay and gain in fantasy what he cannot in reality. Finally, the microspheric play with small miniature life toys and materials should move on to play in the macrosphere and, finally, on to the larger space with his peers, (Erikson, 1950) as we help the child learn to play socio-dramatic play; that is, the playing out with other children roles and themes around Mommies and Daddies, firefighter, mail-person, and the many other social roles that young children experience. (Smilansky, 1968)

If we think back to Tommy, who was posed to strike with the block, we may see him as an asocial person with the inability to be a player or worker with others. Unfortunately, children are not born with this ability, but must learn it during the preschool years. We learn to be social by learning to play many roles. At one moment, we as an adult are a husband, wife, driver of a car, customer, or teacher. Socialization requires the ability to take on a wide variety of roles at appropriate times. (Brissett and Edgley, 1975) So when children are doing dressup social-dramatic play they are not simply "wasting" their time, but are learning to first be a player of roles in fantasy; learning which, at a later time, will enable them to become a worker in reality. (A. Freud, 1965; Smilansky, 1968)

It is well for us to remember that the preschool child is still becoming a socialized being, one in the process of developing a social conscience that will enable him to evaluate his actions in terms of how they affect others. We find that a child's developing conscience at this age is rigid and, consequently, he is repeatedly flooded with the guilt that he feels as a result of his "failures." In fact, Erikson characterized the preschool years as one of Initiative vs. Guilt. (1950) The child thrusts himself into situations where he is seeking social relationships, such as seen in the socio-dramatic play, but when, by adult standards he fails to act as his beloved adults desire him to do he feels guilty for failing them. In the same vein, Piaget has also demonstrated that this guilt also occurs around punishment. To the young child there are no accidental happenings, and when painful accidents do occur, such as a nasty fall, he views this pain as punishment for one's earlier transgressions. (1965)

Because the preschooler is developmentally loaded with guilt feelings and thoughts of imminent punishment, the most destructive form of discipline is to, in our view, "strike the child in the conscience." "See, you have hurt Carol, aren't you ashamed? No one will play with you if you are like this." This form of guilt induction (or Gling) children (Curry, 1971; Wolfgang, 1977) floods the child with fear and guilt, and does not provide him with a direction for an alternative socially acceptable form of behavior. Again, we accept these strong expressions of the child's behavior and, through our intervention, help the child find an acceptable outlet, which is generally a movement through a play release and mastery.

Our purpose here has been to present a different view of aggression in young children, as a natural development phenomenon, and to present a behavioral continuum to view the forms of teacher intrusion that we may employ to help such "difficult" children. And, finally, for those violent children we may use play techniques to channel that agression from the body to toy, toy to micro play with miniature life toys, then to the macrosphere with role play. Finally, through sociodramatic play, the child becomes a worker, able to control, inhibit, or modify the impulses to use given materials aggressively and destructively (not to throw, take apart, to mess, to hoard) and to use them positively and constructively instead. "To build, to plan, to learn, and—in communal life—to share." (A. Freud, 1965)

REFERENCES

Curry, Nancy. Personal communication, 1970.

Erikson, Erik. *Childhood and Society.* New York: Norton, 1950, 182–218.

Freud, Anna. *Normality and Pathology in Childhood.* New York: International Universities Press, 1965.

Frailberg, Selma h. *The Magic Years.* New York: Charles Scribner's Sons, 1959.

Peller, Lilli. "Libidinal Phases, Ego Development and Play." *Psychoanalytic Study of the Child.* 1954. 9, 178-199.

Piaget, Jean. *The Moral Judgment of the Child.* Translated by Marjorie Gabain. New York: The Free Press, 1965.

Piaget, Jean. *The Origins of Intelligence in Children.* New

York: International Universities Press, 1952.

Sapir, Selma S. and Ann C. Nitzburg. *Children with Learning Problems.* New York: Brunner/Mazel Publishers, 1973.

Spitz, Rene. *No and Yes.* New York: International Univer-

sity Press, 1957.

Wolfgang, Charles H. *HELPING aggressive and passive PRESCHOOLERS through PLAY.* Columbus, Ohio: Charles E. Merrill Publishing Company, 1977.

Chapter 45
Identifying Individual Learning Styles & the Instructional Methods and/Or Resources to which Handicapped Early Childhood Youngsters Respond

Rita Dunn, Kenneth Dunn, and Gary Price*

The Need To Diagnose Each Student's Learning Style

We became involved with the phenomenon called "learning style" as an outgrowth of trying to help slowly achieving youngsters narrow the gap between their ability to read and the grade level expectations held for them.

In 1967, the New York State Education Department created The Teacher Reserve, a graduate program designed to develop teachers who were capable of helping "educationally disadvantaged" students to learn (Dunn and Schockley, 1970; 1971). "Mature" persons who had earned a baccalaureate degree in liberal arts areas and who, therefore, had not been exposed to traditional classroom methodology, were recruited into a Master's Degree program to develop innovative instructional strategies during daytime hours and essentially in public school classrooms.

Over a three year period, approximately 600 teachers-in-training, eight college professors, more than 20 classroom teachers, and at least five public school administrators worked together to facilitate learning for children who had not responded well to traditional teaching. Individualization was in its early stages at that time and various kinds of learning activity packages, programmed learning, and games were used and evaluated.

What became apparent was that selected methods appeared to be extremely effective with some youngsters—but failed to produce anything other than minor gains in others. For example, when we used small group strategies, certain children thrived whereas others avoided all peer-oriented studies. When using programmed learning, some youngsters tired easily and could not "sit still" while others would continue using the materials for hours on end, evidencing neither boredom nor fatigue. Games also were intriguing to many—and irritating to others. Some learned rapidly with one technique; others literally despised that method and refused to be enticed into using it after initial experiences. It rapidly became evident that, if we were to help students to become academically successful, we had to develop *different* methods and then, in some way, determine which might appeal to and be effective with selected learners.

An investigation of the research within and outside of the field of education concerned with how children and adults learn revealed a body of knowledge that had been accumulated over an 80-year period repeatedly verifying that students acquire information and skills in many different ways. The literature yielded eighteen categories that, when classified, suggested that learners are affected by their: (a) *immediate environment*, (b) *own emotionality*, c) *sociological needs*, and *physical requirements* (Dunn and Dunn, 1975). We found that learning style is the manner in which at least 18 different elements from the above four basic stimuli affect a person's ability to absorb and retain. The combinations and variations among these elements suggested that few people learn in exactly the same way, just as few people think exactly alike.

Environmental Elements of Learning Style

The environmental elements that affect how much a student is able to achieve at a given time include *sound, light, temperature,* and *design*.

Some people can block out surrounding noises and function effectively in spite of them. Others can adjust to selected sounds, depending on the task. A larger group appears to require virtual silence if the learning to be accomplished requires concentration or is difficult for them. Another group appears to be unable to study or concentrate without discussing the materials to be learned; this group, in effect *requires* sound.

The way in which a room is illuminated also appears to affect the learning process. Whereas some people can function with ease only when the environment is well lit, the same degree of lighting is considered excessive by some and insufficient by others. If lighting is incorrect for the individual, it can prevent concentration either by overstimulating the learner or by lulling him or her into drowsiness.

Temperature is an element that yields easily observable differences in learning ability as the degree of heat varies. Some require a warm environment before they can study; others find that the same amount of warmth that relaxes certain people actually makes them uncomfortable. Selected students can function well only in a cool area, whereas others become "nervous" in the same degree of temperature.

*Dr. Rita Dunn, Professor, Department of Curriculum and Teaching, St. John's University, New York, Dr. Kenneth Dunn, Superintendent of Schools, Hewlett-Wodmere, New York, and Dr. Gary E. Price, Associate Professor, University of Kansas, Lawrence, Kansas.

The way in which an environment is designed also produces differences in the amount of learning that individuals are able to achieve. Certain students indicate that they require a formal study area that includes a desk or table and a chair—such as might be found in a library or a kitchen. Others report that they "cannot sit" in a very traditional area for any length of time and continue to concentrate; these people require a relaxed setting and find that they can continue to work for longer intervals when the furniture and surroundings are informal. This very informality, however, usually causes drowsiness or daydreaming in the group requiring the more rigid design.

Emotional Elements of Learning Style

The emotional elements that affect how much a student is able to achieve at a given time include *motivation, persistence, responsibility,* and the individual's need for *structure* or flexibility.

Most teachers intuitively understand that youngsters who come to school motivated, persistent, responsible, or simply in need of structure should be worked with differently from the unmotivated, the unpersistent, the irresponsible, and the student who should be supervised closely, given short assignments, kept within eyes' sight, and frequently encouraged and praised.

Historically, however, we address each class as a whole and rarely vary the assignments, the requirements, the tests, the instructional methods, or the grading system so that they correspond to what students are *capable* of achieving.

Students who want to learn, who complete assigned tasks, and who accomplish specified objectives, require instructional programs and methods that promote a gradually increasing confrontion with difficult tasks. Those who have short attention spans and few academic interests, who prefer social activities to academic achievement, and who need constant or frequent interaction with an adult, will not profit from participation in a program that permits them to self-select tasks, pace themselves, interact with peers at their discretion, or self-schedule activities. Certainly the student and the program and method(s) to which the student is assigned should be carefully matched.

Sociological Elements of Learning Style

Students react differently to their peers, adults, and the learning process itself. Some prefer to study alone and can achieve more in this manner than when working directly with either other youngsters or adults. Some students require direct and virtually continual interaction with an "authority figure", whether it be the teacher, an expert, an outside resource, or a paraprofessional. There are, however, students who become "uptight" or intimidated by adults; they find they can learn more easily when working with a friend or two or even in a small group. This is true of many students and is often manifested by an inclination to work within a committee structure or on task forces.

Students who profit from close student/teacher interactions should not be assigned to a system wherein independent or peer-group studies are emphasized. Obviously, too, students who successfully achieve through interaction with their classmates and enjoy this process should not be placed in a program that requires either extensive self-teaching or teacher-dominated instruction.

Many students will enjoy variations in the instructional process; teachers can design their methods to include such alternatives. It is necessary, however, to avoid placing students in programs that require a preponderance of specific sociological strategies if the youngster's learning style indicated disharmony with the basic pattern.

Physical Elements of Learning Style

To a major extent students are not free agents; they are controlled by their physical needs. Only the strongly motivated learner can achieve when his physical requirements are at variance with the learning system.

Some people learn well through hearing; for these a lecture, a discussion, a record, or a cassette will facilitate achievement. Some must experience visually what should be learned. Both groups comprise only a portion of the student community, and sometimes their abilities to advance academically through the use of auditory or visual strategies are mutually exclusive; sometimes they are complementary or reinforcing.

Other students experience extensive difficulty when trying to learn without a tactual or kinesthetic involvement. This is often true of youngsters who do not learn to read through either a phonics or word recognition approach. When exposed to tactual or kinesthetic methods however, they often overcome the difficulties they had when taught through auditory or visual techniques. Using a multisensory approach to teaching often will overcome *perceptual* problems that certain students experience in a traditional program emphasizing lecture.

Another physical problem that confronts some students is the need for *"intake"* at regular intervals. Whether this is a physical need to replace the energy being expended by concentration or a means of releasing nervous energy, some students frequently need to eat, drink, chew gum, or even bite on objects while engaged in the learning process. Obviously, a conservative program will not permit breaks for intake, whereas an informal one may.

The *time* when a person is most alert and, therefore, best able to absorb learning varies with the individual. Some students work most effectively early in the morning, others excel later in the day, and still others are proverbial "night owls." A highly structured program divided into time blocks for concentrated study in specific disciplines will not be conducive to achievement for youngsters who may not be alert at the arbitrarily scheduled time. If timing is an important learning style factor for a particular student, his chances for academic success would be improved if he were placed in a program designed so that the subjects with which he experiences the most difficulty can be studied when he is most mentally alert.

Finally, the physical need for *mobility* (apparent in many youngsters) may easily inhibit learning efforts. Students who are not able to remain in their seats or in a restricted environment for long periods of time find it difficult to function in a traditional program. Conversely, youngsters who are at ease in one position for intervals of 45 minutes or longer sometimes find the constant (or frequent) movement that occurs in informal programs disconcerting. Considering the many differences among individuals, before students are assigned to teachers and courses, their learning style profiles should be matched with those programs, methods, and resources whose characteristics complement them (see Table 1).

Implications of Learning Style Differences

Our continuing studies with the development of an instrument to identify learning style differences among youngsters (Dunn, Dunn, and Price, 1977) have accented information which had not been available previously. For example, it is possible to identify which students will function well in a traditional, an individualized, an open, or an alternative program (Dunn and Dunn, 1977). It is also possible to identify which resources (Contract Activity Packages, programmed learning, tapes, instructional packages, films, games, or small-group techniques) will assist individual students to achieve.

We are finding that the majority of students tested are *not* auditory learners—results which certainly do not support the widespread use of the lecture method. It appears that many students are tactual (the need to learn through touching) and/or kinesthetic (whole body activity-oriented, experimental learning). The tendency to learn through the latter two senses appears to decrease with maturity, but at least one third of each high school sample tested exhibited such predispositions; at the elementary levels the proportion was higher.

Application to Early Childhood Pupils

Several years ago a study was conducted with the assistance of St. John's University graduate students involved in a clinical experience in individualizing instruction at the Columbus Avenue Kindergarten Center in Freeport, New York (Dunn, March, 1971.) After three weeks of intensive study, each graduate student was assigned to diagnose a pre-kindergarten or pre-first grade youngster for whom they

were to develop an individual "contract". The subject matter of the contract had to be selected from among several basic topics suitable to early childhood curriculum, e.g., recognition and spelling of the child's own name, the alphabet, color recognition, community helpers, healthful foods, numbers, sequences, shapes, or relative size. The purpose of the first meeting between each graduate student and youngster was to permit diagnosis of the child's level of ability in the topic.

On arrival in Freeport the graduate students were divided among several classes on each of two levels. Approximately one-half of the total pre-kindergarten and pre-first grade population was included. Games were used to provide insight into each youngster's:

- *Functional level* in terms of the curriculum topic. (What did he/she really know?)
- *Experiential level* in terms of his/her ability to use resource alternatives. (Can he/she operate equipment and locate materials?)
- *Motivational level.* (How willing is he/she to learn?)
- *Comprehension level.* (How capable is the youngster of following directions? To what kind of directions does he/she respond—auditory, visual, tactual, or kinesthetic?

The children selected for these first early childhood contracts were: very young (5-7), non-readers, inexperienced with either contracts or independent learning activities, unfamiliar with the graduate students, considered in need of additional readiness experiences by their teachers, and essentially unfamiliar with the mechanics of media equipment operation. These characteristics were obstacles to the implementation of an experimental program of short duration.

Nevertheless, one week after the initial interviews, 57 graduate students returned to Freeport with individually prescribed contract activity packages through which the youngsters could teach themselves. The directions to the child had been recorded on cassette tapes and for each of the contract components (resources, activity and reporting alternatives) the graduate student had developed either originally or commercially-prepared games which the child could play.

We had projected that each child would require a minimum of four sequential experiences with independent learning activities before he/she could function completely without the aid of a teacher. To our amazement more than one-half of the pupils became entirely independent of the graduate student within the first ten minutes of the contract operation. For the most part, these children worked quietly and continuously for 30 to 90 minutes, requiring only occasional assistance. Many did not want to stop the activities after an hour and a half!

Approximately 15 pupils worked in an interested and absorbed manner for the greater part of an hour, but frequently asked questions and required mechanical assistance (operating the tape recorder, locating specific materials, identifying appropriate pages). For these children, fewer initial activities should have been available. Although the valuable element of choice would have been eliminated, the procedures should have been introduced one at a time, eventually building up to a repertoire of alternatives.

We tested the youngsters after the activity period and found most had achieved the curriculum objectives designed for them through the package. For the five or six pupils who required almost constant assistance, we knew that we had to identify alternative methods to which they might respond more positively.

After an additional two years of experimenting with varied teaching strategies we found that many youngsters achieve nicely through contract activity packages, but that some cannot. Approximately one-third of the populations with whom we tested programmed materials appeared to achieve well through that medium. For slowly-achieving, non-auditory, non-reading youngsters, instructional packages appeared to be an extremely effective method.

Through continuing testing and observation, we have been able to identify that students with selected learning style characterists appear to be responsive to selected instructional techniques (see Table 2). Once we have diagnosed early childhood youngsters to identify their individual learning style profiles, it is easy to recommend those methods that are likely to produce academic achievement for those learners.

Application to Handicapped Youngsters

In October, 1975 Judy McCracken (then) Project Coordinator for the EHA Title V1-8 program for the Improvement of Instruction for Low-Incidence Handicapped Children in Ohio wrote to share her reactions to a book that we had written describing the methods that we had been developing and researching. McCracken administered and supervised a statewide program to develop individualization methods for the deaf, legally blind, and multiply handicapped children in Ohio. She was convinced that the strategies we had described were applicable to the special education students in Ohio and wanted us to conduct a series of workshops to share our techniques with the supervisors of the state programs for "low-incidence" handicapped youngsters. We told her that we had never worked with special education students and had no idea of whether the methods, based on their relationship to individual student's learning styles, would be similarly effective when used with handicapped children. She urged us to demonstrate the methods and to permit the approximately 70 Ohio supervisors to form their own judgments.

For a three week period before flying to Ohio, Ken and Rita Dunn visited every special education program available to them.

Teachers of the deaf were observed *shouting* instructions to their charges—in essence trying to teach them through their *weakest* perceptual strength rather than through their stronger senses, e.g., by using visual, tactual, or kinesthetic activities.

Teachers of the near-blind, were witnessed endeavoring to enlarge print —again through the youngsters' *weakest* perceptual strength—rather than using auditory, tactual, and/or visual methods for those youngsters.

Having become sensitive to the identification of learning style characteristics through the extensive observation of student behavior we observed handicapped youngsters demonstrate *identical* predispositions toward the various 18 elements frequently evident among normal, but slowly-achieving youngsters. Hyperactive children were told to "sit still", rather than given an instructional package which permits movement and return to study. Children wearing sweaters were cajoled into removing them—despite the fact that they rubbed their arms to warm themselves after a few moments. Children who gravitated toward their peers to work together were admonished to return to their own places and to complete their assignments. Time and again, handicapped youngsters evidenced similar learning style variations to their counterparts in the regular classes and, unfortunately, their teachers were equally as unaware of their individual differences as were the teachers in the regular schools!

In Ohio we shared our research concerning the 18 elements of learning style and the methods that we believe respond to the various learning style combinations. We never suggested that our experiences would prove viable for handicapped youngsters: we merely demonstrated our approaches and asked for feedback if they considered experimenting with them. We did not find one supervisor who was unwilling to "try" the methods—including the personnel responsible for many schools for deaf, blind, and multiply handicapped children.

During the past year we have enjoyed correspondence and meetings with some of those administrators—people who returned to their institutions and taught their own staffs what we had taught them. In many cases adaptations were made so that the methods were particularly responsive to selected children or groups of children. We have been told repeatedly, ". . .individualization is the only thing that REALLY WORKS for our children!"

Later Judy McCracken became the Director of the East Shore Center in Mentor, Ohio. In November, 1976 we went there to work with 60 special educators (both teachers and supervisors) who teach the retarded, learning disabled, blind, deaf, crippled, autistic or gifted children. This new group in Ohio is slowly introducing the concept of learning style among teachers of handicapped children and are relating their findings to methods that respond to the individual youngsters with whom they want to be successful. The process is slow because it is new; teachers need to

Table 1

DIAGNOSING LEARNING STYLE

ELEMENTS

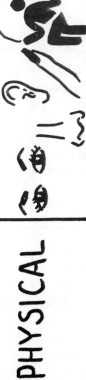

STIMULI				
ENVIRONMENT	SOUND	LIGHT	TEMPERATURE	DESIGN
EMOTIONAL	MOTIVATION	PERSISTENCE	RESPONSIBILITY	STRUCTURE
SOCIOLOGICAL	PEERS	SELF	PAIR	TEAM	ADULT	VARIED
PHYSICAL	PERCEPTUAL	INTAKE	TIME	MOBILITY

Designed by Rita Dunn and Kenneth Dunn

Table 2

Method and/or Resource	Learning Style Characteristics To Which It Responds	Learning Style Characteristics To Which It Does Not Respond	Learning Style Characteristics To Which It Can Be Accommodated
1. **Programed Learning**	Motivation, persistence, responsibility, and a need for structure; a need to work alone, a visually oriented student; when teachers design small-group techniques such as team-learning, circles of knowledge or brain-storming, peer-oriented students may develop an ability to use programs more effectively than if they use them exclusively as individual learners.	A lack of motivation, persistence, or responsibility; a need for flexibility and/or creativity; a need to work with peers or adults; auditory, tactual, or kinesthetic perceptual strengths.	Sound, light, temperature and design; a need for intake, appropriate time of day and a need for mobility.

Note: Where programed learning sequences are accompanied by tapes, they will appeal to auditory learners; when they include films and/or filmstrips, they will reinforce the visually oriented student; when teachers design small-group techniques such as team learning, circle of knowledge, or brainstorming, peer-oriented students may develop an ability to use programs more effectively than if they use them exclusively as individual learners.

Method and/or Resource	Learning Style Characteristics To Which It Responds	Learning Style Characteristics To Which It Does Not Respond	Learning Style Characteristics To Which It Can Be Accommodated
2. **Contract Activity Packages**	A need for sound, and an informal design; motivation, persistence, and reliability; a need to work either alone, with a friend or two or with an adult; all perceptual strengths and/or weaknesses, and the need for mobility.	None	Sound, light, temperature, and design; motivation, persistence, responsibility; sociological needs; perceptual strengths, intake, time of day, and the need for mobility.

Note: Contract Activity Packages respond to all learning style characteristics provided that (1) they are used correctly and (2) multisensory resources are developed as part of them.

Method and/or Resource	Learning Style Characteristics To Which It Responds	Learning Style Characteristics To Which It Does Not Respond	Learning Style Characteristics To Which It Can Be Accommodated
3. **Instructional Packages**	A need for sound or structure; a need to work alone; all perceptual strengths.	A lack of responsibility; a need for peer or adult interactions.	Light, temperature, and design; motivation, persistence; intake, time of day, and mobility.

Note: Because of their multisensory activities, instructional packages are very effective with "slow learners". Unless the curriculum is extremely challenging, they may be boring to high achievers.

Method and/or Resource	Learning Style Characteristics To Which It Responds	Learning Style Characteristics To Which It Does Not Respond	Learning Style Characteristics To Which It Can Be Accommodated
4. **Task Cards** and **Learning Circles**	Motivation, persistence, responsibility, and the need for structure; visual and/or tactual strengths.	A lack of motivation, persistence, responsibility and/or a need for structure; auditory and/or kinesthetic strengths; a need for mobility.	Sound, light, temperature, and design; the need to work alone, with peers, and/or an adult; intake, and time of day
5. **Tapes, Audi Cassettes**	A need for sound; motivation, persistence, responsibility, and a need for structure; a need to work alone; auditory strengths.	A need for silence; a need to work with peers, or an adult; visual, tactual and/or kinesthetic strengths, and a need for mobility.	Light, temperature, and design; intake and time of day.

Designed by Rita Dunn and Kenneth Dunn

experiment with methods with which they had no previous experience. They need to develop the skills of observing individual learning style differences and then prescribing on the basis of their findings. They also need to design and develop contract activity packages, multisensory programmed learning and instructional packages. During the process they are, in a sense, developing new professional identities—but they are also permitting youngsters, who previously labored long and arduously, to learn through "fun" ways that complement their ability to absorb and retain.

Instruments have been designed that diagnose both children's learning styles and teachers' teaching styles (Dunn and Dunn, 1977). The ever-increasing number of malpractice suits being lodged against school systems and their personnel across the country (Dunn, Dunn, and Price, 1977) mandate that educators view Public Law 94-142 as a means for broadening their professional skills and for enhancing the learning opportunities for youngsters who previously were unable to achieve. By diagnosing each student's learning style and then prescribing the method that most complements each student's profile, teachers will be responding to the Federal legislation that mandates individualization knowledgeably and responsibly.

REFERENCES

Rita S. Dunn and Alonzo H. Shockley, Jr. *Better Education Through Community Involvement*. New York: Freeport Public Schools, Pursuant to a U.S. Office of Health, Education, and Welfare Grant under the supervision of the New York State Education Department (1970).

Rita S. Dunn and Alonzo H. Shockley, Jr. *That A Child May Reach: Expanded Education in Freeport*. New York: Freeport Public Schools, under the supervision of the New York State Education Department (1971).

Rita Dunn and Kenneth Dunn. *Educator's Self-Teaching Guide ot Individualizing Instructional Programs*. Nyack, New York: Parker Publishing Company (1975) Chapter 3.

Rita Dunn, Kenneth Dunn, and Gary E. Price. "Diagnosing Learning Styles: A Prescription for Avoiding Malpractice Suits." *Kappan*. Indiana: Phi Delta Kappa (January, 1977) 418-420.

Rita Dunn. "Individualizing Instruction Through Contracts—Does It Work With Very Young Children?" *Audiovisual Instruction*. Washington, D.C.: National Education Association 16, 3 (March, 1971): 78-80.

Rita Dunn and Kenneth Dunn. *Administrator's Guide to New Programs For Faculty Management and Evaluation*. Nyack, New York: Parker Publishing Company (1977) Chapter 3.

Chapter 46

The Readiness Program: For Young Children with Severe Learning Disabilities

Laura Shapiro and Susan Shapiro*

A Model Program For Early Diagnosis and Intervention

The Readiness Program is designed to locate, identify and provide an intervention setting for children from 4 years 9 months to 7 years who exhibit a wide range of serious developmental learning problems. It is a team approach using medical, social and educational experts.

The program began in 1971 with funds granted to the Division of Special Education and Pupil Personnel of the New York City Board of Education. The original program started with 6 classes affiliated with 6 different hospital teams and community agencies. By 1976, the program expanded to 61 classes, 27 teams, some 750 students and a staff of 142.

In the formulation of this service project the following questions were asked:

1. Could we locate and identify the high risk population of 3, 4 and 5 year olds, those with seemingly invisible handicapps, who would perhaps fail in school and society without special help?
2. Could we involve the local hospitals, medical and social agencies to assist in locating these children and to provide on going services, not only to them, but to their parents and to the project staff as well on a voluntary basis?
3. Could we provide a good diagnostic therapeutic school setting for those children?
4. Could we devise a modus operandi – a curriculum based upon the needs and abilities of a heterogeneous handicapped population of 3, 4 and 5 year olds?
5. Would there be a significant or measurable change because of our intervention?
6. When it is time for the child to leave the program, would it be possible to place him in the setting best suited for his needs without any loss of school time?
7. Could we locate and train the staff necessary to carry out this proposal?
8. Would we be able to cut across all of the red tape of the school system, state and federal funding sources, hospital and agency affiliations and meet our stated objectives?

In the following section we shall try to delineate how we set out to achieve these goals.

History and Rationale

In 1966, calls began coming to the New York City Bureau of Speech Improvement seeking help for children in the city Head Start classes who were exhibiting severe speech and language problems. A committee of speech teachers who had experience with this age level was formed to explore the situation. As a result of testing, some 3,600 Head Start children, a demonstration project involving individualized speech therapy and classroom demonstration in language stimulation was initiated in various boroughs. It was decided that many of the children needed more than individualized speech therapy and that they would benefit from a small special class placement rather than a large Head Start group. A pilot project consisting of 2 half day nursery classes was established in Montefiore Hospital with the Speech and Hearing Clinic and the New York City Board of Education Division of Speech Improvement. It soon became clear that speech and language stimulation was only part of the answer and that most of the difficulties the children exhibited were due to other developmental, physical, and/or emotional problems. Simultaneously, a group of experienced teachers and guidance personnel who had worked with the emotionally disturbed population were designing a project to encompass the younger child and include medical affiliations. The two groups combined and the Readiness Program For Disadvantaged Pre School Children With Exceptional Learning Disabilities was launched. The basic philosophy was to provide a good early childhood school setting with input from interdisciplinary teams on an on going basis.

Criteria For Selection

To be considered for admission to the program the applicant must present evidence of the following:
1. Residency in New York City

*Laura Shapiro, M.A., Principal, Readiness Program, Bd. of Education, N.Y.C.

Susan Shapiro, M.A. Doctoral Candidate, Yeshiva Univ. School Psychologist, Educational Assistant, Readiness Program.

2. Be between the ages of 3 years 9 months to 7 years
3. Be Toilet trained
4. Ambulatory
5. Manifestation of developmental lag in speech, language, emotional adjustment, and/or perceptual difficulties.

Referral Procedure

These children may be referred to the program from many sources, the hospital teams and clinics, community and social agencies, school personnel, courts, private physicians, parents, the evaluation and placement units of the New York City Board of Education, day care, head start centers, etc. The referral requests a description of the child's problems with appropriate records, if available, such as the developmental history, medical, neurological, psychiatric, pyschological, and speech and hearing reports. These are sent to the Readiness guidance personnel who evaluate the material, contact the referee, and if the child is appropriate, select the class location.

The child is seen by the teacher for pretesting and to determine which session would most fit his needs If the child has been referred by the class' back-up medical team, or agency, a case conference would have been held to determine his suitability for the program. Parental knowledge and approval is absolutely required before any records are sent and before the child is considered for placement.

Class Population

The central feature of the Readiness Program is that children are not given diagnostic labels upon entry to the program. The population is heterogenous in that the children display a wide range of medical problems, developmental deficits and specific strengths. An individual prescription teaching program is designed for each child based upon educational testing, observations and medical findings. This is periodically up-dated and reviewed by the team and the teacher.

The kindergarten classes consist of one 2½ hour session in the morning and one 2½ hour session in the afternoon, five times weekly with a maximum of 8 students in each group. The Readiness One classes are 5 hours in length and have a maximum of 10 students. There is a licensed special education teacher and an educational assistant in each class.

Educational Staffing

The present staff consists of the following personnel:

*Due to the N.Y.C. Budget Crisis, as of September 1976, only children of legal school age for handicapped, 4 years 9 months are admitted to the program.

1. A special education principal who is responsible for all aspects of the administration, supervision of teachers, students and ancillary staff.
2. A supervisor who assists the principal with the above matters.
3. Two guidance personnel who coordinate all aspects of referrals and placements of students and interact with the medical and social agency teams.
4. One teacher trainer/curriculum developer who assists the teachers with problems of classroom management and curriculum.
5. One teacher coordinator (Bridge to School Program) who implements the Title I proposal in the area of reading and mathematical skills.
6. Seventy-one classroom teachers of special education who work directly with the pupil population:
7. Sixty-two educational assistants who work with students in the classroom.
8. Secretarial staff.
9. Parent advisory council.

The teachers selected for the program have varying backgrounds in the areas of teaching the emotionally disturbed, the neurologically impaired, the speech and language impaired, the retarded, as well as early childhood training and experience. In addition to being carefully selected, they were given extensive in service training and preparation. The training is continuous.

The educational assistants (90%) of whom are college graduates are preparing to enter the teaching or an allied profession. A high proportion of these assistants are male. They were deliberately selected due to the fact that over 85% of our student population is male and most of the teaching staff is female.

Classrooms

Classroom sites were chosen in the general proximity of the medical affiliations. This was to allow for unrestricted observations of pupils in the classroom setting and communication by team members. Several of the classrooms are located in the hospitals. One is in a day care facility, a converted 3 room apartment, one is in a local university, and the rest are in public schools.

Early childhood classrooms have been modified to accommodate the Readiness population. The rooms have been arranged to facilitate both group and individual instruction.

Curriculum

The curriculum designed is based on several factors:
1. *Modification of time allotments* - It has been found that most of the children entering the program have extremely short attention spans. Therefore, the time allotted to each activity (see activity

chart) remains flexible, allowing for the increases in the child's ability to attend to the task.

2. *Initial level of various curricula areas* - It is based on the teacher observations, pre testing, and the child's adaption to the classroom setting.

3. *Individual long and short range goals* - These are required for each child in each aspect of instruction. This individualization is reflected in the teacher's weekly and daily lesson plans

4. *Teacher Creativity* - The teacher is given the freedom to utilize individual skills and talents in the formulation of the lessons, these include music, art, dance, yoga, and crafts.

5. *The Approach* - The teaching approach is basically eclectic depending on the training of the teacher, the orientation of the medical personnel and the needs of the students.

6. *Content* - The curriculum content parallels that of most early childhood classrooms. However, special emphasis is given to language acquisition and expression, body awareness, social interaction and the setting of limits.

7. *Curriculum supervision* - Assistance in planning and selection of materials is provided by the curriculum coordinator/teacher trainer.

A TYPICAL READINESS KINDERGARTEN DAY

TIME	ACTIVITY
9:00—9:05	Arrival, clothing, greetings
9:05—9:45	Work-play period – interest corners (language, perception; motor, social)
9:45—10:00	Group language lesson (expressive, speech improvement)
10:00—10:15	Gross motor training
10:15—10:30	Snack
10:30—10:45	Fine Motor Training
10:45—11:00	Listening Skills (receptive language)
11:00—11:15	Sensory training
11:15—11:30	Cleanup, review, dismissal

A similar format will be followed for afternoon groups (12:30—3:00). It is important to note that the schedule will vary from center to center depending upon the approach of the team assigned and the nature of the learning deprivation of the children. The attached activity chart gives a detailed description of classroom curriculum.

The following chart demonstrates the content, in terms of skills necessary for a child to function in school, of the activities and experiences which will be planned for the children in the preschool program. Task analysis will continue as more and more experiences are planned.

CURRICULUM CHART

Activity Period	Reading Content	Mathematics Content
Large manipulative objects	vocabulary expansion, e.g., big, little, long, house, build fall, under, over, etc.	size, shape, weight, length, width, direction, comparison
	language development; naming, description of sensations	quantity, measures
Kinesthetic materials	color, number words; eye-hand coordination; visual memory; analysis-synthesis; problem solving; visual discriminations	shapes, size, one-to-one correspondence, counting
Group interaction	role playing, social language, social concepts, naming, labeling, classification, comprehension, vocab. develop.	counting, one-to-one correspondence, size, money "pair of shoes", sequence, time concepts
Sensory experiences	language stimulation, color, feeling words	form discrimination, direction (up-down), likeness and difference in shape
Oral expression	relating experiences, relating self to events, object naming, picture identification, pictures are representative of objects, following directions, learning rhymes, understand gestures	rote counting, number concepts, sequence, time concepts
Auditory training	auditory memory, attention span, information processing, following directions, sound differentiation	number stories, critical thinking, sequence
Health education via food	language stimulation, vocabulary building, following directions	liquid and solid measure, one-to-one correspondence, math concepts (more, less, etc.) making judgments, estimating
Gross motor training	spatial orientation, body image, laterality, directionality, motor patterning	concepts (size and shape), (up and down), (high and low) problem solving
Fine motor training	eye-hand coordination, visual tracking, visual constancy, form discrimination figure-ground perception	properties of size, shape, problem solving; judgments
Books	appreciation of literature listening skills, getting ideas, using picture clues, learning to retell story	illustration of concepts, counting books
Environmental experience (walks, trips)	language stimulation, vocabulary, action words	environmental shapes, time concepts, distance concept

Medical Affiliations

The heads of medical departments were contacted personally by the guidance liaison during the initial phase of the program. The response to the request that we co-jointly sponsor a diagnostic therapeutic nursery classroom was positive. The medical teams saw this as an opportunity to place their patients in an educational setting to which they would have access to observe and advise on an on-going basis.

Table of Affiliations

The composition of the medical teams vary. They are interdisciplinary in nature and usually consists of a pediatrician, psychologist, psychiatrist, neurologist, social worker, speech and hearing therapist, and in some cases an occupational therapist. Usually one member of the team acts as primary liaison with the Readiness staff. Their participation is voluntary and on an unpaid basis. The function of the medical team is to:

MEDICAL AND AGENCY AFFILIATONS
OF THE READINESS PROGRAM

MANHATTAN

Babies Hospital
Dept. of Pediatric Neurology

Mt. Sinai Medical Center
Dept. of Child Psychiatry

Metropolitan Hospital
Dept of Child Psychiatry

New York Hospital
Dept. of Pediatrics, Language
& Speech Pathology

Gouverneur Hospital –
Dept. of Pediatrics

Harlem Hospital –
Dept. of Child Psychiatry

Roosevelt Hospital –
Dept. of Child Psychiatry

QUEENS

Elmhurst General Hospital
Dept. of Speech Pathology
& Audiology, Dev. Evalu.
Clinic & Neuromuscular Cl.

Queens General Hospital
Hearing & Speech, Children's
Rehab., Child Psychology &
Pediatrics.
Center for Child Development,
Children's Clinic

QUEENS

Booth Memorial Hospital
Dept of Pediatrics

STATEN ISLAND

Staten Island Development
Disabilities & St. Vincent's Hospital
Dept. of Speech & Hearing
Staten Island Mental Health

BROOKLYN

Brookdale Hospital
Bruner Developmental
Disabilities Center

Cumberland Hospital
Dept. of Child Psychiatry

Maimonides Developmental Center
Children's Program, Developmental
Center

Brooklyn Psychiatric Clinic
Canarsie Mental Health Center

Jewish Board of Guardians
Coney Island Mental Health Center

Downstate-Kings County Hospital
Dept. of Child Psychiatry,
Developmental Evaluation Clinic

Kingsbrook Jewish Medical Center
Learning Disabilities Unit,
Division of Clinical Psychology

BROOKLYN

Brooklyn Jewish Hospital
Dept. of Pediatrics

BRONX

Lincoln Hospital
Children's Evaluation &
Rehabilitation Clinic

Rousso Comprehensive Health Center
Dept of Pediatrics

Fordham Hospital
Child Developmental Center

Morrisania City Hospital
Dept. of Speech Pathology

Rose F. Kennedy
Dept. of Psychology,
Dept. of Speech Pathology

Jacobi Hospital
Dept. of Speech Pathology

Einstein College of Medicine
Children's Evaluation
& Rehabilitation Center

Ittleson Center
Dept. of Psychiatry

Montefiore Hospital
Division of Child Psychiatry
& Speech & Hearing Center

1. Refer cases
2. Participate in case conferences of the children.
3. Provide necessary medical services.
4. Provide evaluations and recommendations for future class placements.
5. Advise the teachers in aspects of behavioral management.
6. Counsel parents.

Since each class is the result of the unique interaction between the medical team and the teaching staff, no two units are alike in pupil composition and/or orientation.

SPECIAL COMPONENTS OF THE READINESS PROGRAM

Bridge to School (Reading and Mathematics)

This component provides individualized and small group instructions in the areas of reading and mathematics. It serves a portion of the Readiness population, the Title I eligibility children, who are deemed ready to profit from such instruction. The 5 itinerant teachers confer with the classroom teachers, observe and pre test the pupils. They then prepare a program for each child selected in both areas. The program is in its 3rd year and the evaluator's findings reported significant gains in the population served.

Speech and Language

Five teachers of Speech Improvement have been added to the staff to provide individualized speech therapy where indicated. They will also give classroom lessons in auditory stimulation, language development and the speech arts.

BiLingual Units

There are 3 bi-lingual (Spanish) Readiness units. One in the Bronx, one in Manhattan, and one in Brooklyn. Children who have little or no working knowledge of English are placed in these units. English is gradually introduced.

In addition to this staff, many members of the Readiness units have a good command of Spanish and its use is encouraged to facilitate learning.

Video

Video tapes have been produced for teacher, medical team, and parent observation. Several tapes were edited for presentation at conventions and workshops. These tapes included detailed studies of particular students which were then presented as illustrative case material at hospital grand rounds. The video tapes proved to be a useful tool in teacher training as well as individual case studies and monitoring of pupil interactions.

Medical Lectures

Another feature of the program has been the inclusion of the Readiness staff members at lectures, meetings and workshops given at the hospitals for the medical personnel. This has enabled the staff to broaden their knowledge in relevant areas of child psychiatry, child neurology and general health care. Provisions are made for the staff to attend and participate at regional professional conferences.

Dissemination of Information

In an effort to stimulate community awareness and participation in the Readiness Program, an active effort was made to disseminate information.

1. Brochures were mailed to all possible referral sources.
2. The staff explained the projects to community groups, local colleges, parent groups, and at Head Start and Day Care Centers.
3. The program was discussed on the local radio station.
4. More formal presentation were made at conventions, colleges, universities, and specialized workshops.

Academic Liaison

Student teachers have been accepted from many of the local colleges and universities. Staff members have been involved in the development of college courses in the area of special education. One Readiness unit is housed in a local university and is equipped with one-way mirrors.

Readiness Program Conferences

The Readiness Program has sponsored three conferences in the past several years to which all medical, community agencies, and educational personnel directly involved with the Readiness Program were invited. The impetus behind the conferences was the desire on the part of the medical teams to meet with each other and to exchange information, ideas and findings. Each conference had a featured guest speaker and several workshops. The workshops included such topics as:

1. Alternate Strategies in Handling the Hyperactive Child.
2. The Differential Diagnosis of the Communication of Aphasic, Autistic, Symbiotic, Deaf and Mentally Retarded Children.
3. Search Battery to Predict Learning Failure at the Pre School Level.
4. Diagnostic & Therapeutic Approaches to Early Intervention.

5. Modes of Parental Participation in the Readiness Program.
6. Clinical Educational Team Functioning with the Readiness Program.
7. How the Board of Education Plans for the Special Child.
8. The Readiness Program - What We Are and What We Do.

Evaluation

In the initial 3 years, the Readiness Program was required to be evaluated by an outside agency. This was to assess the degree to which the stated objectives were met, as well as justify the cost of the program. Each of the evaluation teams recommended that the program not only be continued but expanded, and that all stated objectives had been met.

Funding

The first funding source was a grant under State Urban Education. The amount was increased each year to accommodate more students, staff, and to open more classes. In 1975, the program became an integral part of the Division of Special Education & Pupil Personnel Services. Most of the cost is now paid for from tax levy funds. A small portion of the cost is subsidized by Title VI B - Basic Education For Unserved Needs.

Placement Procedures

When a child is ready to leave the program, a determination is made as to the appropriate placement. The procedure is as follows:
1. All necessary information, as well as a recommendation is obtained from the medical team.
2. The teacher completes an educational evaluation.
3. The material is reviewed by the guidance personnel and principal. It is then sent to the N.Y.C. Board of Education Evaluation & Placement Center. They review the material, see the child, discuss the placement with the parent and the newly formed committees of the handicapped. (see Table 1 which shows the disposition of Readiness children from 1971 through 1976)

Expansion of Program

During the 1975-76 academic year and in consultation with the Executive Director of the Division of Special Education & Pupil Personnel Services, and various special education bureau heads, it was decided that most children in the Readiness kindergarten should be continued for another year in this undifferentiated setting. This decision was hailed by the medical and social agencies as well as by the parents and the Readiness staff. The growth of the children in the various cognitive, social and emotional areas during the initial year of their stay in the Readiness Program had far exceeded our expectations. Another year was needed in this diagnostic setting to ascertain which type of class would best suit their needs for the next portion of their school career.

Thirty (30) Readiness One Classes were open in September 1976 in all boroughs of New York. The day was lengthened to 5½ hours including lunch. (More emphasis is being placed upon the achievement of academic skills, particularly reading and mathematics. (See enclosed schedule) An attempt is being made to include the children in various regular school activities, e.g. assemblies, special events, trips, etc.

The children who were chosen for Readiness One are those whom the teacher and our staff were felt could benefit from an extended day and who were 5 years 9 months of age or older. Placement of children in Readiness One who have not attended Readiness kindergarten must be made by the Evaluation and Placement Bureau.

Conclusion

The Readiness Program has now become a permanent part of the Division of Special Education & Pupil Personnel Services. Our format and use of voluntary medical and social agencies can easily be replicated in all parts of the country.

There are many vital factors which contributed to the success and growth of the program:
1. We have the children at an early age, which is a critical growth period.
2. We have a dedicated and well-trained staff.
3. We have small groups.
4. There is attention paid to the most minute physical disability or ailments.
5. Ongoing, and in some cases daily opportunities for consultation with the clinical team.
6. There is continuous and close parent involvement.
7. There is enough flexibility for the teaching staff to be innovative and creative while keeping the general curriculum and individual goals in mind.
8. There is teacher, parent, team and most important of all, pupil gratification with the program.
9. Encouragement, trust and the freedom to experiment was given by the Executive Director of the Division of Special Education & Pupil Personnel Services to the Program Principal and staff.

Which of the above factors or combination of factors led to the program's growth and success, we don't quite know, but we feel that we must be doing something right!

TABLE I: CATEGORIES OF PLACEMENT OF READINESS GRADUATES*

Classes for:	Jan. '71 June '71	1971 1972	1972 1973	1973 1974	1974 1975	1975 1976
Brain Injured (HC 30 Neurologically Impaired	6	18	35	32	28	32
Emotionally Handicapped (NIEH)				23	23	3
Children With Retarded Mental Development (CRMD)	3	7	18	15	7	15
Classes For Emotionally Handicapped (CEH)		12	34	27	48	13
School For The Deaf	1	1	1	1	1	–
Pre-Placement Program			20	22	26	28
Visually Impaired		1				1
School For Language & Hearing Impaired (P.S. 158)		6	8	21	24	9
Speech Centered Schools			4	9	7	2
State Aid (Private Schools)	3	3	6	8		–
School For Multi-Handicapped			2	2		2
Teacher-Mom Program			5	1	5	9
Hospital School (HC 20)						1
Reg. Kgn. or 1st grade	12	17	30	29	34	16
TOTAL PLACEMENT	24	64	164	190	203	131
Readiness One	Established in Sept. 1976					240
Remained in Readiness Kg.	94	218	135	215	107	266
Total Served in Classes	118	282	299	405	310	729
Screened but not accepted (referred to other sources)	80	86	101	211	95	54

*Approximate

READINESS ONE

DAILY PLAN

9:00 – 9:10	Arrival, clothing, greetings
9:10 – 10:10	Work-play period – interest corners (language, perception, motor, social)
10:10 – 10:30	Group language lesson (expressive, speech improvement)
10:30 – 10:45	Juice – social experience – self-help skills
10:45 – 11:00	Fine Motor Training
11:00 – 11:20	Gross Motor Training
11:20 – 11:45	Listening skills (receptive language)
11:45 – 12:00	Preparation for lunch
12:00 – 12:30	Lunch
12:30 – 1:15	Rest – Library Books – Musical Records
1:15 – 1:30	Sensory Experience
1:30 – 2:00	Clean-up, Evaluation & Review of day, Clothing
2:00	Dismissal

BIBLIOGRAPHY

The following books are recommended readings in the areas of child development and learning disabilities:

Cruickshank, Wm., *The Education of Exceptional Children and Youth*, Prentice-Hall, Englewood Cliffs, N.J., 1967

Curriculum Guide, *Pre Kindergarten and Kindergarten*, Bureau of Curriculum Development, Board of Education, City of New York, 1970

Gessell, Arnold, *The First Five Years of Life*, Harper & Bros., N.Y., 1940

Haeussermann, Elsa, *Developmental Potential of the Pre School Child*, Grune & Stratton, N.Y., 1958

Jedrysek, Klapper, Pope, Wortis, *Psychoeducational Evaluation of the Pre School Child*, A Manual Utilizing the Haeussermann Approach, Grune & Stratton, N.Y., 1972

Kephart, Newell, *The Slow Learner in the Classroom*, Merrill Inc., Ohio, 1960

Myklebust, Helmer & Johnson, Doris, *Learning Disabilities*, Grune & Stratton, N.Y., 1967

Piaget, Jean, *The Origins of Intelligence in Children*, International Universities Press, N.Y., 1952

Valett, Robert E., *The Remediation of Learning Disabilities*, Fearon Publ., Belmont, California, 1967

Chapter 47

An Urban School District Tackles the Problem of Educating Gifted Children in an Early Childhood Setting

Donald Kaplan *

The purpose of this article is to describe the process that took place in one school district of New York City when the question arose: "Are we doing enough for our 4 to 6 year olds with very high academic potential?"

Insofar as the policy and administrative issues are general and not unique to our particular situation, an account of our considerations and decisions may be of value to a district administrator, or the head of a school, wishing to make provisions for children who show indications of being able to learn very rapidly.

As the apple falling for Newton and the steam from the kettle for Watt, a specific experience triggered the interest of our Community Superintendent. A group of outstanding students who attend the specialized high schools of New York City (for students who can do outstanding work in Mathematics and Science) spoke at a City-wide meeting on the topic of improving the education of able children. Without exception the six high school seniors remembered their elementary school experience as boring, and for them, a waste of time. (Ehrlich, 1974)

When asked what they thought would improve matters, they suggested instruction in foreign languages, opportunities to work independently, a curriculum in which they could discover that there were challenges, and that not all learning was easy.

Most of all they wanted to learn at their own pace subject matter that interested them. They did not want to waste time in "busy work" or acquiring facts.

The Superintendent and the writer rode home together after hearing this indictment of how the elementary school program fails to provide for children with superior learning ability. We asked ourselves: "Will the children now in our elementary schools have the same complaints six years from now? Are we offering a challenging and exciting experience in our elementary grades to our most able youngsters?"

At that moment we could not give honest answers. Visits to the twelve K-6 schools in our district yielded several impressions: some schools have classes for superior achievers in grades 4, 5 and 6. Other schools place the children in heterogeneous classes and depend on grouping within the class for instruction in reading and mathematics. Still other schools assign children in classes independently of their reading achievement but schedule reading periods when children report to a group for instruction on the child's level as in the departmental program of high schools.

No school assigned children in the (K-2) lower grades solely on the basis of academic potential. Age, behavior, size were used as criteria.

In our district, as in districts throughout the City, schools offer a program of classes for "Intellectually Gifted Children." These begin in grade 4 and continue through grades 5 and 6. In the junior high schools, the Special Progress classes offer an opportunity for children achieving 2 years above the grade norm in reading, as of grade 6, and 1½ years above in math to complete a 3 year junior high school course in 2 years. An alternative program provides an enriched (more foreign language, math and science) program in 3 years.

It was easy to see that the uncovered area was the Early Childhood years. At grade 4 a child achieving a year or more above his grade average in reading and math would be considered for an IGC class. If none exist in his local school, the District Office will arrange a transfer to the nearest school with an IGC class. As a result of this district practice we felt less concern that the upper elementary grade children with high achievement were not being challenged.

Our focus became the kindergarten, first, second and third grade pupils. Were any of them then being bored? Were any of them wasting opportunities to learn as much as they could that would be useful to them and to society? We obviously did not know. Visiting classes showed some children who could read fluently being given a sequence of phonic drills. A few children in kindergarten and grade one could read as high as third and fourth grade at the start of the school year. What should we do? Place them in a higher grade for the entire day? Place them in an upper grade for reading, or retain them all day in their age-appropriate class for social reasons and ask the teacher to provide individual instruction based on the high achievement of the child?

The last approach is not feasible in schools with large numbers of children who come from homes with socio-economic conditions unfavorable to academic achievement.

---

*Donald Kaplan, Director of Pupil Personnel Services, Community School District #18, Brooklyn, New York.

Teachers tend to use their time with the low achieving children feeling that the most advanced group can progress on their own.

(The solution to providing for the variation in academic achievement in mathematics in School District 18, Brooklyn, is discussed in Garner, et al) (1974)

In some instances teachers may consider using the advanced pupils to help the less advanced readers but this is a questionable solution to the needs of either group.

We looked into the literature and asked our colleagues in other districts for their suggestions as to how they dealt with the problem of challenging high potential children.

THE STATE OF ART: Educating the Gifted & Talented

The Council for Exceptional Children, under contract with the U.S. Office of Education, has made easily available through ERIC a great deal of literature concerning the education of the Gifted & Talented. The ERIC summaries (Boston 1975, pp. 39-40) proved valuable in helping us plan our programs.

The other chief resource that contributed to our thinking and decision making was the National/State Leadership Training Institute on the Gifted & Talented. It was funded by the U.S.O.E., Office of Gifted & Talented in 1972 to meet the recommendation of the Commissioner's Report to Congress (Marland, 1972) that national leadership training institutes be held and a network of consultation and communication be started.

The authors have attended institutes conducted by the N/S LTI G/T and feel that the contribution of the LTI's has been invaluable.

It became clear as we developed our program that we had to choose between two basic approaches: "pull-out" vs. "add-on." In the first case, the children are removed from their regular classes into separate classes in a central location. In the "add-on" approach, their curriculum is enriched using additional instructional materials during special periods each week. A partial "pull-out" approach would involve a resource teacher with special training in working with the Gifted, who would assemble a group from each level and give them special attention for one hour or more each week.

No conclusive studies had been done with 4, 5 and 6 year old children. We had to decide based upon our background of administrative experience and personal value judgments.

Factors we had to consider included: transportation costs, the number of children eligible in each grade, public opinion, staff readiness, etc. We offer our decision fully aware that other administrators will have to reach practical decisions based on the realities of their local situation.

The decision in our district was made easier because of the following:

(1) In past years, 1950 to 1965, one of our thirteen elementary schools had been the designated school in the Borough of Brooklyn to house classes for Gifted children. Youngsters found to have high IQ's (over 130) had been transferred with parental permission to a special track of classes, where French and typing were taught as well as the basic elementary school subjects. This program was halted when the funds for the experiment stopped; but the tradition in the school and the receptivity of the staff remained high. Foreign language instruction and typing were continued for as many children as imaginative scheduling would allow.

(2) A large city school district offers a population of 1.500 to 2.000 children on each grade level. If several districts help in the recruiting for classes to be located centrally, there is a population of 5,000 to 10,000 children on each grade level from which to select.

(3) Transportation factors within an urban center of high population density are such that a 30 minute school bus trip includes most of the target area.

(4) Within our school district, are a number of children whose native tongue is other than English and an even greater number of children from low socio-economic status homes. It would be necessary for the early childhood teachers to emphasize language skills; speaking correctly, listening for retention and comprehension, decoding, etc.

As an aid to making this vital process more rational and manageable, District 18 developed the approach described in (Garnor, 1974). Teacher designed curriculum, teacher written instructional objectives and tests based on mastery of these objectives highlight the program.

In view of the heavy instructional demands made on our teachers we felt it more desirable to "pull-out" our target children and place them in separate classes for the whole day. Of course, they would eat with, use the library with, play games with, and attend assembly programs with the mainstream of the school; but their basic educational experience would be with other Gifted children.

We felt that just as children with special physical conditions are educated in specially equipped rooms and with specially trained teachers, children with special mental strengths deserve rooms, curriculum experiences and teachers trained to help them reach their fullest potential.

The criticism that such a program is contributing to elitism and is undemocratic seems to us to be invalid. We feel each child is entitled to the kind and amount of education that will develop him or her to his or her's highest degree of development.

School District 18 is the center for classes for the Mentally Retarded, Physically Handicapped and Emotionally Handicapped, as well as pre-school children with developmental learning problems.

We needed no persuasion to agree to conduct classes for children with exceptional academic promise. The argument of elitism did not ring true in our schools where for years the settings, the curricula and the teaching strategies have been adopted for the unique learning strengths and deficits of the individual pupils.

Prior to any specific arrangement for starting the class, preparation was carefully made to build public support for the program. Preliminary discussions were held with the School Board and their approval was given to go ahead. Key persons in the community who strongly influence public opinion met with the Superintendent and Director of the Program to share information and to answer all questions and concerns. Most of the community persons consulted agreed with the idea of starting such a program in the district provided that this would not mean overcrowding in any school, diverting available teachers or money to a special group and provided that children in District 18 would have an equal chance for admission to the program.

In 1977, in view of the greatly reduced budget which means larger classes and little, if any, supportive services for the teacher, our 1973 decision for a "pull-out" program seems even wiser.

Recruitment & Selection of Pupils

We were handicapped because we had no idea as to the size of the target population. Until 1964 group intelligence tests were given in the public schools of New York City in grades 1, 3, and 6. The practice was stopped because it was felt that the test results were not accurate for the increasingly large numbers of non-White pupils entering the City system. One result feared was that teachers would assume the results in grade 1 were valid and then not expect more from a Black or Puerto Rican or economically disadvantaged pupil. For low socio-economic status pupils the tests were thought to be inappropriate because of differences between the language and experiences of the populations to be tested on the one hand and the population on which the test was standardized on the other. There is no doubt that some children did poorly on the group measures used because of cultural factors and differences in language experiences in the home. And probably some teachers regarded the first grade mental age measure as fixed and definitive with a self-fulfilling prophecy of failure as the result. (The child is not able to learn up to grade norms therefore I won't have to teach him to achieve up to grade norms.)

Since then no replacement test considered culture fair or not has been introduced into the New York City system. We have no idea how high the incidence is of hidden underachievement, or the number of children who are working at grade level but who can do higher level work. We cannot compare the Mental Age of the child with his Grade Equivalent to see if he is working below expectation.

As a result, teachers have no objective index of expecta-

tion for their children. Children reading on or even above grade in reading and math may be capable of significantly higher achievement, but the teacher and the parents do not know this. (This is a salient argument for criterion reference testing and instruction by objectives.)

In our survey we had found that in our classes for the Gifted above age six were predominantly White, middle-class children. Yet the very bright, culturally different child who finds himself in a regular class often faces extreme difficulty in learning up to his potential.

Gallagher (1964) relates an apocryphal anecdote of a ghetto youngster, Sam, who showed his enthusiasm about an assignment. After school he was confronted by five male classmates, "Hey, Sam, how come you're sucking up to the teach? We don't like guys actin' too smart, do we?" (p. 368)

There is no research data offered to show that peer pressure serves to reduce expression of superior academic ability but it is not inconceivable that the imaginary incident illustrates the problem of a gifted ghetto youngster when he first shows his superior ability.

The research of Frierson cited in Gallagher (1964) found that among two gifted samples, one of upper socio-economic status and the other of lower:

"One of the major efforts to try to answer the question about the characteristics of talented children was conducted by Frierson (1965), who studied four groups of children: two gifted samples, one of upper socio-economic status and the other of low socio-economic status; and two average samples of the same characteristics. A wide variety of personality tests, interest tests, and home information data was collected; comparisons were then made to see whether the differences among the four samples were due more to ability or more to difference in socio-economic status. The primary difference between the two gifted groups from different socio-economic backgrounds was found to be in the dimension of interests and attitudes. There were no major differences between the groups on physical characteristics and few differences obtained on the personality tests. The upper-status gifted spent a great deal more time and had a great deal more interest in reading in recreational hours whereas the lower-status gifted seemed more interested in action and competitive team sports.

A second major question was: Were there differences between the lower-status gifted and the lower-status average student in the same way that differences have been found between the middle-class gifted and average students from comparable backgrounds? Some of the results suggested that the lower-status gifted were more likely to play musical instruments, to aspire to higher-status occupations, read the news sections of the newspaper, and so forth." (p. 369)

Gallagher cited other research that showed gifted children from lower-class homes to have more tension in the family and to be performing substantially lower than their predicted achievement levels. We decided that in our heterogeneous district, locating and placing children from cultural minorities would be a prime concern.

Once our interest in the question of educating the gifted became known, the head of the City-wide program began discussions with our Superintendent towards the goal of establishing a model class in one of our schools to serve the entire borough of Brooklyn. A supportive arm of the central administration of the City school system, the Office of Educational Research, had set up a separate staff and office to focus on the gifted. This was called the Gifted Child Study Project under the coordination of Dr. Virginia Z. Ehrlich. A private source, The Vincent Astor Foundation had offered funds to start classes for 4½ to 5½ year olds on a pilot basis in several boroughs if the school districts would agree to fund them after the first two or three years. (Ehrlich, 1974)

The considerations our school district entertained were: Who selects the children? What standards? What processes? Who selects and supervises the teachers? Who determines curriculum?

In regard to pupil selection our considerations were: The process of selection had to be objective, without bias and such that it could be defended in court if need be. It had to be completely impartial and insulated from political or social pressure. No child should be in the program who did not meet the definition formulated. The process had to be without cost to the families so that the non-middle class pupils would not be at a disadvantage.

We concluded that pupil selection could not be an in-house procedure. Our own staff would be under great pressure. If psychology time was taken for testing then the children with other problems would be deprived of this clinical resource. We thought of the local colleges with Educational Clinics as agencies to approach to arrange cooperation. They would be impartial, professional and not sensitive to the pressure of important personages in our community.

Before we could proceed with any such discussion an offer was made by the Astor Class Program to provide us with a "complete package": selection of pupils, supervision of teachers, operation of classes. This would be done by them with liaison from the district for a period of two to three years. After the program was underway, the district would assume full financial and operational responsibility.

Before we can proceed some technical and definition questions need be discussed. We have so far used vague terms—superior, high potential, gifted, rapid-learning. Just what do we mean by these words?

We are probably familiar with the range of definitions of intelligence. "Intelligence is what the intelligence tests measure."

Intelligence is the ability to solve problems, to adapt.

Similarly, there is a range of definitions of gifted. The top 1% on the Stanford-Binet.

One who is more fully human.

Fortunately, we reached a consensus after reading Martinson (1974) and also the Marland volumes. (1972) We agreed to define as gifted those children who were so far above their classmates in achievement that they could not be taught effectively in the same class. That is, the gifted child was one who would either be wasting his time or taking up an unfair share of the teacher's time until he is in an instructional setting that enables him to function well with other children.

Obviously, this is a matter for judgment and admits of subjectivity. How can we determine whether a 4½ year old is wasting time in kindergarten? How do we detect potential? What does functioning well mean?

The selection process of the Astor Program for our district hinges on personal and social maturity on the one hand and intellectual ability as measured by the Stanford-Binet on the other. The child is interviewed as are the parents. As least two different professionals see the child to appraise his readiness to join a group of rapid children, ages 4½ to 5½.

They ask: Is he free of personal reactions that would interfere with both his and the groups activities?

Does the youngster communicate readily and respond to the communication of others?

What is his attention span and toleration of frustration? Will he delay expression of impulse on an age appropriate level?

In the intellectual area vocabulary development, ability to generalize and to solve problems are measured by the individual intelligence test given by an experienced psychometrist.

For those children who are already reading a wide range inventory of their word recognition is administered.

Drawings and interview data are evaluated for indications of personality trait development.

A child who is able to leave his parents, work in a group, respond to and use language clearly and whose intellectual functioning is in the top 1% of his age mates throughout the country would be considered for the Astor Class Program.

Our district had, to a large extent, passed the responsibility for defining the target and selecting the children onto another organization. Several unresolved questions remained for us in the district:

(1) Would the Black, Haitian, Puerto Rican and other disadvantaged children in our schools or about to enter our schools be tested fairly by the above procedure? Is the Binet valid for the non-middle class population?

(2) Should we not be concerned with a larger group than the top 1%? Should we aim at the top 2 or 3 or 5%?

We did agree emphatically with the focus on 4½ to 5½ year olds with provisions for adding on at least one class each year at the bottom. We did agree with the need to use some objective instrument rather than a check sheet or committee vote as the final selection step.

A search of the literature (Marland, 1972, Martinson, 1974, Gallagher, 1975, p. 27) shows that several states have used the Binet or the WISC with a legislatively defined score, usually 125 or higher. Legally these methods have been upheld.

Our data to date does not convince us that the use of the Stanford-Binet as an individual intelligence test sets up a bias against minority youngsters.

Professionally, we had to ask ourselves, are there any better methods available in regard to locating potential ability among our minority propulation? Were we reaching all gifted children?

An analysis of the number of minority children accepted as compared to the number of non-minority children accepted would need other data that is not available to us such as the number of gifted in the two populations.

Because of the possibility of minority exclusion our district submitted two grant proposals (that were funded) which enabled us to conduct an extensive campaign among Haitian, Spanish speaking and non-White families to ask parents, neighbors and community people to nominate children of high academic promise. The following guidelines were printed in the Spanish and French local newspapers as well as the largest circulation daily newspaper in New York.

As a help to determine whether a child is academically gifted, Dr. Willard Abraham, Chairman of the Department of Special Education at Arizona State University, constructed a giftedness checklist. Some of the items included are:

1. Started to walk and talk before the so-called average child does. While still very young, demonstrated the ability to put words and phrases together.
2. May be somewhat above average for his or her chronological age, in height, weight, physique, and endurance, and in specific measurements like breadth of shoulders, muscular strength, and lung development.
3. Can win rave notices from parents by performing, though not necessarily from a captive audience of visitors! Unusual poise may be one of the first indications of giftedness in some children.
4. Demonstrated by an early interest in time. Talked about yesterday-today-tomorrow, days of the week, then and now, calendars and clocks, at an early age. Showed an awareness of time and relationships.

5. Has a vocabulary beyond other children of the same age or grade, and uses and understands the words in reading, writing, and speaking.
6. Asks questions because he or she really "wants to know," and demonstrates that fact by the later use of information acquired through verbal curiosity.

Parents were surprisingly accurate. Only 2 children out of the 111 who were tested by the author were more than 1 standard deviation away from the cut-off point for consideration.

In addition, all the kindergarten, nursery school teachers and day care workers in the district and surrounding area were given a check sheet and to nominate the most able children in their groups.

When compared with other children in the kindergarten, which of yours pupils possess, to a marked degree, some of the following characteristics? Be particularly observant of the youngest children in the class and of bilingual youngsters. Do not exclude any child because of a speech defect.

(1) Has unusually good vocabulary.
(2) Has ideas which are often very original in one or more areas (i.e., block play, free activities, art, rhythms, sharing.)
(3) Is alert, keenly observant; responds quickly.
(4) Has an unusually good memory.
(5) Has a long attention span.
(6) Recognizes, on his own, some words in books on the browsing table.
(7) Uses longer sentences.
(8) Reasons things out, thinks clearly, recognizes relationships, comprehends meanings. '
(9) Is curious about many activities and places outside immediate environment and/or experience.
(10) Is a leader in several kinds of activities. Is able to influence others to work toward goals.
(11) Sometimes appears to be overly active; often looking for new things to do.
(12) May find ingenious methods of getting his own way, or escaping punishment for circumventing rules.
(13) Has outstanding talent in a special area(s) such as art, music, rhythms, dramatics (indicate area(s) of talent.)

We are still in the process of screening children for the classes.

Once a pool of children is assembled we interview the parents and the children (in their native tongue) to get the developmental history. Children who walk and talk early, who have their first teeth early, and exhibit other evidence of precocious physical development will be tested further.

Once a child is nominated, the following takes place:

If he or she is in a day care center, or nursery school, or class of any kind, his teacher is asked to provide information about his ability to follow directions, to remember things, to solve problems and an appraisal of the child's ability to use language will be made by a member of our staff.

We have not yet reached a decision as to what IQ cut-off point we will use, we do plan to continue with the Stanford-Binet as one part of the entrance process.

In a perfect experimental design we would probably expose all children to the curriculum and teachers of the project. Those who are keeping up (able to function and seem to be enjoying it) would be deemed to be gifted.

In our less than perfect world it is not feasible to place all children in the program. Choices have to be made—some children admitted, some rejected. Our concern is to make every effort to consider as many potentially eligible children as possible, not to keep any possible child out of consideration. Our classes now include 99 children aged 4-7.

Teacher Selection

The Astor Program report (Ehrlich, 1974) describes the process.

Criteria for selecting teachers were quite flexible. They were based on experience, judgment, guides provided in the literature and by the New York City Board of Education, and were determined by the needs and goals of the Astor Program. Basically, these were the guidelines followed:

(1) A New York City Board of Education license was required, or passing of the National Teacher Examination.

(2) Favorable attitude toward gifted children.

(3) Have a warm, stable personality, more than the usual amount of energy, an intellectual curiosity, must be enthusiastic and able to inspire pupils to greater achievement.

(4) Evidence of superior intellect.

(5) Broad range of interests and skills.

(6) Experience with early childhood classes and/or with several levels of teaching.

(7) Willingness to undertake the many allied assignments required in this pioneer effort.

(8) Educational background reflecting a variety of interests and fields of specialization.

In situations where two professionals were assigned to one class, efforts were made to balance temperaments (level of energy, "outgoingness", musical ability, artistic strength, etc.) This was done in regard to teachers and in 1976-77 when paraprofessionals were used, matching one teacher and one paraprofessional as a team for the two new Level 1 Classes.

It would be an exercise in lip service to pretend that all teachers are capable of providing for the gifted population any more than that all teachers can be effective with Brain Injured or Mentally Retarded. At first, it probably seems easier to teach those children who learn quickly. A reading of the section on Curriculum, which appears later in this paper, should dispell this misconception.

By resisting pressure to select teachers strictly on the basis of seniority, we were able to select an excellent staff for our program. We plan to use videotapes to facilitate the exchange of ideas and experience among the project teachers in the different schools.

Curriculum Development

The generalization is heard among educators concerned with curriculum for the gifted that the emphasis should be on process not content. Pupils should not focus on the names of the presidents or vice-presidents but rather the process by which they are selected. The meaning of the data should be more important than the data itself.

The underlying assumptions are that the gifted child will acquire the facts as they are needed. What should be developed in school in a deliberate, planned sequence is a mastery of the tools of learning and thinking.

The Bloom classification scheme (1971) describes, in the Cognitive Domain, the following:

(1) Knowledge (on the lowest level) remembering previously learned material.

(2) Comprehension: Grasp meaning of material.

(3) Application: Ability to use learned materials in new and concrete situations; rules, laws, concepts.

(4) Analysis: Break down material into its component parts so its organizational structure may be understood; content and structure must be understood.

(5) Synthesis: Put parts together to form a new whole, a unique communication (speech, plan, poem).

(6) Evaluation: Ability to judge value of material for given purpose; to be based on definite criteria.

Reading and mathematical skills, use of books and measures, expressive skills, use of symbols, working in groups, critical thinking and sharing—these become the goals.

"As the means for learning the content becomes the vehicle for the student to acquire and/or develop specific skills." (Kaplan, 1974)

Dr. Ehrlich (1974) and the staff of the Astor Program developed a four-faceted curriculum for the 4½ to 5½ year old gifted that concretizes the above goals:

(1) Who am I? The Child in His Time Space. The topic explores the child's identity in relation to himself, to his family, peers, co-workers, immediate social contacts, and also in relation to those who have lived before him and will come after him. It is a view of man in his social, sociological, historical space.

(2) Where Am I? The Child in His Geographical Space. This topic explores the child's geograph-

ical location, in terms of his classroom, school, home, neighborhood, city, state, nation, and the universe.

(3) What am I? The Child in His Environmental Space. This topic explores the natural environment of plants and animals, and the child's interdependence with all living things.

(4) Why am I? The Child in His Physical Space. This topic explores the interdependence of the child with the physical constants of his universe: chemical relationships, physical laws, mathematical equations, etc.

Around these themes are integrated the basic skills of reading, math, scientific concepts, social studies concepts, art and music. Opportunities are made for in-depth exploration by individual children at their interest and ability level.

An inspection of the classroom for the Level 1 children, 4½ to 5½, shows a room with:

(1) A clock so the children can tell and record the time, plan their day by consulting the clock. (Their day included 10 minute segments.)

(2) A thermometer so the temperature could be read and recorded.

(3) Signs indicating the North, South, East and

ASTOR PROGRAM

Daily Schedule

Time	Monday	Tuesday	Wednesday	Thursday	Friday
8:50	Arrival - Discussion and Planning				
9:10	Science/ Art	Social Studies/ Cooking	Mathematics/ Art	Science/ Music	Social Studies/ Mathematics
9:40	Clean-up and Snack				
10:10	Language Arts: S.R.A., Storytelling, Current Events, etc.				
10:40	Physical Activities				
11:10	Evaluation and Discussion of Activities				
11:40	Preparation for Lunch				
11:50	Lunch				
12:20	Clean-up				
12:30	Rest period: Quiet Activities				
1:00	Workshop: Special Projects Dramatics - Puppetry - Tape Recordings - Library New Centers of Interest - Newspaper Neighborhood Walk - Arts and Craft Projects				
1:45	Clean-Up and Departure				
2:00	Dismissal				
Breaks:	Aide 10:40—11:40	Teacher 11:40—12:20	Teacher 12:20—1:10		

ASTOR PROGRAM - GIFTED CHILD STUDIES

LESSON PLANS: _____

School _____   Week of _____

PUPIL GROUP: _____

Broad Goals: (2 columns)

Thinking Skills (2 columns)

Objectives (List and number)

DAY	ACTIVITY	OBJECTIVE
Monday		
Tuesday		
Wednesday		
Thursday		
Friday		

Textbooks, Workbooks, etc.

Resource Materials

Correlation With Other Curriculum Activities

Notes and Outcomes

Teachers _____   _____

West sides of their room so that the children would have precise orientation in describing place.

(4) A pupil prepared printed news chart or journal that told in the words of the pupils their plans for the day, their experiences of the day before and after school and their chief interests.

The vocabulary level of the chart and in the various printed charts throughout the rooms is quite high. I saw words such as "immaculate", "density", "pentagon" and heard them used correctly by the 5 year olds.

The daily schedule on pages 243 and 244 will give some idea of the deliberate effort made to prevent wasting time. The format of the teacher's lesson plan shows the concern for development of thinking skills.

Our school district has been committed to providing an education for every child which takes into account their individual needs, learning styles and abilities. Our success in developing a program for gifted young children is due largely to community involvement from the outset, commitment of school administrators, and many hours of research and planning. We are certain that given a similar commitment, any community can provide for gifted youngsters in a manner suited to their particular resources.

REFERENCES

Boston, Bruce O., *Gifted and Talented—Developing Elementary and Secondary School Programs* - Reston, Virginia: The Council for Exceptional Children - 1975

Bell, Terrel H., United States Commissioner of Education Policy Statement on Gifted and Talented Education, October 7, 1975

Coffey, Kay; Ginsberg, Gina; Lockhart, Carrol; McCartney, DeLois; Nathan, Carol; Wood Keith *Parents Speak on Gifted and Talented Children* Ventura, California: Ventura County Superintendent of Schools Office January, 1976

Coordinating Office for Regional Resource Centers *Non-biased Assessment of Minority Group Children with bias toward none.*, Lexington, Kentucky: CORRC

Dr. Ehrlich, Virginia Z. - *The Astor Program Progress Report*, New York, New York: Gifted Child Studies - June, 1974

Gallagher, James J. *Teaching the Gifted Child* - 2nd Edition. Boston, Massachusetts: Allyn and Bacon, Inc. 1964

Garner, Harvey - Anger, Milton - Trigg, Wayne - *Instructional Support System* in Innovations in Education, A Doctorate Association of New York Educators Series, Dubuque, Iowa: Kendall/Hunt Publishing Company - 1974

Goldberg, Miriam L., *Research on the Talented*, New York: Bureau of Publications, 1965.

Gowan, John Curtis, *Educating the Ablest*, Itasca, Illinois: F.E. Peacock Publishers, Inc., 1971 (pp. 155-160)

Kaplan, Sandra N. *Providing Programs for the Gifted and Talented*, Reston, Virginia: The Council for Exceptional Children, November, 1975.

Marland, S. - *Education of the Gifted & Talented*, Washington, D.C. - Report to the Congress of the United States by the U.S. Commissioner of Education and background papers submitted to the U.S. Office of Education - 1972

Martinson, R. *The Identification of the Gifted and Talented* Los Angeles, California - National/State Leadership Training Institute of the Gifted & Talented - 1973

Martinson, Ruth A. *Identification of the Gifted and Talented*, Ventura, California: Office of the Ventura County Superintendent of Schools, June 1974.

National Advisory Council on the Education of Disadvantaged Children. *1975 Annual Report to the President and the Congress* Washington: NACEDC, 1975

National/State Leadership Training Institute on the Gifted & Talented *New Directions for Gifted Education* - Los Angeles, California: Office of the Ventura County Superintendent of Schools March 1976

Regents of the University of the State of New York *Educating the Gifted and Talented in New York State* Albany: The State Education Department - January 1976

Renzulli, J.S. - *A Guidebook for Evaluating Programs for the Gifted & Talented* - Ventura County, California: Superintendent of Schools, 1975 - N/S LTI Publication

Reynolds, M. - Birch, J. - Tuseth, A. - *Review of Research on Early Admission* - In M. Reynolds (Ed.) *Early School Admission for Mentally Advanced Children* - Reston, Virginia: Council for Exceptional Children, 1962

Sato, Irving S. - Birnbaum, Martin - LoCicero, Jane Early *Developing a Written Plan for the Education of Gifted and Talented Students* - Ventura, California: Office of the Ventura County Superintendent of Schools - June, 1974

Terman, Lewis M. *The Discovery and Encouragement of Exceptional Talent* Yonkers-on-Hudson, New York: World Book Company

U.S. Department of Health, Education and Welfare - Office of Education, *A State's Resource, a State's Responsibility* Albany, New York, Bulletin 1963 No. 34 pp. 58-59

Treffinger, Donald J. & Curl, Clifford D. - *Self Directed Study Guide on the Education of the Gifted and the Talented*, Ventura County, California: Superintendent of Schools Office, August, 1976 - N/S LTI Publication

Chapter 48
Old Myths Are Being Challenged by Down-to-Earth Methods at the University of Washington's Model Preschool for Handicapped Children

Vivian Hedrich*

Of all the handicaps that humanity faces, mental retardation may be the most widely misunderstood. In particular, children with Down's syndrome (mongolism) face a world in which people first wonder what on earth to do with them and then may not expect enough from them.

One encouraging new effort to improve the outlook for Down's and other mentally handicapped children is under way in Seattle at the University of Washington's Model Preschool Center for Handicapped Children. In serving nearly 190 children with a wide range of problems—including more than 60 Down's children from newborn to six years of age—the program concentrates on reaching the youngsters early to get a jump ahead of the adverse effects of retardation.

The children at the Model Preschool are part of approximately three percent of the total population of the country who are mentally retarded. The commonly recognized form is Down's syndrome, a chromosome "accident" that causes mental retardation in about one out of every 640 live births. The statistic leaps higher among mothers over 45 (an estimated one in 50). Today more of these children survive the first difficult months and years of life, even though many suffer from additional serious handicapping conditions.

In addition to the altered brain development, most Down's syndrome children share certain physical characteristics, including poor muscle tone, smaller than normal ears, noses, and hands, eyes that tend to slant upward, and shorter than normal linear growth beginning at about age four. They usually learn to sit, walk, speak, and are toilet trained later than normal, but can learn to dress and feed themselves, play on a swing, swim, and do many other activities typical of childhood. As they grow older their social development tends to be more advanced than their mental development, and they can deal more easily with people and their environment than has traditionally been expected of them.

"We are challenging some persistent myths about mentally handicapped children," Seattle project director Alice Hayden points out, "and attempting to demonstrate that much can be done to accelerate the development of the retarded, especially when intensive help arrives soon after birth. We are especially encouraged about the progress possible when experts in a number of disciplines get together with parents in the proper setting."

The Seattle setting moves toward that idea. Initially funded by the early childhood education program of OE's Bureau of Education for the Handicapped, the Model Preschool is part of the University's Experimental Education Unit, one of four components of the Child Development and Mental Retardation Center, one of the largest and most comprehensive facilities of its type in the country. The rustically modern structure, located on the shores of a scenic ship canal at the south end of the campus, welcomes more than 10,000 visitors each year.

More than six years ago, while the center was still in the planning stage, careful consideration was given to all aspects of children's welfare and safety. All weather instruction and recreation areas promote both indoor and outdoor activities. The latest in multimedia equipment helps to monitor each child's progress. Viewing areas with one-way glass adjoin each classroom. Above all a most important criterion has been met—the center has the atmosphere of a school and not a hospital.

Even the casual visitor soon recognizes that this is an "action place." A large wooden go-cart loaded with clapping and singing toddlers is pushed down the hall by teachers' aides. The group is bound for a play period in the covered courtyard. Classrooms overflow with color displays of children's artwork, huge building blocks, and other manipulative materials. Teachers enthusiastically encourage children— "That's right!" "Good boy!" "Fine try again!"

In one room a teacher sits with several children and unwraps an orange popsicle for them to examine. The three- and four-year-olds quickly name the color of the treat and confirm that it is smooth, cold, and sweet. They enthusiastically join in making orange juice popsicles for the class. Just in doing that, they have demonstrated the ability to discriminate color, texture, temperature, taste, and the motor control needed to pour liquid into special molds without spilling.

---

*Mrs. Vivian Hedrich is a free-lance writer in the Seattle area.

"We believe that these children need a well-balanced program," Dr. Hayden explains. "We have large-group and small-group sessions, teacher-and child-initiated activities, art, music, prereading, and even science. Everything that takes place, however, has a specific objective and each child receives a minimum of ten minutes of concentrated one-to-one instruction every day."

In a small conference room a therapist works with a six-year-old Down's syndrome boy referred to the center by his suburban school district for screening and placement. During the first few minutes the child successfully identifies primary colors by dropping colored tablets into correspondingly colored plastic cups. He also matches animal shapes with pictures on a chart. However, the process is frequently interrupted as his attention wanders and he moves about the room waving his arms and rolling his head aimlessly from side to side. Such random movements probably stem from poor motor control and some emotional complications. According to Dr. Hayden, they are rarely seen among the very youngest children who have been able to get to the center early. Systematic exercise and training has helped them develop control of such movements at a rate that is close to that of normal children.

In the past, children with Down's symdrome were virtually ignored. Their physical characteristics labeled them immediately and everyone assumed they would not live long (many did not survive adolescence), so they were simply tagged noneducable. Today, dismissing any group of children as merely trainable seems unthinkable, says Dr. Hayden.

While most Down's syndrome children are categorized as moderately retarded, J. Doris and S. B. Sarason in their book, *Psychological Problems in Mental Deficiency* show that IQ scores for this population cover a wide range—from severely retarded to dull-normal. However, data gathered on institutionalized Down's children indicate a tendency for IQ scores to decline with age.

Until recently, the prevailing recommendation for many such children was institutionalization to spare families the burdens involved in long-term care. "Although institutions now emphasize group homes and smaller units, it is still apparent that such placement is not the answer to the problems that face society," Dr. Hayden says. She believes that there are a number of reasons for that regression shown by institutionalized children, one of them being separation from their families, from society, and from an environment that promotes normal behavior. Another reason is a failure on the part of society to render early and continuous help.

Following the birth of a Down's syndrome baby, many households are virtually in mourning. Families have to adjust to the embarrassed silence of friends and relatives as well as face their own emotional turmoil. "Parents may feel awkward and fearful of even such elementary tasks as holding the baby," Dr. Hayden says. "One of our first concerns is to encourage interaction with the infant constantly during his waking hours. Enthusiasm is contagious."

In Seattle, parents are involved from the moment their child is seen by the staff. They are trained in many of the instructional procedures used at the school to help their child develop motor and social skills. Parents work in classrooms at least one session each week as observers, data takers, and teaching assistants.

"Being part of the University's Down's syndrome program has really helped me," one mother says. "I have learned specific ways that I can work with my child at home to help him with the skills he is developing at school—matching and sorting, identifying shapes and colors, and so on. Our kitchen provides most of the teaching materials I need. Also, I have a chance to share problems and ideas with other mothers of children the same age as my own. It helps me to be more objective about my child's behavior."

At regular group meetings held at the center, parents may air their concerns, plan programs, and listen to authorities from such fields as nutrition or pediatrics. Videotapes made in the classroom are often shown and followed by group discussions; parents may review tapes of their children over several months to see what progress has been made.

Currently 63 Down's children, including 14 infants, are enrolled in the five year-round classes offered by the preschool. Children are admitted at different ages depending upon when parents first hear of the program. The word usually reaches them through their physician, friends, the news media, or referral by the local school district. All children who apply are admitted at no charge. However, parents are expected to provide transportation for those under three years and to participate in classroom sessions and parent meetings.

While some children are seen as early as two weeks, intensive training does not begin until they are five weeks old. In weekly 30-minute sessions, parents learn about early motor and cognitive development, particularly how to stimulate their young child in the areas of sight and sound. When the baby is about six months old, training turns to self-help skills that require eye-hand coordination. Special aids include crackers and other "finger foods" that the infant can grasp.

"We observe our Down's syndrome children systematically," Dr. Hayden says. "We identify goals for each child's development." She stresses that everyone must be alert to other handicapping conditions. These sometimes develop slowly and might be missed in periodic clinical examinations. But if parents and teachers systematically observe a child's behavior, they can often spot potential problems and thus begin remedial procedures.

Children move through five levels of instruction as they meet the developmental requirements—infant, early preschool, intermediate preschool, advanced preschool, and kindergarten. Each class is staffed by a teacher and an assistant, who helps the teacher identify problems and plan individual programs. Other support personnel assist with physical therapy and communication skills. Children are tested regularly, and their progress measured against the general goal of performing a target skill with 85 percent of better accuracy.

Dr. Hayden points out that the longer children stay in the program, the greater the progress they demonstrate toward developmental norms. But the newcomers also evidence steady improvement. As an example, data from tests given a year apart showed five children new to the kindergarten program had a mean lag of 21 months behind normal development of certain skills, while five children who had been in the program for six to twelve months had a lag of only 5.6 months. The second tests, a year later, showed all of the children had maintained gains or accelerated in their development. The mean IQ for the children who had been in the program over the longer stretch increased from 84.8 to 88. The gain for the other children was from 61 to 74.7. *(Note: Tests used included the Peabody Picture Vocabulary Test, the Denver Developmental Assessment Battery and Screening Test, and inventories developed by the staff and validated in field settings.)*

A kindergarten class added to the Down's syndrome program during the fall of 1973 offers instruction to children in two-hour sessions four days each week. These children not only work on skills they have already learned, but also receive individual instruction in reading, math, and speech. Some specific goals for children in this group are printing their own first names, understanding number concepts from one to five, discriminating and naming all upper and lower case letters of the alphabet, throwing a ball, and walking up and down stairs, alternating feet with each step. In their speech exercises, children are expected to use correctly at least half the words they have shown they understand.

Lessons the project people learned since the beginning make new directions possible. "In the summer of 1974, we successfully phased-in a few normal children to serve as models," says Dr. Hayden. "Their speech, social behaviors, and attention to tasks give handicapped children useful 'clues' that adults cannot so readily provide. Parents of normal children enrolled have been enthusiastic about their children's opportunity to participate.

"A major question in our minds is how well the program will 'travel' to public school special-education classes without the support system we have at the demonstration center," Dr. Hayden continues. "We are concerned too with how well our children will continue to fare in other sur-

roundings and to what extent our approach may be able to serve children who have never had the benefits of intensive early training." Toward that end the center hopes to follow its Down's children as long as it can to ensure appropriate education.

A testing ground for such questions is Seattle's Green Lake Elementary School. There a new primary program was established for Down's children last fall with research funding from the Office of Education's Bureau of Education for the Handicapped. This fall, two classes are made up of Model Preschool graduates with five comparison groups of Down's syndrome children from regular district special-education enrollment.

Ann Sweet, special-education instruction at Green Lake, feels that only "time will tell" how the University-developed techniques will adapt the public school setting. "As a teacher I have been especially impressed with one aspect of the University program that requires only rearranging time," she says. "Each day the teacher or paraprofessional selects target skills from the Down's Syndrome Assessment Form (a list of competencies possible of attainment by the children and developed by the center staff) and concentrates on teaching them to one child for half an hour. This strengthens the child's skill and confidence and helps the teacher get to know individual children well and keep daily records of their progress."

Ms. Sweet feels another worthwhile "spinoff" from the program has been the training of paraprofessional workers. Now a growing number of persons at the school are able to make a substantial contribution to the education of the handicapped.

Currently, the model preschool center serves children from 23 surrounding school districts in the Puget Sound area and many more through the staff's outreach efforts in consultation and training. More than 1,500 undergraduate and graduate students have participated in the University training program and thousands of teachers, paraprofessionals, and parents have attended workshops and received on-site training. Last spring the center's staff helped establish new Down's syndrome programs for children in several States, Canada, and Australia.

Many unanswered questions remain for researchers on the "how and why" of mental retardation and no immediate miracles for easily dealing with it seem likely. Educators like those in Seattle, however, are finding success in a combination of hope and hard work.

Section VI
Critical Issues

Introduction by Bernard Friedman *

An issue can be categorized as significant if it affects great numbers of children or if it has dramatic impact upon the few. The issues discussed in this section are significant both in terms of impact and the large populations involved.

In Diane Divoky's article on child abuse we are informed of the trend requiring teachers to report suspected instances of abuse and neglect. The situation becomes complex when we learn that there is little agreement on what constitutes neglect or abuse. It is possible that the middleclass child who has "everything" is being maltreated too? The author suggests that a lack of teacher expertise in these matters ought to lead teachers away from intervention and toward the kind of political activism that would promote more human social policies.

Cheyney and Adams in their article on the childcare needs of migrants present research findings in the areas of infant mortality, prematurity, nutrition, prenatal care, and maternity age. They conclude with a number of specific recommendations which are designed to combat the conditions which make the migrant mother-to-be a poor reproductive risk.

"Goals and Directions of Bilingual Programs in Early Childhood Years" gives us the sobering information that 13 percent of the population four years old and older are living in households in which languages other than English are spoken. Baecher reminds us that research indicates that 50 percent of a child's total capacity for development is realized by the fourth year. With this information as background, we can readily feel the author's sense of urgency regarding correcting the inadequacies of bilingual education.

The article on day-care facilities for infants and toddlers by Shigaki and Zorn is a careful blend of scholarship and practicality. We are led from theoretical considerations, buttressed by substantial references and a selected bibliography, to information essential as guidelines for curriculum planners and teacher trainers. "Education and Deprivation" presents us with a very readable investigation of the topic covering such areas as the deprivation theory, visual discrimination, auditory discrimination, language formation, and concept formation. The research in this well-documented article leads Ornstein to conclusions which will provoke many interesting discussions.

Professor Black in her article on sex-role development calls upon educators to examine their attitudes with a view toward eliminating those kinds of behaviors which deprive children of optimal growth opportunities. In this connection the author cites interesting and far-reaching examples of preconceived attitudes and generalizations.

Another article in this section deals with the impact of television on children. Dr. Mukerji discusses, among other things, cognitive and affective learning, and the socializing effect as they pertain to television viewing. We are made aware of the vast amount of research being done in this area and of some of the conclusions that can be drawn from this research.

Although the articles in this section are not directly related, nevertheless, they have a common point of view—the necessity to strive for those conditions which will maximize the physical, emotional, and intellectual development of the child. What could be more significant?

*Dr. Bernard Friedman, Guidance Counselor, Pacific High School, New York City Public Schools.

Chapter 49

Education and Deprivation

Allan C. Ornstein *

Interest in the special learning problems of students, and particularly those in the inner city, has been sustained and intense since the early 1960s. Concurrent with this period, the flood of ideas and programs to facilitate learning has been rapid; today, the major outlines of the field are sufficiently clear to permit an organized approach to an understanding of the basic structure of the influence of deprivation upon the achievement of children.

As can be inferred from the current research, the educational deficits that disadvantaged children bring with them to the classroom prevent the schools from working with them effectively. At home, these children are not provided with necessary experiences to explore, manipulate, and discuss—processes which are important for cognitive growth and development—nor do their parents have the time or knowledge to take an active role in teaching them tasks at home that may subsequently facilitate academic achievement and orientate them to the rules and routine of school life. These students consistently perform poorly on tests of scholastic aptitude and achievement which require a language and/or conceptual style.

The purpose of this article is to bring to readers some theoretical insights and knowledge of educating disadvantaged learners, the possible causes and antecedents of observed learning deficits and practical learning problems; the child's social and economic background is a major component in determining his experiences, and such experiences are related to the development of a variety of educationally relevant cognitive skills. In this sense, the child's social and family milieu is an important determinant in his cognitive development, much more than the impact of schools.

As such the concept of deprivation offers one basis for understanding why some children in school perform below grade level and continuously fall further behind. It helps to explain why teachers and schools are often unable to counteract the child's limited environmental experiences—and to subsequently cope with the learning problem of the disadvantaged. It does not follow, however that we let public officials and school systems completely off the hook, rather it suggests that we must be more concerned about the effect home environment has on the development of children and that we must also hold parents responsible for the quality of their children's schooling. Failure to admit to the importance of the home, and to take appropriate educa-tional and social measures will continue to undermine the school program.

The Deprivation Theory

The concept of "cultural deprivation" is an environmentalist's analysis (as opposed to the hereditarian position) of the relationship between the child's experiences and his cognitive growth and development. The relationships are complex and interrelated: suggesting the effects of environment, both quantitative and qualitative experiences, which impact on (1) visual and (2) auditory discrimination, (3) language and (4) concept formation. Each of these four cognitive referents has its own stages of development, but each one effects the others, and therefore, inadequate or adequate development in one area will effect the other areas of development. The four cognitive referents are built on a base of the characteristics of an earlier time; the stages of growth and development have consequences for subsequent stages. For example, if an individual is unable to develop fully a characteristic (say a cognitive one) at a particular stage in life, he usually cannot fully develop that particular characteristic (or the characteristics that are dependent on the prior one) in later stages in life: the idea is well established in biology and studies of animal and infant behavior.***

David Ausubel, (1964, 1968) professor of psychology at the City University of New York, has extended this theory to hypothesize: that there is a tendency for deficits in cognitive development to occur if the child is deprived of necessary stimulation during critical periods when he is maximally susceptible to it in terms of potential capabilities. The corollary of this hypothesis is that individuals who fail to acquire these skills at appropriate times are forever handicapped in attaining them. The reason is that the deficits become irreversible and cumulative in nature, since cur-

*Dr. Allan Ornstein is Associate Professor of Education, Loyola University of Chicago. Printed with permission of the author.

**Adapted from the author's forthcoming text to be published in 1976-77.

***There is some danger in extrapolating from animals to humans or from infants to adults.

rent and future rates of intellectual growth are always based on or limited by the attainment level of development. (New growth, in other words, proceeds from existing growth.) The child who has an existing deficit in growth incurred from past deprivation is less able to profit from new and more advanced levels of environmental stimuli. Thus, irrespective of the adequacy of other factors, except perhaps positive changes in environment, the deficit tends to increase cumulatively and leads to permanent retardation—forming what is called the "cumulative intellectual deficit." (This helps explain the increasing academic retardation of slow or nonreaders as they proceed through school.)

The deprivation theory also holds that early years of development are more important than successive years. Although not all human characteristics reveal the same patterns of development, the most rapid period of development of human characteristics, including cognitive skills, are during the preschool years. For example, Benjamin Bloom (1964) at the University of Chicago presents longitudinal data which strongly suggests that from birth to age 4 the individual develops 50 percent of his potential intelligence, from ages 4-8 he develops another 30 percent, and between ages 8-17 he develops the remaining 20 percent. Supplementary evidence suggests that 33 percent of learning potential takes place by the time the child is age 6, or before he usually enters school, another 17 percent takes place between 6 and 9. The potential for learning is cumulative. As much as 50 percent of learning potential is developed by age 9, 75 percent by age 13, and 100 percent by age 18.

Based on the above estimates for intelligence and learning, home environment is crucial, according to Bloom (1964), not only because of "the large amount of cognitive development which has already taken place before the child enters the first grade but also because of the influence of the home during the elementary school period." These estimates also suggest the very rapid growth of cognitive growth in the early years and the great influence of the early environment (largely home environment) on this development and that all subsequent learning, "is affected and in a large part determined by what the child has (previously) learned." Furthermore, what the child learns in the early and most important years is shaped by what the child has experienced at home. Even the prenatal stages of development effect the child's intellectual development, that is the mother's health and diet and chemical changes related to smoking, alcohol, personality stress, etc. And, it is common knowledge that substantially more lower-income mothers than middle- and upper-income mothers, and more black mothers than white mothers, suffer from poor physical and mental health as well as poor diets.

The theory of deprivation also coincides with the research: a child of low-income status will often suffer from a deprived environment or limited stimuli, which, in turn, negatively effects his opportunities for adequate develop-ment within and among the four aforementioned cognitive referents of development. Conversely, a child of middle- or upper-socioeconomic status usually has an enriched environment or sufficient quantity of high-quality stimuli, which positively effects his opportunities for adequate development within and among these four referents. Thus the child's social class is related to his environmental experiences which subsequently influence his learning capabilities and academic development.

Since the relationships are group patterns, there is room for individual differences among children in both deprived and enriched environments. For example, it is possible for a lower-class child to have an enriched home environment and for his middle-class counterpart to have a deprived home environment. Similarly it does not necessarily mean that all children from deprived environments are going to have limited school abilities while all children from enriched environments are going to have academic success, rather, social class and home enrivonment will handicap or assist children in developing their mental capabilities.

Although the deprivation theory illustrates the importance of environment, this should not be interpreted as acceptance of a one-factor theory in explaining cognitive growth and development. No matter how complex a single-factor can be, there are usually other intervening variables to consider. In this connection, most authorities who subscribe to the deprivation theory, who are in effect staunch environmentalists, agree that hereditary sets limits on individual potential for intellectual growth. (It is further contended that hereditary does not guarantee that this potential will be achieved and it does not, therefore, fix the level of intelligence.) Within the limits of a range, although many authorities cannot agree on what the range is, environment influences the measurement and development of intelligence.

J. McVicker Hunt (1961, 1969) the well-known environmental psychologist from the University of Illinois, has summarized thousands of research studies dealing with intelligence. He alludes to this controversy: the rate of cognitive development "is in substantial part, but certainly not wholly, a function of environmental circumstances." He is unable to determine the interaction between hereditary and environment, but the greater the variety of environmental situations to which the hcild must accommodate his behavioral structures, the more differentiated and mobile he becomes. "Thus, the more new things a child has seen and the more he has heard, the more things he is interested in seeing and hearing." The emphasis on the importance of environment implies the detrimental effects of an impoverished environment; this in turn leads to the concept of "environmental deprivation" or "stimulus deprivation."

The importance of environmental stimuli is better understood by examining the various components and sequences which affect growth and development of cognitive potential. To a large extent the previously mentioned cognitive referents, visual discrimination, auditory discrimination, language formation, and concept formation—provide the framework in which we can better understand the role of environment and how inadequate development in one cognitive area affects the other areas of cognition.

Visual Discrimination

In the home of the disadvantaged, there tends to be a minimum of quantity and quality of stimuli. Cynthia Deutsch (1968) and Martin Deutsch (1971) of New York University contend there is little color variety, few pictures and books, and few household objects. The stimuli that are available tend to be repetitious and lacking in color, shape, and size variations. Although the apartment may be overcrowded and cluttered with objects, the presentation usually lacks organization; it is often chaotic and "noisy" and it often overloads the child. The conflicting and disorganized stimuli often confuse the child, too; he has difficulty in distinguishing relevant stimuli; his range of visual stimuli is obstructed.

According to Martin Deutsch (1973), the lack of diversity of visual stimulation gives the child "few opportunities to manipulate and organize the visual properties of his environment and thus perceptually to organize and discriminate the nuances of the environment." Along with Jerome Bruner (1961) from Harvard University and John Zubek (1969) from the University of Manitoba in Canada it is reported that the child's lack of perceptual development limits his capacity to utilize cues, to extract information and make subsequent classifications and judgments. Similarly, the child makes fewer cognitive decisions and has less opportunity to sustain and use and accumulate knowledge; he experiences few language-symbolic operations and obtains less practice in present and later concepts of visual comparison and relativity. Thus, by virtue of having seen fewer things, he makes fewer specific responses and associatons. Furthermore, since he encounters fewer tasks, he is less able to handle new and potential learning experiences, in the sense that appropriate responses have not yet been learned. For example, a full-size picture of a boy riding a bicycle in the park with trees and grass in the background might be confusing or incomplete. The boy and the bicycle should be relevent stimuli, but to the deprived child it could be submerged by the background of trees and grass or other irrelevent stimuli. The teacher, however, takes it for granted that the child understands the picture—and so starts the child's downhill school spiral.

Learning to write is also linked to the child's perceptual-motor skills. Actually, writing is the substitution of verbal symbols for visual imagery and forms of drawings. According to Herbert Simon and Allen Newell (1970), the child, by learning to write, associates perceptual symbols with internalized representations. Because of limited motor-perceptual development, the child has difficulty discriminating among and writing graphic symbols (o-c or M-W, for example).

The effect of poor visual discrimination is linked with reading retardation, too, for in part reading is based on a form of perceptual discrimination and spatial organization. In this connection, John Guthrie (1973) and Joachim Wohlwill (1970) of Clark University have reviewed the literature and show that readers discriminate among words on the basis of recognizing letters, and that poor readers find it difficult to discriminate on the basis of the shape and form of selected letters and words. For example, again the child may have difficulty in discriminating symbols (o-c or M-W, for example) when reading.

Auditory Discrimination

The child who lives in a slum apartment is usually surrounded by many noises and sounds that lack meaning, at least in terms of learning to discriminate auditory stimuli. People are piled up together in the slum, that is the population is dense on the streets and in apartment dwellings. There is excessive noise from the streets and hallways, television, radios, and phonographs echo loudly, many people may live crowded into one apartment, and there may be several children sleeping in one room. Too much noise in the environment, it has been shown by Cynthia Deutsch (1968) and John Corso (1973) causes the child to "tune out." In addition, they show that the slum child has limited verbal interaction with adults or his parents. He is rarely assisted in listening to verbal responses. In crowded areas with all the daily stresses of living, it is maintained that the conversation, which is directed toward the child is generally noninstructional and few words are multisyllabic.

The child who has limited auditory practice and adult feedback subsequently develops poor attention and memory powers. Attentiveness is also related to the individual's ability to listen and remember what he has experienced, according to Susan Gray and Rupert Klaus (1968) and Jane Raph (1973), lack of sustained auditory contact with a verbally mature parent or significant adult impedes the development of memory; it is by recalling shared experiences with an adult that the child practices and develops his memory and learning experiences. While the middle-class child usually has the benefit of numerous conversational dialogues with verbally mature adults to assist him in his listening and developing of verbal responses and memory, this is not often the case with the lower-class child.

The child raised in a noisy environment, with limited adult conversation directed toward him, will most likely become deficient in auditory discrimination, and subsequently in related speech, language, and reading skills. For example, to learn new words for purposes of speaking or reading means that the individual must listen to and modify speech sounds. He compares his sounds with those of a parent, friend, or teacher, but for the lower-class child the verbal sounds at home and school are often different. The child detects differences and modifies his speech or reading based on what he hears. If the child is familiar with the sounds of the language, and the more practice and feedback he has had with hearing and discriminating previous words and phrases, the more referents he had to build new words and the easier it is to learn the language.

Thus Alan Cohen (1969) and David McNeill (1970) show that in early grades there is a positive relationship between lack of auditory discrimination and poor pronunciation and reading, since phonics play an important role in these learning areas at this age level. To the child with limited auditory facilities, *for four* and *foe* sound alike, and therefore the same, as *can, cane,* and *came.* Similarly, Eric Lennenberg (1970) points out that a sentence of ten words consists of extraordinary detail: "some 60 phonemes. . . characteristized by 9 to 12 distinctive features," and each word broken down into several "intonation stress characteristics." Blind repetition of all these sounds is nearly impossible, since memory is incapable of remembering a list of several of these random verbal characteristics. But when we understand a language, and when we understand its auditory cues, "sequence of phonemes within words and sequences of words within sentences fall within familiar patterns that help organize the stimuli." A child who has not gained facility in auditory discrimination will fail to organize and repeat long sentences. The child may understand the general meaning of the sentence, but when asked to repeat it he is often unable to *accurately* deal with the words and he mixes or provides his own words.

Language Formation

The child's language basically evolves through the label-ling of his environment, that is his describing and reacting to audio-visual stimulation. Learning to speak and use language requires that the child learn to discriminate among the corresponding visual and auditory symbols of words and make proper classifications. What the child perceives and hears serve as a source for understanding what he is verbalizing, as well as for categorizing, stating, and using conceptual referents; by learning the language the child is also able to discriminate and classify various concepts of size, form and sounds. (Berlyne, 1965, and Vygotsky, 1962).

To help the child handle the multiple attributes of words and associate these words with the proper referents, a good deal of exposure to and practice with language is presupposed. For the child, this exposure involves verbal interaction with and feedback from an adult who is significant to the child, e.g., a parent. However, the disadvantaged child's verbal experiences with an adult are often meager in quantity and quality of formal verbal expression; the conversation is often short and functional or authoritarian; the vocabulary is limited in terms of correct English and the meanings are conveyed less in words and more in gestures. In the same vein, there is often little opportunity to engage in games, such as "Peek-a-Boo" and "Pat-a-Cake," hear fairy tales, or get explanations of why the sky is blue or clouds make rain. Both the verbal and emotional encounter restricts the child's verbal skills and subsequent concept formation. A useful but somewhat generalized example of a mother and child at home, the mother trying to stress the reasons for putting away blocks, is illustrated in Table 1; it is based on a classic dialogue purported by the English psychologist Basil Bernstein. (1971).

Table 1
MOTHER AND CHILD AT HOME ILLUSTRATING THE DEVELOPMENT OF LANGUAGE

Case I	Case II
Mother: Put away your blocks.	Mother: Put away your blocks, darling
Child: Why?	Child: Why?
Mother: Put them away	Mother: You have finished playing with them.
Child: Why?	Child: Why?
Mother: They mess up the house.	Mother: Because we should learn to put away our toys when we are finished using them. If the toys are left on the floor, the house will look untidy.
Child: Why	Child: Why?
Mother: I told you to put them away, didn't I	Mother: Now put the blocks away, darling, and don't make such a fuss.

In terms of language development, the child in Case I is disadvantaged relative to the child in Case II. The child in the first case is not given a full explanation of why he should remove his toys from the floor. He does not receive corrective and reinforcing feedback. If this repeatedly occurs, the child may soon stop asking "Why?" In the second case, however, the child has had a better opportunity to learn; he receives full explanations and corrective feedback as well as engages in reasoning and concepts of causality; also, he learns that blocks are toys. In Case I, the mother's vocabulary is limited and categorical. The child perceives few opportunities to listen and learn new words and concepts. He receives little practice in hearing someone speak in elaborate sentences. The emotional relationship between the child and mother seems more authoritarian in that her behavioral demands are abrupt and basically unexplained, and according to the directions the child must do the work alone. The child's change in behavior is brought about by verbal conditioning; the child in this case will often fail to develop facility with the structure of the language and upon entering school is more apt to experience cultural and language shock. In the other case, the mother exposes the child to more words and elaborate sentences. She attempts to satisfy the child's curiosity, in effect stimulating the child to learn new things. Her seemingly warm relationship, and her "we" rather than "you" do it attitude, helps the child develop his cognitive and emotional processes. The child's change in behavior is related to verbal learning; he is learning responsibility and self-discipline, too. Finally, teachers speak with language patters similar to the mother in Case II.

The cumulative deficiency in language formation for the child in Case I, or the disadvantaged child, tends to lead to the development of a restricted language code, or what Bernstein calls "public" language. This is characterized by:

1. Short, grammatically simple, and often incomplete sentences.
2. Simple and repetitive use of conjunctions.
3. Few subordinate clauses.
4. Dislocated subjects and verbs as well as context.
5. Infrequent use of adjectives and adverbs.
6. Infrequent use of pronouns as subjects for conditional clauses.
7. Frequent use of statements to produce illogical conclusions.
8. Frequent use of sequence reinforcers, e.g., "Get it," "Understand."
9. Use of ill-defined idiomatic phrases.
10. A sentence organization of implicit rather than explicit meaning.

On the other hand, the middle-class child speaks a "formal" language in which the characteristic patterns are opposite to the above lower-class language style: accurate grammatical order, a wide range of vocabulary, structure and relationships within and between sentences, and con-

ceptual hierarchy for the organizing of experiences. The original studies of social class language differences of Bernstein were conducted in England, which is a crucial argument for those who disagree with his findings. Nevertheless, his findings have been replicated in this country a number of times, whether the subjects have been black mothers and children (Hess and Shipman, 1965, and Pavenstadt, 1965) or white mothers and children.

The argument for a distinctive black language rests on more subtle and linguistic grounds, rooted in the assumption expounded by Noam Chomsky (1968) of Harvard University that the acquisition of language rests on being placed in the environment of the language, and elaborated and popularized by Joey Dillard (1972) of Yeshiva University who argues that black children possess a different language than the "school register," but one that has direct application to their immediate environment. The argument also has political and social implications: that the school is insensitive to the child's language mode, rather than the student being at fault for not learning, and also corresponds with black cultural pride.

Regardless of the student's ethnicity or racial background, the characteristic patterns of language interaction between lower-class children and adults inhibit the development of standardized language patterns, as well as the vocabulary to register and classify increasing data. The consistent interaction that characterizes middle-class families serves to tell the child when an explanation he has offered is correct or incorrect, to answer his questions about why things are so, and to supply more words and concepts; it is the language used by schools and the larger society—and the language which is recognized to the extent that people judge others in social and job-related contexts.

Concept Formation

Language and thought are closely linked together. Educators agree that conceptual development is in part dependent on language. With the development of language, the child is capable of classifying more stimuli. Language allows the child to make a response, despite spatial or temporal separation from the subject or event. Language permits the child to classify and increase his knowledge, of being able to deal with a variety of stimuli, to label and store up concepts.

Where parents are poorly educated and handicapped by low income, the visual and auditory stimuli at home as well as the parent-child verbal interactions are usually limited. Consequently, the child has less opportunity to learn to label and categorize the various stimuli, to note the difference of these stimuli, and to ask questions and to receive feedback. For example, Hess and Shipman (1965) show that lower-class mothers seem at a loss in giving clear instructions and explanations, as well as motivating their own children to learn about the things they see and hear.

Jerome Bruner and Rose Oliver (1970) and David Elkind (1969) point out that the disadvantaged child's lack of experiences reduce opportunities to link experiences with interpretations, to convert objects and events into abstractions in formulating many abstract relationships and the generalizations needed to identify signals and relate them to previously learned categories.

It is further pointed out that the child who has a disorganized home life often is unable to clearly comprehend the experiences of separateness and difference, or organize and think in a logical order of elaboration. Disorganization at home, plus lack of routine and recognizable sequence of activities recurring in time, result in the child having fewer opportunities to systematize and conceptualize events and to organize a time reference except for the immediate and present—not the past or future. (Dodd and Bourne, 1973 and Wolhill, 1970).

There are several studies (Coleman, 1966 and Rosen, 1956) which show that "sense of control" correlates with class and race. The young middle-class child learns early which of his acts (and later words) will bring about desired results. He internalizes a set of probabilities—reinforced by an organized home life which help him decide the relative merit of several behaviors. Those of which most effectively and most consistently have a high probability of success he practices, thus concurrently gaining mastery over his own skills and environment. As a result, he comes to school with many developed cognitive strategies for problem-solving—most of which corresponds with the new demands of school.

Among the most important coping strategies which the child brings to school is effective language. As Fred Strodtbeck (1964) of Syracuse University contends, power through language is the "hidden curriculum" of the middle-class home. The child has learned that the attainment and maintenance of power are best achieved through words and by conversation, and thus he extends and elaborates his use of words and verbal concepts into a power instrument, one which is as effective at school as it is at home. Where there is reduction of power through words, as in the case of the disadvantaged, the motivation for using words and verbal reasoning are undercut. Not only does the disadvantaged child fail to develop a sense of verbal power or master linguistic complexities, the strategies he develops take on the form of physical strategies—a kind of random striking out both as a response to frustration and as a means of control. Such behavior impedes, rather than promotes, problem solving and cognitive strategies in school.

Great social class differences have also been found in the rate of acquiring the basic differential concepts (big-little, light-dark, near-far). Carl Bereiter and Siegfried Englemann's (1966) controversial approach for teaching preschool and primary grade disadvantaged children is based on this research, that the disadvantaged require experiences with language in a highly structured form—to be drenched with language—in order to conceptualize the world of experience. Their approach, with its emphasis on drill and more drill, does not teach children to raise questions. They contend the child is not ready to be taught in this manner; he must first acquire the rudiments of language to conceptualize.

Many present theories of thinking (say by Jerome Bruner, Robert Gagne, Jean Piaget, and Hilta Taba) are based on sequences and stages of hierarchies of mental development. If there exists little recognizable sequence of activities recurring in time, if there is less opportunity to think in a logical order of elaboration, as in the case of many disadvantaged environments, then at best the child is going to develop different methods and use different cognitive stages or hierarchies to solve the same problem—connoting a learning process based on cultural influence. In many cases, the child is not going to gain facility in conceptual thinking, rather he is going to operate at a low-level, concrete, or possibly rote learning style. This tends to confirm the research by Gerald Lesser (1964) and his associates at Harvard University on cognitive thinking patterns of children of different ethnic and social class backgrounds and of Arthur Jensen (1973) at Berkeley University who argues that the acquisition of concept and rote learning abilities is related to social class variations and black-white differences.

Conclusion

In summarizing the cognitive deficiencies of the disadvantaged child, Ausubel (1963) writes:

It is reasonable to assume that whatever the individual's potentialities are, cognitive development occurs largely in response to a variable range of stimulation . . . . Characteristic of the culturally deprived environment, however, is its restricted range and a less adequate and systematic ordering of stimulation sequences. The effect of this restricted environment includes poor perceptual [and auditory] discrimination skills; inability to use adults as sources of information, correction and reality testing, and as instruments of satisfying curiosity; and an impoverished language system and a paucity of information concepts and relative propositions.

His abstract vocabulary is deficient and his language related knowledge, such as number concepts, self-identity information, and understanding of the physical and geometrical and geographical environment is extremely limited. (pp. 2-3).

Examining the deprivation theory, each social scientist contributes a useful dimension to the understanding of the problem. Some of the data are complimentary, differing in their emphasis and indirectly suggesting different reasons for the major problems of deprivation. Each of the research studies and theories present a logical and consistent piece of the truth in the absence of more definitive and more fully tested explanations. Thus, the various studies, singly and in combination, have given rise to curricular and organizational programs to counteract the deprivation of children. The various programs have not yet provided adequate results, and in many cases there has been failure. Nevertheless the movement toward compensatory education and especially Head Start is a direct result from the hypotheses and research derived from the theory of deprivation.

Although the deprivation theory is criticized by some educators for being culturally biased and for ignoring the cultural systems of students from nonmainstream backgrounds, the alternatives that are advocated rest on a radical alteration of mainstream institutions, a separation theory, and/or an anti-formal educational strategy. Regardless of group ideology, the individual must learn to read and write and to count in our society. In every case in the United States, where groups have overcome poverty and discrimination, they have surmounted these barriers through formal education and by working within mainstream institutions.

Closely related to the criticism of the deprivation theory is the fashionable trend to condemn teachers for their inability to solve the problems of educating the disadvantaged. Not many teachers are familiar with the cultural and social backgrounds of these children, and those who are invariably unable to translate their knowledge into effective instruction. Indeed, there is no evidence that black teachers and administrators can do a better job than their white counterparts in raising achievement levels among black students. (Check the record in schools and in school systems where there is a majority of blacks on the instruction and administrative staff: Southern black schools, Baltimore, Chicago, Detroit, Gary, Philadelphia, Newark, St. Louis, Washington, D.C. etc.).

To blame teachers for their inability to cope with the learning problems of the disadvantaged suggests legitimate frustration on the part of parents, but it also disguises the fact that schools cannot drastically counteract the impact of family life. Society may direct the schools to educate the child, regardless of background or ability, but it cannot perform these functions effectively when the child comes to school with limited skills. This does not mean we should allow public officials and school systems off the hook, rather we must also hold parents responsible for the quality of their children's input and subsequent schooling. Placing total blame on educators for poor student performance, while ignoring family factors, tends to mask the realities and influence of the home and carries with it numerous political motives which can easily lead to unrealistic policies.

BIBLIOGRAPHY

Ausubel, David P. "How Reversible are the Cognitive and Motivational Effects of Cultural Deprivation?" *Urban Education,* Summer 1964, pp. 16–36.

Ausubel, David P. *Educational Psychology: A Cognitive View.* New York: Holt, 1968.

Ausubel, David P. "The Influence of Experience on Intelligence." Paper Read at the NEA Conference on Productive Thinking. Washington, D.C.: May 1963. pp. 2–3.

Bloom, Banjamin. *Stability and Change in Human Characteristics.* New York: Wiley, 1964.

Bruner, Jerome S. "The Cognitive Consequences of Early Sensory Deprivation." In P.D. Solomon (ed.) *Sensory Deprivation.* Cambridge, Mass.: Harvard University Press, 1961. pp. 195–207.

Bruner, Jerome S. and Olver, Rose R. "Development of Equivalence Transformations in Children." In *Cognitive Development in Children: Five Monographs of the Society for Research in Child Development.* Chicago: Society for Research in Child Development, 1970. pp. 243–59.

Berlyne, Daniel E. *Structure and Direction in Thinking.* New York: Wiley, 1965.

Bereiter, Carl and Englemann, Siegfried. *Teaching Disadvantaged Children in the Preschool.* Englewood Cliffs, N.J.: Prentice Hall, 1966.

Bernstein, Basil. "Social Structure, Language, and Learning." In A.H. Passow, M. Goldberg, and A. T. Tannenbaum (eds.) *Education of the Disadvantaged.* New York: Holt, 1967. pp. 225–244. Also see Basil Bernstein. *Class, Codes, and Control.* London: Routledge & Kegan, 1971.

Corso, John F. "Hearing." In B.B. Wolman (ed.) *Handbook of General Psychology.* Englewood Cliffs, N.J.: Prentice Hall, 1973. pp. 348–81.

Cohen, Alan S. *Teach Them To Read.* New York: Random House, 1969.

Chomsky, Noam. *The Sound Pattern of English.* New York: Harper & Row, 1968.

Coleman, Jerome S. *et al.* Equality of Educational Opportunity. Washington, D.C.: U.S. Government Printing Office, 1966.

Dodd, David H. and Bourne, Lyle E. "Thinking and Problem Solving." In B.B. Wolman (ed.) *Handbook of General Psychology.* Englewood Cliffs, N.J.: Prentice-Hall, 1973. pp. 547–66.

Dillard, Joey L. *Black English: Its History and Usage in the United States.* New York: Random House, 1972.

Deutsch, Martin. "Perpsectives on the Education of the Urban child." In A.H. Passow (ed.) *Urban Education in the 1970's.* New York: Teachers College Press, Columbia University, 1971. pp. 103–19.

Deutsch, Martin. "The Disadvantaged Child and the Learning Process." In A.H. Passow (ed.) Education in Depressed Areas. New York: Teachers College Press, Columbia University, 1963, p. 170.

Deutsch, Cynthia P. "Environment and Perception." In M. Deutsch, I. Katz, and A.R. Jensen (eds.) Social Class, Race, and Psychological Development. New York: Holt, 1968. pp. 58-85.

Elkind, David. "Conservation and Concept Formation." In D. Elkind and J.H. Flavell (eds.) Studies in Cognitive Development. New York: Oxford University Press, 1969. pp. 171-90.

Guthrie, John T. "Models of Reading and Reading Disability." Journal of Educational Psychology. August, 1973. pp. 9-18.

Gray, Susan W. and Klaus, Rupert. The Early Training Project for Disadvantaged Children: A Report After Five Years. Chicago: University of Chicago Press, 1968.

Hess, Robert D. and Shipman, Virginia D. "Early Experiences and the Socialization of Cognitive Modes in Children." Child Development, December, 1965. pp. 369-86.

Hunt, J. McVicker. Intelligence and Experience. New York: Ronald Press, 1961. pp. 258-59. Also see J. McVicker Hunt, The Challenge of Incompetence and Poverty. Urban, Ill.: University of Illinois Press, 1969.

Jensen, Arthur R. Genetics and Education. New York: Harper & Row, 1973.

Lesser, Gerald D., Fifer, Gordon, and Clark. Donald H. "Mental Abilities of Children in Different Social and Cultural Groups." Washington, D.C.: U.S. Office of Education, Cooperative Research Project No. 1635, 1964.

Kogan, Kate L. and Wimberger, Herbert C. "Interaction Patterns in Disadvantaged Families." Journal of Clinical Psychology, October 1969. pp. 347-52.

Lennenberg, Eric H. "Speech as a Motor Skill with Speical Reference to Nonaphasic Disorders." In Cognitive Development in Children: Five Monographs of the Society for Research in Child Development. Chicago: Society for Research in Child Development, 1970. p. 401. Also see Eric H. Lennenberg, Noam Chomski, and Otto Mard. Biological Foundations of Language. New York: Wiley, 1967.

McNeill, David. The Acquisition of Language: A Study of Developmental Psycholinguistics. New York: Harper Row, 1970.

Pavenstadt. "A Comparison of the Child-Rearing Environment of Upper-Lower and Very Low-Lower Class Families." American Journal of Orthopsychiatry, January 1965. pp. 92-96.

Rosen, Bernard C. "The Achievement Syndrome: A Psychocultural Dimension of Social Stratification." American Sociological Review, June 1956. pp. 203-11.

Raph, Jane B. "Language Development in Socially Disadvantaged Children." Review of Educational Research, December 1965. pp. 389-400. Also see Milton Schwebel and Jane B. Raph. Piaget in the Classroom. New York: Basic Books, 1973.

Simon, Herbert A. and Newell, Allen. "Computer Simulation of Human Thinking and Problem Solving." In Cognitive Development in Children: Five Monographs of the Society for Research in Child Development. Chicago: SOciety for Research in Child Development, 1970. pp. 113-26.

Strodtbeck, Fred L. "The Hidden Curriculum of the Middle-Class Home." In C.W. Hunnicutt (ed.) Urban Education and Cultural Deprivation. Syracuse, N.Y.: Syracuse University Press, 1964. pp. 15-31.

Vygotsky, Lev S. Thought and Learning. (trans. by E. Kaufman and C. Valtar) New York: Wiley, 1962.

Wohlwill, Joachim F. "From Perception to Interference: A Dimension of Cognitive Development. In Cognitive Development in Children: Five Monographs of the Society for Research in Child Development. Chicago: Society for Research in Child Development, 1970. --. 73-93.

Chapter 50

Program Considerations for Family and Group Day-Care Facilities for Infants and Toddlers

Vera Zorn and Irene Shigaki *

While in the past decade programs for preschool children ages three to five have proliferated, only recently has attention been directed to the provision of child care services for children under the age of three. Given this new direction, a framework for program considerations based on the developmental needs of infants and toddlers is presented below. The social need for child care facilities for very young children is linked to a major shift in the cultural pattern of the United States, i.e., the unusual pace at which women have been entering the job market. While in 1960 women comprised 33% of the labor force, by 1976 that proportion had increased to 40.7% (Lindsey, 1976). Included in the ranks of working women are well over half of the women of child-bearing ages (U.S. Department of Labor, 1975, p. 12). The reasons for this remarkable increase in working women are numerous. Factors such as changes in the family constellation, the women's movement and federal laws increasing hiring opportunities for women have shaped the current social climate, leading to greater acceptability for working women and particularly for working mothers. While it has become a common practice for mothers of schoolage children to return to work, there is also an increase in mothers of very young children entering the labor force. In 1974 it was reported that 32% of the 8 million mothers of children under the age of 3 were employed (U.S. Department of Labor, 1975, p. 25). While most of these young children are cared for in homes usually by a relative, there is still a sizeable lag between the need for and supply of quality care in either center of family settings. (U.S. Department of Labor, 1975, p. 40). Public policy makers and their advisors have begun to take note of these trends and the implications for child care (Fandetti, 1976; Kessen, 1976, p. 67).

Responses to the Social Need for Child Care

At present child care is taking a variety of forms, providing a range of services addressing diverse social needs. The greatest need is child care for working mothers and single parents with operating hours geared to their working day. In addition, there are facilities designed to meet specific needs. School-age adolescent mothers receive child care support while they develop marketable skills which will enable them to maintain the children they are desirous of keeping. Twenty-four hour shelters for children of families in crises, including abused children, are available in some large urban settings to offer support in situations where anonymity often leads to indifference and aid from an extended family or neighbors is lacking. Facilities are available for high risk infants (e.g., Down's syndrome) requiring special educational programs, often with a coordinated parenting program to help parents deal effectively with the unique needs of their child. Parenting programs, another reflection of concern for child care, are growing in number and have been designed for parents of normal children as well. The clientele varies from low-income parents to middle-income parents, including the isolated suburban mother. Parenting programs in high schools for parents of the future are also on the increase. What was once learned about child care through watching and participating with one's extended family is no longer possible in the nuclear family with its usual composition of two children a few years apart in age. The orientation of the various programs differ considerably from direct instruction (Forrester, 1971) to an experientially based model (Brocher, 1971), several programs having been packaged for mass consumption (Brown, 1976).

The focus for this paper, the delineation of a developmental framework within which programs can be designed, is equally applicable to family and group day care facilities. The form of family and group day care facilities vary considerably. For example, in New York City current regulations limit the number of children to a total of five that can be cared for in a licensed family day care situation. It further stipulates that no more than two infants under the age of two can be cared for at any given time by an individual caregiver. Deviations from these regulations can be found in unlicensed family day care settings. Family day care in its broadest sense includes baby-sitting arrangements in which one or more children receive care. Group day care facilities can also vary widely from settings accommodating 20 to 30 youngsters to those geared to as many as 100 chil-

*Dr. Irene S. Shigaki is the Program Coordinator and Dr. Vera Zorn is the Director of the Leadership Program in Group Care of Infants and Toddlers; School of Education, Health, Nursing and Arts Professions at New York University.

dren. Typically, children are grouped by age with infants through age one in one group, toddlers from 12 to 24 months in another, and children from 24 to 36 months in a third. The number of children in each group varies widely, but is commonly between 6 to 15.

Developmental Needs of Infants and Toddlers

Whether the child is cared for in family day care or in group day care, our contention is that it is possible for children to receive quality care from qualified caregivers other than the natural parents. This is possible when there is a clear understanding of the developmental needs of infants and toddlers and a conscious effort on the part of caregivers to meet these needs. These developmental needs, therefore, constitute the non-negotiable base which must be met in any setting concerned with rendering quality care of infants and toddlers. Using the "quality" home as the model for the implementation of quality care, the goal of any group setting becomes offering care which may be different from but not less than that which is found in a quality home. It is recognized that there may be varying definitions of a quality home, just as there are varying philosophies of education. In our pluralistic society this variety is something that we have come to prize. The definition of a quality home is akin to differing approaches to meeting the developmental needs; hence, the model we propose allows the definition of quality to include the quality variations to be found among different ethnic and cultural groups. For example, cultural values concerning toilet training and feeding practices vary. Given differences in philosophy and reordering of priorities in various settings, parents should have the choice from among a range of approaches so that they can select a setting for their child which is most congruent with their set of beliefs and their particular needs. In fact, there is some evidence that effective care of the child outside of the home is positively influenced by the degree of congruence between the philosophy of the facility and the philosophy of the parents (Palmer, 1976).

What are the basic developmental needs that must be addressed in effective care of young children? These needs have been variously defined in such publications as Dittman (1968), Koontz (1974), Russell (1975), Tronick and Greenfield (1973), and Willis and Ricciuti (1975). There is general agreement on the areas involved, though there is some variation in terminology, partially due to the overlapping nature of many of the developmental needs. Central to the well-being of a human is meeting his physiological and health needs including appropriate nutrition, adequate rest, and provisions for elimination. The early years are crucial ones for substantial growth in a variety of areas with a particular emphasis on the child's development of a sense of his own powers to initiate actions and influence the behavior of others. Much growth is attained during the early years in the area of motor development. Gross motor devel-

opment occurs in the child as he moves from reflexive actions to body movements that are under his conscious control such as various forms of locomotion. Fine motor development includes appropriate eye tracking at one or two months to the acquisition of the pincer grasp by about six or seven months. Though cognitive development is inextricably linked to overall development, it is helpful to focus on certain aspects in the cognitive realm. Early sensori-motor activities on the child provide the foundation for later conceptualization. The development of language, both comprehension and expression, serves as mediator and facilitator of cognition. The affective needs as conceptualized here include the emergence of self-esteem and a dynamic between each of the following: attachment and autonomy; trust, security and exploratory behavior; and socialization and the need for privacy. In summary, the developmental needs of young children, as we have labelled them, are as follows:

Physiological
  Nutrition
  Rest
  Elimination
  Health

Motor
  Gross motor
  Fine motor

Cognitive
  Sensori-motor
  Language
  conceptualization

Affective
  Attachment-Autonomy
  Trust, security-Exploratory behavior
  Socialization-Privacy
  Self-esteem

It should be recognized that the specific nature of the developmental needs are expressed differently from age to age. A more specific breakdown of these developmental needs particularly as they are manifested at various points in the young child's life are available by consulting the references cited above. In addition, it is important that the child be viewed in his entirety above and beyond a given need. It has recently been suggested by Katz (1976) that the younger the child the wider the range of functioning the adult is responsible for; hence, our concern and focus should be the "whole child" rather than merely specific aspects of his functioning, e.g., cognitive development. Recognizing the value of such a position, the usefulness of the developmental needs as an explicit comprehensive framework for caregivers of young children is underscored.

A Curriculum Framework

In developing a program for infants and toddlers centering around these developmental needs it is helpful to think though how the quality home is able to meet each need. It is then possible to extrapolate from the quality home model to that of the quality center model. In so doing, the experiences and activities that the center can provide to foster growth in each area can be identified. Guidelines for staffing, use of space, and selection of equipment and materials can be formulated which parallel these experiences and activities. When a series of experiences has been identified as being responsive to the range of needs and to children of differing ages, decisions can be made concerning a general structure supportive of these experiences in areas such as staffing schedules, the daily program, flexibility in the use of space, and multipurpose equipment. An outgrowth of this process would be the identification of components for staff training. This process has been mapped in the flowchart presented in Figure 1.

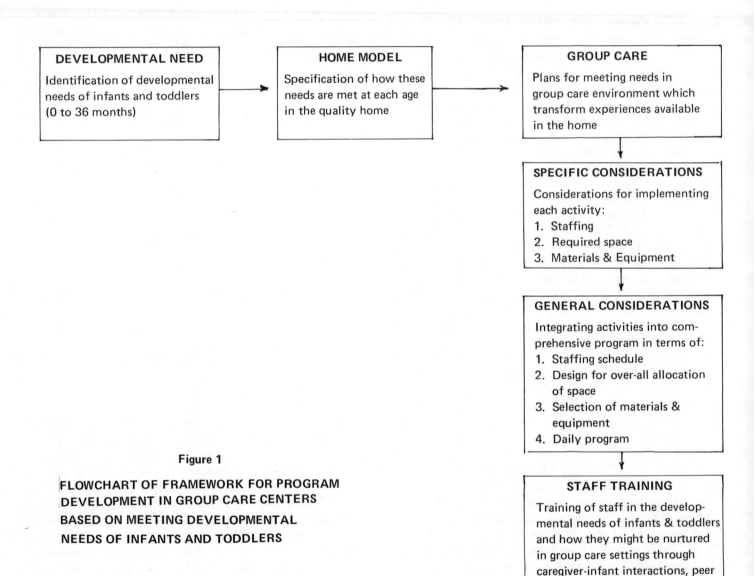

Figure 1

FLOWCHART OF FRAMEWORK FOR PROGRAM DEVELOPMENT IN GROUP CARE CENTERS BASED ON MEETING DEVELOPMENTAL NEEDS OF INFANTS AND TODDLERS

For the purposes of illustration, two examples of specific needs and how they might be fostered are presented in Table 1. The first example is in the motor area and the second deals with affect as they would apply to the needs of a child from 12 to 24 months.

Table 1

RELATING PROGRAM CONSIDERATIONS TO DEVELOPMENTAL NEEDS FOR CHILDREN FROM 12 TO 24 MONTHS

Developmental Need	Provisions in the Home	Provisions in the Center	Guidelines for Staffing	Guidelines for Use of Space	Guidelines for the Selection of Equipment and Materials
	General characteristics:				
	Opportunities to interact with and explore natural living environment	Child-centered environment minimizing potential danger, maximizing opportunities for the child to explore setting	Operates within framework of child's overall development	Child has free access to variety of space including havens for privacy	Environment rich in age-appropriate materials with range of difficulty, appealing to various sensory modalities
			Supportive and facilitating, allowing child to make discoveries as opposed to hovering and restricting. Views child as one who can rather than one who cannot	Allocated, e.g., block area, art materials, book area, music area, areas designated for equipment and materials	Materials rotated to allow for introduction of new and removal of unused to enhance exploration through variation
			Recommended ratio of 1:3 approximately 8 to 10 same age children in group	Open areas for gross motor activities, social interaction, etc. Space is ordered and predictable yet flexible	
Motor Gross motor— begins to run & climb[1]	Opportunities to climb e.g., sofa, large furniture, stairs	Appropriate climbing equipment, with a range of challenges, e.g., varying heights; things to climb, slide, swing, pull, push, etc.	Motor: Understands need for children to be engaged in active play which will facilitate large muscle coordination	Cushioned flooring provided under equipment for safety	Specific equipment available to encourage range of gross motor activities
	Unacollated spaces, e.g., parts of living room, hallway	Floor plan and placement allows for large open spaces			
	Variation of floor surfaces, e.g., linoleum in kitchen carpet in living room	Both carpeted and uncarpeted areas which help define the use of space			
	Availability of both indoor and outdoor space				
Affective Exploratory behavior	Child can engage in activities parallel to his mother, e.g., while mother cooks, child can play with pans	Play areas where a child can explore various familiar objects by modeling through interactions with caregivers	Affective: Understands significance of discovery to child's learning and the importance of 1:1 interactions		
	Child can explore properties of his environment while engaged in routine activities, e.g., waterplay while bathing in company with parent	Provisions for exploring properties of the environment through specially selected equipment, e.g., use of water table in parallel play with peers			
	Potential learnings include: Exploration of child's competence and limitations Respect for the qualities of his environment				

See L. B. Murphy. Individualization of child care and its relation to environment. In L.L. Dittman (Ed.), *Early child care: The new perspectives.* Chicago: Aldine, 1965, p. 89.

As can be seen, in Table 1 the developmental need has been identified in the first column. In the second column are listed the kinds of opportunities that are available in the home to foster growth in each area. In the third column are the provisions that can be made in a quality center paralleling the opportunities available in a quality home. The general characteristics of the home and the center have also been noted. While much of the opportunities available in the home occur naturally in various facets of daily living, the center must consciously plan for similar experiences. To this extent identification of developmental needs becomes the basic guidelines for curriculum planning in the center by helping to alert caregivers to the kinds of experiences which they must provide in order to foster normal growth. The second part of the table focuses on three concerns of the center by identifying guidelines for staffing, for the use of space, and for the selection of equipment and materials. General principles for each of these areas are enumerated which will pertain to most developmental needs together with considerations specific to a given developmental need. The model is offered as an organizing framework within which it is possible to think through how each developmental need is provided for in the quality home, how the same need might be met in the center, and the accompanying implications for staffing, use of space and selection of equipment and materials.

Strengths of Home and Group Care Settings with Implications for Family Day Care

While it is helpful to use the quality home as the model for quality care, it must also be recognized that the home and the group care setting vary in significant ways. Table 2 is an attempt at delineating some of these differences by highlighting the strengths of the home setting juxtaposed against the strengths of the group care setting. It should be noted that the strength of one setting in many cases is offset by a parallel strength of the other setting. For example, while the home includes people in family groupings, in the center peer groupings are common. Hence, the young child has many opportunities to interact with same-age children, contributing to his over-all socialization.

Table 2 should be of particular interest to those engaged in family day care for while such settings are somewhere between the home and group care settings, at its best it can capitalize on the strengths of both. In family day care there is the possibility of a same-age playmate and also the likelihood of family groupings with both older and younger playmates. Likewise, the care of two infants under two plus three children from three to five years can be less demanding than care of five infants under the age of two. Hence, out-of-home ventures can be better accommodated by the family day care mother than the group caregiver.

The above model has been presented not only as a guide-line for curriculum planners and teacher trainers in both family and group day care settings, but also that it might help to dispel the myth that group care of children is necessarily inferior care. Given the changing role of women in our society and the multiplicity of social needs that arise in relation to child care, it is incumbent upon educators to identify means whereby child care can be of the highest quality. In the view of the authors, a curriculum built around a comprehensive view of the developmental needs of young children is one such way of assuring that quality is attained.

REFERENCES AND SELECTED BIBLIOGRAPHY

Brocher, T. Parents' schools. *Psychiatric Communications,* 1971, 13 *(2),* 1-9.

Brown, C. C. It changed my life: A consumer's guide to the four major parent-training programs. *Psychology Today,* November 1976, *10*(6), 47-57+.

Chauncey, H. (Ed.). *Soviet preschool education* (Vol. 1): *Program of instruction.* New York: Holt, Rinehart & Winston, 1969.

Chauncey, H. (Ed.). *Soviet preschool education* (Vol. 2): *Teacher's commentary.* New York: Holt, Rinehart & Winston, 1969.

Dimensions. A journal of the Southern Association on Children Under Six, January 1974, *2*(2).

Dittmann, L. L. (Ed.). *Early child care: The new perspectives.* Chicago: Aldine, 1968.

Elardo, R. & Pagan, B. (Eds.). *Perspectives on infant day care.* Orangeburg, South Carolina: Southern Association on Children Under Six, 1972.

Fandetti, D. V. Day care in working-class ethnic neighborhoods: Implications for social policy. *Child Welfare,* November 1976, *55*(9), 618-626.

Flint, B. M. *The security of infants.* Toronto, Canada: University of Toronto Press, 1959.

Forrester, B. J., *et al. Home visiting with mothers and infants: A procedural manual.* Nashville: George Peabody College for Teachers, Demonstration and Research Center for Early Education, 1971.

Friedlander, B. Z., Sterritt, G. M. & Kirk, G. E. *Exceptional infant* (Vol. 3): *Assessment and intervention.* New York: Brunner/Mazel, 1975.

Frost, J. L. *Understanding and nurturing infant development.* Washington, D.C.: Association for Childhood Education International, 1976.

Goldman, K. S. & Lewis, M. *Child care and public policy: A Case study.* Princeton, New Jersey: Educational Testing Service, Institute for Research in Human Development, 1976.

Grotberg, E. H. (Ed.). *Day care: Resources for decision.* Washington, D.C.: Office of Economic Opportunity,

Table 2

RELATIVE STRENGTHS OF THE HOME AND GROUP CARE SETTINGS
IN CARING FOR INFANTS AND TODDLERS

Strengths of the Home Setting	Strengths of the Group Care Setting
Setting supports the family unit by providing the child with a view of real home life	Provides support system for parents
Grouping of people follows natural patterns of the family	Greater opportunity for peer group interactions
More opportunities for child to relate on a 1:1 basis with a significant adult	May help counter over-attachment
Continuity of caregiving style	Provides child with several adult models
	Staff trained in child development and educational principles
	Interaction with several caregivers may help minimize stranger anxiety
Ease in out-of-home "ventures." Greater potential range of stimulation through encounters with larger environment, e.g., trips to the supermarket, etc.	Enriched environment with built-in safety precautions designed to permit the child maximum exploration of his environment.
	Space allocated for range of activities including vigorous gross motor activities as well as potentially messy activities, e.g., painting, water play, etc.
	Larger variety of age-appropriate materials, possibility of exploring range of curriculum areas, focusing on gross motor, fine motor, cognitive and affective developmental needs
Greater flexibility in scheduling	Scheduling built around the needs of young children by providing for a child-centered day
Greater opportunities for privacy in which to integrate experiences of the day and to foster autonomy	Engenders sense of self apart from the family

Office of Planning, Research and Evaluation, PRE/R, (Undated).

Honig, A. S. & Lally, J. R. *Infant caregiving.* New York: Open Family Press, 1974.

Katz, L. G. *Ethical issues in working with young children.* Paper presented at the meeting of the National Association for the Education of Young Children, Anaheim, California, November 14, 1976.

Kessen, W. Critiques, summary, and remarks on the report and conference proceedings: Implementation of an interactive model. In K. S. Goldman & M. Lewis, *Child care and public policy: A case study.* Princeton, New Jersey: Educational Testing Service, Institute for Research in Human Development, 1976.

Koontz, C. W. *Koontz child developmental program: Training activities for the first 48 months.* Los Angeles. Western Psychological Services, 1974.

Lindsey, R. Women entering job market at an "extraordinary" pace. *The New York Times,* September 12, 1976, pp. 1; 49.

Murphy, L. B. Individualization of child care and its relation to environment. In L. L. Dittmann (Ed.), *Early child care: The new perspectives.* Chicago: Aldine, 1965.

Osborn, J. D. & Osborn, D. K. *Cognitive tasks: An approach for early childhood education.* Athens, Georgio: Education Associates, 1974.

Palmer, S. E. *Children in long-term care: Their experiences and progress.* London: Family and Children's Services of London and Middlesex, 1976.

Pringle, M. K. *The needs of children.* New York: Schocken Books, 1974.

Provence, S. *Guide for the care of infants in groups.* New York: Child Welfare League of America, Inc., 1967.

Rauch, M. D. & Crowell, D. C. *Toward high quality family day care for infants and toddlers: Final report, infant satellite nurseries project.* Honolulu: University of Hawaii, Department of Human Development, 1974.

Russell, F. F. *Identification and management of selected developmental disabilities: A guide for nurses.* (DHEW Publication No. (HSA) 75-5404). Washington, D.C.: U.S. Government Printing Office, 1975.

Sale, J. S., et al. *Final report community family day care project.* Pasadena, California: Pacific Oaks College, 1973.

Smart, M. S. & Smart, R. C. *Infants: Development and relationships.* New York: Macmillan, 1973.

Tronick, E., & Greenfield, P. M. *Infant curriculum.* New York: An Open Family Book, 1973.

U.S. Department of Labor, Employment Standards Administration, Women's Bureau. *1975 Handbook on Women Workers* (Bulletin 297). Washington, D.C.: U.S. Government Printing Office, 1975.

Walters, C. E. (Ed.). *Mother-infant interaction.* New York: Human Sciences Press, 1976.

Willis, A., & Ricciuti, H. *A good beginning for babies: Guidelines for group care.* Washington, D.C.: National Association for the Education of Young Children, 1975.

Chapter 51

The Education of Early Sex-Role Development

Kathryn Norcross Black *

As a female psychologist I have long been interested in the topic of gender differences and their possible precursors in biology or environmental treatment. As the mother of two girls I have observed in real life exemplary occurrences of what research has reported concerning the differential treatment of and expectations for boys and girls and the resultant effects upon children. For example, the following happened when my second daughter was 5. Amanda said, "Oh brother," laughed and then explained, "that's a funny thing to say when you don't have a brother." "Why?" I asked. "Because then I'd have to do what he said. Girls have to do what boys say," and then after a look at my startled face - "Don't they? I thought that's the way it was."

Humans are continually processing and organizing information about the world, making generalizations about their experiences in order to make sense of them and guide their behavior. This is true not only for people such as philosophers and scientists but for all persons no matter what their occupation or age.

Generalizations are sometimes conscious and explicit and sometimes implicit and below the level of awareness. This possibility is especially important to remember when considering generalizations as to the classification of male and female where sometimes generalizations would appear to be more accurately inferred from behavior than from stated beliefs.

This chapter will be especially concerned with what occurs for young girls and boys. It is almost a truism in developmental psychology that the nature of thinking and formulation of generalizations varies with age. Specifically, young children tend to overgeneralize those things they observe to be true "on the average", and ignore probabilities and sometimes obvious empirical exceptions. For example, in a nursery school class it may be the case that the strongest and most aggressive individual is a girl, yet the children when questioned would probably overwhelmingly and without qualifications state that boys are stronger and fight more than girls. This generalization would be in agreement with the mean total observations of the class. Young children and often older children and some adults, appear to reach conclusions as we do in presidential elections; although the differences may be a matter of a few percentage points we still declare one winner.

The first thing we most often note about another person—infant, child, or adult—is their sex. Is it a boy or a girl? From birth onward there are differential reactions as a result of the answer to that question. I shall now report generalized reactions true not for everyone but for some majority of people who in their entirety comprise the socializing agents of our culture. Mothers more often exhibit post partum depression when the baby is a girl than when a boy. If the first child is a boy a longer period of time on the average elapses before a second child is born than if the first child is a girl. That is, it appears that people have another baby sooner when the one already on hand is female rather than male. If a family has two children, both of the same sex, it is more likely that a third child will be born when the first two are girls than when they are boys. Although the literature has suggested that stereotype notions as to appropriate behavior for the sexes may occur to a greater extent in the lower social classes, the above findings do not appear to be restricted to a less educated population. Anecdotally this may be illustrated by a conversation I recently had with a full professor colleague who told me that his secretary was the mother of eight children. When I expressed amazement at the thought he replied explanatorily, "Oh, the first seven were girls." Perhaps a mother's more frequent depression following the birth of a daughter is the result of her awareness that she's going to have to do this again soon!

More clearly, the above data support the interpretation that for at least some proportions of our population boys are valued more highly than girls.

Let us now consider what is known concerning differential expectations for the sexes. Several studies have agreed that adults anticipate that the sexes will differ in some ways. In one study it was found that parents describe boys as more likely to be rough at play, to be noisy, to do dangerous things, and to enjoy mechanical things. Girls are thought more likely to be neat and clean, quiet and reserved, helpful around the house, well-mannered, sensitive to the needs of others, to be easily frightened, and to cry. A study questioning elementary school teachers found that teachers expect that boys will be more aggressive. It is interesting to note that for both parents and teachers the behavior that

*Dr. Kathryn Norcross Black, Associate Professor of Development Psychology, Department of Psychological Science, Purdue University, West Lafayette, Indiana.

they indicated as desirable for the two sexes did not differ. Parents believed that it was important that children not cry frequently, that they be neat and clean, stick up for themselves but not be too aggressive, and so on. (It should be noted here that recent studies asking about desirable characteristics for adults have found that college aged students agreed to a significant extent that these characteristics differed for the sexes. For example, aggressiveness was rated as a desirable characteristic for males but not females, while sensitivity to others feelings was seen as a desirable characteristic for females but not males.)

It is possible that while parents have similar outcome goals in mind for children they accurately see the sexes as coming from different starting places. However, even if it were the case that these generalizations are based on factual mean differences, it seems that such generalizations influence our perceptions of and reaction to specific invidiauals. For example, in one study the same 6 month old baby was sometimes dressed and labelled a boy and sometimes a girl. Persons both interacted with the so-called boy or girl and afterward rated the infant's characteristics. Mean ratings different on such things as "sweet in appearance" and "gentle"; there was indication that the treatment of the baby as a boy was more boisterous than when the baby was thought to be a girl. These findings suggest that we tend to view people as more likely to possess those characteristics considered true of their sex. However, the influence of ascribed sex appears to be more complicated than that according to the findings of a similar research approach which showed films of children in uni-sex clothing and hair styles. Situations were shown in which the children exhibited behaviors, such as aggression and dependence, which are known to be viewed as more characteristic of one sex than the other. The children's behavior was rated by adults for whom a given child was sometimes identified as a boy and sometimes as a girl. There was indeed a difference in rated behavior of the same film depending upon the sex labelling. However, the findings were not that boys were seen as more aggressive than girls but that so-called aggressive behavior was more likely to be noticed and rated high if the actor was thought to be a girl. I believe that behavior such as aggression and dependence may be especially noted at a variety of ages when they run counter to our sex-role stereotyped expectations. For instance, I have now learned that when I am told that a female professional is "tough" or "aggressive" that I may accurately anticipate that she will be about as assertive as the usual male professional.

Finally, differential expectations for the sexes influences from a very early age the areas of achievement orientation and occupation. College attendance is more often anticipated for boys than girls. Not only is the need for employment more often assumed for males than for females but when employment is considered for or by females it is expected that girls will be nurses, dental assistants and secretaries while comparable boys would be doctors, dentists, and businessmen.

As consideration is next given to what is known about the differential treatment of sexes, it should be kept in mind that most of the research has been done with observations of female teachers and parents and that the children observed have most often been white and middle class.

Although as previously indicated there is reason to believe that boys are valued more than girls, overall boys and girls receive the same amount of attention and verbal interaction. However, the fact that boys receive both more positive and negative reactions, feedback that theoretically indicates an attempt to influence behavior, may indicate that parents and teachers are responding to an underlying set that what boys do may be more important in some sense than what girls do.

Ratings and observation of interactions of parents with preschool aged children find that there is no difference in the overall amount of warmth expressed to boys and girls. Interestingly, when elementary school aged children are asked to report on how much affection they have received from their parents, girls more often report more affection. Is this because of inaccurate child perception or a change in parental warmth that develops after public school entrance, a time that has not been directly sutdied? Perhaps it is the case that parents put more achievement pressure on boys once they begin school.

There is evidence at a variety of ages that parents differentially react to those behaviors in children that are considered more appropriate for one sex than another. Parents of preschool aged children in several studies indicated strong negative reactions to such so-called cross-sex activity choices for boys but not for girls. One can understand what this means by imagining the reactions a parent would be likely to have if a girl said she wanted to wear jeans, a cowboy hat, and a gun holster to school one day and compare this to the reactions if a boy said that he wanted to wear a dress and take a doll.

Children become aware of these adult reactions at an early age. It should not be surprising then to learn that when preschool aged children are observed in a free play situation boys are more likely to avoid playing with "girl toys" than girls are to avoid playing with "boy toys". This finding may not be explained away in terms of innate preferences for certain activities since this avoidance is greater when there is an adult physically in the room.

Why are girls allowed some freedom to exhibit so-called masculine behavior while the converse is not allowed for boys? One possibility is that such masculine behaviors are more desirable for behavioral development. It has been found that those girls who in preschool and elementary school had more "masculine" behavior—for example, they were more likely to initiate activities and be competitive— were more likely to have increases in IQ over time. A more likely reason is that adults find it understandable that girls should imitate the more powerful role. Children and adults both are more likely to imitate those who have the power to control rewards. Many children hold the stereotype that only males can control potent resources and it has been experimentally demonstrated that children may not be able to "see" a situation in which mothers are apparently more powerful than fathers. Many families explicitly give power to the person who brings in a salary or who contributes the greater income. My elder daughter recently reported that while visiting a friend the parents had a verbal battle over who would take out the garbage. The disagreement, after many years of marriage, occurred because the wife-mother had recently begun working part time and was feeling aggrieved at not receiving help. The husband-father won the battle not because he was employed full time but because he makes more money and thus claimed (with the children listening) more need for consideration. It is relevant to note here that in 1975 the average wage of employed women was about half that for men and that even when employed at the same responsibility level women on the average were paid less than men.

Not only do children learn that men are more powerful than women, it is also likely that they are exposed to the message that men's abilities are greater than those of women. Three separate kinds of research support this conclusion. Several studies have demonstrated that adults, both male and female, when asked to rate either passages of writing or painted pictures will rate the same work as being of higher quality if a man's name is given as author or artist than if a woman's name is given. It appears that Aurore Dupin was correct in assuming that a name change to George Sand would be more likely to bring her the equal evaluation with men that she desired. A second series of studies have found that from at least late elementary school girls on the average think they are less good than boys. Specifically, although it is usually the case that girls on the average are receiving higher grades in school (through high school), when asked to give an estimate of their intellectual ability girls will tend to underestimate their relative standing while boys will tend to overestimate theirs. Finally, a recent line of research in social psychology has found a difference in the factors used to explain task success for men or women. Briefly put, both men and women tend to attribute successful performance by a male as being due to skill while equivalent performance by a female on the same task is seen to be influenced more by luck. That such beliefs influence one's behavior may be seen by the fact that in both laboratory settings and at fairs males will prefer games requiring skill while females choose games of luck.

What is the source of this differing and denigrating self-evaluation of females? The major learning mechanisms suggested by psychologists are those of reinforcement, both reward and punishment, and of imitation. While the systematic information that we have on the occurrence of punishment for presumed sex-inappropriate behavior suggests that girls are allowed more freedom than boys it may be that this is

so only at the very young ages which have been studied and that later, especially from adolescence, this is changed. It is also possible that imitation is a sufficient mechanism to bring about female compliance. Macoby and Jacklin in their compendium of research studies on *The Psychology of Sex Differences* lists as still an open question and thus a possibility that females are more compliant than males when it comes to following the directions of adults. However, only compliance of both sexes would be needed to perpetuate the distinction modelled by the adults around the child.

Real life, however, is not the only media to which children are exposed. I suggest, as have others, that we should consider the possible role of vicarious reinforcement in and vicarious imitation of the communications of reading material, television, and films. The comparative characterizations of males and females in books have been most frequently and comprehensively studied; however, some consideration to all the media mentioned is given in the various selections of a book entitled, *Sexism and Youth*, edited by Diana Gersoni-Storn.

Three different categories of books have been examined. One category is that of picture books for young children. These are the books which are purchased or borrowed from public libraries by parents or preschool teachers to read to children often while showing them the pictures. These books may be especially potent for several reasons. One is that they are read to children at a time when concepts of sex roles are first forming. The second is suggested from research in cognitive development that the use of pictures may make learning more powerful. A representative study in this area was done by John Stewy and Margaret Higgs.* They examined a selection of books from a children's book collection at an university education library. The books were representative of library collections in general in that they had a range of publication dates and included both award winning and non-award winning books. Some important findings were: while 13% of the books included male characters only, no book dealt with females only. Of the 65% of books that included both men and women in some role, 83% of the women were depicted as "Home-makers", that 17% of the women shown in these books are playing some additional or other occupational role contrasts greatly with the over 50% who are in fact employed outside the home. One wonders to what extent the view presented by books is responsible for the fact that by the time children are 3 or 4 they see the main feminine role as housekeeping and the main masculine role as "breadwinner". These books were also narrow in their depiction of the occupational roles which women did have. Almost 1/3

---

*Stewy, J. and Higgs, M. Girls Grow up to be Mommies: A Study of Sexism in Children's Literature, *School Library Journal*, 1973. Also reprinted in *Issues in Children's Book Selection*, R.R. Bowker Co., 1973, New York.

of the women were shown as teachers. The next two role categories were maids and nurses! There were no female doctors, scientists, or artists. While the depiction of males occupationally was not any more representative of reality— for example, the two most frequent occupational classes were fisherman/sailor and farmer/rancher—men were shown as having much more variation in life activities.

Books for older children have also been examined by a variety of people or feminist groups and their findings are represented in *Youth* and *Issues in Children's Book Selection* (Library Journal Anthology). Three major kinds of questions have been asked. One is the relative extent to which females are portrayed. The second question asks what roles what roles and personality characteristics are demonstrated for the two sexes. And the third question asks what behaviors are awarded and what happens in the story when a nontraditional behavior occurs.

Generally, the answer to the first question is that books primarily about boys outnumber books about girls. For example, the American Library Association's list of Children's Notable Books of 1969 featured males twice as often as females. Merely because a main character is a female does not mean that one will be pleased at what children may learn from a book. I recently found myself in a pediatrician's waiting room and carefully selected a children's book in which a working mother was one of the main characters as well as a male ghost who lived with the family. I was somewhat dismayed to find that the reason the ghost loved mother best of all was—not because she was kind, or intelligent, or charming—but "because she is so pretty." Equally dismaying quotations may be found in Newbury Award Winners over the years. In a 1955 winner a girl asks a boy playmate "Can I go too?" and he replies "No! Girls are no good at jumping. It's a boy's game." In the 1967 book the following was presented in positive terms. "Accept the fact that this is a man's world and learn how to play the game gracefully." A 1969 book began with a non-conformist girl called Al who wears pigtails and doesn't worry about boyfriends. At the end of the book she has reformed, lost weight, had her hair done at a beauty parlor, and is pleased to be popular.

One would hope that this situation in which females are typically ignored, pictured as inept, or as feminine only in restrictive terms would be found only for story books which may be selected or rejected on an optional basis. Unfortunately, surveys of school textbooks indicates that they too demonstrate most of the biases indicated above. Males are more frequently mentioned not only in history and social science textbooks but also in the problems in mathematics books. Once again the roles played by males and females are dissimilar and stereotyped. A 1946 study of third grade readers concluded that the females in the stories were sociable and kind but helpless, less active than males, and uncreative. In 1971 things were still similar with women generally appearing as affectionate, appreciative, charming,

and considerate—certainly desirable traits—but not achieving, creative, or powerful.

Book companies have become aware of the charge of sexism and a number of them are attempting to take measures to change things. However, much of the guideline material issued to authors with respect to this consists of changes in the use of language. Certainly it would seem desirable to cut down or eliminate the use of "he" and its forms as the generic referent to humankind. And it is appropriate to ask that reference be made to "men and women" rather than "men and ladies". But one should be more concerned about the larger issue of the, perhaps unconscious, promulgation of stereotypes that are especially demeaning to females but that limit both males and females.

To this point we have examined the evidence that in our culture boys are more valued and judged by themselves and others in more positive terms than are girls. From what we know of the effects of self-attribution and self-concept— people attempt to match their behavior to their conception of themself—we would predict that females would behave differently than males and that this difference would increase over time and perhaps be greatest after adolescence when one is most concerned with forming a self-identity. This is in fact what happens. In sum, there is strong evidence that differential environments exist for boys and girls and that this is likely to lead to and influence the existence of behavioral sex differences. However, this does not mean that there are no differences between the sexes based on innate factors. To the contrary, as Maccoby and Jacklin conclude, "Biological factors have been most clearly indicated in sex differences in aggression and visual spatial ability" (p. 360), both characteristics which males demonstrate to a greater degree than females. They also conclude there are two more areas of well-demonstrated differences between the sexes with girls having greater verbal ability than boys and boys excelling in mathematical ability.

What, if anything, does the existence of psychological differences between the sexes mean as we consider the development of sex roles? At this point it would be helpful to make some distinctions that occur increasingly in the theoretical literature about sex roles. Sex roles may be separated into both a behavioral component and a personality characteristic component, although we have in the past tended to blur them. Feminity and masculinity should perhaps most usefully refer to attributes rather than behavior. That is, football player Rosie Grier should be able to, and does, do needlepoint without feeling that this negates his maleness; Billie Jean King is a champion tennis player and also an activist woman.

Another clarification with respect to sex roles that is now commonly make is that masculinity and feminity are not opposites such that one must be either masculine or feminine. We typically think of "masculine" characteristics as such things as being active, competent, and assertive while "feminine" characteristics are such things as nurturance and sensitivity to others needs. There is no reason why one could not be both nurturant and competent, both sensitive and assertive. The possession of high degrees of both these masculine and feminine traits has been referred to as androgyny and research suggests that about one third of our population is androgynous. (More information about both theoretical literature and research findings in this field are available in a book of readings entitled, *Beyond Sex Role Stereotypes: Readings Toward a Psychology of Androgyny*, edited by A.G. Kaplan and J.P. Bean).

It has been found that such androgynous individuals are more flexible—that is, have more ready options—in their behavior than do others. Some have also suggested that an androgynous approach to life is a psychologically healthier one, but I do not believe that the evidence is clear on this. This position may be influenced by the value judgment that androgyny is more desirable. In considerations about sex roles it would be helpful to keep in mind that many personal decisions with respect to sex appropriate behaviors and characteristics *are* influenced by values. This means both that there are some limits as to what psychology as a science can tell us should be and also that we should allow individuals the same freedom of choice in this realm as in other value realms with behaviors that don't intrude upon other individuals. Women have felt the psychological pressure of outside disapproval if they choose not to have children or to have children and also work outside the home. At this moment my female students and clients are telling me that they feel some pressure to combine a family and career whether they want to or not. While I still hear stories of parents who become upset if a boy plays with a doll I hear almost as many from people who are trying to rear non-stereotyped girls and who are distressed because their daughter still wants a Barbie doll. In the future many more persons, perhaps especially parents and teachers, will be trying to rear children in what is sometimes called a non-sexist manner. Can this be done? If so, how? Let us now address these questions.

While we do not have much decent evidence on the first question, we do have evidence that differing backgrounds will produce differing views on what is appropriate sex roles. A questionnaire study of college students found that students described males and females differently depending upon whether or not their own mothers had been employed. As a group, students whose mother had not worked outside the home described both males and females with adjectives that fit stereotyped notions while the group whose mothers had worked saw, for example, women as capable of both nurturance and competence and men as capable of both action and tenderness. My students and I are presently gathering data to see if the children of working mothers are more likely to be androgynous. If so, we may expect to see a gradual change in sex role behavior and perhaps our stereotypes as the children of the increasing numbers of working women grow up. It should

not, however, be automatically expected that with a working mother a young child will develop without stereotypes about roles. Anecdotal information from my own children and those of my female colleagues led me to gather systematic information from 4 and 5 year olds attending day care centers. Although all the mothers of these children were working full time they still saw mother primarily in terms of housekeeping functions and child care while the father's role was most often seen in terms of work. This kind of thinking probably comes from a number of reasons. One is that children's thinking at this age appears to be based on concrete experiences as much as verbal statements. Another is the tendency, especially prominet at this stage, to overgeneralize. Thus children may see the mother's role in a limited aspect because this is how they experience their mother at home; although a wife may be working full time it is still the case that she most often assumes the major responsibility for housekeeping and child care. It is also likely that children's conceptions, while most importantly influenced by the people immediately about them, are also derived even from this early age from a wide variety of observational experiences.

With the above reservations in mind let us consider ways one might contribute to children's experiences so that they are more likely to have attributes and beliefs that not only allow but assume equivalent evaluation of the sexes and a wide range of roles and characteristics.

Teachers and parents should first of all examine their own attitudes and behaviors and see what they are communicating to children. Do we assume that men are not capable of sensitivity or child care? If women, do we automatically think and talk of luck as a factor in our success?

In addition to watching one's own example it is as important to observe and help interpret the child's experiences. We need to tell children when they visit their male pediatrician with his female nurse that women are sometimes doctors and men sometimes nurses. We need to say as demonstrate that women are both loving mommies and capable workers while men are both loving daddies and capable workers. We will need to comment upon what they see on television and at the movies. I believe that parents of preschool children should monitor books, movies, and television. At older ages one may wish to give judgments or rewards without prohibitions. My elementary school aged children routinely ask me to watch their favorite television shows and give them my rating of good, so-so, or terrible with explanatory comments. Most libraries now have available yearly lists of non-sexist books. Check these books out for your young children, encourage your older children to read them. A librarian once told me that my daughter's favorite series of books, Nancy Drew, was "not really good literature you know." When I asked Deirdre why she liked them she answered, "She does things; she has an exciting life, You feel like you're there when you read it." Perhaps our evaluation of good books for children should include more than pictorial appeal and literary style.

If we are serious about assisting all children in optimal growth opportunities we may have to protest certain of their experiences: when a preschool visitor leaves nurses caps for girls and stethoscopes for boys; or when an elementary school athletic program has more scheduled time for boys than girls.

In sum, we will need to become assertive *and* caring women, assertive *and* caring men in order to furnish a world in which boys and girls are valued equally and fairly given options in behavior.

Selected Bibliography

Deaux, Kay. *The Behavior of Men and Women.* Harper & Row, 1976.

Gersoni-Stover, D. *Sexism and Youth*, R.R. Bauker, 1974, New York.

Kaplan, A.G. & Bean, J.P. *Beyond Sex-Role Stereotypes*, Little, Brown & Co., 1976, Boston.

Macoby, E. & Jacklin, C. *The Psychology of Sex Differences*, Stanford University Press, 1974, Stanford.

School Library Journal/Library Journal Anthology. Issues in Children's Book Selections. R.R. Banker, 1973, New York.

Eugenia S. Ware

Chapter 52

TV's Impact on Children: A Checkerboard Scene

Rose Mukerji *

Television holdouts are now a rare and endangered species. "We don't even have a TV set" was briefly the badge of the independent-minded spirit withstanding the ubiquitous boob tube or idiot box. More Americans have succumbed to its lure than to any other electrical appliance. Television is now a pervasive and, thereby, a substantial element in our environment.

In our most judicious moments, we acknowledge that our worst fears have not materialized. The haunting possibility that television would pre-empt the teacher's role, and thus the teacher's job, has been laid to rest. The great expectation that television would so revolutionize education in its broadest sense that persistent problems of organized education would be solved has also not come to pass.

Although its potential educational power has not yet been realized, television has had an unmistakable impact on the lives of children. In trying to assess the nature and extent of this impact, researchers no longer have the luxury of studying "before and after TV." Children in the middle years (now in elementary school) have been weaned on television hearing, if not watching. In a brief period of 20 years, children in the early childhood years are now the second TV generation.

This discussion will attempt to sort out the significance of television, and to some extent film, as a medium for influencing learning, both cognitive and affective, and as an agent in the socializing process of children from age 3 to 12. To some extent, distinctions will be made between the two groups of children: early childhood (children 3 to 7) and middle childhood (8 to 12).

In considering TV's impact on children in the early and middle years, it is necessary to take into account all television: commercial, public, and educational or instructional; children's programs and adult programs which they watch; and the inescapable commercials of American television.

There is a growing body of research on various aspects of television. Some studies concentrate on the relative teaching effectiveness of such television techniques as graphics and three-dimensional images. Other studies examine the effect of violence. Still others probe the influence of programs purporting to foster sound values and attitudes.

As a subject that people talk about a great deal, television has generated considerable empirical data about its influence on children. Educators, particularly, derive hypotheses about TV's impact from their strong professional base of learning and child development theory. It is, therefore, reassuring to find that, in summary, television in the lives of children is a complex scene. It is to be expected that contradictory judgments are being made about its influence.

Cognitive Learning

Early, research efforts were designed to measure rather limited informational items, as scores from television and nontelevision instruction were compared. In summary, the findings indicate that television learning of this nature is equal to, or slightly superior to, nontelevision instruction. (Chu, 1967).

More recently, considerable data have been gathered in systematic research in early childhood television learning related to the nationally and internationally broadcast "Sesame Street." Educational Testing Service research shows a positive relationship between amount and frequency of viewing and gains made on items tested: recognition, matching, and labeling of letters and numerals; identification of body parts; and classification by size, form, and function (Lesser, 1974).

It is interesting to note that other independent research findings challenge the interpretation of results presented by ETS. Herbert Sprigle 1972 set out to test two hypotheses suggested by the Research Department of the Children's Television Workshop. Stated as goals these were: 1) "Sesame Street" can prepare poverty-level children for first grade, and 2) it can substantially narrow the achievement gap between the poor and the middle-class child. Sprigle suggests that the "Sesame Street" curriculum did not reach these goals. He adds:

The findings of the two-year study of "Sesame Street" graduates, the findings of the adult/child communication patterns of the program, the examination and evaluation of the philosophy, adult behavior, and attitudes toward learning and children fail

*Rose Mukerji is professor of education, Brooklyn College, City University of New York. Reprinted with the permission of PHI DELTA KAPPAN, January 1876.

to identify any redeeming features of "Sesame Street" as an educational program. The evidence suggests that the label "education" is misleading and deceptive.

One finds little if any controversy about the efficacy of television in enhancing learning for elementary or middle-age children. But there is considerable ferment about the role of television in concept development and cognitive learning by *young* children.

Studies and theory emphasize the centrality of the sensory style of learning among young children. As Milton Schwebel notes, (1973), the seminal work of Piaget makes clear that many diverse and related concrete experiences are required for young children to develop concepts about their world. He states further:

It is absolutely necessary that learners have at their disposal concrete material experiences (and not merely pictures) and that they form their own hypotheses and verify them (or not verify them) themselves through their own active manipulation. The observed activities of others, including those of the teachers, are not formative of new organizations in the child.

It would be simplistic to place the entire burden of the learning process on direct experience. Certainly an important part is played by imitation of others, by stimulating suggestions gained from TV viewing, and by efforts to sort out ideas verbally in a social context. But development of concepts and understanding of relationships by the young child rely primarily on his active structuring in a complex, real environment.

Since much of a child's learning takes place through the medium of play, and since play is a young child's primary vehicle for forming the symbolic meaning of what he is experiencing, there is reason to be concerned about the long hours which some youngster spends in front of the TV set. After all, the time spent watching television is taken from the time when a young child would otherwise play. According to Eleanore E. Maccoby (1951), as long ago as the early days of TV in 1951, approximatley 1½ hours a day shifted from active play to passive viewing. It gives one pause to think of the great increase in TV watching among young children today.

Although to this point the discussion has centered on cognitive learning, it should be noted that the separation of cognitive from affective learning is made only as a convenience for emphasis. Actually, all learning is basically entwined and has components of intellectuality and emotionality. With this understanding, we move on to consider the impact of television on affective learning.

Affective Learning

Three dimensions of affective learning of particular im-

port here are: 1) feelings and emotions, 2) modeling, and 3) fantasy/reality.

Feelings and Emotions – In the early days of television for children, little attention was given to consciously incorporating the subject matter of emotions and feelings, either directly or by implication. Not that this arena was considered unimportant. On the contrary, it was generally agreed that, in the early years, children are trying to manage a crucial aspect of growth in which they begin to understand and to manage their feelings. The demands on them to cope with their feelings in ways acceptable to other people are great.

In response to the question, "Why not feelings and values in instructional television?" I have expressed the view that television *should* deal with a variety of emotions honestly. (Baron, 1974). It should present important feelings such as fear and anxiety as well as those of delight and love. Television, as a channel for dramatic form, is uniquely suited to engaging children in the drama of life, just as outstanding children's books have succeeded in doing.

It is interesting to note that, about 10 years ago, the 1966 Award for Excellence in Children's Programming was awarded by National Educational Television for a program in the "Round-about" series titled "Living or Dead?" The citation spoke of the courage shown in dealing with such a delicate, emotional subject in straightforward, yet sensitive, terms for young viewers age 3 to 5. In an evaluation of this series, "Living or Dead?" (a very controversial program among adults) was mentioned most frequently by children as one they liked, referring to it by their own title, "The Dead Bird." Teachers and parents reported their surprise when many children incorporated the emotional content of the program into their play over an extended period of time.

A long-running early childhood series, "Mister Rogers' Neighborhood,"has as its hallmark the position that children are best served when programming evokes the inner drama of children's feelings. Much of the success of this program rests on children's acceptance of a caring adult who demonstrates that feelings are mentionable as well as manageable.

Programs for elementary children have generally related directly to conventional subject matter while their designers explored more effective ways of presenting these subjects. One outstanding television series, "Inside/Out," is geared to health education but provides a "feelings" approach to the subject. It deals with day-to-day problems and emotions of children from *their* point of view. There are programs on common topics such as the bully, the joker, growing in responsibility and freedom, and competition between brothers and sisters. Included are topics that generally have been hush-hush in school, such as a death in the family, divorce, child abuse, and a crush on the teacher.

The viewers are involved emotionally as well as intellectually in the problems and situations encountered on television. Suggested follow-up discussions and activities make a direct tie between children's viewing and their own ideas, choices, values, and behavior. In the middle year, when the gang or peer group is a powerful molding force, group viewing has a particular advantage because it encourages the interplay of ideas and positions so characteristic of upper-elementary youngsters. In dealing with feelings and emotions, one is naturally led to consider, also, how models of behavior are an integral part of affective learning.

Modeling – The significance of television for both younger and older children rests, in part, on its ability to provide models for their identification and imitation. However, they still need *live* people to help them develop as social beings and to serve as models for identification.

With middle and older children, we need to look at the models which blanket the television scene. What images do they identify with—the dare-devil image of Evel Knievel? The flamboyant dress of the latest rock star? The impossible power of the Six-Million-Dollar Man? The "Kung Fu" hero? The action man on adult drama? One has to answer in the affirmative, and the answer is far from comforting.

In this connection, an ingenious study was carried out by Stanley J. Baron and Timothy P. Meyer. They posed a morally ambiguous problem and asked children to give their own solution. They also asked the children how their favorite television characters would solve it. There was extensive agreement between the two solutions, indicating strong identification with the television model. These findings occur with Urie Bronfenbrenner's theory that children are turning more and more to peers and television characters as behavior models for identification purposes. (Bronfenbrenner, 1970).

On a more positive note, Maccoby (1951), states that the media provide a child with experience free from real-life controls, so that, in attempting to find solutions to a problem, he can try out various modes of action without risking injury or punishment.

Fantasy and Reality – At the same time that television provides models for identification and imitation, it also provides grist for a child's fantasy life. Fantasy is not the same for younger and older children. In the young child, it is intertwined with his developing mode of thinking. He is not able, consistently, to distinguish between fantasy and reality (often a disturbing condition to adults, who are fearful that a youngster is a chronic liar). In this uncertainty, he is only following a normal path of moving from a magical conception of the world to one which is more rational.

In its efforts to engage children's imagination, television has frequently added to a child's confusion by portraying live adults who talk to inanimate objects and expect them to reply. "Mister Rogers' Neighborhood" has, in recent productions, sought to make a clearer distinction between fantasy and reality. Children are invited to "pretend " as the scene shifts from the reality set to the "neighborhood of make-believe." The fact that young children often con-

fuse fantasy and reality is no reason for adults to add further to their confusion through television programming.

When older children create fantasies in which they themselves are active, they do it quite consciously and without confusion. Television can stimulate fantasies which, in turn, may lead to creative and imaginative expression by youngsters. Special effects made possible by television technology offer new and unique visual stimuli which may expand viewers' perceptions. These children can also express their own fantasies through explorational use of the newer media. Television, along with other recreational forms such as drama, fiction, and film, provides a respite from reality. Certainly no one would gainsay the need for fantasy and its attendant aesthetic experience in one's life, provided, of course, that it *is* an aesthetic experience.

On the other hand, there is some indication that fantasies are related to an individual's unfulfilled needs and frustrations. Do fantasies merely reflect frustration, or do they assist in working out solutions to frustrations? There is danger when children retreat from real-life encounters into excessive television fantasy in order to avoid facing problems of reality.

Maccoby (1954) raises another possible danger, suggesting that externally controlled fantasy on television builds up motivation and satisfies it with relatively little delay. One thing that children must learn during the socialization process is to suffer delay in their satisfaction — to keep a motive at work over long periods of time. Maccoby is concerned that mass media experience may run counter to this training and build up habits of premature closure.

In summary, although there can be value in the fantasy nature of identification with television characters for younger and older children alike, they both need to balance their television fantasy encounters against real experiences with live people.

In this brief discussion of television and children's learning in the interrelated cognitive and affective domains, it is clear that the potential and real impact on young and middle children is a checkerboard of positive and negative influences. The same can be said of television as a socializing factor in children's lives.

Socializing Effect

Children's ideas about the social world and how people relate to each other are influenced by television. Thier developing sense of social values also receives some input from television images. Since social behavior is affected by one's emerging ideas and values, it is only natural that, to some extent, television will have a socializing effect on children. Research supports this observation. Children who watch programs depicting interpersonal violence display increased aggressiveness, but television can also encourage socially valued behavior. This discussion will consider some of the research and current points of view concerning television violence and children, as well as pro-social television and children.

Violence — The question of the impact of television violence on children has been one of the most widely studied and discussed aspects of television. In the wake of the assassinations of Robert F. Kennedy and Martin Luther King and during the spread of campus riots, President Lyndon Johnson, in 1968, appointed a National Commission on the Causes and Prevention of Violence, headed by Milton Eisenhower. The commission is not the sole culprit. However, it did conclude that violence on TV encourages violent forms of behavior and fosters moral and social values about violence in daily life which are unacceptable in a civilized society. In one memorable line, it said, "If TV is compared to a meal, programming containing violence clearly is the main course." (Hickey, 1975).

In 1969, Senator John O. Pastore, chairman of the Senate Communications Subcommittee, set in motion the surgeon general's investigation — an exhaustive three-year study costing $1 million — dealing with the impact of televised violence on children. Robert M. Liebert, (1973) a psychologist at the State University of New York and a principal investigator in the study, found:

> The more violence and aggression a youngster sees on TV, regardless of his age, sex, or social background, the more aggressive he is likely to be in his own attitudes and behavior. The effects are not limited to youngsters who are in some way abnormal, but rather were found in large numbers of perfectly normal American children.

This conclusion arises from analysis of more than 50 studies covering the behavior of 10,000 children between the ages of 3 and 19.

Subsequent studies confirm the findings of the 1972 surgeon general's report. Leifer and Roberts, (1972), studying four groups of preschoolers with different treatments, found that young children apparently had difficulty extracting the themes of good or bad *consequences* of aggression and of good or bad *reasons* for aggression from the aggression and counter-aggression in each program. Thus the *amount* of aggression in the program became the significant factor influencing their subsequent behavior.

Despite the surgeon general's report that there are now sufficient data to justify action, not everyone accepted the conclusion. Edith Efron, (1975) a contributing editor of *TV Guide,* speaks out strongly in opposition:

> The sex and violence pack is out again, baying with full throat, blaming crime on network plays. It is a tiresome fact that crime antedates network TV (and she goes back to Cain and Abel to prove it). There is only one reason today to pay the slightest attention to this claque, and that is: It is now brandishing "scien-

tific" that the sight of TV violence can indeed cause real-life violence.

Referring to the measured tones of the research report which deal in tendencies and qualifications rather than in absolutes and unequivocal proof, she adds:

> Now sensible people, facing this kind of intellectual nonsense, will simply put on their hats, go home, and settle down to a jolly evening with "Kojack," "Mannix," "Cannon," and company, who, if they have any virtue in common, [have] the capacity for lucid deduction.

Not unexpectedly, the specter of government censorship began to loom on the horizon. The cry of "civil liberties and censorship" was raised. Frederic Wertham 1975, a psychiatrist known for his long time concern with children and violence, says:

> The battle for civil liberties should not be fought on the backs of children. The argument that protecting children from harmful media exposure is an infringement of civil liberties has no historical foundation. . . . It has never happened in the history of the world that regulations to protect children—be they with regard to child labor, food, drink, arms, sex, publications, entertainment, or plastic toys—have played any role whatsoever in the abridgment of political or civil liberties for adults.

Violence on television continues to be a subject of concern to the television industry. The NBC network president states: "Our Broadcast Standards require that 'violence will be shown only to the extent appropriate to the legitimate development of theme, plot, or characterization. It should not be shown in a context which favors it as a desirable method for solving human problems, for its own sake, for shock effect, or to excess.' " (1975).

In 1975, network broadcasters, as members of the National Association of Broadcasters, ratified an agreement to introduce the "family hour" between 7 and 9 p.m. starting in September. According to Robert D. Wood, president of CBS/TV, it is "an attempt to program a specific part of our schedule so that the whole family can enjoy television together without being disturbed or embarrassed."

This move has been received with some skepticism. It is perceived by most experts as a subtle carte blanche for "business as usual" or, as one writer put it, "gore as before." Despite the passage of years after the surgeon general's report, the 1974 annual report on television violence by George Gerbner and Larry Gross of the Annenberg School of Communications at the University of Pennsylvania states that levels of TV violence have remained unacceptably high. No wonder that skeptics question the impact of the cosmetic Band-aid of a two-hour family slot when radical surgery is required.

Television violence and children should continue to command our concern. However, we must also turn our attention to the potential for pro-social influence through television.

Pro-Social — The early childhood years are ones for reaching out beyond the home and family into more complex and diversified relations with many unpredictable people. Underlying a child's ability to grow as a social person is his capacity for feeling, for empathy, for caring, and for identifying with others. Young children begin this difficult journey of social development; middle children continue it; adults pursue it the rest of their lives.

Can the viewing of pro-social television by children influence them toward pro-social attitudes and behavior? Empirical data in this area are being corroborated by several research studies. For example, regular "Sesame Street" programs showing children and adults sharing and helping each other were used to compare pro-social behavior of children who watched the program with those who did not. It was found that the viewers were more likely to cooperate and share than children who did not view these segments.

In another study with nursery children, Lynette Friedrich (1974): found that

. . . systematic viewing of "Mister Rogers' Neighborhood" effected significant changes in their free play behavior in two areas of personality development: 1) self-regulatory behavior — children increased in task persistence and showed greater ability to carry out responsibility without adult intervention; and 2) pro-social interpersonal behavior — children showed increased cooperative play, increased ability to express feelings, and increased sympathy and help for others. The changes in pro-social interpersonal behavior were significant for children from lower-social-class homes. The increase in self-regulatory behavior was found in the entire sample.

Fostering pro-social attitudes and behavior in children who inescapably live in a multicultural country and world is an urgent responsibility for television. In a recent study commissioned by the Corporation for Public Broadcasting under the auspices of the Advisory Council of National Organizations, one of two underlying recommendations was as follows:

The Corporation for Public Broadcasting should recognize and support the principle of cultural pluralism which is rooted in our common concerns as humans as well as the differences which enhance the strength and diversity of the American people.

It is gratifying to note that progress has been made in educational programs for children in the past 10 years in support of the principle and value of cultural pluralism. An early entry on the national scene was "Roundabout," which had as its central, sustaining character the realistic young black, Jim Jeffers. The "Ripples" series for younger children and the "Inside/Out" series for middle children sustained multi-cultural values throughout. "Big Blue Marble" is a recent series for older children which is made up of segments showing interesting children's activities in various countries. Both "Sesame Street" and "The Electric Company" feature interracial and intercultural casts.

Underlying the multicultural content and multi-ethnic casts of all of these programs is the assumption that these qualities will help develop positive attitudes toward various races and cultures among viewers. This assumption has received some support from recent research. In national studies, children who watched "Sesame Street" for two years had more positive attitudes toward school and members of various races than did children who watched less. (Bogartz, 1970).

Two nationally distributed current series have brought a bilingual, multicultural approach to children's television. They are "Villa Alegre," produced in California, and "Carrascolendas," from Texas. In both cases, the languages used are English and Spanish. "Carrascolendas" states as its principal objective:

To cultivate in each child an awareness of the contributions of his own and other cultures to America, and to provide each child with a rich repertoire of living skills that can enhance his potential for optimally effective living in a multicultural America.

While there is progress in educational and public programming for children, commitment to pro-social themes and multicultural valuing cannot be said to characterize television in general. Commercial television has been severely criticized for its distorted picture of real life. Yet this is what children watch. With what effect?

Leifer (1975) says:

TV, whether or not it accurately reflects our social system, does contribute to forming this social system. At the very least, it helps to socialize a new generation of children into an already existing pattern. To the extent that TV does not reflect reality, it socializes children into a fictitious social system.

Stereotyping — It is to be expected that any medium which must telegraph characters, a story line, and a resolution in a short half-hour or hour will rely on stereotypes and caricatures for quick identification. However, when we examine television stereotypes, we see how prejudicial they can be. For example:

White Americans make up the overwhelming

majority of TV characters. Indians and Africans are barely represented. The typical role of Italians and blacks is an insult to all of us, not only to these groups. And what about the roles of men and women? The TV screen is a sexist screen where the man is not only more evident, but also superior. . .Working women are more often victims of aggression than married women.

And who are the models of success on TV? The clever, highly unorthodox lawyer. . .the brutal police officer. . .the "private eye" operating outside the law. Ordinary workers are frequently depicted as coarse and stupid, there for laughs. (1973).

We object to these distortions; we deplore this stereotyping. At least we say we do. Yet there is a disturbing question that remains to haunt us: Why are these television shows so popular? Why do they continue and multiply season after season? Do we, in our silent hearts, cherish these stereotypes and the excitement of forbidden violence? Are we, by our actions, adding to the negative impact on the checkerboard scene of children and television?

Children as Producers

So far, we have been focusing on children as consumers of television fare, pointing up the tremendous influence, both positive and negative, it has on them. However, there is another facet which deserves attention: children as producers of material using the media of television and film.

Children have traditionally used art media to express who they are and to know more deeply who they are. Too often, in restrictive school settings, they have failed.

Many children are, unfortunately, turned off by their stifling experiences or unfortunate failures with traditional art media. With other media, they have a second chance. Technology has opened channels for children to capture their unique expressions in newer media. Less encumbered by stereotypes, these media can rekindle a child's eagerness to express himself and thereby continue forming himself with a conscious sense of affirmation. (Mukerji, 1973).

Children seem intuitively at home with the unique character of television and film — its all-at-once sound and movement without barriers of time and distance. Perhaps they "know" these dimensions because they are so similar to their own play, which readily defies and controls the limits of time and space.

Having grown up with television, it is not surprising that children all over the country respond enthusiastically by contributing skits, riddles, films, and other "ZOOM-ies" to the unusual children's series, "ZOOM," which incorporates them into the programs. The on-camera children also play a

significant role in putting together this nationally distributed public television show — no small accomplishment for middle and older children.

Within a school setting, the Children's Video Theatre has developed a project for child-created television in the inner city. (LeBaron, 1975). Programs were produced by fifth- and sixth-graders and were shown monthly on local community Antenna Television (CATV). The project reaffirmed that engaging poor achievers in video production can improve academic performance, especially in the language arts.

The demands of television production touch all curriculum areas. Unlike other forms of expression, television and film are group enterprises, requiring social skills and understandings as well as intellectual and aesthetic ones. To conceive, execute, and evaluate anything as complex as television or film making requires children to tap and develop all of their resources. Planning, researching, recording, script writing, making storyboards, learning techniques for handling the technology, scouting and "seeing" locations, interviewing, communicating, selecting, editing, designing, constructing, titling, recording sound and music, coordinating efforts under pressure, adapting, revising, persisting, and sharing the successes and disappointments — all of these come into play in a single television or film production.

Although impressed by its potential, those who have worked with children and media are, nevertheless, aware that it is no easy road leading from failure to success. But, as one creative teacher and her film associate, carrying on a project with 16 children age 5 to 9 (nine of whom were considered failures in school), reported:

As we had suspected, the camera turned out to be an excellent tool. It served not as an end in itself, but rather as a means to help "open up" the children and give them a nonverbal, nonthreatening means to begin to perceive themselves as more worthy and to see themselves in relation to their world: a means to look again, observe, question, differentiate, clarify, and, in the broadest sense, become more effective learners. (Harris, 1973).

These few examples underscore the power of direct involvement in the creative arts, in this case television and film, as an essential means by which children can more fully develop their human potential. Through such involvement, they become not just pawns to be pushed onto positive or negative squares on the checkerboard — they become important players.

Conclusion

The dynamics of the media, and television in particular, are still in a healthy state of flux and development. We are nowhere near approaching a final score where television and children are concerned. That television has a tremendous influence on children is clear. Whether that impact is more positive than negative depends, to some extent, on the determination with which concerned adults help to tilt the balance in favor of children.

BIBLIOGRAPHY

Goodwin C. Chu and Wilbur Schramm, *Learning from Television: What the Research Says* (Washington, D.C.: National Association of Educational Broadcasters, 1967).

Gerald S. Lesser, *Children and Television: Lessons from "Sesame Street"* (New York: Random House, 1974).

Herbert A. Sprigle, "Who Wants To Live on Sesame Street?" *Young Children,* December, 1972.

Milton Schebel and Jane Raph, eds., *Introduction to Piaget in the Classroom* (New York: Basic Books, 1973).

Eleanore E. Maccoby, "Television: Its Impact on School Children," *Public Opinion Quarterly,* Fall, 1951.

Stanley J. Baron and Timothy P. Meyer, "Imitation and Identification," *AV Communication Review,* Summer, 1974.

Urie Bronfenbrenner, *Two Worlds of Childhood* (New York: Russell Sage, 1970).

Eleanore E. Maccoby, "Why Do Children Watch Television?" *Public Opinion Quarterly,* Fall, 1954.

Neil Hickey, "Does TV Violence Affect Our Society? YES," *TV Guide,* June 14–20, 1975.

Robert M. Liebert, John M. Neale, and Emily S. Davidson, *The Early Window: Effects of Television on Children and Youth* (New York: Pergamon Press, 1973).

Aimee Dorr Leifer and Donald F. Roberts, "Children's Responses to Television Violence," in J. P. Murray, E. A. Rubenstein, and G. A. Comstock, eds., *Television and Social Behavior,* vol 2 (Washington, D.C.: U.S. Government Printing Office, 1972).

Edith Efron, "Does TV Violence Affect Our Society? NO," *TV Guide,* June 14–20, 1975.

"Violence!" *TV Guide,* June 14–20, 1975.

D. Lynn McDonald and F. Leon Paulson, *Evaluation of "Sesame Street" Social Goals: The Interpersonal Strategies of Cooperation, Conflict Resolution, and Different Perpsectives,* ERIC Document ED 052824, April, 1971.

Lynette K. Friedrich, "The Use of Television in Early Childhood Education," proceedings of the International Council for Educational Media, Munich, 1974.

Gerry A. Bogatz and Samuel Ball, *The Second Year of "Sesame Street": A Continuing Evaluation* (Princeton, N.J.: Educational Testing Service, 1971).

"Carrascolendas" Television Project, KLRN-TV, Austin, Texas, 1975.

Aimee Dorr Leifer, Neal J. Gordon, and Sherryl Browne Graves, "Children's Television: More than Mere Entertainment," *Harvard Educational Review,* May, 1974.

Rose Mukerji, "Creating and Becoming," in *Children Are Centers for Understanding Media* (Washington, D.C.: Association for Childhood Education International, 1973).

John LeBaron and Louise Kanus, "Child-Created Television in the Inner City," *Elementary School Journal,* April 1975).

Roberta Harris, "A Child's-Eye View," in *Children Are centers for Understanding Media* (Washington, D.C.: Association for Childhood Education International, 1973). □

Chapter 53

Goals and Directions of Bilingual Programs in Early Childhood Years

Richard E. Baecher*

Recent studies by anthropologists, biologists, educators, pediatricians, psychologissts, and others clearly point in one direction. The child's earliest years provide a dynamic context wherein the most rapid physical and cognitive growth takes place. For instance, Bloom (1964, p. 64) has shown that 20 percent of an individual's intellectual growth occurs by age 1 and by the fourth year, 50 percent of the child's total capacity for development is realized.

Burton L. White (1975, p. 108), Director of Harvard's Pre-School Project, maintains that all children from whatever type of family seem to be very much alike during the first year of life, but between 10 and 18 months, life-long differences in competencies emerge. His research leads him to infer that ages 0 to 5 are the human being's best learning period provided that *adult* learning is not viewed as identical to *child* learning. Akers (1972, p. 3) summarized the new focus on childhood in describing its dynamic features:

> the child is learning every moment of his life, sometimes actively and aggressively moving out, at other times assuming a more passive role. He is discovering who and what he is. He is discovering how other people feel about him and what they expect of him, as well as how he feels about them and what he can expect from them. He is continuously searching to understand the world of people and things which surround him and to determine what his own role is in this highly complex situation.

The image of the young child "searching to understand" how he/she is related to the world aptly synthesizes a basic process of early childhood education.

Despite these advances in the field of child development, ambiguity prevails among early childhood specialists. Although such fundamental disciplines as biology and psychology have contributed to our understanding of children's growth, not all of this knowledge can be used specifically in establishing a match between the child's development and an educational program. Sigel (1972, p. 15) has noted that "preschool programs have not agreed upon a body of knowledge or skills that are expected to be transmitted to children." Because an accepted tradition and standards for preschool are lacking, program goals and outcomes usually are determined by the perspectives and preconceptions of early childhood educators. A serious con-

sequence of this ambiguity is that the effectiveness of programs are difficult to compare, thereby limiting replication efforts.

Another limitation gaining more attention from policy makers is that few early childhood programs attempt to match their various program components with the bilingual bicultural characteristics of ethnically diverse children. Some significant findings from the Current Population Survey (Waggoner, 1976, pp. 5–6) underscore this diversity within the United States:

1. 13% of the U.S. population four years and older in July 1975 are living in households in which languages other than English are spoken.
2. Spanish is the most widely spoken language employed in the household after English; there are 8.2 million Spanish speakers in homes with languages other than English.
3. One individual in ten in the U.S. aged four or more resides in a household with a language other than English either as usual or other language, and speaks a language other than English.

Waggoner also found that only 33% of the 4 and 5 year olds who were born abroad, in households where the usual language was other than English, or who usually spoke a language other than English themselves, were in early childhood programs. In addition, only 30% of those who usually communicate in a language other than English were said to be enrolled in or attending school in 1974-75. Among the important implications of these figures is that bilingual children are not participating in preschool programs.

What directions does "bilingual multicultural education" present to early childhood educators? What are the goals of bilingual programs for young children from diverse backgrounds? What competencies must teachers demonstrate in early childhood programs for bilingual children? What techniques can be suggested for practitioners that are derived from bilingual research and allied disciplines?

In this article, I point out some inadequacies of current typologies of bilingual education. I make the case that if bilingual programs are viewed within a social system perspective, more appropriate and congruent models can be

---

*Dr. Richard Baecher, Director of Bilingual Teacher Training Programs, Fordham University.

created for early childhood educators. Such a model includes the 3 interactive elements of individuals, processes, and properties, with specific mention given to: (1) teacher competencies that are unique to the education of Spanish children, (2) the goals of bilingual programs, and (3) description of a bilingual early childhood education set of materials. I conclude with a digest of recommendations for preschool practitioners, based upon some relevant research.

I have used certain terms which need to be made more precise. "Bilingual multicultural education" is the process in which English and other languages and cultures reflecting the life-style of the community are employed as media of instruction (National Advisory Council on Bilingual Education, 1975, p. 8). "Bilingual children" includes those proficient in 2 languages as well as those who will be introduced to English as a second language, i.e., potentially bilingual. Preschool education is used interchangeably with early childhood education and refers to a group setting away from home for children under public school age, i.e., 2-5, and who are under the supervision of licensed public school personnel.

Inadequacy of Certain Bilingual Typologies

A number of descriptive schemes and "typologies" of bilingual schooling have been advanced in the growing body of information pertaining to bilingual multicultural education (Valencia, 1969; Andersson and Boyer, 1970; Fishman and Lovas, 1970; Mackey, 1970; John and Horner, 1971). Because the concept of "bilingual school"' has been employed indiscriminately to cover a wide variety of uses of 2 languages in education, these classification systems attempt to systematically describe the many variables that constitute bilingual school programs. For example, Mackey's typology, by far the most inclusive, consists of 90 basically different patterns of bilingual schooling; Valencia presents 19 basic models. Fishman's typography delineates 4 differing kinds of community and school objectives, ranging from "transitional bilingualism" to "full biliterate bilingualism." One common element that can be abstracted from each model is the ratio of use of the student's 2 languages in a spatial and temporal context. Spatial references might include the pupil's home, school, community, or nation; temporal references are the distribution of the languages from the first to the last year of the school's program. Mackey (1970, p. 603) summarized these classification schemes:

> The component common to all types at all levels is language.....the entire typology may be viewed as a series of patterns of distribution of two or more languages in the education of the learner, within the home, the school, the area, and the nation.

These models are helpful in observing, classifying and quantifying the language variable in the wide range of cur-

rent bilingual programs that are operating in public elementary schools. However, they are inadequate in enabling the practitioner to understand and implement such programs especially at the preschool level.

One obvious reason is the central focus on language use and the serious omission of cognitive and social development variables. One assumption of early childhood programs is that the child's growth is cumulative where early experiences facilitate realization of the individual's capabilities, both in linguistic and non-linguistic symbol formation. Saville-Troike (1976, pp. 14-15) has pointed out that as the child develops whatever specific variety of language is unique to the social environment, he/she "can interpret and use a variety of gestures, facial expressions, and other paralinguistic devices common to their own culture." According to Ramirez and Castaneda (1974, p. 104), the materials, policies and practices of the school need to reflect the incorporation of not only the child's language but also of the culture, values, communication modes, and preferred learning style of the child. Speaking about the Mexican American student population, Valencia (1976, p. 15) states that "no one particular bilingual education curriculum is generalizable." Individual and group differences, then, especially those pertaining to the child's common culture and heritage, must be recognized and attended to in bilingual multicultural programs.

Another weakness of these typologies is the lack of vital information they provide to the decision making process so necessary in the daily implementation of bilingual programs. The issues of *who, what, where, how, when* and *why* of these programs, defining the types of decisions that are required, are not considered. One result is the tendency to act in a fragmentary, piece meal fashion. For instance, recent efforts to introduce change through court mandated means in New York City's education system provides an example of fragmentation. The Aspira decree (Baecher, 1976), in seeking to provide equality of opportunity to Spanish dominant students, centered on the traditional academic disciplines emphasizing the use of the student's dominant language in separate subject areas like science, mathematics and social studies. Recent reports from teachers and administrators involved in these changes indicate increasing unbalance and fragmentation of planning and manpower.

These limitations of current bilingual typologies point out the need to view bilingual education as a social system.

Bilingual Education as a Social System

According to Hill (1972, p. 15), a "system is a defined collection of elements with their interconnections considered over a period of time." Employing the concept of "set" as a powerful analytic tool, one can generate a model of bilingual education viewed as a "social system" Previous attempts by Dworkin (1975) to reconceptualize curriculum as a "social system" were successful in providing a source from which models can be derived.

Careful inspection of bilingual programs shows they include the basic ingredients of a "social system," i.e., a collection of the interactive elements of *persons, processes* and *properties* organized for the purpose of continuing and facilitating the educative experiences of bilingual children. These generic elements of a social system must be seen together as they interact and intersect over a period of time within a certain context. From this perspective bilingual programs manifest their dynamic, changeable features wherein numerous complex factors come into play. Figure 1 represents these 3 interacting elements.

Figure 1.

Bilingual Education as a Social System

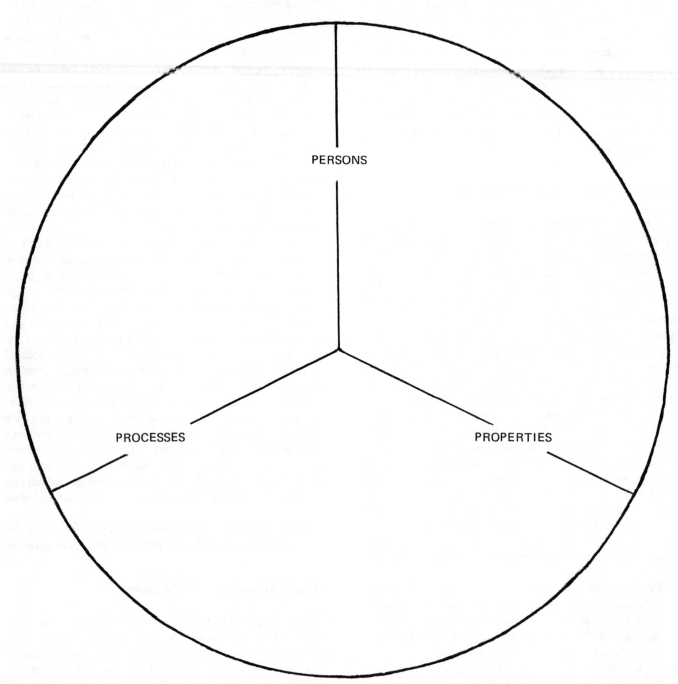

To define the social system pictured here is to identify the persons (teachers, pupils, aides, etc.) involved in the process (actions, methods) of accomplishing the particular goals of bilingual education through a variety of properties (books, media) associated with the system.

"Persons" Element. The term "Persons" is considered to be the individuals participating in the system, e.g., children, teachers, administrators, coordinators, educational assistants, community resource people, and parents. Since a comprehensive description of this aspect would go beyond an article of this nature, I will provide a set of competencies unique to teachers of Spanish speaking children within an early childhood context.

Figure 2.

Distinct Competencies for Early Childhood Teachers of

Mexican American Children

DOMAIN	AREA	INDICATORS (Partial List)
I. Language Proficiency	Enhancing the verbal and interactional behavior of Mexican-American child.	Prospective teacher will: 1. demonstrate fluency in English/Spanish, and in the child's "barrio" colloquialisms; 2. will communicate with the child in the language of his choise and lead him to the acceptance of a second language; 3. will identify and expand basic concepts in Spanish first, then in English.
II. Instructional Methods	Developing curricular activities that will build positive self-concept and self-esteem in Chicano children.	1. provide activities for role playing family members and family situations; 2. arrange for field trips relevant to the child's culture; 3. teach the child folk dancing, songs, and. games in Spanish.
III. School-Community Relations	Developing liaison between the school, parents, and the child.	1. communicate with parents in the language of their choice; 2. utilize parents as resource personnel providing for the demonstration of their talents; 3. ask parents for volunteer assistance in the classroom. (pps. 344–5)

This list of competencies, although incomplete, suggests the types of skills that a teacher working with young Chicano children should demonstrate. They specify the expectations

This list of competencies, although incomplete, suggests the types of skills that a teacher working with young Chicano children should demonstrate. They specify the expectations placed upon teachers who make up one aspect of the "persons" element of bilingual education as a social sytem. A comprehensive analysis would include all the other individuals under this element, with particular attention given to value-orientations, purposive functions, normative structures, and role expectations (Dworkin, 1975, p. 31). Another approach with far-reaching implications for the applied field of education is that of the "Educational Sciences", a conceptual framework proposed by Joseph E. Hill and associates (1971). Drawing upon selected aspects of the educational science of cognitive style, the author has applied this educational framework within a bilingual context whereby practitioners can focus on the strengths of bilingual children (Baecher, 1975).

"Properties" Element. Properties are the contents of the system under consideration. For example, materials of instruction, equipment, textbooks, money, and facilities belong to the properties of the system. A specific illustration of one property employed in bilingual programs might be the *Bilingual Early Childhood Program* (Southwest Educational Development Laboratory, 1970). Consisting of print, visuals, filmstrips, audio cassettes, transparencies, records, manipulatives, games, puzzles, and walking patterns, the BECP was created for 3-5 year old Spanish-speaking children from economically disadvantaged families. The general goals of this instructional program are to: 1) develop the sensory-perceptual skills of the child, 2) increase the child's language skills in both English and Spanish, 3) enhance the child's thinking and reasoning abilities, and 4) help the pupil to develop a positive self-concept. Developmentally oriented, the program is concerned with the general cognitive, psychomotor, and affective stages common to all children. Furthermore, the BECP is sequential, thereby enabling each child to achieve successive levels of competence. The overall assessment of the *Bilingual Early Childhood Program* states that it appears to be the "most comprehensive early childhood program available to bilingual educators (EPIE Report: Number 74, 1976, p. 7). Interacting with the persons and properties elements are the "processes".

"Processes" Element. Process refers to a series of interdependent steps established for the purpose of attaining a particular goal or end. Since purposive behavior is a general characteristic of social systems, the actions and functions of the individuals involved in achieving goals can be considered the processes. Analysis of the processes specific to bilingual programs indicates 3 key distinguishing features. One is the *teaching of language,* or the development

of student proficiency in the use of the language or languages concerned. Emphasis is placed upon developing competence in using language, traditionally called "language arts." A second essential feature is *teaching in the language,* i.e., the languages that make up the bilingual program are employed as media for conducting teaching and learning activities in the subjects being taught. The subjects might include one or all of the following: mathematics, science, social studies, language arts. Since language and culture are inseparable, and since a child's sense of belonging is firmly rooted in part in the cultural heritage of his/her family, biculturalism becomes a necessary aspect of bilingual programs. The bicultural feature may deal with any one of the following:

1. *Poor* or *ethnic-American culture.*
2. *Fundamental* or *monumental* aspects of culture (i.e., culture as a whole vs. studies of selected customs, artifacts or famous people).
3. *Contemporary* as well as *historic* features of culture (as it appears today vs. as it is used to be).
4. various traits of culture, such as material, social, intellectual, aesthetic, and language.

(EPIE Report, 1976, p. x).

These 3 key features (teaching of language, teaching in language, biculturalism) synthesize the processes that constitute the major goals of bilingual programs today.

Some Recommendations

The following digest of recommendations summarizes some major pertinent research findings and their practical implications for teachers of bilingual children. Although necessarily incomplete, it is meant as a guide for the teacher participating in such programs. The reader is encouraged to review the digest in greater depth by consulting the selected references.

Conclusion

In this article, I pointed out certain weaknesses with current typologies of bilingual education and presented the case that bilingual programs be interpreted from a social systems framework. Such a framework enables one to appreciate the dynamic interactions that are unique to bilingual programs, especially as they pertain to early childhood education. The 3 interactive elements of persons, processes, and properties were defined and illustrated with special attention given to preschool programs. Finally, a digest of recommendations was reviewed summarizing some practical implications from bilingual research and insights from allied disciplines.

Figure 3

Suggested Teaching Techniques	Rationale	Selected References
1. Don't criticize children about their grammar. Efforts to teach adult grammar to young children are fruitless and may alienate children.	Children's grammar reflects a consistent, developing system that will mature without specific teaching. Children around the world begin to learn their native language at the same age, in much the same way, and in essentially the same sequence.	Brown, 1973; Carrow, 1971; Saville-Troike, 1973.
2. Create situations in which children want and need to communicate with others concerning things that are relevant and interesting to them. Minimize the role of note memorization and meaningless drill.	Children acquire a second language by a process of "creative construction," i.e., children gradually formulate rules for the speech they hear, guided by innate cognitive mechanisms.	Dulay and Burt, 1972, 1974; Huang, 1971; Milon, 1974; Price, 1968.
3. Don't try to convert the grammar and pronunciation of children who speak a language variety to a standard form of language. Emphasize communication of meaning, i.e., expressing or understanding a concept, with only secondary concern formal correctness.	Pressure won't work at this age. The teacher's objective is to help children learn and verbalize concepts, not to correct their grammar or pronunciation.	Gonzalez, 1975; Saville-Troike, 1976.
4. Don't assume that low-income children are "non-verbal" or that they lack the verbal skills necessary for thinking. Young children can interpret and use a variety of gestures, facial expressions, and other paralinguistic devices common to their own culture.	Language helps children think but it is not a necessary tool for logical thinking. The language chidlren reveal in talking to a teacher may be only a fraction of their evolving competence.	Cazden, 1972; Saville-Troike, 1976.

These recommendations are only a few of the more important ones that seem to have practical implications for teachers of bilingual children in an early childhood context. The reader is encourage to pursue these recommendations in areas beyond language by consulting the selected reference list at the end of this article.

SELECTED BIBLIOGRAPHY

Akers, Milton E. "Prologue: the Why of Early Childhood Education." In Ira Gordon (ed.), *Early Childhood Education.* The 71st. Yearbook of the Study of Education, Part II. Chicago, Ill.: University of Chicago Press, 1972, pp. 2-3.

Andersson, Theodore. "Bilingual Education: The American Experience. *Modern Language Journal* 55 (1971): 427-440.

Andersson, Theodore. "Bilingual Education and Early Childhood." Lecture delivered at Southern Illinois University, May 30, 1974. Available in ERIC microfiche, ED 117 985.

Andersson, Theodore. "A Proposed Investigation of Preschool Biliteracy." Available in ERIC ED 112 668; 1975.

Andersson, Theodore; Boyer, Mildred. (eds.) *Bilingual Schooling in the United States.* Washington, D.C. USGPO, 1970 (2 vols.)

Askins, Billy. "Clovis-Portales Bilingual Early Childhood Program. Third Year Evaluation Study (1974-75). Final Evaluation Report." Available in ERIC, ED 116 812.

Baecher, Richard E. "Focusing on the Strengths of Bilingual Children." In L. Golubchick and B. Persky (eds.) *Innovation In Education,* Dubuque, Iowa: Kendall Hunt Pub. Co., 1975, Chapter 4.

Baecher, Richard E. "The Challenge of the ASPIRA Decree." In L. Golubchick and B. Persky (eds.), *Urban Social, and Educational Issues,* Dubuque, Iowa: Kendall, Hunt Publishing Co., 1976.

Baecher, Richard E. "Bilingual Children and Educational Cognitive Style Analysis." In A. Simoes (ed.), *The Bilingual Child: Research and Analysis of Existing Themes,* N.Y.: Academic Press, 1976.

Berbaum, Marcia. *Early Childhood Programs for Non-English-Speaking Children.* A publication of ERIC clearinghouse on Childhood Education, University of Illinois at Urbana-Champaign. Albany: The University of the State of New York, the State Education Department, 1972.

Bloom, Benjamin S. *Stability and Change in Human Characteristics.* New York: John Wiley and Sons, Inc., 1964.

Brooks, Nelson. "The Meaning of Bilingualism Today." In Earl J. Ogletree and David Garicia, Eds., *Education of the Spanish-Speaking Urban Child: A Book of Readings,* Springfield, Ill.: Charles C. Thomas, 1975, Chapter 29.

Brown, R. *A First Language.* Cambridge, Mass.: Harvard University Press, 1973.

Canham, G. W. *Mother Tongue Teaching.* International Studies in Education 29. Hamburg: UNESCO, Institute for Education, 1969.

Carrow, E. "Comprehension of English and Spanish by Preschool Mexican-American Children." *Modern Language Journal* 55 (1971): 299-306.

Castillo, Max and Cruz, Josue, Jr. "Special Competencies for Teachers of Preschool Chicano Children: Rationale, Content, and Assessment Process." *Young Children,* Sept. 1974, 341-347.

Cazden, C. B. (ed.). *Language in Early Childhood Education.* Washington, D.C.: National Association for the Education of Young Children, 1972.

Dulay, H.D. and Burt, M.K. "Goofing: An Indicator of Children's Second Language Learning Strategies." *Language Learning,* 22 (1972): 235-252.

Dulay, H. C. and Burt, M. K. "Natural Sequences in Child Second Language Acquisition." *Language Learning,* 24 (1974): 37-53.

Dworkin, Leo. "Curriculum as a Social System." *The Educational Scientist,* Vol I, No. 1, Fall, 1975, pp. 27-38.

Evans, E. D. *Contemporary Influences in Early Childhood Education.* New York: Holt, Rinehart and Winston, 1971.

Educational Products Information Exchange Institute (EPIE) Report. *Selector's Guide For Bilingual Education Materials.* Vol. 2, Spanish "branch" Programs. Number 74. EPIE Institute, 463 West Street, N.Y., 1976.

Fishman, Joshua; Lovas, John. "Bilingual Education in Sociolinguistic Perspective." *TESOL Quarterly,* 4 (1970), 215-22.

Fishman, Joshua A. "Bilingual Education: What and Why? "In Alfred C. Aarons, ed., *Florida FL Reporter* Vol. 11, Nos. 1 & 2, Spring/Fall 1973, pp. 13-14, 42-43.

Gonzalez, Gustavo. "La Educacion Bilingue y la Investigacion de la Lengua Infante)." In R. Troike and N. Modiano (eds.), *Proceedings of the First Inter-American Conference on Bilingual Education.* Arlington, VA.: Center for Applied Linguistics, 1975.

Gordon, Ira. J. "An Instructional Theory Approach to the Analysis of Selected Early Childhood Programs." In Ira Gordon (ed.), *Early Childhood Education.* The 71st Yearbook of the Study of Education, Part II. Chicago, Ill.: University of Chicago Press, 1972, pp. 203-228.

Hill, Joseph E. *How Schools Can Apply Systems Analysis.* Bloomington, Indiana: The Phi Delta Kappa Educational Foundation, 1972.

Chapter 54

Early Childhood Education—Native American Style

Leona M. Foerster and Dale Little Soldier*

The education of culturally diverse populations has been the topic of much national publicity during this decade. As society has moved from a melting pot orientation to one of recognizing and encouraging cultural pluralism, increasing attention has been focused upon the schools as agents to promote this culturally pluralistic posture. In the past, the educational achievement of Native Americans has been dismal, indeed. America's first citizens have been second-class citizens when it has come to the educational institution's unwillingness responding to their particular needs.

Statistics gathered in the late 1960's and early 1970's indicated that the average educational level for all Indians was 8.4 years; from grades 8 through 12, the drop-out rate among these students was estimated to be somewhere between 39 to 48 percent; Indian students scored significantly lower on achievement tests than the average white pupil at every grade level; and the lag in achievement appeared to be greater at grade 12 than at grade one (Demmert, 1976, p. 6). As a result of findings like these, efforts were made at the national level to provide financial assistance to upgrade educational opportunities for Indians. Consequently, one of the most promising educational trends to appear on the horizon for Native Americans has been the development and expansion of early childhood programs for Indian pupils which are specifically designed to meet their special needs. It is the purpose of this article to acquaint the reader with what is going on in early childhood education—Native American style. Some of the most noteworthy trends will be examined and several exemplary programs will be discussed.

Perhaps it is important to mention at the beginning that currently many more Indian pupils are being served by early childhood programs than in the past. Part of this increase is due to the expansion of Head Start programs on and off reservations. Also there is a national trend toward providing state-supported kindergartens for all pupils. Indian parents are more receptive to enrolling their children in pre-school programs. It appears that the newer programs are more attractive to parents and they may understand something of the enormous impact of the experiences in the child's early years on future success in school and later in society. For a variety of reasons, early childhood education for Native American pupils is on the increase. This trend in itself might not be too important. However, when one looks at some of the programs which have been developed and examines a sampling of promising practices which are to be found within many of these programs, the reader may perceive something of the really exciting things which are occurring for young Native Americans. And certainly it is about time.

It is important for the reader to be aware of the impact of the Indian Education Act of 1972, (P.L. 92-318, Title IV) upon educational programs for Native Americans. According to Demmert (1976, p. 9) this legislation has accomplished for Indian pupils what the now famous Elementary and Secondary Education Act of 1965 did for the overall student population of this country. Part B of this Act encourages the support of community-based early childhood programs. It stimulates the involvement of Indian parents and communities in the education of their young children. The lack of involvement of Indian parents in the educational institution is considered to be one of the reasons why school programs for Indians have failed so miserably in the past. The current participation of Indian parents in the educative process is considered a great strength and a component which has been absent for too long.

In addition, the involvement of Native American parents in educational programs has been increased through the establishment of Indian advisory boards at local and state levels. Through these advisory boards, input from parents is channelled and utilized in building relevant programs (Foerster and Little Solider, 1975). These boards play a vital role in assessing the special needs of Indian pupils in the local area. Further, the boards may help with the writing of proposals for federal monies under the provisions of the Johnson-O'Malley Act of 1932 or Title IV. Often the advisory boards may help select textbooks and develop culturally relevant curricula on the local or state levels and may serve a monitoring function for programs once they are implemented.

Parent-based early childhood education programs may also serve to stimulate young children (Demmert, 1976). It cannot be denied that the preschool years are crucial in the

---

*Dr. Leona Foerster, Professor of Education, Texas Tech University; Dale Little Soldier, Doctoral student, Texas Tech University and a Mandan/Hidatsa Indian.

development of the young child's cognitive and linguistic abilities. Head Start and kindergarten programs simply may come too late to prevent the early drop out rate of Indian children. Each year the Indian child remains in school, the lag in achievement appears to become greater. As the Native American pupil moves from the child-oriented primary grades to the more subject-matter oriented curriculum of the intermediate grades, the likelihood of this child's dropping out of school increases greatly. Children who enter school lacking the prerequisite skills needed for success seem unable to master these skills sufficiently during the kindergarten and primary grades.

It goes without saying that parents are the child's first and best teachers. Programs which enable Native American parents to gain greater understanding of how young children learn and teach them how to promote the optimal growth, of their children can make an important contribution. It is difficult to speculate about the possible impact of such programs on the future school achievement of pupils. However, these programs offer the *potential* of dramatically reducing the drop out rate of Indian pupils, particularly at the elementary and junior high levels, and of greatly increasing the school achievement of these youngsters.

In the past Indian pupils by and large have suffered from very poor self images. Often the school curriculum does little to correct this image. In fact, it may directly contribute to the problem. Early childhood curriculum projects which take into account the unique heritage of Indian pupils and which promote pride are underway in different parts of the country. Much of this curricular reform is the result of pressures from Indian people themselves to provide something better for their children than what they themselves experienced in school (Tsanusdi, 1976). Attention to feelings and attitudes is considered an important component of many of the programs.

The Bureau of Indian Affairs (BIA) kindergarten curriculum guide used in schools operated by the BIA reflects a bilingual-bicultural approach (1970). The kindergarten is viewed as the bridge between home and school. Attention is given to building upon the strengths that the child brings to school with him including the richness of culture, language and history which are part of the Native American heritage. Cultural differences are viewed as just that—differences, not deficiencies. This represents a long-needed shift in philosophy from an earlier Bureau stance which viewed Indian children as "handicapped" by their home environment.

Learning centers are typically found in early childhood classrooms. Currently efforts are made in many early childhood programs to provide more culturally relevant settings for Indian pupils. For example, the home living center may include kitchen utensils and dishes which are familiar to the child. Dolls may look more like Indian infants than "palefaces." The dress-up corner can include bustles head-

dresses, jewelry and the like which children are used to. Rather than puzzles, pictures and games which reflect things unfamiliar to pupils, the visitor to the Native American early childhood classroom may find rodeo lotto games, pictures of dwellings and scenery found on the reservation, and other materials many of which are teacher-constructed and with which young children can identify immediately and feel comfortable. Cooking experiences may include fry bread, Indian tacos and mutton stew. Books found in the classroom may show settings and situations familiar to the children. Some books may be written in two languages, English and Navajo, for example. Construction activities may include the building of a small wickiup or chickee. Art and music activities, too, may involve experiences familiar to the children.

Churchman, Herman and Hall (1975) have reported the development of a culturally relevant pre-school curriculum for Indian pupils living in the greater Los Angeles area. The curriculum was designed by the Tribal American Consulting Corporation (TAAC) and based on at least two premises. The first of these was that children will learn best in a culturally relevant context. Thus learning materials were developed to demonstrate the richness of tribal history, values and culture. The curriculum was to be implemented employing the traditional Indian communal interaction pattern wherein individuals work cooperatively and share the products of their labor.

The second premise which guided this curriculum development project was that pre-school experiences should prepare the Indian child for success in school. Referring to the work of Bruner, Kagan and White, the authors cited above stress the need for competence in such basic skills as language, problem solving, coping, perception and coordination before the age of five to enable the child to interact positively with the environment. Thus the curriculum materials were designed to tap children's culture and heritage while developing basic skills and promoting growth of a positive self concept.

Curriculum building efforts were made quite complex due to the fact that many tribal groups are represented in the Los Angeles area. Nevertheless, the TACC cultural curriculum for Indian preschools appears to have made some excellent advances in meeting the needs of the culturally diverse Indian population in this area.

The problems of Indians living in large urban areas are complex. Often Native Americans tend to become "lost" in such settings. Maintaining cultural identity may be difficult. Indian Centers in these areas are helping people retain their identity as Indians. As a result of this new solidarity, Indian parents in large urban areas may become more vocal in the future demanding culturally based early childhood programs for their young offspring. The TACC program may help to serve as a model for other programs in large urban areas.

Other noteworthy curriculum projects could be cited, too. The Wisconsin Native American Language and Culture project was set up under title IV of the Indian Education Act (Roth 1976). The major thrust of the project was to preserve the languages of the five Wisconsin tribes (Chippewa, Oneida, Menominee, Potawatomi and Winnebago) by establishing written systems for these languages, developing references and teaching materials for them, and finally teaching these languages and cultures in the schools. Wisconsin Indians who are native speakers of these languages were hired and trained as language teachers and consultants. Linguists were employed to help develop instructional and reference materials. As a result, Indian pupils in Wisconsin beginning with Head Start may have the opportunity to become literate in their native language, to learn more about their heritage and develop a deep sense of prideful identity.

In North Dakota, the American Indian Curricula Development Program, a subsidiary group of the United Tribes of North Dakota Development Corporation, has been involved in a social studies curriculum and teacher training package that is culturally relevant for children in grades K-12 (Gray, 1973). The curriculum includes text material, supplementary booklets, overhead transparencies, slide-tape programs, cassette tapes and a comprehensive teacher's manual. It is an attempt to provide relevance in curriculum for the more than 18,000 Indians living on or near the four United Tribes reservations.

There is no doubt that the project was long needed. Not only has the average family income on these reservations been dreadfully low and unemployment extremely high, but additional problems such as high drop out rate of pupils, below par academic achievement of those who remain in school and an alarming teen-age suicide rate have indicated the need for changes in the education of Indian students. It is hoped that the curriculum relevance provided by the project will encourage greater pupil interest in school, motivation to remain and achieve at a higher level, a more positive self concept, pride and a sense of identity.

North Dakota is not the only state which has made strides in serving the educational needs of young Native Americans. Curriculum projects are under way in most states which have an identifiable Indian population such as Alaska, Montana, Idaho, Washington, California, Arizona, Nevada, Oklahoma and New Mexico. Most of these projects have goals similar to the North Dakota program cited above. In addition to helping Indian pupils learn about their culture, heritage and language, many of these programs provide opportunities for non-Indians to gain more accurate perceptions of Indian peoples and their important contributions to the nation as well as to combat the stereotyped images perpetuated in the media.

No discussion of curriculum would be complete without reference to the many exemplary projects underway on the Navajo reservation. The Rough Rock Demonstration School has developed a myriad of culturally relevant curriculum materials for Navajo pupils. This school was established in 1966 as a community controlled school, a BIA contract school and has served since then as a model for other schools on the reservation. Through its Division of Education, the Navajo nation has promoted educational change on the reservation from early childhood to adult education.

The Navajo Area Language Arts Project (NALAP) has helped with the problems of teaching English to the many Navajo children who enter school speaking Navajo as their prime or sole language. (U.S. Department of the Interior, 1973). A Navajo Social Studies Curriculum project has been completed, too. This project provides a culture-based social studies curriculum for beginners through the eighth grade. These materials were developed to demonstrate to students the many contributions the Indian has made to our nation, to provide insight into the Indian's relationship to other cultures and to enable each child to find a rightful place within society.

The trend nationally seems to be toward earlier diagnosis of the special problems of all children which may affect performance in school. In the past, Indian children with handicapping conditions often remained out of school due to the fact that special education programs for these students were not available. In 1972, a survey of pupils enrolled in BIA schools indicated that a total of 19,540 students was in need of special educational services but that only 3,715 were receiving such services (U.S. Department of the Interior 1973). Since that time, important gains have been made in attempting to meet these needs. For example, the Pine Ridge Agency in South Dakota (Aberdeen Area) was the first agency in the Bureau of Indian Affairs to have a full-time special education coordinator at the agency level and a special education teacher at each of the agency's eight schools. A special education instructional materials center located at the Porcupine School provides the agency area with materials to help meet the special needs of the agency's children.

The Navajo Nation has responded to the needs of its special children, too. Of the more than 60,000 Navajo pupils enrolled in school, it was estimated that 30 percent required some type of special education service (Murphy, 1974). Navajo parents, tribal leaders, community persons and educators have exhibited increased awareness of and concern for the needs of special children. As a result, these needs are being partially met. However, there remains much work to be done to provide services for all children who could profit from them.

The St. Michaels Association for Special Education, located at St. Michaels, Arizona on the reservation opened in September, 1970 and was the first school to offer comprehensive educational, social and medical services for handicapped Navajo children beginning with age 1½

(Murphy, 1974). The Chinle Valley School for Exceptional Children at Chinle, Arizona opened in August, 1973 and was designed to serve trainable children ranging in age from 5 to 15 years.

At the Greasewood Boarding School, also on the Navajo reservation, pupils in grades 1-8 participate in Resource Centers funded under Title I designed to correct specific language disabilities and promote progress in academic skills (Ramey, Sileo and Zongolowicz, 1975). The program at Greasewood has a three-fold thrust. The language development component fosters the acquisition of language skills including listening, oral and written language, articulation, reading skills development and reading comprehension. The conceptual development component deals with number concepts, reasoning, classification skills and general information. The developmental motor skills component encompasses the range of skills involved in gross motor development, sensory-motor integration and perceptual motor skills. The program is individualized, objectives are stated behaviorally and daily logs are maintained for each pupil.

The continued growth of special programs for Indian pupils should aid in halting the dreadful waste of human resources which has occurred in the past when such services were either non-existent for these children or came too late to prevent the maladjustment of pupils, damage to self esteem and early retreat from the educational institution. In this day and age, it is indefensible that any child be denied services which potentially would enable him to become a productive member within his group as well as the greater society.

Perhaps two additional thrusts in early childhood education should be mentioned briefly. They are interrelated. One is the move to provide greater individualization of instruction; the other is the trend toward open education.

Individually Guided Education (IGE) is a refreshingly new approach to education which has come about as a result of research by the Wisconsin Research and Development Center for Cognitive Learning and other educational agencies (U.S. Department of the Interior, 1973). The Institute for the Development of Educational Activities (IDEA) established by the Charles F. Kettering Foundation in 1965 has been instrumental in the national expansion of this program.

IGE schools include the Acomita Day School on the Acoma reservation 60 miles west of Albuquerque, New Mexico, and two other schools at Jemez and Zia in the Albuquerque area (U.S. Department of the Interior, 1973). Pupils have a great deal of physical freedom within these IGE schools. The schools are ungraded and cut across at least two age groups. Work is contracted for and each student draws his assignment from a "contract board." Pupils are responsible for completing their own work. Progress reports are prepared periodically and shared with parents in conferences.

In addition, open education appears to offer a viable alternative to traditional education for many Indian pupils (Foerster and Little Soldier, 1974). Schools for Native American pupils using this approach include the Concho Indian School located near El Reno, Oklahoma, the Rocky Boy Elementary School in Montana and the Finlayson School in Sault Ste. Marie, Michigan. The latter school includes a pre-school program for children ranging in age from 3½ to 6 years. Pre-academic skills are fostered in an open setting which allows pupils to explore and manipulate materials and learn by discovery.

The open classroom setting may provide a better psychological fit for many Indian pupils. Traditional Indian values such as sharing and personal freedom are fostered in this type of classroom context (Foerster and Little Soldier, 1974). Additionally, the greater flexibility is the use of time and the permissiveness characteristic of the open classroom may blend much more effectively with the child rearing practices of many Native Americans. The informal education of the home should be the basis for planning the formal early learning experiences of pupils in school. The open setting may provide greater opportunities for the teacher of young Native American pupils to utilize the strengths these children bring to school with them.

Perhaps it should be mentioned before closing that in attending Indian education meetings one cannot help but be impressed by the enthusiasm, dedication and optimism of the participants. Native American parents, aides, teachers, and administrators are jointed together by the overriding goal of wanting to provide the best experiences possible for young Indian children. Perhaps this is part of the reason for the great strides which have been made recently in early childhood education for these children. Yet this is only a beginning. New challenges arise continually. The reader is encouraged to keep a sharp eye out for newer developments as they occur and are reported in the literature. Early childhood education—Native American style is truly exciting, challenging and rewarding. But for this many children involved, it may mean increased achievement in school as well as richer, fuller, more productive lives later on—very high stakes, indeed.

REFERENCES

Churchman, David, Herman, Joan and Hall, Teresa. "To Know Both Worlds." *Journal of American Indian Education*, 14: 7-12 May, 1975.

Demmert, William G., Jr., "Indian Education: Where and Whither?" *American Education*, 12:6-9, August/September, 1976.

Foerster, Leona M. and Little Soldier, Dale, "Open Education and Native American Values." *Educational*

Leadership, 32: 41-45, October, 1974.

Foerster, Leona M. and Little Soldier, Dale. "What's New and Good in Indian Education Today?" *Educational Leadership*, 33: 192-198, December, 1975.

Gray, Farnum. "Breakthrough in North Dakota." *Learning*, 26: 53-58, January, 1973.

Murphy, Elizabeth A., "The Classroom: Meeting the Needs of the Culturally Different Child—The Navajo Nation." *Exceptional Children.* 40: 601-608, May, 1974.

Ramey, Josephy H., Sileo, Thomas W. and Zongolowicz. "Resource Centers for Children with Learning Disabilities." *Journal of American Indian Education*, 14: 13-20, May, 1975.

Roth, Edith Brill, "Lato: Lats—Hunting in the Indian Languages." *American Education*, 14: 13-20, May, 1975.

Tsanusdi, Tlanuwa. "Native American Children—Values of the Past May be Keys to a Brighter Future." *Dimensions.* 4: 65-69; 77, March, 1976.

U.S. Department of the Interior. *A Kindergarten Curriculum Guide for Indian Children.* Curriculum Bulletin No. 5., Washington, D.C.: Bureau of Indian Affairs, 1970.

U.S. Department of the Interior. *Indian Education Steps to Progress in the 70's*, Washington, D.C.: Bureau of Indian Affairs, 1973.

Superintendent Alfred Melov, NYC School Board 15

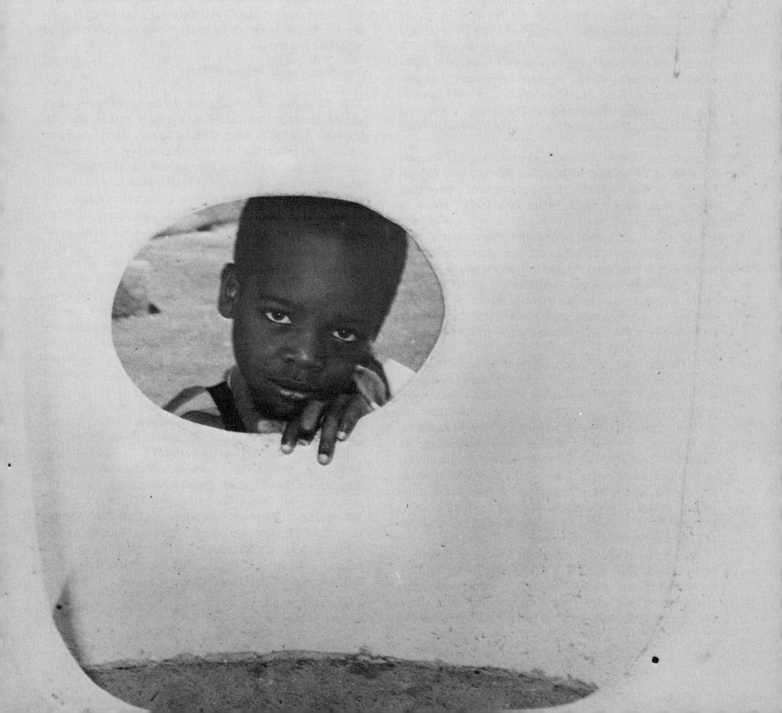

Chapter 55

Child Abuse: Mandate for Teacher Intern Intervention

Diane Divoky*

Ready or not, teachers are being assigned a major role in the national crusade against child abuse now moving at fever pitch. In most states new or updated laws require teachers and other school personnel to report suspected cases of abuse and, often, neglect. In Montgomery County, Maryland, all school employees are required to report physical abuse, sexual abuse and neglect—with the neglected child being one who is ill-clad and dirty, unattended, emotionally disturbed due to friction in the home, emotionally neglected by being denied "normal experiences that produce feelings of being loved," or exposed to unwholesome and demoralizing circumstances. The policy emphasizes that any doubt about reporting should be resolved in favor of the child.

In Adams County, Colorado, elementary grade teachers are told to be on the lookout for children who exhibit reticence in class, aggressive acting-out behavior, poor peer relationships, poor hygienic habits, or a fear of adults. In junior high school, the signs of neglect or abuse include sexual promiscuity and an inability "to conform with school regulations and policies." New Jersey warns its teachers that classroom "signposts" of abuse are "disruptive or aggressive" behavior, "withdrawn or quiet" behavior, "poor attendance or chronic lateness," and dirty and torn clothing. Abusive or neglectful parents, the teachers are told, display a "lack of maturity," "low frustration level" and "impulsive traits."

In the state of New York, teachers are required to report any student whom they have "reasonable cause to suspect" is "maltreated" by a parent: i.e.; the child's "emotional health" has been impaired so that a "substantially diminished psychological or intellectual functioning" can be noted in, for example, the "control of aggressive or self-destructive impulses." *Guidelines for Schools,* the widely distributed child abuse advisory pamphlet of the American Humane Association, says an alert teacher looks for symptoms in the parents as well as in the child: "Are they apathetic or unresponsive?" "Do they fail to participate in school activities or to permit the child to participate?"

At last fall's Child Abuse Training Seminar in Houston—part of the federally funded model program for the identification and referral of abused children by school personnel—the approach was simple: show the gruesome color slides; use dramatic language ("If you were a nine-year-old and your parents were torturing you every night of your life, wouldn't you be grateful to the person who reported you?"); talk about signs like nail biting, thumb sucking, masturbation and uncontrolled urinating; and insist there's no relationship between "abuse" and other kinds of physical force used against children ("Corporal punishment is reasonable and it is meant to teach; abuse is the venting of anger and frustration").

Guidelines Are a "Judgment Thing"

In California, where 120,736 children were reported as abused or neglected in 1974, a school system like the Hayward Unified School District already feels confident about "accepting the moral responsibility to monitor," according to Joan Chambers, administrative director of pupil services, if a teacher sees bruises or some other physical sign of abuse, or hears a child talking about a disruptive incident at home, she arranges for the nurse or other designated staff member to talk to the child to get some indication of what happened and, if warranted, to call a report in directly to the police. Chambers said all reports are supposed to be made directly to one of two police officers with special in-service training in child-abuse cases, but in practice these people are often not around, and any available beat man comes to the school to interrogate the child, remove the clothing, examine the body, and then, perhaps, take the child into protective custody. "Once we've called the police, it's out of our hands," Chambers said.

There are no guidelines as to what signs justify transferring a child from school to the police station—without parental permission. Marks on the buttocks, what one police officer called "overcorrection," is considered "borderline" by that officer. Some school officials admitted they were a bit squeamish about sending a child off in the police car, but one officer disagreed: "Often it's a thrill for the kids to drive off in a police car," she said. "Sometimes I say I'll buy them candy." Margaret Outman, a nurse for the children's centers in the neighboring Oakland schools, concurred: "The children are better through all this than we are."

*Reprinted with permission from Learning Magazine, The Magazine for Creative Teaching, April 1, 1976.

At the station, the child is booked, Polaroid shots are taken of the bare body, and the parents are called. Social agencies are checked by phone to see if the family has a history of problems, because at some point the children's division of the county probation department must decide whether the child will be returned home immediately or put at least temporarily into a children's shelter or foster home. Again, guidelines are fuzzy, a "judgment thing," but the attitude of the parents when they get to the station or shelter—how contrite they seem—is a major factor, two officers said.

Within 36 hours of phoning the police, the school employee must make a written report, including information about the nature of the injuries and the student's statement. Copies of this report go to the police, the probation department, the school district office, the school principal's "confidential" file and, when appropriate, the welfare department. One copy gets sent on to a state register of suspected child abusers, maintained by the Department of Justice.

Even when they are found to be unsubstantiated, these written reports are never removed or expunged from the various agency files. The Hayward school district personnel do not know which of the reports in their own files represent actual abuse and which are false alarms. What services the family receives as a result of reporting and what impact there is on the child aren't known by the school staff, either. "Hopefully, good things come out of reporting," said Chambers, "but there's a possibility that ultimately you may have done more damage, because even the abused child is afraid to lose its family. But our job is to report, to shore up teachers and convince them it's helping and not finking."

The Child Protective Services Act

The message is to look for signs and symptoms and, when in doubt, report. The state laws themselves use both a carrot and a stick to make mandated reporting more palatable: they all grant anonymity as well as immunity against criminal and civil prosecution to those who report suspected cases, and most attach a criminal penalty, usually a misdemeanor, to the failure to report.

And if the Model Child Protective Services Act currently proposed by HEW's Office of Child Development is approved and promulgated by the Secretary of Health, Education and Welfare—and OCD officials are assured it will be—the reporting network will get broader and more active still. The mere existence of the model act, which "seeks to encourage fuller reporting," will move many states still tinkering with their own legislation to adopt it wholesale. Frank Ferro, associate chief of OCD's Children's Bureau, said there will be pressure on states to comply if they want their federal grants.

The model act would require teachers—as well as social workers, daycare workers, podiatrists, religious healers and a raft of other public and private employees who have some contact with children—to report immediately to a single statewide toll-free telephone number "their reasonable suspicions" of parents or other caretakers who abuse or maltreat children. To be reported are those child custodians who create or allow "to be created a substantial risk of physical or mental injury to the child, including excessive corporal punishment" or who fail "to supply the child with adequate food, clothing, shelter, education (as defined by state law), or medical care." The "mental injury" to be reported involves "failure to thrive; ability to think and reason; control of aggressive or self-destructive impulses; acting out or misbehavior, including incorrigibility, ungovernability, or habitual truancy."

Under the model act, the teacher would first call in a report and then immediately notify the principal or his agent, who would take color photos and, if medically indicated, have a radiological examination of the child be performed. Once the report was made to the hotline, it would be transmitted—ideally by facsimile telecopier—to the local social service agency. (Local school officials could also use the statewide number—and a remote-access computer terminal—to check out a parent's record of prior reports in order to decide whether to report "suspicious circumstances" or not.) After the report, the action begins. The child protective service worker or police officer can take the child into protective custody without the consent of the parents if there's an imminent danger to the child's health. A thorough investigation ensues. If the parents refuse to give the protective service access to the child or the home or to allow the child to be removed from the home or to accept the "service plan" of the agency, court proceedings or other legal action can be taken against them.

A New Institution Is Born

The model law, and the growing campaign against child abuse it will cap, possibly represents the most extensive system of intervention into the lives of families that this nation has yet conceived. What began as an intensive but very limited movement in the early '60's to save physically battered and ravaged children—usually preschoolers—from death or permanent physical damage is suddenly a national social welfare system, complete with data banks, a whole new army of social workers, and enormous legal authority, capable of subtly and not so subtly directing parents and guardians as to how they will raise and treat their children. Teachers and other mandated reporters are installed as snoops; everyone else is permitted to play the game, with their reports given equal status. Local social workers, bestowed the new title of "child protective service team," become instant experts on family dynamics, with the capability of working up "appropriate service plans" that will heal wounded families and relieve the strains of poverty. If the family declines the plan, it can be referred to the police or criminal court.

And the model act is not a lonely example of overkill. Brian G. Fraser, attorney for the federally funded National Center for the Prevention and Treatment of Child Abuse and Neglect in Denver, has suggested a national computer to hook up all the state data banks "so that abusive and potentially abusive parents may be tracked as they move across the country." Dr. C. Henry Kempe of the University of Colorado School of Medicine, the father of the "battered child syndrome," has suggested a national policy of health visitors who would regularly visit every home to check on the well-being of young children.

The overreaching thrust of the model act—and similarly ambitious plans—has not met with universal approval. Senator Walter F. Mondale of Minnesota, the author of the 1974 Child Abuse Prevention and Treatment Act, which set the stage for the current crusade, has expressed his "deep concern" about the model, noting that resources are not available for the problem of "child neglect," and that the act may be unevenly applied to poor families and minorities. Mondale stated that the intention of his legislation was "to address the problems of the most severely threatened and abused children in this country," quite a different goal from that now being pursued. "I feel so strongly about this that, if HEW should decide to promulgate the law in its present form, I would personally write to all of our state legislatures and recommend that it not be adopted."

Judge James Lincoln, chairman of the Neglected Children's Committee of the National Council of Juvenile Court Judges, is equally critical of the model's inclusion of "mental injury" and "neglect" and of its information-maintenance procedures. Lincoln has recommended its postponement and has backed instead a much more limited model system for the handling of physical child-abuse cases to be published by the Justice Department. And 12 members of the model act's own advisory committee have damned the model as being "the Trojan Horse of child protective services," so zealously broad "as to preclude effective delivery of services to those acutely in need or prevention of serious injury to children. Coercive intervention into family life in vaguely defined situations of suspected neglect and maltreatment is inappropriate to a social service agency and violates due process of law....The provisions governing access to information in the central register are inadequate to protect the privacy of families and children."

But while the model act gets battered about, the child-abuse industry grows and grows. HEW's National Center on Child Abuse and Neglect spent some $19 million in 1975, and a raft of other agencies, from the Health Resources Administration to the Law Enforcement Assistance Admin-

istration, have money in child abuse. Because the field has become a pork barrel for researchers and clinicians in an otherwise hungry era, any number of social scientists and private consultants are busy designing scales and tests to uncover potentially abusive or neglectful parents, indexes and schemes to note the early warning signs, and blueprints for prevention.

What has allowed the best-intentioned of social programs—salvaging the battered child from the truly psychopathic or incompetent parent and reclaiming the most dysfunctional of families—to turn so rapidly into both a glamor industry and an ominous threat to our civil liberties and family autonomy is a number of myths that have caught on in the highly charged environment that surrounds the child-abuse issue. The myths—interfering with any true understanding of who the child abusers are, what abuse is, the extent of the problem and the possibilities for curbing it—don't necessarily support one another; in fact, at times they seem in total conflict. But each has contributed, in its time, to a precipitate growth in the campaign against child abuse.

Who Is the Child Abuser?

The first-born of the myths, the one that initially fixed public attention and wrath on child abusers, depicted child abuse as an aberration in a culture that generally treats children very well, and child abusers as deviants—usually pathological misfits—in an otherwise healthy population of parents. The "battered child syndrome"—first explored in the early '60s—certainly suggested extremes of behavior and personality, and early conclusions about abuse were drawn from a small sample of those families involved in severe attacks on their children. Presentations of the child-abuse phenomenon, whether before a Senate subcommittee or in the popular press, were hallmarked by full-color photos of the ravaged bodies of babies and toddlers and sensational stories of sadists and torturers who happened to be parents. Indeed, emotion-packed voices, like that of Dr. Vincent Fontana, director of the Mayor's Task Force on Child Abuse insist that "the important battle continues between the child murderer and the child saver."

But as early as the late '60s, the results of the first and still only reliable nationwide survey of child abuse (conducted at Brandeis University with U.S. Children's Bureau funds) were indicating, according to its chief researcher, professor of social policy David G. Gil, that "violence against children is not a rare occurrence, but may be endemic in our society because of a child-rearing philosophy which sanctions, and even encourages, the use of physical force in disciplining children. Furthermore. . . .abuse of children committed or tolerated by society as a whole, by permitting millions of children to grow up under conditions of severe deprivation, (is) a much more serious social problem than abusive acts toward children committed by individual caretakers." Gil also found that "children living in deprived circumstances were, for a variety of reasons, more likely than other children to be subjected to abusive acts by their caretakers," and that such acts are triggered by the strains and frustrations of poverty.

"Finally," Gil noted, "the study revealed that children are being abused both physically and emotionally not only in their own homes, but also in the public domain, in schools, and in other child-care settings, especially those schools and institutions that serve children from economically depressed neighborhoods." He concluded that "the dynamics of child abuse were thus found to be deeply rooted in the fabric of our culture. Consequently, the widespread notion that this destructive phenomenon was primarily a symptom of individual psychopathology appeared to be too narrow an interpretation of the wide spectrum of child abuse." Gil's recommendations were to attack all violence at its source by changing the prevailing practices of disciplining children and to work to eliminate poverty.

A brand-new study by Elizabeth Elmer of the University of Pittsburgh takes the relationship between abuse and poverty one step further. In comparing three groups of lower-class children—one of abused children, one of youngsters who'd suffered accidents, and one with no history of abuse or accidents—she found a large percentage of the entire sample had serious problems in speech, emotional development and school achievement. These problems "were distributed quite evenly among abuse, accident and comparison children. The entire sample...appeared sad and fearful....Mothers' reports indicated that the families, whether abuse, accident or comparison, experienced constant violence, both environmental and personal. It must be concluded that the effects of abuse on child development are insignificant compared to membership in the lower classes."

James Kent, a pediatric psychologist who leads the research and demonstration child-abuse team at Los Angeles' Children's Hospital, admits that the child-abuse issue is a "red herring." "Getting beaten is the least of these kids' problems," he said. "The bones will mend and the bruises will heal. It's everything else that goes on in their lives and in their families that's overwhelming." Sit in on a disposition of abuse cases at the hospital, and the talk is of parents without education, jobs, a telephone to break thier isolation, or bus fare to get a child to a clinic for orthopedic shoes; of mothers of five who already are old in their early 20s; of people who spend their days being tossed from one social agency to another, who finally turn on each other in their frustration and anger.

But the abuse issue is popular in this time when our social policy is such that benign neglect is the answer to poverty and when our former good intentions about coming to terms with hunger and ghetto schools and hopelessness in our society seem all but forgotten. As Gil said, looking at the relationship between poverty and child

abuse: "Public and professional concern with child abuse in individual homes tends to exceed by far the concern with this massive, collective abuse of children by society as a whole. Could it be that the oversensationalized interest in the former serves as a smoke screen to cover up society's destructive inaction with respect to the latter? Are abusive parents perhaps seized upon as convenient scapegoats to expiate society's collective guilt for abusing countless numbers of its young?"

If few wanted to hear Gil's argument that poverty breeds abuse, fewer still wanted to heed his words about attacking the sanctioning of violence—especially violence against children—at its roots. There is a long tradition to overcome: infanticide, abandonment, exploitation, maimings, child labor and brutal beatings are all part of our cultural legacy. Bizarre punishments seen as "for the good of the child" are woven into our history. Even today, children are the only persons in society who legally do not have the right to what Gil calls "the dignity of their bodies."

In 1970, Dr. Brandt F. Steele, professor of psychiatry at the University of Colorado Medical Center and a leader in the child-abuse movement, wrote that violence is endemic to our society, that "individuals as well as various cultural and social groups tend to use aggression and violence that they consider good or right to enforce their good and right standards." Among these are sane parents who really believe—as their parents did—that they are teaching their child right from wrong and respect for authority with beatings and physical punishment. "If we are really to understand the mechanisms of violence and how to control it in our culture, we must pay attention much more than we have in the past to those moral forces within us that tell us to direct violence in certain ways, and that enable us all to do evil under the guise of doing good."

In 1973, Dr. E. F. Lenoski, director of the Pediatric Emergency Center at the University of Southern California Medical Center in Los Angeles, told a Senate subcommittee: "The flood of venom that has spewed forth from many authors has painted the perpetrators of abuse to children as only fit for the gallows or some other similar fate.... I would agree with those who have written and spoken out that between 5 and 10 percent of the people who are involved in child abuse are mentally ill. . . . The remainder of child abusers appear to be essentially normal, intact human beings."

Is There a Child Abuse Epidemic?

The myth of the child abuser as derranged sadist has lost some credibility, but only to be replaced by an opposite notion: that we are all potential abusers and that child abuse is a raging and terrifying epidemic in the land. Gil had said early on that the "quantity and quality of abuse as a serious social problem has been exaggerated"; that more than half of abused children received only cuts and bruises; that abuse does not "constitute a major social problem"; and that "even if allowance is made for the gross under-reporting of fatalities, physical abuse cannot be considered a major killer and maimer of children."

Yet the myth of an epidemic of abuse, with all its attendant hysteria, keeps growing. Often the hysteria is engendered by those who have the responsibility of knowing better. A case in point: on November 30, 1975, the Sunday *New York Times* ran a story headed "*Child Abuse Rate Called 'Epidemic.'*" The subhead: "U.S. Says Fifth of the Million Annual Victims Die." The lead sentence: "More than a million American children suffer physical abuse or neglect each year, and at least one in five of the young victims die from their mistreatment, the government announced today." Many other papers across the nation ran similar stories, all taken from a United Press International release. The "government" speaking here was Douglas Besharov, director of HEW's National Center on Child Abuse and Neglect and author of the Model Protective Services Act. Besides announcing that at least 200,000 children die each year from child abuse, Besharov was quoted as saying that statistics indicate that 1.6 million cases of abuse and neglect are reported each year, that more than a million of these are substantiated, and that about three fourths of the neglect reports come from people in the same cultural life as those accused, eliminating any cultural bias in reporting.

The statement that 200,000 children a year die from child abuse should have been taken for what it was—a ludicrous charge (620 deaths were verified in 1974). The other assertions, all inaccurate and unfounded, could have been, and in fact were, taken at face value by the unsuspecting. Besharov had told the reporter that all his statistics came from the American Humane Association, which has a contract with the National Center to compile reporting statistics. The people at AHA, who had been working as repidly as possible to put together a responsible statistical estimate for release in 1975, described Besharov's statements as "groundless" and "excessive." "We have no idea what Doug is talking about," one staff member said succinctly.

In spite of assurances from Besharov's staff that at least the 200,000 deaths figure would be corrected in the *Times*, no correction ever came. Instead, Walter Cronkite picked up the startling statistics as the basis for a feature on the CBS nightly news the following day, and practitioners in the field began to use them as reliable data, thus further alarming the public groundlessly.

When Is a Child Abused or Neglected?

One of the major problems in gathering real statistics is, of course, the absence of a meaningful definition of abuse or neglect. In spite of the myth that all of us can recognize abuse or neglect on its face, that there are universally understood standards of acceptable treatment of children, neglect and maltreatment—and even abuse—are almost impossible to define. Are the four children of the welfare mother who all sleep in a single bunk bed under lead-based peeling paint neglected? Or is the middle-class child in the tense home so perfectly appointed with fragile art objects and white carpets that he can't function as a child the victim of maltreatment? Or are both, and a lot cf children in between, whose parenting doesn't live up to some utopian ideal? Are children in understaffed day-care centers or authoritarian boarding schools neglected? Is corporal punishment in the schools abusive? (Authorities such as Gertrude Williams, editor of the *Journal of Clinical Child Psychology*, think so.) Is the abusive parent the one who doesn't let his child participate in neighborhood activities, or the one who forces his boy to make it in Little League?

Is the child of an alcoholic parent automatically an abused child? One child may fall apart in such a stressful environment; his sibling may cope quite nicely. As Norman Polansky, professor of social work and sociology at the University of Georgia and perhaps the most respected authority on neglect, notes: "The environment's impact, after all, is experienced as 'stressful' only as it impinges on individual feelings." Psychologist Sheldon White, an authority on child development at Harvard University, adds: "Neither theory nor research has specified the exact mechanisms by which a child's development and his family functioning are linked." Polansky describes attempts to define neglect as "premature and scientifically presumptuous," pointing out what other researchers have also observed: that neglect is "inevitably relative," depending on the knowledge and state of child development and care as well as the wherewithal of any community; and that "children of disorganized, multiproblem American families are nearly all better off than those now starving in Africa's drought countries."

Besides, as Michael Wald, professor of the Stanford Law School and an authority on juvenile law, explains, "We cannot predict the consequences for a child of growing up in a home environment that lacks affection or stimulation or with a parent who suffers from alcoholism, drug addiction, mental illness, or retardation....In fact, by focusing solely on parental behavior, child-care workers often ignore the many strengths a given child may be deriving from his environment...The complexity of the process by which a child relates to any environment defies any attempt to draft laws solely in terms of environmental influences."

Even serious physical abuse, apparently the most specific and incontrovertible form of maltreatment, is not always easy for doctors to identify, much less nonmedical persons. In what was to be "a simple, straightforward study of clearly abused children and clearly abusive families" funded by the National Institute of Mental Health, researcher Elizabeth Elmer of the Pittsburgh Parental Stress Center found the "totally unexpected": that of 33 children who met the "powerful criteria for admission to the study"—multiple bone injuries acquired at early ages when the children couldn't "propel themselves into positions of danger" and "a history of neglect or abuse"—four had not, in fact, been abused, and for seven others, the evidence was inconclusive. Elmer calls for the "painstaking" evaluation of suspected abuse cases and describes the psychological damage suffered by parents and children as the result of erroneous accusations by the hospital staff: "It cannot be emphasized too strongly that false accusations of the parents can be harmful in the extreme."

Richard J. Gelles, professor of sociology and anthropology at the University of Rhode Island, agrees with Elmer, and suggests that what has been taken as the personality characteristics of child abusers—anxiety and depression—may actually be the results of being publicly labeled as abusers: "At least it ought to be recognized that the effects of being labeled an abuser may be more damaging to the individual caretaker and his or her child than is the actual instance of abuse."

Can We, Should We, Intervene?

The extensive reporting networks now in the planning are based on the most preposterous myth of all: that beneficial and significant social intervention will automatically follow identification. Again and again, child-abuse authorities stress that a reporting system is only justified by the benefits and services to families which are triggered by reporting. Yet there is simply no evidence to suggest that intervention is both possible and good, that enormously expensive public services can save families.

One hears much from the media about a few high-powered, well-funded demonstration projects that seem to be having some success in treating a carefully selected group of abusive parents. For example, the Children's Trauma Center, part of the Oakland (Calif.) Children's Hospital, has a $387,000 annual budget, a highly trained, full-time staff of 15, plus two consultants and a large volunteer corps, to service some 175 cases a year. Their reabuse rate is under 10 percent.

But no comparable funding or expertise is—or can be expected to be—available in most other communities. And the Trauma Center deals exclusively with the abusing parent. For the much larger group of neglectful parents, the outlook is more bleak. According to the newsletter *Child Protection Report,* "Parents Anonymous (the self-help group for abusive parents) and other organizations which have attempted to involve neglectful parents in their group experiences report little or no success." Leonard Lieber, the founder of Parents Anonymous and a former social worker, stated that neglecting parents need more individual attention over much longer periods of time than abusive parents: "Neglecting families characteristically express infantile behavior problems, and it becomes a problem of raising the

parents all over again from infancy. We're talking in terms of a time period that can extend from five to ten years, and even then, when the support system is withdrawn, the family often regresses to where it was before."

Professor Polansky—in addition to painting in elegant detail the totally ineffective "rituals in which welfare workers participate with their clients," the neglecting parents—makes a powerful case that "half measures may be worse than nothing," dismisses most conventional forms of intervention as useless, and suggests some radical steps which would be loathsome to those who take the Constitution seriously. He endorses the early and permanent removal of children from homes where there is "even persuasive evidence" of abuse, substantial prison terms for abusive parents, the promotion of sterilizations subsidized by the government, and institutional placement of many neglecting mothers.

Short of this side of 1984, the outlook for stepped-up intervention is dim for a number of reasons: it assumes proven methods that we haven't begun to find; it would cost staggering amounts; and it just might do more to undermine our social fabric than the problem of abuse itself.

Arguing for parental autonomy and against coercive intervention except in cases where a child evidences serious physical or emotional damage, Professor Wald states that "there is substantial evidence that, except in cases involving very seriously harmed children, we are unable to improve a child's situation through coercive state intervention. In fact, under current practice, coercive intervention frequently results in placing a child in a more detrimental situation than he would be in without intervention. This is true whether intervention results in removal of the child from his home or 'only' in mandating that his parents accept services as a condition of continued custody."

Carefully documenting the detrimental effects of institutional or foster home placement, the at best ineffective and often harmful attempts of social workers to provide services, and the vagaries of the system by which the government makes decisions about intervention, Wald concludes that "we lack sufficient knowledge and agreement about child development and 'proper' parenting to justify either the state's undertaking the functions now assumed a more extensive role in monitoring parental decision-making....If the law required all parents to provide a home environment that maximized the opportunity for their children to realize that inherent potentials, intervention might be necessary in most American homes."

Wald continues: "Such a system is possible. According to one observer, in the Soviet Union, 'when mothers take their babies to the clinics, they are given quizzes to see if they are doing the "right thing." Workers are frequently sent into the home to observe the parents' relationship with each other—and with their children.' Given the plight of many children, it is tempting to adopt policies along these lines. However, the history of failure of previous state efforts to improve children's lives through substitute parenting demands rejection of this notion."

"Finally," Wald suggests, "adopting a policy of minimal coercive intervention may encourage the creation of more extensive services available on a voluntary basis to all families. Hopefully, this will improve the well-being of many more children than now are aided through the almost haphazard application of neglect laws....It should be remembered that our societal commitment to child welfare has not extended to guaranteeing all families adequate income to assure that all children can receive basic nutritional and medical care, adequate housing, or any of the other advantages we would like parents to provide. Nor have governmental bodies been willing to make day care, homemakers, or other services available to all who would use them voluntarily. Yet every study shows a strong correlation between neglect and poverty. In a society that is committed to protecting individual freedom and privacy, it is preferable to attempt to solve problems by noncoercive methods."

What Role Should the Teacher Play?

No one, of course, would advocate leaving children who are suffering severe physical or emotional damage to the mercy of their abusive caretakers. Clearly, there is a group of children whose very existence depends on the state's ability to intervene rapidly and skillfully. But these children are almost always the very young, who will not come to the attention of those mandated to report under the new schemes, and they are just the children who may very well be lost in the rush to identify and service hundreds of thousands of families who are—in one way or another—delinquent or deviant in their child-rearing practices. Services, expertise and funds are limited; the existing social agencies can do only so much repair work. Better to husband the available resources for those in the most urgent need than to diffuse it in creating a vast new bureaucracy with slim prospects of helping anybody.

Teachers, like all those who work intimately with children, can see flaws and deficiencies in the nurturing and home environments of many of their students. There is a tendency to want to move in and save the child, to reconstruct the family. The instinct is natural; but the doing is something else entirely. Few teachers have the expertise to do little more than guess, let alone determine, whether a truant or a shabbily dressed child, a rebellious or withdrawn child, is an abused child. And few social workers assigned to intervene in such cases can do more than perform holding operations.

If teachers really care about the quality of life of their youngsters, there are, however, a number of steps they might take. They can call for a rejection of the overly broad reporting laws and demand narrowly focused laws that, as Senator Mondale recommends, "address the problems of the most severely threatened and abused children in this country." At the same time, they can fight for the voluntary child welfare services—day care, homemakers, parent-support services—that are now available to few families. They can lead the way in promoting the social policies that would guarantee that no child would go hungry, ill-clothed or poorly housed, and that no parent would live day in and day out under stresses that finally turn them against their children.

Chapter 56

Child Care Needs of Migrant Children

Arnold B. Cheyney and Georgia B. Adams*

TYPHOID!!!

Surely this scourge of the past had been eradicated by the marvels of medical research. But not so. Typhoid fever struck down 193 migrant men, women, and children in the early months of 1973. Farmworker families at the South Side Dade Labor Camp in South Florida suffered disease, agony, fear, and economic loss.

A little known story in the Annual Narrative Report of the Executive Director of the Redlands Christian Migrant Association, Wendall Rollasons (1973), graphically portrays what the vigilance of individuals can accomplish when concern for children is paramount in their thinking.

We think it no coincidence that nary a child who regularly attended our South Dade Labor Camp Day Care Center was stricken with typhoid. Mathematically, ten per cent of our youngsters should have been felled by the disease—that's the percentage of the entire camp population which was hit. At least eight of our infants and toddlers were saved by something.

And that something, in our view, was RCMA's registered nurse, Mrs. Ethelene Himberg. At her direction—and vigorously supported by the center director, Mrs. Ethel Lee Strachan, our children and staff went on a "boiled water only" regime at least two weeks prior to appearance of the first typhoid case. Mrs. Himberg, herself a former public health nurse with years of experience in the camps, had become alarmed at the number of diarrhea cases reported to her. She decided to take direct action. All water faucets at the center were disconnected to prevent youngsters from sneaking a drink. All water in the center was boiled. We had no hard evidence then (and none since) that camp water was the culprit, but taking these precautions was viewed as a logical place to begin....

Speculation? Certainly.

But the stark fact remains that none of the youngsters regularly attending the RCMA day care center were hit with typhoid.

Migrant children are the deprived of the deprived. The literature is full of evidence that the migrant worker and his children qualify as members of that group of humanity variously labeled as culturally or socially deprived, disadvantaged, different or just plain poor.

Specifically, we see the child care needs of migrant children being given priority before birth. The research described in this paper indicates that medical and nutritional aid can make a major difference in later physical and intellectual functioning. To wait until school age to attach migrant children's needs is senseless.

The deadening influence of poverty on mental ability begins at the moment of conception. This environmental damage during the reproductive cycle is organic in nature and, therefore, likely to be permanent. As a result of such factors as her own lifelong poor health care, faulty nutrition, and minimal education, the disadvantaged expectant mother is a poor reproductive risk. The migrant, from conception to death, is at physical risk with respect to a whole spectrum of physical hazards which may produce intellectual deficit and academic failure (Birch and Gussow, 1970).

The migrant child who is apathetic because of hunger or malnutrition, whose sequence of prior experiences has been interrupted by acute or chronic illness, whose perceptions and ability to organize have been affected by previous exposure to risks of damage to the central nervous system, cannot be expected to respond in an academic situation in the same way as a child who has not been exposed to these experiences.

Infant Mortality

The infant death rate of a given population is an indication of the medical risk to which that population is exposed. Birch and Gussow (1970) described the high infant mortality rate among the poor and Browning and Northcut (1961) confirmed this high mortality rate among the migrant population.

In identifying a population with a high rate of infant loss, we are also describing a group in whose surviving

*Arnold B. Cheyney, Professor of Education, University of Miami; Georgia B. Adams, Assistant Superintendent, Montgomery County Schools, Troy, North Carolina. Reprinted with permission from CONTEMPORARY EDUCATION, published by the School of Education, Indiana State University, Terre Haute, Volume XLV, Number 4, Summer 1974.

children we can expect to find a higher-than-average prevalence of central nervous system involvement resulting from the hazards prevalent in gestation, birth, and early life. Almost every complication of the pre, neo-, and post-natal periods which is potentially damaging to children is excessively present in the economically depressed population and particularly those that are poor and non-white. Organic damage due to disease and poor nutrition, for example, both during the reproductive cycle and after the child is born, occurs among the poor much more frequently than among other classes.

Prematurity

The migrant population is a high-risk group for premature births and other perinatal disorders. These conditions are historically associated with central nervous system disorders. Evidence seems to show that the highest rate of prematurity and brain damage is associated with disorders in the first three months of pregnancy. Often the normal diet and activity level of the disadvantaged mother is not sufficient to protect the developing embryo at this stage.

Prematurity is more clearly associated with a wide range of insult to the central nervous system than with any other complication of pregnancy. A close association exists both between prematurity and retardation and between poverty and prematurity. In fact, in the premature infant, mental retardation is ten times more likely to appear than in the full-term infant (Hurley, 1969).

Studies by Drillen, Pasamanick, and Wortis found a relationship between prematurity and behavior disorders. Decreased birth weight was associated with an increasing proportion of chidren judged "unsettled or maladjusted" by their teachers (Olser and Cooke, 1965).

Work by Guttmacher (Osler and Cooke, 1965) showed that the patient most likely to have a premature infant is a young Negro woman in her first pregnancy who has received little or no prenatal care, who comes from an underpriviledged group, who works hard and eats poorly. These characteristics of pregnancy are true for the black migrant mother as well as those of Mexican-American and Anglo ethnic origin (Browning and Northcutt, 1961).

Nutrition

Many migrant children do not achieve well academically. A faulty diet, low in critically important vitamins and minerals, can cause serious damage to an infant's brain. Many physicians, nutritionists, and physiologists agree that such poor nutrition can result in academic retardation. This retardation is not the result of accident, disease or injury, but the repercussions of environmental deprivation and the effects of poverty (Coles, 1970; Hurley, 1969). Centuries ago it was recognized that poor diet caused depressed intellectual performance. In modern time the lethargy, dullness,

and pseudo-mental retardation of many poor children can be ascribed to this same factor (Dayton, 1969).

As is so often true for children of poverty, one inadequacy—food—leads to another. Missing nutrients in the migrant child's system weaken his physical and emotional ability to overcome his problem. A further chain reaction results when money must be spent unexpectedly for clothing, medical expenses, or automobile maintenance. There is, usually, only one source from which that money can come—the amount allocated for food. The result is the withholding of the elements of a proper diet from already malnourished bodies (Bagdikian, 1964).

Nelson (1967) described a "vicious triangle" which links infantile diarrhea, brain damage, and malnutrition. This may account for mental retardation among children far more than is realized. The dehydration of infantile diarrheal disease can contribute to permanent central nervous system damage. Equally significant are data suggesting a link between malnutrition and intestinal infection.

In the San Joaquin Valley in 1960, shigellosis (a form of dysentery) ran rampant among the migrant population. In a short time twenty-eight babies died of dehydration and malnutrition (Moore, 1965).

According to Dayton (1969) maternal malnutrition is known to be associated with increased rates of morbidity during pregnancy. Evidence is increasing that nutritional experiences of a potential mother before conception may also be extremely important to subsequent intra-uterine growth. Where malnutrition occurs in critical periods of the potential mother's development, such as adolescence, future generations may be affected. Suboptimal diet during pregnancy is thus added to a lifetime of poor feeding as another of the potential risks for reproductive casualty to which poverty exposes the migrant mother. Osler and Cook (1965) cited numerous studies which reflect the ultimate effect of maternal nutrition upon the subsequent offspring. In one of the studies conducted by Thompkins, 750 patients were given "advice and vitamins" as a part of their prenatal care. In these 750 pregnancies there were no premature births.

Prenatal Care

According to Cowles (1967) pregnant poor women, who have the greatest need for prenatal care, get very little. They have a high incidence of anemia, malnutrition, chronic vascular disease, toxemia, contracted pelves, and premature labor.

The most serious of the migrant maternal health problems with reference to retardation are disorders of the geni-to-urinary system. Browning and Northcutt (1961) found that such disorders occur in from ten to twenty percent of the migrant population. While venereal disease, especially syphilis, is a major problem, the greatest need is prenatal care. The study showed low hemoglobin and extremes of blood pressures to be prevalent among pregnant migrant women. These conditions existed in combination with the problem of frequent pregnancies, lack of prenatal care, and insufficient funds for private medical care.

Patients without prenatal care have much higher rates of prematurity, complications of delivery, prenatal, neonatal, and maternal death than do women who receive continuing care at relatively good levels during their reproductive years (Hurley, 1969). Women who receive inadequate prenatal care also fail to receive adequate care during, after, or between deliveries.

Maternity Age and Parity

The migrant mother differs from the non-migrant in the early age at which she begins her productive life, in the late age at which she ends it, and in the total number of pregnancies which she completes during her total period of fertility (Browning and Northcutt, 1961).

Poor women, and, especially, poor non-white women, begin child-bearing younger, and repeat it more rapidly than the non-poor and white women. They are more apt to continue producing children into the older ages and higher birth orders where the rates of complication are strikingly high (Osler and Cooke, 1965).

Recommendations

The research discussed in this paper is only the tip of an iceberg. But individuals who are aware and care can intervene and make a difference in the lives of migrant children, as evidenced by the nurse during the typhoid epidemic in the opening illustration.

We recommend the following course of action be taken to provide migrant children a chance for developing more fully their capacities:

1. Medical care and advice for future mothers, mothers and children must be given in the immediate vicinity of the camps if not within the camps. One way this can be done is through mobile trailer medical clinics. All too often it is difficult, if not impossible, for migrant mothers and their children to get to physicians who live at some distance from the camps.

2. Day Care Centers should be built at the migrant camps to handle children whose mothers are working in the fields. These centers should incorporate a Career Development Program through which migrant mothers could be trained to deal with children in groups. Ultimately, these centers would be staffed and administered by migrants who would then have an employment alternative to the fields.

3. In conjunction with the medical and Day Care Centers, there should be an agency that would be responsible for training migrant mothers in preparation of basic foods to effect a more balanced and nutritional diet for migrant children.

Only by reaching migrant children before they are born can we affect their later lives.

BIBLIOGRAPHY

Bagdikian, B.H. *In the midst of plenty.* New York: New American Library, 1964.

Birch, H.G. and Gussow, J.D. *Disadvantaged children.* New York: Harcourt, Brace & World, 1970.

Browning, R. H. and Northcutt, Jr., T. J. On the season. Florida State Board of Health Monograph, 1961 No. 2.

Cheyney, A. B. (ed.) *The ripe harvest.* Coral Gables, Florida: University of Miami Press, 1972.

Coles, R. *Teachers and the children of poverty.* The Potomac Institute, 1970.

Coles, R. *Migrants sharecroppers, mountaineers.* Boston: Little, Brown. 1971.

Cowles, M. *Perspectives in the education of disadvantaged children.* Cleveland: World Publishing Co., 1967.

Dayton, D. H. Early malnutrition and human development. *Children,* 1969, *16,* 210-217.

Greene, S. E. *The education of migrant children.* Washington, D.C.: Department of Rural Education of the National Education Association of the U.S., 1954.

Hurley, R. *Poverty and mental retardation.* New York: Vintage Books, 1969.

Kleinert, E. J. *Migrant children in Florida — Vols. I and II.* Coral Gables: University of Miami, 1968-69.

Matthiessen, P. Sal si puedes: *Cesar Chavez and the new American Revolution.* New York: Dell, 1973.

Moore, T. Slaves for rent. *Atlantic Monthly,* 1965, *215,* No. 5, 109-22.

Nelson, J. D. Infantile diarrhea and neurological deficit. *Hospital Practice,* 1967, July.

National Committee on the Education of Migrant Children. *Wednesday's children.* New York: 1971.

Osler, S. F. and Cooke, R. E. (ed.) *The biosocial basis of mental retardation.* Baltimore, Maryland: John Hopkins, 1965.

Pinnie, A. F. (ed.) *Another disadvantaged dimension: educating the migrant child.* Cheyney, Pennsylvania: Cheyney State College, 1969.

Rollason, Wendall. *Annual narrative report of the executive director-1973.* Homestead, Florida: Redlands Christian Migrant Association, 1973.

Samora, J. *Los mojados: the wetback story.* Notre Dame: University of Notre Dame Press, 1971.

Steiner, S. *La raza: the Mexican Americans.* New York: Harper and Row, 1970.

Sutton, E. *Knowing and teaching the migrant child.* Washington D.C.: National Education Association, 1962.

Wright, D. *They harvest despair.* Boston: Beacon Press, 1965.

Section VII

Parent Education and the Family

Introduction by Regina Persky*

No one will deny that parenting is a difficult task. Conscientious parents fumble and grope in their attempts to bring up their children as well as possible. The style they employ varies from individual to individual depending on their own backgrounds, experiences, and childhood family interactions. Paradoxically today's greater awareness of the difficulties involved in child rearing, instead of making the task easier, tends to make it more anxiety producing and confusing. Contradictions in the plethora of literature as to the correct degree of permissiveness has thoroughly confused well-intentioned parents. Coupled with the prolific growth of mental-health concepts and new terminology, young parents are burdened with the tremendous responsibilities of redefining their roles.

Role identity as popularized by William Glasser, characterizes today's women as they ride the crest of a social revolution fostered by the Women's Liberation Movement. Whether or not they believe in the movement, they are caught in the current which forces them to reassess their goals, priorities, and role functions. Womens' Lib, economic conditions, and better education have resulted in a greater number of women entering into the work force. While striving for better living conditions, many working moms are saddled with a great deal of guilt as to whether they have abandoned their children at too early an age. Conversely, many women who stay at home are concerned with the possibility that they have not fulfilled their own potential. This role confusion caused by rapid social change has disoriented both fathers and mothers alike. As a result, we have witnessed a generation characterized by many disillusioned, unhappy, and drug-addicted youngsters. Social upheaval often results in the sweeping away of old values without replacing them. This vacuum often leads to a breakdown of authority and a decline in morality.

These negative manifestations have resulted in many parents seeking professional services. The schools experiencing similar difficulties with these same children have been attempting to enter into a partnership with parents in order to improve conditions. One of the approaches has been the implementation of parent workshops. One important aspect that they focus on is opening new lines of communication between parents and children. Child psychologists such as Haim Ginott, Thomas Gordon, and Rudolf Dreikurs are discussed in relation to their approaches concerning discipline, sibling rivalry, negative behavior, and other problems.

Dr. Spock is still the parents' bible in dealing with children's health and stages of development. Unfortunately, in spite of having all of this available material, many parents still unrealistically expect children to behave in line with adult standards. Adults all too often forget that young children are basically self-centered, not always ready to share, want instant gratification, and have a code of ethics that serves their immediate needs.

The ways in which children mature, develop the ability to make decisions, assume responsibility, acquire values, and develop their own identities in becoming self-confident autonomous individuals is an ongoing life-time journey. They learn through limitation and emulation of parents, communication, and experience. Success lays down the foundation for more success. Parents share the joy of satisfaction when a little child does something for himself for the first time such as turn on a light, put on socks, ride a bike, or make a new friend. As success takes place at the initial stages, the foundation is set for future successes in the hierarchy of development.

Even in its embryonic stages, parent education holds tremendous potential for present and future generations. Through parent sensitivity much misery and confusion can be avoided. By serving in a supportive role, parents can help their children grow and develop to their fullest individual potentials.

The articles in the following section discuss the cooperative efforts made by parents and educators to unify home and school so that they support and reinforce each other.

*Regina Persky, Early Childhood Teacher, New York City Public Schools.

Chapter 57

The Changing American Family

Urie Bronfenbrenner*

Americans like to talk a lot about "progress," improving the quality of life," and "meeting the challenges of tomorrow." All these depend on our ability to raise today's children well. The future belongs to those countries that make their primary commitment to the cultivation of the minds, character and creative vigor of the young. Therefore, the United States should take the upbringings of its children at least as seriously as it does landing on the moon or Mars.

In the upbringing of today's children numerous factors play a role: their neighborhood or town, schools, friends, religious institutions, games, work, the television and films they watch, the papers, advertising, magazines and books they read, role models, and their family. But in the recent years nearly every line of social and psychological research points to the family as the foremost influence in what we might call "character formation," "cultural education," or "upbringing."

That the family is the central institution comes as no surprise to most anthropologists, ethnic patriarchs, or social historians because the family is the only social institution that is present in every single village, tribe, people or nation-state we know throughout history. But that the family is the core institution in every society may startle and annoy many contemporary Americans. For most of us it is the individual that is the chief social unit. We speak of the individual vs. the state, individual achievement, support for disadvantaged individuals, the rights of individuals, finding ourselves as individuals. It's always the individual with "the government" a weak second. The family is not currently a social unit we value or support.

This fact is reflected in the scholarly research of the United States. Until recently there has been only sporadic research on the history, significance, or changes in the family. And it is reflected in our national, local, and business policies, where a father, mother, son, and daughter are usually treated as four individuals rather than as a family.

Thus at a time when our nation more than ever needs a public-spirited and enlightened young, and when the best new research is pointing to the critical role of the family, our nation pays little attention to the family as a key social unit, and there are mounting indications that the American family as we know it is falling apart.

Several times in the past century observers have wailed about the decline of the family. Historian Charles Thwing, for example, wrote in his 1913 book on the family: "The individual has come to be regarded as the crown and centre of social and legal order. The family, as an institution of prime importance, has passed away." But what has happened in the United States since the 1950s really adds up to a rapid and radical change in American family life. And the consequences for the young, and for society as a whole, are approaching the calamitous.

There was a kind of family stability in the late 1940s and early 1950s. The extended family still existed in places; one out of 10 families had another adult relative living under its roof. After the shakeout year of 1946, the divorce rate was quite low, especially among families with young children. Only one mother in four was working outside the home. And fewer than 4 percent of all children born were illegitimate. Parents fought for a better education for their children, kicking off a school and college-building boom. Television, which became commercially available to households in 1948, was almost unknown. Mass magazines wrote of "togetherness" and radio soap operas featured families. Hollywood made films about young Andy Hardy, Shirley Temple and Dorothy from Kansas, who went to see the Wizard of Oz but longed to return to her family.

In the past 25 years, however, the change has been dramatic. The dimensions of this change can be illustrated by some data about two categories: the number of parents and other adult relatives in the home, and the amount of attention that parents devote to genuine relationships with their children.

As for adults in the home, there has been a further decline in the number of grandmothers, uncles, or unmarried sisters in the home. From roughly 10 percent of all homes having a third or fourth adult in 1950, the percentage has dropped to half that. Compared to 50 years ago, the change is even more considerable. For example, in the 1920s

*Urie Bronfenbrenner is one of the nation's foremost experts on child development and one of the founders of the federal Head Start program. He is a professor at State University of New York (SUNY). This article is from the fall 1976 issue of the SUNY magazine Search. Reprinted with permission of AFL-CIO *American Federationist.*

half the households in Massachusetts included at least one adult besides the parents; today the figure is 4 percent.

That leaves Mom and Dad. But Mom is increasingly not found at home either because she's out working, as well as attending meetings or shopping several nights a week. In 1975 for the first time in American history a majority of the nation's mothers with school-age children—ages 6 to 17—held jobs outside the home. In fact, women with school-age children show the highest labor force participation rate, 54 percent, compared with 28 percent in 1950.

For pre-school children the change is more startling. In 1975, 39 percent of mothers of children under six were working, more than three times as many as in 1948. As for mothers with tiny infants, children under three, nearly one in three is working—an amazing jump from 1950.

Of course, the increase of women in the workforce is one of the most significant social and economic facts of our time. While the number of working husbands has risen from 29.8 million to 37.8 million between 1947 and 1975, or 27 percent, the number of working wives has shot up from 6.5 million to 19.8 million, or 205 percent—nearly 10 times the increase among working husbands. It began before the so-called women's liberation movement, and has unquestionably brought many new opportunities and greater satisfaction to numerous wives and mothers. But it has also had a major impact on American child-rearing.

The parents have not only been leaving the home to work; they have increasingly been disappearing. The number of children under 18 living with only one of their parents—now one out of six—has almost doubled in the past 25 years. And the change has been most rapid for children under six years old. In 1974, 13 percent of all infants under three—nearly 1 million babies—lived with only one parent.

Three of the main contributors to the rise of one-parent homes have been divorces, illegitimate births, and desertions.

The divorce rate has risen appreciably in the past 25 years, but especially since the early 1960s. Last year for the first time in U.S. history the number of divorces exceeded 1 million—twice the number of a decade earlier, and almost three times that of 1950. Nearly 40 percent of all marriages now end in divorce; 3 of 10 women separate from their husbands before the age of 30. The number of children from divorced families is twice that of a decade ago.

True, the remarriage rate has been going up too, but it lags far behind the divorce rate. Also, more divorces can mean that there is more affection between married couples now than in 1950, when unhappy couples tended to stay together regardless. But a growing number of divorces are now accompanied by a new phenomenon: the unwillingness of either parent to take custody of the children.

Next to divorce, illegitimate births are the fastest growing contributor to one-parent homes. In the past 25 years the rate of illegitimacy has more than doubled, from 4 per 100 live births to 10 per 100 live births. And in addition to the more than 350,000 babies born out of wedlock last year, another 65,000 pregnancies were halted by abortions to teenagers alone. Thus, a growing number of children are being born to unmarried women, 80 percent of them under 25 years old.

As for desertions, the male has long been a frequent deserter of his wife and children—male desertion accounted for 49 percent of divorces in the United States in 1900—and males continue to flee. But wives have begun deserting in far greater numbers too. Police department reports are suddenly full of notices of missing mothers, and detective bureaus indicate a quantum leap in the number of runaway wives.

Single-parenthood is especially common among the poor, although it's becoming more frequent among the lower- and upper-middle classes. And it is particularly prevalent among black Americans, many of whom are poor. In 1974 only 56 percent of all black children under 18 lived with both parents, down from 71 percent in 1965. (Recent research by Herbert Gutmann and others has found that until recently, black families have been more stable than many believed.) Specifically, between 1960 and 1970 the percentage of single-parent families among blacks increased at a rate five times that for whites—a baffling fact since it was a period of considerable economic and education gains for blacks. Today, the proportion of single-parent families among blacks is three times that of whites.

Two things are noteworthy, however. White families are being fragmented progressively as well as black families. And middle-class families are now approaching the social disintegration of lower-class families a decade ago.

The other broad category of change is the amount of attention that one or both parents give to affectionate child-raising when the children and adults are not separated by school or work. Here, too, there has been a sharp decline.

With demands of a job that sometimes claim the evening hours and weekends, with increasing time spent commuting and caring for automobiles, with entertaining and social visits as well as meetings and community obligations, parents spend less and less time working, playing, reading and talking with their children. More and more children come home to an empty house or apartment.

In some homes a child spends more evenings with a passive, uninterested babysitter than a participating parent. One study of middle-class fathers of one-year-old infants found that they spent an average of only 20 minutes a day with their babies. When a recording microphone was attached, to each infant's shirt, the data indicated that in terms of true, intimate interaction between father and child the average daily time together was 38 seconds. One survey I did of child rearing practices in the United States over the past 25 years reveals a decrease in all spheres of interaction between parents and their children.(The same trend is appearing in Europe, studies show.)

An increasing number of parents enroll their children in day care centers—enrollment doubled between 1965 and 1975 alone—and then preschools. And they sit them in front of television. It is estimated by experts that pre-school children—under six—spend an average 50 hours a week watching TV. By the time the average American youngster graduates from high school he has spent more hours watching the television screen than he has spent in school, or in any other activity except sleeping.

Gone increasingly are family picnics, long Sunday dinners, children and parents working together fixing the house, preparing meals, hiking in the woods, singing and dancing with other families or friends. And we are paying a price for this growing inattention, even hostility, to our children.

Accidents among children appear to be increasing. Accidents are now the chief cause of death for persons under 18, and about 15 million days of school are lost annually because of accidental injuries to youngsters.

Child abuse by parents has become a national problem. A 1970 survey projected that at least 2 million battered-child cases a year may be found annually now; nearly 200,000 infants and children a year are being killed by their supposed caretakers. A more gruesome trend shows that the killing of infants under 1 year of age has been in-creasing since 1957. The infanticide rate has risen from 3.1 per 100,000 in 1957 to 4.7 per 100,000 in 1970. Sadly, 90 percent of these incidents take place right in the home; the most severe injuries occur in single-parent homes; and many brutalities are inflicted by the frazzled mother herself.

It is not only the parents of children who are neglecting them. Society does so too. As the 1970 White House Conference on Children reported: "A host of factors conspire to isolate children from the rest of society. The fragmenta-tion of the extended family, the separation of residential and business areas, the disappearance of neighborhoods, zoning ordinances, occupational mobility, child labor laws, the abolishment of the apprentice system, consolidated schools, television, separate patterns of social life for different age groups, the working mother, the delegation of child care to specialists—all these manifestations of progress operate to decrease opportunity and incentive for meaningful contact between children and persons older or younger than themselves."

James Coleman's fine 1974 study, "Youth: Transition to Adulthood," documented the same new conditions.

Nor should all the blame fall on the heads of the parents themselves. In many ways, the crux of the problem is not the battered child but the battered parent. The same 1970 Report to the President also said: "In today's world parents find themselves at the mercy of a society which imposes pressures and priorities that allow neither time nor place for meaningful activities and relations between children and adults, which downgrade the role of parents and the functions of parenthood, and which prevent the parent from doing things he wants to do as a guide, friend, and companion to his children...The frustrations are greatest for the family of poverty where the capacity for human re-sponse is crippled by hunger, cold, filth, sickness, and despair."

What has replaced the parents, relatives, neighbors and other caring adults? Three things primarily: television, peer groups (same-age cliques or gangs) and loneliness. A recent study found that at every age level, children today show a greater dependency on their age-mates then they did 10 years ago. And, increasing numbers of lonely "latch-key children" are growing up with almost no care at all, often running away—at the rate of more than 1 million a year now—to join colonies of other solitary juveniles and to experiment with drugs, crime, sex, religious cults, and the sheer restless busy-ness of Kerouac-like movement over the American landscape. These so-called "latch-key child-ren" contribute far out of proportion to the ranks of young persons who have reading problems, or are dropouts, drug users and juvenile delinquents.

What is not often recognized is that the social fabric which so many feel is tearing around them is to large extent a result of the deteriorating family life and the conditions that undermine declining care for our children. Look at what has been happening to America's youth.

The first consequence is that many of them die at birth or soon thereafter. America, the richest, most advanced scientific and medical country in the world, stands 17th among nations in combating infant mortality. The offspring of young, black mothers face an especially frightful pros-pect; babies of black mothers are today still dying at the rate that white babies died in the 1940s.

Crime in America is increasingly a youth problem. Crimes by children—those under 18—have been growing at a higher rate than the juvenile population. According to FBI data, arrests of children for serious crimes—murder, assault, robbery and rape—have jumped about 200 percent in the past 15 years, and arrests for lesser crimes—larceny, burglary, auto theft, forgery—have doubled. Arrests for juvenile prostitution have increased 286 percent, those for traffick-ing and use of drugs 4,600 percent.

This increase of crime by children is three times that of adults over the same period. In 1973 1.7 million children were arrested for criminal actions—one fourth of the total arrests in that year. At the present rate, one out of every nine teenagers can be expected to appear in court before the age of 18. And since many criminal offenders tend to be repeaters, the depressing prospect is for an expanded adult criminal population in the years ahead. And crime is already costing Americans an estimated $80 billion a year.

School vandalism has become in some areas as American as apple pie, soft drinks and aspirin. A good deal of the blame put on teachers for failing to instruct our youth adequately belongs with parents and their increasingly resentful and violent children, and on the rest of us for failing to give both our teachers and our families adequate support, especially of the non-monetary kind.

The suicide rate for young people aged 15 to 19 has more than tripled in less than 20 years, leaping from 2.3 per 100.000 in 1956 to 7.1 in 1974; and in recent years there has been an increase in suicides among younger children, some as young as 10. Suicide is now the third leading cause of death among young American whites; the rate for young blacks is lower but increasing faster. For young American black males, homicide is now the leading cause of death. Death from violence in some form—suicide, homicide, auto and other accidents—now accounts for two of three deaths of those between 5 and 18. The self-destructiveness of our children has become a truly serious problem.

Well known by now is the decline in academic capability among the nation's young during the past 15 years or so. According to the College Entrance Examination Board, in the past 12 years average scores on the scholastic aptitude tests have dropped 44 points (from 478 to 434) in the verbal skills amd 30 points (from 502 to 472) in math, on a scale of 200 to 800. Teachers and professors have in recent years become alarmed at what they experience as their student's growing inability to write decently, refusal to be rigorous in their work, and inability to use common sense reasoning about everyday adult affairs of life.

In a 1976 Gallup Poll conducted for the Phi Delta Kappan, a professional education journal, two-thirds of the sampled Americans blamed parents for these test score declines because they did not provide enough attention, help and supervision for their children. And an impressive series of investigations, most notably by James Coleman and Christopher Jencks, have demonstrated that it is not so much the schools that determine academic achievement or character as a student's family life and the conditions undergirding a strong life within the family: employment, health services, work schedules, child care, neighbors who care, and the like.

In addition, the alienation, antisocial behavior, and disorientation of the young have made an ever larger minority of them unemployable, without training or self-discipline. Half the unemployment in our country today is among young persons under 25 years old.

What are we as a nation to do?

I conducted a study recently for the National Academy of Sciences that tried to determine how successful all of America's early intervention programs such as Head Start, really were. The results, sad to admit, were disappointing—except in places or in programs that involved the parents in the effort.

It's transparent now that the family is a critically important institution in shaping our children's minds, values, and behavior. But it's equally clear that the American family is disintegrating. That's what I'd call a collision course for our society. It must be reversed. But how?

Without attempting concrete suggestions, I would like to offer a few thoughts. I think the main causes of the change in family life are three in number—our attitudes, our socio-technical structure and our national rules and policy. So perhaps our remedies need to take three paths.

Attitudes- American has temporarily lost its balance. Today what matters most for many people is their own growth and happiness, their own self-fulfillment, doing their own thing, finding ourselves. We seem to be sunk in individualism. We so much want to "make it" for ourselves that we have almost stopped being a caring society that cares for others. We seem to be hesitant about making a commitment to anyone or anything, including our own flesh and blood.

To be sure, individualism has helped bring about extraordinary solo efforts by many Americans—in art, science, business and other areas. But we have entered a period of history when we need to put other, neglected values on the scale too. We have many other traditions in the American past: our social welfare schemes; our great public education system; our way of helping our neighbors—or foreign peoples—in times of catastrophe; our volunteer organizations that Alexis de Tocqueville found so outstanding; our scholarships and other help for the poor but able; and our quickness in extending friendship and care to strangers. Like individualism, they too are American traits; and we should draw upon them also. It's a matter of more balanced attitudes.

The healthy growth of each child requires a commitment of love, care and attention from someone. Neighbors, day care leaders, and school teachers can help, but most of the enduring, irrational involvement and intimate activities must come from parents. No one else can ever care so much or so continually. We need to get out of ourselves and into the lives of our children more than we do.

Socio-technical structure. This includes the network of work schemes, social dances, travel patterns, telephones and other social patterns and apparatus that conduce us to separate and fragment rather than come together. We need to reshape parts of this socio-technical structure to meet the needs of today's parents and children.

As a nation we are superb at scientific technology. In this area we are pragmatic. We try new things to see if they work. But when it comes to social technology, we are stuffy, rigid, pessimistic. We often refuse to try little experiments in human affairs to see if our society can be more harmonious, and our children happier. Little things, like more part-time work schemes to allow mothers, students and fathers to have more flexible schedules for greater human contact, seem so difficult.

Our welfare system is a disaster, actively abetting the dissolution of our families. It's chaotic and was designed by no one. Do we re-design it? No, we prefer to continue to muddle through even though the cost in human lives is staggering.

I would suggest that the United States can no longer afford to be so methodical, precise, pragmatic and research-oriented solely in its technological advances, and continue to be so sloppy, neglectful, cautious and fatalistic in its social programs.

National rules and policy. The United States is now the only industrialized nation that does not insure health care or a minimum income for every family with young children, and the only one that has not yet established a program of child care services for working mothers. In the controversial gun control legislation we support the rights of each individual to bear arms but not the rights of our people—or our police—against being shot to death more easily each year. We care more fervently about keeping our wilderness wild, our favorite fishing holes intact, and football than we do about the condition of our families or the gradually spreading cancer among our children.

In our taxes, our plane fares, or our government welfare policies we pay close attention to each individual's privileges and pay little attention to family rates or policies that would help build more cohesive families. We are not only "far out" in some of our individual behavior; among the advanced nations of the world the United States is "far out" in its national permissiveness toward individuals and its national neglect of the upbringing of its children.

Obviously, we cannot go back to the family life of an earlier age—nor should we wish to do so, given some of the old-time family's inequalities and authoritarian practices. But we can design and put into practice new attitudes and structures appropriate for our time. Among all the talk about returning to decency and fundamental values after Vietnam and Watergate, none ought to be more dear than that of a renewed concentration on the proper care, instruction, guidance, and values of America's young people and the families in which they are raised.

The bodies, minds and emotional health of our children demand it. And the ability of our country to cope with its awesome future demands it.

Chapter 58

So What Did You Learn in School Today?

Estelle Wolk*

Brows furrowed, blue eyes questioning, Josh, four years old, asks, "How come you just let us play and you don't teach us nothing?" I smile to myself as I finish buttoning his coat and think back on the morning.

The last few weeks the class has been preparing their snacks making many things that contain eggs. Today we made hard boiled eggs. Well that's what we adults call them. Josh discovered that hard boiled eggs are not hard at all. To open the egg, he tapped it on the side of the bowl as if it were a raw egg. He now found that he had to peel off the shell. The clear liquid had become firm and white, but where was the yellow? "Look," he said as he squeezed it, "It squooshes." Whether something is hard or soft is a relative term and I learned to be careful of my terminology. What he found out was that the cooked egg was different. So different that the yolk now popped out and rolled across the table much to his delight.

The rest of the morning he painted letting his blue paint run into his yellow paint and then brushing it together. He played with the color paddles holding the yellow and blue paddles together in front of his eyes and making "green monsters" out of the other children. He played with blocks; ran out of double blocks; tried to take one from a peer; was rebuffed; complained to the teacher; the teacher asked what other way he could build the same thing; discovered two unit blocks equalled the same as the double block. His eyes shone. Josh played outside riding in a car informing the children that he had a car fixit shop and before long he had a group of customers and other mechanics with him.

As he left, his mother greated him. "So what did you learn in school today?" "Nothing," he replied. "We just played again." This question mirrors the results and product oriented parental attitude toward learning. The process of learning which comprises elements of growth and development and is idiosyncratic receives much less parental attention.

How do we learn? Let me count the ways...Elizabeth Barrett Browning has made us cognizant of the many facets and ways to love and educators are faced with how to enlighten parents about the many ways to learn. Before an educator can do this, he must take a close look at the difference between what he says, how he feels, and what he does. When he says that he views learning as a process of involvement, exploration, and discovery rather than "teacher tells-child learns", his behavior should correspond to his words. How he feels about the child's capacity and ability to learn, about the child being instrumental in his own learning will be displayed by his behavior toward children. When his actions in the classroom foster a relationship of mutual trust between the teacher and the children and enhance the development of internal locus of control of children, he is on his way to being in tune in philosophy and practice. This educator, with a high degree of openness, will have an open and trusting attitude toward parents.

Being aware of their individual differences and concerns, he sets out through the use of various methods to demonstrate to parents the educational purposes and the inherent value of materials both in their orthodox and unorthodox uses. A combination of conferences, workshops, and classroom visits help to ease the concern that Josh's original question echos by displaying the high degree of organization and structure necessary to accomplish a flexible curriculum, one that facilitates cognitive achievement within the socio-emotional domain. This program for parents must be ongoing because learning takes time whether for children or for adults.

The Plowden Report stresses the importance of time. "...allowance to each child for the time necessary for his own individual mental synthesizing."[1] Barth's assumption thirteen reads, "Concept formation proceeds very slowly."[2] This is one area that adults find difficult no matter how "open" they are. The dichotomy of what is known intellectually and what is felt and done shows up most in this area. Educators being part of our culture are caught up with everyone else in our merry-go-round society which turns faster and faster merging what we see into a huge blur. The value of speed and instant gratification are reflected in the facets of everyday life. We have instant foods to cater to our tastes; we have just to press a button to have light, radio or television for visual and auditory gratification. Need company? Pick up the telephone; hop in the car. Parents expect instant readers. Teachers want instant feedback on experiences. Arbitrary norms are set up and child-

---

*Estelle Work, Nursery School Teacher, Hebrew Educational Society.

ren are expected to gratify adult expectations. The acceleration of our external clocks has put us on a collision course with the child's internal clock. We must keep our goals in perspective at all times and resist the impulse for immediate results.

Basically the message we want to communicate to parents is that a child learns not only with his head but with all parts of his body. When he catches a ball or walks on the balance beam, he is developing eye hand coordination. When he sews, he is developing directionality. When he constructs with blocks, he is developing laterality and noting configuration. When he does a puzzle, it aids in figure ground perception. Each time he uses his thumb and forefinger to pick something up, he develops those fine muscles necessary for turning the pages of a book. Each time he interacts with peers, expresses his feelings, listens to a story, or tells something in class, he adds to his storehouse of ideas and experiences. Every child needs his own amount of time to fill his storehouse and every child will fill it in his own way.

We want parents to know that little feet taking little steps take a long time but that each little step well taken is surely a giant step!

FOOTNOTES

Lillian Weber (1971) in "The Rationale of Informal Education" uses the Plowden Report among others to discuss how children learn as reported in the *Open Classroom Reader* (p. 151).

Roland Barth (1972) advises that a shortage of time is a consequence of an abundant society and until adults know more about how children think and learn, the child is a better judge of his needs with respect to time. (p. 31).

BIBLIOGRAPHY

Barth, Roland S. *Open Education and the American School.* New York: Agathon Press, Inc., 1972.
Silberman, Chalres E. *The Open Classroom Reader.* New York: Random House, 1973.

Chapter 59

When a Child Begins School

Luleen S. Anderson*

This September more than six million 5- and 6-year olds will make their first significant venture into foreign territory: they will leave home to begin kindergarten or first grade. That a large percentage of them adjust to school with a minimum of difficulty is a tribute to the resiliency of the young child. Unfortunately, parents, who play a major role in this drama, seldom receive the support they need to help both themselves and their child effectively handle this new experience.

When the child leaves home comfortably and is eager for the new experiences school will bring, everything is lovely. But when the child becomes anxious and fearful or refuses to go to school — or if he or she goes amid such emotional scenes that both the child and parent are physically and emotionally drained — something has gone awry. Unless the situation receives immediate attention, a temporary crisis may become a chronic problem. (This may lead to what is usually called "school avoidance" or "school phobia" — terms which simply mean that for one reason or another, the child is anxious about the separation from home and is afraid to go to school.)

What can parents do to help their child take this developmental step forward? First, parents should understand that there are certain tasks which must be mastered at certain ages. No matter what our age, each of us has a job to do — a task or tasks to master. Each period of life brings its own challenges and stresses — from infancy, when the baby must learn to trust his world and the helping people in it, to young adulthood, when the young person must decide on career goals and lifestyles. The building blocks for sound personality development involve the successful mastery of these tasks at each level of growth and development.

Thus, the 5- or 6-year-old has a major job: to go to school. In order to do this — a task society has set for him or her — the child must successfully master three earlier tasks. First, he or she must make the shift from dependency upon parents and the home to dependency upon peers and other adults. This means that the school-age child must allow other people to meet many of his needs and to relate to him in meaningful fashion. How easily this task is mastered depends in large measure upon how secure and trusting his early relationships have been, and how unambivalent his parents are about supporting his new venture.

The second task of the child entering school is the management of separation anxiety. For most children this is accomplished with a minimum of anxiety or distress. For others, however, the threat of the loss of mother is terribly frightening and extremely stressful, both for the child and for the mother. Separation anxiety is one of the most painful experiences a child can have. Often for mothers, who can see no logical reason for it, it is a most baffling experience.

Finally, the school-age child must learn to accept the authority of other adults, namely, the teacher, principal and other support personnel in the school. This acceptance is made easier if the child has had a healthy dose of basic trust through his early relationships with other helping adults.

These, then, are the young child's jobs. But parents have their job, too, and that is to do everything they can to make it possible for the child to deal effectively with his or her new experiences. How can parents do this? In response to questions from many parents, I began three years ago, in the late spring, to meet with parents of preschoolers to discuss how they could help prepare their children for entry into school. Here are some practical suggestions — some "dos" and "don'ts" — which we discussed and which have proven effective for many parents:

- Don't make the beginning of school a topic of daily conversation during the summer months. Don't belabor the issue — or, as one child said to his over-zealous mother, "Don't make a federal case out of it!"

- Do treat going to school as part of the normal course of events, something that is expected and something that parents casually accept that the child will be doing (with some support and encouragement).

- Don't allow older children to frighten or tease the younger child with tales of how awful school is. If necessary, speak with the older children privately about their responsibility in helping the younger child to go to school without fear. Try to make the older children your allies.

*Dr. Luleen S. Anderson, is coordinator of Psychological Services and Elementary Guidance for the Quincy Public Schools, Quincy, Massachusetts. Reprinted from New York Teacher Magazine.

If a teasing child is a neighborhood bully over whom you have no control, invite your child to trust *your* perceptions about what school will be like, rather than accepting what the older child has to say on the subject.

- Do answer honestly all questions the child asks about school and what to expect. Knowing the number of days he will attend, the length of time he will be away from home, how he will get back and forth to school — all are important, for a child may be made anxious by uncertainty and needs to know details in order to master his anxiety. Many schools hold orientation sessions for parents and children to acquaint them with school staff members, the classroom the child will be attending and school procedures.

  Working mothers and fathers will also want to make certain that the child knows the arrangement for before- and/or after-school care.

- Don't give the impression that there is any choice about whether or not to attend school. Children will often say, "I'm not going," or "They can't make me." These comments should be responded to calmly and reassuringly, letting the child know that you understand his concerns about this new situation but that you know he will be able to handle it — and that all children have to go to school. You may want to add that there is a law (or rule) which requires that children attend school. At five and six, children are already learning to respect and appreciate laws and rules. The point is not to waiver; the wise parent does not offer a choice which he cannot or will not honor. The mother who wants a child to eat eggs does not say, "Would you like an egg for breakfast?" Instead, she asks casually, "How would you like your egg this morning: fried, scrambled or boiled?" Don't argue the issue of school attendance. A calm, matter-of-fact, positive attitude is your goal.

- Do communicate to the child that you appreciate the effort he or she is making to do what is being asked, and that you will do your part to make it as easy as possible for the child to meet this new responsibility. There are many possibilities for communicating this support: "Would you prefer your new shoes or your sneakers for the first day of school?" "What dessert would you like in your lunch box?" "Think of something special you'd like us to do when you get home." The basic idea here is to find ways of acknowledging the child's efforts and to give the child some say-so — some control — over the situation, whenever possible.

- Do make transportation plans clear to the child. If he or she is to walk to school, walk the route together once or twice before school begins or walk him to school and meet him there after classes have ended the first day or so. If there are other children from your neighborhood who are his age and who are walking, see if your child and a friend could walk together.

Don't set a pattern of walking into the classroom. and wait until the child gets seated. This may lead to tears or clingy behavior, which gets the child off on the wrong foot with other children, who then may tease him, thus adding to the problem. Goodbyes are best said at home or in the school yard.

If a child is transported to school by bus, help the child identify the type of vehicle and, if possible, take a bus ride with the child prior to the first day of school to alleviate some anxiety. If there are other children whom you know waiting for the bus, introduce your child to them. Older children may be encouraged to watch over younger ones. Once the bus arrives, be direct; say goodbye and allow the child to board by himself. If the child does cry, be assured that in most cases the tears will usually disppear before the bus is out of sight.

- Don't try to force the child to be exuberant about going to school. It is natural for a child not to be ecstatic about giving up a comfortable and safe relationship at home for the uncertain territory of school. Allow, even encourage, him to express all his feelings about school. One good way of allowing children to let off steam is through fantasy — and you need not be afraid of granting in fantasy that which you cannot grant in reality. In other words, acknowledge a child's right to wish for things or to wish that things were different, even when you cannot allow the wish to be fulfilled. For example, when the up-tight 6-year-old says, the day before school begins, "I wish nobody ever invented schools or teachers," the wise parent will understand the underlying concern in such a statement and respond, perhaps in the following fashion:

  "It would be fun, wouldn't it, if we could just stay home and play all day and have nobody telling us what to do. Some days I feel that way, too. But we can't do all the things we'd like to, even though it's fun to think about the idea."

  Sometimes just being able to say whatever is on his or her mind and to discover that the words are heard and the feelings are accepted is both calming and reassuring to a child.

- Many non-working mothers look forward to the free time they will have once their child enters school. However, don't tell the child how much fun you are going to be having while he or she is in school. Do let the child know that while he is doing his job at school, you will be doing yours. Mentioning of concrete tasks can be very reassuring to the child. "While you're in school today, I'll do the laundry and vacuuming so we can have some time together when you get home."

  Working mothers often make special arrangements which allow them to be home the first day or two when their child returns from school. When this is not possible, other ways of giving a little extra attention can be found, such as a telephone call from work to the child who has just completed his first day at school, or an arrangement to do something special with the child later in the day when the mother returns home from work.

● Do create a normal routine atmosphere at home the first few days of school. This does not mean that you deny or avoid the uniqueness of the first day of school but, on the other hand, don't give the child the impression that his leaving for his first day of school is of the same magnitude as Lindbergh's solo flight over the Atlantic. One such family of a 5-year-old arrived en masse at the school for the child's first day, formed a line on the sidewalk and waved and cried as their movie camera recorded his slow disappearance into the school! The parent's responsibility is to provide reassuring support when needed, but otherwise to "play it cool."

● Don't assume that all of the anxiety associated with a child's entry into school is the child's. Parents — especially mothers — may experience some anciety of their own over their child's moving into a new era. This is understandable, for the mother has to give up some of her control of the child to school authorities and to share her child's teaching and upbringing with others. Often she also has major readjustments to make in her own life if she now has a large portion of her time free.

Mothers need to separate their own anxiety from that of the child's. A mother's worry and tension are highly contagious and the young child quickly perceives and responds to them. I encourage mothers to acknowledge and accept their own feelings and reactions, get the youngster off to school — and then to relax and share their feelings with a friend, going off to school represents a developmental phase for parents as well as children. Parents should be aware that sending a child off to school can be anxiety-provoking for them. Each parent maintains many childhood memories, both positive and negative, about school. A child's entry into school seems to reactivate for some parents the feelings they had when they started school themselves, particularly feelings associated with negative experiences — which, perhaps, leave the deepest impression. Therefore, remembering their school experiences, parents may have ambivalent feelings concerning their child's new experience. Since the parents' reaction to the child's early school experiences is of critical importance to his or her early school adjustment, parents might profit by reviewing their own anxieties and satisfactions regarding their school entry experiences.

By the time their first child begins school, most parents have been away from the educational system for a number of years. When their child enters kindergarten or first grade, parents see a school that has probably changed considerably from what they remember. It would be helpful if parents could see this as a positive opportunity to reacquaint themselves with the educational system and to get to know the school staff members and other parents involved in their child's school.

While the focus here has been on the child entering kindergarten or first grade, we must realize that, for increasing numbers of children, kindergarten does not represent their first school experience. Today many children attend nursery schools, day care centers and other preschool programs. A happy preschool experience may promote a comfortable transition into kindergarten; however, kindergarten is *not* a repeat of nursery school. As one very bright second-grader explained when asked about the differences between nursery school and kindergarten, "Well, most anybody can make it in nursery school. But when you go to *real* school, you're not so sure you can learn everything and make good grades."

Parents whose children have adjusted well to preschool are often surprised that they may experience separation anxiety when they approach kindergarten or first grade. This repetition of emotional experience is an important developmental phenomenon. These children have endured the initial separation from home to receive the gratification of new experiences and friends, and they have dealt with their first major loss of persons outside their home. Children who have attended preschool and are entering kindergarten are, in effect, being asked to risk separation again for new horizons which have not been defined.

If parents do enroll a child in a preschool program, they should, if possible, select one which is as compatible as possible with the school their child will later attend. If the parents themselves are aware of whatever major differences exist, they can forewarn the child and, thus, help him to cope with them. The intention of preschool programs should be to provide a bridge between home and the world, one which might help children toward a kindergarten adjustment without infringing on local kindergarten experiences.

What happens if, after all this good planning and careful handling, the big day arrives and the child begins to cry or to complain of being sick? Parents should grit their teeth, fight back the annoyance and PUSH. This means that the child is to go even if tears flow. Usually the "moment of truth" occurs at the point of separation between mother and child. Once this separation is made, the child usually recovers quickly and has a successful day. Many a mother or father who feels terrible all day because the child left in tears would be reassured if they could know that the tears have usually subsided before the child had gone two blocks away, and that the teacher was unaware that the child had experienced difficulty in getting to school that day. In a situation such as this, the first few days are critical. With firm, patient, reassuring handling of the child by parents and teachers, this fearful, tearful behavior usually disappears within a few days. By then the child has learned to feel comfortable away from home; he has learned to trust his teacher and has made some new friends; and he has learned that some interesting, exciting things go on in his classroom. What is important for the child's *emotional* health is that with support he or she has mastered a fear — has learned to cope — and, in the process, has learned to feel good inside about himself and secure in his world.

In rare instances when this smooth process does not occur, when the anxiety does not abate after a few days and the child's fearfulness and feelings of distress continue to mount, the child may be developing a more serious problem. At this point, parents should seek pro-

fessional advice by asking for a consultation with the school guidance counselor, if the school has such a person, or other school personnel. A consultation with the family doctor or pediatrician might also be considered. However, for most children who have experienced basically stable and supportive relationships prior to entering school, and whose parents have dealt successfully with their own ambivalent feelings about the child's entry into school, their upset — if obvious at all — usually disappears quickly, particularly if the techniques described here are used consistently by parents and other supportive persons.

NYC Board of Education, Office of Continuing Education

Chapter 60

Rearing Children to Meet the Challenge of Change

Dan W. Dodson*

As parents, we desire for our children a better world than the one in which we now live. Most of us want them to take heritage we are passing on to them and together with those of their generation from all lands, move beyond where we are now to a more creative life. We hope our sons and daughters will be:

> Tall men—Sun crowned men
> Men who can keep their heads when
> those about them are losing theirs.

For our children to grow into this kind of citizenship requires our help. We know our children must possess great ideals, for "without vision a people perish." But they must not become so rigid and inflexible they can accept no differences or change. They must learn to live in a world in which both change and differences are important facts of life.

What can we as parents do to help our children meet the challenge of change and differences?

1. We can help our children see and understand how group differences come about.

All children are born and reared in groups: families, churches, neighborhoods and nations. Such groups provide a culture in which a way of life is learned. Trager and Yarrow found in the study of small children in Philadelphia that at an early age, children were quite conscious of their differences as Protestants, Catholics, Jews, etc. The groups in which they were reared had taught them early to perceive their differences.

We are born into groups which predispose us, favorably and unfavorably, toward both people and things. Many of these social habits and ways of thinking are necessary and useful. Some are harmful and dangerous, both to ourselves and others. Children who will be capable of meeting the challenges of today and tomorrow will not only have to unlearn many of the erroneous conceptions they now have about other people, but will need to acquire, as well, a questioning attitude as to *what is reality*, in order to insure that the cultural porthole through which they first learned to view the world does not permanently distort their vision.

In This Undertaking What Is The Parent's Role?

We can examine what are the stereotypes and prejudgments we are inculcating in our children. "Have we tested them against reality for ourselves?" "Are we sure they are sound?" One of the greatest joys of parenthood is experienced during that stage of our children's lives when they begin to behave in line with family tradition—provided, of course, that tradition is worth emulation. As our children mirror us, their family, in their attitudes and behavior towards others, are we proud of what they mirror? Our children can do much more to take their responsible places in society if they do not have to spend a large share of their adult lives unlearning, the hard way, things they have learned from us as parents.

We may well ask ourselves, "Are we free of prejudices towards peoples of other races, creeds, or groups?" "Do we, ourselves, feel strange, insecure, and rigid when thrown in company with peoples of backgrounds other than our own?" or "Do we feel comfortable with most?"

Our children learn—in our homes, our schools, our neighborhoods, our churches, or our groups—*what they live* and not necessarily what they are taught. It does little good to teach respect for Jews, for instance, if those who teach refuse to live in neighborhoods with Jews. It does little good to teach us about the Brotherhood of Man if the brother who is Negro is refused opportunity to worship with his coreligionists who are white. Children are quick to detect our insincerities.

A heavy responsibility rests on us as parents to find ways in which our children can get to know children of different backgrounds who possess deep and basic differences, and also to know people who may be different in some respects, but have large areas of common interest with us.

We may well ask ourselves how our children will ever be able to make decisions about world affairs if they never know intimately people who are different from themselves. For instance, what are the handicaps for one who never had a child of another race for a playmate, a classmate, a neighbor or a fellow worshipper? The same could be said for other group differences such as creed, social class or nationality. As adults we are the principle bearers to our children of all that is the history, the meaning of life, the

---

*Dr. Dan Dodson, Professor Emeritus, New York University.

values, hopes and aspirations of the groups to which we belong. Some of this, however, may be dead tonnage and may be dangerous to ourselves and others.

Undoubtedly we would all do our children a real service if we could rid our own lives of those biases toward other groups which result from our misinformation, faulty logic and limited experience.

2. We can help our children become secure in their own group so they do not feel threatened when they come in contact with people of other groups.

All people have a need to belong to some groups and feel they are secure in their belonging. The social climbers who are not comfortable in their feeling that they are accepted by the social class to which they aspire are more likely to respect rigidly the amenities of that class than are those who are comfortable. Many superpatriots are people who are unsure of their relationship to their country—sometimes second and third generation people. Some have observed there is no race prejudice in the South that exceeds that of some persons from the North who migrated there and aspire to be accepted by the Southern society. Such manifestations of insecure membership in basic groups are varied.

Still another group insecurity was observed by Kurt Lewin among minority groups as "group self hate." Here the person tends to reject his own group and its culture and idealize the culture of other groups. Kenneth and Mamie Clark did a study in which they presented Negro children with white and colored dolls and asked questions about them. These children tended to identify the white dolls as the clean ones, the nice ones, the good ones; the colored dolls they identified as the dirty ones, the bad ones, etc. Such rejection of one's own group, and the idealization of the other, limits the capacity to appraise situations objectively and to make mature decisions. Pre-judgments are already "triggered" which will sway decisions out of line with what the facts in the case might otherwise warrant.

Another group insecurity might be called the "chip on the shoulder." When a person is insecure he must continually test out whether he is really accepted. Often there can never be proof enough, so in his anxiety he makes a nuisance of himself by demanding that his acceptance be proved. Almost every minority group has been accused at some stage of being "pushy"—because so many of its members have been caught in this type of insecurity. It should be remembered, however, that it is not minority group individuals alone who behave in this fashion. Many from majority groups do so, for the behavior is occasioned by one's feeling of relationship to his group, and not his ethnic background.

What Can Parents Do About This Problem?

a) The first and most important thing is to make their children loved, wanted, and happy members of their own

family. Indeed, many would say that all the difficulties outlined above stem from lack of such a relationship. In hundreds of ways every day, children are learning images of themselves as people. This includes what the parents "image" as the status of the family, as well as the image the child acquires of himself as a person. "What would your grandmother say?" clearly represents concern about the family status. "What's your name?" "Whose little girl are you?" "Who is mama's little man?" All are terms of endearment and affection heard over and over in the home. They are helping the child develop a conception of himself.

Some of these roles become invidious. "We are better than the Joneses." "Tom is the smartest child of the family," "Eleanor is the prettiest." "Lois is the friendliest." Through these images, the child may come to feel that he is not loved as much, or does not belong in the same way as others, and the ground is laid for deep-seated personality problems that tend to persist through life. We all say every personality is unique and creative unto itself, yet we as parents too often compare one child with another, to the disadvantage of uniqueness. Only one step removed from derogatory comparison of one child with another, our family with the neighbors', or our house with the neighbors', is the comparison of our race with the next, our religion with the next, and our nationality group with the next.

Compare we must. All of us must be proud of who we are and what we are. But to feel we are better than others because we are different is dangerous. It is grand to be able to say, "I have the best mother in the world." It is awful to say, "My mother is better than your mother." *The base on which all other personality maturity is laid is a happy, secure relationship to one's parents and family.*

b) We can help our children understand the history of the groups to which they belong so that they can appreciate their own heritage. No person can meet people of other groups and feel he is their equal without feeling secure in his own heritage. This led one Negro leader some years ago to exclaim, "The thing that would help our children more than anything else would be a good dose of ancestry." It was a way of saying that the white group would not accept the Negro person as an equal until the Negro person could accept himself as an equal. One major part of feeling equal is to be proud of one's heritage. The appreciation of this fact led Negro educators to institute Negro History Week, to emphasize what has been omitted from most text books, namely the creative role Negroes have played in the historical past.

An understanding of this need to feel secure in their heritage led the British to supply children who were being evacuated during World War II with a little volume containing some of the precious documents of English history—the Magna Carta, passages from the King James version of the Bible, Shakespeare, Browning, etc. Hence, wherever they went, there would be a part of their hearts which would be "forever England."

Bettleheim and others have concluded that a large portion of the social disorganization in America among second generation persons is due to the rapid shift from old world cultures to those of the new world. In the transition the "thread of historic continuity" has been severed in the personality of the individual.

We have helped a person when we have enabled him to appreciate his own cultural heritage. He will not need to "withdraw" with feelings of inferiority or "stick his chin out" in aggression, or shield his basic lack of inner security about "who he is."

A Negro mother in St. Louis admonished her child on his first morning of attendance at the desegrated school: "Don't try to act superior. Only inferior people try to act like there are people beneath them. Prove your worth; people will accept you, that is, the decent ones will." (Valen, p. 33).

Secutity in one's heritage can be achieved by repeating the legends about the family—who they are, what they have stood for, and what has been their travail, their aspirations, their disappointments. It can include study of one's religious heritage—not in a chauvinistic way, but in a quest to understand the search for God and man's relation to Him. It might include a study of other religions also, not to prove one better than another, but to help children understand some of the depth and richness of this search of man for the Highest.

Security in one's heritage can also be developed by a study of culture so that children understand that all peoples have culture, some more complex than others, but all with many points to recommend them. They could be helped to understand that differences of culture do not mean cultural inferiorities; that to all peoples their own culture is as precious as life itself. An examination of some types of cultural conflict would reveal that the complex task of preserving cultural differences and basic values is difficult for all of us as our culture changes.

In this day of extreme mobility of American people, when children are often far removed from their grandparents, uncles and aunts, etc., understanding one's family is not easy. Neither is it easy to maintain strong group identification of other kinds. This places an even greater responsibility upon parents.

3. We can help our children grow into emotional maturity so they do not use prejudice and hostility as a crutch for their own personality inadequacies.

A stable and creative world will not be achieved by unstable, emotionally arrested personalities. Frustration leads to hostile, aggressive behavior or to withdrawal and self-destructive reactions. Sometimes when there is a less privileged group around, the frustration is projected toward them in hostile, aggressive behavior. The Commissioner of Investigations of New York City prepared a report in 1944 on some 27 cases of anti-Semitic behavior, where the cul-

prits had been caught and case histories prepared on them. When one realized the frustration and rejection in the lives of these youths, he could understand that had their hostility not been channeled toward a minority group, it would no doubt have led to juvenile delinquency of some other sort. It so happened that in the communities where they lived, anti-Semitism was very great. Without doubt, for some, these anti-Semitic behaviors were among the very few of their activities for which they had ever received community approbation.

We cannot, even if we so desire, shield our children from disappointments. The task is rather to shield them from "overpowering frustration," and teach them to use frustration for creative ends. Good schools now provide not only games and activities of a physical nature, but clays, finger paints—material that can be destroyed—on which small children work off their aggressions harmlessly. As they grow older, they are provided with shops where frustrations can be vented on woodwork, plastics, and other less destructible materials. The child is thus taught patience as a part of maturity. In each instance the astute educator is providing growth experiences toward a type of citizenship needed in a modern world by siphoning off anti-social hostilities and destructive aggression from human relations and channeling their expression to harmless, valueless materials. Gradually these are sublimated, or substituted for, to the end that frustration becomes a drive to socially useful purposes.

We know that people look for a scapegoat. It is much easier to blame one's faults and failures on someone else than it is to accept responsibility for one's self. Only the mature person can accept responsibility for his own shortcomings. The blood spilled to defeat Nazism—which sought in a helpless minority, the Jews, a scapegoat for collective frustrations—should be a reminder of the price we pay when bias towards groups becomes a crutch for personality deficiencies resulting from sick or immature emotional life.

What Can Parents Do?

Any of the above suggestions, of course, which contribute to healthy personality develop self-adequacy. The fundamental psychological point is that when an emotional drive is blocked, it may result in a variety of dangers. The wise parent will help find ways through which such frustrations can be dealt with to achieve good mental health. High among the things we can do is to examine our own "levels of anticipation" for our children. We want our children to reflect credit upon the family. All children, however, cannot make the honor roll in school, make the football team or win the scholarship to college. It is perhaps our own personal parental anxieties, that ours will not show up as well, that are most devastating of all for children. Above all else we should help them to understand that we love them whether they achieve their (and our) expectations or not. This makes it easier for them to accept their own limitations.

We can help them rationalize their disappointments and find substitutes for their "dream ships that didn't come in." We can encourage them to test, constantly, their aspirations so that they neither aspire to that which is beyond reality nor do they underaspire. If there is anything worse than getting hurt by aspiring too high, it is perhaps in never aspiring at all, never lifting the eyes to the vistas on the distant horizon and reaching for them. Lastly, we can teach them to take their defeats in good sportsmanship and profit from the disappointing experiences—using them as stepping stones to greater growth and achievement. It was Peter the Great who, when he was being defeated by the armies of Europe exclaimed: "They will beat us until they teach us how to fight, and then we will defeat them." Mature people learn from their failures as well as from their successes.

4. We can teach children to make decisions and to accept the moral obligations of their choices.

At birth our children are helpless and decisions are made for them. They should ultimately become persons capable of making responsible choices for themselves and accepting the responsibilities involved. Making decisions is not easy. All of us find times when we would like to have a "psychological papa" decide for us.

While we constantly use consultants, experts, and seek advice, after all the advice is in a mature individual must make his own decisions for himself. The pages of history are full of instances where nations, races, labor groups and others have entrusted the decision-making to others, to their regret. Charlatans maintain themselves in office by persuading people that danger is so imminent that they must not wait for decision-making to take place; they must simply follow. This relieves the average citizen of the responsibility for the choices made, and thereby relieves him of any feeling of guilt because of consequences.

The birthright of free men is their right of decision-making, and their hope is in the soundness of their collective judgments. Their greatest safeguard is in the growth of decision-making capacity and in moral insight which comes as they grapple with the problems which involve their destiny. There can be no moral growth unless there is responsibility for choices made.

What Can Parents Do?

As parents we have to steer a course between two extremes in this relationship. We must recognize social immaturity and not force children to make decisions beyond their capacities. We must not shield them from decision-making to the extent that their capacity to decide is stunted. One would not allow a small child to imperil his life by such action as jumping out of a high window, even though he desired to do it.

A technique of psychotherapy now popular is called non-directive. Here the therapist in the role of an authority simply asks questions that push the patient toward a clarification of his own problems, a formulation of his own goals and the ability to reach his own decisions. In the era of the authoritarian family, where father "wore the breeches," there was a tendency for father or the "father-figure" to make the decisions. He could never be challenged, regardless of how galling his decisions were for the remainder of the family. Children, and sometimes wives, obeyed not from an understanding of why he wanted a thing done, but simply because he said so. In the democratic family, parents still resort to authority, but they measure their leadership more by how fast their children come to behave from self-made decisions which are based on solid knowledge of why they should act as they do. Parents increasingly lead their children with age and experience, to make their own decisions, by assisting them to assess all the possibilities and implications of their own decisions.

5. We can encourage children to learn the art and skill of handling relationships.

The skillful handling of group differences in the years ahead will perhaps be the most essential art we as a people will need to acquire. The nature of conflict arising over differences must be understood; ways of preserving differences which people feel are essential, and skill of social process must be found.

"Come, let us reason together," has been for a long time a familiar phrase to men of good will. In recent years we have seen the growth of the mediator in labor relations, and in other types of continuing conflict. We have developed skills such as how to participate in discussion, how to respect differences, how to learn that there are things about which honest people must agree they disagree. We are learning that there are rarely issues which are black or white, right or wrong. Most often there are shades of gray in between. The art of compromise; the skill to select limited objectives when groups are in conflict; stress upon what groups have in common while they are battling over items of differences; negotiation, conciliation, and adjudication—these are skills we need to practice from early childhood.

As Parents—

We can help our children with these skills if we make our own home a training place for democracy. Many families set aside a time each week for a family conference. Here the expression of differences, gripes, frustration and criticisms is encouraged. Wise parents know it is better to let them come out than to repress them. Group decisions are reached, conflicts resolved, and goals reformulated. Out of these experiences come children who respect the right of other people to differ, and who have skills for dealing with difference—to meet the challenge of change. Thus practice of responsible citizenship begins in the home, and extends as members of the family move outside the home.

6. We can work with the neighbors to create "community" where ours and our neighbors' children will have demonstrated to them how the good life can be achieved without sacrificing basic differences.

None of us can do the best job of rearing our children without the help of neighbors and neighbors' children. The climate of the community in which we live frequently is such that much of the positive we do in human relations is neutralized by it. Our community is the first place where our children meet people of other groups than their own family. This can foster moral and spiritual growth and development, or it can be deleterious. It is something any of us, with a little effort, can do something about. What can we do?

(1) We can see that all the children of our community have adequate services such as good schools, good recreation, adequate programs in agencies and organizations that will give them direction, values, and sublimation for their aggressions.

(2) We can work with our friends and neighbors to build understanding in youth as to what are the sanctions of behavior in the community, so there is a respect for the limits of authority established by the group.

All persons need to understand clearly what the community will stand for, and what it will not stand for as desirable behavior. Beyond what is right and wrong is the other problem of what can one get away with. Many people know what they should declare as income tax, for instance. They frequently declare, however, that which they cannot "get away with." Educators know when a substitute teacher is sent into a classroom, there will be little work done the first day. The children will be trying the new teacher out to see how far they can go. So it is in community. Youths are continuously testing the perimeters of authority. If they find vacillation or equivocation, they are headed for trouble. If police wink at certain kinds of behavior, if they do not enforce the law among all alike, if there is inconsistency among parents as to when children shall come home from parties, if there is open discrimination or flouting of the civil rights of some of the people of the community, the youth may find difficulty discerning what his role should be. A democracy does not mean the absence of authority. It means that the seat of authority is the people. Every citizen has a role in helping establish what is the authority of his community and nation. This responsibility no citizen can escape. He may decide to abdicate his responsibility, but he cannot abdicate the moral consequences attendant upon his choices.

It is here that we face the acid test of citizenship. Almost every parent wants the very best for his own children. Sometimes he is much less concerned about what his neighbor's children get— especially if the neighbor is of some other group identification. It is here we are called upon to show that we mean what we say about our concern for all the children of the community. From this starting point we ultimately have to ask it about all the children of the world. It is here that we have to show that we believe in the principle of difference. In so many instances we are willing to help if those served will become like us. If we really believe in people, we must be willing to help without controlling and have faith enough to believe that if people are allowed to grow to maturity, unique in their own heritage, they will not only have richer lives themselves, but will enrich the lives of everyone else.

Community forces either work toward a way of life which will aid children to understand each other, or they work against it. Agencies such as the National Conference of Christians and Jews, Mayor's Committee on Good Will, and other national and local groups are working in countless communities to achieve a helpful climate of life. Support of these agencies would be a great help in many instances.

Toward Brotherhood

The attempt in this statement has been to deal with problems of difference. However, we have many more things in common than we have differences. Practically all of us believe that spiritually we are brothers. Most of us believe that there are potentials in each of us, which are unique to us alone, if there could only be found the magic to unleash them. Some of us are afraid to see that creativeness unleashed in some part of the people. We feel threatened by it. This is immaturity on our part.

We can help our children 1) to respect the dignity and worth of human personality, although it may differ from their own radically, 2) we can brush the faulty pre-conceptions from their eyes, so they see and learn to correct their vision, 3) we can give them a firm grounding in their own heritage so they neither quail nor overcompensate for their own background, 4) we can help them to acquire a basic emotional stability, so their decisions will not be clouded by their own maladjustments, 5) we can train them in decision-making, so they will not sell their democratic birthright, 6) we can assist them to acquire the arts and skills of negotiation, so they learn how to wait out the reconciling differences, and 7) add to these the ability to create communities more conducive to growth and development. We shall continue to have our differences. They will not be "watered down." But to our spiritual kinship will be added the skills and maturity with which to forge ever new and more creative designs of life.

Chapter 61

The Family: The Young Child's Earliest Educator

Jane Attanucci and Barbara Kaban*

During the first six years of life, before the child enters a school setting, many dramatic changes occur. The child masters the use of his body, masters the use of spoken language, develops a wider range of cognitive abilities and becomes a fairly sophisticated social being. In the past, very little reliable information or training had been available to parents so that they could understand and/or enhance the development of their young child. In the past decade, however, there has been a growing interest on the part of parents and educators in these early years.

The Harvard Preschool Project has been studying the development of children between the ages of birth and six years since 1965. Our mandate was easy to express: learn how to structure the experiences of the first six years of life so that a child might be optimally prepared for formal education. Such a goal leads to a consideration of two problem areas: (1) what is human competence in 6 year old children, and (2) how do we learn the details of the interactions between early experience and the development of such competence?

We undertook an extensive library search, reviewing all research projects concerning children three to six years of age since 1900. Nowhere in the literature could we find a detailed description to a healthy, well developed six year old. We decided to follow the lead of the European ethologists (Lorenz, Tinbergen etc.) and observe children in their natural environments. Initially we selected as broad an array of types of preschool children as we could. Our original sample consisted of 400 three, four, and five year old children living in eastern Massachusetts who attended seventeen kindergartens and nursery schools. On the basis of extensive independent observations by fifteen staff members and the teachers of these children, and also on the basis of their performance on objective tests such as the Wechsler Intelligence Scale for Children and tests of motor and sensory capacities, we isolated fifty-one children. Half were judged to be very high on overall competence, able to cope in superior fashion with anything they met, day in day out. The other half were judged to be free from gross pathology but generally of very low competence. We then proceeded to observe these children each week for a period of eight months. We gathered some 1,100 protocols on the typical moment-to-moment activities of these children, mostly in the institutions, but also in their homes. At the end of the observation period, we selected the thirteen most talented and thirteen least talented children. Through intensive discussions by our staff of twenty people, we compiled a list of abilities that seemed to distinguish the two groups. The list, along with short definitions, follows.

Social Abilities

1. *To Get and Maintain the Attention of Adults in Socially Acceptable Ways*
   The ability to get the attention of an adult through the use of various strategies (e.g., moves toward and stands/sits near A; touches A; calls to A; shows something to A; tells something to A.)

2. *To Use Adults as Resources*
   The ability to make use of an adult in order to obtain something by means of a verbal request or demand or a physical demonstration of his need. His object may be to gain information, assistance, or food, and he may demonstrate this by declaring what he wants, making a request, making a demand, or by gesturing, acting out, or pointing.

3. *To Express Both Affection and Hostility to Adults*
   The ability to express affection and/or hostility through verbal and/or physical means (e.g., friendly statements, such as "I like you," "You're nice," or hugging A; statements of dislike, such as "I hate you," "You're bad," hitting A, or physically resisting A).

4. *To Lead and Follow Peers*
   The ability to assume control in peer-related activities; e.g., to give suggestions, to orient and direct, to set oneself up as a model for limitation. The ability to follow the lead of others; e.g., to follow suggestions.

5. *To Express Both Affection and Hostilily to Peers*
   The ability to express an affection and/or hostility to peers through verbal or physical means.

*Barbara Kaban, Assistant Director, Harvard Lilly Program for parent education; Jane Attanucci, Research Coordinator, Harvard Lilly Program for Parent Education.

6. *To Compete with Peers*
   The ability to exhibit interpersonal competition.

7. *To Praise Oneself and/or Show Pride in
   One's Accomplishments*
   The ability to express pride in something he has created, owns, or possesses at the moment, or something he is in the process of doing or has done.

8. *To Involve Oneself in Adult Role-Playing Behaviors or to
   Otherwise Express the Desire to Grow Up*
   To act out a typical adult activity or verbally express a desire to grow up.

Nonsocial Abilities

1. *Linguistic Competence; i.e., grammatical capacity, vocabulary, articulation, and extensive use of expressed language*
   Self-explanatory.

2. *Intellectual Competence*
   a) The ability to sense dissonance or note discrepancies
   This is a critical faculty on the part of the child, an ability to indicate one's awareness of discrepancies, inconsistencies, and other forms of irregularity in the environment. It is almost always expressed verbally, but occasionally takes nonverbal forms as well. It is observable whenever a child comments upon some noticed irregularity. The effect that generally accompanies it usually involves mild confusion, a look of discovery, or a display of righteousness, in pointing out and correcting the irregularity.
   b) The ability to anticipate consequences
   This is the ability to anticipate a probable effect, on or sequence to, whatever is currently occupying the attention of the child. It is usually expressed verbally, but also takes nonverbal forms. It can take place in a social context or in relative isolation. It is not simply an awareness of a future event—e.g., "Tomorrow is Thursday"—but must somehow relate that event to a present condition. The relationship may be either causal—e.g., "If X, then Y"—or sequential—e.g., "Now 1, next 2." The second half of each relationship *must* be an anticipated future outcome. It cannot actually occur until after the child anticipates its occurrence.
   c) The ability to deal with abstractions; i.e., numbers, letters, rules
   To use abstract concepts and symbols in ways that require building upon what is concretely present, and showing mental organization of what is perceived. The term *concept* means "a mental state or process that refers to more than one object or experience"; the term *symbol* means "an object, expression, or responsive activity that replaces and becomes a representative substi-

tute for another.
   d) The ability to take the perspective of another
   To show an understanding of how things look to another person whose position in space is different from the subject's, or to show an understanding of a person's emotional state or mental attitude when they are different from the subject's. (The opposite of egocentricity.)
   e) The ability to make interesting associations
   When presented with visible scenes, objects, or verbal descriptions, a person with this ability shows a capacity to produce related kinds of objects or themes from either his own realm of past experience or some imagined experience. These productions are characterized by the ingenuity of the relationships or the elaborateness of the representation. Another form is the ability to build upon these events by assigning new and interesting labels or building coherent stories around the presented elements.

3. *Executive Abilities*
   a) The ability to plan and carry out multistep activities
   This designation applies to largely self-directed activities, rather than activities in which the child is guided. At earlier ages, it would develop through gradual refinement of the use of means-ends relationships and the ability to plan and execute longer sequences.
   b) The ability to use resources effectively
   The ability to select and organize materials and/or people to solve problems. An additional feature is the recognition of unusual uses of such resources.

4. *Attentional Ability—Dual Focus*
   The ability to attend to two things simultaneously or in rapid alternation; i.e., the ability to concentrate on a proximal task and remain aware of peripheral happenings; the ability to talk while doing.

Again, using the method of group discussions of each child based on extensive observational records and objective test scores, we examined the issue of the growth of competence as we had defined it. Our staff came to a remarkable conclusion. Our well developed three year olds looked more like well developed four to six year olds on our target abilities than did our older but poorly developing children. If we had to guess which group would have done better in first grade had the competent 3 year olds and the older but less competent five and six year olds entered the following year, we would have chosen the competent 3 year olds.

The implications of this judgment of the remarkable level of achievement of some 3 year olds were most important for the project. If most of the qualities that distinguish outstanding six year olds can be achieved in large measure by age three, the focus of the project could be narrowed dramatically. We rather abruptly found ourselves concentrating on the zero-to-three age range.

The Longitudinal Study

The primary purpose of our longitudinal study was to search for environmental factors that play important causal roles in the early development of human competence. We observed two sets of families as they reared their children during their second and third years of life. The sample consisted of 39 families, 25 predicted to raise well developing children, 14 predicted to raise poorly developing children.[1] The children were from a variety of religions and ethnic backgrounds and ranged in socio-economic status on the Hollingshead-Redlich (1958) Scales from I through V (See Table I). In addition to testing for general development at 12 and 24 months (using the Bayley Scales of Infant Development), we also periodically assessed the young child's ability to understand language, the ability to sense discre-

Table 1

Subject Characteristics

	1–Year–Olds				
SES Score[2]	I	II	III	IV	V
Predicted to develop very well[3]					
A'S – Boys	5	3	5	0	0
– Girls	5	2	5	0	0
Predicted to develop less well					
C's – Boys	1	0	3	4	1
– Girls	0	0	2	2	1

pancies, and the capacity for abstract thinking.[4] We also gathered observational data on the child's social interactions[5] and on the stream of experience (some of this data will be reported below).

The instrument for the quantitative analysis of the stream of experience is called the Task instrument.[6] We observe children as they go about their normal activities, tape recording a continuous series of remarks describing what the child is trying to do from moment to moment, while writing other relevant information about stimulating factors, impediments, and success or failure. After ten minutes of such recording, with the duration of the tasks timed to the second with stopwatches, we play back the tape and code the record during the next twenty minutes. Three such cycles are a normal half-day's work. The instrument consists of thirty-seven categories, with several multiple combinations.[7]

Task data was collected when the children were 12 to 15 months, 18 to 21 months, 24 to 27 months, and 30 to 33 months. The following discussion will emphasize the data from the second year of life.

Experiences of One-Year Olds: 12-15 months and 18-21 months

The task instrument provides data on the moment-to-moment experiences of our one-year old subjects. First, the data reveals a preponderance of nonsocial tasks. Regardless of competence, children spend far more time interacting with the physical world than in social exchanges. At 12-to-15 months, the median percents of total duration are 89.7% for nonsocial tasks, versus 10.3% for social tasks. By 18-to-21 months, the figures are 83.8% for non-social and 16.2% for social. These findings are corroborated by the work of C. Wenar (1972) and A.K. Clarke-Stewart (1973) in that they, too, find infants at home spending more time in nonsocial activities.

A closely related finding is that, for the most part, our one-year olds initiated their own experiences. The task-initiation data shows, again regardless of competence, that our one-year old children initiated 86.5% (median percent duration– of their own tasks at 12-to-15 months and 87.7% at 18-to-21 months. Furthermore, when tasks are divided into nonsocial and social categories, the same trend prevails with nonsocial tasks self-initiated 91.6% of the time at 12-to-15 months, 93.0% at 18-to-21 months, and social tasks self-initiated slightly less: 60.2% of the time at 12-to-15 and 58.9% at 18-to-21 months. The mother initiates 39.5% of social tasks at 12-to-15 months and 34.0% at 18-to-21 months most often to elicit cooperation from the child (*to cooperate*).[8]

Experiences Associated with the Development of Competence

The central purpose of our natural longitudinal experiment was to identify experiences that maximally contribute to the development of competence in children. We selected our sample of children so as to heighten the probability that we would be studying some children who were devel-

Table 2

Correlation Among Tasks at 12–15 months and Achieved Levels of Competence at 3 years ($N_s = 19$)

	Percent Time[10] Spent in Activity	Correlation with Overall Competence at Three Years of Age
Social Tasks		
All Social Tasks	10.3	- .49*
To please	0.1	- .40
To cooperate	2.8	- .01
To procure a service	1.0	- .46*
To gain attention	2.2	- .46*
To maintain social contact	2.2	- .19
To assert self	0.5	.05
Nonsocial Tasks		
To eat	4.4	- .04
To gain information (visual)	16.0	-.49*
To gain information (visual auditory)	6.0	- .27
live language directed to the child	1.7	.78***
overheard language	0.8	- .33
mechanical language	0.2	.20
Nontask	12.2	.42
To pass time	3.4	.33
To prepare for activity	1.4	- .25
To procure an object	3.3	.48*
To gain pleasure	0.0	.11
To ease discomfort	0.6	.21
To restore order	0.7	- .11
To operate a mechanism	0.0	.12
To explore	12.8	- .06
Mastery	8.7	.40
gross	6.7	.40
fine	2.4	.01
To eat and gain info. (v)	4.2	- .62**
To eat and gain info (v & a)		- .30
live language directed to the child	0.1	- .36

*p ⩽ .05
**p ⩽ .01
***p ⩽ .001
Spearman Rank Correlation

Table 3

Correlation Among Tasks at 18-21 months
and Achieved Levels of Competence at 3 years
(N_s = 19)

	Percent Time [11] Spent in Activity (Group Median)	Correlation with Overall Competence at Three Years of Age
Social Tasks		
All Social Tasks	16.2	- .37
To please	0.0	- .50*
To cooperate	4.6	- .34
To gain approval	0.0	- .41
To procure a service	1.0	- .45*
To gain attention	2.0	- .11
To maintain social contact	2.8	.22
To direct	0.1	- .53*
To assert self	1.5	.00
To enjoy pets	0.0	.22
Nonsocial Tasks		
To eat	10.3	.51*
To gain information (visual)	10.6	- .25
To gain information (visual auditory)	6.0	- .17
live language directed to the child	1.4	- .36
overheard language	1.3	- .13
mechanical language	0.0	- .15
Sesame Street	0.0	- .34
Nontask	11.8	.61**
To pass time	3.2	- .16
To prepare for activity	2.0	- .51*
To procure an object	3.1	- .40
To engage in large muscle activity	0.0	- .36
To imitate	0.0	.09
To pretend	1.5	- .06
To ease discomfort	0.4	- .02
To restore order	0.6	- .80***
To operate a mechanism	0.2	- .24
To explore	6.6	- .16
Mastery	11.4	- .29
gross	2.4	- .05
fine	3.9	- .42
verbal	0.1	- .34
To eat and gain info. (v)	1.9	.04

*$p \leqslant .05$
**$p \leqslant .01$
***$p \leqslant .001$
Spearman Rank Correlation

oping very well and others who would develop much lower levels of competence. Since groups of such children usually look similar in achievement at about 12 months of age and gradually differ in achievement sometime later in the second year of life (see also Halper, 1969; Shaefer, 1968), data on their experiences before they diverge around two years of age interest us most.

Correlations of task experiences during the second year of life and the levels of overall competence achieved by our subjects at 3 years of age are presented in Tables 2 and 3.[9] These relationships between early experiences and competence of a combined social and intellectual nature at 3 years of age served as the basis for our recommendations to parents.

At 12-15 months, the total of all social tasks correlates rather strongly with competence at 3 years of age with well-developing children having a considerably greater amount of social experience than those not developing well. Consistent with previous remarks about the balance of social and nonsocial interests, the social tasks total only 10.3% of the time. However, this correlation speaks strongly for the importance of early social experiences.

The individual social tasks of *to procure a service*[12] and *to gain attention*[13] are also considerably predictive. *To procure a service,* at this age in particular, represents the emergence of the dimension of competence we refer to as *to use an adult as a resource* and is indicative of competence throughout the first 6 years of life.

Turning to nonsocial tasks, the most predominant activity of the children during the 12 to 15 month period was *gaining information through steady staring*[14] with well-developing children watching more often. The education value of steady staring is not simply interpreted. However, such a behavior indicates an ability for focused attention upon people and things of interest in the surrounding environment. Concurrently, *to eat and gain information visually*[15] predicts later competence occurring more frequently in well developing children.

Live language directed to the child[16] correlates most strongly with later competence. Obviously language plays a key role in intellectual and social development. However, few parents realize that a child begins to understand language as early as 8 or 9 months of age and that this direct input to the child is an essential ingredient in the experiences of the well-developing child.

To procure an object[17] is a more common task among less well-developing children. The meaning of this finding is difficult for us to formulate without further study.

Though the correlations do not reach statistical significance, *nontask*[18], *and gross motor mastery*[19] deserve mention as they are relatively frequent activities during the 12 to 15 month age period.

Nontask represents 12.2% of the time and the correlation indicates a trend for poorly developing children to experience more empty time. Similarly, poorly developing children tend to spend more time practicing gross motor activities such as climbing up stairs and onto furniture.

Toward the end of the second year at 18 to 21 months, the total of social tasks increases somewhat (from 10.3 to 16.2%) and indicates a trend of well-developing children continuing to have more social experience. *To procure a service* remains a significant predictor of competence. Similarly, the relatively rare task of *directing another*[20] is evidence of a well-developing child.

Among the nonsocial tasks, *nontask* behavior which consists of desultory scanning and aimless wandering predicts lower levels of achieved competence. The less-well developing child spends more time in nonproductive aimless behavior.

Less capable children *eat*[21] more during the 18 to 21 month period. The children at 18 to 21 months are in the middle of a period of negativistic behavior and are generally more difficult to handle. Poorly developing children were routinely given food as a last resort by their pratnes when they simply could not control their misbehavior.

Preparing for activity[22] and the relatively rare task of *restoring order*[23] correlate with high levels of later achievement. These behaviors are most typically observed in well-developing children at this age.

Exploration[24] and *mastery* occupy considerable amounts of time in the child's second year and are of special interest as they are activities observed in every infant we have ever studied. During the 12 to 15 month properties of its objects. By 18 to 21 months, the emphasis of their interactions with the physical environment shift to *mastery* behaviors (11.4%), often involving fine motor coordination in the well-developing child.

Effective Child Rearing Practices

Effective parents, as evidenced from the natural longitudinal experiment, essentially perform three major functions for their children in a manner which distinguishes them from other parents. They serve to design the child's world, to consult for the child, and to discipline the child.

Parents design the child's world most appropriately by making the living area as safe as possible for the naive, newly crawling or walking child and then providing maximum access to the home. Designing is, therefore, not a complicated task which requires professional training but rather the provision of access to the world which is of greatest interest to the child—the home. Setting up a kitchen cabinet with safe household objects is one example of a valuable design feature. Opportunities for looking out the windows or playing with water are other easily available activities in the home. By appropriately setting up the child's environment, the parent encourages a proper balance in the child's major interests: the parent, the world around him and the mastery of his body.

Parents act as consultants for their children by being readily available to respond to their overtures. This is characterized by a pattern of responding to the child's requests which consist of the following steps. Frist, they respond rather quickly to the child, rarely keeping the child waiting. On those occasions when the parent must keep the child waiting they have preceded that wait with the words, "I'm busy now, I'll be with you soon," or some equivalent. Then, once they turn to the child they pause to identify the child's interest of the moment. (This task is fortunately quite easy to do in the first years of life). They then provide what is needed; whether it is comfort, or the unsticking of a couple of stuck items, a compliment, or an indication of their own excitement. This service is usually accompanied by some words and an occasional related idea on the topic at hand. When appropriate they will teach some sort of realistic limit about the activity, for example pointing out that mother's tea is too hot and the child should drink his milk. Then, the child is allowed to return to his or her private explorations. Such responses take twenty to forty seconds and occur dozens of times each day in the lives of children developing well. They are the core teaching situations involved in good development and are a substantial part of the important early social interchanges that discriminate between well developed and poorly developed children.

Finally, parents set realistic limits for their children. They attempt to be firm and consistent while simultaneously showing their love and respect for the child's interests. Effective parents recognize the different stages in their child's development and vary the types of discipline they use in infancy and toddlerhood. Usually, children between 8 and 13 months can be easily distracted away from misbehavior. Children 13 to 18 months require distraction and physical removal from the situation, while children between 18 and 24 months require firm and consistent verbal restriction in addition to other tactics.

Our recommendations to parents are compatible with the quantitative data we have on the specific experiences of children. Of course a much greater expansion of the ideas along with experimental confirmation is needed. All we have so far are hypotheses because they are based on natural observations rather than a true experiment. Experimental testing is currently being executed and will be reported in a later publication.

NOTES

[1] The predictions of competence were based upon teachers' and staff ratings of the social and nonsocial competence of a school-aged sibling.

[2] Hollingshead-Redlich scale.

[3] The predicted and achieved levels of competence did correlate with SES such that the most competent 3 year olds were generally from higher SES levels. In another publication (*Experience and Environment: Major Influences in the Development of the Young Child,* Vol. II) we provide additional analyses with SES controlled. The findings do not change dramatically.

[4] The development of these assessment procedures was the work of: Mary Mokler, Jane Marmor and Burton White; Barbara Koslowski and Burton White; Ellen Cardone Banks and Burton White.

[5] The development of this assessment device was the work of Daniel Ogilive, Bernice Shapiro, and Jolinda Taylor.

[6] The development of this instrument was the work of Kitty Riley Clark, Andrew Cohn, Cherry Wedgewood Collins, Barbara Kaban and Burton L. White.

[7] The definitions of the categories are presented in *Experience and Environment: Major Influences on the Development of the Young Child,* Vol. I. We will present only the definitions of those task experiences discussed here.

[8] *To Cooperate:* To comply with another's directive when there is little evidence that the compliance is unwilling. To listen, when brief demands are made on one's attention.

[9] These tables are only part of a more extensive analysis of the data. The authors refer the reader to White, B.L. et al., *Experience and Environment: Major Influences on the Development of the Young Child,* Vol. II, in press.

[10] To gauge the psychological significance of these data, one must consider both the level of statistical significance of the correlation and the amount of time spent in the particular activity. In some instances common tasks seem to bear a strong relationship to later competence (to gain information, visual 12-15 months) and in other cases a correlation is statistically significant but the experience occurs rarely at that time in the child's life (to please, 18-21 months).

[11] To gauge the psychological significance of these data, one must consider both the level of statistical significance of the correlation and the amount of time spent in the particular activity. In some instances common tasks seem to bear a strong relationship to later competence (to eat, 18-21 months) and in other cases a correlation is statistically significant but the experience occurs rarely at that time in the child's life (to please, 18-21 months).

[12] *To Procure A Service:* To try to obtain aid from another.

[13] *To Gain Attention/To Achieve Social Contact:* a) to join a group; b) to initiate social contact; c) to maximize the chance of being noticed.

[14] *To Gain Information Through Steady Staring:* Sustained visual inquiry directed toward a specific object or person.

[15] *To Eat and Gain Information (Visual):* Eating and sustained visual inquiry.

[16] *Live Language Directed to the Child:* To attend to language from any source. To gain information through looking and listening when the prime interest is on the context of information being made available.

[17] *To Procure an Object:* To get something, not as an instrumental task for constructing a product, but as a task per se. If procuring an object in order to use it for constructing a product, or for any purpose, takes longer than 15 seconds, it is coded as focal.

[18] *Nontask Behavior:* To remain in place and not dwell on any specific object (e.g., desultory scanning, sitting with eyes closed, or holding a blank stare), or to wander aimlessly from one location to another.

[19] *To Improve a Developing Motor, Intellectual, or Verbal Skill:* To improve a developing motor, intellectual, or verbal skill is typically distinguished by the redundancy of S's behavior (i.e., repeats the same sequence of actions again and again) and by less-than-masterful skill in performing the activity in question.

[20] *To Dominate to Direct or Lead:* To play the leader role or to demonstrate a process to others or advise others; in short, to direct a specific activity of others.

[21] *To Eat:* To ingest food or drink.

[22] *To Prepare for an Activity:* To perform the socially prescribed activities or sequence of actions that a child carries out almost automatically owing to previous experience and/or practice, in order to prepare for something that the child anticipates.

[23] *To Restore Order:* To return things to a previously acceptable state but not for the purpose of easing discomfort, pleasing another, or preparing for an activity.

[24] *To Explore:* To explore materials, objects, activities, people. To investigate the properties or nature of materials, objects, activities, or people through touch, taste, vision, etc. Experimenting with an object or material's possibilities by adding to it or taking something away from it as the primary concern, rather than for the purpose of con-

structing a product or because of interest in the process per se, as is evident in *to pretend.*

BIBLIOGRAPHY

Clarke-Stewart, A.K. "Interaction Between Mothers and Their Young Children: Characteristics and Consequences." Monograph of the Society for Research in Child Development, 1973, Serial No. 153, 38; 6-7.

Halpern, Florence. "The Mental Development of Black Rural Southern Children Aged One Week to Thirty-six Months." Paper presented at the Society for Research in Child Development at Santa Monica, California, March, 1969.

Hollingshead, A.B. and Redlich, F.C. *Social Class and Mental Illness.* New York: John Wiley & Sons, Inc., 1958.

Shaefer, Earl S. "Intellectual Stimulation of Culturally-Deprived Infants." Excerpted from Mental Health Grant Proposal MH-09224-01. Laboratory of Psychology, National Institute of Mental Health, 1968.

Wenar, C. "Executive Competence and Spontaneous Social Behavior in One-Year-Olds." *Child Development,* 1972, 43: 256-260.

White, B.L., Watts, J.C. Kaban, B., Mamor, J. Shapiro, B., and Barnett, I. *Experience and Environment: Major Influences on the Development of the Young Child.* Englewood Cliffs, N.J.: Prentice Hall, Inc., 1973.

SELECTED BIBLIOGRAPHY

Murphy, Lois. *Personality in Young Children,* Vol. II. New York: Basic Books, Inc., 1956.

Stone, J. and Church, J. *Childhood and Adolescence: A Psychology of the Growing Person.* New York: Random House, 1964.

White, B.L., et al. *Experience and Environment: Major Influences on the Development of the Young Child,* Vol. 1. Englewood Cliffs, N.J.: Prentice-Hall, Inc., 1973.

White, B.L. *The First Three Years of Life.* Englewood Cliffs, N.J.: Prentice-Hall, Inc., 1975.

Chapter 62

Family-Community Involvement in Teacher Education

Dorothy Rich*

Two urgent questions for all of us in education today are these:

1. How can we translate the mounting research on the importance of the home on children's school success into practical action?
2. How can we involve the community meaningfully in the education action?

Seeking and providing some of the answers to these questions is the mission of the non-profit, Washington-based Home and School Institute which is devoted to the development of home-school-community partnership programs in education.

Sharing the research rationale for these programs and a sampling of the HSI approaches that translate this research into reading action and then involve the community in the work is the thrust of this article.

Research Rationale

The research data of the last decade on the importance of the home as the critical institution determining a child's success in formidable. In study after study, from the head-line-making work of Bloom, Coleman, and Jencks, to the lesser known but significant findings of the early childhood intervention projects, the home and the community have been identified as vital influences on student school success.

A growing volume of research over the past few years has documented the need for more information on the building of a home-school educational partnership, especially in the "regular" grades which have received less attention up to this time than have the preschool years.

What is known now, on the basis of conclusions from the available data, supports the concept and practice of the involvement of parents as teachers of their children. Summarizing this basic approach, the Stanford School of Education reports that, as a group, the programs using the model of parents as tutors (as contrasted to the models of parent as advisor or the parent as para professional) have "consistently produced significant immediate gains in children's scores and school performance and seemed to alter in a positive direction the teaching behavior of parents.

What is not yet clear is exactly what are the specific features of the model which work to produce the higher achievement results. There is as yet a weak relationship between the major intervention and the children's outcomes.

This can be seen as a somewhat frustrating situation at this time. We know that something is happening in terms of raising children's achievement in the parents-as-teachers model. We know that achievement is occurring, using a variety of strategies within the model. Yet, we have not yet been able to isolate the significant variables in the treatment—if indeed, significant variables in any one strategy do exist.

It may well be that what is really happening to produce children's achievement gains in the model is that the interaction between parent and child, which is directly related to the education of the child, has enhanced the total family process and motivated the parent and child to talk and to do more with one another; and thus, these interactions in themselves may have raised the child's achievement.

We do know that programs designed to promote parent participation in the education of their children create effects which may contribute in different ways to the success (or failure) of this work. These include: a) an increase in the parents' awareness of their child's behavior and their influence on him/her; b) a more systematic focusing on the parent-child interaction or intellectual activities; c) an increase in the level of verbal interaction between parents and children; d) an increase in the amount of parent feedback and responsiveness to children.

If one couples these effects with the growth in parental interest in children's education, as indicated in the Gallup Polls, a finding that may well emerge as more research is conducted is that the specific details of the treatment itself may not be all that important. This may be a very promising finding.

The data indicates that families are interested in getting involved in their children's education when the activities they are asked to do are specific, practical and geared to the basic skills achievement of their children. On the basis of this finding and on the basis of the body of research data which points so promisingly to the parent-as-tutor model,

*Dr. Dorothy Rich, Director, Home & School Institute, Trinity College, Washington, D.C. Copyright by Dorothy Rich, 1976.

what may be found as more intervention strategies are studied, is that almost any school outreach approach to promote parent-child interaction at home around academic-centered activities will work to bring about children's achievement gains.

All programs which involve parents as active teachers of their children provide a type of social reinforcement in the form of increased attention, both to the parent from the school and from the parent to the child. All of the programs convey a sense of excitement, newness, commitment, enthusiasm and perhaps most of all—caring.

The concept that a smorgasbord of strategies, all using the basic framework of the parent-as-teacher model, can all work to build children's achievement is a most hopeful sign! A dream that can be realized.

From Dream to Action—One Approach:

The Home and School Institute Programs – A Description

The overall goal of all HSI programs is to raise children's abilities as learners and to build adult competencies as teachers—through specific, easy, not to low cost, practical ways that share educational accountability between home and school.

The Home and School Institute began in 1965 with its first Creative Parent-Success for Children courses in which adults learned more about becoming more active participants in their children's learning, outside of the usual classroom situation. In 1970, in order to reach a wider number of parents and other adults, HSI began in-service programs for educators to help them work effectively with parents and community resources. In 1972, these efforts were consolidated umbrella of the Home and School Institute, Inc.

HSI moves into action primarily using the research rationale as the base for a variety of training programs for teachers and community adults.

The School and Parent-Community Involvement graduate education programs of HSI began in 1971, with four pioneering participants. By fall 1976, over 1,000 educators, parents, teenagers, and "ordinary taxpayers" had taken part in at least one aspect of the total program. The School and Parent-Community Involvement programs became a full-fledged master's degree concentration in 1974 and its graduates include the vice-president of the Prince Georges County, Md. School Board, teachers who are now in administrative positions in the Community Schools, housewives who wanted to get back into education but not necessarily into the classroom—they're doing parent-school-community work for local, state and Federal education projects; and good teachers who wanted to become better by developing home-school partnership programs for their classrooms.

A core component of all HSI programs is the design and use of Home Learning Activities. All participants prepare recipe-style activities to help families become more effective teachers of their children at home. The school is the institutional delivery agent, the source, of the Activities, prepared as often as possible, with the school "family"—the parents, community adults, teenagers, and teachers working together. The activities are designed to supplement, not to duplicate the school, even in basic 3 R skills.

HSI's ten years of experience with these home learning recipes at the "regular" grade levels—from kindergarten right through the secondary grades—have shown that parents/caregivers don't need a license or even a college background to be good home teachers; they don't need fancy equipment or even a lot of time. They have what they need: the materials available around any home and the desire to help their children achieve. Our role is in helping schools help families mobilize and express these abilities and resources.

HSI Research: HELP-Home Educational Learning Program

During the school year 1974–75, eight first grade classes—218 children—participated in an HSI Washington area study designed to find out whether sending home a series of Home Learning Lab Activities would increase student achievement in reading and math over a control group of classes which did not experience this "treatment."

The treatment consisted of eight activities describing ways that the family working together at home could reinforce and supplement reading and math: ways that used home resources; they were not typical schoolwork.

The activities were each written "recipe-style" on one sheet of paper. They were short, easy activities—involving for example, grocery lists for math and newspaper sport columns for reading, ordinary items found at home. Anyone over the age of 10—brothers, sisters, grandparents, friends—could work with the first grader on the activity.

The treatment, designed by teachers in the HSI/Trinity School and Parent-Community Involvement program, were sent home from school (preceded only by a letter of explanation) one every two weeks, for a period of 16 weeks. This design was developed so that it could be completely replicable by any teacher or school system: it involved no extra monies, no extra personnel and very little time. No additional meetings of any kind were set between parents and teachers; all participation was to be voluntary with no effect on the child's in-school grades.

The classes were from all over the Washington area; from inner city to suburb. Two classes in the treatment group had a majority of black children; one class in the control group was composed of all black children. (The study did not set out to test for differences between blacks and whites in reacting to the treatment.) The teachers in the study had all volunteered to be part of the project: half were randomly assigned to the treatment group; half to the control.

The pre- and post-testing measure used in the study was the McGraw-Hill Comprehensive Test of Basic Skills, Form S, Level B. The Archdiocese Schools of the Washington area were used for the study because of the need for relatively quick recruitment of teachers and the need to tie in with an ongoing testing program without restraints on disseminating the results.

Major result: The treatment group, using the HSI-based activities, did achieve significantly higher scores in reading (at .05 level of significance) than the classes in the control group. However, the treatment group did not achieve significantly higher scores in the area of mathematics.

Serendipity Findings: between The study did not set out to test for differences in effect black and white students, but in looking over the data, it was clear that there were differences. The predominantly black classes in the treatment group did significantly better than the predominantly black class in the control group in both reading and mathematics.

The predominantly black classes in the treatment group did significantly better than the predominantly white classes in the treatment group in reading. However, the scores between these groups in math, while indicating a trend in the direction of difference (at .057) did not quite achieve significance. More research using larger samples of black and white students will be needed to examine these differences.

Both black and white families did approximately the same number of activities: 6.5 out of the 8 offered. Of the 89 families in the treatment group, 79 families did five or more of the activities.

The frequency of use, activity by activity, 1–8, showed that math-oriented activities were done more often than reading activities. The data suggests that people will tend to do short (under 15 minutes) math activities over longer (over 15 minutes) reading activities.

Mothers far outdistanced father and "others" in their involvement in working with children at home. The "others" (who could be anyone in the home or community 10 years old or older) worked substantially more with the children than did the fathers. Only mothers participated in all eight activities.

Thus, what this HSI study has pointed to is a strategy to help train teachers to help parents and others in their roles as teachers at home.

It would appear that both wider research in this area is needed along with changes in teachers training and re-training. Graduate education institutions, in order to put the research into practice will want to consider incorporating home outreach strategies to assist parents as educators, to build a working educational partnership and thus to enhance in the process the entire school community relationship.

Just as some questions were answered by this HSI study, many more were raised.

The greater strengths of the model were these:
1. The study showed some evidence of a significant rise in children's reading achievement.
2. Families willingly participated in the activities with their children.
3. The project involved no extra monies, no extra personnel and very little time, aside from the initial training of the teachers involved.

Among the questions was this one:

Could this model be workable in a public school getting on a city-wide basis?

Replicating the Help Model

In 1975-76, HSI began on-site training programs for educators, away from its home base in Washington. Thus far, these programs have taken place in Fresno, California; Baltimore, Maryland; and in Benton Harbor, Michigan.

The significance of the Benton Harbor Project HELP for school year 1976-77 is that it involves the city's Title I schools and is focused on Home Learning Activities. HELP enlarges on the HSI research of 1974-75 by providing for a systematic outreach to the home during the school year of a series of Home Learning Activities in an action research program to determine the impact of these activities on first grade reading achievement.

These are not a ready-made set of activities. The HSI Benton Harbor model provides for joint development by local teachers and parents of the activities which they felt would work in their community. The nature of the activities, the number to be used in the "treatment," the communication materials about the program, the data reporting system—all were jointly designed and tested by the project participants.

Among the final treatment activities selected for the program were these two examples:

"Name of Activity:	The Grocery Bag
Why Do It:	To help your child develop an awareness of things that go together.
Materials Needed:	Items from the kitchen, bathroom, or living room. A large bag.
"How to Do It:	You select four (4) items, three that go together and one that does not belong in the group. Examples: spoon, fork, knife, and a potholder. Put them in a large bag. Your child should not see you do this. Have your child

reach into the bag, take each object out, one at a time and tell you its name. Then have him/her tell you the object that does not belong in the group. Example: the potholder because you can't eat with it. You may want to use three bathroom objects and one from the kitchen. Or choose clothing items such as shoes, belt and put in an ashtray as the item that does not belong.

Time: Continue the activity for 5 to 15 minutes.

Evaluation: If your child can name the objects and tell you which object does not belong, the activity is successful."

"Name of Activity: Spaghetti Letters

Why Do it: To help your child name and make the letters of the alphabet.

Materials Needed: 1/One (1) cup of cooked spaghetti (no sauce). Hint – to keep spaghetti fron being 'sticky' keep it in a bowl of cool water.

                     2/ A cookie sheet or some flat surface.

                     3/ Alphabet letters at the bottom of this sheet.

How to Do It: 1/ Child points to the letter you name (give help if needed).

                     2/ Child shapes letter he just named using the spaghetti pieces. Hint: spaghetti is wiggly—letters won't be perfect.

Time Needed: Do as many letters as you can in ten (10) minutes; on another day you can review letters or start on a new one.

Evaluation: If your child can identify the letters he/she makes in other places—examples, on signs, in magazines, in stores, etc., then the activity is successful."

Basically, what the Home Learning Lab treatment provides is a situation in which families become directly involved in the education of their child. While it has been noted in this discussion that research has not yet pinpointed the specific relationship between specific treatments and achievement effects, it may well be that what is happening in school outreach to the home via Home Learning Activities is an enhancement of the family process itself. It may not matter what the specific activity is or in what order it is presented. What may ultimately matter is that the child, through this work, comes to realize that the family values education and schooling, and the family, through this outreach from the school, comes to realize that the school really cares about the family and the achievement of the child. Thus, the school is providing a plan of practical action, rather than just words, for families to help build student motivation and achievement.

It may well be, in not too many years, that educators and parents will be able to pick from a stockpile of readily available, no cost, easy to do home treatment strategies to enhance children's learning.

101 Activities for Building More Effective School-Community Involvement

Home Learning Activities are but one approach. There are a variety of other ways in which schools can enhance the school-community relationship and the family process. The HSI publication, *101 Activities for Building More Effective School-Community Involvement,* details in recipe-format 101 other ways to reach out from the schools to families. These ways follow the HSI mission of helping schools use what they already have—they are activities that involve little to no additional costs, little time and no additional staffing.

Here is a sampling of some of the 101 Activities:

Family of the Week

Using the school bulletin board or newsletter, here's a way to make a special fuss about parents and others who are doing special things for the school. Pull out the snapshots, spell all the family names in big bold print, mention the family's involvement in neighborhood activities: all of this fosters better communication and good feelings among the various people associated with the school.

Guest Cards for Grandparents

Grandparents and neighborhood senior citizens are special people who can play and should play an important role in the school. So, why not extend to them special, personalized open-door visiting cards. And, make these cards available also for the community people who should be coming in to see the school in action—the school's neighbors, the drivers of school supply trucks, etc.

Community Information Boards

Share news of community resources parents and school neighbors might not ordinarily know about: garage sales, special local outings, parks' events, new regulations on food stamps or welfare rules, etc. This is most appreciated information: for foreign parents, it's helpful to have this material translated into other languages.

Parent Buddies: "Habla Espanol?"

For new parents in the community—try pairing them with a parent buddy to welcome them, to accompany them to the first school meetings, to introduce them around. This is especially welcomed by foreign-speaking parents.

Chance to Talk Back: Suggestion Box

Place a suggestion box in an easily accessible place but in a position that can be used by parents without necessarily being seen by the front office personnel. Parents appreciate this anonymity. Have several different kinds of response cards available—for new ideas, for reactions to school practices, etc. Check the box often and respond in the school newsletter to all suggestions—on actions taken, committees taking up ideas, etc.

New PTA Meeting Hours

Why not take advantage of the cocktail hour for a new PTA meeting time? Start the meeting at 6, bring a casserole or crackers and be home at 8:30 instead of 11 PM. This may spark new membership and avoid the competition between the meeting and what's on TV.

Community Thank You

Did your school receive a new tape recorder last week? a new flagpole? Whatever it was, why not extend a thank you to the community that made it possible. From an upper story of the school, fly a large thank you banner so that all who pass the school can feel the pride of giving and the thanks of the children and staff.

Parents Place in the School

With decreasing enrollment, you may have an empty classroom to use for a Parent's Place. Convert that room (with furniture borrowed from the community) into a room where parents visiting the school can take off their shoes and get comfortable: services that can be provided in

the Parents' Place can include baby and child care, book and toy lending materials for home use, sewing materials, typing/office equipment, washing machine/dryer. Community businesses are often willing to donate useful items in return for a tax deduction. Staff members can use the room so that parents and teachers can meet informally together.

These are but a few of the many ways educators can reach out with a helping hand to families and help themselves to improved school-community relations building the probability of higher achievement for the children as well.

The value of the change which can be effected through HELP and all of these related school-community activities is that this change offers the potential for self-perpetrating and growing development of school-community services. The training for educators which involves the community can be seen as a "seed" from which more change, more initiative, more materials and imagination can grow in the future. The parents affected by the programs will be on their jobs for some time to come, just like the teachers. Parental involvement in teacher training will have a growth ripple effect at home on all the children, including those yet to be born. Changes in attitudes and actual behavior between parents and teachers, between parents and their children, offer the greatest potential for wide-ranging, lasting growing change. . .this is an investment in people, not in hardware.

Note: (*101 Activities* is available from HSI, Trinity College, Washington, D.C. 20017)

SELECTED BIBLIOGRAPHY

Benton Harbor Area Schools/Home and School Institute, *Project H.E.L.P.* Home Educational Learning Program, Benton, Harbor, Michigan: Title I ESEA, August 1976.

Bloom, Benjamin, *Stability and Change in Human Characteristics.* New York: John Wiley, 1964.

Bronfenbrenner, Urie, *Is Early Intervention Effective?* Washington: U.S. Government Printing Office, 1974.

Coleman, James et al, *Equality and Educational Opportunity.* Washington: U.S. Government Printing Office, 1966.

Goodson, Barbara and Robert D., *Parents as Teachers of Young Children:* An Evaluative Review of Some Contemporary Concepts and Programs. Palo Alto: Stanford University Press, 1975.

Gallup, George, "The Public Looks at the Public Schools." *Today's Education* 64 May/June 1976: 66-70. *Eighth Annual survey of the Public's Attitudes towards the Public Schools.* Princeton: Public Opinion Surveys, Inc. 1976.

Jencks, Christopher et al. Inequality: *A Reassessment of the Effect of Family and Schooling in America.* Boston: Basic Books, 1972.

Lazar, J. and Chapman, J. *A Review of the Present Status and Future Research Needs of Programs to Develop Parenting Skills.* Washington: Social Research Group, George Washington University, 1972.

Masla, John and Royster, Preston. *Community Involvement in Teacher Education:* A Study of the Models. Washington: ERIC Clearinghouse on Teacher Education, 1976.

Rich, Dorothy. *"The Relationship of the Home Learning Lab Technique to First Grade Student Achievement.* Washington: Ed. D. Dissertation, The Catholic University of America, 1976.

Rich, Dorothy and Mattox, Beverly. *101 Activities for Building More Effective School-Community Involvement.* Washington: The Home and School Institute, 1976.

Superintendent Alfred Melov, NYC School Board 15

Chapter 63

Parents, Teachers, and Early Education

Judith A. Schickedanz*

Parent involvement in education is receiving increased emphasis today. The beginnings of the current interest probably stem from several sources. First, there is the recent evidence from research on early childhood education intervention programs which suggests that gains made by children are maintained to a greater extent when parents are involved in the program than when they are not (Schaefer, 1972). Proponents of parent involvement in early education who base their arguments on this evidence advocate involvement because it seems to increase the benefits a child will receive from a program.

A second source of interest in parental involvement is the ethnic group pride and power that have emerged during the last decade. Traditionally, schools have reflected the dominant culture in American society. This had made it difficult for children from minority ethnic groups to excel in school or maintain their ethnic identity (Edelman, 1974; Hess, Beckum, Knowles, and Miller, 1971; Knitzer, 1972). From this perspective, parental involvement is seen as a way to change the decision-making structure of the school in order that minority group values and goals may be represented.

The women's movement and the rise of day care have probably contributed to the interest in parent involvement too. Although day care has a long history in the United States, the dominant pattern and view has been that young children are the responsibility of the family. Day care, when used, was a "next best" alternative for those families who "defaulted" on their responsibility. This traditional view has gradually changed, and more and more families are sharing the care of children with non-family members such as the staff of a day care center (Steinfels, 1973). This change in the demand for day care has in turn changed the power relationships between clients (parents) and institutions (day care centers). As long as day care was restricted to families who could not provide for their children, and as long as the mainstream American family did not use it, the clients could easily be viewed as incompetent and unworthy of having any say about what others might think was best for their children. However, as day care is utilized more by people who are defining their own reasons for wanting it, the client as incompetent or "deficient" is an idea that is beginning to fade. Parents are having their say about the schools for their young children, and one would expect that the demand for input might increase even more as the age of entry into day care extends downward. One might also expect that this practice in participation during the preschool years will have an effect on how parents will wish to relate to the public schools when their children enter them.

Finally, parent involvement in education has probably received impetus from the general "anti-expert" mood that can be found in the United States today. Professionals in education are not the only targets of increased public scrutiny. Professionals in medicine, government, and military and religious groups have been targets too. The growth of professionalism and bureaucracy has led many people to doubt the sincerity of professionals. The fear is that professionals will act in terms of their own self-interest or the interest of the profession rather than in terms of the people they supposedly serve. For some people, then, parent involvement is a vehicle for getting inside the school for the purpose of reminding the school personnel of parental and community interests.

Although in most cases, each of the above conditions developed rather independently of any other, they all emerged as issues during the same period of time, and therefore, have come to exert a collective influence toward increasing the demand for parental involvement that is quite substantial. The meaning of parent involvement and the form it takes will vary depending on the issues that are important with regard to it's development in a particular school.

Levels of Parent Involvement

There are many ways parents can be involved in their

*Dr. Judith A. Schickedanz, Assistant Professor of Education, Boston University.

young child's education. The way(s) a particular early childhood program involves parents indicates something about the issues that formed the basis for parent involvement, and how parents and the school view each other's roles.

For our purposes here, levels of parental involvement will be defined in terms of the degree to which the involvement alters the role of the teacher as "expert" and the role of the school personnel as "decision-makers." To the extent that parent involvement tasks do not alter these roles and functions, it will be considered low involvement. To the extent that parent involvement tasks do alter these relationships, it will be considered high involvement (Figure 1).

Figure 1.

teacher as expert school as decision-maker		teachers *and* parents have expertise parents *and* school make decisions
Level One Low involvement	Level Two	Level Three high involvement

The reader should note that in this framework, high and low involvement are not related to frequency of involvement or to amount of time spent by the parent. Rather, level of involvement is determined by the kinds of activities in which parents are involved. The nature of the role relationships between parents and schools is the crucial factor.

It should also be noted that the framework itself cannot be used to determine the "ideal" or "best" level of parental involvement. What is best or ideal will differ, of course, depending on the values and goals of the people involved in a particular school, and the extent to which there is agreement between groups within a school regarding roles.

Ways in Which Parents are Involved in Education

Parent activities or tasks can be grouped into categories that correspond to the three levels of involvement represented above in Figure 1. Typically, schools that involve parents in high-involvement tasks also involve parents in low-involvement tasks. This accumulation is not represented in the listing below. In order to avoid redundancy, only the new tasks which characterize the particular level will be listed.

Level One

Level one is characterized by parental activities that do not challenge the expertise of the teacher or the decision-making power of the school. The teacher-produced class or school *newsletter* which informs parents about school life would be a level-one activity. *Parent meetings* called for the purpose of informing parents about their child's class or school would also fall within level one, as would any *individual parent conferences.* The *provision* or snack items such as juice and crackers by parents is another example of a level-one task, as is the *donation of waste items* such as egg cartons, scraps of cloth, string or newspapers.

All of the above quite literally keep parents out of the special territory of the teacher and the school. Information is obtained by parents secondhand, from the school personnel themselves. Clearly, all of the activities fall on the side of low invonvement as involvement is defined here.

Level Two

Level two is characterized by parental presence and participation in the educational setting. *Parent visitation* and *observation* in the classroom would occur at this level. The use of parents as *volunteers* would also be consistent with this level. Parent volunteers might help children cook soup or make puppets, or they might drive for a field trip or perform clerical or housekeeping tasks in the classroom.

While parents are represented physically in the educational setting at this level and have a chance to obtain information about their child's school experiences firsthand, what goes on in the classroom is determined largely by the teacher and the school. The teacher is still viewed as the key to the education of the child. The parent is seen and utilized as a source of help for enrichment or for routine tasks. This additional man or womanpower frees the teacher to perform more of the tasks that she was specially trained to perform.

Level Three

Level three is characterized by activities that involve parents in teaching their own children and in making decisions concerning educational policy. Parents may in fact serve as volunteer helpers in the classroom at this level, but the duties assigned to them are not trivial. Although the teacher may at first have much more expertise in teaching than many of the parents, she considers it her responsibility to help parents develop expertise too. Work, therefore, is not organized to maintain the differences in skill between the parent and the teacher, but to decrease them instead.

Parents may also be involved in workshops or meetings designed to help them learn about teaching their children. Meetings and workshops are also used to communicate to parents about the tremendous amount of influence they have on their young children, and how important it is for them to become effective teachers of their children.

At this level, parents also are members of school policy councils or governing boards. Such membership gives parents a real voice in running a school or program. Parents have a say in the curriculum, the budget, the staff and so on.

As can be seen, the role of teacher as "expert" and the role of school as "decision-maker" are altered in level three. In a sense, the teacher is still the expert, but the expertise is no longer guarded. It is actively shared with parents, and it is hoped that they will develop expertise from which their children will benefit.

Summary

Demands for parent involvement in education have been increasing during the last few years. The form that involvement takes varies depending on the specific conditions in a particular school and community. Forms of involvement can be categorized in terms of the extent to which they alter the view of teacher as "expert" and the view of school as "decision-maker."

Teachers in early childhood are apt to experience stronger demands for parental involvement than teachers of older children. Whatever the source of the motivation to become involved, the assumed vulnerability of the very young child would serve as an additional impetus for these parents. Although the role relationships found at level three might appear to be a drastic change from those that are traditionally found in schools, early childhood education has a long history of this kind of involvement. Parent cooperative nursery schools which began in the United States early in the 1900's (Braun, 1972) have been organized around just such relationships. Some of the federally funded programs that have been started during the last decade utilize this structure to a great extent also. Home Start and Parent-Child Centers would be examples of such programs (Pieper, 1970).

As public schools begin to provide more programs for young children, it might be expected that parents will demand to be involved in these to as great an extent as they have demanded to be involved in programs outside the public school. In the long run, relationships traditionally found in the public schools might give way to different ones.

SELECTED BIBLIOGRAPHY

Braun, Samuel J. *History and Theory of Early Childhood Education.* Worthington, Ohio: Charles Jones Publishing Company, 1972.

Edelman, Marian. *Children Out of School in America.* Washington, D.C.: Washington Research Project, Inc., Children's Defense Fund, 1972.

Hess, Robert; Beckum, Leonard; Knowles, Ruby; and Miller, Ruth. "Parent-Training Programs and Community Involvement in Day Care." In *Day Care: Resources for Decisions,* edited by Edith Grotberg. Washington, D.C.: Office of Economic Opportunity, 1971.

Honig, Alice. *Parent Involvement in Early Childhood Education.* Washington, D.C.: National Association for the Education of Young Children, 1975.

Knitzer, Jane. "Parental Involvement: The Elixir of Change." In *Early Childhood Development Programs and Services: Planning for Action,* edited by Dennis McFadden. Washington, D.C.: National Association for the Education of Young Children, 1972.

Lane, Mary. *Education for Parenting.* Washington, D.C.: National Association for the Education of Young Children, 1975.

Miller, Bette; and Wilhurst, Ann. *Parents and Volunteers in the Classroom: A Handbook for Teachers.* San Francisco: R and E Associates, 1975.

Pieper, Alice. "Parent and Child Centers—Impetus, Implementation, In-Depth View," *Young Children,* 1970, 26:70–76.

Schaeffer, Earl S. "Parents as Educators: Evidence from Cross-Sectional, Longitudinal and Intervention Research." *Young Children,* April 1972, 27:227–239.

Steinfels, Margaret O'Brien. *Who's Minding the Children? The History and Politics of Day Care in America.* New York: Simon and Schuster, 1973.

Weiser, Margaret. "Parental Responsibility in the Teaching of Reading." *Young Children,* May 1974, 29:225–230.

Section VIII

Professionalism and Teacher Education

Introduction by Arnold Raisner*

"When I die, I hope it will be my good fortune to go where Miss Blake will meet me and lead me to my seat."

—Bernard M. Baruch

Such was the poignant life-long image of the early-grade teacher held by a sophisticated friend of kings, and advisor to presidents. Is there anyone among us who does not retain at least a misty image of his or her early-grade teacher? There is a magic in the ether of the early childhood classroom. Real fairies and goblins stitch and weave the world of half-dreams to the fabric of reality. We remember the patterns, the textures, and the colors of the life that was confirmed as "real" by the "Miss Blakes" who led us to our places.

Roles, goals, skills, tasks, competencies. . .these are just words, words which we use in defining our programs and in directing our efforts. These words, however, can be powerful when they profile several ideas or stand as milestones on a road which leads us to a new area of thought or understanding. The authors of the succeeding sections of this text have welded personal experience and understanding with the talent to tell and share. Each focuses his or her effort on the relationships between teacher and pupil: Who should the teacher be? How shall we teach the teacher? What should he or she do? What results should we expect, and how do we know when the training and the effort match the need and the purpose.?

In recent years, thought and technology have attracted the enlightened attention of our educators. Proponents of new ideas and their detracting critics have burst in upon our awareness as never before. Somehow, the critical period of early childhood has been leading the growing edge of educational innovation. Educational philosophers and psychologists have reopened the questions of how our children learn and why they learn. Teachers and administrators have followed with strategies and structures which attempt to meet the new thought and mood.

The following chapters are sculpted to meet the educated consumers' need for understanding the product and the powers of early childhood education. In America, education is ultimately controlled and directed by the thought and impulse of the lay community. They, in the final analysis, recognize the flash of tinsel programs that may represent attractive ideas not yet rooted in the practical groundwork of experience. They test the teachers' consistency; his or her ability to carry out the long-range purposes of education, and the viability of processes which seek to provide respite for past failures and frustrations.

The surest safeguard against continued misguided support of impractical programs or philosophies is the sanity and endurance of the professional teachers. They are the guardians of the values and processes that we hold sacred—not rigid, not inflexible, yet not fickle nor flighty. Their selection, training, and support will be the theme of the following sections.

*Dr. Arnold Raisner, Community Superintendent, Community School District #28, New York City.

Chapter 64

Who Should Work with Young Children?

Lillian B. Graham and Blanche A. Persky*

It is the intent of this article to discuss the necessity for providing specialized preparation for care takers of infants and toddlers at all levels of responsibility.

Before we consider to whom the responsibility for the care of young children should be handed over, and certainly before we look at what kind of training, if any, should be given to these people we must look at the children themselves.

Growth in the early years consists of complex and rapid change in every phase of development. All of these phases are interdependent and each is important. Physical growth, social and emotional development and cognition may be thought of as separate entities, but are actually dependent aspects af the whole person. Therefore, it becomes crucial that the child's early environment concern itself with each aspect of his development.

Researchers and practitioners concerned with the lives of young children agree that the quality of the child's life from the time he is born—the quality of his experiences and his relationships—are critical to a determination of the kind of person he becomes.

There are those who are convinced that early experiences and environment create irreversible conditions which mold the adult person. If one subscribes to this point of view it becomes impossible to overestimate the importance of the quality of care. In large measure the quality of care depends on the qualities of the adults and of their preparation for responsibilties.

On the other hand, there are researchers and practitioners who find that gaps can be overcome and effects of negative experiences reversed through subsequent positive experiences and conditions. The question that confronts us is: Since the preventive aspects of positive early experiences are more desirable, more effective, more humane, more likely to lead to success, and are even more economical than the remediation procedures which are only sometimes successful, should we not then focus on providing positive, developmental early experiences?

It is universally agreed that the infant and toddler should live in an active, nurturing and stimulating environment, whether it be with his own family in his own home or in an outside care giving situation.
What should this environment be like?
The typical surroundings should provide for a safe, clean

setting, adequate space, good lighting, heat and ventilation and materials for exploration and manipulation.

Provision for the child's good health should include good nutrition, ongoing medical care and attention, appropriate clothing, personal cleanliness and hygiene and the sound health of the adults who are with him.

The assessment of a desirable physical environment is relatively non-controversial and, under normal circumstances, not very difficult to attain. The basic conditions for good health are lacking for many children and their families, although their basic essentials are also universally accepted.

This universality of acceptance of what children need is not present when there is consideration of *who* should care for them. The controversial question is—Is traning for care giving responsibilities essential? Or, are there persons who by the innate nature of their personalities and 'love for children' are ipso-facto 'qualified'? Representing this point of view are those who are convinced that unless specific observable damage is done by care givers the child does not suffer.

The establishment of the child's emotional security and the beginnings of socialization are the most critical developmental tasks of infants and toddlers. The people who work with young children are the key factors in determining whether a child succeeds in the mastery of these developmental tasks.

We believe that thorough preparation of the care giver, or lack of it, does matter. The following are examples of situations in which the approach of a well prepared care giver is likely to differ from that of a person who is well meaning, but who lacks the knowledge needed for maximizing the child's learning opportunities.

Children need to develop independence, responsibility and self control. The development of these strengths begins in the earliest years. The uninformed care giver, in the interest of efficiency, is likely to get the child dressed as quickly as possible, without

*Dr. Lillie B. Graham, Assistant Professor, LaGuardia Community College, City University of New York.
*Dr. Blanche A. Persky, Professor Emeritus, New York University.

involving him in the process. She does this in order to get on with what she, the adult, considers to be a more important activity. The knowledgeable and trained person will recognize the cognitive and emotional learnings inherent in dressing oneself and will provide the time, the setting, and the atmosphere in which a child is encouraged to be independent and to enjoy his sense of achievement—e.g. to dress himself.

The untrained person, recognizing the importance of establishing rapport and communication with a child will show a book to a toddler and ask, "Do you like the pretty pictures?" She does not realize that a question asked in this way boxes the child into a "yes" or "no" response. The person who understands that there is a relationship between thought and language and that verbal interaction can promote thinking skills will word her comments so that they evoke a more thoughtful and complex response—e.g. "Why do you think the puppy is running after the little boy?" This can be the beginning of a conversation and an exchange of ideas rather than a simple question and answer episode.

The uninformed individual, not understanding the stages in the development of socialization, will expect a toddler to share a toy he brings from home and may complain to the parent about the child's failure to do so. The knowledgeable adult, familiar with stages and processes of socialization, will understand that the toddler is egocentric and requires the security of possession before he can share. Her expectations will be consistent with this and she will be able to help the parent have reasonable and appropriate expectations.

The uninformed person is likely to shy away from the use of materials such as water, finger paint or sand because they are difficult to manage and time consuming and messy to clean up. The individual who has had training becomes aware of the values of sensory experiences for both emotional and cognitive development; she learns techniques and procedures for their effective use and learning potential.

Illustrations such as these cannot be considered definite evidence for the value of training for work with infants and toddlers. They do, however, highlight some of the areas in which training has significance.

At this point the comments of Mrs. Minerva Jorn are relevant. Mrs. Jorn is Senior Consultant, Early Childhood Education, and Coordinator of Infant Group Programs, New York City.

"You ask, "Where is the evidence that a well prepared and informed adult can and does facilitate and promote intellectual, emotional, social and physical growth?' We in the early childhood education field feel it, know it and see it. It is real and it is based on solid experience of trained, sensitive teachers, accumulated day by day, month by month and year by year. It is evidence based on the experience of teachers who understand development and how learning takes place and who know where each child is in his development. They know when to step in and help and when to stand by, alert, to allow a child to work and when to stand by, alert, to allow a child to work out a problem for himself; who know how to encourage and allow a child to experience trial and error, discovery, frustration and achievement, and to value himself and others. More than ever today we need adults who understand how to nourish humanistic values."

"Yes, the evidence is there, but we have failed to document it. Even the use of anecdotal records which could have been coded, would have produced the evidence. Now our urgent task is to find acceptable research methods and funds to document what we already know."

We share Mrs. Jorn's feelings of urgency about the need for documentation of the greater values to children of care from adults who have had specialized training. There are at the present time a few programs which are designed to prepare personnel for varying levels of responsibility in infant-toddler care and education. If our premise of the need for such programs is to be validated there must be built into each of them an ongoing evaluation of the effectiveness of care giving programs staffed by people who have been trained, as compared with those programs whose staffs have not had such training.

We know that the kinds of experiences we provide for young children have a profound effect on the nature of society. In our comments we have made a beginning in validating the premise that the people who care for young children are the most important components of their environment and that people who are educated and trained to provide this care will be more effective in creating a rich and nurturing environment for children. We know that there is a price to be paid for such achievement, but we must determine and live by our priorities.

Under present economic conditions it has become the norm to place emphasis upon cost as the primary criterion for acceptance and implementation of ideas, regardless of their significance in the improvement of life.

It is heartening to know that there is a resurgence of concern with basic human rights and dignity, as exemplified by these statements made by our national leaders:

"We believe it should be the birthright of every American child—every child—to have the fullest possible opportunity to share in the best of American life." Excerpt from the nomination acceptance speech of Vice-President Walter F. Mondale at the Democratic National Convention, July 15, 1976.

"We can have an America that provides excellence in education for my child and your child, and every child." Excerpt from the nomination acceptance speech of President James E. Carter at the Democratic National Convention, July 15, 1976.

BIBLIOGRAPHY

Brazelton, T. B., *Infants and Mother. Differences in Development.* New York: Delacorte Press, 1969.

Erikson, E.H., *Childhood and Society.* New York: W. W. Norton, Second Edition, 1963.

Frank. L. K., *On the Importance of Infancy.* New York: Random House, 1966.

Gordon, Ira J., *Baby Learning Through Baby Play.* New York: St. Martin's Press, 1970.

Hoberman, S., Persky, B. and Williams, Barbara G. "Report of a Field Study Using a Critical Task Behavior-Anchored Instrument to Evaluate the Competence of Child Development Workers." National Committee on Employment of Youth, 145 E. 32 Street, New York, 1975.

Keister, M. B., "The Good Life for Infants and Toddlers." National Association for the Education of Young Children, 1834 Connecticut Avenue, Washington, D. C., 1970.

National Association for the Education of Young Children. *The Infants We Care For.* Edited by Laura L. Dittman, Washington, D.C. 1973.

Provence, Sally, *Guide for the Care of Infants in Groups.* New York: Child Welfare League of America, 1967.

White, Burton, L., *The First Three Years of Life.* Englewood Cliffs, N.J.: Prentice Hall, 1975.

Chapter 65

Early Childhood Education and Teacher Education: A Search for Consistency

Bernard Spodek*

In early childhood education today there are a number of program models available. Such programs as the Becker-Engelmann program or the behavior analysis approach or the "British Infant School" model are distinct approaches to early childhood education that can be represented as models. Often these programs are analyzed according to the school of psychology (whether of learning or development) that each program represents. A better way of analyzing the programs might be in terms of the view of man that is manifest in each program.

To view early childhood programs as reflective of a view of man rather than simply as reflective of a psychological theory is to view each education program as an extension of an ideology. Educational programs differ not only in a technical sense, but also in an essential moral sense. While most educational programs share some goals, the differences in goals that exist are based upon value preferences. Even the choice of means for achieving common goals may suggest a moral act.

Kohlberg (1972) has discussed the value bases of different educational approaches as ideologies.

> Prescription of educational practice cannot be derived from psychological theory or science alone. In addition to theoretical assumptions about how children learn or develop (the psychological theory component), educational ideologies include value assumptions about what is educationally good or worthwhile. To call a pattern of educational thought an ideology is to indicate it is a fairly systematic combination of a theory about psychological and social fact with a set of value principles. (pp. 463-4)

Kohlberg identifies three ideological strains in contemporary educational programs — romanticism, cultural transmission, and progressivism.

> Romantics hold that what comes from within the child is the most important aspect of development; therefore the pedagogical environment should be permissive enough to allow the inner "good" (abilities and social virtues) to unfold and the inner "bad" to come under control. Thus teaching the child the ideas and attitudes of others through rote or drill would result in meaningless learning and the suppression of

inner spontaneous tendencies of positive value. (p. 451)

> Traditional educators believe that their primary task is the transmission to the present generation of bodies of information and of rules or values collected in the past; they believe that the educator's job is the direct instruction of such information and rules. The important emphasis, however, is not on the sanctity of the past, but on the view that educating consists of transmitting knowledge, skills, and social and moral rules of the culture. Knowledge and rules may be rapidly changing or they may be static. In either case, however, it is assumed that education is the transmission of the culturally given. (p. 452)

> As an educational ideology, progressivism holds that education should nourish the child's natural interaction with a developing society or environment. Unlike the romantics, the progressives do not assume that development is the unfolding of an innate pattern or that the primary aim of education is to create an unconflicted environment able to foster healthy development. Instead, they define development as a progression through invariant ordered sequential stages. The educational goal is the eventual attainment of a higher level or stage of development in adulthood, not merely the healthy functioning of the child at a present level. (p. 454)

Within Kohlberg's system of ideologies most traditional nursery school programs which are based upon maturational or psychodynamic principles, contemporary open education programs as well as a range of programs and school and nonschool organizational frameworks for education would be labeled "romantc." Programs based upon behavior analysis techniques as well as the Becker-Engelman program are considered by Kohlberg as concerned with "cultural transmission," while programs based upon Piagetian principles could be labeled "progressive."

Hitt (1969) has suggested that the conflict in psychology

*Dr. Bernard Spodek, Professor of Early Childhood Education, University of Illinois, Chicago. Reprinted with permission from YOUNG CHILDREN, March 1975.

for many years has been between those scholars who adhere to a phenomenological view of man and those who adhere to a behavioral view of man. Hitt has characterized these two views as follows:

> The behaviorist views man as a passive organism governed by external stimuli. Man can be manipulated through proper control of these stimuli. Moreover, the laws that govern man are essentially the same laws as the laws that govern all natural phenomena of the world; hence it is assumed that the scientific method used by the physical scientist is equally appropriate to the study of man. The phenomenologist views man as the source of acts; he is free to choose in each situation. The essence of man is inside of man; he is controlled by his own consciousness. The most appropriate methodology for the study of man is phenomenology, which begins in the world of experience. (p. 657)

Using Hitt's conceptions of behaviorism and phenomenology as polar ends of an ideological continuum, one can range early childhood education programs from behavior analysis programs on one end to open education programs on the other end, with other educational models ranging as different positions between them (see Spodek 1973).

James Macdonald (1973) has presented a third view of curriculum ideologies. Macdonald has identified three different human interests which are reflected in educational programs. These interests are essentially ideologies since they are statements of values as well as theories. Macdonald's system includes control interests, consensus interests, and liberation interests.

> The basic human interests have a language which accompanies them. Wherever such terms as objectives, systems, (or delivery systems), quality control, efficiency, effectiveness, criterion referenced evaluation, etc., are used to the exclusion of others, it is clearly in the interest of control. The control syndrome operates with a clear idea of preordinate goals and evaluation procedures and organized experiences in light of goals and evaluation. Most individualization is in the interest of control.
>
> Consensus interest oriented programs are much more prone to talk about immersion or initiation into the important areas of our culture. They further quite frequently deal with activities and goals or purposes rather than specific objectives. Activities are usually groups of common ones. Competency is certified by the completion of courses and programs at an acceptable level and standardized tests or other expert validation are utilized.
>
> Liberation interest oriented programs talk more about ranges of alternative experiences from which

emerging purposes which reflect and develop needs and interests are continuously emerging. Student choice is central to these proposals. The organization of time, space and resources is considered fluid and flexible with considerable emphasis upon self direction and self evaluation. The adults are talked about as guides, helpers and resource persons. Human relationships are seen as A with B rather than the more authority oriented A/B relationships in the other two. This kind of program is often referred to as personalized (in comparison to group or individualized). The basic distinction between personalized and individualized is the recognition of the student as a moral agent (i.e. chooser of goals and means to achieve them). (p. 5)

Using the Macdonald framework, most traditional educational programs, including those at the nursery school and kindergarten level, could be considered to be based upon consensus interests. Educational models using programmed instruction, behavior analysis, or prescribed patterns of interactions could be considered to be based upon control interests. Open education, as well as much that is advocated by the free school movement and by many community-based education groups, could be identified as liberation interest programs. Most attempts at individualizing instruction and providing for differentiated staffing patterns are developed in the interest of control rather than liberation.

Of the three systems of educational thought presented, the Macdonald framework appears to be the most productive. Kohlberg's view of ideologies tends to oversimplify commonalities. His "romanticism" category contains too many approaches that are essentially different from one another. In addition, progressive education contains both elements of romanticism and cultural transmission making the difference between these two categories questionable. Many other criticisms of Kohlberg's presentation can also be raised. The Hitt framework can be easily subsumed into the Macdonald one which contains other elements within it essential to the understanding of educational proposals.

Teacher Training and Ideology

Just as educational programs for young children can be analyzed for their ideological base, so can teacher-training programs. Most existing programs of teacher preparation can be conceived of as manifesting consensus interest. These programs put students through a series of common experiences, normally conceived of as courses. The completion of a sequence of courses generally leads to a recommendation for certification. Seldom are behavioral competencies specified; rather, general goals are presented. One seldom finds significant opportunities for individualization in these programs, nor are the students' emerging interests considered.

Innovations in teacher education have moved in two distinct directions: toward control-oriented programs and toward liberation-oriented programs. Proposals for alternative programs are based not only upon evidence about what is a more effective program of teacher education but also upon a moral conviction of what kind of educational experience is more worthy for the teacher-student as a person. Some teacher educators suggest the utilization of a "systems" approach to teacher training requiring a behavioral base. Others reject the determination of goals as specific observable behaviors and suggest a more phenomenological approach, stressing the greater involvement of the prospective teacher in his own education and a more personalized approach to training.

The "systems" approach to teacher education requires that teaching competencies be clearly specified and trained for directly. Performance-based criteria for determining effectiveness in teaching is the basis for the programs. Such a systems-oriented approach has been taken by nine models of elementary teacher education, including preschool education, supported by the U.S. Office of Education.

The systems approach used in these models includes determining the "problems universe," defining the subsystems or units within the system, determining alternative procedures for the accomplishment of goals, selecting the best from among alternatives, and implementing the system (Klay and LeBaron 1970). In order to create adequate evaluation procedures, goals of the component instructional units need to be identified in terms of specific observable behaviors.

Behavioral objectives have been identified for each of the above programs. Rosenshine and Furst (1973) have criticized the use of performance criteria in these models since the source of the criteria selected has not been described. In addition, the validity of the criteria used is questionable. There are a number of ways in which these criteria could be validated. One way is through comparison with an ideal model or an explicit value framework. The degree of consistency between the framework and the criteria would determine validity. An empirical determination of what happens to teachers (and their students) who manifest the terminal behavior could also be used as a validating strategy. Outcome measures would still need to be related to a value framework. In any case, educational research has not yet identified a repertoire of teaching skills that have particular effects on cognitive or affective achievement in students, leaving up in the air the whole question of whether any set of teaching behaviors is worth eliciting through any training program.

An Alternative Approach to Teacher Education

A different approach to change in teacher education is related to the increasing involvement of students in their own education. Combs (1965) identified five characteristics of the effective teacher: (a) rich, extensive, and available perceptions of his field, (b) accurate perceptions of what people are like, (c) perception of self leading to adequacy, (d) accurate perceptions of the purposes and processes of learning, and (e) personal perceptions about appropriate methods for carrying out purposes. Growing out of these characteristics, Combs suggests a program that helps students develop richer and more personal perceptions of themselves, others, and the educational process. Specific behaviors are not defined as the goals of the program, and, indeed, such a program would lead to an increased diversity of behaviors by its graduates.

It may very well be that programs developed from these two models might be unequally effective in preparing teachers. It may also be that these programs would turn out different kinds of teachers with different teacher behaviors, understandings, and values. In fact, such ought to be the case if they are implemented effectively.

Which would produce a better teacher? Such a judgment is hard to make and would be based as much upon ideological considerations, including one's personal view of man. The fact that one approach to teacher education is being advocated generally by funding agencies and certification agencies in the United States today, and that this approach represents control interests, has many educational and political implications.

We presently have a number of different models of early childhood education operating. It is doubtful whether any single program, based upon any one point of view, could adequately serve all program models. A program such as the Becker-Engelmann approach requires a teacher to use prescribed materials in prespecified ways. Training a teacher for this program requires the patterning of specific behaviors and the teacher's continued adherence to one method, one set of materials, and one set of behaviors. Were a teacher preparing to enter such a program helped to seek alternatives, to look for personal meanings in classroom settings, and to arrange for educational activities based upon children's desires and interest, the result would be either conflict or the sabotaging of an educational model.

Similarly, there are no prespecified behaviors that can be predetermined for an open classroom teacher. The teacher needs to become sensitive and observant of children's behaviors, to have skills that allow him or her to use a range of educational alternatives, and to behave in an honest, warm, responsive way in class. While competencies can be listed for such a teacher, the behavioral manifestations of these competencies would be so varied and so different from person to person, and from setting to setting, that no prespecifications can be made even though their existence could be assessed. In addition, a program that focused on the shaping of particular behaviors would convey to the teacher values that were antagonistic to the program, again resulting in conflict or sabotage.

It would seem, therefore, that just as there are variations in programs of early childhood education, there need to be variations in programs of teacher education. Not only would the particular ideology of the program of a teacher education institution need to be considered in designing such programs, but the particular model of early childhood education for which the teacher is being prepared would also need to be considered. Programs of teacher education would need to be consistent in educational view with the programs of childhood education to which they would be related.

REFERENCES

Combs, A.W. *The Professional Education of Teachers*, Boston: Ally and Bacon, 1965.

Hitt, W.H. "Two Models of Man." *American Psychologist* 23 (July 1969): 651–658.

Klatt, J., and LeBaron, W. *A Short Summary of Ten Model Teacher Educational Programs.* Washington: U.S. Government Printing Office, 1970.

Kohlberg, L., and Mayer, R. "Development as the Aim of Education." *Harvard Education Review* 42 (1972): 449–496.

Macdonald, J.B. *Potential Relationship of Human Interests, Language, and Orientation to Curriculum Thinking.* Paper presented at meeting of The American Educational Research Association., New Orleans, Louisiana, February 28, 1973.

Rosenshine, B., and Furst, N. "Research on Teacher Performance Criteria." In *Research on Teacher Education: A Symposium*, edited by B. O. Smith, Englewood Cliffs, NJ: Prentice-Hall, 1971.

Spodek, B. Early Childhood Ed*ucation.* Englewood Cliffs, NJ: Prentice-Hall, 1973.

Chapter 66

Goal-Directed Teaching in Action-Based Learning Environments

Sydney L. Schwartz*

Traditionally, one of the fundamental goals in Early Childhood Education has been to conform the teaching environment to the learning environment. The natural learning environment of young children is an active one, with children moving about, interacting with other children, with adults and with materials. For the non-professional, this has created great confusion about the curriculum or program of the schools which serve children before first grade, nursery school, head start, day care and kindergarten. The untrained eye of the parents, lay boards and representatives of the funding agencies see these programs of active children as "just play". The extensive literature justifying the value of play and active learning for young children acts as testimonial to the fact that not only non-professionals but also professional find it difficult to view an early childhood setting of active children as a justifiable educational program.[1] However, conforming the teaching environment to children's natural learning styles requires this kind of active involvement of children with a variety of materials on their own terms. Setting up an action-based learning environment for young children DOES NOT mean the abondoning of instructional goals, but rather the development of instructional goals that are most likely to relate to where the children are able to focus their energy and where the goals are most likely to have long term influence on the learners.

When one walks into a grade school classroom, it is usually comparatively easy to identify the instructional goal of the moment, such as recognizing alphabet letters, practicing handwriting skills, memorizing addition facts or practicing phonics skills. What facilitates the recognition of the instructional goal is the physical arrangement of the classroom, with children seated at desks, while clusters of children are doing the same thing and the teacher inputs clearly focus on the instructional activity in progress. In an action-based learning environment, children are rarely seated in an orderly pattern; they are rarely producing the same actions and the teacher's inputs are varied, directed to different children. Consequently, it takes a skilled professional to identify the instructional goals and to specify the ways in which the teacher is achieving the goals. Similarly, it takes a skilled professional to plan for and implement instructional goals that fit together in an action-based program. For example, in a three year old classroom during the first few days of school, a teacher was observed pursuing the following behavior:

The teacher moved from table to table, sitting with each child at a table and briefly chatting about the actions of the child. As the teacher moved from the table area toward the block area, one child approached the teacher carrying a long block, saying, "OHHH. OHHH." His body language simultaneously indicated that he perceived the block to be heavy. The teacher responded, "It is heavy, isn't it?" The child moved away from the teacher repeating, "Yeah. Heavy. Heavy. Heavy." As he repeated the word heavy, he slowly raised and lowered the block he was carrying. The teacher moved to the rabbit cage, where two children were making squealing sounds as they approached and withdrew from the cage repeatedly. The teacher focused the children's attention on the rabbit's nose, by the combined question-direction strategy of "What's happening to his nose? Look at his nose." The approach-withdrawal behavior of the children ceased, along with the squealing as they stopped to look at the rabbit's nose. The teacher next focused attention on the rabbit's food and the way he was eating. Ultimately, the children responded to the teacher question and demonstration about how the fur feels by tentatively placing one finger through the cage onto the back of the rabbit.

This competent young teacher was teaching in a familiar pattern of a program that builds the teaching sequences on the interest and involvement of the children. Yet, beyond explaining that she was fostering children's adjustment to school by helping them feel comfortable with the people, materials and animal, it would be difficult for the teacher to explain her goals in terms of the world's understanding of curriculum. In reality, some very important and familiar curriculum goals were being served by this teaching interaction, but it was not being done in a familiar way. A familiar goal in teaching is "to expand children's vocabulary in

*Dr. Sydney L. Schwartz, Associate Professor, Dept. of Elementary & Early Childhood Education, Queens College, CUNY

terms of descriptive language". The most familiar way to teach a term such as "heavy" is by lecture-demonstration followed by a battery of test questions.[2] That is, the teacher shows a collection of objects or pictures of objects and explains or discusses the relative weight of the objects with the children. After the discussion, children are asked to demonstrate understanding by identifying the heavy objects and the light objects in the collection.

What is rarely understood by those unfamiliar with young children is that the formalized instructional activity with teacher lecture-demonstration-test strategies requires that the learners have prior understanding of the subject matter which is then reaffirmed through the lecture approach. A child's notion of heavier-lighter is essentially acquired through many experiences which allows the learner to sort out his perceptions of comparative heaviness. Although the formalized lesson fits the popular notion of teaching, such a lesson can only succeed if the learners have had considerable opportunity to develop the prior understandings of heavy-light through direct experience. From a developmental perspective, one of the first steps in sorting out one's understandings of heaviness is to discover what objects you can lift and what objects you can't lift. Through experience, finer and finer distinctions are made as the learner discovers which of the liftable objects are hard to lift and which are easy to lift. In the earlier illustration of the teaching-learning interaction in the three year old program, the teacher was verifying for the child his growing notion of heaviness at the level of "hard to lift."

The teacher behavior of verbalizing selected aspects of what the child is experiencing, as illustrated above, is one of a major vehicles of curriculum in an action-based learning environment. Since children engaged in activities are always experiencing multiple learnings at any one point in time, the challenge of selecting one aspect of the learning experience to foster the development of instructional goals becomes complex and demanding. Consequently, one major task in achieving teaching competence at the early childhood level is to develop the skills of specifying and selecting instructional goals in order to implement an integrated and continuous program which may be explained in curriculum terms. To achieve these skills requires clarification of understandings about (a) the nature of goals, (b) the variety of teaching strategies available to the teacher and the aspects of the program in which the strategies are used, and (c) the scope and sequence of curriculum in all areas as related to child development and learning.

The Nature of Goals

Over the past decade, extensive attention has been directed toward the notion of behavioral objectives or behavioral goals, which is translated to mean teaching goals or instructional goals.[3] In reality, behavioral objects are short-term goals stated specifically so that outcomes of instruction can be observed. For example, a behavioral goal in a lesson on alphabet letters might be "Children recognize the first ten letters of the alphabet when displayed on cards." Another behavioral goal related to alphabet letters at a more introductory level might be, "Children match the letters of their name to name cards."[4] When goals are stated specifically, it is possible to evaluate outcomes of teaching or degree of learner progress toward the goal. In the reverse, when goals are not specified, there is no way to analyze the relationship between procedures and outcomes. That is, if goals are not planned, the outcomes become accidental, occurring by chance. In the prior illustration of the teacher of three-year-olds, the teaching response, "It is heavy." reflects a clear understanding of the use of behavioral objectives as part of the design of teaching in an action-based learning environment.

From the perspective of a group of professionals in early childhood and humanistic education, the use of behavioral objectives has caused serious concern.[5] The conflict which has developed centers on the question of whether such objectives violate the goals of action-based learning and whether precise goals are, by definition, unacceptable in a humanistic environment where learner interests dominate development of learning activities. The problem is an outgrowth of a lack of awareness of the relationship between short-term goals, i.e. behavioral objectives, and long-term goals. Long-term goals are the basic foundation of decision-making in teaching. Short-term goals are steppingstones along the path toward long-term goals. What is undesirable is the isolation of the behavioral goal, or short-term goal, from the long-term goals. For example, an appropriate short-term goal might be "Children practice comparing gross differences in weight and use descriptive terms of heavier and lighter." This short-term goal, which may be achieved in one instructional interaction serves the long-term goals of (a) using the skills of inquiry to identify the properties of objects,—science curriculum, and (b) expanding vocabulary and language meanings,—oral language development and reading readiness curriculum. If, in the process of developing the instructional activity, the children begin to examine properties other than that of weight, the teacher is challenged to adapt the episode to serve the long-term goals, which always take precedent over short-term goals as a basis for decision-making in the process of teaching. A misunderstanding of the function of short-term goals may lead to teaching decisions which interfere with long-term goals.

The same rules of relationship apply to instructional goals in the social development sphere as apply to the conventional curriculum areas. Unless the short-term, immediate goals are viewed in relationship to the long-term, distance goals, decisions can be made which inhibit continuous growth rather than foster it for the learners. One common concern in teaching young children is to develop the social skills of communication, that is, the skill of interacting with peers within a group discussion context. Interaction requires both the ability to listen to what the classmate is saying and to contribute to the subject being discussed. A short-term instructional goal, a steppingstone to the ultimate goal, is usually identified as "learning to take turns." If this goal is pursued as simply learning to wait while the other person talks, the end goal of interaction is not likely to ever be achieved. Such teacher statements as "Wait your turn.", "Johnny is talking now. You will have to wait." and "You must raise your hand if you want to speak.", focus only on the management demands of the teacher for orderly speaking in turn, but not on the learning goals for children, the active listening to another's ideas and perceptions. Interaction skills require actively tuning in to what the other person is saying and not just passively waiting for a quiet spot to begin speaking. Teachers find themselves unwittingly caught in the web of dictating procedures of who will speak next, maintaining quiet until the speaker completes his statements and generally guiding the management of the activity rather than facilitating interaction based on content. When the goal of the teacher terminates at the level of how the procedure will work, i.e. taking turns, there is little expectation that the more important concerns will ever become a dominant factor in teaching decisions. If a teacher is concerned about the lack of continuity between listening and speaking within the group, several levels of decision making are required. One level is in terms of the size of the discussion group, reducing this size to eliminate the continual need to monitor taking turns and noise level. Another level is in terms of selection of discussion topics which lead toward exchange of ideas and experiences or perceptions rather than monologues.

Teaching Strategies and Program Context

There are three basic contexts within which instructional goals are pursued in a program serving young children. These are (a) total group instructional context, (b) small group and individual teaching-learning context and (c) routines and transitions of the program. In an action-based learning environment, the small group and individual context combined with the routines and transitions consumes the bulk of the teaching time available. The amount of total group activity is confined to brief periods and constitutes a small percentage of in-school time.

Within these contexts, children are engaged in learning at the level of acquiring new learning, practicing learning in repetitive fashion and/or applying learning. The teaching decisions about what forms of teaching behavior to use stems from an understanding of what kinds of learning behavior is most likely to occur. Perhaps the easiest context to predict the level of learning is in the routines and transitions where children are asked to produce behaviors that they know, and the actions are highly repetitive. For example, one common routine in early childhood classrooms is

that of snack. In this routine, the children are asked to repeatedly produce the same behaviors of sitting down at tables, distributing utensils, distributing food, discarding waste, cleaning and straightening tables. The behaviors most commonly produced by the teacher within this routine is that of giving directions to facilitate the management of the routine. It is not likely that a teacher can expect to successfully introduce much new learning during the routines and transition periods. However, it is quite possible to consider more extensive application of prior learnings as instructional goals are clearly identified. Teachers have already discovered that the beginning skills of name recognition and picture reading can be the focus of practice application by the use of helper charts, attendance recording charts and children's activity charts. In the instance of using charts, the difference between repetitive practice and application rests in the fact that the names on the chart are continuously changing, and children cannot automatically expect to find their name in the same position on the chart daily. They must find their names at different points on the chart and then read the chart for indiction of the job to be completed.

As the teacher shifts the form of the learning task from straight repetitive practice, as in distributing milk and straws, the teacher behavior of giving directions can shift to asking questions which focus on the process of the routine. That is, if there is a helper chart which signals the responsibilities of the children to perform the separate steps in the routine, the teaching task rests in focusing the children's attention on finding out what their tasks are rather than having the teacher continuously giving verbal directions on who is to do what task and how to do it. As the children actively participate in applying what they know, the follow-up teaching behavior may take the form of reinforcing the children's skills of applying learning. If the routine is limited to the more common practice of asking children to obediently follow teacher directions, the only teacher reinforcement possible is that of praise for obedience. In early childhood teaching-learning settings, obedience is a terminal goal which does not serve the broad range of instructional-curriculum goals.

In sharp contrast to routines and transitions, the period of small group and individual teaching-learning activity is reflective of great diversity in both children's behavior and teacher behavior. The greatest challenge to the teacher, to identify how to fit learning goals with teaching goals, occurs during this period of greatest diversity in children's activity. The teacher engages with children within this period under two different conditions, by teacher choice to engage the child in interaction or by child invitation to engage the teacher in interaction. If the child invites the teacher to participate, the form of teaching behavior is essentially dictated by the child's invitation. For example, if the child who is building a boat at the woodworking table asks the teacher to help him get two pieces of wood joined together, the teaching behavior is circumscribed by the teacher's need to find out what approaches to the problem have already been tried by the child. Once the unsuccessful attempts have been reviewed, it is possible to generate alternate approaches. Whether the teacher asks the child, "What have you tried?", or asks a series of repeated questions, "Have you tried this way?", the most natural first step in the interaction is the questioning one by the teacher. The second step in the interaction is for the teacher to identify whether the problem is one of lack of understanding of spatial relationships, lack of understanding of the properties of the materials or lack of skill with the tools. The third step poses the teaching decision of whether to offer a suggestion, to elicit from the child another way to try to solve the problem, or to compensate for the lack of skill with tools by doing for or with him. This final decision is dependent upon teacher assessment of the level of difficulty of the problem and the child's tolerance for further problem solving at the moment.

If the teacher decides to engage the child, this occurs by entering the child's on-going activity without invitation from the learner, or inviting the learner to participate in a teacher designed activity. Entering a child's on-going activity without invitation poses complex decision-making for the teacher. The teacher has the option to enter the learner's activity as a participant, as is often done when children are role-playing family members and familiar workers within the immediate economic and social community. Another option the teacher has is to add some information to the situation, as might happen when the teacher notices that a block structure might collapse and decides to focus children's attention on the impending problem by such a statement as "Your building looks very shaky." Whether the teacher joins children's activities as a temporary participant or offers children unsolicited information, the foundation for the teaching decision rests in the goals selected.[6]

The more commonly selected option the teacher has during the activity period is that of planning for small group and individual instructional interactions. It is usually easier for the teacher to coordinate the selection of the instructional goal in this kind of planning than it is for the on-going interactions where the teacher contributes to children's activities. When inviting the learners to participate in a teacher designed activity, the teacher has the opportunity to draw from a broad range of curriculum goals and may introduce new learnings, build practice opportunities and plan for application of learnings in project type activities. Just as the teacher may select goals at the level of new learnings, practice or application, there is an active decision to be made relative to the thrust of the teaching approach. While all teacher interactions include a variety of teachings behaviors, an analysis of the type of instructional goal leads to a decision of the type of teaching role or thrust to be developed. That is, if the instructional goal is the acquisition of new learning, the primary thrust of the teaching behavior

will be the giving of information either through verbal explanation and/or demonstration and modelling. An example of a goal focusing on new learning is "Children find out how to use a hammer." In this instance, the learning goal is designed to be served by teacher explanation and demonstration. If the instructional goal is focused on practicing newly acquired learnings through repeated behaviors, the teaching behavior is most likely to be that of giving directions in the establishing of some gameful activity which engages the learner in the selected practice. An example of a goal for repetitive practice is "Children match colors for same and different and practice labelling the match colors." In this instance, a gameful activity would call forth repeated behaviors for the learner in terms of placing matching colors together as in a game such as lotto. In addition to explaining how the activity works, the teacher behavior is likely to include continual reinforcement as the teacher reaffirms for the learner the color matches that have been completed and the color labels applied to the matching activity.

If the instructional goal assumes knowledge and skill acquisition and is selected to foster the application of acquired learnings, the teacher role will be less dominant, as the children engage in the problem solving which accompanies project activities. An example of the instructional goal that focuses on application of learning is, "Children design and construct humorous masks using craft materials." As the children pursue this activity, the teacher behavior will tend to reflect diverse sub-goals, as children seek help based upon limitations in skills in understandings. At this application level, it is reasonable to expect that children will evidence irregularity in mastery of skills and understandings. That is, one child may have limited understanding about the properties of a particular material he has selected for use and the teacher behavior, through narrative recall and questioning, helps the learner verify the properties of the material as 'cannot be torn evenly, must be cut', 'cannot be glued, must be stapled'. Another child may have limited measurement skills and may need help in figuring out how to position the eye holes in the mask. In this case, the teacher behavior may become collaborative as measurement skills are applied to the task.

In essence, teacher behaviors and teacher role are selected based on the form of the instructional goal and the design of the learning opportunity. Probably the most difficult challenge facing teachers of young children is one of modifying the dominant teaching behavior of asking testing-type questions. The use of the questioning technique to encourage children to talk about what they know strongly stimulates the learner to organize what he knows. The use of the questioning technique when it is clear that children do not know the desired information poses serious limitations to successful teaching-learning interactions.

Curriculum Sequence and Child Development

The curriculum sequence and the development of the children offers the most clearly visible basis for identifying instructional goals. Each curriculum area has available lists of scope and sequence.[7] A study of curriculum for young children indicates that two factors affect teaching decisions on goals, the scope of the content area and the stages of child development related to the sequence. As children acquire the specific learnings identified in a curriculum sequence, teacher knowledge of stages of children's development determines whether to proceed to the next goal in the sequence or to remain at the same goal level and develop practice opportunities and application activities. As a way of illustrating the range of decisions posed for the teacher, one sequence in mathematics, the prenumber sequence, is illustrated in terms of the teaching decisions posed and the alternatives available to pursue the goal-directed teaching in the action-based environment.

In order to count successfully, the learnings that must be achieved can be stated as follows:

a. skill of matching one for one, or maintaining one to one correspondence between two sets,

b. skill of stating the number names in order,

c. maintaining the concept of set, distinguishing what items are included in a set and what items are not,

d. a developed notion of 'more' and 'less' in comparison of sets with gross differences in size.

There seems to be little evidence that these four learnings need to be sequenced, but it is clear that these learnings must be achieved as a prerequisite to successful beginning counting. Each item listed above can legitimately be considered an instructional goal for children who have not yet mastered beginning counting. The term preprequisite learning means that the learning occurs as separate and distinct, not attached to counting drill practice. That is, children learn to match one-for-one in a variety of ways without using number, such as matching socks, or one straw for one milk container, or one glass for one person, or one hat for one head. Once it is established that an instructional goal is "Children practice the skills of one to one matching with objects in the classroom.", the teacher can develop teaching sequences in all three contexts of the program, in routines, in small group and individual activity and in the large group instructional context. In routines, tasks can be assigned to the children in food set-up periods, clean-up periods and arrival and departure periods that feature matching sets of items. In small group activity, playful-gameful activities can be devised that require one-to-one matching as part of the game, such as lotto games in which one marker is used to cover each space. As the teacher meets children engaged in their own self-selected activity, the teacher can reinforce matching activity when it occurs. For example, if a child manipulated attribute blocks by placing one circular-shaped block on top of one rectangular-shaped block in repeated

series, a teacher comment about this activity serves to reinforce the one-to-one matching learning being practiced as well as the geometry learnings.

Similarly, in fostering learnings toward the goal of "Children stabilize notions of set by creating sets and distinguising members from non-members", the same types of teaching decisions are made. Where children spontaneously engage in the learning practice, the teaching role serves to reinforce the learning by comments and conversation. Where children require stimulation to engage in the learning, small group instructional activities are developed to attract the child to try out the activity and engage in the learning practice. Where children have initial skills, the routine activities can draw upon these skills by the assignment of children to complete the chores in such a way that the skills are practiced.

An instructional goal which often creates conflict between professionals is "Children recite the number names in order." There is little defense for mindless recitation in any educational setting, much less one that claims to build learning through action. However, toward this goal some legitimate activities can be directed. Children thoroughly enjoy chants, rhymes, songs and repetitive refrains. The pursuit of such activities as chanting and rhyming serves goals connected with language mastery, which is partly built on great familiarity with language sounds, rhythm patterns and melodic patterns of speech. The number names are often learned spontaneously by younger children as they imitate older children bouncing balls, jumping rope and playing hide and seek games. Using the activity of chants with and without music, accompanied by motoric activity, the appropriate order of number names can readily be learned, ready to be used later to apply number thinking to set when the concerns are for finding out "how many" occur appropriate in the curriculum sequence.

The role of diagnosis in decision-making about instrucional goals is ever-present. Where children demonstrate stability in the acquisition of learning, the appropriate goal selection is usually the next goal in the sequence. However, it is not uncommon to be deceived by children's performance and to assume stability where stability does not exist. Consequently, it is strongly recommended that the applied level of learning activity be considered essential in the program to assure continuous monitoring of pacing of progress in moving through the sequence of instructional goals in any given curriculum area. For example, it is very common for young children to demonstrate successful counting skills up to seven or eight and then become unstable. The instability in this skill may reflect itself in the loss of the ability to sustain the notion of set when more items are included, or it may be the loss of ability to sustain one-to-one correspondence above the level of seven, or the loss of the ability to organize the larger set as having a beginning and end for counting purposes. The task, in terms of teaching, is to develop activity for the learner in the area which has been demonstrated as unstable. If the learner loses the ability to sustain one-to-one correspondence with larger sets, matching sets is the kind of practice required, without the focus on number. Gameful activities that require matching one bead with one block for sets of 7 to 15 objects or a skill activity which uses tally marks in boxes to record frequency illustrate the kind of activity which uses the matching practice without number. The importance of diagnosis as a guide to teaching decisions cannot be underestimated. But knowing what the learner needs and finding ways to engage the learner are separate teaching decisions which are dependent, one upon the other. If the task is too complex, but the form of the activity is very engrossing, the learner may be doomed to frustration, seeking to perform an activity for which he does not have the skills. If the task is well selected in terms of the learner's development, but the form of the activity is very uninteresting to the learner, he is not likely to engage long enough to achieve the learning goal.

Summary

It is strongly suggested in this article that the identification of learning goals is a major steppingstone to the development of viable and defensible programs serving young children. It is further suggested that the identification and pursuit of teaching-learning goals supports action-based learning rather than violates it. The teacher's ability to specify the goals which guide teaching decisions in planning and process is an evergrowing skill which is dependent upon continuous growth in understanding of curriculum content, child development and the dynamics of teaching.

NOTES

[1] The literature on children's play focuses on play as a dominant form of children's learning behavior and includes theoretical constructs, research and curriculum guides. For a selected listing of suggested readings, see the bibliography.

[2] Although extensive research has been done on the strategies of teaching, comparatively little is available on teaching roles and strategies in action-based learning environments. A list of suggested readings on describing and analyzing teaching behavior in early childhood classrooms is provided in the bibliography.

[3] For a list of suggested readings on developing behavioral objectives, see bibliography.

[4] For a full sequence of instructional goals in seven curriculum areas, see Robison, H.F. & Schwartz, S.L. *Learning At An Early Age, Vol. 2,* Englewood Cliffs, N.J., Prentice-Hall, 1972.

[5] One example of the type of dialogue reflecting this conflict is, "Behavioral Objectives: New Ways to Fail Children?" by Sarah Moskovitz, in *Young Children,* April, 1973.

[6] For further reading on contributing to children's activities, see listing in bibliography.

[7] Robison, H.F. & Schwartz, S.L. op.cit.

SELECTED BIBLIOGRAPHY

Children's Play

Almy, Millie (ed.), *Early Childhood Play,* New York, Selected Academic Readings, 1968.

Almy, Millie, "Spontaneous Play: An Avenue for Intellectual Development", *Bulletin of the Institute for Child Study,* 1966, 28, No. 2.

Ellis, Michael, J., *Why People Play,* Englewood Cliffs, N.J., Prentice-Hall, 1973.

Hartley, Ruth E. and Goldenson, Robert M., *The Complete Book of Children's Play,* New York, Crowell, (Rev. Ed.), 1963.

Herron, R. and Sutton-Smith, Brian, *Child's Play,* New York, Wiley, 1971.

Millar, Susanna, *The Psychology of Play,* Baltimore, Md., Pelican Books, 1968.

Spodek, Bernard, "The Problem of Play: Educational or Recreational?" in *Play as a Learning Medium* edited by Doris Sponseller, Washington, D.C., National Association for the Education of Young Children, 1974.

Sponseller, Doris, "Why is Play a Learning Medium?" in *Play as a Learning Medium,* Washington, D.C., National Association for the Education of Young Children, 1974.

Sutton-Smith, Brian, "The Playful Modes of Knowing", in *Play: The Child Strives Toward Self-realization* edited by Georgia Engstrom, Washington, D.C., National Association of Education of Young Children, 1971.

The Study of Teaching Behavior

Joyce, Bruce & Weil, Marsha, *Models of Teaching,* Englewood Cliffs, N.J., Prentice-Hall, 1972.

Katz, Lillian G., "Teaching in Preschools: Roles and Goals", *Children,* 1970, 17, 42-48.

Robison, Helen F. & Schwartz, S.L., *Learning At An Early Age, Volume I,* Englewood Cliffs, N.J., Prentice-Hall, 1974. Ch. 4.

Developing Behavioral Objectives

Burns, R.W., *New Approaches to Behavioral Objectives,* Dubuque, Iowa, Wm. C. Brown Publ., 1972.

Mager, R.F. and Pipe, P., *Analyzing Performance Problems,* Belmont, Calif., Fearon Publishers, 1970.

Mager, R.F. *Preparing Instructional Objectives,* Belmont, Cal., Fearon Publishers, 1962.

**Contributing to Children's
Self-selected Activities**

Kleve, G.L., *Educational Objectives and Learning Activities For Early Childhood Education,* University Microfilms, 1970.

Robison, Helen F., "The Decline of Play in Urban Kindergartens", *Young Children,* August, 1971.

Smilansky, Sara, *The Effect of Sociodramatic Play in Disadvantaged Preschool Children,* N.Y., John Wiley and Sons, Inc., 1968.

BIBLIOGRAPHY

Moskovitz, Sarah, "Behavioral Objectives: New Ways to Fail Children?" *Young Children,* April, 1973.

Robison, Helen F. & Schwartz, Sydney L., *Learning At an Early Age, Volume 2, A Curriculum for Young Children.* Englewood Cliffs, N.J., Prentice-Hall, 1972.

Center for Library, Media and Telecommunications NYC Board of Education

Chapter 67

An Approach to Competency Based Teacher Preparation in Early Childhood Education

Adelle Jacobs and Laura Bursak*

As an outgrowth of demands for teacher accountability in education, there has developed a strong movement toward competency-based teacher education and certification. The purpose of teacher preparation programs has always been the development of competent teachers—this is not new. What is new is the call for reformulation of preparatory programs in terms that delineate specifically the kinds of performances considered basic to effective teaching, that specify strategies designed to provide for their development, and that spell out assessment techniques to measure attainment of the specific performances. A major change in certification procedures is also being called for. Instead of being based on the kinds of college courses taken and the number of credits earned, competency-based certification would depend upon the demonstrated achievement of specified competencies.

In our view, this reformulation of teacher preparation and certification must take a "holistic or global" approach (Combs, 1972) rather than one based solely upon discrete behaviors. The goal should be the development of teachers who have the requisite knowledge, attitudes and skills for facilitating children's cognitive, affective, and psychomotor development, and who, in addition to being well-informed, are "creative, flexible, open to experience, responsible for themselves and others, and guided by positive goals and purposes." (Combs, 1972, p. 12). Toward this end, the following competencies are proposed as appropriate for teachers of young children.

The prospective teacher should be able to state objectives upon which an educational program for young children in a democratic society may be based.

The prospective teacher should be able to articulate a philosophy of early childhood education.

The prospective teacher should have an understanding and acceptance of himself as a person and an awareness of his attitudes toward and relationships with others.

The prospective teacher should be able to identify and describe the stages of social, emotional, and intellectual development of children from birth through eight years of age according to specific theories of personality and intellectual development.

The prospective teacher should be able to describe the impact of societal factors on a young child's school experience.

The prospective teacher should be able to describe the teacher's role in fostering intellectual, social, emotional, and physical development.

The prospective teacher should be able to assess individual differences in intellectual, social, emotional, and physical development.

The prospective teacher should be able to articulate criteria for selecting appropriate curriculum content, methods, and materials for nursery, kindergarten, and primary grade children.

The prospective teacher should be able to plan safe, appropriate early childhood environments using space, equipment, and materials to foster intellectual, social, emotional, and physical development consonant with developmental theory.

The prospective teacher should be able to integrate mathematics, science, social studies, reading, language arts, and expressive arts into a cohesive educational program.

The prospective teacher should be able to plan for individuals and for groups of children, both for short range and for longer periods.

The prospective teacher should be able to plan a program for parent involvement and for home-school corporation.

*Dr. Adelle Jacobs, Assistant Professor of Education, York College, CUNY. Dr. Laura Bursuk, Assistant Professor of Education, York College, CUNY.

The prospective teacher should be able to identify educational resources in the community and describe some ways of using these.

The prospective teacher should be able to analyze and critique existing programs for children, using educational objectives, developmental theory, and educational philosophy as criteria.

The prospective teacher should be able to demonstrate behaviors which support cognitive and affective development of children during college field work and student teaching situations.

To provide students with opportunities for the development of these competencies, the following areas of study are proposed.

Self-Understanding for Teachers: In order to help young children develop self-understanding and self-acceptance, teachers themselves must have a positive feeling of self. As Combs (1965) has noted, "The production of effective teachers will require helping each student to explore and discover his personal meanings about subject matter, people, purposes, and learning, about methods and about himself." (p. 28). Opportunities should be provided within the framework of the teacher's preparatory program for such experiences.

Child Development: Since an understanding of the total development of young children is necessary for planning and implementing appropriate educational programs, a study of child development is basic to the teacher's preparation. This should include study of the normal growth and development of children from birth through eight years of age: physical, emotional, social and intellectual aspects of development and the roles of endowment, maturation, environment, and experience. Research findings and their implications for the education of young children should be studied, with particular attention to the contributions of Piaget, Erikson, Isaacs, among others.

The Young Child in His Envrionment: Since societal factors have a strong and multi-faceted impact on a young child's school experience, an understanding of these factors is crucial. This entails study of the educational implications of the style and content of the young child's daily life in his particular environment (urban, suburban, rural), including the role of significant adults at home and at school. Physical, psychological, environment, and cultural factors as they affect his attitudes, behavior, and learning are important understandings for teachers. The experiences, feelings, values, strengths, and needs of young children, as influenced by their backgrounds, should be explored in relation to program development and instructional practices of the teacher.

Language Arts: Language development is a pivotal aspect of the total development of the young child. The teacher must understand her role in providing appropriate opportunities for extending and enriching the language with which the child comes to school. For such understanding, study of language development as it relates to intellectual, social, and emotional growth in young children is important. The interrelationship of listening, speaking, writing, and reading and ways in which teachers may facilitate development in these areas should be stressed.

Literature for Young Children: Good literature enriches children's lives in many ways. Read for information, for pleasure, for the deepening understanding of a mood or concept, or for the aesthetic experience of poetry, literature may extend self-understanding and the understanding of others. It may contribute to the development of imagination, sensitivity, and values, and provide language experiences of high quality. Young children "will learn early to look to literature for truth and wisdom as well as for aesthetic impact, with respectful curiosity for the many faces of the human relationship and the foibles and wonders of man. . ." (Jacobs, 1965, p. 5). It is important for prospective teachers to be familiar with the broad range of literary material for young children and to develop and use appropriate criteria for evaluation and selection.

Reading skills in Early Childhood Education: There is overwhelming concern and continuing controversy regarding the pros and cons of early reading instruction, the suitability of different approaches and methodologies, and the variety of programs whose developers claim are the "solution to the reading problem." Teachers have to be able to make knowledgeable decisions in regard to the many, and often contradictory, claims made by the protagonists of various points of view. They need an understanding of the nature of reading and the reading process, and of the numerous factors involved (physical, perceptual, intellectual, language, emotional, social, and school factors). Competency in the teaching of specific reading skills in developmental sequences appropriate for individual children should be developed through a study of theory and practice related to the development of pre-reading and reading skills in nursery school, kindergarten, and the primary grades. Diagnostic and corrective teaching competencies should also be developed.

Mathematics, Science, and Social Studies in Early Childhood Education: To bring order to the understanding of their physical and social world, young children need opportunities for direct experiences with people and things, and help in interpreting their experiences. Prospective teachers should become knowledgeable about appropriate objectives, content, methods, and materials for helping children develop modes of inquiry, critical thinking, problem-solving techniques, and values, as well as concepts and skills—all of which constitute the substance of mathematics, science and social learning. The role of the teacher in facilitating children's development in these areas should be considered along with ways of integrating subject matter content with other areas of the program, stressing concrete, first-hand experiences and learning through discovery.

The Expressive Arts in Early Childhood Education: Children need opportunities for free, creative expression of their ideas and feelings in their own unique and personal styles, and in non-verbal as well as verbal modes. The teacher must provide an environment which is aesthetic as well as emotionally safe, in order to foster such expression. She must offer many opportunities, a variety of media, support, and guidance in order to facilitate a growing perception and control in the use of media. Suggested for prospective teachers is a multidisciplinary approach to music, movement, and art experiences, with stress on ways of providing opportunities for exploration, experimentation, and personal expression as well as for perceptual and motor development.

Working with Parents: Positive relationships between parents and teachers, between home and school, are vital in providing for harmony and continuity in the lives of young children. In order to foster such relationships, prospective teachers need to learn ways of working with parents for mutual understanding and support. Helping parents to become aware of the goals, content, and values of the early childhood education program is one aspect of teacher-parent interaction. Prospective teachers must learn ways of sharing insights and information about individual children and about young children in general, and about the contributions parents can make to the teacher's understanding of particular children and of children in a given community. In addition, they must learn techniques of involving parents in their programs: parent-teacher meetings and workshops, discussion groups, conferences, written communications.

Although, for purposes of clarity and discussion, specific competencies and areas of study have been treated separately, a holistic approach is considered by the writers to be basic to sound teacher preparation. Opportunity must be provided in the program for integrating into a coherent whole insights, content, and methods so that they do not remain isolated segments. This would include consideration of appropriate goals, development of a philosophy of early childhood education, and the role of play in the total development of the young child.

Organization of the school environment in terms of space, equipment, time, age groupings, and personnel patterns, as well as integration of subject matter must be considered. Since planning for individual, small groups, and total groups on both short range and long range bases is an important teacher function, skill in observing children and keeping records should be developed toward this end. Prospective teachers, in addition to learning ways of relating effectively to parents, must learn to use community resources as a means of providing continuity in the life of a young child.

A multi-faceted field work component should be part of the entire ongoing teacher preparation program so that theory and practice can be meaningfully meshed. In addition to field work relating to curriculum and teaching, it is suggested that students have practical experiences which might include home visits, parent conferences, and involvement with community agencies.

Developers of particular teacher preparation programs may wish to break down further the competencies delineated in this article, detailed according to their views. Strategies for achieving competencies would also be determined by program developers. Possibilities in this regard include traditional courses, instructional modules, independent study, field work, or any combination of these.

Assessment techniques are another aspect to be considered in relation to competency-based teacher education. These may vary from one competency to another, and from one program to another, but in all instances should be evaluated and refined with experience.

Our overriding concern is that teacher education programs do not become primarily interested and involved in minutiae, leading to a fragmented approach. A good competency-based program must offer each student the needed opportunities to grow toward becoming a "whole teacher" for "whole children". Attributes such as wisdom, sensitivity, kindness, supportiveness, flexibility, tolerance for ambiguity and for change, spontaneity, creativity, and a sense of humor are vital for teachers of young children. Although these cannot be taught *per se,* programs of teacher education must strive to nurture these. We must be wary of adopting an "engineering approach," a charge often leveled by critics of the concept of competency-based teacher education. Humanism is crucial to teacher effectiveness. It must be paramount when planning for teacher development.

BIBLIOGRAPHY

Arthur W. Combs, *Educational Accountability: Beyond Behavioral Objectives.* Washington, D.C.: Association for Supervision and Curriculum Development, 1972.

Arthur W. Combs, *The Professional Education of Teachers.* Boston: Allyn and Bacon, Inc., 1965.

Leland B. Jacobs, ed., *Using Literature with Young Children.* New York: Teachers College Press, Teachers College, Columbia University, 1965, p. 5.

Chapter 68
Just Another Pair of Hands?
The Role of the Assistant Teacher
in Early Childhood Programs

Paula L. Zajan*

Introduction

One of the more innovating practices that has been part of the educational scene during the past fifteen years, has been the employment of community based personnel in educational programs. Although school aides had been hired previously to supervise lunchroom activities, or for yard patrol, collection of monies and other clerical chores, the practice of employing men and women from the immediate community to participate in classroom activities under the direction of a teacher with the hope of encouraging these workers to move up the career ladder into more responsible and professional positions was indeed a new approach. The purpose of this article is to present a brief account of how and why these programs started; to describe the role of the assistant teacher in early childhood programs; to examine the impact of community based personnel working as assistant teachers; and finally to look at where the programs are currently and where they may be going.

Background of the Assistant Teacher Program

The decade of the sixties has been described as a time of dissension, controversy over the Vietnam war and increasing alienation and unrest on the part of many young people. But it also has been described as a time of great social progress, a time when the ills of poverty and racism could be attacked as in a war. Indeed, President Lyndon Johnson declared a "war on poverty" and from his statement and the subsequent legislation (The Economic Opportunity Act of 1964 and Title I of the elementary and Secondary Act of 1965) many social programs to help the poor and the minorities were created. One of the most publicized and well known of these programs was "Operation Head Start", a preschool program for children living in urban and rural poverty areas. Because the federal guidelines called for "maximum feasible participation of residents of the areas and members of the groups served", (U.S. Congress, Senate Committee on Labor and Public Welfare) those who set up local Head Start programs were mandated to include community members both in the planning and operation of such programs.

The involvement of parents in their children's education has always been part and parcel of the early childhood philosophy. The awareness that the professional can learn from the parent, especially in areas where the teacher is not of the same socioeconomic group or cultural or ethnic background, was not a new way of thinking for the well trained early childhood specialist. With young children, it is especially important to make the transition from home to school as positive an experience as possible and close communication between parent and teacher is a necessary ingredient in accomplishing this.

What was new, however, was including community members and parents in the actual organizing of the program and providing employment in the program for many of these same people. The utilization of community persons as school aides, clerical aides, etc. had been a relatively common occurrence in the 1950'ies but it was not until the early 1960'ies that a body of literature emerged calling for a new career concept. This is best described by Pearl and Riessman as

> The creation of jobs normally allotted to highly
> trained professionals or technicians, but which could
> be performed by the unskilled, inexperienced and
> relatively untrained worker; (Pearl and Riessman,
> 1965)

This meant that paraprofessionals not only would be assistants in the classroom under the direction of the professionals, ie. credentialed teachers, but fully functioning members of the team working directly with children and their parents. Implicit in this definition of paraprofessional was the goal of not only providing entry level positions at minimum pay but encouraging upward mobility on the career ladder through on-the-job training, an opportunity to further one's formal education, and ultimately to assume full responsibility as a professional.

Although the term paraprofessional is used to cover the broad category of these workers, they are usually referred to as educational assistants, or assistant teachers or teacher aides. The differences in title may, in some localities, denote differences in educational preparation and/or on-the-job experience.

*Dr. Paula L. Zajan, Professor and Director of the Early Childhood Program, Hostos Community College, City University of New York.

The assistants or aides who were chosen to participate in these programs were usually persons living in the neighborhood or community. Men were encouraged to become assistants and many did so but most of the assistants were women. Assistants were generally part of the predominant ethnic or cultural group of that neighborhood and therefore well aware of the cultural and social resources available in the area. They knew the families of the children who attended the school or center and, in fact, were often the parents of children attending the program.

Although they might be lacking formal education, degrees or credentials, these workers possessed a wealth of practical experiences and community "know-how" that supplemented and enriched the classroom teacher's expertise. The teachers and their assistants were able to form a strong team to help children and their families derive maximum benefit from the school experience.

The concept of utilizing the skills and experiences of community personnel in early childhood programs has become a widely accepted practice in public school early childhood programs, day care centers, Head Start programs, etc. The paraprofessional plays a vital role in these programs and functions on many different levels. Professionals who have never worked as members of such a team may look upon the assistant as just another pair of hands for the teacher. Experience has shown that the assistant is much more than that.

The Role of The Assistant Teacher

The Assistant Teacher is a fully functioning member of the early childhood staff who brings to the program a variety of skills, experiences, and attitudes. His/her duties are many and varied and decidedly not limited to monitorial or housekeeping chores. He/she assists the teacher in setting out the materials to be used during the day and in preparing the room. Before the children arrive, there may be time for the teacher and assistant to discuss the plans for the day or talk over the solution to some problems of the previous day. As the children enter the classroom, the teacher and assistant greet them and their parents giving special attention to those who may want a bit of help or a private word or two. This is also an opportunity to talk briefly with parents.

Throughout the day's activities the aide is there to assist the teacher and children in countless ways. Assistants are encouraged to sit with individuals or small groups of children, encouraging them to talk, listening to them when they do and providing that special bit of individual attention and help so many of the children need. During story time, for example, an assistant may take an individual child or small group aside for their own story or some other activity if they are unable to sit with the larger group. This may be particularly necessary if some of the children do not understand English. In situations where the assistant is bilingual, she may serve a very important function in helping children feel comfortable in a group where they do not speak the dominant language. He/she will also help these children as they begin to learn English, giving them opportunities to speak and helping them with vocabulary and language usage. He/she will also share with the entire group the customs, stories, songs, holiday celebrations of her culture thus enriching the activities for all.

The assistant plays an important role in helping to carry out the everyday routines. He/she will help the children during clean-up time, at snack time and particularly at lunch, preparing the room, and helping the children serve the lunch. Throughout the meal, he/she will sit with a small group to encourage good eating habits and relaxed conversation. It is also a time to reinforce language by discussing the categories of foods, the tastes, smells, colors, shapes, etc. If lunch is followed by a rest period, the assistant will help the teacher and children set out the cots and then assist in quieting the children. At this time, a hug, a word or two, a bit of comfort will go a long way in helping restless or anxious children relax. During outdoor play or neighborhood walks, the assistant is there to aid the teacher in following safety routines and participating in the activities with the children.

In addition to all the daily routines and activities, the assistant must be alert to many other factors such as the health and safety of the children. This would include knowledge of what to do in case of illness, accident or other crises, major or minor. He/she must be aware of the many conditions in the room, on the playground, or on trips in order to provide a healthy and safe learning environment and must work hand in hand with the teacher at all times to anticipate situations that may lead to accidents or unhealthy conditions.

The assistant serves as an important link between the program or school and the parents. Often the assistant may be told information of a confidential nature either by school personnel or by parents which must be used with discretion and good judgment. The assistant may also be in a position where he/she must interpret the program or school's philosophy and goals to the parents. The assistant's role as interpreter of the school to the community, and of the community to the school is a particularly sensitive one.

The effective assistant teacher functions on many different levels throughout the day, each one important in its own way and serving the needs of the program staff, the children, and their families.

The Impact of Community Based Personnel

As in any situation that deals primarily with human relationships and interaction among people with differing responsibilities, attitudes and skills, problems are bound to arise. Some of these are organizational in nature and require better planning and implementation to be solved, but others are more deep-seated and demand attitudinal changes and a deeper feeling of mutual trust.

The whole question of job roles is a thorny one. Although the centers/schools usually have job descriptions, they are not the complete answer as each situation presents its own problems and must, of necessity, provide its own answers. A broad outline of the duties and responsibilities as well as thorough training for both teachers and paraprofessionals, appears to be the best solution. The question of "who does what" is not the only problem. Situations exist where the assistant, more mature, experienced or forceful than the novice or less assertive teacher, may attempt to dominate the team. There can be disagreements as to how children are to be disciplined; whether the aide can initiate activities without discussing or planning with the teacher; how the assistant should talk to the children; whether the aide should discuss children's behavior and progress with the parents; how the aide can be corrected if he/she is excessively late, unwilling to work, disagreeable to the children, etc. For many teachers, the presence of another adult in the room has required an adjustment that some teachers have found difficult to accept.

The paraprofessional worker also faces various problems which are detrimental to his/her morale and effective functioning within the program. One must be aware that the assistant usually has had limited experienee in a work situation and minimal educational background. To thrust such a person into a center/school situation where on-the-job training may be haphazard and to expect from such a person the sensitivity and knowledge required to be effective is unrealistic. Frequently, the talents and skills of paraprofessionals are not used to their fullest and the aide may feel that he/she is expected to do only the more menial tasks. It sometimes happens that the paraprofessional feels equal to the teacher in terms of skills and effectiveness and may resent the low wages and lack of status.

Of course not all problems are present in every center/school nor to the same degree and while there are many variations of the problems mentioned above, there is no doubt that the presence of paraprofessionals has added another dimension to early childhood programs.

If the early childhood program is one that encourages the development of each child, then it is necessary that the adult-child ratio be small, preferably one adult to five children. Young children especially those who are educationally and economically disadvantaged, need the attention of an adult, someone to talk with, someone who will listen to them, someone to encourage and support them. The center/school may be the only place in a child's life where he can receive this attention.

For the teacher, additional "hands" can mean time to give to individuals and small groups of children, opportunity to carry on a fuller, richer program and help in arranging the physical environment. She is able to use her profession-al skills more effectively and assumes a new leadership role within the classroom.

To function effectively, all personnel must work together as members of a team for the benefit of the children. The teacher, as professional leader of this team assumes the responsibility for planning, coordinating and supervising the activities of those who will be working directly with her. She is aware that as she directs these activities, she is training those who work with her in the attitudes, skills and procedures that are necessary to provide an optimum learning environment.

In addition to their contributions to early childhood programs, paraprofessionals can themselves gain from their experiences. For some, it may mean financial security and opportunity for advanced study and preparation for a career; for others, an opportunity to be of service, a direct link between the community and the center/school.

Current Status of Assistant Teachers in Early Childhood Programs

Paraprofessionals have been widely recognized and accepted for their contributions to the field of education. During the past decade the number of teacher assistants has increased dramatically but whether the original goals of the career ladder are being fulfilled is questionable. (Cohen). Although many paraprofessionals who are affiliated with government agencies and/or unions such as the United Federation of Teachers have benefited in terms of higher salaries, better benefits and opportunity for advanced study, their number is small in comparison with the many thousands of teacher assistants who earn minimum hourly wages and have little or no opportunity for further advancement. In addition, the reduction of Federal funds and the budgetary constraints that now obtain in most large urban municipalities have lessened the opportunities for even entry level positions and have, in many cases, eliminated or reduced the programs. It has also led to the practice of filling positions by more credentialed persons who were unable to find jobs equivalent to their preparation and/or experience.

The future of the paraprofessional program depends on factors such as an upsurge in the general economy, political support both nationally and locally and a restructuring of the entire human service field so that they can be more responsive to practitioner and comsumer alike (Cohen).

Conclusion

The past decade has shown that community persons serving as paraprofessionals in early childhood programs have contributed immeasurably to the quality of these programs. Not only have the children, parents and professionals gained but the paraprofessionals themselves. For them, it has been an opportunity to become financially independent, to use their skills in worthwhile and satisfying work and in many instances to continue their own educations and move up the career ladder.

As more women seek employment, the need for expansion of child care service is obvious and compelling. There are men and women who are willing and able to provide these services. It now remains for Federal, state, and local governments together with educational institutions and agencies to provide the means.

BIBLIOGRAPHY

Cohen, Robert. *"New Careers" A Decade Later.* (N.Y.: New York University Education Quarterly, Fall 1976), p. 5, p. 11.

Gattman, Eric and Hendricks, William. *The Other Teacher.* (Belmont, California: Wadsworth Publishing Co., Inc., 1973).

Pearl, Arthur and Riessman, Frank. *New Careers for the Poor.* (N.Y.: The Macmillan Company, 1973).

U.S. Congress, Senate, Committee on Labor and Public Welfare, *The Economic Opportunity Act of 1964.* A compilation of Materials Relevant to S2642 Prepared for the Select Sub-Committee on Poverty (Washington: Government Printing Office, 1964), Title I, Part A, Section 202 (3).

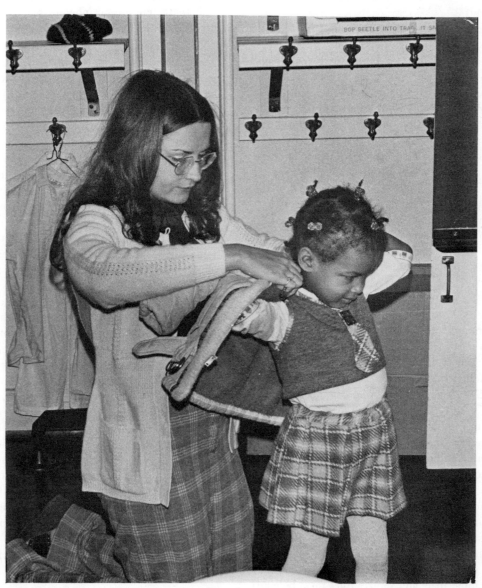

American Federation of Teachers

Chapter 69

The Need for More Male Early Childhood Teachers

Bruce R. Shames*

"What do you do for a living?" asks a new acquaintance.
"I'm a teacher," answers the male nursery school teacher.
"What do you teach?"
"I teach nursery school."
"You mean you teach such young children?" (Said in a disbelieving way)
"Yes." (feeling embarrassed and inadequate)

This is the scenario that often occurs with male early childhood teachers and provides some insight into why there are so few men in this field. There is a subtle yet clearly communicated attitude on the part of many people in our society that men who go into early childhood education are somewhat peculiar and this is manifested in numerous myths that denigrate this profession and the people in it, particularly males. First of all, it is believed that caring for young children is primarily within the province and scope of the woman's function in society and hence, any man who does this is considered strange. Secondly, nursery school teachers get paid very little and since it is believed that it is the man's role to be the family bread-winner, a man, by going into this profession and receiving very low pay, must have made this occupational choice due to the fact that he probably could not succeed in other more "male" oriented and socially acceptable positions. In addition, the amount of monetary compensation is one measure of the level of status that our society gives to various occupations and it is apparent, when using this criterion, early childhood education is considered quite low. George Bernard Shaw's saying, "He who can, does; he who cannot, teaches," aptly describes our society's attitude toward teachers in general and holds doubly true for male early childhood teachers. The low pay given to nursery school teachers in conjunction with society's myths and attitudes that accord such low status to men in this field accounts for so few men in early childhood education. This is very unfortunate for there should be more men teaching young children.

Although most educators recognize the need for more early childhood teachers it is interesting that two divergent philosophies are used to support this goal. Some feel that separate, conventional male and female roles must be clarified to children (Mathew, pp. 532-3) while others believe that we should indicate to children that there should not be separate sex roles (Weistein, p. 143). Since it is through identification with both adult males and females that children learn sex roles or lack of these roles (Taylor, p. 1220) more male contact with young children will either reinforce conventional sex roles by providing a male example or indicate that there are no inherent sex roles since one sex can function in the traditional role of the other.

Regardless of the social philosophy used to justify the need for more male early childhood teachers there is a valid psychological reason. For our society to produce adequately functioning adults young children (both boys and girls) must learn to interact with men and women. Our society's family structure is so varied that it is hard to find a typical pattern. This results in classrooms that are filled with children who live with only one parent in comparison to the other because of employment requirements or have limited adult-child interaction in general leaving much of this necessary contact to the schools which provide predominantly female-child interaction for young children. Numerous other patterns that also cause many children to receive an imbalance in their contact with adult males and females are apparent. Children live and are going to live in a society that is populated with half males and half females and in order to learn to deal successfully in such a milieu and have satisfying interpersonal relationships they should begin by dealing with both sexes from the beginning. Whether they are to learn conventional sex roles or lack of sex roles is a matter of philosophy. However, children should have interaction with both men and women if they are to become psychologically healthy (Hetherington, p. 84). and having this interaction as young children will increase their chances of leading successful and satisfying lives as adults.

Concerning society's myths and derogatory attitudes towards male early childhood teachers a vicious cycle has developed that counters a tendency that may encourage more men to enter this profession. If there were an increase in the amount of male early childhood teachers the more it would become a socially acceptable profession for males for once something becomes more ordinary it naturally becomes less strange. However, the fact that it is

*Bruce R. Shames, Assistant Principal at P.S. 120, Queens, New York City Board of Education.

considered odd for males to be in this profession is a discouraging influence thereby lessening the likelihood that more males will enter and hence make it more acceptable. This cycle should and can be broken. The negative attitudes of society toward male early childhood teachers are probably breaking down for people appear more accepting of the unconventional in general (Bardwick, p. 156). But there is no doubt that the pace of change in this area is slow and only economic factors can hasten it.

Monetary gain, being a powerful motivator in our society, would encourage more men to overcome these denegrating attitudes on the part of the society and break the cycle. In addition, there is no just reason for nursery school teachers to get paid less than other teachers for the position is certainly as important and takes just as much skill as teaching older children.

Traditional sex roles that are still predominant at present in our society foster the belief that women are not primarily the economic supporters of the family and are to be dependent upon their husbands in this regard (Gove, p. 52). In addition the sex role beliefs determine that care of young children is in the province of the woman's role. The linking of these two traditional sex role tenets together result in early childhood educators receiving very low pay. This is unjust and the salaries should be increased not only to encourage more men to enter the profession or so that these men can support their families (it may be just as important for women to support their families— Seaman, pp. 286-7) but because early childhood educators warrant it due to the nature of their occupation. The women in the field are being exploited and it is up to the profession to work toward righting this injustice. A beneficial side effect of justice in this area would be the entrance of more men into the field.

The profession and the people in it are worth more to our society than they are paid. Early childhood education is critical, especially now, with our family patterns weakening and in a state of change (Toffler, p. 238). The arguments made for having more male nursery school teachers due to these pattern changes are just as cogent for emphasizing early childhood ecucation in general. Previously, "typical" patterns involving the nuclear or more extended families fulfilled the role of providing early childhood education. But with more and more of these breaking down the functioning of schools in this area is all the more important. There is general acceptance now that early education is not only necessary for children of poverty so that they can overcome disadvantages but also for the "shortchanged" middle income children (National School Public Relations Association, P. 214). Early childhood education involves nurturing human beings at a crucial time in their development (Akers, p. 3). The importance of early development as it influences the future is generally accepted (Shane, pp. 367-90) and it is probably the most formative and hence, most important years as far as education is concerned

(Dottrens, p. 156). It is up to professional organizations to inform the public of this and lobby politically to place early childhood education as a national priority. Only then will more money be appropriated, pay raised, more status accorded and our young children get the teachers they deserve—including more men.

NOTES

[1] A personal survey of nursery school teaching salaries in the New York City area by the author supports an unpublished survey by Jane Schwertfeger (Ann Arbor: University of Michigan School of Education, 1972) which indicates the very low salaries paid to full-time nursery school teachers—$3,000 to $7,000 per year with most getting below $5,000.

BIBLIOGRAPHY

Akers, Merton E. "Prologue: The Why of Early Childhood Education." In *Early Childhood Education, The 71st Yearbook of the National Society for The Study of Education, Part II.* edited by Ira J. Gordon. Chicago: National Society for the Study of Education, 1972, pp. 1-12.

Bardwick, Judith N. and Elizabeth Donavan. "Ambivalence: The Socialization of Women." In *Women in a Sexist Society*, edited by Vivian Gornick and Barbara K. Moran. New York: Basic Books, Inc., 1971, pp. 147-57.

Dottrens, Robert. *Primary School Curriculum.* France: UNESCO, 1962.

Gove, Walter R. and Jeannette F. Tudor. "Adult Sex Roles and Mental Illness." In *Changing Women in a Changing Society*, edited by Joan Huber. Chicago: University of Chicago Press, 1973, pp. 50-73.

Greer, Germaine. *The Female Eunich.* New York: McGraw-Hill Book Co., 1971.

Hetherington, Eileen Mavis. "Personality Development." In *Encyclopedia of Education, Vol. 7.* New York: Growell-Collier Education Corp., 1971, pp. 76-86.

Mathew, Esther R. "Occupational Counseling for Women." In *Encyclopedia of Education, Vol 2.* New York: Growell-Collier Education Corp., 1971, pp. 532-40.

National School Pubic Relations Association. *Education, USA*, Vol. 17, No. 37 (May 12,1975). Washington, D.C.: National School Public Relations Association.

Schwertfeger, Jane. Unpublished survey. Ann Arbor: University of Michigan, School of Education, 1972.

Seaman, Barbara. *Free and Female.* Greenwhich, Conn.: Fawcett Pub., Inc., 1972.

Shane, Harold G. "Implications of Early Childhood Education for Lifelong Learning." In *Early Childhood Education, the 71st Yearbook of the National Society for the Study of Education, Part II*, edited be Ira J. Gordon. Chicago: National Society for the Study of Education, 1972, pp. 367-90.

Taylor, Lorna E. "Sex Differences." In *Encyclopedia of Educational Research, 4th Edition*, edited by Robert

L. Ebel. New York: Macmillan and Co., 1969, pp. 1217-1221.

Toffler, Alvin. *Future Shock.* New York: Bantam Books, 1970.

Weisstein, Naomi. "Psychology Constructs the Female." In *Women in Sexist Society*, edited by Vivian Gornick and Barbara K. Moran. New York: Basic Books, Inc., 1971, pp. 133-46.

Superintendent Alfred Melov, NYC School Board 15

Chapter 70

The Role of the Manager
of Early Childhood Programs

Alicia I. Pagano*

Introduction

The phenomenal growth and sophistication of early childhood programs in the past decade has brought about the emergence of a new level of organizational management—the manager of early childhood programs. This management position has evolved as a result of the realization of the importance of the early years for child development based on new research and knowledge, the need for quality day care programs for children of working parents, and open public support for a variety of preschool programs. Some of the questions that have arisen as a result of this new professional field are as follows: What is the role of the manager of these programs? Does the management of early childhood programs require special expertise? Is the management of early education and child care different from the management of other levels of education? Do programs under varying auspices (profit and nonprofit) require different managerial skills? What are the areas of management for these programs? Does this position require interdisciplinary knowledge with expertise in child development and early learning as well as in management? What are the directions for the future of managers and administrators of early childhood programs? Concerned educators, parents, medical and social workers are asking these questions.

A clearer definition of the role of the director of these programs is essential if early childhood programs are to build upon previous and current research relating to child development and to management theory for future programs of improved quality.

History of Early Childhood Program Management

Formal early childhood programs began almost 200 years ago as women and children were beginning to work in factories and as the changes in knowledge of child education and health brought about an emphasis upon childhood as a distinct and important time in an individual's life. This concern for specialized care of children within institutional structures occurred concurrently with the development of large industrial corporations and the building of an organizational society (Hays, 1972) as well as the beginnings of the professionalization of management. "New institutions for the care and education of young children developed rapidly during the early decades of the Nineteenth Century, both in England and on the continent" (Forest, 1927, p. 62).

Robert Owen, a British industrialist and management theoretician, was one of the first individuals to establish *infant schools* for the education of preschool children. As the manager of the New Lanark Cotton Spinning Mills in Scotland, he saw many children of the employees and he was concerned with the position of these children whose "parent's resources were limited and whose mothers worked" (Forest, 1927, p. 68). He gave impetus to the Infant School Movement in the 1880's which spread to England, Europe, and the United States. Infant schools were organized to assist the family in the tasks of educating their children. The schools were especially directed to meet the needs of the poor. They included physical, social, moral, religious, and intellectual training.

The beginning of the objective study of young children by John Comenius, John Locke, and Jean Jacques Rousseau and others brought about a philosophy of education directing attention to child development. The work of Rousseau preceded Pestalozzi's and Froebel's effort to develop educational theory for young children and to structure organized preschool programs based on theory.

The first organization of early childhood education, the *kindergarten*, had its beginning with Froebel who is usually considered the "father of the kindergarten". Froebel's institutions were small and informal. His management plan included toys and games that had spiritual as well as educational implications. Although many people criticized his mystical outlook, his materials were used by many and his organizational method was the foundation for the Kindergarten Movement. In America, the first kindergarten for English-speaking children was started in Boston in 1860 by Miss Elizabeth Peabody. Miss Peabody recognized her need for further training to manage a kindergarten and she went abroad in 1867 to study the kindergarten system and Froebel's education principles. In 1873, under the leadership of Miss Susan Blow and Dr. W.T.

*Dr. Alicia L. Pagano, Assistant Professor, Division of Teacher Education, Medgar Evers College, CUNY.

Harris, the kindergarten became part of the public school system in St. Louis. As the kindergarten movement grew, additional training for leadership was considered essential. Miss Patty Smith Hill became recognized as one of the outstanding educators training kindergarten teachers (Hewes, 1976). Historically, kindergarten organizations have had aims that have been primarily educational under public, philanthropic and private sponshorship.

Day care programs for young children are an outgrowth of the concept of the infant schools in England. Through the years, their services have changed according to societal needs and on the basis of new knowledge about children's growth and development. The first day nursery in the United States, a precursor of today's day care centers, was opened in 1854 in connection with New York Nursery and Child's Hospital of New York City (Forest, 1927). The purpose of this nursery was the care of children of working mothers. Day care organizations have flourished during times of national need and diminished in number at the end of periods of national crisis. These organizations were prevalent at the turn of the century in many cities. The Settlement Houses in New York City and other communities administered child care programs as part of their services to the immigrants (Fein and Clarke-Stewart, 1973). Day care organizations grew during the depression years of the 1930's with government sponsorship to provide employment and to care for children of families in need (Hymes, 1975). Again, during World War II, day care centers were organized to care for children of mothers working in war plants (Lazar and Rosenberg, 1971). These programs were becoming more sophisticated and offered care and education based on the technologies of the day. One of the outstanding programs of this era was managed by the Kaiser shipbuilding corporation. It was operated on a 24-hour basis and met the needs of both the children and the parents employed in the plant. After the war, most of these programs ceased to operate. In the 1960's, day care organizations began to increase in numbers again because of social concerns for children of working mothers and renewed interest in the importance of early childhood for broader social participation of the poor in society. Project Headstart is an example of a program inaugurated by the federal government because of a recognition of "responsibility for the inequalities of opportunity among pre-school children" (J. McVicker Hunt, 1971). Day care programs are managed by welfare, proprietary, corporations, colleges, churches, franchises, and other organizations. While the goals of day care centers have tended toward physical care and safety, many programs are now directed toward total development of the child.

Nursery schools are the most recent organization for early childhood in the United States. They were first organized after the turn of the Century. They drew on the knowledge of the progressive kindergarten movement and were based upon scientific interest in child development

and mental hygiene. They have had a distinctively educational aim which has been broader than kindergarten in that it included every phase of education rather than primarily promoting the children's cognitive development. Nursery schools have emphasized a close relation to the home and parent education in "development of the child in courses of study and intense observation of him at home and in school" (Fein and Clarke-Stewart, 1973). Individual nursery schools vary widely in their goals and methodology. Several types of nursery schools include the research centers to increase knowledge about children, privately owned organizations, and philanthropic centers. Today some pre-kindergarten programs in public schools have goals and programs similar to nursery schools.

During the beginning years of the growth of child care and child education organizations, little concern was given to the management aspects of the programs. The individual organizations were small, relationships with the broader society were not complex, and management problems were not recognized as significant. Rather, the leaders began with the knowledge and skills in a educational discipline and concentrated upon its rapidly growing knowledge base. These dominant concerns were the physical and education programs leading to child development goals.

However, as society became more complex, organization and management theory in both business and the public sector developed into a separate field of study. These new managerial studies, begun around the turn of the century, made it possible to look at complex organizations in a dynamic society and to determine effective methods for administering them. Knowledge of management for large, private corporations and public institutions also included the management of education systems. More recently, the interest in quality education and the desire for accountability in early childhood programs requires that management theory and practices be consciously applied to early childhood programs.

Early childhood programs as complex organizations have come of age in our society. They are interrelated with numerous other organizations through certification procedures, funding, and provision of services (Lazar, 1971). These organizations need appropriate and skillful management. Effective leadership will determine the ability of these organizations to meet their goals and to survive as useful institutions in our society. Therefore, it is important to define the role of the manager or director in these diverse programs and to describe responsibilities and necessary skills in a variety of settings.

Definition of a Manager

Management is a process of coordinating human and material resources toward the accomplishment of an objective (Kast and Rosenzweig, 1970). It is the responsiblity of a manager to bring together the necessary resources of an organization so the goal of the organization can be reached with the greatest efficiency. Directors and administrators of early childhood programs are actually managers, although they are sometimes identified as "early childhood educators" (Almy, 1975, p. 3). They are responsible for making certain the people in the organization are operating in the most effective way to meet personal goals within the constraints of organizational objectives. Directors are also responsible for making certain the material resources are used advantageously in the organization. The materials resources include the finances, the building, the equipment, and the teaching materials in the classroom.

Early childhood organizations are service oriented. That is, they provide personal and social service rather than produce a product as does the automotive industry or a shoe factory. Although the specific services of the organizations vary, the general service provided is directed toward quality care and/or quality child development. In addition, early childhood organizations are labor intensive. This means that they use people to meet the goals of the organization rather than using a large amount of capital or technical equipment. Although teachers use educational technology, and doctors, dentists, and other medical specialists rely on sophisticated machines for diagnosis and treatment, the primary means for delivering quality child care is through human endeavor.

The organizational structure of early childhood programs has great variation as does the type of funding for these programs. This diversity results in several levels of management that make it difficult to define the scope of responsibility for leadership. In small, privately-owned organizations the manager is completely responsible for the program. However, in most organizations, the manager is responsible to a board of directors, a board of education, or a corporate manager. Many types of early childhood programs exist today under the varying auspices and organizational form. Some are for profit and others are nonprofit. Some programs exist as a subsystem of a larger organization. For example, day care centers in large corporations. Public programs under the sponsorship of federal, state, and local governments include Head Start, day care, preschool, kindergartens in public schools, and special programs affiliated with social services and health care. In addition, other nonprofit programs operate as cooperatives, in connection with colleges or hospitals, or as part of church organizations. The entrepreneurial programs are investor owned and operate for profit. These proprietary programs include a variety of day care and nursery schools ranging from tiny organizations individually operated in an owner's home to large corporations with franchises throughout the United States and abroad. All these types of organizations require management. The question then arises as to whether or not the management skills are the same for all of these organizations. Let us begin to answer this question by looking at the areas of management identifiable in all programs.

The following areas for management expertise are required in all early childhood programs:
1. Programming
2. Planning budgets
3. Personnel direction
4. Parent involvement
5. Politics and public relations

These are the FIVE P's of management for early childhood programs. The manager or director must apply management functions of setting objectives, directing, and evaluating in each of these five areas. A focus on this level of management will provide an insight into early childhood management. As we establish the role of the center director in each of the five areas essential managing an early childhood program we will also determine the expertise required to accomplish the related tasks.

Programming

The program of an early childhood organization is the central service the organization offers to the clients or users. This includes the education curriculum as well as the health and social services. Each of these activities must be planned in advance and carefully coordinated to meet the needs of the children and their families. A good program is based upon child development theory and will be designed to provide experiences that promote intellectual, emotional, social, and physical growth and development. As stated earlier, the goals of programs for young children are varied. "The diversity of programs encompassed in early childhood education reflects new knowledge of the early years and a variety of attempts to apply that knowledge effectively" (Almay, 1975, p. 3). Some programs place first priority on the safety and physical well-being of the children. Others give major emphasis to intellectual development and academic skills. Many programs seek to provide a comprehensive service with care in all of the above areas. Usually, the programs reflect the needs of the children and the type of care required to supplement the care provided by the family.

The goals of an early childhood organization are determined and stated at the time the organization begins operation. However, all organizations are dynamic and the program will change to reflect new research on child development, new techniques for child care, the increase or decrease in financial resources, and changing needs in the community.

The director is responsible for implementing the current program. To do this, the director may delegate responsibilities to other persons within the organization. For example, the education program may be placed under the jurisdiction of an educational director. The services of medical care will be carried out by a nurse, physician or other professional. In most commercially operated franchises, the curriculum focus and general program suggestions are mailed to each individual organization on a monthly basis. The manager is responsible for planning staff meetings and directing the teaching staff to implement this curriculum. In a public school program the curriculum areas are specified in the curriculum guide and the administrator oversees the teaching according to the guide.

The center director is responsible for operating an on-going program for children in a manner that contributes to their growth and development and is in accordance with the goals of the program. This includes maintaining a physical environment that conforms to government and agency standards of safety and sanitation.

The director often assists, and in many organizations is responsible for, planning future programs as well as implementing the current program. Program planning generally occurs on an annual basis in conjunction with planning the budget. In addition, evaluation procedures for assessing the effectiveness of the program are the responsibility of the director (DHEW Publication No. OCD 73-20, 1971).

The variety of programs indicates that the manager will have varying responsibility for planning and implementing programs and for recommending changes within the program guidelines. However, all programs have a commonality. That is, the role of the manager is to coordinate the resources in the organization to implement the program goals. In order to carry out these responsibilities, the manager of an early childhood program must have depth knowledge of both child development and management procedures. The director needs background knowledge of child psychology and learning theory in order to plan programs. It is important that the director know how children learn and grow and to be cognizant of methods for planning optimum learning environments to facilitate daily activities. The director must be able to supervise other people and to get them to work together harmoniously. Some people appear to have these skills intuitively; but new knowledge in management theory is necessary for efficient management of quality programs in today's complex and rapidly changing society. The skills needed to manage the program require interdisciplinary knowledge (Almy, 1975) of the social sciences and their applications for effective program development and administration.

Planning Budgets

Financial stability is one of the most pressing problems in the operation of an early childhood program. The finest ideas and the best intentions to provide a quality program for young children will be meaningless without a firm, realistic fiscal basis. In all organizations financial viability is essential to smooth and continued operations. Many small businesses begin without a good understanding of budgets and finances only to discontinue within one or two years for lack of funds. The role of the manager often included the complexities of planning an annual budget as well as operating on the basis of this budget.

A budget is one type of statement of the program of an organization. It defines the goals in monetary terms and it provides a guideline for management during the year for which it has been designed. A budget is both a managerial planning and control tool. Sophisticated technologies for planning cost-effective programs to determine the best use of funds and the amount of funding required to operate an organization at a specified level are available today. Such techniques as break-even analysis can assist the manager in determining the fee basis or the number of children a center can effectively serve. Effective utilization of resources is important, especially in a decade of competing choices for available funds. Larger cities are taking action to measure output through financial accountability in day care programs that use public funding. Management options must be evaluated against the goals of the organization and the standards of quality care. One of the problems in predicting costs is the analysis of cost per child enrolled with the cost per child attendance. The profit seeking organizations do not leave this figure to chance. They have calculated and clearly specified a cost per child in attendance so the director can analyze cost in daily and monthly figures. Both profit and nonprofit organizations must plan and follow a budget. The not-for-profit corporation must be able to live within the budget determined by grants, gifts, and public allocations. The profit organization must be able to obtain operating expenses, capital expenses, and a reasonable profit through fees.

The managerial skills for budgeting are largely in the area of finance and accounting. Some marketing skills are also desirable for managing public relations and advertisement of the program.

Personnel Direction

The staff of the early childhood program is the foundation for the operation. All early childhood programs are organizations of high human intensity rather than capital or machine intensity. It is the knowledge and the skills and the cooperative efforts of the staff that makes the program successful. The manager's skills in personnel direction are very important. Explicit and relevant recruitment, selection and hiring policies are the first steps in ensuring a good program. Staff must be hired in accordance with the needs of the program and the skills of the current personnel. The goals of the individual staff members will need to be in line with the goals of the organization or there will be a high turnover, and dissatisfaction among employees will result. Personnel conflicts will cause discontinuities, unsatisfactory experiences for the children, and a program that is less than effective.

In addition to hiring new staff, the manager is also responsible for giving direction to present employees to promote productivity based upon skills and to ensure continued professional and personal development. To do this, the manager must know the abilities of the staff, their current activities and their future goals.

Good communication within the organization is important. Communication patterns are usually the result of the leadership style of the manager. If the director is open and democratic in interactions with the staff, there is usually excellent communication between staff members and a high level of feedback to the director. Under these conditions, the manager can be aware of the continuity of the program and will be prepared to make the best decisions for the future.

Evaluation of the staff in terms of the goals of the organization is one of the responsibilities of the manager. Evaluation can provide an opportunity for staff development and a reassessment of the goals of the individual within the context of the goals of the organization. Evaluation provides an opportunity for assessing and encouraging the growth of each and all staff members.

The skills necessary for leadership and direction of personnel include understanding of human relations, motivation in life and the work place, styles of leadership and a broad knowledge of organization requirements for providing quality service for children and their families.

Parent Involvement

The Constitution of the United States places the responsibility of education at the State level so local communities will have the dominant voice in the education of their children. Throughout the history of the United States, parents have exercised the right and the responsibility to be involved in programs affecting their children. Bronfenbrenner (1973) stated that the family is still considered the most important influence on the small child. The importance of the family is paramount in American child care and education.

Early childhood programs have always been recognized as a supplement to, and not a replacement for, family care and education. This holds for public kindergartens and for nursery schools of a proprietary nature as well as comprehensive day care programs supported by public funds. Parent involvement ranges from the minimal responsibility of making a choice of merely enrolling the child to an active parent participating in formulating policy and program operation. Ira Gordon (1970) lists six levels of parent involvement in early childhood programs:

1. Parents as an audience (passive role—conferences, newsletters, etc.)
2. Parents as a reference (active role—insights and perspectives on their child)
3. Parents as the teacher of the child
4. Parents as volunteers in the classroom

5. Parents as trained/paid aides
6. Parents as participants in the decision-making process

The responsibility of the manager of the early childhood programs varies greatly in the area of parent involvement. In a nonprofit day care program such as Headstart, parent involvement is a requirement by legislation, and parents are actively encouraged to participate in the decision making process and in other levels of operation. The director of these programs works closely with the parents to promote high levels of interaction in health, education, and social services of the center.

In the proprietary organizations, parent involvement is generally within the range of levels one and two of Gordon's scale. The manager of these programs is more like a mediator who seeks to keep open communications between the staff of the center and the parents. This provides an exchange of information which affects the child's development and the smooth operation of the organization. Many managers of proprietary organizations seek to increase parental involvement because they recognize its value for the child and for the parent-child relationship. They try to motivate parents through written information, suggestions for parent-child activities at home based on experiences in the center, educational films, and regular parent meetings.

To successfully work with parents, the manager requires a knowledge of appropriate educational materials and activities for parents, creative methods to motivate parents toward involvement, and a patient attitude to understand the many conflicting pressures of society that cause parents stress.

Politics and Public Relations

Early childhood organizations exist in a complex and changing society. Many interacts that affect the operation of the organization take place outside the center. For example, licensing for operating early childhood education programs and for day care programs is a function of the state and some local levels of government. Financing of many programs are the result of legislation. Early childhood organizations purchase materials from companies in the communities in which they operate. Medical and social organizations provide services for children and their families. The role of the manager in relating to the external environment is one of coordinating the resources of the larger community with the resources of the early childhood organization.

Since early childhood programs are varied and have a multiplicity of settings and objectives, it is often necessary to explain the importance of early childhood and the programs for the education and care of young children. The importance of these programs is just gaining recognition and their purpose and content need to be outlined. This activity may be considered political action. The community boards of health and social services can be encouraged to cooperate in the assistance of young children's programs. Often beneficial legislation results from political actions of parents, educators and other professionals concerned with the development of young children.

The essential managerial skills are a political awareness, knowledge of legislation that affects children and communities plus some marketing and community relations skills.

Conclusions

The well-trained manager of early childhood programs is emerging into an identifiable professional position with recognizable roles, tasks, and skills necessary for the position. These competencies are based upon interdisciplinary knowledge and skills. They are grounded in child psychology and learning theory as well as management theory. As society seeks to refine early childhood programs and obtain a greater degree of accountability in the management of programs and budgets, the managerial skills are becoming more essential. People who are planning to work in this profession may look forward to a dual preparation similar to the requirements for elementary school principals and other administrators in public education positions. Alert and ambitious students are enrolling at the universities and colleges that are designing curriculums to meet the requirements for this emerging position.

Bibliography

Almy, M. *The Early Childhood Educator at Work*. New York: McGraw-Hill Book Company, 1975.

Avrin, C. and G. Sassen. *Corporations and Child Care*. Cambridge, Mass.: Women's Research Action Project, 1974.

Boguslawski, D. *Guide for Establishing and Operating Day Care Centers for Young Children*. New York: Child Welfare League of America, Inc. 1966.

Bronfenbrenner, U. In appearance before Subcommittee on Children and Youth of Senate Labor and Public Welfare Committee as reported in *Report of Pre-School Education*, October 3, 1973, pp. 3-6.

Child Welfare League of America. *Standards for Day Care Service*. New York, 1969.

Fein, G. and A. Clarke-Stewart. *Day Care in Context*. New York: John Wiley & Sons, 1973.

Forest, I. Preschool Education: *A Historical and Critical Study*. New York: The Macmillan Company, 1927.

Gordon, I. Developing Parent Power, In *Critical Issues in Research Related to Disadvantaged Children*, edited by E. Grotberg. Princeton, N.J.: Educational Testing Service, 1969a.

Hays, S.P. The New Organizational Society. *In Building the Organizational Society*, edited by Jerry Israel. New York: The Free Press, 1972.

Hewes, D. Patty Smith Hill: Pioneer for Young Children. In *Young Children*. May, 1976.

Hunt, J.M. Foreword. *In Day Care: Resources for Decisions*, edited by E. Grotberg. Washington: Superintendent of Documents, OEO Pamplet 6106-1, 1971.

Hymes, J.L. *Early Childhood Education: An Introduction to the Profession*. Washington: The National Association for the Education of Young Children, 1975.

Kast, F. and Rosenzweig, J. *Organization and Management: A Systems Approach*. New York: McGraw-Hill Book Company, 1970.

Lazar, I. Delivery Systems. In *Day Care: Resources for Decisions*, edited by E. Grotberg. Washington: Superintendent of Documents, OEO Pamphlet 6106-1, 1971.

Lazar I. and N. Rosenberg. Day Care in America. In *Day Care: Resources for Decisions*, edited by E. Grotberg. Washington: Superintendent of Documents, OEO Pamphlet 6106-1, 1971.

Office of Child Development. *Day Care Administration*, DHEW Publication No. (OCE) 73-20, 1971.

Spodek, B. *Teaching in the Early Years*. Englewood Cliffs, N.J.: Prentice-Hall, 1972.

Stevens, J. and E. King. *Administering Early Childhood Education Programs*. Boston: Little, Brown and Company, 1976.

Pagano, A.L. Art is Young. *Day Care and Early Education*, April, 1975.

Section IX

International Early Childhood Education Programs

Introduction by Carl Erdberg*

Currently, there is a great deal of interest in early childhood education in the United States; perhaps more than at any time in our history. Early childhood education abroad traditionally has had a considerable measure of input in structuring philosophy and methodology in our country; e.g. the work of a Pestalozzi, a Montessori, or a Piaget.

The attempt to build a Great Society in our country in recent years had as one of its pillars the Headstart program. A major purpose of the aptly named Headstart was to do just that; namely to give educationally disadvantaged young children a proper and much-needed foundation for educational success in their later schooling.

There are other examples in the United States of newer areas of interest in child welfare; e.g. child advocacy organizations, national movements to prevent child abuse, and new legislation to protect children. Perhaps we shall see proposed a Child Rights Amendment to the Constitution, as we are now witnessing with the E.R.A. for women.

The concept of zero population growth will, no doubt, be a factor in increasing interest in early childhood education as an area for which future teachers will train. As the number of K-12 students diminishes, the concept of Educare, which provides education "from cradle to the grave," will blossom.

The relationship of proper nutrition to learning receptivity will also be a factor in turning to early childhood (even prenatal) education, to help us give a proper foundation to the future adolescents and adults of our nation.

Without doubt, the advancement of women toward their rightful places in society may mean an expansion of early childhood education as large numbers of women seek part-time or full-time employment to develop their careers.

With such expansion envisaged it makes a great deal of sense to study early childhood programs abroad to take notice of the positive elements we can import to our shores; e.g. Moral Education, not necessarily mainland China's style, but a curriculum tailored to include the finest elements of the thinking of Kohlberg and Simon; public nursery education after close study of the Kibbutz approach, in addition to outstanding nursery school programs in other countries; Persky's statement that most international day-care programs are universal and non-means tested; his statement that early education is under the aegis of the education department rather than the health or welfare department as is frequently the case in the United States. Rederer's insightful statement that a child is "answered attentively each time he tries to say something in early childhood classes in the Soviet Union"; Davidson's pointing out that Scandinavia tries to recruit men, as well as women, to teach the youngest school children. She also tells us that parents are paid two days salary if they miss work to attend school conferences. The fact that pregnant mothers receive prenatal care and free hospital delivery service is also a matter worth mentioning, as is the mainstreaming which takes place for children in need of special education in Scandinavia.

For bilingual practitioners it might be worth a trip to Denmark—the first country to organize a public education system—to see how their system operates.

A final word about the concern for happiness in school as a major aim of early childhood educationists in the Soviet Union. Shouldn't that be a universal major aim in our early childhood classes, as well?

In regard to the Soviet Union, an issue which might be debatable is that of a drive to structure curriculum along cognitive lines at a rather early age. In Israel, the matter of multi-age groups in some of the Kibbutzim does not fit in easily with Piagetian chronological invariance.

Thus, there is much food for thought in the ensuing articles. A personal visit on the part of each of us involved would even be more advantageous.

*Dr. Carl Erdberg, Professor, Department of Administration and Supervision, Pace University.

Chapter 71

The Kibbutz: An Educational Model for Early Childhood Development Programs

Leonard H. Golubchick *

Group care for young children is one of the United States' most pressing needs. As great numbers of women enter the labor force and seek to combine family life with a career, it is evident that a national policy with clearcut guidelines must be established. At present a wide variety of programs exist and their philosophies, goals, curriculum, staffing patterns, credentialing of personnel, and health and safety standards are as different as the various forms of group care. Such programs should be under the jurisdiction of the public schools with professionally trained teachers, paraprofessionals, and administrators. A major advantage of early childhood development programs will be the alleviation of family circumstances which cause deprivation in the child and promote full cognitive growth and socialization.

The Kibbutz (Israeli communal farms) exemplifies the kind of programs and techniques which can be utilized in the formation and organization of early childhood developmental programs in the United States. It is on the Kibbutz where the school is a miniature of Kibbutz society; it is here where the early childhood program is not separated from the education system and which is staffed by trained teachers, administrators, and nurses (*Metapelots*).

Bruno Bettelheim (1969) and Peter Neubauer (1965) suggest that the Kibbutz has important implications for theories of Human Development; and that, in studying the Kibbutz we can learn how to formulate methods of community care programs for young children. This becomes decisive in terms of developing all day community child care centers particularly for working mothers and as a potential method for freeing welfare mothers so that they might find employment. The Kibbutz could also give us insights into dealing with the disadvantaged child by mitigating the circumstances which cause this problem.

In order to understand the Kibbutz early childhood program it is vital to understand what is a Kibbutz.

The Kibbutz is a communal agricultural society which is based upon Marxian Socialism. The Kibbutz is a voluntary society in which all property is communally owned. Most Kibbutzim also engage in industrial production. Today there are over 250 Kibbutzim which have a total population of approximately 100,000 or about 4% of the Israeli population. The Kibbutz with the Moshave (cooperative farms where the means of production are owned communally but in which there is private enterprise) form the backbone of Israeli agriculture. The Kibbutz movement has had an impact on every aspect of life in Israel. For example, the choice of where to establish a new Kibbutz is concerned with the question of national security and policy over and above its economic or personal convenience. Due to historical circumstances there are three major Kibbutz federations which are aligned to different political parties. There is a fourth Kibbutz movement composed of members who are orthodox in terms of religion.

Moreover, the Kibbutz of today is heterogeneous in terms of age, family status, and social groups and those who come at different times of its development from varying backgrounds. The Kibbutz has governmental support and maintains a standard of living comparable to that of urban workers.

Structure of the Kibbutz

The number of Kibbutz members varies from 150-500 (a few have as many as 2,000). In addition to members, the Kibbutz population consists of member's children, their elderly parents, as well as various youth groups which receive training on the Kibbutz.

The Kibbutz members live in cottages consisting of one to two rooms which also contain a small kitchen. Single persons live in one room flats and children live with their peers in children cottages. There is a communal dining hall for main meals and there is a communal social hall as well as a theatre.

The Kibbutz is a democratic community based upon the principles of equality, labor, collectivism, responsibility, self-sacrifice, and voluntarism. Decisions involving all matters of Kibbutz life are made by a majority vote of Kibbutz members (as in New England Town Meetings). The general assembly of Kibbutzniks is the "supreme body of the Kibbutz". The members elect office holders who are responsible to them and who are responsive to them. The Secretariat coordinates all economic and

*Dr. Leonard H. Golubchick, President of the National Doctorate Association; Chairman of the Board, Doctorate Association of New York Educators; Administrator, New York City Public Schools.

social activities. The Secretariat is the main committee which heads all other committees. The Secretariat also resolves all problems which cannot be settled by committees.

Every Kibbutznik works in a branch of the Kibbutz. There is a work committee which is responsible for the scheduling and rotation of positions at each branch. There are no bosses since Kibbutzniks work out of responsibility. Workers in each branch ascertain the needs of each branch and plan for the following year. There is a branch manager who is elected by the workers each year. He is responsible for the functioning of the branch and to see that equipment is maintained. Today, the branch manager usually has special training in the area of the Kibbutz they manage.

The Kibbutz maintains a rich cultural life and is extremely culture conscious; in fact, the Kibbutz has been called an "island of culture". The Kibbutz maintains sizeable libraries, discussion groups, choirs, orchestras and art and photographic exhibits. The Kibbutz publishes literary journals, several newspapers and owns publishing houses. Some of the best known Israeli artists and writers are Kibbutz members.

The Kibbutz movement or Kibbutz federations maintain banking enterprises, factories, trucking and food processing corporations and teacher-training institutes.

Kibbutz Education

"Collective Education" is the term used by the Kibbutz to refer to its method of child rearing. Collective education or communal child rearing developed within the context of the overall Kibbutz ideology. A basic tenet of Kibbutz or collective education is that there are two emotional centers in the life of the child. The family and the children's houses in which the children live and grow up with other Kibbutz youngsters. The Kibbutz system is designed to maximize the love between parent and child and to minimize conflicts, and to eliminate ambivalent feelings in parent-child relationships "which characterize the Oedipus conflict" (Sprio, 1968, p. 15). For the "child does not feel himself economically dependent upon his parents; the metapelots are the primary disciplinarians; the child interacts primarily with his peers; and parent and child meet under optimal conditions with the minimum of stress (Spiro, pp. 15-16). Moshe Kerem (1970) indicates that the Kibbutz educational system in the early years was "dictated by physical circumstances and the desire of women to work full-time in the economy" (p. 243). Now this education has become institutionalized. This system it is believed by Kibbutz educators, is the best way to teach the habits of cooperation and communal living from the earliest age.

The fundamental aim of Kibbutz education is to maintain the Kibbutz values of labor, equality, collectivism, democracy, and voluntarism. The overall goals of the Kibbutz education system is to perpetuate the Kibbutz society (its values and ideology) and to integrate the child fully into the Kibbutz system which includes its moral, social, and economic life. Basic to this is the transmission of the values: the worth of work and to be a good *chaver* (Kibbutznik or comrade).

Mordechai Segal (1970) summarizes the "well-defined educational theory and practices" that "reflect the Kibbutz philosophy of life" (p. 275). This includes:

a) full-egalitarian democracy in education, coupled with an individualized approach...

b) an educational program...based on systematic analysis of the environment, tackling of emerging problems... structuring a healthy, vital, well-socialized outlook on life.

c) an integrative, active, both pupil and group-centered method, not overridden by skill training, not dominated by examination.

d) a 'home' atmosphere with simple unencumbered friendly relations, educators being addressed by first name, discipline stemming from affective identification with children's home and educator, as well as from traditional or ad hoc collective judgements, attitudes, and standards of the group.

e) home and school considered a socially structured entity...

f) all education embued with social aims of historical movement (pp. 275-76).

The Kibbutz school is a Kibbutz society in miniature where Kibbutz ideals of humanism, social living, social responsibility, social consciousness, pride, loyality, acceptance, tolerance, self-reliance, self-identification as well as identification with one's family, and internalization of group norms and values are transmitted, transformed into action, and integrated into one's psyche.

Another unique aspect of the Kibbutz school is the relationship between the teacher and parent and teacher and student. The parents recognize their right in the socialization of their child and the teacher recognizes that right as well, unlike in many American school situations where teachers are expected to be *"In Loco Parentis"* or parent substitutes. On the Kibbutz the teacher is respected by the parents as a person who is interested in educating their children and in their welfare; and he is respected as a professional. Overall, the teacher is considered as an *educator* and not just a teacher. As such the teacher is responsible for educating the whole child: socially, emotionally, as well as intellectually. The students view their teacher as a helping person who is interested in their welfare and interested in them as human beings. The teacher does not represent an authoritarian figure since he is not allowed to punish the child (parents and teachers do not hit children). Discipline emanates from the group as group pressure is applied by fellow students, Kibbutz morality, and internalization of Kibbutz ideals. Thus discipline in the Kibbutz school comes from the peer group where the unwritten law of the Kibbutz established codes of behavior and self discipline.

The uniqueness of collective education is in the Children's Houses which are designed to meet the needs of small groups. Deprivation (physical and psychological) is non-existent since the child is able to fully develop his cognitive ability; i.e., auditory and visual discrimination, and language and concept formation. The Children's House provides fully for the child's development of motor ability which contributes to his independence. The peer relationship enables the child to develop fully intellectually and socially.

The Kibbutz divides its educational system into the infants' house, the toddlers' house, the kindergarten, the junior children's community (elementary school) and the secondary school-junior high school-high school (known as the *mosad*). For the purposes of this article, we will concern ourselves with the infants' house to the kindergarten.

Infancy to Kindergarten

The children of the Kibbutz live from birth onward in the children's houses* where they are taken care of by trained members of the Kibbutz. These persons are called *metapelot(s)*.

The literal meaning of the word metapelet (plural: *metapelot*) is "the one who takes care" of the child—the nurse. The metapelet is in charge of the infants' house and its residents. She is responsible for the infants' house in terms of housekeeping chores as well as nursing chores. At one time it was not customary for the parents to visit the babies and the kindergartens except at night. Today parents visit whenever they like. In some cases the metapelet puts the children to bed in others the parents do this. Overall, the metapelet provides care, education and socialization. The metapelet is at the side of the nursing mother and she instructs and advises mothers in the carrying out of maternal tasks like feeding and bathing. The Kibbutz has the lowest infant mortality rate in the world due to such careful attention provided the infant.

The role of the metapelet for the toddler and the kindergarten age children is in assisting the children to live together, to communicate with each other, to share things, and in teaching hygenics, proper table manners, eating habits, overall socialization, and "the way of human relationships".

An important concept is the permanency of the metapelet. The metapelet usually stays with one group of children from the last year in the infants' house to the end of kindergarten. Another metapelet stays with one group

*Some Kibbutzim are experimenting by letting children stay in the parents' house till age six.

from the time the children enter the elementary school to the end of the sixth grade.

Levin (1970) has cogently pointed out that:

...the metapelet, therefore is doing a complementary job as regards to the child, and an instructor's job as regards to the mother. Here and there it is a corrective or regulating task. The difference in the child's relations to the two maternal images, lies in the intensity of his emotional relationships; it is more intense to the mother...The existence of several caretaker images arouses in the child various expectations from each of them. In our opinion, this is of vital importance in the process of socialization.

From my own observations during my stay on a Kibbutz the infant was able to discern the mother from the metapelet.

Peter Neubauer (1965) has observed in terms of the child rearing methods employed by the Kibbutz that:

In spite of the fact that the literature had led many of us to expect that we would discover deprivation in the young child of the Kibbutz, we did not find evidence to confirm these anticipations. On the contrary, we were quite impressed by the strength of the family influence on the children's development, and by this unique example of how family life can even by integrated—to its own advantage—into a system of collective child care. *The geographic distance between parental quarters and children's home is a wholly inadequate measure of the quality of the emotional relationships between parent and child* (p. 315). The Kibbutz never set out to offer the child-rearing functions; on the contrary, its goal was to develop a collective care program. This in itself is of decisive importance, since it eliminates at once the 'traditional' dichotomy of 'family care or community care'.

The intensity of the mother's participation, and the stability of the metapelet's involvement; the long-term programming, continuity of contact and stability of the social structure—all these provide the essential ingredients for a more successful, new form of communal care (p. 317).

On most Kibbutzim the infants' house could accomodate as many as twenty children from birth to approximately fifteen months. The building usually has two sections— one for newly born and one for those who have been weaned. During the first six weeks of life the infant's mother is relieved entirely from her work so that she can exclusively devote herself to feeding and taking care of her baby. After this period, the mother's hours of work start at four hours a day and is increased to a full seven hours by the time the baby is one year old. The mother breastfeeds and/or feeds, changes, plays and puts the baby to sleep. The metapelet looks after the baby when the mother is not there and gives advice to young inexperienced mothers. It can be noted that the metapelet receives intensive training at the Kibbutz Teacher Training Seminary in Oranim, Israel.

There is great flexibility in the infants' house so as to meet individual needs. For example, if the baby is crying at night or is restless, the mother can sleep in a special room in the infants' house so as to be close to the baby. Also, there is a night watchman, one for every children's house, who remains on duty all night. Also, parents can see their babies any time they want and the babies are taken to the parents' house everyday for family gatherings; thus the parents' room becomes a place of major importance. The parents, the metapelet, the group, and the Kibbutz itself makes up the educational environment of the child.

After fifteen months the infants are moved as a group (usually six children) to the toddlers' house. A permanent metapelet, who has worked with the children during their last few months in the infants' house, accompanies the group and takes full responsibility of the group.

The Toddlers' House usually contains two groups of six children, but some Kibbutzim have to maintain more than two groups. The children usually remain in the Toddlers' House for approximately three years—till the child reaches four years of age. The Toddlers' House is equipped to meet all of the child's needs. There are bedrooms that sleep four to six children; playrooms equipped with toys, games, and art supplies and picture books; a dining room; and an enclosed outside yard which is adjacent to the living quarters.

In the Toddlers' House the children learn how to live together; they learn the rudiments of collective behavior and socialization. They learn how to play with others, to share, to communicate, and to dress themselves. They are toilet trained, taught proper eating and hygenic habits as well as discipline.

Beginning at three years of age a coordinated program of walks, hikes, story-telling and group-singing, and organized games and crafts supplement spontaneous and individual play. The metapelet is with the children most of the day with the exception of when the children visit their parents. This is from 4:00 P.M. to 7:00 P.M. This is a time on the Kibbutz when the whole family, including all siblings, gather in the parents' house. The parents keep the children's toys in a special corner of the house—"the children's corner". During this time, the parents (and other relatives like grandparents) are totally involved with their children. This is where the quality of the relationships is such that it makes for a psychological healthy human being, which is unmatched in other societies.

At 7:00 P.M., the parents walk their children back to the Toddlers' House where the metapelet prepares the children for bed. Most parents come by at night to put their children to bed.

During the first year the two groups of six children that have been living side by side are combined and are joined by a third group of six children, to make up the complement of the kindergarten.

Thus, by age four or five the children enter the kindergarten as a peer group. The group consists of eighteen to twenty youngsters. The kindergarten allows for systematic development of the physical and sensory capacities of the youngsters. The children are allowed free time for free play, to visit their parents at work, and to explore their environment. The kindergarten combines play and learning as well as personal, family, and group experiences. There are many organized collective activities like gymnastics, music, art, crafts, and acting. There are organized excursions through the Kibbutz with visits to the barns, fields, factories, laundry, and dining hall. There is also nature study of the flora and fauna of the area. These excursions become topics for storytelling, drawings, discussions, and creative activity at evening gatherings. The coordination of activities are related to the child's experiences. This method is a lead-up to the "project method" of education which predominates in the primary grades.

During the last year of kindergarten, which includes ages six to seven, the children are taught the rudiments of reading, writing, and arithmetic— which is usually mastered by the age of eight. The last year of kindergarten is called the "transitional kindergarten" and it replaces the first grade. Teaching is individualized, but more emphasis is now placed upon discipline, the obligations of the child to the group, mutual aid and group solidarity. During this period the children remain closely attached to their parents' room and the family circle.

Organization of the Kibbutz kindergarten is not uniform in the three major Kibbutz Federations. Some prefer a uniform age group while others prefer multi-age groups. The "mixed kindergarten" can have children ranging in age from as low as two to as high as seven. Rabin (1965) points out that the:

> ...advocates of this multi-age kindergarten feel that it provides for a continuity in the kindergarten 'culture'. Not all children are moved en masse from the kindergarten into the second grade;...(p. 20).

In the "mixed kindergarten" the older children can serve as role models for the younger ones, the older children will gain a sense of responsibility, and there will be broader experience in interpersonal relationships.

Summary

The implications of communal child rearing as practiced on the Kibbutz are of great significance for American educators attemting to deal with the problems of establishing early childhood developmental programs. Moreover, Kibbutz practices can also give us insights into methods of dealing with "cultural deprivation". Samuel Golan (1958) points out that:

> We believe that the experience of collective education may add its own modest contribution to the sol-tion may add its own modest contribution to the solu-common to modern society throughout the world (p. 549).

Thus, we can gain insight into the transformation of a personality in accordance with a specific ideology so as to produce a community ideology which would engender cultural continuity and cultural conformity. The theoretical question arises: Are we able to shape the life space of an individual so that a new man and a new society can be created?

Golan (1958) believes that human relations reflect different life conditions and they change as society changes. Thus, one's life space can be molded to produce a new kind of man imbued (as in the case of the Kibbutz) with an ideology of social consciousness, sacrifice, equality, democracy, freedom, and collectivism.

In terms of American educational problems, we might be able to short-circuit the factors which lead to educational deprivation through a carefully designed early childhood developmental program. Since the child's social, economic, and family milieu are the major determinants in his cognitive development, we might be able to counteract these factors which result in the child's limited environmental experiences (and consequently lead to deprivation) by immersing the child into a totally rich environment. At the same time, we might also provide special seminars and experiences for the parents so that the home environment might also be improved at the same time; and which would reinforce the experiences of the child. Thereby, we will be able to have an impact upon the child's experiences which would affect his cognitive and developmental growth. Implicit in this would be an impact upon the child's visual and auditory discrimination, and language and concept formation. Each of these cognitive referents are developed at different stages, but one cannot be developed until the other is developed.

Moreover, programs for the young child, as in the Kibbutz model, will enhance the socialization process. Early childhood developmental programs can only succeed if staffed by professionally trained individuals who are warm and affective. Rather than expending funds on new facilities and on training new personnel, it would be much more efficacious to utilize existing public school facilities (which have space due to declining enrollments) and public school teachers and administrators (who have spent many years of training in dealing with young children). Walter Mondale congently puts the need for a national education policy when he stated at the American Federa-

tion of Teachers Convention on August 16, 1976, that:

> There is no issue before America today that is more critical than the one we discuss here today, for they involve the country's most precious heritage, our most precious resource, namely our children. The investment we make as a nation in the education of our country will determine profoundly the kind of country that we will have over not just the next decade but the next century as well...
> ...I have spent most of my adult life trying to learn, trying to understand, and trying to unravel the mystery why in this land of wealth and strength it is possible for millions of children, through no fault of their own, to be denied an equal chance for the fullness of American life. We must stop that, we must end it and the key to it is a national program of effective education for every child in America.

BIBLIOGRAPHY

Bettleheim, Bruno, *The Children of the Dream*, N.Y.: Macmillan, 1969.

Golan, Shmuel, "Behavior Research in Collective Settlements in Israel: Collective Education in the Kibbutz", *American Journal of Orthopsychiatry*, 28 (1958), pp. 549-556.

Golan, Shmuel, ed., *Collective Education In the Kibbutz*, Tel-Aviv: Education Dept. of Kibbutz Artzi, Hashomer Hatzair, 1961.

Golubchick, Leonard, *Comparison of Attitudes of Kibbutz Reared and Non-Kibbutz Reared High School Students*, Ph.D. Dissertation, New York University, 1972.

Jarus, A., Marcus, J., Oren, J., and Rapaport, Ch., eds., *Children and Families in Israel: Some Mental Health Perspectives*. N.Y.; Gordon and Breach, 1970.

Leon, Dan. *The Kibbutz: A New Way of Life*, London: Pergammon Press, 1969.

Levin, Gideon, "The Child and His Family in the Kibbutz: Infancy and His Early Childhood", in *Children and Families in Israel*, Eds. Jarus, *et al.*, N.Y.: Gordon and Breach, 1970, pp. 263-278.

Mondale, Walter, speech at American Federation of Teachers, August 16, 1976.

Neubauer, Peter, ed., *Children in Collectives: Child Rearing Aims and Practices in the Kibbutz*. Springfield, Ill.,: Charles C. Thomas, publisher, 1965.

Rabin, A. I., *Growing Up In The Kibbutz*, N.Y.: Springer Publishing Co., 1965.

Segal, Mordechai, "The Child and His Family in the Kibbutz: School Age", in *Children and Families in Israel*, Ed., Jarus, *et al.*, N.Y.: Gordon and Breach, 1970, pp. 271-283.

Spiro, Melford. *Children of the Kibbutz*, 4th ed., N.Y.: Shocken, 1968.

Chapter 72

An International Overview of Child Care Programs

Barry Persky*

The countries studied represent a broad spectrum of political ideologies, economic philosphies, and cultural differences. Yet, there are universal concerns that transcend geographical boundaries and man-made borders. Economic and social pressures that triggered the explosive growth in "out-of-home" child care here in the United States during the decade of the 60's similarly characterized the nine nations studied: Canada, France, Germany, Israel, Poland, Sweden, England, United States and Yugoslavia. The common forces contributing to this increased demand for expanded child care services in these countries are:

(a) the increased number of one-parent, female headed family breadwinners;

(b) the trend away from the extended family constellation;

(c) inflationary economic conditions fostering the entry of more women with very young children back into the labor force;

(d) the women's liberation movement providing viable alternatives to kinder, kuche and kirche by opening up new avenues of employment;

(e) an increased concern by parents as to the importance of early educational intervention to avoid later cumulative educational deficits experienced extensively by minorities, immigrants, and the urban poor.

Preschool coverage on a full day and part-day basis is already very wide-spread in most of the countries. Future projections stress universal coverage for all children between 3 and compulsary school age. Where formal resources are in short supply—and this would therefore be applicable to most of the programs within the nine countries studied, the single, major criterion for eligibility for entry into such programs is: presumptive social need. Although the rank order of priority may differ from country to country, preference is given to children falling into the following categories:

(a) children of working mothers or full-time students;

(b) children of one-parent families;

(c) children of immigrant families;

(d) children of socially, economically, and/or culturally deprived or disadvantaged families;

(e) abused or neglected children.

Within all the preceding categories, priority is given to children from low-income families. Ironically enough, current research (Kahn & Kamerman, 1975) indicates that the clamor for increased facilities is being made by middle class parents whose children are enjoying the highest rate of usage within existing programs.

These findings lend support to a proliferation of research findings (Deutsch, 1968), (Sprigle, 1972) and (Schwebel, 1973) alleging that our own Head Start Programs and television productions such as Sesame Street are not hitting their intended target populations.* These high quality programs have proven a boon to the middle class, but have done little to eliminate the educational gap existing between lower-class children and middle-class children after entry into elementary school. Several rationales have been advanced to account for the failure of lower-class children to fully capitalize on the educational opportunities afforded them through these programs. Among these are Schwebel (1973) who notes that children learn best through their own concrete experiences and not through the vicarious experiences of teachers or television personalities. Birch and Gussow (1970) posit the theory that many youngsters come from homes so hostile to life that the scars they bear will be impairments of their physical and mental health. When learning experiences are made available to this type of child, he will not be fully able to exploit them. Martin Deutsch (1968) points out the lack of provision for follow-up programs necessary to maximize the gains made by disadvantaged youngsters after Head Start. The gains that were initially made were soon dissipated within the mainstream of the first and second grades.

The predominant goals in child-care programs are:

(a) For programs serving children under age 3: custodial—the care and protection of young children;

(b) for programs serving children aged 3 and over: educational (and to a lesser extent social).

The programs have been structured into either two consecutive, age-related systems (0-3; 3-6), for the most part under separate ministries (welfare or health education) or

Adapted from Child-care Programs in Nine Countries, Kahn and Kamerman DHEW Publication No. 30080.
*Dr. Barry Persky, President of the Doctorate Association of New York Educators and Chairman of the Committee on the Handicapped, District 15, New York City.

two parallel systems with preschool beginning in the mean range covered by day care (e.g. day care 0-6; kindergarten 3-6). This generally leads to poor coordination between the systems with consequent problems for children and their families resulting from the lack of articulation.

Most child-care programs are publicly funded, either directly or by purchase of service through voluntary agencies. The extent or public subsidy for child-care programs is very high in all countries, and there is no relationship between economic costs and even the maximum fee charged. Most programs are universal and nonmeans tested although they may employ income criteria as the basis for sliding-fee payments. Almost all programs involve some fee payment by parents. Where fees are charged they range from low to lower. It is interesting to note that where private school programs exist, fees for such care are not much higher than the fees of nonprofit programs. There is insufficient existant data to compare the quality of delivery of service. However, a uniform characteristic of the operating costs of child-care programs in all countries is that 70-80 percent of the costs is attributed to expenditures for staff.

There is inconsistency between countries and no consensus regarding the nature of training, qualifications for child-care staff, and ratio of staff to children in care. In general, care for children under age 3 is described as requiring particularly high staff-child ratios (1:5 or at most 1:8, although in Israel it is as high as 1:15, but this includes 3-5 year olds also). For 3-6 year olds the range is enormous, from 1:10 to 1:40 in the French écoles maternelles. Training for kindergarten programs stress teacher training and qualification, day care/crèche programs stress nursing and/or child development, and few qualifications are required and/or little training is available for family-day-care mothers in any country.

The current debate in each country tends to cluster around six general themes regarding future directions in child-care programs.

1. Should child-care programs be designed and operated to meet children's needs, parents' needs, or both? If both, what happens when there is conflict?

   Are organized child-care programs designed to compensate children for socio-cultural deprivation of family life, or just to provide custodial care while the mother works?

2. Should available funds be invested in supplementing programs for school-age children, in expanding preschool care for children aged 3-5, or in expanding care for children under 3 (infants and toddlers).

3. In considering the unmet need and demand for additional facilities, what parameters should be set?

   All children under compulsary school age (C.S.A.). All children between the ages of 3 and C.S.A. All children under C.S.A. who live in certain communities—or in certain types of families; e.g. working mothers.

4. Is child care a specialized type of program to be developed and operated independently of all other children's programs? Is it part of the child-welfare system generally, or the health system, or the education system?

5. Which ministry or department should be responsible for child-care programs: welfare, health, or education? What should be included in good program curricula? What kinds of standards should there be and how will they be enforced? Should programs be financed by direct support of the programs themselves? By indirect support by aiding the users through vouchers or by supplementing child-care allowances for low-income working mothers?

6. The future direction for child-care programs: What is planned, projected, stressed, and why?

As one can readily see by this overview, the universal concerns of child-care are quite similar within the nine countries studied. The present and future problems they face vary only slightly. Economic and social forces are indeed international in scope and affect all political ideologies. Our children, our most precious resource, are very much dependent upon global trends.

Chapter 73

An Overview of Early Childhood Programs in Some Western European Countries

Gilbert R. Austin*

There have been two particularly important periods of time in the development of early childhood education in Europe. The first one took place between 1750 and 1830; the second between 1890 and the present day.

The person who is most commonly given the credit for being the father of the concept of early childhood education is the French philosopher and reformer, Jean Jacques Rousseau (1712-1778).

Rousseau is credited with being the discoverer of "childhood" as a result of his writing *Emile* in 1762 and *The Social Contract* in 1767. Both books called attention to the importance of the concept of childhood. Rousseau believed that childhood was a unique time and that a child during this period should not be considered just a small adult. He was one of the first philosophers to point out the relationship between society, the home and problems of education.

Emile has often been called the charter of childhood, for it laid down a plan for education to make an ordinary child morally responsible and intellectually capable.

Rousseau offers six guiding principles to education:

1. Education is growth; it should be a natural process.
2. Education should be paedocentric, which means that it must be directed primarily to the child and our teaching adapted to his needs. We must consider the utility of what is being taught for nothing is useful and good for him which is unbefitting his age.
3. Education is for liberty and happiness of the child. Freedom of the individual is the most precious ideal.
4. Education should be through experience. Children are to learn by doing. They are to learn by activity, through first hand experience.
5. Education is for individual development.
6. Education is for society or at least for social awareness. The ultimate aim of this kind of education is for the child to take his place as a responsible citizen in the society.

Johann Heinrich Pestalozzi (1746-1827) was one of the first to put Rousseau's ideas into practice by creating an actual early childhood education center. Pestalozzi, a Swiss teacher and philosopher, was much moved by the terrible living conditions under which young children in Switzerland existed. He worked very hard in the city of Zurich attempting to help these children. It was there that he wrote his famous book *The Evening Hours of a Hermit*. In 1805 he founded the early childhood education centre at Yverdon which soon became internationally famous for the methods he used in instructing young children; also, it soon became the place to go to learn to be a teacher.

Froebel (1782-1853), a German educator, is acknowledged to be the father of kindergarten. In 1808 he worked and studied under Pestalozzi at the school at Yverdon. He opened his first kindergarten in Blankenburg in Thuringen in 1837. Froebel was moved to open his first kindergarten in reaction to the very bad conditions prevalent in the child-minding institutions found in many German cities. Froebel's major contribution to early childhood education is the concept of play. He believed that in play we have the fullest expression of the child's nature and this should be the means of the child's education. "Play", declared Froebel, "is the great game of life itself in its beginning". Froebelian kindergartens therefore stress the great importance of play, of letting children explore their own environment and learn from it.

To accomplish this he designed many teaching materials. Some of the earliest of these were the three forms: The sphere, the cube and the cylinder. These he called the basic "gifts". The spheres were balls which the children rolled and tossed; the cubes were used as building blocks; and the cylinders were mediating forms between the other two, to be used as either stationary or movable elements in the play. Many other "gifts" were created. Squares, triangles, sticks, rings were soon added to the original three. The basic aim of Froebel's kindergarten was not knowledge about things, especially not verbalism, but rather the use of things for the accomplishment of the child's purposes.

Froebel's psychology was based upon four fundamental ideas:

1. Education is a natural process.
2. The child is an organism or organic whole which through a creative self-activity develops according to natural laws.

---

*Dr. Gilbert R. Austin, Professor of Education, University of Maryland.

3. The individual is an organic part of society.

4. The universe as a whole is an organism of which all lesser organisms are members.

Therefore creative self-activity through social participation is the basis of Froebel's psychology.

The aims and objectives of the teacher and those concerned with operating the kindergarten were to provide an environment which was as rich and stimulating as possible for the children so that they might fully develop their innate potential.

It is important to note that all three of these philosopher-educators were moved by their moral consciences to attempt to aid children who they saw living in terribly deprived and disadvantaged conditions.

Several points seem to emerge most importantly from this review of the first phase. First, the work of Rousseau was basic to the discovery and identity of childhood as a special time. Then the contribution of Pestalozzi was to identify the kinds of activities which were important for educating young children, particularly through the use of objects and sense impressions. Finally, Froebel put the ideas of Rousseau and Pestalozzi together in creating the kindergarten.

The second period of time, extending from 1890 to the present day, produced a new group of educators concerned with the education of young children. They tend much more to be implementers of the ideas of Rousseau, Pestlozzi and Froebel than original creators of new concepts. This is not to suggest that they did not make important contributions to early childhood education, only that in general they tended to expand the ideas of these three earlier educators. We shall trace this development in five European countries chosen because of their different developmental patterns.

Froebel's teachings and the spread of his kindergarten proceeded quite rapidly in Germany until 1857 when they were suppressed by the Prussian Government as radical teachings. For a lengthy period of time kindergarten was banned in Prussia and looked upon with great suspicion in other German states. The kindergarten movement in Germany as a result has grown slowly ever since and is almost entirely run on the basis of private sponsorship, i.e., the church.

The beginning of concern for early childhood education in France preceded our established starting date for this period by some one hundred years. Jean Frederic Oberlin (1740-1829), an Alsatian Lutheran pastor, opened one of the first pre-elementary schools in France. His teachings and beliefs drew heavily on the work of Rousseau; he created a number of schools called *ecóles à tricoter* (knitting schools). At about the same time, another group of pre-schools were opened in France called *salles d'asile* (place of refuge, a sanctuary). Starting with this base France has, since the time of Oberlin, consistently maintained and expanded its pre-school system. Today it has one of the largest and most complete pre-school systems in the world. France is also an important example of a country that maintained its orientation of pre-schools for the poor. It was not until after the Second World War that attendance at the *ecole maternelle* became particularly important for children of the middle class. Attendance at a pre-school is provided at no cost to the parents.

The French pre-schools did not change very much from child-minding institutions until the beginning of the 20th century when an *inspectrice générale* named Pauline Kergomard demonstrated what a rich and varied curriculum could be offered to young children in the *ecole maternelle*. Pauline Kergomard not only drew heavily on the teachings of Rousseau, Pestalozzi, Froebel and Oberlin; she also used the work of Binet and Freinet of France, Spencer of the United States, Claparede and Decroly of Belgium and Montessori of Italy.

In Great Britain Robert Owens (1771-1858), a socialist reformer and manager of a number of cotton mills, was first to introduce pre-school education. He opened a pre-school in Lanark, Scotland, near his mill in 1816. Owens was much influenced by the teachings of Rousseau and Pestalozzi and felt that the early years were very important. Froebel's teachings were also readily accepted in the United Kingdom, and in 1875 a Froebelian society was founded.

In the 1920's and 30's the best-known persons in England concerned with early childhood education were Margaret McMillan and Susan Isaacs. Both held a strong Froebelian point of view about pre-school. By the mid-twenties and thirties most pre-school education in England and Wales was being offered to the children of the middle class rather than the working poor. Pre-school during this period emphasized the importance of social and emotional growth and did not stress cognitive learning.

Pre-school education began in the early 1800's in the Netherlands. The first schools were known as *Bewaarshold* (minding schools) and they had primarily a psychohygienic (medical care and control) concern for young children. This was coupled with a strong religious conviction that the training of children should begin at a very young age. The Dutch have maintained over the years a relatively extensive pre-school system.

In the early part of the 20th century the teachings of Froebel and subsequently those of Montessori became important in the Netherlands. From 1930 through 1950 the most important early childhood educator was Langeveld. He viewed the family as the basic educational unit, teaching that it sets many of the basic conditions on which later education can be built and arguing for close family-school ties. The Dutch pre-school is quite unstructured, and the children are free to create their own learning centers.

Belgium has a history relatively similar to that of France. In 1825 a society was created which build pre-schools called *salles d'asile* (place of refuge) for the children of the poor. Belgium has since then maintained this orientation for providing pre-school education for the poor. The teachings of Froebel in the early 1900's were augmented by Montessori in the 1920's and in 1950 by Decroly. Decroly (1871-1932) was a Belgian physician who became interested in the problems of young children. His most famous saying is "l'enseignement pour la vie, par la vie" (Education for life, by living). Decroly is sometimes called the John Dewey of Belgium. The Belgian pre-school, like the French, is quite carefully planned and structured and is oriented toward primary school readiness.

In Italy in 1835 a Catholic priest, Abate Ferrante Aporti, having become discouraged with the problems of attempting to educate poor children in the elementary school, established the first pre-primary school. He concluded from this experience that the years before children came to elementary school were particularly important.

In 1895 the Agazzi sisters developed their method of educating young children through the development of curricula based upon what the children had in their pockets. The Agazzi sisters, each year in each class, built what they called a museum, based on the interesting objects the children brought into the classroom.

Maria Montessori carried pre-school education to new heights when, in 1912, she wrote her famous book, *The Method of Scientific Teaching*. Dr. Montessori brought to pre-school education a great deal of scientific talent and scientific principles of research. She, like all other educators mentioned in this article, felt that it was through the senses that the young learned best. She created a vast number of teaching materials that were carefully graded in degree of difficulty. To use this material well a teacher must be trained in the Montessori method.

We have traced briefly the development of early childhood education over the past 200 years and have identified for five countries leaders in the area of early childhood education in the last 100 years. The aims and objectives of these original designers of early childhood education were to provide childcare and education for children who were the products of the early European industrial slums or of the turmoils of war that marched back and forth across the face of Europe during this period of time.

The present increasing demand for early childhood education is seen as a reflection of a changing society and a concern for the democratization and comprehensiveness of education.

The rest of this article is concerned with a documentation of present early childhood education programs as they exist in eight countries: Belgium, Canada, France, Germany (F.R.), Italy, the Netherlands, Sweden, England and Wales. The countries were chosen because they were judged to be representative of a wide cross-section of practices in early childhood education.

Early childhood education is administered in many ways. In Belgium and France the administration is highly centralized at the national level. Both countries have

adopted a set of guidelines suggesting how early childhood education is to be organized and administered. These suggest what kinds of activities should be taking place in the school and an inspectorate system ensures that the guidelines are being followed. In the Netherlands the national administration does not control the curriculum of the pre-school but it does pay for the cost of running the schools and therefore its effective control is quite strong. In both Canada and Germany (F.R.) education is controlled by the regional government which has laid down guidelines for the organization and administration of early childhood education. In both Canada and Germany regions do cooperate with each other through the use of co-ordination committees. In England and Wales early childhood education is by law a local concern. The Department of Education and Science has created general guidelines which it hopes will be of assistance to the local educational agencies in creating ECE centres. The Department also provides inspectors who are responsible for observing what is going on in early childhood education programs and who offer help. Both Sweden and Italy have a strong Central Ministry of Education but since the great majority of pre-school education is financed at the local level, the real control lies there.

In all of the eight countries studied, there are extensive early childhood education programs in the private sector. All privately organized programs are in general subject to the rules and regulations laid down about physical facilities and the physical safety of the children by the national, regional or local educational authority. In general, however, private schools are much freer to conduct the educational program they want than are educators in the public sector.

Financial support of pre-school education in the eight countries is closely related to administrative responsibility. In Belgium, France and the Netherlands most of the money (90-95%) comes from the national government. In general, in these three countries, the local or regional authorities are responsible for the construction and maintenance of buildings, the national government reimbursing them for a portion of these capital costs, which ranges from 40 to 80 percent. In Canada and Germany (F.R.) the national government makes little contribution to pre-school education. Most of the money is raised at the regional or local level or aid by the parents. In England and Wales, Sweden, and Italy, most of the money is raised at the local level. In the school year 1970-71 the per pupil cost of pre-school education in these eight countries ranged from a high of 621 U.S. dollars in Sweden to a low of 110 U.S. dollars in France.

There are long waiting lists in most countries for the limited number of places available in pre-schools. For this reason priority is given to the children of working mothers, unmarried mothers, one-parent families, large and disorganized low-income families and families with long-term sickness.

In the pre-primary sector, the number of children enrolled in 1960-61 was 4.5 million. In 1970-71, this had risen to 6.8 million. It should be borne in mind that in this study no definition of pre-primary education was given. Each country has its own definition of it and its own age range for pre-school education. Table 1 presents the percentage of children by single year age group who were attending some form of pre-primary education in 1970-71.

The number of teachers involved in pre-primary education increased between 1960 and 1970 by 55,890. This fact has led to a decline in the pupil/teacher ratio from 34.0 in 1960 to 30.3 in 1970. In France, the ratio of children to any one teacher is 43:1. In England and Wales it is 19:1.

TABLE I

Percentage of Pre-school Pupils in Attendance by Single Year of Age Two-Six, 1970–71

Age	Belgium	Canada	England and Wales	France	Germany (F.R.)	Italy	Netherlands	Sweden
6	99	99	99	99	95	99	99	70
5	99	85E	99	99	70E	85E	95	25E
4	95	25E	20E	84	35E	60E	80E	10E
3	90	5E	5E	55	10E	20E	5E	2E
2	15E	1E	1E	15	1E	1E	1E	1E

E = Estimated from available data.

There is a great variety of training and certification practices for pre-primary teachers in the countries studied. The qualifications required are as follows:

Sweden - Completion of Comprehensive school; two years of training in teacher training college.

France - Completion of lower secondary school; four years of training; with baccalaureate two years of training in teachers college plus examination.

Italy - Completion of lower secondary school; three years of training in teacher training college plus examination.

Germany - Certificate of lower secondary school; two years of vocational school.

United Kingdom - Completion of secondary school; three years of training in teacher training college.

Netherlands - Completion of a four-year course in secondary modern school; three years of training in teacher training college.

Belgium - Completion of lower secondary school; two to four years at teacher training college.

Canada - Pre-primary teachers' certificates offered after a minimum of one year of training beyond junior or senior matriculation in high school, except in British Columbia and Alberta where teacher education is only given at university and teachers' certificates are given after a minimum of two years.

The organization of pre-school education across the eight countries was similar in the sense that all countries gathered together groups of children in physical facilities called pre-schools and provided them with teachers. The differences are found in such things as permissible age of entry (Belgium, France and Sweden, age two; England and Wales, age three; Canada, Germany, Italy, and the Netherlands, age four) as well as the age of leaving (England and Wales, age five; the others age six, except Sweden, age seven). Most countries grouped their pre-school children by single or double year age group, i.e. three and four year olds together. Sweden is a notable exception, where they have recently started trying out what they call sibling groups, which may span five years of age.

Pre-school education in seven of the eight countries is organized in separate facilities from the primary school. In Belgium pre-schools are commonly attached to primary schools. This physical separation seems only to make stronger the lack of communication between the pre-school and the primary school. Many educators feel that the level of communication must be improved to smooth the transition for the child from pre-primary to primary school.

Most pre-primary schools have similar physical facilities, viz., large tables for the children to work and play on, small chairs for them to sit in groups round the teacher, and carpets to work on. For the younger children, provision is made for taking naps in the afternoon. There are usually many small boxes or cupboards along the wall for the children to keep their drawings and books in, large wall space for the children to paint on or to display their work, and there may be climbing bars, water tables, sand tables, different kinds of plants, small animals and birds and as wide a selection of toys as funds will permit.

The instructional methods used in the pre-primary

schools are quite different, the difference arising as a result of two factors—the pupil/teacher ratio and the aims and objectives of the pre-primary school. At one end of the continuum we found countries like France and Italy, with high pupil/teacher ratios—43:1 and 37:1 respectively—and tending to a structured academically oriented program. At the other end are England and Wales and Canada with lower pupil/teacher ratios—19:1 and 25:1 respectively—and tending to an unstructured child-oriented program. These differences also reflect the traditions of early childhood education in the different countries named. France, for instance, has a tradition of providing child care for poor children which has evolved over the years into the present pre-primary system. While in England and Wales pre-school provision for the poor reached a high point in 1900 (41 percent of the three and four year olds) it has since declined to 15 percent of that age group in 1971, with the majority coming from middle class homes. In recent years, one of the major concerns in some of the countries reported here is how to achieve in their pre-primary programs a balance between programs which are almost totally devoted to free play and discovery and ones that are more structured and whose principal aim is to prepare children for entrance into primary school.

Pre-primary education since its creation has been concerned with the social and emotional adjustment of young children. The problems of social adjustment for children born into the present day nuclear family are becoming increasingly difficult. The changing life styles for both men and women have also created additional emotional problems for children when both parents are away from the home most of the day. Sweden is an example of a country which has chosen to put its major emphasis on social and emotional development. The Swedes believe that what is most important for their society is people who, as adults, can live at peace with the neighbors. Here, too, the development of a positive self-concept or self-image is stressed.

In each of the eight countries there are research activities, both sponsored by the governments and taking place in individual universities. In Belgium a national research project has as its aims to diagnose and recommend compensatory programs for children from infancy to seven years of age who suffer from socio-cultural handicaps. This project is being conducted on an inter-university basis at Brussels, Ghent, Liege and Mons. Its main objectives are:

(1) to determine the origin of affective and cognitive handicaps traceable to socio-economic and cultural conditions and to identify the prerequisite skills that primary school calls for so that these may be made available to disadvantaged children;

(2) to define the theoretical base and optimal forms of pre-school education, in particular to prevent handicaps.

In the last ten years there has been a great deal of research done in Canada on the problems of educating young children. Ryan, who has compiled a good review of research (1971), recommends an increased emphasis upon the operational specificity of programs, evaluative investigations of intervention programs. The French Ministry of Education is particularly interested in the area of pre-school education and the application of Piaget's theories of learning. In 1968 the French Ministry set up the Centre de Recherche de l'Education specialisee et de l'Adaptation Scholaire. The Centre is studying a variety of problems concerned with educating young children. The major center in Italy concerned with research on early childhood education is the Centre Didattico Nazionale per la Scuola Materna, located in Brescia. In Germany, the initiatives for educational-research projects have come from the research establishments and universities, from educational authorities, foundations, the German Education Council and the Science Council. In the area of pre-school education the leading centre of activity is the Deutsches Jugendinstitut, located in Munich.

In the Netherlands a number of researchers are working at the Universities of Utrecht and Amsterdam. Kohnstamm (1970) studied the effects of providing additional stimulation in nursery school for the development of toddlers. The study compared children at a nursery school with a group of matched, non-attending children, and indicated that the nursery school experience was positive and stimulating. A series of studies at the University of Utrecht concerned a family program in which the mother was concerned with in-school development of language and thought program. These programs were evaluated by de Vries (1971) and his general conclusion is that immediately after the programs there were positive effects. In Sweden, the research done by Stukat (1971) and his colleagues at the University of Gothenburg has been concerned with cognitive development. Their findings are similar to those in the United States in which a structured, carefully planned pre-school program results in more learning taking place on the part of pre-school children. The United Kingdom's most famous piece of research on education is the Plowden Report (1967) which indicated, as did the Coleman Report (1966) in the United States, that the greatest single factor in determining a pupil's success in school was the quality of the home background. Based on the findings and recommendations of the Plowden Report a number of projects concerned with pre-school education were set up. Halsey (Davie et al 1972) commenting on his evaluation of some of these pre-school projects, states:

"We have come to three general conclusions about pre-schooling from our experiences over three years in four districts. The first is that pre-schooling is the most effective educational instrument for applying the principle of positive discrimination and this conviction rests partly on the theory that primary and secondary educational attainment has its social foundations in the child's experience in the pre-school years and partly on the evidence that positive discrimination at the pre-school level can have a multiplying effect on the overwhelmingly important educative influences of the family and the peer group to which the child belongs. Second, pre-schooling is a point of entry into the development of the community school. It is the point at which, properly understood, the networks of family and formal education can most easily be linked. Third, there is no unique blueprinting of either organization or content which could be applied mechanically as national policy. On the contrary, the essential pre-requisite is correct diagnosis of the needs of individual children and of particular Educational Priority Areas."

The pre-primary population identified in this article are children who range in age from two to six years; they come from a wide variety of socio-economic and cultural backgrounds. The children are attending pre-primary school for a wide variety of reasons, the chief ones being:

(1) Parents' increased awareness of the general value of education.
(2) Demand for equality of educational opportunity.
(3) The importance of early childhood education as contributing to the family's role in educating children or come from one parent families.
(4) Changing social attitudes. A need for children to learn how to live and play together in a co-operative manner. Particular emphasis here is placed on the emotional, social, nutritional and educational goals in their broadest sense.
(5) A concern for the intellectual aspects of pre-primary education. This has only emerged recently, but it is receiving an increasing amount of attention.

In all of the countries there are a variety of programs and research projects in process which are concerned with aiding the children of the poor, the isolated or recent immigrants. These programs and research projects tend to emphasize cognitive development. There are few evaluation results available about them but where they are available they tend to indicate that programs which are structured and carefully planned are those which are most successful. Any results from an examination of long term effects are in close agreement with the findings of the Head Start study in the United States, which clearly indicate that without a follow-through program into the primary school, most of the benefits from pre-primary education are apparently lost.

REFERENCES

Austin, G. and Antonsen, K., A Review of Pre-school Educational Efforts in Five Countries, OECD, 1971.
Austin, G. Early Childhood Education in Eight OECD Countries, 1972.
Bereiter, C. Pre-School programs for the disadvantaged: Five Experimental Approaches to Early Childhood Education. Stanley, J.C. (Ed.). Johns Hopkins University Press, 1972.
Bernstein, B., Education Cannot Compensate for Society. New Society 26.2. 1970.
Blackstone, T., A Fair Start—The Provision of Pre-school Education. Allen Lane, The Penguin Press, 1971.
Bloom, B. Stability and Change in Human Characteristics. New York, N.Y. John Wiley and Sons, Inc. 1964.
van Calcar, C., Development of Compensatory Early Childhood Education. Bernard van Leer Foundation, Cursem/pe/12. The Hague, 3rd November, 1972.
Coleman, J., Equality of Educational Opportunity. Washinton, D.C., U.S. Government Printing Office, 1966.
Coulon, M. La Planification de l'enseignement en Belgique: Universite libre de Bruxelles, Institut de Sociologie, 1966.
Crellin, E. Kellmer, Pringle, M.L., West, P., Born Illegimate: Social and Educational Implications, a Report by National Children's Bureau, John Gardner Ltd., 1971.
Davie, R., Butler, N., Goldstein, H., Halsey, A.H., From Birth to Seven: A Report of the National Child Development Study. William Clowes and Sons, Ltd., 1972. Educational Priority: E.P.A. problems and policies. Vol. 1, Her Majesty's Stationery Office, October, 1972.
Herbiniere, Lebert S., l'Education des parents d'enfants d'age prescolaire par la cooperation entre la famille et les educatrices des jeunes enfants, OMEP.
Hoenisch, N., Niggemeyer, E., Zimmer, J., Vorschulkinder, Stuttgart, 1969, 239 pp.
Hunt, J., Intelligence and Experience. New York, N.Y. Ronald Press Co. 1961.
Husen, T., International Study of Achievement in Mathematics, Vol. I and II. Almquist and Wiksell, Stockholm, 1967.
Kohnstamm, G.A., The Language and Thought Programme, University of Utrecht, Utrecht, 1969.
Kohnstamm, G.A., Project Compensation Programme, Department of Education, University of Utrecht, dated 12th December, 1968.
de Landsheere, G., Pour une nouvelle formation des maitresses de jardins d'enfants necessite d'une reforme seminaire internationale, OMEP, Liege, Sept., 1967.
Libotte, M., Thirion, A.M. Les stimulations, dans Journee d'etude sur la prevention dans la premiere enfance (1971) a paraitre dans Acta Psychiatrica Belgica.
Orlando, D. Pedagogia dell'infanzia e Scuola materna Brescia, Ed. La Scuola 1970 (Collana 'Infanzia e Educazione).
Parisi, D. Socioculturel influences on language abilities at the beginning of school education. Estratto da: Giornate Internazionali di Socio-linquistica, Roma

15-17 Settembre 1969.

Plowden, B. Children and their Primary Schools. Her Majesty's Stationery Office, 1, II, 1967.

Reid, T.E. Education as social intervention in the Cycle of Canadian Poverty, in The Best of Times/The Worst of Times, contemporary issues in Canadian Education. Holt, Rinehart and Winston of Canada, Toronto, Montreal, 1972.

Ryan, T. Poverty and Early Education in Canada. Carelton

University, 1971, in press.

Stukat, K.G., Sverund, K.A. Nursery School Project. The Institute of Educational Psychology, Gothenburg School of Education, Stencil 1971.

de Vries, A.K., Pre-school Education and Development Psychology. Research into the age group 2-7 years in the Netherlands, Utrecht, 1971. Report of the Federal Government on Education, 1970, Bildungsbericht, 1970. Germany (F.R.).

Jack L. Mahan

Chapter 74

Preschool and Elementary Education in Scandinavia Today

Adele Davidson *

The first word heard at a recent summer Preschool and Elementary Education Seminar in Scandanavia was "Valkommen" and throughout the tour of Helsinki, Stockholm, Oslo, and Copenhagen this word of welcome resounded many times. The tour schedule was very full and included visits to children's libraries, recreation centers (open before and after school), kindergartens, playgrounds, social agencies, National Boards of Education, day nurseries. educational innovation centers, and elementary schools.

You migh ask, "Is there anything to see during the summer? Are schools open?" The regular school holiday in Scandinavia starts in June and ends about August 10th. Day nurseries function throughout the year, though not at full capacity during the summer months. The government strongly encourages women to work. Stipends are paid periodically for each child, and, by law, women are permitted paid time off from work to have children. Priorities which govern the intake of children to a day care center are: a) one parent families; b) families with ill health; c) families with low income; d) where children would benefit in other ways, e.g. social needs.

Children start formal elementary school in the first grade at age seven. Some elementary schools have kindergarten classes for six year olds and there are projected plans to increase the number of these classes so that all eligible children can attend. Out of ninety schools in Copenhagen, thirty now have kindergartens. The classes are half day sessions after which children of working parents are transported to day nurseries or after-school recreation centers to round out the full day session until mothers or fathers return from work.

Throughout our tour (arranged by Det Danske Selskab— the Danish Institute for Information about Denmark and Cultural Cooperation with other Nations) we heard about the challenges to educators, of parents pressuring for earlier formal instruction, of changing populations, of shrinking registers in urban areas, or underutilized schools, of the need for multi-lingual curriculums, of difficulties with school boards, and of budget cuts. The seminar participants, which included Educators from Australia, Canada, United States, Egypt, Iran and Switzerland, shared their experiences with similar challenges and problems. Several representatives voiced a need for and a shortage of trained, experienced mature teachers, especially men, for young children's

schools.

Young children in Scandinavia are treasured and provisions are made for space for large muscle activities both out-of-doors and indoors. Space is opened in newer schools to permit freedom of movement from class to class and from activity to activity. Gymnasiums, filled with every conceivable type of equipment, and large swimming pools in some centers focus on the physical development of young bodies. Young children bathe nude in park fountains, in pools and on beaches.

Nutritional snacks and lunches served in the schools use whole grains. Fruit is fresh and canned food is minimally used. Food services varies—delivered cooked, frozen or cooked in school. It is deemed important that food be prepared in the pre-school because there is so much that children can learn from the preparation.

Playgrounds are creatively designed, each with different features. One had a simulated rock mountain to teach children to climb mountains. Adventure playgrounds make use of found materials to make functional buildings which the children use. Many playground structures are made by parents.

Recreation, free time, or leisure centers are available to all school-age children before 8:30 A.M. and after 3 P.M. Children relax, play games, do woodwork, chat, write, and put on plays. Snacks and sometimes suppers are served. Centers are open from 6:30 A,M. until 6:30 P.M. and if needed, on school days, holidays and Saturdays. Children are supervised, occupied and safe while parents are at work.

Dental and medical services are provided to all children in the schools. Children are summoned from their classes for dental or medical care. When a child between six months and twelve years is ill and cannot attend a day-care center, parents can call for a children's nurse to come to the home.

DAY-CARE CENTERS: Children between 6 months and 7 years of age are welcome to the day-care centers in the daytime, when their parents are at work or school. They are taken care of by trained personnel who make sure that they

*Adele Davidson, Supervisor of Early Childhood Education, New York Education, New York City Board of Education.

have their proper meals and rest periods, and are given opportunities to play with other children and learn many things. The parents are always welcome to visit the center. Its personnel are anxious to have positive and active relations with parents, since this gives them a better chance to contribute to the positive development of the children. A child who is introduced to a day-care center is allowed a certain period (about 2 weeks) of gradual adjustment to life at the center. The first few days they are accompanied by one of their parents and stay only for a brief while, gradually extending their visits. This gives the child a chance to get used to the new environment, the new friends and the personnel. The child will then feel secure when the parents are gone during the day.

NURSERY SCHOOLS: Nursery schools are open 3 hours a day Mondays through Fridays, normally between 9 A.M. and noon, or between 1 P.M. and 4 P.M. No fees are charged.

DAY-CARE HOMES: The Day-Care Home is a private home that received one or more children aged between 6 months and 12 years while the parents are working or studying. The person who attends the children is called a day-care parent. This is child care in a family environment. The child is received by the family and offered meals, rest and various activities. Children between 4 and 6 usually spend 3 hours a day at a nursery school and the rest of the day in a day-care home.

GUIDED FAMILY DAY-CARE: A Pre-School teacher works with married women who take care of children in the homes. They are called Day Mothers. Some day mothers are Pre-School teachers who have children.

The seminar participants met in Helsinki, Finland to begin to learn about the cultures and educational systems in the four countries comprising Scandinavia.

Finland's kindergartens are intended to support and supplement the child's upbringing at home by providing him with activities suitable to his age and development. They also have a social role in that they cater to the children of poor people.

Legislation came into force on the first of April, 1973— a Day Care Act. The Act allows for the development of various forms of Day Care service:

1. Care of children in day-care homes;
2. The care of children in private homes called family day-care;
3. The direction and supervision of children's games and activities both indoors and outdoors in special restricted areas such as playgrounds.

Kaija Jyhlia from the National Board of Schools in Finland in a report "Pre-School Children in Finland" states:

"Among the most important scientifically proved observations concerning early education is the dependence of later development on the educational experiences of early childhood."

Young children are increasingly receiving the support,

through the Day Care Act, or guided experiences and social living situations. (One sees a day mother wheeling three children in a carriage in the company of two or three other day mothers (with their charges).

The new housing that is being built provides protected outdoor space for planned playgrounds for children.

The main library in Helsinki serves children and adults with books, records, puppetry, concerts and listening centers. Rooms are available to reserve for a length of time for study and for research. The very modern architecture is surrounded by landscaped spacious grounds and the picture windows frame beautiful garden views. What a joy to spend time here! Mothers sat and read to their young children, older children sat in an upholstered circular area using earphones. Some children used puppets. The atmosphere was relaxed and books were beautifully displayed.

The increase to 70% of working mothers of school children intensifies the need for more day care for young children.

Sweden has almost no illiteracy —nearly every person can read and write. Education is compulsory to the age of 15. The Swedish people place great value on education. Teachers are among the highest paid workers. Training for teaching is very thorough and an apprenticeship must be served. Pre-school teachers must take additional courses to teach in elementary schools.

Parents are very actively involved in the schools. In the elementary schools they serve on advisory committees to choose texts. In day nurseries they collect materials for the school and have special days set aside for cleaning. Employed parents are paid salary two days a year to attend educational conferences.

Classroom environments in model schools such as the Peter Lykke Skolem in Copenhagen are very colorful, comfortable, and conducive to learning. Model communities like Tapiola in Finland, Ski in Norway, Taby in Sweden, take great pride in their innovative schools Educators from all the Scandinavian Ministries of Education meet in Sweden regularly to share, compare, and report on various investigations.

Though 7 years is the age of admission to the first grade, 6-year-olds are admitted if they pass a very difficult test. It is reported that not many do. Grades 1—3 is known as the junior level, middle level is grades 4—8, and senior level is grades 7—9. The Swedish Education Act was passed in 1962 and entitles all children to attend comprehensive school for 9 years. It is compulsory to attend school to age 16. Further education is provided according to interest and ability.

Pupils are given the opportunity to draw and paint from their very first day in school. In grade 3, two new subjects are introduced, namely, English and handicraft. Handicraft includes textile work, woodwork, and metal work for all pupils. All comprehensive pupils continue to study English up to grade 9.

In 1975, the first Preschool Law was passed. It states that all 6 year old children in Sweden should be offered preschool education. Special needs, language or physical handicaps, children from homes with working parents, one-parent families, low income families, or families with ill health are to be considered first. Boarding schools are provided for retarded children.

All pregnant mothers receive free prenatal care and free hospital delivery service. Child allowances are payable to parents of all children until they reach the age of 16. In comprehensive schools, all children receive free tuition and transportation. Laplanders, because of travel difficulties, also receive free lodging. Menus for the meals served are printed in the local newspapers and thereby must meet public criticism. Local elementary schools choose their own curricula in order to meet special group needs. In Sweden, the children keep all their books so they can work with them during vacation periods and provide a permanent record at home of their school progress.

According to the Education Act, no students are transferred from one class to another because of scholastic performance. Tracking is never practiced. It is becoming less and less common to organize special remedial classes for students with difficulties. Such students are divided into smaller groups within the larger class or assistant teachers are engaged during "resource hours". Homework is assigned only sporadically. Although class enrollments at the junior level may not exceed 25 pupils, thirty are allowed at the middle and senior levels.

Sweden has many single parent families who need child care assistance. However, marriage is once again reported becoming more fashionable. There are many day care centers accommodating children from 6 months to 7 years of age.

The centers visited by the seminar were spacious, equipped with beautifully designed doll corner areas, cooking centers, blocks, outdoor sandboxes and climbing equipment.

The very young children's centers had indoor cribs, outdoor sheltered carriages on a porch and also a row of carriages in the open. Trained nurses diapered, fed, and played lovingly with the babies.

All children in the centers were given opportunities for lots of large muscle climbing, tumbling on mats, and freedom to explore space in many ways. Swedish gymnastics are part of the school curriculum.

The need for children to move about is respected. Even in the elementary schools children studied for a period, then played, then studied and played again. Children were learning to respect each other in their play contacts.

Many children travel long distances because of the lack of schools in outlying districts. Some can only go to school three days a week. In Norway there are ambulent pre-

schools where the teacher drives a car or even a snowmobile to mountain cottages. The teacher may stay 3 weeks, leave materials, then travel on. There are also some buses equipped as playrooms that travel to areas and hold classes.

In Oslo, 25,000 of the children have a place in kindergarten. By 1981, they expect to have places for 10,000 children. Children can start school (first grade) at 7 years of age or wait another year or two. In Norway, women's attitudes toward work and the family is different than in Finland and Sweden because Norway is becoming industrialized much more slowly. In more and more families two parents are working and, when asked, 65% wanted some kind of day care.

On June 6, 1975 a law was passed for preschool services with the aim of finding room for all Norwegian children. In 1976 a law was passed allowing all handicapped children to be included in regular classes. Integration of the handicapped child in regular preschool classes is an educational goal if the child can benefit from such placement. Teachers must receive training to work with integrated classes. Play libraries are attached to library or psychological centers to serve the special needs of children who have no place in other schools. In Ski, Norway there is a program practicing reverse integration—putting normal children into a new modern school (with a swimming pool) for the retarded and handicapped.

The last country we visited was Denmark. In the inner-city schools of Copenhagen the population was integrated with children from Turkey, India, Pakistan, Czechoslovakia, Africa, Spain, Greece, Poland and America. Most were children of parents employed in the city. Their visas are issued for several years and return to their native lands is planned. The children are put in special classes to master the Danish language but there are also instructors on staff to aid the children in retaining their mother tongue and ethnic identification. Some home language instructors service several schools and often are foreign students or people attached to the various embassies.

The Danish King in 1814 ordered every Dane, rich or poor, to go to school and so Denmark was the first country in the world to have compulsory free public education for every citizen. It is one of the most literate nations in the world because education is compulsory from the age of 7 to 14.

The Church and the State are one in Denmark and we witnessed religious instruction in a first-grade classroom in Copenhagen. The religion taught is mainly in the form of ethics and morals from the Old and New Testaments. We observed the story of creation dramatized by the children, at their level, and with individual interpretations. The male teacher played the violin to accompany the songs and creative movement. He also simply illustrated the story using colored chalk and the electric lights for the sun. Though the language was Danish the story was clear to us. The first-grade children, of two classes, both with male teachers enjoyed sharing the experiences. The third teacher was a woman who had been the children's kindergarten teacher of the previous year. Kindergarten starts one month later than the rest of the school while the teacher is assigned to assist with the children's adjustment to first grade. There were about 40 children in the combined class. The stated aims of the Danish primary school are to promote and develop the children's natural capacities and aptitudes, to strengthen their character, and give them useful knowledge.

The Peter Lykke Skolen (primary school) on the outskirts of Copenhagen is built to promote and develop children's natural capacities and aptitudes. The classrooms were on either side of a large open area used for individual pursuits using materials in the bookcases in this area. The building has a large center hall and three extensions in the form of an E. Children could be seen through the large long windows as they examined, with their teachers, water they had scooped from the pools. The walks were lined with various shrubs and flowers. There was an exchange of excitement in discovery which only a stimulating environment can produce.

Specialized classrooms for singing, music, woodwork, science, home economics, and handicrafts open off the main corridor. A staircase in each room leads to an upper platform for small group dramatizations or other work. The long windows and wide bright corridors furnished with modern chairs give a relaxed feeling. Children move easily, lunch on their open sandwiches and drink the milk which is provided. This is a model school and is in sharp physical contrast to the inner city school but the ease of movement and common feeling of respect is present in both situations. In both schools, the inspector (teacher) and the assistant inspector (teacher aide) had class assignments in reading and math. The arrival pattern is also the same. Children do not line up but come to school and proceed to their classes.

The kindergarten children in the inner city school had a little book (Kontactbok). The book must go home in the child's briefcase each night (every child has a briefcase). The teacher writes notes to the parent each time she needs to and the parent writes to the teacher. The book continues with the child to the next grade for continued communication.

The stated objectives of Scandinavian education are to provide pupils with knowledge and fundamental skills necessary in a modern society—to bring children up to be open-minded, productive and independent thinking human beings. All Ministries of Education stated that they had problems with measuring achievement in cognitive growth and questioned how to measure and even whether to measure. They are concerned with the problems in measuring affective gains. They are awaiting the reports of the investigations using different methods. Children and the problems of educators are obviously the same throughout the world.

A refreshing look at children learning to play together and communicate on many levels so that they can continue to learn together—That's Scandinavia!

Chapter 75

Early Childhood Education in the Soviet Union

Virginia Rederer *

A recognition of the importance of early childhood is a mark of the educational systems of both the United States and the Union of Soviet Socialist Republics. The chief educational officers of both super powers acknowledge that the experiences of the earliest years of life exert a lasting impact on the character and personality of its citizens. It is worthwhile, then, to examine in close detail the educational program set forth for Soviet children.

As a background for this investigation, it is helpful to keep in mind as a reference point some principles of American early education. Unlike the Soviet system with an official program designed for nationwide implementation, American early childhood programs are diversified and decentralized. Early childhood programs in the United States are conducted with a great variety in educational methodology and program scope. Furthermore, the appropriate age for children to participate in organized programs is viewed differently by American and Soviet educators. The Soviet guidelines provide for detailed, systematic intervention in the life of the infant from two months, while few American children are introduced to nursery school experiences before three years of age.

The program objectives for early childhood education show a remarkable similarity in both nations. American and Soviet educators both subscribe to goals of encouraging full individual development in all areas: physical, intellectual, emotional, and social. Both systems also recognize the contribution early experiences can provide in orienting children to participation in national life. The Soviet manual contains repeated statements on the importance of training children to participate fully in the collective. American programs, on the contrary, seek to bring children into the democratic process.

This basic difference in the nature of society is reflected in the methods of instruction. Soviet teachers are reminded to impress upon children from the earliest age to share toys, to help each other, and to participate in the work of adults. American programs give greater priority to helping children identify their own talents and achieve their individual potential.

In addition, American early education permits children to discover concepts within their own time pattern. Russian educators, on the other hand, are urged to teach everything as early as they can. All areas of development are system-atically organized into levels of difficulty, and children are instructed in each component as soon as possible.

In 1959, the Communist Party of the Soviet Union approved the creation of preschool institutions for children from two months to seven years, and commissioned the Academy of Pedagogical Sciences and the Academy of Medical Science to prepare a new and detailed curriculum for these institutions. This curriculum was first published in 1962, and then in a revised edition in 1965. The 1965 edition has been translated under the direction of Henry Chauncey of the Educational Testing Service. This article summarizes the program as outlined in this two volume work, *Program of Instruction*, which sets forth the curriculum in detail, and *Teacher's Commentary*, which provides a guide for carrying out the program.

From Birth to One Year. Physical characteristics of the child from birth to twelve months are noted, and a daily schedule for the organization of the child's life is set forth in great detail. Although there are specific recommendations for such activities as the number of feedings, the length of intervals between feedings, the length of each waking period, and the number and length of naps, these recommendations are to be used as a point of departure. The program states, "It is extremely important to systematically check whether the schedule corresponds to the condition and capabilities of the baby, and to make changes in the schedule in case it does not correspond." (*Program of Instruction*, p. 9). The nursery staff, however, are expected to structure the environment so that the babies are likely to respond to the schedule by playing, eating, and falling asleep at appropriate times.

This positive intervention is a keynote of Soviet early education. Every opportunity to stimulate the baby's developing abilities is utilized. For example, the program directs, "When feeding babies over six months old, the nurse names the motions and actions which the child makes and the objects connected with eating, and thus strives to control the baby's behavior verbally." (*Program of Instruction*, p. 11).

---

*Dr. Virginia Rederer, Special Assistant to the Chancellor, Board of Education, New York City.

Not only the baby's motor development and language skill, but also his emotional reaction is a proper area of concern. The teacher-nurse is urged to try to evoke smiles, sounds, and typical lively moments by playing with the baby and by talking and singing to him affectionately.

Socialization of babies begins early. Soviet infants from two months on are placed in large high playpens with five to seven other babies, well spread out, so the babies do not get in each other's way. The teacher-nurses are reminded to encourage the babies to smile and play with each other. Games to arouse the babies' interest in each other are played.

Music forms an important part in Soviet pre-school life. From the first months, teachers are encouraged to hum songs to the babies. Babies as young as four to six months old are grouped to listen to songs and to clap to music. The teacher-nurse dances with a baby in her arms to encourage a pleasant emotional response to music.

From One to Two. In the second year of life, objectives for the Soviet child involve continued physical growth, an active, cheerful disposition, early training in neatness and self-sufficiency, and the development of basic locomotor skills. A daily schedule is recommended with feeding at regulated time, and alternation of sleep and active periods.

Self-reliance is emphasized in the second year. The child is expected to feed himself with a spoon, to take his shoes and socks off, to wash his hands, and to express his requests by gesture or by words.

The second year is a period of intensive speech development. The staff is urged to utilize every moment of close contact with the child for speech, to answer the child attentively when he attempts to speak and to try to prolong the conversation.

In play activities during the second year, children are encouraged to illustrate events in daily life, and work activities of adults. The teacher-nurse staff is expected to demonstrate the use of such toys as trucks and dolls to the children, and to actively participate in the games.

Early training in responding to the requests of adults is considered important. Children as young as fourteen months are expected to listen to the nurse, look at objects as they are presented, and respond appropriately.

During the second year, physical skills are improved through exercises in walking, running, crawling, and throwing balls. Calisthenics and active games are scheduled two or three times weekly.

Activities to improve perception and coordination are also planned. Children are taught to put rings on a rod, to open and close boxes, and to build a tower with blocks.

Musical training is also planned two or three times a week to help children to listen attentively to the melody and words of a song, to imitate the sounds, to repeat simple words and syllables, and to perform appropriate dance movements. The teacher-nurse is instructed to prepare these activities in advance, to listen to recordings of the songs, and to rehearse the dance movements.

From Two to Three. The third year marks a transition from the infant group to the first preschool group. To ease this period of transition for the children, the teachers are instructed to get acquainted with the incoming group by observing the children at play, by chatting with them, and by conferring with the present teacher. Written reports with data on children's development are forwarded to the preschool teacher. Visits by staff members to pupil's homes are also recommended to help establish mutual cooperation between parents and staff.

Good social relationships between children and staff are strongly emphasized. Children are taught to play together, to assist younger children and to respond to requests from adults. Children are also taught to develop stable behavior and self-sufficiency through such responsibilities as assisting staff members to set lunch tables.

The development of speech ability continues as a major goal for the three year olds. Teachers of three year olds are reminded to utilize the routines of dressing, eating, and washing to help children develop speech abilities. Children are encouraged to discuss the work of adults, natural phenomena, and animals, and to ask questions related to daily happenings.

Children's play becomes more complex and varied in the third year. In the morning session, children first play independently with familiar toys, and then join in activities organized by the teacher. In the afternoon, the teacher introduces new toys, and demonstrates ways of playing with them to the children. Puppet shows, slides, and dramatizations are suggested.

Under the teacher's guidance, the children progress from discovery to planned play. They establish an objective, such as, "I'll build a hill for my cars." They are also able to organize games on a more sustained basis in the housekeeping corner, and the construction corner. Through play activities, the children become accustomed to sharing toys with each other.

Games with educational toys are scheduled once or twice weekly to develop recognition of colors and shapes, and fundamental number, time, and space concepts. Children group wooden balls or rods according to color, they find the missing part of a toy, or they assemble a puzzle.

Play with water and sand is encouraged as a pleasant activity for the children, and as a means for teaching children the properties of these materials, and the qualities of "wet", "dry", "damp", and "warm".

Simple literary and artistic works are also introduced. Appropriate rhymes, jingles, folk stories, and poems are suggested in the *Teacher's Commentary*, p. 110-115.

The objectives for the physical education of children in the third year involve attainment of greater coordination and agility in running, crawling, and jumping. Special equipment, such as ladders, balance boards, swings, and bikes are recommended. Active, energetic games are scheduled daily for both indoor and outdoor play.

Drawing and modeling activities are encouraged as aids in the development of perception and memory. Familiar objects are observed for general shape, dimensions, and outlines. The teacher is urged to help the child recognize any resemblance between his drawing and real objects. Instruction in drawing and in modeling is introduced gradually by the teacher as she participates in the activity.

The teacher also plays an active role in helping the children use building material. *The Teacher's Commentary* (p. 124) recommends, "At the beginning of the year, having organized a group of six to eight children, the teacher builds in their presence not a huge but an interesting structure—a house, a bridge, or a tower—calls upon the children to participate to a certain extent, and organizes games centered upon the construction." The children are encouraged to build independently such structures as towers, houses for dolls and toy animals, or a ramp for cars.

Musical training in the third year is provided twice weekly by a music teacher assisted by the regular teacher. In addition, daily songs, circle dances, and movements to music, such as marching and running, are scheduled daily.

From Three to Four. By this age, children are expected to be self-reliant in eating, washing, and dressing. Children also participate as fully as possible in the chores of the nursery. They tidy the playroom, set the table, help the teacher prepare materials for the activities, tend the plants and animals, and help the teachers take care of the playground.

Play activities are designed to help the children develop friendly, cooperative relationships with each other, and to develop speech, cognitive, and imaginative abilities. Role-playing games in small groups are encouraged.

Outdoor play is utilized not only to develop physical coordination but to increase relationships among the children of various ages. Teachers are encouraged to plan a schedule which will realize educational objectives in a way consistent with the interests and abilities of the children. For example, the *Program of Instruction* (p. 57) outlines the following schedule for cold winter days:

As they come out for the outdoor recreation period (in subgroups), the children play active games and role-playing games—They run, sleigh ride, play "Horses," take dolls for rides, etc. It is important that all the children are active and do a lot of moving about. Then the teacher organizes active games with rules for the whole group or for several children at a time (five to eight). In the intervals between games, observations are made (a snowfall, winter birds and how to feed them, transportation...). The children are given simple tasks to perform, for example, to shovel snow together and transport it on sleighs to a given spot.

The curriculum set forth in the *Program of Instruction* becomes more specific, as the children enter their fourth year. In some areas, objectives and activities are indicated on a quarterly basis, with the notation that skills introduced in one quarter are to be continued and refined in succeeding quarters.

For orientation to the environment, the children acquire knowledge concerning familiar household objects, work routines, local transportation patterns, common farm and domestic animals, and local plants and birds.

Drawing, modeling, cutting and pasting, and construction activities are outlined quarter by quarter in the *Program of Instruction* (pp. 65-67). By the end of the fourth quarter, children can draw and model familiar objects, such as wagons, flowers, or trees, paste an object with two or three parts, and build simple structures.

For computation, the children are taught to recognize the equality of groups and to use expressions "just as many as," "equal," "more/less," "one by one," and "more than one."

Musical training for both singing and rhythmic movements is provided. The children are helped to pronounce words of a song, to carry a tune correctly, and to sing with the teacher and alone. Circle games and dances are taught with running, spinning, stamping, and jumping steps. Children also perform movements with flags, scarves, and tambourines (*Program of Instruction*, p. 68).

Physical development is outlined with specific detail in each quarter. By the end of the year, children can walk and run in formation, throw balls into a basket, walk along a log, and climb on gymnastic apparatus. Specific exercises for muscle development in shoulders, legs, and torso are also prescribed.

National holidays, the First of May, the Seventh of November, and International Women's Day, March 8, are celebrated with parties and dramatic presentations.

From Four to Five. Further development of physical skills, speech, artistic abilities, and moral training is expected. Children start to grasp simple cause-effect relationships. Self-sufficiency in dressing, care of clothes, personal hygiene, and eating is expected. Work responsibilities increase, as children are assigned regular dining room duties, such as setting the table or distributing food.

Concept development continues, as the children increase their understanding of such temporal and spatial concepts as today, yesterday, tomorrow, here, there, above, below, near, far. Seasonal weather changes are also noticed, and the daily work activities of adults are discussed. The children explore the kindergarten, and take trips to observe buses, trains, ships, and planes.

Outdoor play is scheduled daily, with appropriate activities. In winter, children are taught to ski, to throw snowballs at a target, and to sleigh ride. In summer, tricycles and swings are provided, and ball games are organized.

Role-playing games, especially "Family," "Kindergarten," and "Holiday," are important at this age, and help to develop the children's attitudes towards each other and towards adults.

Construction activities become more complex, as the children begin to plan their building in advance. With teacher guidance, the children can build trains, bridges, doll houses, and garages.

Active circle games with definite rules are also popular. The teacher is expected to join with the children in such games as "Bear in the Forest" and "The Rabbit Sits and Sits."

Children learn to recognize domestic and farm animals, their habits, and their usefulness to man. They learn to identify characteristics of birds, fish, frogs, beetles, and butterflies. Children observe seasonal changes in plants, and learn to identify garden and wild flowers. They plant seeds and bulbs, and are able to distinguish common fruits and vegetables.

Computation activities include naming the cardinal numbers up to five, comparing collections of objects, distinguishing right from left, and subtracting objects up to five from a group.

One activity period weekly is devoted to drawing and modeling instruction; building activities are scheduled daily. Specific activities are outlined in the *Program of Instruction* (pp. 90-92). By the end of the year, children can draw pictures, use scissors correctly, model familiar objects, and build buses and doll houses.

Musical training in singing and rhythmic movement continues. The children are taught to hold notes when singing, and to sing with and without instrumental accompaniment. They learn to move according to the tempo and dynamics of music. Circle dances are more complex, with heel-toe steps, clapping, and spins.

Physical development is emphasized with definite activities indicated for each quarter (*Program of Instruction*, pp. 95-98). By the end of the year, the children can run zigzag, along inclined boards and in a column. They can climb under a pipe and over a log, and can throw a sandbag with both right and left hand. Exercises for shoulder, leg, and torso muscles are also planned.

Sleigh riding, skiing, tricycle riding, and playing in shallow water are sports enjoyed by five year olds.

The national holidays are celebrated, with children participating in the preparations.

From Five to Six. The *Program of Instruction* indicates the children now begin to show respect for the work of people around them, they wish to assist adults and friends, and they desire to participate in a common undertaking, especially when the activity is for the collective (p. 101). Children are now given more responsibility for organizing the work themselves, distributing the various tasks, and arranging job priorities. Children are also encouraged to work on their own initiative and to evaluate the quality of their own work.

Habits of personal hygiene should be instilled, so children wash themselves without reminders, use proper table manners, including correct use of a knife and fork, and care for their clothes and hair.

Themes for play now extend beyond the immediate experiences of the children. The children pretend to be workers on a collective farm or airplane pilots, or train engineers. Two play activities are conducted daily, the first activity for 20 to 35 minutes, and the second activity for 15 to 20 minutes.

Outdoor play activities are designed to develop friendly relationships among the children, and to strengthen physical health. Games involve running, jumping, climbing, and throwing. Ball playing, jump rope, hoops, cycling, roller skating, and swings are all organized, with the teacher instructed to see that children engage in a variety of play activities, and to be sure toys and gymnastic equipment are used properly. Action games with an element of competition between groups are played.

Role-playing games are encouraged to develop relationships among children, and to deepen perspective on the role of adults. "House," "Store," and "Our Street" are popular.

Dramatization games help develop expressive speech and help children share a common interest in books, fairy tales, and songs.

Construction activities now involve many more materials: snow, sand, clay, boxes, boards. The children build ships, railroad stations, kindergartens. The teacher "stimulates the children's efforts...", she draws the children's attention to the most interesting structures, helps them to add details, demonstrates specific techniques, and challenges them to build according to a drawing, sketch, or description" (*Program of Instruction*, p. 111).

Games with educational toys help develop concepts and skills in classification and generalization.

The program includes three kinds of work activities: routine housework, work with nature, and handicraft. For routine housekeeping routines, the children set out dishes and silverware, prepare and clean up for pasting, modeling, and painting activities, and participate in cleaning the playground. In plant cultivation, the children plant, weed, and water indoor plants and outdoor gardens, they care for domestic animals, and feed birds. For handicraft, the children learn to make simple objects from paper, wood, and cloth. For example, little bags or boxes for seeds and New Year's tree decorations might be made.

Activities to acquaint the children with the environment are outlined quarter by quarter in the *Program of Instruction* (pp. 115-118). Children observe seasonal changes in weather, plants, and animals. They observe preparation of food and clothing. They plan trips to construction sites, and learn about means of transportation. They enjoy celebrating national holidays.

Instruction in mathematics follows the systematic, sequential approach started in earlier years. The concept of number as the power index of a set is further developed. Instruction is based on the comparison of sets and the establishment of one-to-one correspondence up to ten.

In drawing, painting, modeling, and construction activities, the objectives include development of powers of observation and refinement of conceptions of shapes, positions and characteristics of objects. Children paint scenes from nature, they model figures in proportion, they build structures from photographs, and they cooperate on decorative projects for the playroom.

Physical development for children from five to six years old is an important element in the pre-school program. The children of this age can orient themselves in space, distinguish various directions, and maintain balance. They can catch balls, do a running high jump, and play tag. Muscle exercises and drills continue. Sleigh riding, and skiing downhill are enjoyed. Children learn to ride a two-wheel bike, and to float in shallow water.

The objectives for musical training are directed to the development of a sense of rhythm. To accomplish this, a musical repertory of national folk songs and dances, works of Soviet composers, and classical works is recommended. The children learn to sing at different tempos, and to respond rhythmically to contrasts in music. They also learn simple dance steps with partners.

School Preparatory Group. The total experience of the kindergarten must prepare children for new responsibilities. The transition from kindergarten to school must achieve a unified educational program. The role of activities increases, and more stable relationships grow among the children. The children learn to organize projects, and rudimentary collective procedures emerge.

Preparation for reading and writing begins, with a gradual introduction of the sounds and letters in the Russian alphabet in one activity a week. Aural discrimination activities are scheduled twice weekly. The children learn the meaning of a sentence, a word, a syllable, a sound, and a letter. Finally, the children start to use a notebook to trace designs with a ruler and to write the basic elements of letters.

National holidays to celebrate Soviet patriots and achievements are observed in the kindergarten. Both the *Program of Instruction* (p.138) and the *Teacher's Commentary* (p. 196) emphasize that children must be involved in happy experiences associated with these national holidays. The holiday must be a source of joy to the children. The *Teacher's Commentary* (pp. 197-198) states, "The children remember for a long time those assemblies which are organized for all the groups together on the grounds of the kindergarten: the winter festival with Grandfather Frost, sleigh riding on decorated sleighs or in troikas, lively active games, and the summer holiday with athletic events, round dances, singing, and dancing."

Children's birthdays are celebrated, with a festive birthday cake and small presents for children during the month. This observance helps increase friendship of children for each other.

Work activities of the children involve more complex responsibilities and high standards for performance. The children participate in routine housework, cultivation of plants, and care of the animals. Handicrafts with wood, paper, and cloth are scheduled. The general working atmosphere should be friendly, well-organized, and cooperative. Respect for workers must be inculcated. Labor for the good of all must be considered a joy, an absorbing activity. Every effort is made to develop in the children patterns of social behavior and personality characteristics of the Soviet people.

Objectives in mathematics include reinforcement of skills in counting up to ten, and understanding of such concepts as: greater-less; smaller-larger; wider-narrower; taller-shorter; lighter-heavier; thicker-thinner. Children also have practice for writing numbers, and for identifying geometric forms. Simple problem solving is also introduced on the basis of the children's personal experiences. The operational symbols for addition, subtraction, and equality are taught, and children practice adding and subtracting by units.

Drawing, painting, modeling, and construction activities provide an opportunity for the children to develop perception and visual memory; to stimulate creative imagination; and to increase appreciation for color and form. The children draw and paint scenes from nature and from literary works, they model figures to scale, they cut silhouettes and symmetrical forms, and they work collectively to construct toys and models of houses and machines.

Activities for physical development are designed to improve gracefulness, skill, and coordination. Spatial orientation and sense of balance also develop. The children enjoy running obstacle courses, dodging and chasing, broad jumping, throwing balls at moving targets, and climbing ladders.

Exercises for shoulder, leg, and torso are scheduled, and sports are emphasized. Children are taught to pick up objects while sleigh riding down a hill, to ski on trails and cross-country; to ice skate; to ride a bike without help; and to float in shallow water.

Singing and rhythmic movements improve, as the children develop an ear for melody and a sense of subtle differentiation in music. The repertory of familiar musical works is increased, and children distinguish dances, lullabies, and marches. More dance steps are taught, including polka dances and tap dances, and children are encouraged to use these steps in improvising original dances.

The entire pre-school program concludes with a morning party the end of August to mark the child's entrance into school. He has had the benefit of a carefully organized program from the first two months of life, and he is now ready for formal schooling. His experiences have been designed for continuity with school activities and with the closely associated communist youth organizations; the Octobrists (grades 1 through 3, ages 7-9), the Pioneers (grades 4 through 8, ages 10-15), and the Young Communist League for young adults. He has been guided skillfully through a structured program with the objective of developing the ideal Soviet citizen.

BIBLIOGRAPHY

Chauncey, Henry, editor. *Soviet Preschool Education, Volume I: Program of Instruction.* New York: Holt, Rinehart, Winston, 1969.

Soviet Preschool Education, Volume II: *Teacher's Commentary.* New York: Holt, Rinehart, Winston, 1969.

Chapter 76

Curriculum Practices in Preschool and Primary Schools in the People's Republic of China

Alfred L. Karlson*

Introduction

In January of 1975 I participated in a month long study tour of educational settings in the People's Republic of China. I traveled with twenty Americans, all specialists in preschool or primary school education. Some of us were classroom teachers, others teacher trainers, and others worked in universities. We were a diverse group and represented a broad political and experiential background. In our travels we were in the countryside and urban centers. Although we spent most of our time in schools and teacher training centers, we also visited factories, work places, hospitals, farms museums, parks, cultural events, the Shanghai docks, neighborhoods, stores, and people's homes. Much of our time was spent in seminars or discussion groups with teachers, school administrators, and the children. Geographically our tour was limited to the north and central part of the country. We were in the cities of Peking, Tientsein, Nanking, Soochow and Shanghai. We traveled by air from the United States entering the country from Japan (Tokyo to Peking) and then by train from city to city. In each city we were escorted by the travel service, Luxshinge, who provided translators, hotel and food services and bus transportation to the educational sites. The travel services also planned our itinerary, arranging for school visits and our busy daily schedules. We had some free time for moving about on our own althouth this was limited. In general the staff of the travel service was helpful and flexible, attempting to meet our various requests. For example, we were eager to see special education in practice and they arranged for us to see a school for the deaf in Shanghai. In any case, it is important to remember that the educational settings we observed were from a limited sample, although we saw several.

The following paper is divided into six sections—the philosophy and aims of current Chinese education; curriculum practices in the preschool and the primary school; the middle school; teacher training institutions; the little red soldiers and the children's palaces; and, some concluding observations. Emphasis is on factual information told to our groups in meetings with the Chinese school committee members, children and teachers.

The Philosophy and Aims of Current Chinese Education

At all levels of education practice the guiding philosophy is that of Maoist political ideology. The aim of education is to teach revolutionary struggle, to help build a new socialist man, and to teach a form of morality that encourages selflessness and services to others. To achieve these goals educational practice is encouraged not to be made separate from theory. Theory is always to be put into practice, and there must be no false distinction between theory and practice. Educational practices also must follow three directions: moral, physical and intellectual development.

The overall purpose of education in the People's Republic of China was described most clearly to us by Talitha Gurlach, an American born woman who had been a Y.W.C.A. worker in China and has become one of the famous Chinese "one hundred percenters." In a meeting in Shanghai with our group she stated that the overall goal of Chinese educational practice was to stamp out the last vestiges of bourgeois ideology in the thoughts of the people and to create a new socialist man committed to selfless thought and to the good of the whole, not just a few.

Examples of the purposes and goals of the current educational philosophy could be seen everywhere. In all classrooms there were pictures of Mao, often flanked by slogans such as "Serve the People" or "Learn by Doing." The notion that the educational process should not separate theory and practice was evidenced as workers from factories lectured in the classroom, and parts of school days were given over to productive labor. For example, students took time out from lessons to build a building to house a new classroom, or in shop classes students manufactured electrical coils used in actual production for motors. In one primary school ten and twelve year olds folded cardboard t's in a production line fashion for an hour each day. These were then used by a toothpaste factory nearby for packaging.

Moral education was also clearly in evidence. In the preschool and primary school grades children acted out plays

*Dr. Alfred Karlson, Assistant Professor, Program in Human Development, University of Massachusetts.

and stories that had "lessons" in them. For example, the children in a Peking Preschool acted out the story of the sheep and the bad wolf. Each child had a part and recited lines and moved wooden figures of the sheep around on a table with the appropriate scenery. The story was of a poor heard of sheep suffering attack by an evil wolf who often appeared in the skin of a dead sheep. The sheep banned together to discuss a strategy. They could see that their strength was in numbers and solidarity and they banned together to remove their enemy.

Moral education was also stressed in the content of language lessons that told of the lives of the hero's of the revolution or in ways that the people of the communes worked out their differences.

Physical education was a primary part of every school curriculum and young children through college age all participated in various kinds of dancing, traditional Chinese martial arts, western sports such as basketball and gymnastics, and of course ping pong. Everywhere we were given demonstrations of the children's abilities and strengths in the area of physical skills, and the performances were outstanding.

Curriculum Practices in the Preschool and Primary Schools

In modern day China everyone works (man and woman) who is able, and therefore child care services are provided from infancy on. Many children are cared for in groups by grandparents, and there are neighborhood and factory day care services for workers. Children are cared for during the eight hour shift that the mother works. Nursing babies are fed by their mothers on regularly scheduled breaks. In most day care centers there is a high ratio of workers to children, about one to eight. Workers appear to be in constant interaction with children. By American standards the centers have few toys, but activities center more around people to people interactions. Two and three year olds learn songs, group games, clean up skills, and other group activities that require few props. Most Chinese preschool children, however, live in rural communes and villages where the family structure is still intact and there children are cared for in the home.

At the age of four nearly half of all Chinese children begin kindergarten. The curriculum stresses physical development, games, relay races, gymnastic exercises, some art: paper folding, drawing and clay modeling, and some rudimentary language skills. But most of the formal schooling is given over to the learning and performance of playlets and song and dance stories, all that have a lesson in them.

Modern Chinese children begin formal primary school at the age of seven and continue for five years. They learn basic reading, writing and computational skills and have science lessons (intellectual development). They continue with gymnastics, sports and music and dance for physical development and begin more formal moral education by studying the tennats of Maoist teachings.

The primary schooling appears to be very formal. Classes have forty to fifty children, and children sit quietly in pairs paying careful attention to the teacher. Lessons involve group recitations and group seat work. Choral reading is very popular in language lessons with all children reading out loud at the top of their voices.

The Middle School

After five years of primary schooling most children enter into the Middle School. Here the curriculum becomes more specialized and there is a new emphasis on science, and foreign languages are taught. The middle school curriculum was very strongly affected by the turbulence during the Great Proletarian Cultural Revolution. It was felt by many that these schools had become too formal and there was too much emphasis on the individual student's career in a profession or the government. Currently Maoist teachings are most strongly stressed and students spend more time in programs that involve nearby factories, or spend some of their time in special commune schools during their formal education, where they learn to respect manual labor and the life of the farm workers. It well may be that with the changes in government, following the recent death of Mao Tse-tung, the middle school curriculum will undergo more modifications.

The Teacher Training Institute

Because our group was made up of early childhood and elementary school specialists, our visits to places of higher learning were limited to teaching training institutes where young men and women learned to be preschool and primary school teachers.

At all educational levels when individuals are asked the question "What do you want to do when you are an adult?" their response is, "I wish to serve in the way that I am needed." At the age of seventeen all men and women are assigned to work in a factory or in a farm setting for two years. None go straight from the middle school to a university, teacher training institute or medical school. During this period individuals are assessed by responsible members of the neighborhood party as to who should go on for future education and who should continue to work in the countryside or in the factory. Therefore, all students at the teacher training institute were selected by the party to participate in this experience.

The course of study lasts two years with half of the last year given over to a practical experience under a master teacher in an operating preschool or primary school. Students took classroom instruction in reading, science and math methods, music and physical education. In one classroom we observed students constructing their own visual aids or instructors aids for geometry. In music classes students composed songs to be sung by the children. This additional student responsibility was seen as an innovation after the cultural revolution, because it was felt that students needed a stronger voice in deciding their education. A further innovation was reported to us by students and faculty. It was said that since the cultural revolution students had become free to question the authority of the teachers.

After graduation from the teacher training institute, new teachers are assigned places of work as vacancies come open. Extra curricular activities are planned for students which include intramural sports and political study groups.

The Little Red Soldiers and The Children's Palace

As in the Soviet Union and Cuba the Chinese have a nationally sponsored youth program. It is called The Little Red Soldiers. This is a citizenship training organization with adult leaders. Children are selected by their peers to be members beginning in the second grade. Little Red Soldiers meet for one to two hours every day after school in special study groups where they learn Maoist ideology, practice military drill, produce musical plays and pageants and do sports. Their organization is also service oriented for it is the job of the Little Red Soldiers to help the slower children with their schoolwork and to set the correct moral tone of the classroom and school by leading their lives by good example showing the others the way. By the end of primary school almost all children have been voted into membership in the organization. Elected leaders of the Little Red Soldiers also participate in school committee meetings.

In each major city we visited a Children's Palace. These are large buildings that house after school programs sponsored by the Little Red Soldiers. Study groups, gymnastics, sports, music, practice to become para medicals, and military drill are all offered. The children themselves decide who is to attend, but adult youth leaders help organize the programs.

Concluding Remarks

First of all, these observations go beyond the facts I have reported from the tour and are more speculative, but are not contradictory to the views of others on the tour and have also been corroborated by a group of American psychologists who had previously participated in a similar tour. To the American observer the direct teaching of values and an emphasis on learning the correct value system is antithetical to our stated belief of teaching the individual to think for himself. It is beyond the scope of this paper to compare the effectiveness of the two very different sociopolitical systems of the United States and The People's Republic of China, however, it is clear to even the most naive observer that many of the educational practices in China more clearly deserve the term indoctrinational, and therefore may have serious limiting consequences when alternative solutions to future problems may become needed.

Secondarily to the direct training of values, is the formal pedagogical style in which, from an early age, children do choral reading, group recitation and rehearse and perform playlets. I do not want to give the impression that this appears to be oppressive in any way. It does not. It simply appears formal. In a primary school art class, for example, children all copy the same picture of Tien An Min Square. On in English class children read in unison. One abacus lesson stands out in particular: The teacher held up a flash card with the problem. The children responded with a clatter of moving and then hands went up. The teacher called on several different children who shouted out the correct answer from their independent calculations.

A third striking feature is the emphasis on physical training. Children spend much of their school time practicing formal physical fitness training. This is seen in gymnastic exercises and games, such as running relays, doing song and dance routines. These appeared to me to always be at an exceptionally high performance level. These observations all clearly fit in with Mao's doctrines of physical, moral and intellectual development, and these three observations are hardly speculative. From what I can tell, they are also similar to the observations of others.

A final observation, however, is more puzzling and has to do with school behavior of children that Jack Kounin and other educational psychologists call with-it-ness. In all of the school settings in which we observed, children, even down to age three, appeared to be alert, tuned in, and paying attention to the ongoing activities. This was true also of the children as they watched their peers perform in playlets, or when others were reciting in front of the class. There appeared to this observer little evidence that children were restive under a familiar oppressive regime of "school," as we have sometimes characterized in our society. We frequently remarked on how well the children perfomed, how alert they were, and how happy they seemed. How is it that the children seem so at ease in their performances, so well-disciplined, so eager? Our guides felt that this stemmed from a feeling of confidence and trust in their country. They were pleased to see us judge the children so positively and equally pleased to use the children's behavior as evidence of the success of the goals of the educational system. Clearly, this was only part of the picture. Children in China are also experiencing an era of incomparable prosperity, especially in contrast to the time previous 1949. It seems clear too, that parents' family life, now also prosperous, supports the child. Everywhere children appeared well-fed, well-clothed, and well-cared for. In all of the time of our tour I never saw a child scolded, reprimanded or even spoken harshly to. Responsible children often attended our seminars and responded to our questions. The attitudes teachers, as professionals, expressed toward the children was loving, kind and understanding. Once in a performance of a playlet a child forgot her lines. The teachers waited patiently and smiled and the child proceeded. In one primary school we visited the children appeared a little wild—the principal's attitude was tolerant and humanistic—they need to run off some energy on the play yard. "You know how children are, don't you?" she said.

A final statement about these observations: I do not wish to join the ranks of instant American Sinologists who return from tours of China and view children in China with awe and jealousy; nor do I want to rail against the uniformity and limited political rhetoric they are being taught. I simply want, on making good a promise made to the members of the travel services and Chinese school teachers I met, to share some of my observations with you.